PREACHING THE LECTIONARY

A Workbook for Year C

Also by Perry H. Biddle, Jr.

Preaching the Lectionary
A Workbook for Year A

Preaching the Lectionary
A Workbook for Year B

PREACHING THE LECTIONARY

A Workbook for Year C

PERRY H. BIDDLE, Jr., Editor

Westminster/John Knox Press
Louisville, Kentucky

© 1991 Perry H. Biddle, Jr.

All rights reserved—no part of this book may be reproduced in any form without permission in writing from the publisher, except by a reviewer who wishes to quote brief passages in connection with a review in magazine or newspaper.

Unless otherwise indicated, scripture quotations are from the Revised Standard Version of the Bible, copyrighted 1946, 1952, © 1971, 1973 by the Division of Christian Education of the National Council of the Churches of Christ in the U.S.A., and are used by permission.

Scripture quotations marked NRSV are from the New Revised Standard Version of the Bible, copyright © 1989 by the Division of Christian Education of the National Council of the Churches of Christ in the U.S.A., and are used by permission.

Scripture quotations marked NEB are from *The New English Bible,* © The Delegates of the Oxford University Press and The Syndics of the Cambridge University Press, 1961, 1970. Used by permission.

Scripture quotations marked TEV are from the *Good News Bible: The Bible in Today's English Version.* Old Testament: copyright © American Bible Society, 1976; New Testament: copyright © American Bible Society, 1966, 1971, 1976.

Scripture quotations marked JB are from *The Jerusalem Bible,* copyright © 1966, 1967, 1968 by Darton, Longman & Todd, Ltd., and Doubleday & Co., Inc. Used by permission of the publishers.

Scripture quotations marked PHILLIPS are from *The New Testament in Modern English,* revised edition, translated by J. B. Phillips. © J. B. Phillips 1958, 1960, 1972. Used by permission of Macmillan Publishing Co.

Scripture quotations from translations found in the Anchor Bible Commentary series are copyright © 1965, 1987 by Doubleday, a division of Bantam Doubleday Dell Publishing Group.

Material on page 17 is reprinted in altered form from "Preparing to Preach," in *Hallelujah!* No. 6, a publication of the Section on Worship of the General Board of Discipleship of The United Methodist Church, by permission of the General Board of Discipleship of the United Methodist Church.

Book design by Gene Harris

First edition

Published by Westminster/John Knox Press
Louisville, Kentucky

PRINTED IN THE UNITED STATES OF AMERICA

9 8 7 6 5 4 3 2 1

Library of Congress Cataloging-in-Publication Data

Preaching the lectionary : a workbook for year C / Perry H. Biddle,
   Jr., editor.
        p.   cm.
   Includes bibliographical references.
   ISBN 0-664-25160-9

   1. Preaching.   2. Bible—Homiletical use.   3. Common lectionary.
4. Lectionaries.   I. Biddle, Perry H., 1932–   .
BV4211.2.P7375   1991
251'.0076—dc20   91-276

DEDICATED TO

JOHN R. KILLINGER, JR.

FAITHFUL FRIEND

INSPIRING TEACHER

MENTOR IN WRITING

Contents

Preface

I have been very gratified by the generally positive reception of my two earlier workbooks in this series for Years A and B. While recovering from a serious auto accident on August 24, 1989, I proposed to the editors of Westminster/John Knox Press that since I would be unable to write the workbook for Year C alone, we invite four gifted and experienced writers to write a quarter's materials each for this workbook. I discussed this plan with my friend and colleague Bill Tuck when he gave me pastoral care in the hospitals in Louisville, Kentucky. He was supportive of the concept of an edited workbook, and I was very pleased when he accepted the invitation of the publisher to be one of the writers.

I am especially pleased that this workbook offers the broad perspective of four writers: two men, two women, two Presbyterian (U.S.A.) ministers, one United Methodist minister, and one Southern Baptist minister. Each one has a unique perspective on the lectionary texts and on preaching. One writer teaches preaching and another has taught preaching before going on to the pastorate. One writer directs the continuing education program of a seminary, and the fourth writer is a former editor and writer of curriculum materials.

Dr. Barbara Bate is the writer for the Advent/Christmas/Epiphany season. She teaches preaching at Drew University. A former professor of rhetoric and communication in Illinois, she entered the seminary world as a student at the age of forty. She became a seminary faculty member in preaching in 1987. In addition to Drew University Theological School, she has taught at Princeton Theological Seminary and in the Doctor of Ministry Program in Preaching at the Chicago Cluster of Theological Schools. She has won awards for preaching, for teaching, and for public speaking. She has completed two books, *Communication and the Sexes* and *Women Communicating,* and she continues to write on the topics of preaching, communication, and gender. She is an active lay member of the United Methodist Church, a frequent guest preacher, a keyboard musician, and the mother of an elementary school daughter.

Dr. William Tuck, who is from the free church tradition and appreciates the lectionary, is pastor of St. Matthew's Baptist Church in Louisville, Kentucky. He has written for the Lent/Easter/Pentecost cycle. Dr. Tuck, a native of Virginia, has pastored churches in Virginia and Louisiana and has served as Professor of Christian Preaching at Southern Baptist Theological Seminary for five years, where he continues to serve as an adjunct professor. An author of five books, his latest is *The Way for All Seasons.* He has edited several books, including *Ministry: An Ecumenical Challenge,* contributed to numerous collections, and written articles for many journals. He is a member of the Academy of Homiletics, the Academy of Parish Clergy, and serves as Book Review Editor for their journal. He received the Man and Boy Award from the Bristol Boys Club, the Doctor of Divinity degree from the University of Richmond and was made a Walter Pope Binns Fellow by William Jewell College. He gave the 1990 lectures on preaching at Wake Forest University. Dr. Tuck is married and the father of two grown children.

Rev. Sara Covin Juengst is Director of Continuing Education at Columbia Theological Seminary. She has written for Trinity Sunday through Pentecost 14. While in seminary, she was awarded the Presbytery of St. Andrews preaching award for the best sermon of the academic year. She has served the church as a campus minister, Christian educator, missionary in Zaire, and as staff associate for the Presbyterian Church (U.S.A.) in international mission. She is the author of a children's book, *Silver Ships, Green Fields,* and numerous curriculum pieces for the Presbyterian Church (U.S.A.). She has traveled widely and has led study tours to France, Switzerland, the U.S.S.R., China, England, Scotland, Jamaica, Costa Rica, and Haiti.

Dr. John C. Purdy, a former Presbyterian pastor and editor of Presbyterian church school resources, has written for Pentecost 15 through Christ the King. His interest in the

10 lectionary stems from both occupations. As a preacher, he dealt with the weekly task of selecting and interpreting appropriate passages of scripture. As an editor, he was responsible for the development of a series of educational resources that were lectionary related. He is the author of two books *Parables at Work* and *Returning God's Call.*

I am especially grateful to Harold Twiss, editorial consultant for Westminster/John Knox Press who has edited all three volumes in this series of workbooks. He has been very cooperative and supportive all through the three-year project, as well as being a demanding and precise editor.

I hope that you, the working pastor, will find this workbook a useful tool as you prepare to preach each week—bringing a fresh word from God to God's people. Preaching is indeed "truth through personality" and I hope this workbook will enable you to discover God's truth for your congregation so that through the medium of your personality, you may proclaim that truth with *boldness, joy, and love.*

September 14, 1990
Old Hickory, Tennessee

P. H. B., Jr.

Introduction

This workbook is designed by a working pastor for use by working pastors in preparing to preach one or more times each week. While many of us hesitate to write in our books, this one invites you to write in its margins and underline passages as you use it week by week. Take a few minutes to become familiar with its design and intended purpose. Too often we attempt futilely to use a new gadget and *then* turn to the instructions to find out why it doesn't work! By purchasing this book you have made a commitment to improve your preaching skills. Find out what it has to offer before digging in to develop a sermon for a particular Sunday.

Weekly Materials

Step 1. The scripture for each Sunday is listed at the beginning of the material for each week, including a psalm appropriate for singing or reading or for use as a responsive reading. (No commentary is offered on the psalms, however.) Many readings are prescribed by the Consultation on Common Texts, an ecumenical body. When there are no variations from this reading, no symbol is placed after it. However, when there are variations,

(C) indicates the Common Lectionary reading,
(L) indicates the Lutheran reading,
(RC) indicates the Roman Catholic reading, and
(E) indicates the Episcopal reading.

Often the only difference is the length of the reading or the omission of verses. The commentary always deals with the longer passage; you, as the preacher, have the option of selecting the shorter pericope if this is preferable. Be sure to read the passages preceding and following the pericope in order to see it in its context. There may be times when you will want to read in the service *more* than the lectionary calls for, in order to give the full sense of a pas-

sage. You should be aggressive in asking why the shapers of the lectionary omitted certain verses, particularly those dealing with judgment and eternal punishment. By doing this, you will help preserve the meaning of the passage as we have received it.

Step 2. The **Meditation on the Texts** is designed to help you "pray through the scriptures" in preparation for reading the commentary. Listen for God's word as you meditate on the scripture. In addition to reading the meditation, it is helpful to read the lectionary selections and pray for God's wisdom and guidance in handling the texts and preparing to preach.

Step 3. Now make a copy of the **Preparing to Preach Worksheet** found at the end of this section and fill it out, following the suggestions that immediately precede it. This should be done *before* going to commentaries, because the commentaries may answer questions you have not asked or may blur your vision of a question that should be asked. By first working through the worksheet you will gain critically important insights into what to look for in your commentary work and related study. This exercise will help you examine three vital aspects of the preaching task: (1) the world of the living word; (2) the world of you, the preacher, and (3) the world of the community.

Step 4. Next, turn to the **Commentary on the Texts** in the workbook and, after reading it over, consult two or more commentaries; several are suggested under Preaching Resources for Year C. While studying other commentaries, you may want to make notes in the margins of this workbook. Among other tools, you will need Bible wordbooks, a Bible dictionary, a concordance, the original Hebrew or Greek texts if you are able to work in them, and an atlas of the Bible lands. Write notes gleaned from this study in your workbook or on a separate pad as your sermon preparation moves forward. Doing this study early in the week—Monday or Tuesday—will give you adequate time to reflect on the texts during the week and to let your subconscious mind ruminate on the meaning of the passage and its application for the congregation. Artists are very much aware of the need for time in which to let the creative process take place before painting a scene, composing a poem, or writing a chapter of a novel. Preachers, who rely on the guidance of the Holy Spirit in sermon preparation, should also allow time for the Spirit to work in the creative process.

Read the commentary for all the texts for a particular Sunday even though you select only one for the basis of the sermon. When a text has been used on another Sunday as well, you will find cross references to that treatment. Note the boldface type identifying suggestions for **additional study** and **the sermon.** Also, read the section entitled **Theological Reflection,** which gives a brief summary of each passage and seeks to relate common themes.

Step 5. The **Children's Message** is usually based on one of the passages from the lectionary. In most cases, you will need to flesh out the suggestions for the talk. They are not object lessons, nor do they seek to draw a moral from the text. Rather, the message seeks to enable the children to think with the preacher about some aspect of church life or life in general in the light of scripture teaching. The relationship developed between preacher and children is a very important aspect of the message.

Step 6. The hymns suggested for each Sunday are related to one or more of the lectionary texts. In many cases, the writers have suggested some contemporary hymns in addition to the more traditional hymns. Full publication information about the books containing the newer hymns will be found in the Preaching Resources for Year C. Read or sing the hymns as another way of reflecting on the themes of the lectionary selections. Many hymnals have a listing of hymns according to the scripture passages on which they are based. This is an additional resource for shaping the worship in following the theme of the sermon. The *Handbook of the Christian Year,* edited by Hoyt L. Hickman and others, is useful in planning worship throughout the Christian year.

Other Materials

In addition to the materials for each week, this workbook includes an **Overview of the Gospel of Luke.** After reading this section, you will benefit from reading one or more similar introductions to Luke in order to get a better grasp of this Gospel's structure and themes and the audience for whom it was written. We need to remember that the Gospels were written to be *heard;* someone would read them aloud in a worship service or group study of scripture because few people could read and write.

A bibliographic listing of additional commentaries and other resources appears in the section titled **Preaching Resources for Year C.**

Celebrating the Christian Year introduces the two centers of the Christian year: Advent/Christmas/Epiphany and Lent/Easter/Pentecost. These two centers developed independently in the history of the church in different times and places. A valuable tool to use in preparation for following the lectionary is the *Handbook for the Common Lectionary,* edited by Peter C. Bower. It describes the two basic patterns for text selection for lectionaries, explains the advantages and disadvantages of using a lectionary, gives brief summaries of the texts for each Sunday, and suggests hymns, anthems, and musical settings for the psalms.

Shaping a More Creative Message

One church that used a computer for designing each Sunday's worship bulletin habitually put instructions for worshipers down the left-hand side, indicating when to "stand," "sit," or "kneel." One day an unauthorized person got into the computer memory and put an additional cue to the congregation just to the left of the sermon: "Sleep!"

One of the chief criticisms from sermon listeners is that sermons are boring, more likely to induce sleep than to make one sit up and take notice. One reason for this is that sermons are often predictable. The sermon with three points and a poem (which was a standard homiletical product in the past) usually engaged the congregation in a rational argument. The scripture text was reduced to a proposition, which was developed into a neat three-point message, each point leading logically to the next. The sermon ended with a conclusion and often a poem or a hymn stanza on the theme.

This stock homiletic developed during the eighteenth and nineteenth centuries at the same time that the scientific method was further developed, and it is no accident that a rationalistic, objective approach to preaching resulted. A topic was isolated for study, all too often on Saturday night. A general deduction followed by a descriptive statement and some illustrations was shaped into a sermon. One professor I had in seminary confessed that when he was preaching during the 1920s he would have given $5 on many a Saturday night for a good illustration. The preacher might also exercise some sanctified imagination in altering the rational points of the sermon. Thus a romantic notion of inspiration was wedded to a rational methodology, the homiletic still found in most books on preaching.

However, a fresh new approach has appeared in the homiletical world in recent years. David Buttrick has stated the case for this new approach better than anyone else in *Homiletic.* This book on how language forms in human consciousness, and what this has to say about the way in which sermons are shaped, is extremely valuable.

Buttrick asks four things of the scripture passage. What is its form? What is the plot, structure, or shape of the passage? What is the field of concern? What is its logic of movement? The passage is viewed as a moving picture rather than a proposition containing religious truth according to the rationalistic approach. The preacher asks: What is the world this scripture addresses and what is the passage trying to do?

This dynamic approach to scripture and preaching sees sermons as plotted sequences of language units. However, the "movements" of the sermon need not follow the sequence of moves found in a biblical passage. Nor is the sermon bound by the biblical form. Buttrick says the preacher should be a combination of poet, exegete, and theologian.

Images are critical in this method of preaching, images that not only form in the consciousness but motivate the hearer to do something. The human psyche is ever in flux, made up of a movement of images of many kinds, both visual and nonvisual. Our goals as persons come out of this flow of moving imagery. We cannot underestimate the power of images in shaping our values,

hopes, and future. The prophets describe the new age which God is bringing about. God is a God of the future who is drawing us forward through images of the new Eden when the kingdom is consummated.

People enjoy hearing and telling stories because of the power the stories have to form memorable images. The point of view of the sermon, as in fiction, is very important. For this reason you should be cautious about using the pronoun "I" in the sermon, since this causes a shift in the point of view from third person to first.

At the end of each commentary on a lectionary passage there are a few sentences suggesting possible moves the sermon may take that are influenced by the scripture. Only the preacher who knows the congregation, the scripture passage, and himself or herself can properly develop a sermon for a congregation. However, the suggested moves may serve as a foil, against which you will react as you wrestle with the text, or as a catalyst to help bring a sermon into being. This paragraph at the end might be compared to a jump start for a car. It is intended to get you going so you can develop the sermon on your own.

One of the many advantages of following the lectionary in preaching is that it enables you to plan ahead. Many preachers find that keeping a file for each Sunday with text and theme for six weeks in advance allows them to collect images, illustrations, and ideas for the sermon. This also allows for advance planning with the church musician(s) and the worship committee. This file would include illustrations the minister has gathered from conversations and observation of life. Other illustrations may be gathered from reading novels and short stories, attending plays, and watching movies and selected television programs that give insights into the contemporary mind and values. You may want to make up illustrations as Jesus made up parables, indicating in some way to the congregation that these are not factual stories. Keeping a notebook for each year with observations, stories, and images can be a valuable resource for more creative preaching. You may use only 40 percent of the material, but what is used will be fresher and more interesting than canned illustrations from sermon illustration books.

A sense of humor is important in creative preaching. The most effective humor often comes spontaneously from a playful mind-set. Playing around in the mind with an idea or image can enable you to come up with a fresh view of a problem or issue or of the way the Gospel speaks to you. This playfulness should also be combined with the focus of one's thinking, relating images and illustrations to a particular theme or thrust of the sermon. Sermons must be dynamic and moving if they are to move the hearers. Humor can crack a door in a closed mind and enable a fresh point of view to enter. Humor, of course, should be used sparingly and for a purpose; it should not simply be humor for humor's sake. That preacher demeans the pulpit who tries to compete with stand-up comedians or late-night television show hosts in making people laugh. Jokes do not work in sermons, because jokes are not open-ended, to hook on to what follows, but are a closed system with a beginning, a middle, and an end.

Creative preaching depends ultimately upon our listening to God speaking in and through scripture to us as preachers who interpret the message for our hearers. This calls for an openness to God in prayer, meditation on scripture, and seeing where and how God is working in human events today as well as in past history. Preachers would do well to look for places where God is working and call God's people to join in working for justice, peace, and love. In an interview with Bishop Desmond Tutu in South Africa a few years ago we prayed for "the hot spots of the world." We should pray for these hot spots. Creative preaching calls for helping people to see the world through the eyes of faith and become engaged in the work of the kingdom here and now.

The lectionary should be used as a tool for preaching rather than as a legalistic system to which the preacher must adhere. For example, during the nonfestival season, from Pentecost to the end of the church year, the preacher may choose to develop a series of sermons on the Lord's Prayer, on the Apostles' Creed, on the Ten Commandments, or on a book or section of the Bible. This is another way of becoming more creative in preaching. A series should run from two to seven sermons. Or after preaching through the Gospel lessons one year during the nonfestival season, the preacher may preach next on the epistle lessons and on the third cycle of Year C preach from the Old Testament lessons. The lectionary was created by a particular group of Christians, and thus it reflects their own view of scripture and Christian thought. The preacher should be aware of this limitation and seek to supplement the lectionary by preaching on the minor prophets, Esther, and other passages that the lectionary passes over or treats only briefly. The lament and complaint psalms should also be included.

The greatest challenge for the preacher is to do justice to the biblical material in applying it to current concerns of the congregation. Only you, the preacher in your particular congregation, know the *Sitz im Leben,* the place in life, and can shape the sermon so that it is a faithful proclamation of God's word to your hearers. The workbook's philosophy of seeing the scriptures and sermon as dynamic, moving process rather than as static, propositional truth can enable you to keep the sermon crackling with excitement from beginning to end.

Seek to engage your hearers in asking, What is the message of this scripture for our lives as a congregation and for my life in particular? This is the thrust of the parables Jesus told. The listener was caught up in a simple story that had a hook and offered a challenge to make a decision for or against the kingdom of God. The parable of the waiting father (prodigal son) is a prime example of what faithful preaching should do. The parable concludes without telling us whether or not the elder brother repented and went in to the feast that had been prepared for the prodigal son. Each hearer must respond to the challenge: Will I repent and enter God's kingdom and fellowship with brothers and sisters at God's banquet of love? Another aspect of being creative in preaching is responding to events in the congregation, the community, and the world through an "occasional sermon." This may call for breaking with the lectionary for one or more Sundays. However, if the sermon is based on a Gospel text, you might continue the regular lectionary readings for the epistle and the Old Testament, explaining what is being done. This might be the case on a special Sunday like Mother's Day or in response to a community crisis or other event. While the lectionary is a very helpful guide for preaching through the scriptures, it should not become an obstacle to following the leading of the Holy Spirit in preaching for special occasions.

While some people seem to be inspired

most by deadlines and by the necessity of producing a sermon, a piece of art, or a novel, many people find this kind of pressure counterproductive. They become too anxious and cannot do their best. Starting early in the week to study for the sermon, and allowing the sermon idea to roll around in the mind while they attend to other pastoral work, frees them to be their most creative. Each preacher must work out her or his own system for sermon preparation. But whatever the process, it should enable you to find satisfaction, a sense of affirmation in obeying God's call to preach, and even occasional joy in the task! We do best those things which we like to do and which reinforce us in what we are doing. The preacher who dreads the task of preaching after doing it for a few years should probably consider another expression of ministry. Few preachers earn much money, but they have the privilege, as one professor of preaching put it, of ''rolling in the scriptures'' each week, a privilege allowed few other Christians by time or energy.

Moving from Text to Sermon

The following suggestions for shaping the sermon in the light of the world of scripture, the world of the preacher, and the world of the community are adapted from *Hallelujah!* No. 6 (1988), in an article by Rev. Michael Williams and Rev. Andy Langford of the Section on Worship of the General Board of Discipleship of the United Methodist Church. Use the worksheet at the end of this introduction to answer these questions. (Permission is granted to copy this material, in whole or in part, from *Hallelujah!*)

The World of the Living Word (Scripture)

After you select the text for the sermon, read it aloud with passion, as if reading to the congregation who will hear it later. Then answer the following questions on a copy of the form that follows this section.

1. Where is the event taking place and what is the setting in which the scripture arose?
2. When did the scripture occur, the time and occasion?
3. Who are the characters in the text? What people (and other parts of creation) are present, both seen and unseen?
4. What objects are present? Examine the narrative and list both seen and unseen things found in it.
5. What is the sequence of scenes or themes? In what order do the events or ideas occur?
6. What strikes you as strange or unexpected in the passage?
7. What words appear to be most important? Are any unusual verbs, nouns, or catch phrases used?
8. Why was this passage written? What caused the writing, and why did the community of faith preserve it?
9. Do you find an invitation in the scripture? Is it explicit or implicit to the audience?

The World of the Preacher

Again, read the scripture aloud using the voices of the different characters in the text. Ask yourself the following questions and note them on the form that follows.

1. With which characters do I identify most closely? With which am I most comfortable? With which am I most uncomfortable?
2. When have I experienced this scripture, if ever? Do I have life experiences that parallel this text?
3. What is my reaction to the text? What feelings and thoughts are produced by the situation related in the text?
4. What is God inviting me to be or to do through this text? How do I hear God's call to me through it?

The World of the Community

Listen to the scripture as a member of your congregation would and then answer the following questions, seeking to relate your community to the scripture. Try to include the whole of the church universal in your community.

1. When have individuals in my community experienced an event similar to this text? Are there persons in my community who have lived or now live this story?
2. When does or did my community as a corporate body experience a similar event?
3. When does or did my community ex-

16

perience this scripture through its shared oral tradition? In my community are there stories that are parallel to this text?

4. When does or did my community experience this event through its culture? Are there media (books, TV, movies) that are familiar to my community which parallel this scripture?
5. What is or was my community's reaction to this event and how do or did people respond?
6. How does God invite my community through this text, and what grace does God offer my community through it?

Review the answers you gave to the foregoing questions. Then ask yourself: What more do I need to know about the scriptures? What perceptions do I need to evaluate? What more do I need to know about myself and what perceptions do I need to evaluate? What more do I need to know about my community and what perceptions of it do I need to evaluate? Seek answers and write them on your worksheet.

Having followed this process, next select the sermon focus. It may be the basic image, thrust, theme, statement, or impact that guides the sermon and will direct the service. State this focus in a short declarative sentence. If you do this several weeks in advance you will then be able to collect ideas and illustrations for the sermon and place them in a folder. (A period of eight weeks in advance is advocated by Williams and Langford.) Then select other aspects of the worship and persons to participate in it. Select visuals.

Additional guidance for preaching may be found in *Preaching Pilgrims,* by Michael E. Williams. This is a self-study book for preachers using a variety of approaches to preaching.

The preacher following the lectionary might use the foregoing process and share insights with a lectionary preaching group that meets weekly to share insights and illustrations on the text. For guidance in working in a lectionary preaching group, see *Preaching Peers,* by Michael E. Williams. Many ecumenical lectionary preaching groups of two to seven preachers are finding this a stimulating method of sermon preparation.

Preparing to Preach Worksheet

It is suggested that you make several copies of this form at one time, using one for each sermon.

Date: _____ Day of the Christian Year: _____

Scripture: _____

World of the Living Word

Where:

When:

Characters:

Objects:

Sequence:

The Unexpected:

Words:

Why:

Invitation:

World of the Preacher

Characters:

Experiences:

Reactions:

Invitation:

World of the Community

Personal Experiences:

Community Experiences:

Oral Traditions:

Culture:

Reactions:

Invitation:

Sermon Focus

Overview of the Gospel of Luke

The preacher is urged to read through the Gospel of Luke using this brief introduction as a guide to better understanding the Gospel and its message for today. It would also be helpful to read commentaries listed in Preaching Resources for Year C, especially those by Caird, Craddock, Ellis, and Fitzmyer.

Author

Scholars generally agree that Luke the physician who accompanied Paul (Col. 4:14; 2 Tim. 4:11; Philemon 24) is the author of the Gospel of Luke. While some recent scholars have questioned Luke's authorship, this writer accepts Luke's authorship of both the Gospel and Acts, which is the sequel to it. Luke was writing against the heretics of his day who challenged the orthodox faith but did not know who wrote their ''gospels.'' Irenaeus, who became bishop of Lyon about 178 C.E. asserted that Luke the companion of Paul was the author of the Gospel of Luke. The use of medical language and concern for illness and cures points to the author's being a physician. However, other writers who were not physicians used medical terms.

Date

While the date of the writing of Luke is not easy to determine, it seems safe to put it sometime in the last third of the first century. Most scholars today date it either 60–65 C.E. or 70–90 C.E. Some even narrow the date to 80 C.E. However, since Luke-Acts does not mention the destruction of Jerusalem which took place in 70 C.E., it seems an earlier date than 70 C.E. is more probable.

Place of Writing

We cannot be certain of the place where Luke was written, but one external source says it was inspired by the Holy Spirit and was written for the most part in the region of Achaia. It was intended for general circulation among Gentiles.

Outline of Luke

A brief outline of the Gospel of Luke is as follows:

1. Preface (1:1–4)
2. Prophecies of future greatness (1:5–4:14)
3. Jesus is anointed with the Holy Spirit (4:16–9:50)
4. Guidance on the journey (9:51–19:44)
5. Jesus' death and vindication (19:45–24:53)

An alternate outline is as follows:

1. Preface (1:1–4)
2. Birth and infancy stories of John the Baptist and Jesus (1:5–2:52)
3. Ministry in Galilee (3:1–9:50)
4. Jesus' journey toward Jerusalem which goes through Samaria (9:51–19:48)
5. Ministry in Jerusalem (chs. 20–21)
6. Account of Jesus' passion and resurrection (chs. 22–24)

We should remember that the Greek manuscript of Luke was not punctuated or divided into paragraphs or divisions. Thus outlines are imposed on the Gospel, opening the way for many variations.

Luke, in writing his Gospel, has included, excluded, and ordered the material he used in accordance with his overall goals. Luke writes a continuation of the acts of God recorded in the Hebrew Scriptures, and continues this theme in his Book of Acts.

Some scholars suggest that the structure of the Gospel is itself symbolic, and it may have liturgical meaning. For example, note the "eighth day" motif found in the eight meal scenes and elsewhere.

We should note that Luke, following the tradition of the writers of the Old Testament, can and does move his materials around without regard for their chronological sequence. He also alters the geographical setting of several episodes. Examples of such altering are found in the temptations, the healing at Jericho, and the prophecy of Peter's denial.

As you read the Gospel be conscious of the way in which Luke subordinated chronological and geographical matters to the theological and literary motifs of his Gospel.

Some Emphases and Themes for Sermons on Luke

A number of special emphases in Luke's Gospel speak to contemporary concerns and needs. The following are among those to which the preacher will want to be alert in studying the Gospel:

The interest in *stories about women* should be particularly noted by the preacher in the light of the current women's movement with its concern for justice and equality. Note especially the portrait Luke gives of the Virgin, Elizabeth, Anna, the widow of Nain, the repentant prostitute, and the women from Galilee who minister to Jesus and the disciples. Recall also Mary and Martha and the women mentioned in the parables of the lost coin and unjust judge. Reflect on the fact that the same interest is also shown in the Acts in the accounts of Tabitha, Priscilla, Lydia, and Philip's four daughters. Women lamented Jesus' death and told the apostles of the empty tomb. In reading Luke-Acts, we see a continuing interest of Luke in the role of women in the early church—a role that carries over from the relationship women had with Jesus.

The theme of *universalism* runs throughout the Gospel. Look for it especially in Jesus' sermon at Nazareth, the references to the widow of Zarephath, and the story of Naaman, the Syrian leper. The universalistic thrust is pointed up by Luke's tracing Jesus' genealogy back to Adam, the father of the human race. Note also accounts of commending despised people such as the Samaritans, and promises that the Gentiles will have an opportunity to accept the gospel. The new place of importance women have among Jesus' followers also underlines the universal thrust of Luke's Gospel.

Luke's Gospel shows a special concern for *social relationships.* This is found especially in the Beatitudes which are addressed to the poor, and the woes directed to the rich. Note also the illustrations from finance—particularly in the parables such as the rich fool, the two debtors, the tower builder, the pounds, and the rich man and Lazarus. There is a concern for the right use of wealth in the Gospel in social relationships. This speaks to the American culture today with its growing number of homeless people and the growing gap between the rich and the poor. Recall Jesus' birth in a humble setting to poor parents and his saying he came to preach "good news to the poor" (4:18). Note also the mention of almsgiving and frequent references to lodging and entertainment.

Luke's Gospel also reveals Jesus' *deep concern for outcasts* and *sinners.* There seems to be a paradoxical love for sinners coupled with a confident hope of their forgiveness and amendment.

Another theme the preacher should note is the emphasis on *the Holy Spirit, prayer, and joy.* The angels announce to the shepherds at Jesus' birth "good news of a great joy which will come to all the people" (2:10). Luke has seventeen references to the Holy Spirit in his Gospel and fifty-seven in the Book of Acts. Compare this with six references to the Spirit in Mark and twelve in Matthew. Note especially the work of the Spirit in the introductory chapter of Luke. Jesus promises the gift of the Spirit to the disciples (24:49). This focus on the Spirit carries over into Acts. Luke also stresses the role of prayer in Jesus' life and in the life of the early church. Notice how Jesus prayed at critical points in his life and ministry, and his last words from the cross were a prayer. Jesus' teaching on prayer is found in many of the parables such as the Pharisee and the tax collector, the unjust judge, and the importunate friend.

Luke shows a special interest in the *resurrection appearance* of Jesus, both in the Gospel and in Acts. He tells of Jesus' appearance on the road to Emmaus, and to the disciples in Jerusalem.

Luke's Gospel stresses both the *graciousness* and the *severity* of the demands of Jesus. Recall that at Nazareth all spoke well of Jesus and wondered at his gracious words. He shows tenderness and compassion toward repentant sinners, but Jesus also demands undivided loyalty to himself. He also calls for complete renunciation as indicated in the parable of the rash king (14:33). Note also the saying on salt (14:34–35) which is a more absolute and searching one than the sayings in Mark and Matthew.

Luke stresses Jesus as both the *Christ* (Messiah) and *Lord*. Luke uses the title "the Lord" at least eighteen times, and in Acts it is used in various combinations some fifty times. While Luke recognizes the Sonship of Jesus, he does not stress it as do Paul and John.

A final theme to be noted is Luke's emphasis on the *Passion*. Luke's Gospel resembles Mark in this respect, but shows a greater interest in its tragic aspects. Jesus is portrayed by Luke as the divine Son and Lord who in obedience to God whom he called Father fulfills a ministry of grace which reaches its peak in the sufferings, death, and resurrection. The preacher will want to be especially aware of this emphasis in preaching from Luke's Gospel.

The preacher will note other themes in Luke's Gospel, but the above emphases should be particularly noted as he or she preaches from this Gospel during Year C.

Preaching Resources for Year C

(* = highly recommended)

Commentaries on the Gospel of Luke

*Caird, G. B. *The Gospel of St. Luke.* Pelican New Testament Commentaries. Baltimore: Penguin Books, 1963.

*Craddock, Fred B. *Luke.* Interpretation series. Louisville, Ky.: Westminster/John Knox Press, 1990.

*Ellis, E. Earle. *The Gospel of Luke.* New Century Bible Commentary. Grand Rapids: Wm. B. Eerdmans Publishing Co., 1967.

*Fitzmyer, Joseph A., ed. and tr. *The Gospel According to Luke* I–IX and X–XXIV. Anchor Bible, vols. 28 and 28A. Garden City, N.Y.: Doubleday & Co., 1981; 1985.

The Interpreter's Bible. Vol. 8. George A. Buttrick and others, eds. Nashville: Abingdon Press, 1952.

Kee, Howard Clark, and others. *The Gospels. Interpreter's Concise Commentary.* Vol. 6. Nashville: Abingdon Press, 1983.

Additional Commentaries and Resources for Bible Study

Achtemeier, Elizabeth. *Preaching from the Old Testament.* Louisville, Ky.: Westminster/John Knox Press, 1989.

Barrett, Charles V. *The First Epistle to the Corinthians.* Harper New Testament Commentary. San Francisco: Harper & Row, 1968.

———. *The Second Epistle to the Corinthians.* Harper New Testament Commentary. San Francisco: Harper & Row, 1974.

*Brown, Raymond E. *The Gospel According to John.* Anchor Bible. 2 vols. Garden City, N.Y.: Doubleday & Co., 1966, 1970.

Cox, James W., ed. *Biblical Preaching: An Expositor's Treasury.* Philadelphia: Westminster Press, 1983.

Craddock, Fred B., John Hayes, and Carl Holladay. *Preaching the New Common Lectionary,* Year C. 3 vols. Nashville: Abingdon Press, 1984, 1987, 1988.

*Crenshaw, James L. *Story and Faith: A Guide to the Old Testament.* New York: Macmillan Publishing Co., 1986.

Fuller, Reginald H. *Preaching the Lectionary: The Word of God for the Church Today.* Rev. ed. Includes cycles A, B, C. Collegeville, Minn.: Liturgical Press, 1984.

The Interpreter's Bible: The Holy Scriptures in the King James and Revised Standard Versions. George A. Buttrick, commentary editor, and others. 12 vols. Nashville: Abingdon Press, 1951–1957. Pertinent volumes.

*Jeremias, Joachim. *New Testament Theology.* New York: Charles Scribner's Sons, 1971.

Laymon, Charles M., ed. *Interpreter's Concise Commentary.* 8 vols. Nashville: Abingdon Press, 1971–. Pertinent volumes.

McCurley, Foster R. *Proclaiming the Promise.* Philadelphia: Fortress Press, 1974.

Old Testament Library. Philadelphia: Westminster Press, 1961–. Pertinent volumes.

Plaut, W. G. *The Torah: A Modern Commentary.* New York: Union of American Hebrew Congregations, 1981.

Proclamation 3, Series C. Philadelphia: Fortress Press, 1984.

One-Volume Commentaries

*Black, Matthew, and H. H. Rowley, eds. *Peake's Commentary on the Bible.* New York: Thomas Nelson & Sons, 1962.

*Brown, Raymond E., and others, eds. *The Jerome Biblical Commentary.* Rev. ed. Englewood Cliffs, N.J.: Prentice-Hall, 1986.

Allen, Horace T., Jr. *A Handbook for the Lectionary.* Philadelphia: Geneva Press, 1980.
*Bower, Peter C. *Handbook for the Common Lectionary.* Philadelphia: Geneva Press, 1987.
Common Lectionary: The Lectionary Proposed by the Consultation on Common Texts. New York: Church Hymnal Corp., 1983.
*Hickman, Hoyt L., and others, eds. *Handbook of the Christian Year.* Nashville: Abingdon Press, 1986.
An Inclusive-Language Lectionary: Readings for Year C. Rev. ed. New York: Pilgrim Press, 1988.
Old, Hughes Oliphant. *Guides to the Reformed Tradition: Worship.* Atlanta: John Knox Press, 1985.

Recommended Translations

The New Oxford Annotated Bible with the Apocrypha, Expanded Edition, Revised Standard Version. Edited by Herbert G. May and Bruce M. Metzger. New York: Oxford University Press, 1977.
New Revised Standard Version Bible. New York: Division of Christian Education of the National Council of the Churches of Christ in the United States of America, 1989.

Other Resources

Burghardt, Walter J. *Preaching: The Art and the Craft.* Mahwah, N.J.: Paulist Press, 1987.
*Buttrick, David G. *Homiletic: Moves and Structures.* Philadelphia: Fortress Press, 1987.
Craddock, Fred B. *As One Without Authority.* 3d ed. Nashville: Abingdon Press, 1979.
*———. *Preaching.* Nashville: Abingdon Press, 1985.
Davis, Henry Grady. *Design for Preaching.* Philadelphia: Muhlenberg Press, 1958.
Efird, James M. *How to Interpret the Bible.* Atlanta: John Knox Press, 1984.
Fant, Clyde E. *Preaching for Today.* San Francisco: Harper & Row, 1977.
Hallelujah! No. 6. Nashville: General Board of Discipleship, United Methodist Church, 1988.
Keck, Leander E. *The Bible in the Pulpit: The Renewal of Biblical Preaching.* Nashville: Abingdon Press, 1978.
McKim, Donald K., ed. *A Guide to Contemporary Hermeneutics: Major Trends in Biblical Interpretation.* Grand Rapids: Wm. B. Eerdmans Publishing Co., 1986.
Smith, D. Moody. *Interpreting the Gospels for Preaching.* Philadelphia: Fortress Press, 1980.
*Williams, Michael E. *Preaching Peers.* Nashville: Discipleship Resources, 1987.
*———. *Preaching Pilgrims.* Nashville: Discipleship Resources, 1988.

Contemporary Hymnals

(Please note that many of the contemporary alternative selections listed in this volume will be found in the new hymnals published by some of the major denominations in recent years.)
Avery, Richard, and Donald Marsh. *Songs and Carols.* Vol. 8. Port Jervis, N.Y.: Proclamation Publications, 1979.
Bock, Fred, ed. *Hymns for the Family of God.* Nashville: Paragon Associates, 1976.
Huber, Jane Parker. *A Singing Faith.* Philadelphia: Westminster Press, 1986.
Hymns for the Living Church. Carol Stream, Ill.: Hope Publishing Co., 1974.
Rejoice in the Lord. Grand Rapids: Wm. B. Eerdmans Publishing Co., 1985.
Songs of Zion. Nashville: Abingdon Press, 1981.
Troeger, Thomas, and Carol Doran. *New Hymns for the Lectionary.* New York: Oxford University Press, 1986.
Wren, Brian. *Praising a Mystery.* Carol Stream, Ill.: Hope Publishing Co., 1986.
Young, Carlton R., ed. *Choirbook for Saints and Singers.* Carol Stream, Ill.: Hope Publishing Co., Agape.

Celebrating the Christian Year

Almost all Christians follow the Christian year to some extent. Some observe only Christmas and Easter; others follow the church calendar from the first Sunday of Advent all the way through the year to Christ the King Sunday. The growing use of the Christian year in planning worship and preaching is a result of the modern liturgical movement, which continues to influence both Protestant and Roman Catholic worship.

The lectionaries used in this workbook are based on the Christian calendar, which begins with the first Sunday of Advent, the Sunday nearest to November 30. We may divide the Christian year into two roughly equal parts: the special seasons that celebrate events in sacred history, and what is called ordinary time, the "Sundays of the year." The special or festal seasons begin with the first Sunday of Advent and continue through the feast of Epiphany, they pick up again with Ash Wednesday and go through the Day of Pentecost. The Sundays after Epiphany and after Pentecost are called ordinary time, with the following exceptions. The Sunday after Epiphany is known as the Baptism of Our Lord, and in some churches the last Sunday of that season is known as the Transfiguration of Our Lord, the first Sunday after Pentecost is called Trinity Sunday, and the final Sunday of the church year is called Christ the King.

During much of ordinary time we find readings of scripture in sequence. In Year C, the Gospel of Luke is used in this way. Note that the Gospel of John and other books of the New and Old Testaments are read where they seem most appropriate, and the psalms generally are harmonized with the lessons. However, the Common Lectionary follows a course reading during ordinary time in the Old Testament lessons and so does not usually have a common theme with the Gospel, while the Lutheran readings in the Old Testament are chosen for their relevance to the Gospel reading. The preacher should be aware of the differences in the lectionaries and not try to force the readings for a particular Sunday to harmonize when they do not do so.

The origin of the lectionary seems to go back to a time in Judaism after Jesus' ministry when there were two readings for each Sabbath, one from Torah (the Pentateuch) and one from the Prophets. Some Jewish scholars think this practice existed as early as Jesus' ministry, and Luke may have assumed that Jesus was reading a proscribed reading at Nazareth as recorded in Luke 4:18–19. History does not tell us exactly how or when lectionaries came into use in the Christian church, but some scholars think that Mark, Matthew, and John were shaped on the plan of the Jewish liturgical year and were intended to be read in sequence. The earliest lectionaries in the Western Church date from the fifth century as certain books of the Bible came to be associated with specific seasons of the year. There were gradual changes during the Middle Ages, and various lectionaries emerged, but all of these were similar to one another and were based on a one-year cycle. This eliminated many passages from being read. John Calvin advocated reading a single passage in each service, a custom many Reformed churches follow, while the more radical Protestant churches rejected lectionaries entirely. But following Vatican II and the modern liturgical renewal, many ministers and churches are adopting the practice of following the lectionary for some if not all of the Christian year. The major reason for doing this is to enable the congregation to hear many parts of the Bible read in public in a systematic fashion over the three-year cycle of Years A, B, and C. A church may begin following the lectionary at any time and need not wait until Year A or even until Advent 1 to do so. However, the congregation should be prepared for the use of the lectionary, and appropriate explanations should be given.

The Common Lectionary, noted as (C) in this workbook, was prepared by the North American Committee on Calendar and Lectionary. The Consultation on Common Texts, an association of representatives of most of the major denominations of the United States and Canada, has commended the present Common Lectionary for use until 1992. Some adjustments may be made in readings after that time. Where there are longer and shorter readings in this workbook, the longer one is used, leaving you, the preacher, the option of selecting the reading of your denomination, which may be shorter.

Both the Jewish and Christian lectionaries reveal a tendency common to many religions to have a cycle of annual festivals and fasts. In primitive religions there were myths about the eternal return of the seasons, and one goal of religion was to ensure that this cycle was observed properly. Following the cycle of the Christian year is helpful both psychologically and educationally for preacher and people. But rather than seeing the cycle as a mere repetition of the same texts and celebrations, we should view the cycle each year as a kind of *spiral* moving toward Christ, fostering growth and greater faithfulness in the Christian life. The cycle of the Christian year reminds us that there is an aspect of the Christian faith that stays the same, while the structure of worship and sermon and the church's life is apt to change over the years. One purpose of the lectionary is to help Christians see by faith that in scripture we have one continuous story of God's dealing with the human race which reveals God's nature and purpose. The ultimate purpose of all preaching and worship, of course, is to unite us more fully to God through Christ.

Color alone can often be a most effective symbol for use in the worship setting. We should understand that such visual symbols are more than mere decorations. They serve as visual proclamations of the gospel. The meaning of the colors of the year should be given the worshipers in either written or spoken form. Often a visual image will remain in the worshiper's mind long after spoken words are forgotten. Visual aspects of worship should be chosen with care; they can be an integral part of the service and not just decoration.

While the colors used on specific days and seasons were first formally set forth in 1570 in the reformed missal under Pius V, a few changes have been made in recent times. The colors of the Christian year are as follows (see J. G. Davies, ed., *The Westminster Dictionary of Worship,* p. 140; Philadelphia: Westminster Press, 1972).

Advent to Christmas Eve	Violet/Blue/Black
Christmas to Epiphany	White/Gold
Sundays after Epiphany	Green
Septuagesima to Ash Wednesday	Violet/Blue/Black
Throughout Lent	Veiling of colors
Passion Sunday to Easter Eve	Red/Rose
Easter	White/Gold
Pentecost	Red
Trinity	White/Gold
Sundays after Trinity	Green
Ordinary weekdays	Green
Blessed Virgin Mary	White/Red
Apostles, evangelists, martyrs	Red
Saints (except martyrs)	White/Yellow
Baptism/confirmation	White/Red
Ordination/marriage	White
Funeral	Violet/Blue/Black
Dedication of a church	White

In the Roman Catholic Church the post-Vatican II *Ordo Missae* (1969) in general reaffirmed the current practice:

White for Easter, Christmas, feasts of Christ (other than the Passion), All Saints, feast of Mary, and so forth.

Red for Passion/Palm Sunday, Good Friday, Pentecost, feasts of the Passion of Christ and of martyrs.

Violet for Advent and Lent and possibly for funeral masses in place of black.

Rose for Gaudete Sunday and Laetare Sunday.

Green for other times.

For additional suggestions for use of liturgical colors and visual effects in the Christian year, see Hoyt Hickman and others, *Handbook of the Christian Year,* p. 36. It notes that purples, grays, and blues may be used for seasons of a preparatory and penitential character, while white and gold are used for celebrating joyous seasons and events that have a special christological emphasis.

The Seasons of Advent and Christmas/Epiphany

There is a powerful word in the theology of the seasons of Advent and Christmas/ Epiphany, which are viewed here as a unity. The underlying theology unites the celebration of the expectation and birth of Jesus, and the waiting for his return, with his life, suffering, death, and resurrection. The incarnation and the atonement cannot be separated; they are both aspects of God's saving action in Christ Jesus. The purpose of Jesus' birth was to make God known to all humanity through Jesus' life, death, and resurrection.

The central message of this season is expressed in the words of John's Gospel: "The Word became flesh and dwelt among us" (John 1:14). We learn from church history that the original special day of this season was not Christmas but Epiphany. This was the day for celebrating the manifestation (epiphany) of God's light and power in Christ. Along with Easter and Pentecost, it was the third great celebration of the Christian calendar for the church, beginning around the fifth century. The focus in the earliest lectionaries and sermons for Epiphany was placed on John 1:1–2:11. Among the themes associated with Epiphany were light, Jesus' advent (coming) into the world, his baptism, and the miracle of changing water into wine at Cana. The one theme running like a red thread through all these events was the affirmation that God was in Christ manifesting God to human beings to the end of the world.

Advent

Color: Purple.

The season of Advent begins with the fourth Sunday before Christmas, which is the Sunday nearest November 30, and continues to Christmas Eve. The season combines themes of both threat and promise. Its primary concern is eschatology, or the events of the End, including Christ's return in glory, the last judgment, and the consummation of the kingdom.

Advent looks both backward to Jesus' first coming at Bethlehem and forward to his coming again at the End. Thus we begin the Christian year by reflecting on the End of history. Consider the message of the many Advent hymns that have a note of threat and promise, in contrast to Christmas carols. Their emphasis fits the direction of the readings and sermons of Advent, which deal not so much with preparation for Christmas as with the *expectation* of Christ's return in glory to rule, judge, and save. The prayer of this season is expressed in the phrases of the Lord's Prayer: "Thy kingdom come, thy will be done, on earth." There is a strong prophetic note in this season announcing judgment upon evil, combined with an emphasis on hope and the expectation of Christ's coming reign in glory.

Some leaders of denominational worship programs suggest that Advent hymns may be sung *before* Advent begins, that is, on the Sundays of November when sermons deal with the End time and the coming rule of Christ as King. Then, during the Advent season proper, appropriate Christmas hymns and carols may be interspersed with Advent hymns. Not to sing Christmas hymns during Advent, as liturgical purists insist, is to confine the singing of Christmas carols and hymns to Christmas Eve and Christmas Day only. A compromise might be to sing only Advent hymns on the first Sunday of Advent and then intersperse Christmas hymns with Advent hymns on the other three Sundays.

Christmas

Color: White, yellow, and gold, and combinations of these.

The color of white signifies joy and is used for Christmas Eve and Christmas Day. The Christmas celebration begins on Christmas Eve (which is counted as an integral part of the following day, as Jews do with the Jewish Sabbath). Many congregations celebrate on Christmas Eve with a candlelight Communion service and again with worship and Communion on Christmas Day. Christmas should focus on the incarnation and its meaning. The celebration should not become a sentimental service of child worship but should connect the incarnation with the atonement. The Christ who was born was born to die as our redeemer. Preaching during this season should lift up the joy that Christ brings into our lives by forgiving our sins and giving us eternal life. This joy, a gift of the Holy Spirit, is independent of outward circumstances and passes all understanding. The fulfillment of Old Testament prophecies of Messiah in the birth of Jesus highlights God's continuing plan of salvation.

In the hymn "O Little Town of Bethlehem" the words "Cast out our sin, and enter in, be born in us today" are a prayer for Christmas. The goal of preaching in this season is to enable people to so hear the gracious word of God that they may invite the living Christ to be born anew in their lives.

In the time between Christmas and Epiphany some early churches celebrated the Sacrament of Baptism, with an emphasis second only to that of the Easter Vigil and the Great Fifty Days. In the Roman Catholic tradition, the feasts of martyrs and saints are observed during this time, which reminds us of the connection between Christmas/Epiphany and our dying to sin and being raised to new life in Christ.

Epiphany

Color: White, gold, and yellow for Epiphany Day, the Baptism of Our Lord, and the Transfiguration of Our Lord.
Green is used on other Sundays of Epiphany.

The word "epiphany" comes from a Greek word meaning "manifestation." The thrust of this day and season is the revelation of God in Jesus Christ, the Light of the World. White, which is used during this season, symbolizes joy and celebration. Green, which is also used, symbolizes growth in our knowledge and love of God in Christ. Epiphany Day itself is a celebration of the act of Jesus manifesting God to the world. The Wise Men, who represent the whole human race, come bearing precious gifts, and Jesus manifests God to them. It is a day of splendor and light. Two events also associated with Epiphany are Jesus' baptism and the wedding at Cana.

January 6 was chosen as Epiphany Day because it was the winter solstice in the East and it was on this day that the birth of the sun-god was celebrated. Later, Christians substituted Epiphany for the solstice, and Jesus is sometimes referred to as the Sun of Righteousness, carrying out this symbol of light and the return of more sunlight. No wonder light and its rebirth are ancient themes of Epiphany.

One way to celebrate this season of more light is through a renewed emphasis on evangelism. Christ, the Sun of Righteousness, shines in the darkness of this world's evil to cast it out. Notice that the focus of Transfiguration is on worship as the disciples experienced worship on that occasion.

Two symbols that may be used effectively are the Epiphany star and candle. The star represents the star that guided the Wise Men to the stable and that can guide us to the Christ-child. The candle sends forth light into a world of darkness and gives its light by burning itself up. Thus we find in the burning candle a symbol of Christ himself who "burned himself out" on the cross as the Light of the World.

Notice that the number of weeks in Epiphany depends upon the date of Easter. Thus the length of the season may vary. It may consist of six to nine Sundays, since the former pre-Lenten season of three Sundays was incorporated into Epiphany in the new lectionary.

Advent 1

Psalm 25:1–10 (C)

Jeremiah 33:14–16 (C) (L) (RC)
Zechariah 14:4–9 (E)

1 Thessalonians 3:9–13 (C) (L) (E)
1 Thessalonians 3:12–4:2 (RC)

Luke 21:25–36 (C) (L)
Luke 21:25–31 (E)
Luke 21:25–28, 34–36 (RC)

Meditation on the Texts

Holy One, in this amazing Advent season you lead each of us on a journey—into the known story of Christ's birth, and toward an awareness of the unknown details of your plans for us. We can feel the excitement of the promised coming of Jesus Christ. We can delight in the thought that all flesh shall again have the chance to see the salvation of God. At the same time we may become aware of our fear and trembling in the face of the final promise, for it is a promise to bring the whole world under the holy judgment of God. Looking within ourselves at our personal reactions to this season, we are better able to look to you and to each other with a mature and realistic hope.

While studying and preparing to preach in this season, may I seek to have the confidence of a beleaguered Paul as he writes to his beloved people of Thessalonica. May I be openhearted and bold in the spirit of John the Baptizer, who knew that every mountain, valley, and road on earth would be altered by the presence of the One who came after him. May I be able to respond in a new way to the hearing and the knowing of these complex and wondrous words of your people.

May all of us await your presence with clean, honest, and watchful hearts. Amen.

Commentary on the Texts

Luke 21:25–36 (C) (L)

Luke 21:25–31 (E)

Luke 21:25–28, 34–36 (RC)

The Advent season begins not with a cradle to be filled, but with a cosmos to be set right. Luke the Gospel writer predominates throughout year C of the three-year cycle of readings. Of all the Gospel accounts of Advent, Christmas, and Epiphany, Luke most completely spans the spatial, temporal, and societal range of the Christian message. In the first two chapters of his Gospel he presents an intimate drama of parents, relatives, and newborn. In the readings for Advent 1, taken from a much later part of Luke's Gospel, chapter 21, our attention is hurried from one level of interest to another: from cosmic dislocations to the growing of local trees, and finally to the need for personal discipline and alertness in waiting for the ultimate day of the Lord.

Luke 21 is often called the Olivet Discourse because in Matthew's account Jesus is sitting on the Mount of Olives when he answers the disciples' questions about the future. Luke moves the location of this discussion from the mountain to the temple and widens the audience to an unspecified "some" and "they." Presumably this denotes a wider circle of Jesus' followers listening to his words.

Jesus is called "Teacher," so they begin to ask him to address the central questions of eschatology: "When will this be?" (the destruction of the temple) and "What will be the sign when this is about to take place?" One can imagine the wise young sage sitting among eager listeners, uttering words that describe a future in turmoil. Somehow it is likely that Jesus the teacher also conveyed the confidence that every event would be, as always, in the hands of God. From vs. 13 through 19 there is the affirmation that followers would be instructed and protected in the midst of difficulty. Verses 18 and 19 are explicit: "But not a hair of your head will perish. By your endurance you will gain your lives." This context of reassurance is important to note before reading the nearly twenty lines of prophecy that follow.

By setting forth a dramatic eschatological passage at the start of the church year, the preparers of common texts have given the church no escape route into a cozy, private waiting room near the manger. The prophecy carries with it a mixture of hope, danger, and ambiguity. In the fig tree segment, which is included in all but the Roman Catholic lectionary, the quality of natural process predominates: the growth of trees as the summer approaches is a regular and expected sign of God's kingdom. In the verses immediately preceding vs. 29–31 there is more of a mix of moods: there will be "distress of nations" and the people will be "fainting with fear"; yet believers are encouraged to "look up and raise your heads, because your redemption is drawing near." Notice that Luke omits the phraseology of both Mark and Matthew, who portray Jesus as promising that either the Son of Man or his angels will "gather his elect from the four winds." Luke's cosmic prophet takes a more immediate, even intimate, approach to his listeners, de-emphasizing which people will win and which will lose, and emphasizing instead the necessary personal response: "Look up and raise your heads, for your redemption is near." It is a timely message for Luke's community, but also a timeless message for all believers. Living in the realm of God means living in the presence of hope and redemption, whatever the external circumstances.

Part of the prophecy in Luke 21 has come true. The temple has been destroyed, and Jerusalem has been subjected to a long series of sieges. Part of the prophecy is still awaited. In the Roman Catholic lection the line is omitted which promises that "this generation will not pass away till all has taken place" (v. 32). This omission may allow the leaders of worship in the Roman Catholic Church to avoid the question as to whether Jesus' words should be taken as literally accurate. Verse 33, however, has a wider connotation than v. 32, and it is a potential meaning that can be attested to by any professing Christian in the late twentieth century: "Heaven and earth will pass away, but my words will not pass away." All the Synoptic Gospels include the statement in v. 33.

How are we expected to respond to this Gospel message for Advent 1? Are we to be frightened at the cosmic reversals to come, pleased at the prospect of redemption for believers, apprehensive at standing before the Son of Man, or confused at the mixture of promises and threats in this prophecy? Why are we hearing this eschatological passage at the start of Advent? According to Luke, an attitude of serious attention is the most appropriate response. The future times may well provoke worry, as Luke—alone among all four Gospel writers—indicates. "Watch at all times, praying that you may have strength to escape all these things that will take place, and to stand before the Son of man" (v. 36). The social dimension of Luke's approach probably lies behind v. 36, with its image of destruction of the fainthearted. Luke's Jesus calls for personal courage, not hiding from the evils of the world, at this pivotal time of crisis and opportunity.

The preacher can move in several directions in developing this rich and complex Gospel material. One choice is to develop the psychological dimension of these verses. It is helpful to recognize in preparing to preach the Advent 1 Gospel text that visions of the future carry for most people both promise and threat. Having their ambivalence named and identified as under the watchful eye of a loving creator can reduce some of the guilty stress with which many people move into the Christmas season. Another potential choice for the preacher is to move from the images of destruction to the image of the Second Advent of Christ. This promotes a wider image of the infant birth to come, allowing it to exist as part of a true and yet difficult narrative. A third possibility for the preacher is to focus on the central idea of being watchful. Worshipers can consider what it took for the disciples and other followers to concentrate their attention on Jesus' words. We can all think today about what it takes to keep one's mind and heart on the coming of Jesus to redeem and empower the whole created world, instead of losing our alertness in the face of secular distractions and temptations. In general, the most lively prospects for dealing with the material from Luke 21 will emerge if the preacher is alert to paradox, contradiction, and the unexpected. The future is important in Luke 21 on the cosmic, the sociopolitical, and the psychological levels; enabling people to move imaginatively across those boundaries may give them more of a sense of participation in the Advent narrative on their own terms.

Jeremiah 33:14–16 (C) (L) (RC)

This passage, part of a section that is absent from the Septuagint (Jer. 33:14–26), is closely modeled on an earlier passage from Jeremiah 23. Scholars assume that Jeremiah 23:5–6 were the words of the original prophet Jeremiah. A later disciple reiterated Jeremiah's statement of promise during the long exile, quoting God's promise as a way to reaffirm to the people that the God of their ancestors had not forgotten them: "I will cause a righteous Branch to spring forth for David" (v. 15; cf. 23:5). Hearing the echo of the earlier promise was particularly important to people whose first hopes of returning home had long ago evaporated. Judah and Jerusalem, battered and vulnerable at the time of the writing of Jeremiah 33, are imaged forth as strong, secure, and productive.

This brief passage in Jeremiah presents a clear image of a redeemed future. The promised branch of the house of David is often treated as a prefiguring of Christ. Though the passage in Jeremiah focuses on a specific historical future rather than on the coming of Jesus Christ, it still illustrates the power of prophecy and promise to help people survive times of despair.

The preacher can choose to concentrate on the prefiguring of Christ in this passage, either through the literary connection or the genealogical links between David, Jesse, and Jesus. Another direction may be more productive, however. The conditions of the Hebrew people in exile and the function of a vision of the future in keeping them going can become vivid to worshipers in relation to corporate and individual struggles in their own or others' lives. The absence of hope is strongly correlated with the medical onset of death. On the other hand, having a window into a possible future is one way to breathe and thus survive in the dark.

Zechariah 14:4–9 (E)

The prophet Zechariah offers another image of the cosmic world as linked to the immediate and personal. In this passage God is portrayed initially as a successful warrior, and we are given an image of the deity as standing astride and splitting the Mount of Olives. This earlier style of God-talk in the Hebrew Scriptures depicts an anthropomorphic deity, a giant whose actions bring large-scale changes. Thus the rivers flow separately down each side of the split mountain, and frightened people flee from the quake.

Just after this giant-narrative come statements that evoke the language of Jesus preaching in the Gospels: "living waters shall flow out of Jerusalem," and "there shall be continuous day," "neither cold nor frost," and "on that day the LORD will be one and the LORD's name one" (vs. 6–9 passim). The promise of Jerusalem's redemption is central to Zechariah; so is the promise that the world as a whole will have a new prospect of calm and unity.

Responding to this passage, **the preacher** might do well to look at the contrasting descriptions of deity that it presents. In the Advent season there is typically a concentration on what God has done and will do; it is appropriate at this time to consider at least briefly what is the portrayal of that God who promises and reverses and redeems and judges. The anthropomorphic God fits an old and even primitive theology, one that is still held by a great many believers. The second set of images, of water and oneness and continuous day, carries a more spiritual symbolism. It can be helpful to enable worshipers to reflect on their own images of the deity, as they look toward the birth of the one called the Messiah and the Son of God.

1 Thessalonians 3:12–4:2 (RC)

The primary importance of this passage as an Advent text is that it shows Paul continuing to think and pray about faithful people he could not often visit. He knew them best by the reports of Timothy concerning their well-being. He delighted in the news he received of their faith and love, while expressing a concern that their faith be solidified (v. 10). He prays for the church at Thessalonica in behalf of the Father, Jesus, and "the saints," who represent Paul's synonym for the angels rather than representing the people of the early church. Most important, Paul refers to "the coming of our Lord Jesus," the return of the Christ, an event that was for Paul and many others an imminent prospect.

The fact of the church's existence is important in any season of the church year. It is especially significant now in the Advent and Christmas seasons, when so many Christians think of the private story of Jesus' birth apart from the church's presence and mission in the world.

The preacher can enliven this passage for worshipers by comparing Paul's sentiments toward the Thessalonians with those of spiritual and ecclesiastical leaders who can affirm and encourage people in struggling local churches. Whether the hope of Christ's return is immediate or long-range, the fact of hope and its capacity to bring cooperative action can be emphasized in a community of believers. Also, the preacher can use this passage to illuminate the idea that one can prepare appropriately in the Advent season by acting in love and following the guidance of brothers and sisters in the faith.

Theological Reflection

Starting Advent with a cosmic disruption is simply a way of saying that the coming of Jesus Christ was and is the most world-changing event in history. Luke's entire Gospel begins with the story on a small scale, but he later joins the cosmic and the personal dimensions with confidence and power.

Jeremiah offers a pointed example of the hope for a righteous king to rule over the world, but it is not until Luke that the promise of a king, the demands of human discipleship, and the irreversible alterations of the world as a whole become intertwined. Even with Zechariah, the prophecy has a breathtaking scale. Modern people schooled in science may scoff at some of Zechariah's statements, but their importance goes beyond their technical accuracy.

The birth of Jesus Christ is a cleft in the world's landscape and its history that cannot be undone. The issue for every Christian at Advent is, What am I going to do in response to this news and this promise? What are we as the body of Christ going to do in response? Not to respond at all is tantamount to being unconscious—or spiritually dead.

Personal study in preparation for preaching will be aided by working with the writings of Joseph Fitzmyer: both *The Gospel According to Luke* in the Anchor Bible and *Luke the Theologian* (Mahwah, N.J.: Paulist Press, 1989) are likely to be helpful.

Children's Message

Begin with a question: How can you tell that something is a promise?

Gather in answers: for example, a promise is a serious statement saying that something good for you is going to happen. Give an example from experience, such as, When I was five years old I was told I would have to wear glasses for a long time because of a weak eye muscle. I hated wearing glasses, but the eye doctor promised me that if I wore the glasses every day I would not need them by the time I was going to high school. The promise seemed so far away as to be impossible to keep, or even to remember. But at fourteen years of age I went to the doctor who told me the glasses were no longer needed. Everyone in my family rejoiced.

God makes and keeps promises too. That is a major way we know God. God has made and kept promises, sometimes called covenants, with the people of God for many centuries, since long before the time Christ was alive. Keeping promises is one way that you can tell God loves us. Some of God's promises are talked about in the scriptures for today. Whose birth was promised to the people of God? Yes, Jesus' birth was promised. Was the promise kept? Yes, as you know, the birth of Jesus has already happened, long ago. In the season called Advent—or "the coming"—we especially remember Jesus' birth and we get ready for celebrating it in the church. Other promises from God, such as the promise that the whole world would see Jesus Christ returning someday, are promises we are still waiting to see happen. Christians believe in the truth of God's promises.

What about the promises in your life? What promises are you waiting to see kept right now? (Wait for answers: they may be presents, trips, new privileges with growing up. Use all answers, and repeat them so that adults and children can hear them clearly.) Those are some pretty exciting things to be looking forward to.

Whatever you are waiting for, the Bible makes it clear that God keeps God's promises to human beings. So believing in God's promises makes people happier and more hopeful.

Today, will you remember how wonderful a promise can be, especially a promise from God?

Hymns for Advent 1

God of Our Life, Through All the Circling Years; Send Your Word, O Lord (Imakoma and Hanaoka); O Come, O Come, Emmanuel.

Advent 2

Psalm 126

Baruch 5:1–9 (C) (RC) (E)
Malachi 3:1–4 (alt. C) (L)
Malachi 3:1–11 (E)

Philippians 1:3–11 (C) (L)
Philippians 1:1–11 (E)
Philippians 1:4–6, 8–11 (RC)

Luke 3:1–6

Meditation on the Texts

God of insight and challenge, bring these passages into a clear light, so that they will be understood and used in accordance with your purposes by your church. You have brought intelligence into the lives of your people in many ways: not only through the Gospel writers and the early Hebrew writers but also in the imaginations of the many people who have read these words and interpreted your will for us. You continue to foster our growth in mind and spirit, and to surprise us into new insights about your created world and its possibilities. In particular, you bring new light to this time of waiting and personal preparation for the birth of the Christ-child.

Help me today to hear and identify with John the Baptizer, and to recognize in his desert of aloneness a place for my own reflecting on and preaching your word. Help me to hear the sorrow of those like the widow Jerusalem whose children seem lost to them forever, and help me to speak a word of convincing comfort and hope to all those people who mourn the past and fear the future. Help me to participate in the task of the messenger called Malachi, who called for a purification of the people's worship so that they would be able to receive the blessing of God's reign. Help me to see and hear the kindnesses of the people in my community who resemble the Philippians, so that I can better identify with Paul in his gratitude and love toward them in their continuing care and righteousness.

Most of all, help me this day to imagine the joy of Christ's birth, and at the same time to lift up the claim of Christ's coming on each of us and on all of our futures. Amen.

Commentary on the Texts

Luke 3:1–6

If the Lukan passage for Advent 1 looks toward a cosmic future of the people of God, the passage for Advent 2 is a more direct look at history and a more inward look into the souls of believers.

John the Baptizer is introduced according to the secular fashion of Luke's day by naming the various rulers of that region in that year. To us as modern listeners, however, the series of names is not just a list of strangers. The naming of men like Pilate, Herod, Caiaphas, and Zechariah produces in modern ears echoes from the holy story that will unfold in this season and beyond this season.

The priest Zechariah is John's father, and he is related by marriage to Mary the mother of Jesus. His name evokes Jesus' birth story, a story that the evangelist Luke emphasizes much more than any of the other Gospel writers. For those who have become familiar over time with Matthew's Gospel, the name of Herod the king will remind them of his duplicity in ordering the Wise Men to worship the babe, when Herod actually planned to destroy that very baby. The other two leaders, Pilate and the high priest Caiaphas, participated in the later chapter of Jesus' persecution and trial in Jerusalem.

The presence of all these men in the midst of the introduction of John the Baptist, a man intent on preparing his audience for Christ's coming, is an important foreshadowing of the larger story of Christ's confrontation with earthly powers and its cost in his death on the cross. As in the First Sunday of Advent, the preliminaries to the Christmas story forbid us a simpleminded response to the birth of a newborn babe. Instead they demand that everyone who would celebrate Jesus' birth purify the self in repentance and humility, as the only authentic way to make ready the path of Jesus Christ into one's soul.

Luke's language of preparation is borrowed from Isaiah 40. Language similar to that of Isaiah is also found in the Baruch passage for this Sunday, as noted below. Luke makes small but significant shifts in meaning in his adaptation of the earlier prophet. Whereas the wilderness in Isaiah was to be the place to prepare the way of the Lord, in Luke wilderness is the home of the prophet John himself, who emerges to call the people of the city and the village to make straight their own souls in preparation for Christ.

The image of changing the topography of the created world is extreme, even in modern times when explosives have altered the shape of mountains and rivers. For any beings anywhere to change the whole landscape to make the "way of the Lord" smooth and straight is a profound tribute, and a profoundly difficult one to produce. The likely purpose, particularly as presented by Luke, is to portray dramatically the alteration in the personal soul, its priorities and its hidden places, that a total confrontation with the gospel of Jesus Christ can produce. The last line in this passage is important in lifting up the inclusive vision extending from Isaiah through Luke. Isaiah's words have been translated "And the glory of the LORD shall be revealed, and all flesh shall see it together." Luke's version is shorter, but it is compatible with the earlier one: "All flesh shall see the salvation of God" (v. 6). This is a Gospel not only for individual confessing sinners, but for an entire world being redeemed.

In preaching from this passage, **the preacher** has a chance to build on the worshipers' knowledge of the Christian drama as a whole—not only the birth of Christ but also the ministry, trial, death, and resurrection of this world-changing being. By reaffirming the seriousness of John the Baptist's message in the light of the life and sacrifice of Jesus Christ, a minister can offer a solid counterweight to the narrow or materialistic approaches to the Christmas season. The preacher can delight with others in the fulfilled promise of Jesus' coming. The preacher can also serve as a role model for personal reflection and recommitment in response to the Advent Gospel message. The mixture of solemnity and celebration represented by this passage is an opportunity to integrate those two motives, both in the worship event and in the life of the church outside worship.

Baruch 5:1–9 (C) (RC) (E)

The long and tortuous waiting period for a redeeming leader and a day of release are often noted as characteristic of many of the Hebrew Scriptures, whether or not they explicitly promise the coming of the Lord. The book called Baruch is linked to the Book of Daniel in style, to the prophet Jeremiah through the personal contact of the two men, and to other writers in its historical context. Thus this apocryphal book is a key thread in the weaving of Old Testament history, worship, and prophecy.

Baruch 5:1–9 has a different mood from any of the other pericopes for this Sunday. These verses have been called by some scholars part of a poem of consolation. Presented in a poetic style, the prophetic voice speaks to Jerusalem as the mother of many children who have been led away by enemies but are now about to return home in glory. Jerusalem herself is affirmed with the promise that God will forever call her name "Peace of righteousness and glory of godliness" (Bar. 5:4a). Nature gathers together to protect and honor mother Jerusalem. The world as a whole responds to God's ordering voice, so that Israel's welfare and happiness will be assured:

> For God has ordered that every
>   high mountain and the
>   everlasting hills be made low
> and the valley filled up, to
>   make level ground,
>   so that Israel may walk safely in
>   the glory of God.
>   Baruch 5:7

The level ground promised by the prophet will allow all the children of Israel to come home in comfort and pleasure. The final verse of this passage illuminates the meaning of the Hebrew word *shalom,* for peace in the context of justice is the heart of Baruch's promise. God promises to lead Israel forward with joy, in the light of God's glory, and with the mercy and righteousness that come from God alone. The mood of this passage matches inward calm and security with the rewards of being a righteous community.

It is important to note that the happy and expansive spirit of Baruch 5:1–9 is in strong contrast to earlier sections of the same book. The prophet says in 4:5–6, for example, ''It was not for destruction that you were sold to the nations, but you were handed over to your enemies because you angered God.'' The people of Israel were rightly punished for their sins, but as today's lection reveals, they were capable of being redeemed into a wonderful future.

The preacher can bring this material from Baruch into the world of serious promise that appears in the Second Sunday of Advent. The contrast between a sinful past and a gloriously liberated future is vivid in these verses. Moreover, there is a quality of personal and pastoral caring in these lines that can serve as a balance for the less personal and perhaps more intimidating prophetic words of John the Baptist in Luke 3:1–6. To personify Jerusalem or Israel or Chicago or Newark is to be able to speak of relationship between God and human beings rather than to be limited to abstract theological concepts. The prophets knew what they were doing.

Malachi 3:1–4 (alt. C) (L)

Malachi 3:1–11 (E)

The lectionary passage from Malachi shares the ambivalent mood of hope and apprehension that has already been identified in the readings for Advent 1. In Malachi (Hebrew: ''my messenger'') God's messenger is being sent to prepare the way for the era of a restored temple and a renewed worshiping community. In response to the expected preparation, the Lord will appear suddenly in the temple.

This last book of the canonical Old Testament was probably written during the fifth century B.C.E. The lection for this Sunday is typically cited as a preview or prediction of the prophetic ministry of John the Baptist, but the meaning of the present passage can profitably be examined in its own right.

After the rather upbeat announcement of the ''messenger of the covenant in whom you delight,'' v. 2 brings in a more somber side of the announced changes: ''But who can endure the day of his coming, and who can stand when he appears?'' The two verses that follow develop two vivid sensory similes for the purifying action of God: God is like the refiner's fire and God is like fullers' soap. Both items come from the Palestinians' daily life, for gold and silver were melted down to produce decoration, and fullers' soap was used to bleach impurities and unwanted colors out of cloth. Human beings, and particularly the priests of the temple, are depicted here as God's metal and cloth, the raw material for appropriate worship and ethical living. Since the author of Malachi had an antipathy toward the ''sons of Levi'' of the Zadokite priesthood, the use of images like fire and lye soap might have been a way to call forth a blessing in the most unpleasant way possible. In any case, the initiative here is God's, for it is God alone who will be able to purify the religious leaders so that their worship will once again be acceptable to Yahweh.

The Book of Malachi in general has its eye on both the public and the private worlds. While concerned with the proper forms of sacrifice in cultic worship, the author also brings in the ethical issues attached to individual relationships. In 2:13–17 as an example, the situation of husbands being unfaithful to the wives of their youth is cited as a barrier to meaningful worship. God is proclaimed as being scornful of the faithless worshiper's voluminous tears and lengthy words. The echo can be heard of an earlier prophet, who saw righteousness as the foundation of right worship.

In preaching from the Malachi text, one might build on the idea of God as refining and washing human beings in preparation of our minds and our senses for the birth of Christ. Also, the parallel linking of the public world of worship and the private choices of individuals is apparent in Malachi and in the words of John the Baptist. Finally, the promise of a new era, with its risks as well as its benefits, appears at the start of Malachi 3.

Philippians 1:3–11 (C) (L)

Philippians 1:1–11 (E)

Philippians 1:4–6, 8–11 (RC)

Paul's letter to this faithful community, geographically located in what is now part of Greece, offers us a word portrait of a strong relationship between a hard-pressed missionary and a benefactor church. This is important as a lection for Advent 2 because it explicitly lifts up the church, as a human institution founded on the life and death of Jesus Christ and defended by Paul throughout his journeys.

As in other New Testament writings, the promise of the day of Christ Jesus here again reminds us of the time-bound and yet timeless quality of the church's faith. The church at Philippi sent Paul financial gifts to support his work. They heard from him both directly and from others about his own imprisonments, beatings, and other types of significant setbacks. Amid all this they remained supportive of his work, apparently believing as Paul himself did that Christ's return in glory was likely to occur at any time. Though their hope for Christ's return was not borne out by historical fact, their love and support exemplify the kind of discipleship that present churches, and particularly many of their pastors, would like to experience.

The passage beginning with v. 1 includes Paul's ritual salutation to "all the saints" and to the leaders of the local church. It is a reminder that he was aware of the structures of leadership and followership which were always in the process of development and often in conflict.

When beginning with v. 3, this lection starts with a prayer of thanksgiving that is heartfelt, not only because of the generosity of the people at Philippi, but because the time in prison has allowed Paul to reflect at length on those many people who have made his work worthwhile. The Roman Catholic lection leaves out Paul's personal circumstances, with the result that the prayer appears more general and less conditioned by the letter writer's circumstances.

A temptation faces **the preacher** who attempts to respond to this passage from the pulpit. It is the temptation to say to one's community, "Here is a first-century church that did right in supporting the work of their leader; you should be more like that!" A more constructive response would be to bring into the present context the kinds of empowerment that a community's continuing support provides to persons who are in long-term struggle. For example, there are families who jointly keep vigils for their hospitalized members; there are musical and athletic group members who build up the newer members over time by reinforcement and rejoicing in the new members' success; and there are contributors to social causes who support an individual's effort to complete marathons or lengthy walking trips. These are secular examples, but any one of them could make clear to a modern set of parishioners the level and extent of interpersonal commitment which Paul describes as crucial to his survival and continuation in evangelical work. Finally, the preacher may need to make a judgment as to whether the inclusion of Paul's prison circumstances strengthens or weakens the power of this letter of personal thanksgiving. Since all the worshipers of any denomination live their lives within particular circumstances, it may be helpful to make Paul more understandable as a dedicated human servant of God by enabling his physical circumstances to be known as part of the background for his thankfulness.

Theological Reflection

Personal conversion changes the whole landscape of personal experience. This truth is a miracle as noteworthy as the changing of mountains and valleys into a straight path, for Jesus (in Luke 3), for Israel's children (in Baruch 5), for God (in Isaiah 40). Such a miracle seems to have been the goal of John the Baptizer as he called to people from his isolation in the desert. To prepare for the birth and life and claims of Jesus Christ means to seek out inner integrity, as in the call of John and Malachi It can happen only if one is open to miraculous changes in the geographical and social landscape (depicted in Luke, Baruch, and Philippians) that characterized Israel's history and the first-century Christian church as well.

Children's Message

There is a song many children sing during the weeks before Christmas. The chorus starts out like this, ''You better watch out . . . '' (This is best sung, if you yourself can do it with passable accuracy.)

Ask the children what lines come after that. Many of them will respond immediately with ''you better not cry, Better not pout, I'm telling you why . . . '' Ask the children what they think those song lyrics are about, and some will probably say that it's because Santa Claus wants them to be good, or that they themselves want to be good so that they will get the presents they want for Christmas.

Jesus loves you, as Santa Claus does; but Jesus isn't exactly like Santa Claus. Jesus came to save the whole world, not just to be generous to children. There is something in this song that brings the two together. It is the idea of preparing ourselves for something wonderful. The song says to watch out, not to cry or pout. John the Baptist, who came ahead of Jesus, said, ''Look inside yourselves and say no to sins, yes to making kind and honest things happen in your life.'' In both cases it isn't enough just to sit around and wait for the Christmas gifts to fall into your lap. What you and I do every day can help us be ready for God's good gifts, or not to be ready. Think of something you can do this week that will make it easier for Jesus to arrive here (and maybe please Santa Claus as well).

Hymns for Advent 2

O Promised One of Israel (*A Singing Faith*); Break Forth, O Living Light of God; Come, Thou Long-Expected Jesus; Battle Hymn of the Republic.

Canticle, Isaiah 12:2–6 (C)   **Philippians 4:4–9 (C)**
                                    Philippians 4:4–7 (L) (RC) (E)

Zephaniah 3:14–20 (C) (E)
Zephaniah 3:14–18a (L) (RC)   **Luke 3:7–18 (C) (L) (E)**
                                    Luke 3:10–18 (RC)

Meditation on the Texts

O God of steadfast love, whose anger at our pride and injustice is more than equaled by your delight in our renewal, help us to hear the unshakeable power of your word this day. As we come closer and closer to the anniversary of the birth of Christ Jesus, we are claimed by the charge of John the Baptist, who calls his listeners to act ethically in daily life, and not to claim privilege as the sons and daughters of Abraham.

We are people of privilege, O God. We barely know how to put aside our concerns with status and money and success for long enough to hear your words of challenge and rejoicing. Lacking a crisis as long and deep as the Babylonian exile, we fall into believing that stubbing a toe or a late-delivered letter is a prime example of suffering. Paul's writing to the Philippians from his imprisonment is a reminder of the real tribulations that others endure; so is the passage of rejoicing from Zephaniah, coming as it does after many verses that prophesy the day of the wrath of the Lord.

I know that your love for us is a strong love, a constant love, and a love capable of chastising as well as healing the beloved. I ask your help this day in realizing within myself, and in showing to the people, the freedom that comes from knowing that we are loved—loved too much to be ignored by our God. True rejoicing comes when one is led back from the place of the lost. True preparation for the birth of Christ comes when those who prepare are able to live in the awareness of life and death and resurrection.

May this Advent help to bring us, your people, to a clearer knowledge of ourselves as we prepare, and of you as we listen to your bracing and encouraging word. Amen.

Commentary on the Texts

Luke 3:7–18 (C) (L) (E)

Luke 3:10–18 (RC)

This prophetic message of John the Baptizer to the multitude has three distinct sections in its Common Lectionary version: (1) John confronts the listeners with their presumptuous belief that they are God's favored ones because of being the children of Abraham; (2) John answers several questions from the listeners by setting forth ethical choices that should be made if one wants to bear good fruit; (3) John responds to the surmises that he is the Christ by separating himself from that rumor and promising that the words of Christ will have the dual power to baptize with both fire and the Holy Spirit. Each of these sections deserves attention before looking at the pericope as a whole.

Luke has John the Baptizer saying to "the multitudes" the dramatic phrase "You brood of vipers!" The words are identical to those of John quoted in Matthew 3:7, but the contexts differ. Matthew depicts the audience for this phrase as the Pharisees and Sadducees who had come to be baptized—sectarian Jews who hoped to further their personal religious status through acts such as baptism. In contrast, Luke's John is speaking to everyone when he calls out his confrontation. No one, whether priest or laborer or official, has a claim to special status or security at the time of the wrath of God to come. Luke's eye is on the egalitarian will of God, and any created being, human or tree, can be cut down if its fruits do not reflect well on its creator. A single humbling sentence, taken from the Q source, makes it clear that no religious group can consider itself the exclusive chosen ones: ''God is able from these stones to raise up children to Abraham.''

The ethical heart of John the Baptizer's preaching comes in vs. 10–14, where he answers the perennial question of those who preach and many of those who come to hear preaching, ''What then shall we do?'' John answers concretely, both in terms of the actions to be taken and various groups of people who have specific opportunities to act rightly or wrongly. In Luke's Gospel, alone of all the Gospel accounts, John the Baptizer begins with a social welfare proposal so radical (in both senses) as to make the affluent parishioner squirm: you should share your extra coat with a person who has none and your extra food with those who have none. There are no qualifiers in this proposal, and no escape routes. John goes on to respond to the various occupational groups asking him what they can do to bear good fruit. The tax collectors or publicans, widely known to siphon off part of the citizens' tax payments for their own profit, are given another simple admonition: take only what you are required to collect, no more. To the soldiers, who were also in a position to use their occupation for personal advancement, John answers in a way that fits late-twentieth-century officers with chilling appropriateness: give up violence, false accusation, extortion of witnesses, and discontent over wages. Despite being an isolate in the wilderness, Luke's John must have known of the temptations to abuse of power that faced public figures such as the soldiers and tax collectors. His answers acknowledge the struggles such people face, but the answers also require from their listeners a new humility and discipline.

Luke alone records the multitude as asking John the Baptist whether he was the Christ. The question of John's identity was one that surfaced and resurfaced repeatedly, especially in the writings of Luke-Acts, for example, Luke 1:5–80; 9:18–22; Acts 18:24–28; 19:1–7. What emerges is an emphatic series of assertions that John is not the Christ. John states that Jesus will baptize not with water, but with fire and the Spirit; that John himself is not worthy to be the slave of the one who is to follow; and that Jesus will bring judgment in his hand to separate the wheat from the chaff. Though John explicitly abases himself in these statements, he is at the same time speaking with the assurance of a prophet; so that his very confidence can itself serve as a part of the good news that Luke attributes to John in v. 18. For the multitude, to hear words of fairness, truth, and promise from one such as John the Baptizer could produce a bracing, adult hopefulness.

The image of John the Baptizer in popular sources is that of a big, loud, glaring near-bully—a person who would not hesitate to enter a fight. Luke 3:7–9 brings John the preacher to the forefront because of this portrayal, so different as it is from the popular views of Jesus among the crowds. But when the passage read begins with v. 10, as in the Roman Catholic lection, the image of John as a dominant personality recedes somewhat and his calls to ethical and egalitarian conduct come to center stage.

The material describing John's background, preaching, and later imprisonment should be recognized as a whole unit of narrative, beginning with Luke 3:1 and extending through v. 18. Acknowledging this unit in Luke's writing allows listeners to recognize John's part in the larger gospel message, and to see individual parts of the longer passage in the context of the whole unit. For example, the apocalyptic note in the longer version of this passage for Advent 3 is struck by the word ''therefore'' at the start of v. 7. It is the prospect of ''the salvation of God'' appearing to all flesh (v. 6) that requires the truth be told about false privilege and exclusive cultic relationships with the Holy One.

The preacher has many prospects for sermon development from this passage in Luke 3. In addition to the opportunity to bring out the wider setting for the passage that has been mentioned above, there is the chance to lift up the ethical simplicity of John's calls for right action, applicable at any time in the church year but especially timely in the weeks before Christmas, when getting and spending become so central to so many people. The notion of Jesus as baptizing with fire and the Spirit is another theme that can be used to pull Advent away from the infant worship which tends to gut the social conscience of the church. Finally, John's confrontive label ''vipers'' has the power to convict any of us who seek by some historical or genealogical or ethnic means to claim personal importance—including clergy, business leaders, community volunteers, and sports coaches. John's words, difficult as they are to hear, ask us to ask ourselves, "Does any one of my statuses make me better?" The answer is clear; it does not.

Zephaniah 3:14–20 (C) (E)

Zephaniah 3:14–18a (L) (RC)

The prophet Zephaniah is thought to have lived during the latter half of the seventh century B.C.E. His prophetic activities occurred while Josiah was king of Judah (640–609 B.C.E.), during the domination of Assyria over the smaller states and Josiah's rebellion against that domination. Zephaniah's prophecies are fifty to one hundred years later than the time of Isaiah and Micah (c. 701 B.C.E.). Zephaniah's prophecies employ the much earlier concept of the coming day of the Lord to remind the idolatrous people of Judah that they have corrupted their worship through venerating foreign gods. Zephaniah 1 and 2 delineate this corruption and its consequences in vivid detail.

In contrast, the lectionary passage for this Sunday from the prophet Zephaniah could not be more positive or more different in tone from both Luke 3:7–9 and Zephaniah 1 and 2. Delight is everywhere in the last chapter of Zephaniah. The new people of God enjoy a pervasive mood of happiness, the spirit of festival, freedom from war, and the very presence of the warrior-God who will no longer fight them, but live peacefully in their presence. Zephaniah 3 was certainly written years after the first two chapters. It may have been composed for a remnant of the faithful people of Judah. The phrase "daughter of Zion" probably refers to Zion (or Jerusalem) considered as a young woman. The fact of nearly identical phrasings in vs. 19 and 20—"renown in all the earth" and "renowned and praised among all the peoples of the earth"—may mean that two different endings were composed for this hymn of joy.

The preacher might note that this passage is used for the Easter Vigil as well as for Advent 3. Its celebrative mood and its explicit release from judgments, oppressors, and disaster make it a wonderful moment in the corporate dance of faith.

Philippians 4:4–9 (C)

Philippians 4:4–7 (L) (RC) (E)

This section of the letter to Paul's generous benefactors is focused primarily on advice about acting out one's faith. In that respect it is similar to the preaching of John the Baptizer in Luke 3; but one significant difference is that Paul urges the faithful of Philippi to follow his lead: "What you have learned and received and heard and seen in me, do; and the God of peace will be with you." In contrast John's admonitions stand alone, without personal references to John's own practice. Paul's advice is also striking in the rhythm it conveys between the faithful person's action and the response-ability of God. For example, in v. 6 the believers are told to let their requests be known to God "by prayer and supplication with thanksgiving." God's peace will keep their hearts and minds centered on Christ Jesus. In v. 9 the Philippians are told to do all that they have seen and heard and learned from Paul; thus the God of peace will be with them. When the shortest version of this passage is read (vs. 4–7), the four verses have the quality of a concise program for keeping oneself on the track spiritually: Rejoice, pray, and let it go. The Lord is at hand: whether thought to be immediately present in space or about to return in time, the Lord is in charge of our spiritual journeys.

In the longer versions of the pericope (4:4–13) the life of the faithful is not portrayed as simple, however much the repeated word "Rejoice!" might ring in a listener's mind. As Paul knew well, the external circumstances of life do not fall easily into place just because one prays or is free from anxiety. Given that fact, the response Paul makes is to do a basic form of mind control. He concentrates on the positive ideas and events available to him, and he keeps always in his mind the strength he derives from his commitment to Christ. "I can do all things in him who strengthens me.'' Believing this frees one from a rugged and damaging individualism.

Preaching from this passage allows the preacher to build on what will be strong familiarity among the parishioners. It is wise not simply to paraphrase Paul's words, which are unusually clear and well phrased in this instance. Instead, a move into a contemporary context might give more sensory power to Paul's concepts. As an example, both psychologists and physicians know that the images one fixes the mind on can have the power to build personal confidence and improve the body's immune response, or to do the opposite in either case. What Paul offers is a biblical counterpart to positive thinking, made more potent by the fact that he himself has had to endure privation and physical hardship before offering his admonition to ''rejoice!'' Another direction for preaching would be to illuminate the rhythm of the believer's prayer and peaceful response to prayer; this might serve as a balance for the child's notion, ''I prayed for it, so I'm sure God will give it to me.'' Being able to avoid the anxiety of wondering how God will dispose of events is as freeing as the unrealistic idea of controlling the outcome oneself. For **further exploration** of ideas related to rejoicing, control, and faith, see Wayne Bradley Robinson, *The Transforming Power of the Bible (New York: Pilgrim Press, 1984).*

Theological Reflection

The emotional range in human religious experience and the nature of the God who is with human beings in that experience are at the heart of this week's lections. On the surface the three passages are highly different. Zephaniah depicts a Jerusalem being brought into a festival of delight by its warrior-God; Paul tells his beloved community to endure all things without anxiety, as he has learned to do; and Luke's John the Baptizer starts by challenging an overconfident audience to make ethical choices, and ends by limiting his own importance as compared to that of Jesus Christ, the one who is to follow.

It is useful to keep in mind that human beings are inclined to assess our experience by what happens to us from the outside. The verses from Zephaniah allow this kind of approach, focusing as they do on the day of festival and the renown to come to the people of God from all over the earth; but in both Philippians 4 and Luke 3 the trajectory of the passages is not toward what happens to the believers but what the believers make happen, out of a central personal core of truth and faithfulness. As in the earlier two Sundays of Advent, the outside world is always at hand, but the primary challenge is turning to the righteous core of one's being, particularly in its relationship to an always faithful and ever-loving God.

Children's Message

You might begin this message with a question that nobody is required to answer: I'm wondering if any of you have had the experience that I had as a child—a time when you did something wrong, something you knew for sure was wrong, and you hoped with all your heart that no one would find out about it. Does that sound at all familiar? You don't have to say so out loud. If anything like that has happened to you, you'll probably know what I mean when I tell this story. I can tell mine because my parents aren't sitting out there watching and listening.

(Proceed with a story of your own; it could take shape like this one.) One time I told a big lie to my friends in school. I did it to get attention and to feel important, but it didn't work. The others asked me questions I couldn't answer, and after a while I could tell they didn't believe my lie. But they did tell their parents what I said, and the parents went to *my* parents and told them. My parents found me hiding in my bedroom, and they told me they were really angry with me. Then they told me how important the truth was, and after a while I felt okay enough to promise them that I wouldn't tell any more lies. The funny thing was that I found I was actually happy they found out what I did, and I was glad they talked with me about lies and truth. It made me feel important to them—more important than the lie had made me feel.

Two of the passages from the Bible for today are about good news that comes from people called prophets who told God's people when they were doing wrong, and told them to change their ways. Maybe it's hard to imagine good news coming from someone who is angry at what you have done. But God never stops caring about what people do, and about what they think and feel. The *really* good news is that God, through Jesus Christ and the Spirit, is always watching out for us and making sure that we don't get lost—whether by lying, or stealing, or saying mean things. God tells us that nothing can take away the good news that we are loved, every minute of every day.

Will you remember that good news today, and all this week? Perhaps you can also tell some others the good news that you love them, and that you care about what they do. Try it out!

Hymns for Advent 3

Hail to the Lord's Anointed; Is Every Time a Threshold Time? (*A Singing Faith*); Seek the Lord; On Jordan's Bank the Baptist's Cry.

Advent 4

Psalm 80:1–7 (C)   **Hebrews 10:5–10**

Micah 5:2–5a (C)   **Luke 1:39–55 (C)**
Micah 5:2–4 (L) (E)   **Luke 1:39–45 (L) (RC)**
Micah 5:1–4a (RC)   **Luke 1:39–49 (E)**

Meditation on the Texts

Spirit of God, you enable us to feel the approach of the Christ, especially on this last Sunday which marks his coming to earth and our preparation to meet him.

Help us to imagine the mixture of emotions that must have emerged in Elizabeth, whose pregnancy late in life meant an amazing opportunity to bring into a priestly family a gospel prophet. Help us to enter into the consciousness of the young Mary as she rushed to see her elder relative and then paused to express her strength of faith through a song of joy and justice. Help us also to recognize in Micah the hope of religious and national renewal through the peace-giving heir of David, a hope that modern prophets and leaders still hold in the light of the birth of Jesus. Finally, help us to hear through the words to the Hebrews a ringing affirmation of the embodied life of Jesus Christ, and through those words an affirmation of the embodied life of Christians everywhere, meeting each other not just in ideas and visions, but in the concrete circumstances of caring about and working with each other throughout our lives.

As we walk together toward the night that commemorates the birth of Jesus, help us to hear the echoes of these prophets and disciples, and to hear in them the voices of joy and justice for our own time. Amen.

Commentary on the Texts

Luke 1:39–55 (C)

Luke 1:39–45 (L) (RC)

Luke 1:39–49 (E)

Unlike most passages in the lectionary, this one brings together two women of faith in a doubly delicious shared experience: not only giving birth but giving birth as the chosen bearers of God's embodied will. The meeting of Elizabeth and Mary in Luke 1 is a striking mixture of homely events and divine purposes. As already noted in relation to the earlier weeks of Advent, this mixture of life experiences—the private and the public, the individual and the corporate, the time-bound and the timeless—is a clear reminder that God's presence is without limits, and goes beyond the bounds of human expectations. Luke in particular celebrates paradox, as in the joining of lowly servant and royal ruler; so the recounting of this section of the Advent-Christmas story shows a narrator's special relish.

Historically, both Mary and Elizabeth were most likely residents of the hill country of Judea, though only Elizabeth's home is referred to in v. 39 as being in the hill country. As Luke has mentioned earlier in chapter 1, Elizabeth is the child of a priestly family, a daughter of Aaron, in addition to being married to one of the temple priests, Zechariah. She shares with earlier women in the scriptures (Sarah, Rebekah, Rachel, Hannah, and the wife of Manoah) the soul-wrenching pain and shame of being childless for many years. While we do not know her exact age, it is likely that she was Mary's elder by as much as four decades. Elizabeth is referred to as the kinswoman of Mary; the two were probably cousins. Their difference in age and situation is as noteworthy as their being relatives: Mary is betrothed but not yet married, and probably as young as fourteen or fifteen years old, while Elizabeth is what might be called today a "matronly woman" in her forties or fifties, with a secure social and economic standing from her husband's family background and her own.

The differences between the two women are emphasized because they highlight the wonderfully unpredictable nature of the Gospel narrative in Luke 1. Mary goes "with haste" to visit Elizabeth after learning from the angel Gabriel that Elizabeth "in her old age" has miraculously conceived a son and is already six months pregnant. Interestingly, the narrative does not indicate that Mary was told that Elizabeth's son is to be John the Baptist, the forerunner of Jesus. Renita Weems has suggested that Mary's motive for rushing to Elizabeth may have been the longing to talk with someone who might understand Mary's strange visitor and the amazing news she has been given.

> "How do you defend a blessing you cannot explain?" she asked herself. Besides, who would believe her? Joseph? Absolutely not. The townswomen? Hardly. Elizabeth, her relative? Perhaps.*

The meeting of the two women is an encounter of two lively human beings, even as it is the vehicle for demonstrating the strong and distinct images of discipleship that both of them offer to the modern church.

Elizabeth's song to Mary in vs. 42–45 is the song of a prophet and the mother-to-be of a prophet. She names Mary as the mother of our Lord; she names the leaping of the child in her womb as the prophet John's acknowledgment of the coming of Jesus; and she names Mary's action in coming to her as proof of Mary's faithfulness as a disciple. She honors the woman who by all worldly standards should be honoring Elizabeth herself. Her song of praise is then answered by Mary's own praise-song, which extends the themes of blessedness and joy into wider realms of history and social critique. The Lutheran and Roman Catholic lectionaries end the passage with Elizabeth's song to Mary. Doing so heightens the prophetic quality of Elizabeth's words, and perhaps that of the quickening of the prophet baby as well. This way of marking the passage also emphasizes the faith of Elizabeth in her veneration of Mary as the mother of Jesus Christ.

Mary's song, typically called the Magnificat because of its first word in Latin, is part of a long tradition of songs of praise and thanksgiving that appear in the Psalms and in other sections of the Hebrew Scriptures. The Magnificat can be compared most notably with the Song of Hannah, which appears in 1 Samuel 2:1–10. Since the life story of the woman Hannah appears to be more similar to the life of Elizabeth than that of young Mary, a few scholars have thought it likely that Elizabeth rather than Mary sang the original Magnificat; but there is no strong argument for this attribution on the basis of the Lukan text. Hannah was a barren woman of faith, who went to the temple at Shiloh to pray for the birth of a son. She promised in her prayer to dedicate a son granted to her to the service of the Lord, for as long as he would live. The Song of Hannah is her prayer-song of praise and thanksgiving, sung in worship when she brings her young son Samuel to the temple.

One feature of biblical literature that deserves recalling here is the frequent quotation of earlier passages of scripture by later speakers and writers—not only by Jesus and the apostle Paul but by the prophets and the various Gospel writers as well. The Magnificat and the Song of Hannah share several features of both content and poetic form, an indication of the interwoven nature of the Holy Word. Both poems begin with a personal expression of gratitude for God's favor; both extol the might of God; both deal extensively with the reversals produced by the work of God—the rich become poor, those of low degree are exalted, the hungry are well fed, and the arrogant are put down. The social critique represented by this series of reversals is often taken as surprising coming from the mouth of the youthful Mary, but seen against the backdrop of the Hannah tradition and the psalms which connect personal salvation and social change, the Magnificat emerges as a marker of salvation history as well as a wonderful song of personal joy.

---

*Renita Weems, *Just a Sister Away* (San Diego: LuraMedia, 1988), p. 118.

In the Episcopal lectionary the passage ends at v. 49. This boundary brings to the forefront the worshipful quality of Mary's words. She exalts the power of God, particularly in contrast to her low estate, and she recognizes that marvelous things have been done for her. These are the words of a hymn of praise, and coming from the very young Mary they denote an impressive discipleship.

In its longest version, the Common Lectionary passage extends from Mary's hastening to the home of Elizabeth through the entirety of the Magnificat song. This allows reader and listener to focus on both the human interchange of the two women and the two praise-songs. But even this version of the pericope omits the last verse of Luke's narrative, and thus the opportunity is missed of balancing the spiritual center, represented by Elizabeth's and Mary's two songs, with its human context, in which both pregnancy and friendship are celebrated. Mary stayed with Elizabeth for three months (v. 56). Her return home may have been just before the birth of John or just after the birth; we are not told. Luke chooses to round off the narrative of announcement and celebration with a simple word of solidarity between the women over an extended period of time. It is a detail worth recalling today, in an era of the instantaneous and the temporary.

For **the preacher,** this passage in any of its forms offers a striking example of the female discipleship which has been submerged in much biblical scholarship during the church's history. The preacher can choose to move from either one of the human dramas in which the two women are engaged toward the magnetic event of the announced births and their galvanizing force in the world. An effort to illuminate the meeting of the two women might even include having two women from the congregation read the words of the two women. Another useful approach would be to develop the parallels and contrasts between the songs of Mary and of Hannah, highlighting the ways that the Gospel adds new meaning to the experience of centuries earlier. **Two resources for further study** in this comparative approach are A. D. Ritterspach, ''Rhetorical Criticism and the Song of Hannah,'' in *Rhetorical Criticism: Essays in Honor of James Muilenburg,* ed. Jared J. Jackson and Martin Kessler (Pittsburgh: Pickwick Press, 1974), pp. 68–74; and Ralph W. Klein, *1 Samuel,* in *The Word Biblical Commentary,* vol. 10 (Waco, Tex.: Word Books, 1983).

A final word about the use of this passage by the preacher comes from the work of feminist biblical scholars, many of whom have urged that preachers permit their imaginations to address the spaces between what is made explicit and what is reasonable to believe, in texts such as the Luke 1:39–56 section concerning the interaction of Mary and Elizabeth. Luke presents the two women to the church and the world without many details, but the women are clearly presented as embodied human beings, happy to be women, and not as disembodied functionaries that exist only to sing timeless songs of faith. Their embodiment as women is one of the major gifts of this passage, and it is a gift not to be lost or squandered.

Micah 5:2–5a (C)

Micah 5:2–4 (L) (E)

Micah 5:1–4a (RC)

We know little about Micah of Moresheth, except that he lived in Judah during the reign of three Judean kings, between 742 and 698 B.C.E. Much of that era was dominated by crises brought on by expansion of the Assyrian Empire. In particular, the attack in 701 B.C.E. led to the killing of many, and the city of Jerusalem barely escaped destruction. Micah's prophecy takes account of these events, describing the retribution of a God defamed by idolatry. In this Micah shows a similarity to Hosea; Micah is also compared to Isaiah, because both prophets believed in Jerusalem as the holy center of the world, and in the dynasty of Davidic kings as the best hope for the future.

Micah warned the people of Zion that their wrongdoing would double back on them. He denounced the greedy who tricked neighbors out of their land, the smooth liars who preached allegedly good news to the helpless, and the ''justice'' administrators who symbolically "eat the flesh of my people" (3:3). For Micah the judgment of God is appropriate, and inescapable.

Micah 4 and 5 are strikingly different from the mood of the first three chapters described above. This fact, as well as differences in language, has led some scholars to conclude that chapters 4–7 of Micah came from a century or two later than Micah's own lifetime. At a later time Jerusalem had been attacked and then sent into exile by the Babylonians, and people were looking back idealistically to the Davidic line of kings while being ruled by outsiders.

Today's verses from Micah—whether delineated as 5:2–5a or as 5:1–4—are important because they were appropriated first by Matthew (2:1 and 2:5, and quoting from Micah in 2:6) and then by later readers, as a prophecy of the birth of Jesus in Bethlehem. Though the predominant view of historians is that Jesus' family was from the town of Nazareth, Micah's words paint such a vivid picture of Bethlehem and its shepherd-king that this location has been the primary focus of imagery in poetry and song. The fact that King David's family home was Bethlehem (1 Sam. 16:1) tightens the geographical connection between David and Jesus, though there are mentions by every Gospel writer of Jesus as a Nazarene and of Nazareth as the place where he grew up.

As important as the references to Bethlehem in the present passage is the image of the shepherd who will "feed his flock in the strength of the LORD," and the prediction that this humble leader will nevertheless be known as "great to the ends of the earth." As so often in the Advent material, paradoxes are central. This shepherd will come from modest Bethlehem, but will carry the marks of the ancient history of God's people. Further, the humble shepherd will have the power of the Almighty, allowing the people long besieged to come home again in security. Most pertinent to Advent 4, this renewal is dependent on a single birth—"when she who is in travail has brought forth" (5:3a).

The Roman Catholic version of this lection includes the first verse of the chapter, which recounts the current state of siege brought about by either the Assyrians in 701 B.C.E. or by the Babylonians a century later. The passage ends with v. 4a, before the statement that "they shall dwell secure," thus bringing out the struggle from which the hope for a leader has come, but without ending the passage in the confidence that earthly peace will ensue simply because the leader has been born. In the other three versions of the lection, the reference to the current siege is omitted, but the statement about security is retained; this shifts the emphasis slightly, to a more pastoral focus.

The act of giving birth is central in all versions of the passage from Micah. The oracle has been taken literally in many circles as a prediction of the birth of Jesus. **The preacher** would be wise to mention, however, that even if it is not read as a precise prediction of the birth of Jesus Christ, this brief passage from Micah still shows the power of a long-held hope for one who would be both mighty and peaceful. As in the case of other prophetic materials, the preacher could develop briefly the historical setting for this lection, and then reflect on its parallel with modern forms of "siege"—cultural, economic, and mass-mediated as well as political versions—and the resulting longing people feel for security and a new form of leader. The Hebrew Scriptures are rich with language and images that depict human struggle moving toward, against, and away from the divine. Illuminating that struggle allows worshipers to feel the connections between the biblical world and their own.

Hebrews 10:5–10

This book is more an argument than an epistle. Its anonymous author was almost certainly not Paul, for reference is made (2:3–4) to the author's being of a later generation than those who had heard Jesus directly. The Book of Hebrews is intended to make a coherent case for the Christian revelation, particularly in the light of the truths of the Hebrew Scriptures. The passage for Advent 4 is an effective partner to the Gospel account of Elizabeth and Mary, because it also centers on the embodied nature of Christ. In this instance the focus is on Christ's sacrifice for humanity, portrayed in a dialogue (somewhat awkward to modern ears) which involves "Christ" and "God" in the process of affirming the heavenly choice of a body for the earthly redeemer rather than burnt offerings, the more ancient form of sacrifice. Despite the difference of its orientation, looking toward the cross instead of toward Christ's birth, this passage about Christ's sacrifice has in it some of the same language of obedience that is seen in both Elizabeth and Mary in Luke 1.

One irony about Hebrews 10 is that its argument is founded on a Greek mistranslation of the Hebrew "open ear" in Psalm 40:6 into *sōma*, which means "body" in English. The psalmist contrasted the tradition of animal sacrifices with God's gift to human beings of the ability to hear, to listen to God's will for themselves. By making the body the central image in the present passage, the author dramatizes the physical death of Christ. In contrast, another statement attributed to Christ in various encounters with believers and skeptics is more directly in keeping with the meaning of the psalm: "Let anyone with ears to hear listen!" (Luke 14:35; Matt. 13:9; Mark 4:9, NRSV). **For a further analysis** of the operation of that and similar phrases, see George A. Kennedy, *New Testament Interpretation Through Rhetorical Criticism* (Chapel Hill, N.C.: University of North Carolina Press, 1984).

One opportunity for **the preacher** using Hebrews 10:5–10 is to develop the theme of obedience across the Hebrews and Luke passages for this day. Another is to make the connection between the experiences of celebration and sacrifice, with the goal of grounding the joy of Advent in the awareness of the costs of furthering the realm of God. A third possibility is to consider the connections between gift and sacrifice that are made available in any of the readings for this day.

Theological Reflection

The themes of celebration, obedience, and solidarity loom large on this last Sunday before Christmas. The meeting of the two women is also a meeting of the concrete promise of Christ's birth with the enlarged message of human liberation under the eye of God. This fact makes the lection from Luke 1 rich with promise for preaching. When we add the prophetic fervor of Micah, turning the pain of judgment into pastoral hope, the celebrative vision is given even more scope and depth. And with the passage in Hebrews bringing into focus the ultimate sacrifice of Christ, we are brought squarely into an Advent for adult believers, its realism coexisting with its happiness and hope.

Children's Message

You can start by asking the children to think about any time that someone in their family has done something special that everyone was happy about. You may give examples. Maybe it was like one of these things: finishing something big that you were working on, winning a prize in a contest, coming home after a long time, or married children in the family having their first baby. (Let any of the children add their own responses, and acknowledge each of them.)

Today's passage from the Gospel writer Luke is about a celebration too. It is not a big party, with dozens of people and balloons and a decorated cake, but it is still a real celebration. It all happens because two women are going to have babies. I happen to think that all babies are special, and that they are a gift from God, but these two particular women were going to have babies that were *very* special. Do you have any idea who either of these babies might have been? (Wait for answers, and go ahead if none is offered.)

The babies were Jesus and John the Baptist. John was the messenger of God who told people to get ready for the coming of Jesus. The celebration happened when angels came to Mary, the mother of Jesus, and Elizabeth, the mother of John the Baptist, to tell them they would be the lucky parents of God's chosen leaders on earth. And Mary and Elizabeth really celebrated. Wouldn't you? They sang songs of happiness to each other, and they stayed together for a long time, many weeks, getting ready for the birth of these two wonderful babies. I'll bet they had a fine time waiting together for these two amazing births.

In this next week we'll be celebrating Jesus' birth, here at this church. While we do it, your parents and friends may be remembering how special it has been to have *you* come into their world.

Babies are special, and so are the people that they grow up to be. Jesus, the child of God, was a very special baby, who grew up to be the one who led all the people toward love and justice. That's quite a lot to celebrate, and Mary and Elizabeth knew it was a big thing. So let's all celebrate, as they did, the coming of Jesus now, by saying together, very loud, "*Welcome, Jesus!*" Say those words after I say the words, "And we all say, *Welcome, Jesus!*"

Hymns for Advent 4

Lo, How a Rose E'er Blooming; Come, My Way, My Truth, My Life; Let All Mortal Flesh Keep Silence; Hark, What a Sound.

Christmas 1

Psalm 111 (C)

1 Samuel 2:18–20, 26 (C)
1 Samuel 1:20–22, 24–28 (RC)
Jeremiah 31:10–13 (L)
Isaiah 61:10–62:3 (E)

Colossians 3:12–17 (C)
Hebrews 2:10–18 (L)
1 John 3:1–2, 21–24 (RC)
Galatians 3:23–25; 4:4–7 (E)

Luke 2:41–52 (C) (L) (RC)
John 1:1–18 (E)

Meditation on the Texts

O Bringer of New Life, we come to you with awe at the gift of the Christ-child to the world, and to us. It is almost beyond imagining that the event of an infant's birth could contribute to reversing the course of history. Yet you have always shown us that you see the universe from both the smallest and the largest conceivable perspective, all at once. And you ask the same of us—to recognize the holy in the hay of a cow's stall and to look for personal meaning in a star.

This week is a time to give attention to the impact on the watchers and hearers of the holy moment of birth. In my personal study and reflection on these texts, may I feel my own responses in an authentic way as I try to gather in the truth from these writers of scripture. May I allow to come within myself the idea of Christ being made of the same nature as my own, according to the writer of the Hebrews. May I consider how I might really know what it is like to have the peace of Christ rule in my heart, as Paul urged the people of Colossae. May I exult in the presence of God as if I were bedecked like a bride or a bridegroom, according to the words of Isaiah. Above all, may I experience the sense of profound and exuberant newness in the light of the living presence of Christ in my life, and may I communicate that newness by the way I encounter every person in my path.

In this season between the birth of Jesus and his transfiguration, may all of us remain alert to our experiences of having been transfigured—changed in our being as well as in our appearing—by the gift of Christ Jesus to the world. Amen.

Commentary on the Texts

Luke 2:41–52 (C) (L) (RC)

For Christmas 1 the lection from Luke 2 moves precipitously away from the manger scene and into the precocious development of the young Jesus. The story, which takes the literary form of a legend, presents in vivid relief the contrast between Jesus' potential life within a particular family—a family about which we are told almost nothing in any of the canonical scriptures—and his life as a young interlocutor with his Jewish elders in the temple.

Luke 2:41–52 is the sole transition story in the canonical Gospels, coming between the infancy narrative and the mature ministry of preaching, healing, and teaching that is developed by Luke in chapters 4 through 21. In contrast to the many apocryphal stories of Jesus' supernatural exploits as a child, this story appears quiet, understated. Its particular function is to help modern believers imagine a youthful Jesus growing on his way, rather than to present to Luke's audience only a gap of three decades between his birth and his mission with the twelve chosen disciples.

Mary and Joseph with Jesus, age twelve, were, like others from Galilee, pilgrims to

Jerusalem for the annual Passover feast. There were probably a sizable number of people traveling to Jerusalem from the north and then back home after the Passover festivities. Thus the image (v. 44) of a caravan with many adults and many children, large enough that the boy Jesus might have been thought to be riding for a while with others, is a plausible explanation for the parents' losing track of their child.

Luke treats all the participants in this narrative with respect. Mary and Joseph are not portrayed as if they had been irresponsible to be separated from their son; travel by a community in that time was not at all like isolated family outings in the United States of the late twentieth century. The parents are said to be anxious about their son, and to tell him so. But their son is also portrayed as having a reasonable explanation for his actions. He is already operating in kairos, in God's time frame rather than in a human one, and he assumes that his sojourn "in my Father's house" (v. 49) is the most logical action for one who had entered the lives of Mary and Joseph as he had done, a dozen years earlier. The problem, of course, is that the two sides of this dialogue are in two different frames of reference. The parents do not understand what their son is doing; the son does not understand why his earthly parents do not understand. In spite of this lack of rapport, their immediate situation is resolved. Jesus agrees to go with his parents back to Nazareth, for the time being, and Mary chooses to reflect on the event to herself (as she had done before, 2:19) for the time being.

The word "transitional" is an important descriptor for this story: besides marking Jesus' literal youth as a period of time, it is a narrative means of reminding its audience that Jesus was both a human being and a divine force beyond human limits. When Jesus refers to "Father" we are told that his parents did not know what to make of his saying, but believers recognize that the relationship between Jesus and the one he later called "Abba" was both like and unlike any earthly relationship between parent and child. One other transitional element of this story comes from the close parallel of v. 52 and its Hebrew scriptural counterpart: Jesus is compared to the young Samuel, who grew in stature and in favor with both God and human beings (1 Sam. 2:26). Though Luke is not as intent on connections with the Jewish community as Matthew, Luke does end the story with this reminder that Jesus is in a line with the law and the judges.

The preacher can address this narrative with a horizontal or a vertical focus, each with its separate benefits. The horizontal focus gives attention to the family relationships described, and the significance of Jesus' human qualities for understanding him in the ministry and sacrifice that ensue. The vertical focus gives particular attention to the early evidence of Jesus as a rabbi, and as one for whom the "family" is that of the faithful ones rather than those who are linked by household. In addition, there is a background element in the story that is often overlooked, and that is the religious community depicted through the travelers from Nazareth. This is not a story of isolated individuals: Jesus, his earthly parents, the temple teachers, and the Nazareth pilgrims are all woven in various ways into a religious community that is maintained through obedience and discussion and problem solving. This offers another way to see the Christmas season as other than a tidy or even trivial miniature.

John 1:1–18 (E)

The Prologue to John is distinctive as a text for a Christmas Sunday, for it begins at the level of cosmic and philosophical truth, not historical narrative. Whereas the writer of this Gospel names John (the Baptist) early (v. 6) as a man sent from God, only in the seventeenth of eighteen verses does it cite by name Jesus Christ, the one in whom the Word has become flesh.

In the Episcopal Church, three services for Christmas Day are included in the schedule of lectionary readings. In the first service the traditional Christmas story in Luke 2:1–14, with an optional addition of vs. 15–20, and in the second service Luke 2:15–20, with an optional addition of vs. 1–14, would be read. For the third Christmas Day service, John 1:1–14 is specified as the Gospel reading. Thus the jump from the Advent encounter of Mary and Elizabeth to the Logos of John is not as abrupt as might be imagined. Nevertheless, it is clear that the choice of a more general and theological passage for Christmas 1 draws the attention of worshipers toward a more expansive and reflective look at the source, life, and meaning of Jesus Christ than is the case when worshipers hear Luke's story about the twelve-year-old Jesus tarrying in the temple.

In its complete form, The Prologue to John is a summary of the coming of Christ and its meaning for believers. The Prologue is in four sections. The first (vs. 1–5) describes in a poetic cadence the Word in creation, joined with the ideas of light and life. The fact that "Word" (*logos*) is used here without a qualifier in Greek, without a phrase such as "the Word of the Lord," gives the idea of God's speech a different, independent existence that appears to be unique in scripture. Some observers have noticed a double meaning in the statement, "The light shines in the darkness, and the darkness has not overcome it"; the Greek verb for "overcome" can be translated as "comprehend," with the connotation that those in the dark may not so much fight the Light as to be unable to perceive it for what it is. (See below about preaching on light and dark as metaphors.)

In the second section of the Prologue, the light metaphor from the first section shines on a particular person, John the Baptizer (vs. 6–8), whose identity is made clear primarily by his indirect relation to the light. Verses 7–8, plus v. 15, suggest that the question about John's identity still had currency in the last third of the first century C.E. John the Baptizer was crucial as witness, a term used twice in this Prologue. Given the later timing of John's Gospel as a whole, one who had been an eyewitness to Jesus would have particular import.

The third section (vs. 9–13) alludes to Christ as "the true light" and evokes both his struggle and his power. The allusion to all those who became "children of God, . . . born . . . of God," through Christ, suggests that the writer is endeavoring to solidify Christ as the locus of belief for an audience one or two generations after his immediate presence. In any case, the impact of the life of Christ is appropriate for believers to hear on the Sunday immediately after the celebration of his birth.

The fourth and final section of the Prologue (vs. 14–18) is a creed: the Word became flesh, the believers beheld his glory, John witnessed to his superiority, grace was given which transcended the law, and God became known through Christ. It is hard to imagine a more condensed set of belief statements.

The preacher in using this Prologue would do well to hold it in dynamic tension with the concrete Christmas narrative, as a way of uniting the Word—the Prologue itself—and the flesh—the embodied story of Jesus' birth. The writer of John keeps a grasp on facts of history such as Jesus and John the Baptist both being misunderstood. A useful connection can be made between these misunderstandings and the ease with which the church and the world can misunderstand the coming of Christ.

One thought about light and dark in preaching: the African-American churches in particular have called attention to the slippery uses of dark or black as symbols for evil. It is important to be sensitive to those problematic connotations, even where no racial language is used, in scriptural passages where light is idealized and dark is treated as inferior or dangerous. We can make a distinction between facts—such as day being light and night being dark—and problematic images of personal and group identity.

1 Samuel 2:18–20, 26 (C)

The last line in Luke's story of young Jesus in the temple quotes 1 Samuel 2:26, a tribute to the virtue of the young man who would become the first of the judges. Verses 18–20 in this story about Samuel depict another set of faithful parents like Mary and Joseph, making their yearly religious pilgrimage. But in the case of Samuel, the boy is already living away from home while in religious service. Thus, in contrast to the plaints of Jesus' worried parents, Samuel receives each year the gift of a robe from his mother Hannah. The fact that he wears a linen ephod links him with David, for it is a religious trapping uniquely believed to link the wearer with God.

1 Samuel 1:20–22, 24–28 (RC)

This lection portrays the actual birth of Samuel, "in due time," and the strength of his mother Hannah's vow that she would bring him to the temple to serve God. Hannah's practicality emerges in her bringing to the temple at Shiloh not only her son but three sacrifices—a bull, flour, and wine. If people wish to press for parallelism between this Old Testament story and the infancy account in Luke, it is possible to recognize the two scheduled births, the three gifts, and the expectations that the child will serve God. One difference, however, is that Hannah is cited as talking to Eli at the temple about the vow she has made and is keeping, while Mary is cited after the birth as keeping her thoughts in her heart—quiet for a time, though as John notes in the Cana account, capable of speaking in public as well

Preaching from this passage may be made easier by the fact that listeners will already know the Luke story quite well. To bring out some of the parallels and contrasts in the story of Samuel may help people to think of the scale of Jesus' connection to the saga of the judges in the Hebrew Scriptures, while making visible Jesus' departure from the model of a single individual's service in the temple.

Jeremiah 31:10–13 (L)

See also Christmas 2, (C) (E).

"And they shall be radiant over the goodness of the LORD" (v. 12). This is the promise of the prophet Jeremiah, who has in many other instances put his attention on dire prophecies rather than radiant hopes. The land will change, the people will come back, the young will be inspired by what they see. So the writer hopes, and so hopes the church which comes together again after the frequent Christmas "blitz" to pick up the pieces of who we are and what we believe. This echo of promise from a source so often perceived as negative can act as a verbal compass for the time when worshipers often need a pointed word about what the coming of Christ is capable of accomplishing in the world and in the soul.

Isaiah 61:10–62:3 (E)

See also Christmas 2, (L).

This pericope is full of delight and celebration, sentiments perfectly fitting the First Sunday after Christmas. The joy felt by the writer is personal, but not only personal. One may feel like a bride or bridegroom, but to seek the vindication of the beloved poor in a beleaguered Zion is to move into the realm of justice to an entire community. The naturalness of God's actions emerges in the garden metaphors; there is the prospect of new shoots appearing in full view of all nations. Further, the giving of a new name to Jerusalem by the Lord is a dramatic way to say that in the light of the Lord's presence the whole identity of the beloved ones has changed forever.

Preaching this passage needs to be done in keeping with its celebrative mood, while also taking account of the radical claim for change that these verses present. As verification, Jesus' quoting of the verses just prior to the present passage was seen as a radical act by listeners in the temple (Luke 4).

Colossians 3:12–17 (C)

This passage gives guidance for life in the light of Christ. Paul's advice in this section contrasts the qualities of the new morality, produced by personal dwelling in the presence of Christ's forgiving love, with the qualities of the old "morality" which promoted lying, anger, and other forms of falseness.

To preach on this passage it is essential that the general qualities are drawn toward concrete, experienced realities known to the listeners, because general concepts alone will not be remembered long even by attentive listeners. The best link to the Christmas story in Luke may be that like the shepherds we may be changed forever by what we have seen, and by what has been said to us about that vision.

Hebrews 2:10–18 (L)

Hebrews in general is an argument for various points of Christian doctrine. In the case of Christmas 1 the doctrine need not be deep or abstruse. The key point in this passage is that Jesus Christ is the high priest for all the descendants of Abraham. The christological paradox, offered forthrightly throughout this passage, is that Jesus "partook of the same nature" (v. 14) and treated as "brethren" the very children whose sins he suffered to remove.

In terms of **preaching,** these verses remind of Jesus' coming to earth as a flesh-and-blood human being, while they also indicate a priestly calling for the Human One, to destroy the power of death through death itself.

1 John 3:1–2, 21–24 (RC)

The first part of this pericope is centered on the fact that we have been made God's children through Christ. Interestingly, it does not stay with that point, but allows for the possibility that "what we shall be" will change and that we will somehow be like Christ when the End time occurs. More important than exactly what will happen later, according to this writer, is the idea that once made children of God we cannot lose this status.

The second, separate part of this pericope takes a different angle on the same idea—that God has made us God's children, and that even our uncertainty or mistakes cannot destroy that relationship. From the standpoint of **preaching,** this idea is of great significance, for it seems that many people think they can be removed from God's favor for even trivial reasons. A major cause of individuals' moving away from the church, many report, is that they have felt judged and thereby made unacceptable to God and to others in the church. So the idea of relationship to God as unchangeable and everlasting may need more emphasis than has been thought. Appropriately, the passage ends with the love commandment, and the connection between keeping the commandments and staying within the realm of the Spirit. Distinguishing between the spirit and the letter of God's law can be another helpful act of instruction by preachers.

Galatians 3:23–25; 4:4–7 (E)

See also Pentecost 5, (C).

The image of being imprisoned by the law is vivid here, but it must be acknowledged that Paul himself was a student of the law and not inclined to ignore its power. Instead, he uses this opportunity to explore the paradox that Jesus was born under the law, and born under the natural law of bodily birth from a woman, and at the same time that Jesus is the means for faith to free believers from imprisonment to legalism. Most of the Galatians to whom he writes are Gentiles, troubled by both the legalistic Judaizers and the gnostic libertines, so Paul is intent on giving them a clear and persuasive reminder of the gift of Jesus Christ and its power to change their lives.

Noteworthy here is Paul's frequent pattern of spinning out an argument by a quick step-by-step progression. Through Christ's birth, he says, we have all been (1) adopted as sons (children) of God, and if that is true, we have been (2) given the spirit of Jesus, the Son, in our hearts, and if that is true, we are (3) the heirs of God. This form of argument could be countered by other claims, to be sure, but in this case it serves to bolster new believers who may have lost confidence in the face of attacks and counterattacks on their beliefs.

The preacher can lift up the central idea in this passage, of being God's adopted children in contrast to being slaves in a household, either by the literal experience of slavery and being freed in American history, or by the various kinds of slavery that people encounter (to food, drugs, negative relationships, gambling, and the contrasting experience of liberation.

Theological Reflection

This array of messages reflects the array of interpretations of the meaning of the Christ event for individuals and the church. Luke leads us to think of the youthful Christ moving into the world of the temple. John tells us that the cosmic light has come into this world as the Word of God became flesh in our midst. The Hebrew writers lift up the natural and personal changes which God brings forth, while the epistle writers urge on their communities new life choices in the light of Christ's past and future coming. In widely varying ways, these writers embody the truth that Christ alters the world, the community, and the soul.

Children's Message

I have a story to tell you. I'm pretty sure that this story really happened, quite a while ago; it was told to me by someone else. A little girl went to dinner with her father and mother to a restaurant where they had never been before. Her father told the waitress what he wanted to eat, her mother said what she wanted, and then the father told the waitress what the little girl would have—without looking at her or asking her. The waitress waited politely till the father had finished, then turned to the little girl and said, "What will you have for dinner?" The little girl was *very* surprised—you could even say shocked—but she finally answered in a small voice, "I'd like a hamburger and French fries and a glass of milk, please." The waitress smiled at her, wrote down the order, and went off to the kitchen. Then the little girl looked after the waitress and said, mostly to herself, "She thinks I'm *real!*"

Do you like that story? (Wait for responses.) I do. The reason I like it so much is that it seems like the way God is acting toward us by giving us the gift of Jesus. God thinks we are *real,* enough to have this wonderful friend and helper and leader in our world—even if we haven't always been perfect enough to deserve his coming. That's really something, isn't it? I think God hopes we will be so happy and so confident because of being loved this much that we will pass on the happiness and love and good actions in the world, wherever we go—to school, to playgrounds, to friends' houses, and home to our own house and family.

This week, whenever things are just a little bit hard for you, will you try to say to yourself, "Well, God thinks I'm *real* and I'm wonderful." Say it with me now (everyone!)—"God thinks I'm *real* and I'm wonderful." God thinks that every one of us is real, and that everyone—you, I, all of us—is wonderful enough to have Jesus Christ as our gift.

Enjoy that feeling. OK?

Hymns for Christmas 1

Break Forth, O Beauteous Heavenly Light; The Sheep Stood Stunned in Sudden Light (*New Hymns for the Lectionary*); The First One Ever.

Christmas 2

Psalm 147:12–20 (C)   Ephesians 1:3–6, 15–18 (C) (L) (RC)
                            Ephesians 1:3–6, 15–19a (E)
Jeremiah 31:7–14 (C) (E)
Isaiah 61:10–62:3 (L)   John 1:1–18 (C) (L) (RC)
Sirach 24:1–2, 8–12 (RC)   Matthew 2:13–15, 19–23 (E)

Meditation on the Texts

Send us wisdom on this day, O God of knowledge and truth. Help us to absorb the meaning of your appearance on this earth, and to recognize your continuing claim on our minds and hearts. We tend to see you only in fleeting glimpses, while we gaze at length on the world's glitter and glow. On this Sunday of the Christmas season, keep our eyes on the star that brought the shepherds and the Magi to the Christ-child. At the same time, keep us alert to the false worshipers like Herod, who would speak of a celebration but destroy the actual presence of the Christ.

As I study the passages for this week, may the eyes of my heart be enlightened; may the light of the star, shining on the light of the world, enter into my being in a new way. I know some words, some stories almost too well; help me to come to them as a reader of a new language, as if the words had just been translated into a form I could understand with my whole being. Finally, let me be open to the wisdom that comes when knowledge and love are merged. Let the wisdom I am able to encounter in these words become a gift to those with whom I speak, a gift we will all choose to share in wider and wider circles. Amen.

Commentary on the Texts

John 1:1–18 (C) (L) (RC)

See also Christmas 1, (E).

For Christmas 2 the churches are well positioned to move toward the philosophical implications of Christ's coming to the world. Specifically, the theme of wisdom is in front of us, both in terms of Christ as embodied Wisdom (cf. Sirach 24 below) and in terms of the wisdom that becomes available to human beings when we submit ourselves to the awesome experience of Christ's revelatory presence.

Many worshipers will be surprised to learn that the Prologue to John has its polemical as well as its philosophical side. One can almost imagine the writer of this Gospel standing facing a wondrous light, holding up one open hand to receive the light of wisdom, while using the other hand to fend off one of the followers of John the Baptist. The fact that the Prologue can be read in such a way that the partisan struggle between Jesus followers and John followers is not apparent is a tribute to the author's rhetorical ability. In this Prologue John is called a witness, and he calls himself a witness, to the One who is greater than he. Thus John the Baptizer is given the final word that limits his own claim to Messiahship.

For **preachers** who want to use this Prologue in preaching, it would be helpful to find ways to bring to life its hymnic quality. A reading of successive verses by several chosen individuals, or a choral reading by a small group, or simply a responsive reading of alternate verses by people on one side of the aisle and then the other—any of these can be ways to help people hear more fully, and in a literally more embodied way, these words that have such direct and profound power. Terms like *logos* and "wisdom" tend to remain abstract and distant for many who hear them in the church. The act of speaking a powerful word can reverse that trend.

Matthew 2:13–15, 19–23 (E)

The story of the flight of Jesus and his parents into Egypt is offered only in the Gospel of Matthew; thus we experience a departure from the Gospel of Luke for this week's Gospel reading in the Episcopal lectionary. This tiny story is one of the most easily visualized stories in all of the Gospels, and because of this it is often drawn or painted in religious materials.

The Episcopal lectionary includes only the flight, but not the intervening material (one could call it a subplot) about Herod's rage and the resulting massacre of male infants in Bethlehem. The result is that the focus is on one story, but again it is a story that paradoxically joins the most private family unit and a large-scale political struggle that crosses both national and religious boundaries.

Structurally this story follows several requirements of form that fit Matthew's interest in the way the coming of Christ fulfills God's plan for salvation. First, the flight occurs after Joseph has had one of the three dreams or visits by an angel that guide his actions in behalf of Mary and the infant. Second, the story has two verses that act as fulfillment citations, verifying that the event carries out the will of God as stated by the prophets: "Out of Egypt have I called my son" and "He shall be called a Nazarene." If Matthew was trying to show his community that Jesus was the founder of the New Israel, these links would be essential. Finally, the third element in the story that seems to have been of interest to Matthew is the motif of danger, hiding, and relief that was well known from the birth story of Moses and to some extent in the Exodus saga as well. Letting the old stories echo into the new ones is a major activity for believers, and Matthew does this with an apparent concern for his listeners' self-perceptions in relation to history.

For readers and listeners to this passage, there is another more psychological dimension to the story of the flight into Egypt. Coming away from Bethlehem, from the infant narrative, is coming away from a celebration and into another reality. One can admire the baby and delight in the gift of its presence, but at some point one must get up from a kneeling position and go off to other places—perhaps to tell the story to someone who will scoff or ignore it, perhaps to be quiet and to wait for another believer to come forth, perhaps to become embroiled in the getting and spending and worrying of daily life, unable to hold on to the sense of celebration at all.

The political dimension of Jesus' birth marches out, toward both the pulpit and the pews, in this passage from Matthew. It is up to **the preacher** whether that wider dimension is allowed to appear at this point in the church year, instead of being submerged in a more private portrayal of Mary, Joseph, and Jesus as a small band of temporary nomads. That Jesus was unwelcome—with a few exceptions—both early and later in his life is an inescapable fact.

The choice of Nazareth as the place for Jesus' youth has become well known through the appellation "Jesus of Nazareth" and the frequently used label "Nazarenes" for Christians. Though Matthew and the Gospel of John both refer to the prophets as naming Nazareth or the Nazarene as labels for Jesus, no specific mention of either term is made in the Hebrew Scriptures. The derogatory reference by Nathanael—"Can anything good come out of Nazareth?" (John 1:46)—indicates that the little village near a trade route was not a noteworthy place to call home, though its lack of pagan artifacts suggest that it may have been a place of piety.

Jeremiah 31:7–14 (C) (E)

See also Christmas 1, (L).

A redeemed and joyful community is imaged forth in this passage. Jeremiah prophesies a time of gathering in of the lost flocks of Zion, who will travel home and then enjoy a time of merrymaking and dance in the light of their new time of freedom. This passage comes from what is called the Book of Consolation (chs. 30–31) in Jeremiah. Though much of the book is later, this section probably came from the seventh century B.C.E., and its allusion to "the north country" probably meant Assyria, where many northerners had been taken by force.

The language of this passage is rich with sensory elements: the blind, the lame, the woman with child; singing aloud on the height of Zion; exulting in the grain, wine, and oil; and being like a watered garden because of the nurturance of the Lord. While the essential message is one of happiness, the mention of weeping is a reminder of the pain that the Israelites had had to endure before coming home to the garden and the dancing.

The preacher may point out one of the links between this section of Jeremiah and the Christmas story: the simile of God as the shepherd keeping a flock. Another less obvious parallel is in the youthfulness of the happy people of God: there are mentions of the maidens, the young men, and the young of the flock and the herd. As a whole this prophecy suggests some of the excitement of the early Advent passages, now expanded into fulfillment.

Isaiah 61:10–62:3 (L)

See also Christmas 1, (E).

As in the passage from Jeremiah 31 cited earlier, the image of the garden is visible in this passage. The image is appropriate because it indicates that the growth of righteousness and praise springs up naturally under God's rule. Another use of natural material is the citation of the speaker as a bridegroom or bride covered with salvation and righteousness. We can note that the speaker is treated as analogous to either bride or groom, perhaps implying that God's gifts are given openly to both sexes. The images of bride and groom continue into the next chapter, beyond the scope of the present pericope.

The second half of this passage (62:1–3) conveys the urgency of God's vindication of Zion. "I will not keep silent" says the prophet, until the vindication is widely known and a new name is bestowed on the chosen people. Interestingly, the new names are those of private emotions and personal relationships, evoking the personal quality of God's relationship with the Israelites. Changes of name are markers of changes in identity. Another personal detail is the use of the first person pronoun; it is one indication of the difference between Second Isaiah and Third Isaiah, for the former contained primarily community hymns rather than the words of an individual. The royal diadem in the hand of God is the headdress denoting God's kingship; the fact that it is in God's hand suggests that God's sovereignty is being won through the redemption of God's people.

One approach for **the preacher** using this passage is to live with the idea of Zion, and the modern people of God, being called by a new name. The power of naming harks back to the power of the Word, Logos, and Wisdom emerging from the mouth of God. Named as a Christian, my being and my presence to others are both changed.

Sirach 24:1–2, 8–12 (RC)

This apocryphal book has many names: Greek manuscripts name it The Wisdom of Jesus the Son of Sirach, the Syriac text calls it The Wisdom of Bar Sira (after its author Ben Sira), many Western Christians call it Ecclesiasticus, and one tenth-century scholar calls it The Book of Discipline and Instruction. The book as a whole recalls both the prophetic and the wisdom literature, but most particularly Job, Proverbs, and Ecclesiastes. The author's grandson translated the book into Greek, citing the importance of the book's practical wisdom and its importance in helping Jews live in obedience to Mosaic law. Ben Sira probably wrote the original book between 200 and 180 B.C.E., at a time of struggle leading up to the Maccabean revolt.

Wisdom in Sirach is positioned between Hellenic and Judaic thought, with the balance finally in the direction of revelation as the true wisdom. Knowledge is valued, but the fear of God is primary. Wisdom in this book is also an allegorical character, one who speaks of and for herself. The lection for this Sunday presents Wisdom as a forthright speaker in her own behalf, as the Creator's emissary to the people of Jacob and Israel, finding "a place for my tent" (v. 8) among an honored people. The mix of the concrete and the timeless is striking in this passage, for along with the tent, the dwelling, territory, and the city we find repeated language about eternity. Wisdom is both a palpable experience for Ben Sira and something far beyond human grasp and control.

Various scholars have examined the use of the female imagery for Wisdom. It is a tradition not unique to Sirach, though it is noteworthy in this book because the author's treatment of actual women in the book is highly negative. **For further study** of the wisdom tradition among both Jews and Christians, consider the work of Susan A. Cady, Marian Ronan, and Hal Taussig, *Sophia: The Future of Feminist Spirituality* (San Francisco: Harper & Row, 1986) and their second book, *Wisdom's Feast: Sophia in Study and Celebration* (San Francisco: Harper & Row, 1989).

As a text for the Second Sunday after Christmas, this reading offers an image of revelation that links the incarnation of Jesus with the wisdom tradition that was operative in his time. Jesus Christ is both a palpable human being and, as Christine Smith has written, "a parable of God" (*Weaving the Sermon,* pp. 84–86; Louisville, Ky.: Westminster/John Knox Press, 1989)—not capable of being fixed in meaning, but clearly a link between the human and the divine. Christ as Wisdom may be hard to grasp in cognitive terms, but Christ as revealing the wisdom of the divine can be a liberating image.

For **the preacher** this passage has intriguing possibilities for creativity, and at least one potential minefield. It is intriguing to look more closely at Jesus as bringing Wisdom to the earth through his birth, ministry, death, and resurrection. It is also worth considering the tension between the earthly tent and the eternal, both in terms of Christ's presence at Christmastide and our own experiences of our lives with each other. A third possibility is also a risk: the passage in Sirach talks of the *people* of Zion as God's inheritance, but there is also the connotation of the place, Jerusalem, and more widely, Israel, as the inheritance of the people themselves. That second meaning is at the heart of the Zionist struggle for the specific section of land now called Israel. Thus, it makes a great deal of difference whether you read Sirach 24 as providing a particular plot of land as an inheritance to one set of people, or read it as God's rendering the people into an inheritance to God. The Melkite Christian priest Elias Chacour has written eloquently about this struggle because of living his life in and around Galilee; see his *Blood Brothers* (Grand Rapids: Zondervan Publishing House, 1985).

Ephesians 1:3–6, 15–18 (C) (L) (RC)

Ephesians 1:3–6, 15–19a (E)

While Paul's authorship of this brief letter is not beyond dispute, the letter seems to be a fine summary of Paul's beliefs about the church and the roots of belief. The present passage has two particular directions: vs. 3–6 are a prayer of blessing to God, incorporating the idea of God's predestined love for human beings; and vs. 15–18 (or 19a, a more logical boundary) are a prayer for wisdom and revelation among the Ephesians.

The first part of this passage includes the phrase "heavenly places"—wording that appears also in Ephesians 1:20 and 2:6, 3:10, 6:12, and similar to that which appears in Philippians 3:20. This phrase denotes the realm in which Christ rules after his resurrection, sharing this realm with those raised into new life with him, and continuing to wage spiritual warfare against the powers of darkness and evil. The status of believers as children of God through grace is one of Paul's most dominant themes.

Verses 15–18 extend the prayer of blessing into the present and future, honoring the Ephesians and wishing for them the mixture of wisdom and revelation that was seen above in the selection from Sirach. Two particularly appealing phrases occur in this section of the pericope. The first is "having the eyes of your hearts enlightened" (v. 18), a wonderful way of referring to one's spiritual discernment by uniting images of truth and feeling. The second striking phrase occurs in the longer version of this pericope, in v. 19a: "and what is the immeasurable greatness of his power in us who believe" unites the cosmic scope of God's power and the immediacy of personal commitment to the gospel. These two instances make theological statements in language that can be grasped and remembered by nontheologians.

Preachers dealing with this passage would be well advised to follow the guidance of the lectionary committees, who chose (wisely in this writer's view) to tie the cosmic affirmation to the experience and hopes of the local community. Several phrases in this passage warrant extended treatment. It may be more effective to pick as a center a single phrase that has strong meaning for the preacher than to try to run through the entire pericope in summary fashion. As an example, one might ask, When in my life have I found the eyes of my heart to be enlightened, and what did that do to my Christian faith?

Theological Reflection

Though there are statements about the deity in this week's passages, the main direction of these readings is toward the believers' capacity to discern, to absorb, and then to live by the embodied truth that comes in the Christmas narrative. Herod is offered as an example of one who could not stand the truth, and the Ephesians are cited as disciples called to live the truth in the church. The passages in Jeremiah, Isaiah, and implicitly in Sirach show forth the celebrative response to the truth, and it is essential that Western Christians not lose awareness of the necessary role of delight in the corporate life of the church. The Prologue to John stands as a beacon in the midst of all of this, saying simply and profoundly that the Word was, and is, and forever shall be at the heart of spiritual life.

Children's Message

What do you think it takes to be a wise person? Do you know anyone you think of as a wise person? What does that person do that seems wise, that seems to you to show wisdom? (Allow time for answers, and pull out a quality or a phrase from each.)

I've been thinking about this idea of wisdom, because Wisdom is a character in the Bible readings for this week. Did you notice that I called Wisdom a *character* in the Bible? Now, I don't want to give you the wrong idea: this isn't a character like Batman or the Little Mermaid. Some of the people who wrote our Bible considered Wisdom to be one of the most essential qualities of God, what made God God. Wisdom was a feature of God so important that it was given a name, as a woman, someone who could give people the power to think right and make good decisions when they were faithful to God.

Wisdom in the Bible is a gift that God gives to certain people and groups of people. It is a wonderful gift that can be used to help other people, and to bring people closer to God and the church by helping them use their minds well.

How many of you have seen Mr. Rogers on television? He has an imaginary land, ruled by King Friday, a puppet king, and visited by various human and puppet characters. Sometimes one of the humans gets to be the Wisdom person—the one who has figured out what King Friday doesn't realize—and sometimes the Queen is the Wisdom person, quietly saying what she has noticed about the problem that needs to be solved.

I've known a number of wise people in my life, but the one I think of most is my Grandmother Latta, my mother's mother. She never pointed a finger at me, never told me I *had* to do certain things or I'd be a terrible child. When I asked her questions about why things happened and what she thought, she always gave me an answer and always listened to my words and my feelings. Grandmother was my version of Wisdom; she knew what was right and what was wrong, she knew that some people were more honest and friendly than others, and she knew that you could get along a little better if you were courteous to people, even the ones who weren't your favorites. I learned from her that life was pretty good, and that caring about people was worth the trouble.

You may or may not have met the people who are going to be your own Wisdom people in your life. Keep an eye out for them. We need the help of Wisdom, and it can come in any size body, at any age. Isaiah once said, "And a little child shall lead them." *You* could be one of the Wisdom people for other people!

Hymns for Christmas 2

The Hands That First Held Mary's Child (*New Hymns for the Lectionary*); Jesus Comes Today (*Praising a Mystery*); Angels, from the Realms of Glory; Woman in the Night.

(Epiphany 1)

Psalm 29 (C)   **Acts 8:14–17 (C)**
                                     Acts 10:34–38 (L) (E)
Isaiah 61:1–4 (C)   **Titus 2:11–14; 3:4–7 (RC)**
Isaiah 42:1–7 (L)
Isaiah 40:1–5, 9–11 (RC)   **Luke 3:15–17, 21–22**
Isaiah 42:1–9 (E)

Meditation on the Texts

God of light and fire and living water, we look for you in the world around us, and we often do not know whom we see and hear. We speak of your Holy Spirit, hoping that it will come to us and abide with us, but we often lose touch with your Spirit as we come and go in daily life. On this day of Epiphany, when your presence is manifested through a baptism into the Holy Spirit and through the proclamation of God's favor, we have a new opportunity to absorb the truth of your presence and your ministry to us on this earth. We thank you for these signs of truth and power.

As I prepare to preach on this Sunday of the Baptism of Our Lord, may I be open to a renewed sense of my own baptism into the community of faith. May I hear Isaiah's call to be a servant, and to seek justice and liberation of all the oppressed. May I stand with Paul and Peter and Priscilla and Aquila, beholding the grace in Jesus Christ and conveying its power to other disciples. May I have the integrity of John the Baptizer, able to speak with strength, and willing to submit myself to being a true witness to Jesus Christ. In my studies and my preaching, may I experience the tangible presence of the triune God, and may I remain confident in the power of the gospel to change lives. Amen.

Commentary on the Texts

Luke 3:15–17, 21–22

As mentioned earlier in the material for Advent 3, John the Baptizer recognized both the importance of witnessing to the coming of the Lord and his own subordination as witness to the One whose way he was preparing. In the current pericope for this Sunday, called both Epiphany and the Baptism of Our Lord, the perspective of the witness is underscored. The idea of epiphany centers on the notions of revealing, appearance, and manifestation—and all of these are terms that come into the various lections chosen for this Sunday. Behind the language is a phenomenon difficult to put into words: it is the fact of knowing the truth of the presence of someone or something, encountering that which cannot be ignored or denied or mistaken for something else. John the Baptizer in this respect is like each of us as modern believers. He is a witness to the revelation of God in Jesus Christ. He sees what we can see only by means of his witness; he hears what we can hear only through his witness; and thus he has the position of receiving and recording in our behalf the presence and power of Christ.

In v. 17, John prophesies that the One who comes will separate the wheat from the chaff as a farmer does when threshing grain. The images are visual and powerful—the winnowing fork and the burning of the chaff—with a strength that connotes judgment. Since wind and fire are symbols of the Holy Spirit in Luke's writing (see Acts 2:2–3), the residual message in this part of the passage may be that the Holy Spirit is to judge more than to counsel. This would be in keeping with the Hebrew connotation of prophet.

What Luke reports in vs. 21–22 is the baptism of Jesus along with a crowd of other people, and the crucial aftermath of that baptism. Jesus is not set apart as a visiting dignitary, but instead undergoes the same baptism that others undergo in the presence of John. The Greek phrase that has been translated "had been baptized" denotes the act of undergoing immersion, or immersing oneself. This suggests, as does the Greek of Mark 1:9, that John was the witness to many baptisms including that of Jesus, but that John was not the administrator of the baptism himself. Jesus immersed himself along with many other people, all of them witnessed by John.

The second section of this Sunday's Gospel passage is quite different with regard to its time and space perspective. It comes after we are already told that John is in prison, so it is a kind of flashback. It has both private and public elements. On the one hand, Jesus is said to be in prayer after baptism when the skies open. Also, the heavenly voice says, "Thou art my beloved Son," a direct address to Jesus, not the crowd. On the other hand, the bodily form of a dove descends upon him, and this is presumably visible to everyone present. So the Epiphany, the manifestation of Jesus empowered with the Holy Spirit, is both a public event and a private experience. The same can be said of the experience of the manifest Christ as a phenomenon for modern believers. To lose the personal, prayerful element is to risk becoming detached from spirituality. To limit the Epiphany to a private possession is to leave behind the responsibility of ministry and evangelism.

This split pericope allows **the preacher** to emphasize the prophecy of John, with its vivid and even intimidating metaphor of the wheat and the chaff. A more upbeat option is to examine the public baptism and the proclamation which follows as the manifestation of Jesus' call and claim to royal servanthood. Since Jesus was baptized with the people, the event confirms our own call to servanthood. The Spirit comes embodied from the heavens to empower Jesus, and Jesus himself comes embodied into our world to empower us. This passage offers an opportunity to unite the vertical (God to human) and the horizontal (human to human) aspects of the moment of Baptism-Epiphany.

Isaiah 61:1–4 (C)

This passage is well known in its New Testament version, as quoted by Jesus in his first synagogue sermon in Nazareth. (Luke 4:18–19, the Lucan version of this material, appears later in the lectionary for Epiphany 3.) In both New and Old Testament versions one of the key elements is the persona of the preacher: this speaker has a clear and unified social agenda, to liberate the righteous poor and reverse their ill fortune, and the speaker is confident that the announced good news will come true. There is some debate as to whether these verses come from Second Isaiah or Third Isaiah; the portrayal of the speaker suggests Third Isaiah as the more likely. Some scholars note that the uses of both "day of vengeance" and "year of the LORD's favor" suggest a lack of specificity in the stated promises, but this does not seem unusual or problematic in a prophetic utterance. One can recall Dr. Martin Luther King, Jr.'s speech "I Have a Dream," in which no specific date is given for the resolution of the problem of racism in the United States. The vision itself is necessary to motivate caring persons into action.

The word "anointing" traditionally refers to the anointing of royalty, but in this case it may have more of the connotation of being appointed to a task. The prophet's essential task is to empower those in need: first to enable them to move away from mourning and into a perspective of gladness and praise, and then to empower them into being the strong and righteous fruits of God's nurture. The inclusion in this pericope of v. 4, even though it actually starts a new strophe, accentuates the idea that God's "righteous oaks" are intended to act, to repair and renew a damaged and hurting world. Righteousness is not a matter of private perfection, but a dedication to just action in the world beyond the individual being.

This passage has the kind of poetic power that deserves lively and careful reading from the pulpit or the lectern. **The preacher** can build on the fact that the prophecy comes from a confident, dedicated messenger of God, and that it offers an ultimately practical message of hope and constructive action for the church and the world.

Isaiah 42:1–9 (E)

This material develops the notion of the Servant to God and to the nations. While the language includes singular pronouns, there is the strong implication that a nation as a whole can be called to act as God's servant. The qualities of the servant are striking in their stringence, yet in their reasonableness. The servant, having been given the Spirit, is expected to work faithfully toward justice, to be nonviolent (honoring the bruised weed and the dimly burning wick), to liberate those in prison and those who are blind (compare Isaiah 61), to work quietly, and to persevere in the face of difficulty.

Having developed a character study of the ideal servant, individual or nation, the rest of this pericope completes the partnership by dealing with the nature of the God who claims the servant. God is an intimate partner: "I have taken you by the hand and kept you" (v. 6b). God is also the one who has created the universe (v. 5) and the one who chooses to allow the servant to have prior knowledge of events yet to come (v. 9).

This passage does not deal directly with baptism, but it does offer a perspective on God's manifestation through relating to humanity in a particular context. **For preaching,** the material dealing with the actions of the servant and the actions of God in empowering the servant have a very good chance of reaching listeners in their concerns with questions of vocation and the accessibility of God in their lives.

Isaiah 40:1–5, 9–11 (RC)

This selection offers a vivid and varied message, part of which has already been heard in the Roman Catholic Church during Advent 2, through its paraphase in Luke 3. In the longer pericope in Isaiah, the prophetic action goes in three distinct yet related directions: (1) Emissaries of Yahweh are told to bring comfort to Jerusalem after her long suffering; (2) a voice of an emissary calls in the wilderness for the straight way of the Lord, promising that the "glory of the LORD shall be revealed" (v. 5); (3) Jerusalem is called to go up to a high mountain and shout out the words "Behold your God!" (v. 9). While the structure of these subsections is not tight, they in effect circle around the phenomenon of the revelation of God's being and care. In this way, the passage bears on Epiphany. God is revealed to Jerusalem through comfort and tenderness, God is revealed to the people of Israel through the altering of creation, and with Jerusalem's help, God will be revealed to Israel and the nations through proclamation and from the acts of a shepherd. God is known wherever and whenever God chooses, and God chooses individual human beings and whole nations to make God known.

Acts 8:14–17 (C)

In this pericope as much as any for this Sunday, the link between baptism and the presence of the Holy Spirit is brought to the forefront. The context for this passage is the work of Philip in reaching out to the Gentiles in Samaria. Many people had been converted to belief in Jesus Christ, a source of happiness to the remaining disciples both in and outside of Jerusalem. At this period of time the persecutions of believers had led most Christians to flee from Jerusalem; but Peter and John remained, in the role of organizational leaders of the fledgling church. Word of Philip's success reached them, and Peter and John went to the city of Samaria to reinforce his work.

The report by Luke is clear: Philip could baptize new believers, but his preaching had not elicited the Holy Spirit. The key difference was the laying on of hands by the apostles. When Peter and John prayed for the Samaritans and laid their hands on them, the Holy Spirit came to them. It was a Pentecostal experience, perhaps accompanied by speaking in tongues and prophesying. It is important to note that, as in the other Lucan account (Luke 3:21–22), the act of being in prayer along with the act of physically touching the new convert produced the blessing of the presence of the Holy Spirit. Prayer was required as evidence of the believer's move toward God, in effect a precondition for the appearance of the Spirit to that individual.

The awkwardness of this passage, from an egalitarian point of view, is that it diminishes the power of the work of Philip, who was clearly an effective preacher: "and the multitudes with one accord gave heed to what was said by Philip" (Acts 8:6). On the other hand, it may be important to recognize that the coming of the Spirit is not entirely predictable for those who preach the word. An attitude of humility and a continuing posture of prayer toward the act of preaching may be an appropriate response to this particular story. Whether one believes that the Spirit is manifested only to those who are ordained within a particular church body is an area of debate that goes beyond the present passage. **For preaching,** it is worthwhile in any case to reflect seriously on one's actual beliefs about the Holy Spirit and its appearances.

Acts 10:34–38 (L) (E)

See also Easter Day, (C) (E).

This passage offers an excerpt of Peter's sermon to Cornelius in the home of this new convert in Caesarea. Cornelius is a Roman centurion and the third Gentile convert to be identified in the Book of Acts. The situation is both private and public, for Cornelius has called together many of his friends and relatives in honor of Simon Peter's visit.

Peter's attitude as a speaker harks back to the approach of the speaker in Isaiah 61: confident, clear, and without hesitation in his role as spokesperson for God. He states that he perceives God as impartial, an important prologue because Peter himself has had to grow into that belief. Then he goes on to review the settings in which Christ's "good news of peace" has been proclaimed up to this time. He reiterates both the baptism preached by John and Christ's anointing with the Holy Spirit "and with power" (v. 38). These two related but distinct phenomena are enlisted as proof of the truth of the Christian claim and the basis for Jesus' ability to heal, to win followers, and to do good. The foundation for all these assertions is simple: "for God was with him" (v. 38).

The ties between this truncated sermon and Luke's other report in chapter 3 of his Gospel are obvious. Baptism, of Jesus and of other believers, is the mark of new life. The anointing with the Holy Spirit empowered Jesus to do all that was necessary in his life and ministry. Peter's task in this setting is to recite the essential story of Jesus' actions, power, and impact, so that this story will be told again and again by those who hear him. It suggests the title of the old hymn, "I Love to Tell the Story." The gospel can only be spread if individuals and groups and communities decide to tell that story without ceasing.

For more insights on this topic see Clarice J. Martin, "Tongues of Fire: Studies in the Acts of the Apostles," in *Horizons,* 1990–91 (Louisville, Ky.: Presbyterian Church (U.S.A.)).

Titus 2:11–14; 3:4–7 (RC)

Along with the two letters to Timothy, this letter probably was written in the latter two decades of the first century C.E. It may have come from the pen of a secretary to Paul, or from someone who took Paul's notes and completed the letter with materials known to be compatible with Paul's approach. In any event, the present passage from Titus makes a connection familiar in the epistles between the glory of God and the ethical obligations of the Christian life. The context for this call to right action is a hopeful awaiting of the second coming of Jesus Christ. From the standpoint of a reading for Epiphany, the most pertinent phrase is v. 11, "For the grace of God has appeared," an affirmation of the manifestation of the Godhead in the presence of Jesus Christ among human beings. The implication here is that the only way that we can apprehend the grace of God is in the embodiment of Jesus and (one might add) of those whose lives Jesus has touched and changed forever.

For preaching, an idea worth noting from this passage is that Jesus came to purify a people for himself. At times the focus on the suffering of the cross can turn our attention away from the idea that Jesus was in the business of empowerment, equipping people to be "zealous for good deeds" (v. 14) and to help in bringing forth the glory of God in this world.

Theological Reflection

This Sunday, as the title suggests, has two directions: the Baptism of Jesus and the Epiphany, or the manifestation of God to humanity. As the analyses above have meant to suggest, the two are related, though the reader's or preacher's emphasis may be on one or the other. How one or many of us receive the appearance of God is what differentiates believers from those who may observe sensory data but discount them. Over and over again in these accounts, the prophets and preachers have tried to say what they knew and had seen, making the news as vivid and relevant as it could be, but knowing that others might or might not believe it.

A literary source may shed light on the experience we are calling Epiphany. James Joyce's *A Portrait of the Artist as a Young Man* (New York: Viking Press, 1964) centers on a young man, Stephen Daedalus, who wants to understand life and experience its essence—to grab what he calls the "quidditas," or the whatness, of what happens to him. He finds the quidditas elusive, and the search for ultimate essence both fascinating and frustrating. One distinction between the quidditas in this short novel and the Epiphany of the church year is that the Christian gospel, and thereby the church, takes account of the fact that the essence of experience does not lie within human control. It is interactive, and it is finally available only through the gift of clarity, a gift of the Holy Spirit. The same principle of reality both present and transcendent holds true in attempting to understand how Jesus Christ might have been baptized in the presence of John the Baptizer. It was an act that bonded him to human beings but at the same time marked him as the embodiment of a transcendent God, made manifest to humanity and the church.

Children's Message

Has anybody here ever heard of a person named Helen Keller? (Wait for responses, and use what material you can.)

She was a very bright little girl who was born in 1880. Because of an illness she had when she was younger than any of you are now, she was unable to hear and unable to see for the rest of her life. People used to say that someone was deaf and dumb if the person was unable to hear or to talk. The "dumb" part usually meant that the person was thought to be stupid if he or she couldn't talk to other people. Well, Helen wasn't stupid at all, but she couldn't talk. That is, not until a teacher came to live with her family. The teacher was Annie Sullivan, a young woman who was nearly blind herself.

Annie started from her first day with Helen Keller to try to teach Helen the letters of the alphabet, and to show Helen how letters went together to make words.

How many of you know the letters of the alphabet? Great. And how many of you know whole words? How many know this word? (Hold up a card with the word "water.")

It took months and months, and quite a bit of fighting and yelling, for Annie to get Helen to concentrate on one word—the word "water." She took Helen to the outdoor water pump, and spelled the letters into Helen's hand, again and again and again. And one day, all of a sudden, Helen *got it!* She knew that the wet liquid on her hand and the letters W A T E R were the same!

Today in the Christian church, we celebrate our own chance to be like Helen Keller. Jesus has come to us to show us what "living water" is—the loving-kindness of God that has come to earth in the form of Jesus of Nazareth. God tried and tried to show us what this loving-kindness was, but the people kept not knowing—not seeing and hearing. But Jesus was brought to earth to be a person of love and kindness, so that finally we could *see* and *hear* what God is like, and how God cares for us.

On this special day we remember what it is like to see and hear who Jesus really is, and how God really loves all of us. That's the living water, the water of overflowing love. The next time you see water running, think of little Helen Keller, and think of the flowing love of Jesus. Will you do that?

Hymns for Epiphany 1

Christ, Whose Glory Fills the Skies; Testimony (*Songs and Carols,* vol. 8); Christ, When for Us You Were Baptized; There's a Spirit in the Air.

Epiphany 2

Ordinary Time 2

Psalm 36:5–10 (C)   **1 Corinthians 12:1–11 (C) (L) (E)**
                         1 Corinthians 12:4–11 (RC)
Isaiah 62:1–5
                         John 2:1–11

Meditation on the Texts

O God, faithful and eternal lover of your people, you have brought us this day into the realm of celebration. We can see ourselves in the midst of an exuberant wedding celebration and feel the gratitude of those who drink new wine from an unexpected benefactor. We can identify ourselves with the symbolic wedding between your loving self and your beloved Israel, in language that tells us how deep and how endless your commitment to our welfare must be. We can absorb the importance of the varied gifts you have bestowed on your servants, so that each of us can bring your blessings in our own unique fashion to all others we may encounter.

In preparing to preach on this Second Sunday after Epiphany, may I know how fully you are engaged with me, with the church, and with the world. May I be honest, as was the writer of Third Isaiah, about my frustration that your will is so rarely done on the earth. May I be forthright, as I examine Paul's words to the Corinthians, in countering the words that appear to be your gospel but actually turn people away from it. May I hold on to the sense of celebration that comes whenever the resurrected Christ enters my thoughts with the aid of the Holy Spirit. May I be truly a guest at this celebration, whenever I lead worship among your people, so that they too will know they are welcome and honored and entitled to the blessed new wine. Amen.

Commentary on the Texts

John 2:1–11

This passage is widely known as the sole account of the first sign or miracle of Jesus. Most commentators identify Jesus' act of changing the water into wine at the wedding celebration at Cana as Jesus' first manifestation of divine power. Thus it is an appropriate lection for the season of Epiphany. The passage has also been used to justify various other views. Some readers say that it shows Jesus as being in favor of marriage rather than celibacy, and others conclude that the story shows the Savior's acceptance of social drinking. In any event, the story itself is appealing on the human level, and noteworthy in showing Jesus as part of a family and community celebration rather than as healing, preaching, or debating religious law with opponents.

The village of Cana in Galilee is mentioned only by John, in chapters 2, 4, and 21. Modern churches four miles northeast of Nazareth claim to be the location of Cana, but an unexcavated hill, nine miles from Nazareth, Khirbet Qana, is a more likely choice.

The Cana story comes immediately after a series of brief scenes showing John the Baptizer repeatedly meeting and pointing out the importantly named one who was to follow him—"the Lamb of God" and "Son of God." This series of meetings portrays John as leading his own disciples toward Jesus, and those disciples are shown as moving toward Jesus at least as much as Jesus is shown seeking out the disciples. The phrase "the next day" is used three times (1:29, 35, 43), underlining the short amount of time within which the followers of John the Baptizer had been effectively passed along to Jesus the Messiah. When the Cana narrative begins, the introductory phrase is "On the third day" (2:1) which does not make immediate sense chronologically but may have been for John the writer a symbolic parallel to the timing of the resurrection (see John 2:20–21 for another resurrection parallel).

Scholars have traditionally focused attention on the miraculous aspects of the story. The very fact that one hundred to one hundred fifty gallons of water were obtained by the servants is in itself an unusual occurrence, in addition to the fact that the wine became available to the wedding guests without any visible act of touching by Jesus. The unobtrusiveness of his action suggests a sign meant to be confirmation for the new disciples, rather than a dramatic miracle meant to impress a wider audience.

More recent analyses of this story focus on the progress of the story itself and the relationship between the adult Jesus and his mother (elsewhere known as Mary, but never thus named in John's Gospel). Mary's part in the story has traditionally been minimized in the light of the concern to show Jesus' action as glorifying God. Several recent scholars have noted that the event reveals a partnership between Jesus and Mary, showing the adult Mary as both sensitive mother and faithful disciple. **See, for example,** Rachel Conrad Wahlberg, *Jesus and the Freed Woman* (New York: Paulist Press, 1978); Evelyn and Frank Stagg, *Woman in the World of Jesus* (Philadelphia: Westminster Press, 1978); Denise Lardner Carmody, *Biblical Woman: Contemporary Reflections on Scriptural Texts* (New York: Crossroad, 1988); and Letty M. Russell, ed., *Feminist Interpretation of the Bible* (Philadelphia: Westminster Press, 1985).

The portrayal of the mother of Jesus as active in the Cana event is in keeping with John the Evangelist's consistently egalitarian treatment of women throughout his Gospel: John 4:7–42, the Samaritan woman; 8:3–11, the woman caught in adultery; 11:1–28, Martha grieving for Lazarus; 12:1–8, Mary of Bethany anointing Jesus' feet; and 20:1–18, Mary of Magdala at the empty tomb. More often than the physician Luke, John the Evangelist presents women's stories at length, showing women in ways that transcend their social and economic status in the Jewish household and community. Thus Mary's status at the wedding feast is not likely to have been an accidental detail for John. It is she who is mentioned first as present at the wedding, with Jesus and his disciples "also . . . invited" (2:2). She also is in a position to know that the wine had run out, perhaps because of being close to the celebrating family.

The relationship between Jesus and his mother in this story has brought forth varying interpretations. A crux in this matter is his brief speech to her, "O woman, what have you to do with me? My hour has not yet come" (v. 4). Three points of language can be clarified: (1) "Woman" or "O woman" would not be an unusual phrasing between two adults; it is somewhat formal, but not in itself disrespectful. (2) "What have you to do with me?" can also be translated "What to me and to you, woman," possibly connoting a response of distraction while being more involved with another concern, such as his new followers. (3) The "hour" in John is a term used frequently and intended to connote Jesus' appointed time of death and resurrection. In any case, we can hear the sound of some tension between the two; and Mary responds to it with a calm, unobtrusive request to the servants to "do whatever he tells you" (v. 5). She is not offended by Jesus' response to her, and she keeps her attention on seeing that the task is completed, with Jesus officially in command. Some respondents to this passage wonder if Mary was acting in a surreptitious or manipulative way; but others say that she sounds like a mother who knows that an intimate's "No" can turn into a "Yes" if not put under pressure. Those who remember Mary's Advent song The Magnificat can hear the echo of her praise, that God has "exalted those of low degree . . . [and] filled the hungry with good things" (Luke 1:52–53).

The boundary of this pericope should be noted as an interpretation in itself. Verse 12 states that Jesus went down to Capernaum, with his mother, brothers, and disciples, staying there for a few days. The fact that all lectionaries omit this sentence forces the passage away from the historical and interpersonal realities within which Jesus as well as his family and disciples functioned. While this choice highlights the miraculous quality of the event at Cana, it leaves out what John the Evangelist seems to have intended the church to know, namely, that Jesus was related to others and that early in his public ministry his human connections were viable along with his heavenly mission.

For the preacher lifting up this passage, it is important to avoid the temptation to polarize the passage, arguing that *either* this is the story of the first of Jesus' miracles *or* it is an account of a son dealing in some fashion with his mother (also a disciple) about when and how his public ministry would begin. The passage is rich with both concrete moments of speech and theological meaning. One can allow both Jesus and his mother to be visible as faithful persons, even while the dimension of Christ's glory is also respected. Such an approach can bring new meaning to many worshipers and provide an example of the joining of the divine and human.

Isaiah 62:1–5

This passage of Third Isaiah is fitting for Epiphany 2 because, like John 2, it refers to marriage. In this instance marriage is the metaphor for the right relationship between God and Israel, who will be married to a rejoicing God and will be called thenceforth "My delight is in her" (v. 4). But before the marriage delight is presented, the writer must express his anger that Jerusalem has not yet been vindicated, and her lands not yet restored to their rightful state. This material was written after the exile was over, and in the light of the not-yet-completed promise of God. The issue is not only restoration before the people of Israel, but being vindicated before all the nations of the world. The writer is angry, yet assertive about the vision still to be fulfilled.

This passage is rich with symbolic language. Being called by a new name is equivalent to being given a new identity in relationship to the namer, that is, God. The contrast between the name "Forsaken" and "My delight is in her" is essentially the difference between aloneness in struggle and confidence in the care of the divine. The marriage language recurs in both Hebrew Scriptures and New Testament, here with particularly intimate and joyous terminology. Symbolic "marriage" between humanity and God is not a relationship of distant awe but a close, committed bond of knowing and affirmation. Verses 3–4 add the dimension of royalty, as noted earlier in the material for Christmas 2.

For preaching, this passage offers an opportunity to lift up the dual experiences of the prophet's anger at what has been blocked and delight at the prospect of what can still be attained. Worshipers often believe that anger is not present in the Bible, and certainly not condoned, but Third Isaiah embodies the form of anger that arises from hope and energy blocked from fulfillment. This experience needs to be expressed somewhere if the anger is to be transcended and replaced by positive emotions. Dealing with these phenomena in preaching is a contribution to realism and constructive action in the church as well as in private relationships.

1 Corinthians 12:1–11 (C) (L) (E)

1 Corinthians 12:4–11 (RC)

This is the first of many lections that have been taken from 1 Corinthians 12–15. The material in these chapters focuses on the Holy Spirit and the spirits that can appear in the church in problematic ways. Using these materials in the season of Epiphany highlights the place of the church in appropriating gifts and resolving conflicts in expressions of faith.

The church at Corinth functioned within a cosmopolitan trading city, full of variety in sociological backgrounds, religious histories, and perspectives on morality. Paul as a missionary had already written to the church at Corinth before the official "First Letter," as indicated by references to earlier discussions, debates, and inquiries. Gnosticism had its power in that community, as did Jewish Hellenistic wisdom theology. The latter was especially pertinent to questions about the Spirit, for Hellenistic Christians tended to see themselves as rising above the body through wisdom (*sophia*) and thereby becoming "spiritual persons." Paul apparently did not see them that way, but he wanted to instruct them accurately about the Holy Spirit so that they would mature in the Christian faith.

The pericope for this Sunday can begin at either v. 1 or v. 4. Beginning at v. 1, one can hear Paul responding to the Corinthians as a careful and circumspect instructor. People who had called themselves pneumatics or spiritual persons had gone too far in presuming they could discern the workings of the Holy Spirit, so Paul gives a concrete example to these learners in the faith: no one can curse Jesus and be speaking by the Spirit, only the phrase "Jesus is Lord" (v. 3) can be said by the true guidance of the Holy Spirit. The words said are thus as important as the claim to speak by the Spirit.

Verses 4–11 deal with the variety of spiritual gifts inspired by God. This section probably arose out of a situation of competition and envy among the Corinthians—a situation not hard to imagine from the perspective of late-twentieth-century church life. Three facets of the gifts should be noted: (1) The variety of gifts is both asserted and demonstrated by a listing of nine distinct gifts, including the last two related to speaking in tongues. It is likely that Paul's listing of wisdom, knowledge, and faith as the first three and tongues and the interpretation of tongues as the last two was based on the writer's value judgment. (2) All these gifts have a common source of inspiration in the Holy Spirit, so they are not random expressions by individuals. (3) For Paul, highly significant, these gifts are all meant for the common good, for the building up of the community. Tongues can have potentially positive value or they can divide a faith community because of the difficulty in interpreting them and incorporating their insights into the understanding of all the local believers. This last point would have been especially relevant in Corinth, where diverse groups probably operated in ignorance of or in conflict with other groups.

Paul's use of the word "faith" may have been centered on the community at Corinth, for it seems to mean an intensity of faith expression within the church. This use of "faith" might connote a helpful gift if one having it was strong enough to draw others toward the Christian gospel. However, as with the other gifts, if an application of a gift became an individualistic dramatization of skill or superiority, it would not build up the church as a whole and would thus contribute to dividing the community already in existence. Paul is writing to the people of Corinth to guard against just such a possibility.

Preaching from this passage can be relatively easy, for the parallel between the multiplicity of forces in Corinth and the situations in most communities allows many people to find an identification between themselves and the Corinthians. More specifically, the existence of several gifts, all honored by God but often differentiated in value by human beings, can be dealt with as a current parallel to the biblical problem. One might ask people which gift they believe they have, if any, and then ask which gift they wish they had or envy another individual for having. The important move in such a sermon is to respect the diversity of gifts as God-given, and then to consider how to implement one's gifts appropriately for the common good. For Western Christians, trying *not* to compare the relative merits of different gifts is a major challenge, and one worth undertaking.

Theological Reflection

The intimacy of God's presence with humanity is bodied forth in each of the passages for this Sunday. Isaiah is intimate with God both through the anger expressed at Jerusalem's continuing struggle and through the array of names bestowed on the other as bride and royal diadem. John tells an intimate story of mother and son, attending a wedding and showing God's power through an immediate and friendly transfer of one element into another. Paul is also intimate with the Corinthians as he tries to wean them from a false view of the Spirit and to help them honor the variety of gifts that they may have in the service of the young church. In all these passages, God is available to those who believe, wanting grace and happiness to occur for them. God is manifest as one who cares, commits, restores, and bestows, always in ways that can benefit the community as a whole as well as the individual.

Children's Message

One thing about growing up is that you become more and more able to do things for yourself. My little girl used to have a book that was called, in fact, *I Can Do It Myself.* It had all sorts of pictures of Bert and Ernie from "Sesame Street" showing that they could do things for themselves—things like putting on their own clothes, tying their own shoes, combing their own hair, picking up their toys, and straightening up their bed. How many of you put on your own clothes? How many tie your own shoes? How many pick up your toys? That's great. Now how many of you buy and cook your own food? How many of you drive yourself to school or church? So it looks like you can do quite a few things for yourself, but not everything. You need help to get along.

Do you think God needs help to get along? How many say yes, and how many say no? (Leave time for both, and encourage and take account of both answers.) I think you're both right. I think that God is mightier and wiser than any woman or man who lives on the earth, and God is strong like the wind and the fire and all the powers of the earth. So the "no" people have a point. But the Bible tells us clearly that God has always wanted to have a people to love and to help God make the world a more loving and fair and open kind of place for all people to live in. God came to earth in the form of Jesus, and gave us ideas about what we could do to help God's plan. Some people helped, some didn't, and some who were afraid of Jesus and God's power tried to kill him; but the power of Jesus does not die. Do you know why? Because of people who believe and speak the truth about the Christian life and who help right things to happen and to spread. So you "yes" people are correct too, because God needs you and me to keep goodness and truth and love going in the world.

In the story for today Jesus was able to do something helpful at a wedding, helping people who were very thirsty, and his mother, Mary, also helped by suggesting what was needed and by telling the servants to do what Jesus said. Those were not big actions, but they were actions that really helped. Mary knew before Jesus was born that she was to help in God's plan, and at the wedding she helped it along. Sometimes people imagine that to be one of God's helpers, or disciples, you have to be a hero, doing something that everyone will know about. But you don't. All you have to do is to listen to what Jesus says about the help he needs, and to be ready to do it. That's called being faithful, being a good friend and helper to Jesus. Will you keep listening to Jesus so you can help God's plan too?

Hymns for Epiphany 2

How Can We Name a Love; Fill Thou My Life, O Lord My God; Lord, You Give the Great Commission; Spirit of God, Descend Upon My Heart.

Epiphany 3

Ordinary Time 3

Psalm 19:7–14 (C)

Nehemiah 8:1–4a, 5–6, 8–10 (C)
Nehemiah 8:2–4a, 5–6, 8–10 (RC)
Nehemiah 8:2–10 (E)
Isaiah 61:1–6 (L)

1 Corinthians 12:12–30 (C) (RC)
1 Corinthians 12:12–21, 26–27 (L)
1 Corinthians 12:12–27 (E)

Luke 4:14–21 (C) (L) (E)
Luke 1:1–4; 4:14–21 (RC)

Meditation on the Texts

God of past and future, we come to you this Sunday with the hope that you will enlighten the present. We come with mixed emotions, knowing that you have always intended to heal the afflicted, free the captives, and give sight to the blind, including all those who are imprisoned or blinded in ways no one else may identify. We ourselves are part of situations and systems that do not free anyone, but in fact make us captive of our wants and our fears. We believe in joining the effort to bring equality and fairness and abundant life to all your children, but we sometimes are immobilized, weeping at your law instead of seeing its power to grant life. We want to be part of a church that is full of life, openhearted to the stranger, conscious of human struggle, and committed to justice and peace in the world. We know we tend to be competitive even in the church, but with the guidance of your Spirit we hope to discern the gifts and talents you give to each member of your body.

As I consider the possibilities for preaching from the passages from the scriptures for this week, O God, help me to imagine the church at its best—full of diverse gifts that are equally respected, founded on doctrine that is constructive and clear, and open to celebration and surprise in the leading of your Spirit and the revealing of your power. Enable me to feel the authority of the call to ministry, and at the same time the humility of needing many other people to be able to carry out that ministry. Carry the law into my pulpit as a structure for my faith, and bring the wine to your table as a gift for our heavenly wedding. Amen.

Commentary on the Texts

Luke 4:14–21 (C) (L) (E)

Luke 1:1–4; 4:14–21 (RC)

Luke has been called the most skillful literary artist among those who wrote about the life and times of Jesus Christ. Luke's prologue (1:1–4) is a major source of evidence for that claim. Modern writers are urged never to write a single sentence with multiple thoughts embedded in multiple clauses, but somehow Luke's words to Theophilus emerge with relative clarity despite being presented in one long and complicated sentence. The rhythm of Luke's unusual first sentence conveys both the writer's own intelligence and a respect for the person receiving the message. Theophilus may have been a Roman official; it is also possible that the name theo-philus was a construction to denote a "lover of God." The prologue alludes to other narratives about Jesus. There were many in circulation at the time of Luke's writing, though we can be sure only that Luke used the account written by John Mark. Luke's concern is to be "orderly," to give maximum use to the records of "eyewitnesses and ministers of the word," and to winnow through the various tales to find "the truth" about the things which "have been accomplished among us." This language denotes a writer with the skills and the ethical viewpoint of a social science researcher. Luke has those qualities, but he is also intent on writing a coherent and magnetic story for a public audience. The prologue indicates that he takes that task seriously, with awareness of controversy in his surroundings and with what appears to be pleasure in the opportunity to tell the most important story he knows in his own way.

Luke 4:14–21, unlike the prologue to the Gospel of Luke, is not in itself a complete unit. It begins immediately after Luke's account of Jesus' temptation in the wilderness. Jesus is said to have returned to Galilee, traveled to various synagogues in the vicinity, and garnered the approving notice of many people in the surrounding towns. The next narrative unit is actually made up of vs. 16–30, in which Jesus reads and proclaims in the temple at Nazareth, receives the interested reactions of townspeople, and responds to them with other scripturally based claims that lead the people to reject him. Luke's time frame in this entire account differs from that of both Mark and Matthew, who place Jesus' rejection in Nazareth much later in his ministry. In contrast, Luke may be trying to demonstrate that Jesus as an adult encountered conflict within the community of his roots from the earliest moment in his adult ministry.

The four subsections of the pericope vs. 14–21 are (1) vs. 14–15, marking the transition from the wilderness into the world of teaching and "being glorified by all"; (2) vs. 16–17, placing Jesus in the synagogue of Nazareth, where he is asked to read from the Hebrew Scriptures; (3) vs. 18–19, the words read from Isaiah 61, an accurate though selective quotation; (4) vs. 20–21, Jesus' sitting down after the reading and the first statement in his preaching to the local congregation. This summary reveals that Jesus is depicted straightforwardly as a Jew, one who observes faithfully the cultic expectations of his family's faith. Luke also makes clear that Jesus returned from the wilderness, as he entered it, "in the power of the Spirit." The presence and power of the Holy Spirit will remain central in Luke's Gospel account and also in Luke-Acts when describing the growth of the first-century church. Finally, this summary of the four sections shows the dramatic coherence that Luke has produced in his narrative. He wants his receivers to comprehend and recall the story that is becoming their own story.

The reading from Isaiah 61 as recorded by Luke is accurate in its general approach but changed in some details from the original. The quotation begins with the Spirit of the Lord authorizing the prophet to proclaim good news and do righteous actions. The recipients of the proclamation and the actions are the disenfranchised—of Isaiah's world, of Nazareth, and by implication, of our own: the poor, the blind, the oppressed, the imprisoned. Interestingly, two verses from the Isaiah passage which have disappeared from Luke are Isaiah 61:1c, "He has sent me to bind up the brokenhearted," and Isaiah 61:2b, which (as translated) completes a thought after "to proclaim the year of the Lord's favor"—the completion is "and the day of vengeance of our God." The first statement has been left out of the RSV, though it was in the KJV. The reason for this change is not clear. The second omission may have to do with Luke's choice of focus in recounting Christ's first sermon setting. Leaving out "the day of vengeance" would allow for a clearer differentiation from John the Baptizer's preaching, and more of a focus on healing, as Luke the physician may have preferred.

The "acceptable year of the Lord" or "the year of the Lord's favor" can be treated as a symbol of the messianic age. It also evokes the idea of the Year of Jubilee, when all debts are repaid and all relationships righted under the eye of a forgiving God.

Jesus' sitting down was in keeping with the Jewish tradition that the reader of scripture would stand, and then the one who interpreted the scripture would sit down. The fact of all eyes being on Jesus can be taken as a mark of respect and admiration, since we had earlier been told that his teachings in the synagogues had been "glorified by all." Since vs. 22–30 of this pericope are being treated next Sunday, it is wise to avoid a sneak preview at this point into the more negative response of the people. One can say fairly that at the point Jesus began to preach, the people were attentive to his words.

"Today" is a powerful word in this passage. Jesus announces that the scripture setting forth God's social agenda through the Anointed One is now in effect. Without saying explicitly "I am the Messiah," Jesus has said that he is taking on the work of the prophetic servant, work that must be done with actual suffering people in an immediately present world. The agenda is no longer hypothetical, it is actual.

Preaching this passage allows the preacher to treat Jesus accurately as a practicing Jew with a reformer's sensibility. Congregations would do well to absorb the information in these verses about ancient synagogue worship, while recognizing at the same time that Jesus probably had a lover's quarrel with his own religious tradition. The quoting of Hebrew Scriptures in the New Testament is another area in which worshipers have a chance to develop a stronger awareness of the interpenetration of parts of the Bible. Using both pericopes from Isaiah and Luke, as the Lutheran lectionary allows, is a way to promote more of this awareness. A sermon on this passage can also illuminate Jesus' sermon as a statement not of the completion of God's work in the world, but of the immediacy of that work for those who are baptized into the Spirit. It is important that people not misinterpret the "Today —has been fulfilled" statement as a claim that God has done all that is necessary, leaving no further tasks for God's people to perform. One more option: the preacher may choose to make overt connections between Jesus' act of reading and preaching and the comparable acts that occur in the present church. The relation between a scriptural text and its interpretation is not, as most preachers know, a foregone conclusion. Further, the degree to which people expect to listen actively to the sermons they hear warrants discussion. Openness by the preacher about this issue from the pulpit can foster such discussion.

Nehemiah 8:1–4a, 5–6, 8–10 (C)

Nehemiah 8:2–4a, 5–6, 8–10 (RC)

Nehemiah 8:2–10 (E)

This section of the Book of Nehemiah focuses on Ezra, a postexilic priest who traced his genealogy back to Aaron. The present material may have come from Ezra's own memoir, which was combined by a later writer with the memoir of Nehemiah so that the careers of these two leaders would be seen as intertwined by the readers of these records.

The law and the people's response to the law form the heart of this passage. Ezra is asked by the returning Israelites to present the law of Moses to them in the public square. The ritual significance of the moment is made clear by the details: the date and hour, the presence of women and "all who could hear with understanding," the high wooden pulpit constructed especially for the event, the thirteen named officials on either side of Ezra, and the active verbal and physical responses of the people before and after the reading. Ezra is assisted by thirteen additional men, who were probably Levites, in bringing the interpretation of the law to the people as they sat in their places. The "Amens" and the emotional reactions of the people evoke the expressiveness of modern African-American churches, where the entire worship event involves an active participation by the lay people as well as the pastor. The group of people adding interpretation of the law suggests that the event was an educational as well as a cultic event: people were intended to learn and appropriate what they heard.

People hearing the law mourned and wept. Some scholars say that they wept for their sins; another possibility is that they wept in pain for their years in exile and for the promises of God that had at last been fulfilled. The writer in Nehemiah reports that the worship leaders urged the people not to grieve, "for the joy of the LORD is your strength" (v. 10).

For us in modern worship, this passage offers an unusual portrait of people in worship at a pivotal moment in their lives together. The array of people aiding in worship is noteworthy in itself. While the Common and Roman Catholic lectionaries save the reader of scripture from pronouncing many Hebrew names, what is lost thereby is the richness of the naming of individuals who would have been honored by this important task on the day when the law of Moses was read to all in the square. Worship that treats parishioners as passive members of an audience is not in keeping with this enlivened worship event in Jerusalem.

Isaiah 61:1–6 (L)

The first four verses of this lection have already appeared for Epiphany 1, (C). In this slightly longer version for the Lutheran lectionary, the idea of the anointing by the Spirit is expanded into a portrayal of the ministry of Zion to the whole world. The process moves from a call to healing and renewal in vs. 1–3, through the rebuilding of the nation in v. 4, and into the international arena of public ministry in vs. 5–6. This poetic message deals with both priests and the wider community of the faithful, in a spirit of gladness, respect, and renewal. Thus it is fitting as an Epiphany text, and a reminder of Jesus' knowledge of the ancient texts as bolstering his own ministry to the Jewish community, and ultimately to the Gentiles as well.

1 Corinthians 12:12–30 (C) (RC)

1 Corinthians 12:12–21, 26–27 (L)

1 Corinthians 12:12–27 (E)

The section of Paul's letter to Corinth that appears in today's readings is part of a much longer unit of thought, which begins at 12:1 with the question "Now concerning spiritual gifts" and ends at 14:40 with the admonition "but all things should be done decently and in order." In the center of this long unit, bounded on either side by extended discussions about spiritual gifts in the church, is the familiar passage about love as the aim of all human striving. The rhetorical purpose of Paul's letter is to persuade the people to shift or expand their thinking in response to his friendship, his eyewitness status among the faithful, and his carefully wrought rhetoric. **For further aid** in understanding the rhetoric of New Testament epistles, see chapter 7 of Thomas G. Long's *Preaching and the Literary Forms of the Bible* (Philadelphia: Fortress Press, 1989).

Crucial to the progress of thought in the present passage is the paradoxical relationship between the one and the many. Paul is interested in the growth and effectiveness of the new church, and a strong linkage between individuals and the faith community as a whole is essential. Paul develops that linkage by the structure of his rhetoric. In every sentence between v. 12 and v. 30, there is an allusion to the connection, be it tension-laden or peaceful, between variety and unity. Individual ethnic backgrounds, separate parts of the body, and particular roles in the church are each placed in relation to a larger whole. The first whole is baptism by the Spirit; the second is the image of the healthy body; and the third is the church.

Paul employs several concrete and visible images of body parts to further his argument for cooperation and unity. One may find his dramatization far-fetched at times: "The eye cannot say to the hand, 'I have no need of you' "(v. 21a); but for Paul's audience, the fable of the body as having lively, speaking parts would have been familiar. Moreover, the idea of the body as integral to the human being was part of the background of Paul's thought, and the idea of Christ's bodily resurrection as making possible the resurrection of human beings was part of Paul's theology. Thus a distinction can be made between the view of the body in 1 Corinthians 12 and the dichotomy spirit versus flesh, in which Paul is concerned with the human addiction to sinful activities (Gal. 5:19–21).

The central idea of this passage is the organic relationship between individuals and the body of Christ as a whole. Paul moves from baptism through the human body and finally to the church as an organic unit. In this last section Paul explicitly names eight activities corresponding to various spiritual gifts. As in the earlier passage from chapter 12, used for Epiphany 2, Paul lists the gift of tongues last of all. As was noted, speaking in tongues does not necessarily edify other members of a church. In terms of today's focus on unity, a similar limitation may have concerned Paul about tongues, since it is hard to maintain unity when people cannot communicate with each other.

The various denominational boundaries for this passage have varying effects on the meaning of the passage. The Lutheran lection omits vs. 22–25 and ends the passage with v. 27. The result of this setting of the boundaries is that hierarchy, by which one body part or one gift for the church is ranked more highly than another, is not given attention. A more egalitarian image of the church results. The Episcopal lection shares the omission of the church's list of gifts and expectations and the rhetorical questions such as "Do all possess gifts of healing?" However, the Episcopal lection leaves in vs. 22–25, the section that offers a cryptic view of body parts as having greater and lesser amounts of honor or unpresentability. Both the Common and the Roman Catholic lections in this instance include all the above material, so that Paul's argument is allowed to progress as he constructed it, with both local and universal references.

Preaching from this passage may be done most easily by taking Paul's examples from the church and analyzing how a church functions with fewer roles being filled. The problem of finding lay leaders in the church is a widespread concern today. Making the bridge from Paul's time to our own will be easy. As for the body parts, one could become creative in this case by designating body parts as interests or skills: the ear as the counselor, the foot as the jogger, the mouth as the salesperson or public speaker, the head as the professor. Then one could ask how long each one can function without needing the help of any other. Much as it may seem appealing to be independent of anyone else's control, it would not be appealing to be unable to live through a day because of the lack of cooperation from others. Simply discussing how a family prepares a meal or goes on a trip will help to reveal the role of interdependence.

Theological Reflection

While on the surface the readings for this Sunday are highly diverse, they all build images and concepts bearing on the identity, growth, and mission of the church. Luke 4 brings Isaiah's vision of healing and liberation forward into a synagogue in Nazareth, where the Spirit-anointed Christ can announce the present truth of the ancient words. Paul in writing to the Corinthians keeps driving at the truth that diversity is not only a fact and a problem but actually a resource for the community if the varying gifts of the Spirit are all respected. In the Nehemiah passage, Ezra's reading of the Mosaic law, asked for by the recently returned exiles, is an example of the ancient church acting like a community with diverse gifts, diverse emotions, and yet a unified commitment to follow God's commands for their lives.

Children's Message

How many of you have ever played or watched a team sport like soccer or baseball or basketball? How many of you ever play a game like hide-and-seek? One of the things that makes a game work is a set of rules. They may not be very fancy rules, but the game won't work unless everyone knows them and plays by them. For example, think of the rules for hide-and-seek—what are you supposed to do, and what are you supposed not to do? (Items: there is a base; one person who is It stands there and counts to a certain number while others hide; some places are out of bounds as hiding places; and the people in hiding try to get back to the base before the one who is It.) Now this game works out only if different people agree to do different things. If all hide, no one is left to look for them!

The apostle Paul figured out that the church works something like a game, with different people doing different things. If all the people wanted to preach, there would be no one to hear. If every child wanted to teach church school, there would be no students to learn the Bible stories. Paul told the people he knew that God gave us different gifts so that we would be able to work together, to act like a team and play well with one another. Does that sound like a good idea?

The next time you play a game and people disagree about who is going to do what, remember that both the church and the playground are places where we need people to be different, and to work it out together.

Hymns for Epiphany 3

We Are Living, We Are Dwelling; "Your Kingdom Come," Great God We Pray (*A Singing Faith*); I Know Who Holds Tomorrow (*Songs of Zion*); There's a Wideness in God's Mercy.

Epiphany 4

Ordinary Time 4

Psalm 71:1-6 (C)

Jeremiah 1:4-10 (C) (L) (E)
Jeremiah 1:4-5, 17-19 (RC)

1 Corinthians 13:1-13 (C)
1 Corinthians 12:27-13:13 (L)
1 Corinthians 12:31-13:13 (RC)
1 Corinthians 14:12b-20 (E)

Luke 4:21-30 (C) (RC)
Luke 4:21-32 (L) (E)

Meditation on the Texts

O Holy One, to whom we are known as a mother knows her infant and as a lover knows the beloved, come into our presence this day. We know that we have been claimed by you since before our births. We know that you have stayed with us through the most terrible of trials, and have remained with us in the sheer emptiness of loss. You recognize our tendency to be in conflict, and our hesitancy to speak up for you. You called to frightened young Jeremiah, assuring him that he would not have to speak alone, and that he would be a messenger for you. You called forth the apostle Paul, assuring him that there was a principle of love larger than any one gift, and more eternal than any one individual life. You called to the people as Jesus spoke in the temple of Nazareth, showing them that the scriptures they quoted were the guide to justice and peace for the wider world. You knew there would be conflict, but you have never sought an easy peace.

May God help me, as I prepare to preach from these texts, to be free from seeking an easy peace. May I hear the hesitation of Jeremiah, yet know at the same time that the Word is above all earthly powers. May I empathize with the struggle of those worshipers in Nazareth, while standing confidently behind the gospel that is sent forth to the world. May I recognize the dimness of my own vision, yet try to see God's vision as I listen to God's word. Most of all, I ask that I be known of God as I would have others be known of God, so that we all experience the freedom of being children and the empowerment of being strong and capable adults, in a world ruled by agape-love and shalom-justice. Amen.

Commentary on the Texts

Luke 4:21-30 (C) (RC)

Luke 4:21-32 (L) (E)

Today's lection continues the drama in Nazareth that was begun in the Gospel reading for Epiphany 3. The mood changes significantly between the passage read last Sunday and the present passage. Verse 21 overlaps both readings; it is both the interpretive conclusion to Jesus' reading and the introduction (a fact to be recognized only in retrospect) of his sermon. Biblical commentators do not agree about the emotional tone to attribute to v. 22, but it seems reasonable to this writer that Jesus' listeners would be attentive and curious, proud that a man from their own community was now a rabbi, but not altogether sure what to make of his claim that the scriptural words had been fulfilled "today."

The question asked by the listeners in v. 22, "Is not this Joseph's son?," appears on the face of it to be a typical query of townspeople who are trying to relate what they perceive of an adult child to what they know of the parents. In this instance, however, there is an added dimension. Joseph is and is not Jesus' father. That is a fact that Luke's Jesus has already affirmed in the earlier story of young Jesus visiting the temple, the place he called "my father's house." Luke is aware of the tension between the human roots of Jesus and the heavenly parent who has called and claimed Jesus. So the moment of reading and interpreting the scriptures is not the same for Jesus as it would be for any of the other men in the synagogue who would have been permitted to read and comment. According to Luke this is the pivotal moment when Jesus ceases to be "one of us" within the town of Nazareth, because he chooses to differentiate himself. This moment of differentiation becomes clear in the present passage by virtue of two actions: Jesus demonstrates an acute awareness of the distance between the townspeople's image of him and his vocation on earth; and Jesus uses the very scriptures upon which the people depend to show them their vision of faith and mission is too small.

In vs. 23 and 24, Jesus effectively predicts the response he will receive. First, he quotes a proverb that indicates their likely expectation that he will perform for them in the short run, or anchor his ministry among them in the long run. His exploits in Capernaum are known to them, and they may be assuming that he owes them no less. Then Jesus himself turns the emotional direction toward a more negative response, by saying in terms that befit a prophet, "no prophet is acceptable in his own country" (v. 24). Thus Jesus himself has preempted the listeners' response by this point, asserting what he expects from them from the viewpoints of both proverb and prophecy. One is reminded of the statement quoted by Matthew, "I have not come to bring peace, but a sword" (Matt. 10:34).

We can assume that every verse in the present pericope had meaning for the evangelist-writer and that the order of events as presented was intentional. Although many readers conclude that Jesus was victimized in Nazareth by a vindictive mob, it seems more reasonable to conclude that Luke wanted his audience to see Jesus as aware of his mission and his destiny from the start and capable of helping people to convict themselves of bias, self-centeredness, and limited vision.

Having inserted a wedge between himself and his hometown listeners, Jesus proceeds to tell two scriptural stories of people outside the Jewish community who have been served by God's messengers in the past. In the case of the widow of Zarephath and Naaman the Syrian, each person helped was a foreigner, chosen by Elijah or Elisha for special treatment in contrast to all the local people waiting to be helped. Hearing those stories in the local synagogue from a man who has already taken his God-given talents elsewhere, a listener in Nazareth might at the very least feel excluded, and at the most feel insulted. Jesus was telling them the stories from their own scriptures, apparently not to give comfort but to rub salt in the wound of exclusion.

From a rhetorical standpoint, the passage as a whole is noteworthy in three respects: (1) Jesus does not say "I" but speaks obliquely; (2) he sets up a conflict which the people act out after he has spoken; and (3) once the expected conflict occurs he is able despite his notoriety to slip away. Luke as writer is emphasizing Jesus' ministry in a symbolic microcosm. Jesus is shown as having a clear view of his message and its reception, but Jesus is not shown as in concrete personal risk or having to develop strategies for disappearing in a crowd. Luke presents here a microcosm of Jesus' journey toward the cross, leaving his readers to make the symbolic connection between the earlier rejection by local townspeople and the later rejection by the Jews of whom he was called "King."

Verses 31 and 32, which depict Jesus as going (back) down to Capernaum and teaching with authority, are included in the passage in the Lutheran and Episcopal lectionaries. The effect of the added verses is to show that Jesus had authority in some settings if not in Nazareth, and to underscore his success in gathering interested people. This addition moderates the element of foreshadowing that emerges when the passage stops with v. 30; instead it brings out the difference between one local community's negative response to Jesus' teaching and another's positive response.

For preaching, this passage is centrally concerned with the relationship between local and personal relationships and the larger, often conflicting tasks of ministry to which Christians are called. It is important to assert Jesus' active part in this scene of increasing conflict. It is also important to deal with the insider-outsider distinction that Jesus makes parabolically and that the audience clearly heard as an attack on them: the insiders unexpectedly become the outsiders, and the outsiders become the insiders. Applying this to the modern world, how do contemporary churches deal with boundaries and limits? How do we hear prophetic words, and what response do we make to the prophet? **Ideas related** to this latter point are examined at greater length in Thomas D. Hanks, *God So Loved the Third World: The Biblical Vocabulary of Oppression* (Maryknoll, N.Y.: Orbis Books, 1983).

Jeremiah 1:4–10 (C) (L) (E)

Jeremiah 1:4–5, 17–19 (RC)

The Book of Jeremiah was written in a time when the power of the Assyrians was waning and the power of Babylon was rising. This lengthy book of prose and poetry is personal as well as prophetic—not only in the number and extent of biographical materials that are included along with its oracles but also in the inclusion of personal complaints or laments that occur in no other prophetic book. This fact points up the relational and dialogical aspect of the prophetic role: Jeremiah the historical prophet, who is also known as Jeremiah the character in this literary text, interacts with Yahweh-God and with the people. They are interdependent, because in neither of these cases can the prophet operate alone. In this context the introduction to the Book of Jeremiah can be seen as both conventional (compare the calls of Moses and Isaiah) and specific to its circumstances.

The key themes of God's call to Jeremiah are these:

1. God "knew" Jeremiah even before Jeremiah was conceived, and consecrated him before birth, implying a relationship of intimacy and covenant that goes beyond human time measurements.

2. God appointed Jeremiah to be a prophet to the nations—not just to Judah and Israel, as was more customary.

3. God knows that Jeremiah will hesitate on the basis of his youth and his awkwardness in speaking, but God will be with the prophet at all times and will give him the words to speak.

4. God's words show foreknowledge of opposition to the prophet, for God promises "to deliver you."

5. God's touch grants Jeremiah spiritual power over all the nations and kingdoms. The implication is that the truth will free both the people and their prophet; there is no mention of other kinds of political or military power that accompany the prophetic call.

Throughout this passage the attachment of God to Jeremiah, and ultimately of Jeremiah to God, is vivid and immediate. It is hard to imagine a dialogue between a human and God that would have deeper evidence of love on the part of God and of an honest vulnerability on the part of the one called. The idea of attachment to God and the conceptions of the God to whom human beings attach themselves are discussed usefully by Gordon D. Kaufman in *The Theological Imagination: Constructing the Concept of God* (Philadelphia: Westminster Press, 1981).

From the standpoint of **preaching**, this passage has a large measure of psychological realism which can be tapped from the pulpit. The paradox of strength in weakness emerges clearly from this passage. Jeremiah feels young and inarticulate, and we learn of nothing that would improve his prospects except for the call, which is likely to produce conflict rather than adulation. Yet God promises to set Jeremiah over the whole world by means of the prophetic word. While most people do not experience a direct call to preach to all the nations, many feel called by God to do something for which their strength seems to be inadequate. Many who are faithful church members shrink from leadership or from speaking during worship, believing that there are "natural speakers" who could do the task much better than they. Jeremiah's call is a fine counterexample. Jeremiah was not known to God because of perfect skills or absolute confidence, but simply because God loved and chose him. The empowerment of God's confidence and the claim that God's word needs human mouths to speak it are worthy messages to glean from Jeremiah for the contemporary church.

1 Corinthians 13:1–13 (C)

1 Corinthians 12:27–13:13 (L)

1 Corinthians 12:31–13:13 (RC)

The famous passage on love in 1 Corinthians 13 is usually detached from its moorings in Paul's letter as a whole, with the result that it is often romanticized or allegorized and thereby of little use to the church. The material for this Sunday's epistle lesson occurs in between two full chapters of material that deal with spiritual gifts, their uses, and their relationship to the body of Christ as a whole. From this perspective, Paul's words about agape-love are not abstractions, but rather a reframing of the debate about roles and behaviors. The Lutheran version of this pericope keeps alive the connection between life in the church and the agape-love principle, by beginning with Paul's central claim in v. 27, that we are all "the body of Christ and individually members of it." To a lesser extent, the Roman Catholic version of the lection draws the reader's attention to the material beyond chapter 13, by beginning with an intriguing conjunction: "But earnestly desire the higher gifts" (v. 31).

In 1 Corinthians 13, Paul develops the idea of agape-love as a guiding principle for human action. To live and work cooperatively with each other, human beings need to have some compass to consult when differences in preference or gift or belief occur. Without this, as vs. 1–3 reveal, there will be no power in the enactment of individual gifts.

The rhetorical tool of defining by negation is used by Paul to good purpose in this passage. Negation is used first in vs. 1–3 to show the other gifts which become useless if they are not exercised in a spirit of love. Negation is used another way in vs. 4–7, where a small number of positive qualities of love is mixed with a larger number of things that agape-love is not, and does not do. Negation is used in a third way when Paul's discussion becomes more eschatological: the way we know that love will not end is to know all the other gifts and experiences that will end: prophecy, tongues, even knowledge. Negation is even implied in the last section of the definition, where knowledge is shown to be limited in the child, and limited in every adult, who can know only dimly and in part.

Paul writes as if the truth of the agape-love principle cannot be grasped tightly, but only approached hesitantly and with humility. Scholars have debated about whether he wrote as an individual struggling with his own practice of agape-love, or instead constructed a hypothetical believer with all the gifts but none of the insight of what the practice of love entails. In either case, Paul is realistic in avoiding a categorical, tight definition and application of self-giving love in the church. He develops instead a philosophical perspective within which individuals can ask themselves about the extent to which they are treating others in the church in a self-giving and growth-affirming way.

Preachers would do well to follow Paul in his oblique approach to the idea of self-giving love; a narrative in which love is not named but is at issue may be more empowering for worshipers than to hear the general words defined analytically and without context. The preacher is also advised to look at the wider context of the church as Paul intended his receivers to do.

1 Corinthians 14:12b–20 (E)

In this Episcopal lection Paul continues the extended discussion about gifts and their uses in the church. Particularly important in this pericope is the concern for gifts as edifying other members of the body of Christ: "strive to excel in building up the church" begins the passage (v. 12b). Paul contrasts the gift of tongues and the use of the mind; since the two do not naturally go together (since speaking in tongues is an ecstatic gift), one should pray for the mind to interpret what has been said. The church at Corinth was divided over the use of tongues by some members; Paul responds by asserting that he too has the gift of tongues, but that he is more concerned to educate other members than to demonstrate the extent of his own gift. We may note, however, that he says he speaks in tongues "more than you all" (v. 18), so he can call for their limited use not on the basis of weakness, but on the basis of other goals. Here as in the earlier sections of chapters 12 and 14, Paul has an eye on the growth and effectiveness of the church as a whole, operating at a time when its practices were scrutinized and its survival questioned. In this sense Paul's words are timely for the church in the late twentieth century, when the future of the church is questioned by many and the treatment of some members by others deserves to be examined with care.

Preachers can bring up this passage not as judges of their parishioners, but as brothers and sisters also struggling with how to edify and empower each other for the life of faith.

Theological Reflection

Each of the lections for Epiphany 4 relates to this season through the idea of knowing and being known. God is made known to the prophet Jeremiah, whose task it is to make God's will known to the wider community. Jeremiah is known to God in the intimacy of his fear, and the support given by God to the fearful one reveals the depth of their covenant. In 1 Corinthians, Paul digs deeper than the level of the local controversy over spiritual gifts, to bring forth the guiding principle of the gospel, a way by which human beings can be known to each other and to God without guile and without fear. If Paul was including self-examination in the passage on love, rather than presenting a hypothetical person's thoughts and feelings, such self-disclosure would indicate that the apostle was letting himself be known to the Corinthian community in ways that would make him more accountable to them and would make them more trusting of him. The evangelist Luke offers the most complex version of knowing and being known, for Jesus was ostensibly already "known" to his family, neighbors, and friends in Nazareth before he preached in the synagogue. His interpretation of the Hebrew Scriptures undercut the confidence of others that they knew "Joseph's son," and in the resulting interpersonal distance Jesus was able to distinguish himself as committed to all the nations, rather than being limited to the Jewish community alone. This is not a prophet afraid to speak, as was true of the young Jeremiah, but a prophet who knows exactly what must be said and what it will cost the speaker—later in Jerusalem if not now in Nazareth.

The idea of being known, in the biblical world as well as in our own, has its risks and complications, but these passages give evidence that to be known of God and to be willing to be known of other humans will offer experiences without parallel. To be revealed to God, and to have God revealed in one's life, are events of abiding significance and empowering impact.

Children's Message

Have you ever been asked to do something that you didn't feel ready to do? (Possible examples are riding a bike without training wheels, cutting one's own food, saying hello on the telephone, saying "I'm sorry" to another child.) How did you feel when you were asked to do this thing? (Wait for answers.) If any of you felt scared, you weren't alone. (The preacher can continue with an experience such as the following one; other possible examples are athletic competitions, school plays, or demonstrating a skill for neighbors or relatives.) When I was growing up, taking piano lessons meant you had to play a piece in a recital at the end of the spring. I never wanted to do that. My hands got cold and sweaty, my face got flushed, and I felt as if I couldn't remember any of the notes I was supposed to play. At other times it was fun to play the piano, but at recital time, I wished I would get sick and miss the whole thing.

Some of the most important messengers for God in the Bible were frightened about doing something important too—even something God had asked them to do. Moses, for example, asked God to send some other person to lead the people out of Egypt. Moses said he didn't speak well enough, but I think that he was just plain scared. God gave Moses the help of his brother Aaron, and the two of them led the people. Another prophet, Jeremiah, was asked by God to speak to the people about God's will for them; God wanted him to become God's messenger for life. Jeremiah said the same thing as Moses, "I don't know how to speak." He also said he was too young to be God's messenger. Do you think that Jeremiah was frightened about having this big job for God? (Wait.) I do. But

God said to Jeremiah, as God said earlier to Moses, "I will be with you." God promised not to leave these messengers alone when they were doing hard tasks for God.

The next time you have to do something that seems too hard for you, or something you have never done before on your own, you can remember what God said to Jeremiah and to Moses: "I will be with you," and you can pray to God to hold you and protect you when you need help. Let's pray to God for help now.

Dear God, you know that we sometimes have to do new things or big things that frighten us. Keep us with you so that we will not be afraid. Help us to know that you are strong and that we are strong as your children, as Jesus taught us. Amen.

Hymns for Epiphany 4

Holy Spirit, Storm of Love (*Praising a Mystery*); O for a Faith That Will Not Shrink (*Hymns for the Living Church*); The Church of Christ, in Every Age; Strong Son of God, Immortal Love.

Epiphany 5

Ordinary Time 5

Psalm 138 (C)

Isaiah 6:1–8 (C) (L)
Isaiah 6:1–2a, 3–8 (RC)
Judges 6:11–24a (E)

1 Corinthians 15:1–11 (C) (RC) (E)
1 Corinthians 14:12b–20 (L)

Luke 5:1–11

Meditation on the Texts

Word of Life, you call us into being. You call us into our true vocation, to be your servants and your messengers to the whole world. You call us into self-examination, wherein we are likely to see our shortcomings and our misdirections with horrifying clarity. Then you call to us with the essential word of reassurance. You remind us that we are never alone, and that you are always with us when the most difficult challenges lie ahead. You call to us with the scriptural witnesses, who bring back to us vividly the pictures of the empty tomb, the women who proclaimed the resurrection, the disciples gathering renewed strength for spreading the resurrection message, and the apostles like Paul whose lives have been changed radically and permanently by an encounter with you.

O God, you call me to preach your Word. May I not be afraid to answer with a word of truth. May I realize that the truth may not always be popular, and that it may at times divide those who listen. May I, like Isaiah and Gideon and Peter and Paul, know my own sinfulness in the face of a perfect God. But may I also, like each of these people and many others, move from awe to courage. May I stand up and say "Send me," even if the message is one that will convict me as well as those I love in the church. May I be free of the will to success, and instead bound to your call to speak shalom. As Jesus Christ came to the earth to speak the truth, no matter its cost, no matter its reception. Amen.

Commentary on the Texts

Luke 5:1–11

This passage has two interesting elements of context. (1) Its timing in Luke is different from that of any of the other three Gospel writers. Matthew and Mark put the call very early, before Jesus has become widely known (Matt. 4:18–22; Mark 1:16–20). John includes a similar account of a miraculous catch of fish, but he places it after the resurrection (John 21:1–8). Luke places the story after Jesus has been to Galilee and to Capernaum, so that the present version understandably has Jesus preaching to large numbers of people and using the boat to find some distance from the crowd. (2) Luke's uses of names are somewhat idiosyncratic. He calls the Sea of Galilee the Lake of Gennesaret. He refers to Peter as Simon, and later (v. 8) Simon Peter, a practice that suggests that Luke assumed his audience would already know Simon Peter. Luke omits mentioning Andrew, the brother of Peter, when telling the story of calling the fishermen. Both the use of names and the timing of the story can be accounted for by Luke's requirements for the story itself. For this tale about the calling of the disciples to have maximum impact, it would need to be situated where it was most logical; Jesus would have needed helpers after he had had some success in attracting audiences. Also, the account of the men fishing lists the three men usually trusted in Jesus' inner circle. These three names would have the most impact for Luke's audience because of the other parts they were to play in the drama of Jesus' ministry, particularly in the pivotal event of the Transfiguration (Luke 9:28–36, the Gospel lection for four weeks from now).

Luke's call narrative begins with Jesus acting as a rabbi, just as he had in the synagogue at Nazareth: sitting down to teach. This time he is sitting in Peter's boat, a more mundane location, but Christ's presence makes every location holy. The fact that he has picked Simon Peter's boat to borrow is in keeping with the prominent role Peter has in Luke's Gospel and the other Gospels. Evidence that Peter is treated as the leader is found in Jesus' instructing him to put the nets back in the water, Peter's initial response of resistance followed by a willingness to comply "at your word" (v. 5b), and Peter's later self-judgment in the face of his realization of Jesus' power and authority. Luke makes Simon Peter highly visible in this narrative, both as leader and as a self-critical individual, so that he carries weight both as the most prominent disciple and as a representative of everyone who is eager to follow Jesus but at the same time intimidated by the Lord.

Throughout the Bible there are instances of people seeing God in some form and being awed or frightened by the experience. This event, while more indirect in phrasing, is in keeping with that tradition. When Simon Peter sees all the fish—enough to break his nets and nearly sink his boat—he knows that no natural power could produce that result. He knows he is in the presence of God, and is appropriately "astonished" by that fact. This is an updated version of the tradition from the exodus (Ex. 33:20–23), one that specified Yahweh could only be seen going away. In the present narrative Peter becomes sure that God is present only after he has seen the fish he and his partners have caught. Seeing the power that has already been demonstrated, he now knows of the gap between his own limitations and the power of God. This section of the narrative echoes Moses bemoaning his poor speech, Isaiah his youth, and Gideon the weakness of his clan and himself. Peter acts as if he cannot stand the gap between his own moral being and the revelation of Jesus. Like many people facing what seems better than they can imagine themselves being or doing, Peter tries to push Jesus away so he will be less aware of his sinfulness. But the God he deals with is a God of grace; Jesus offers to be with Peter and the other first disciples and to show them how to catch live human beings.

Some writers believe that because of Peter's "Depart from me" message this entire narrative was meant to be a postresurrection story, taking into account Peter's three denials of Jesus; but it is not necessary to assume that later misdeed to account for Peter's response to Jesus. A great many people, perhaps most, are uncomfortable in the presence of someone who is very different from and clearly superior to themselves. Even in matters as small as appearance, highly attractive people can unwittingly produce depression in those who fervently wish to be like them and cannot. Evidence throughout the Gospels suggests that Peter had high expectations for his own behavior. For him to be proved wrong about his own profession was to be undercut to an extreme degree. Once he realized the source of the miracle, his responses were to worship like a child at Jesus' knee and to make an effort to be cleansed of his sins. He and the others were reassured by Jesus' promise to give them a new vocation.

There is a parallel in worship to the process just described as occurring to Simon Peter. In the first phase of worship, praise and adoration, the people express joy in the presence of God. The very awareness of God brings forth an awareness of the not-God or anti-God in ourselves; so the prayer of confession is parallel to Peter's self-judgment in Luke 5. This is followed by the assurance of pardon, echoed in Jesus' "Do not be afraid." The movement toward dedication to serving Christ is the modern parallel to Christ's call and the men's decision to leave their old vocation and follow him. Rey O'Day and Edward A. Powers describe a pattern similar to this in *Theatre of the Spirit: A Worship Handbook* (New York: Pilgrim Press, 1980). In some churches an explicit call to the altar gives worshipers an opportunity to relinquish old patterns and make a personal and public commitment to Jesus Christ. But even in churches without that specific tradition, there is value in inviting listeners to appropriate the gospel message and make an active response to it. A recent writer from the United Methodist tradition argues for a direct invitation to believers to respond to the word; see O. Dean Martin, *Invite: Preaching for Response* (Nashville: Discipleship Resources, 1987).

Beyond the implications for preaching and worship already suggested above, **this passage offers preachers** a chance to think further about preaching as related to evangelism. Evangelism requires that a person have an experience of God that abides and continues to nourish his or her faith. As in the case of the three fishermen, it is best done as a cooperative effort. And as Jesus indicates in his promise to Peter and the others, it asks of the participant certainty about the goal: catching people alive, and helping them to remain so, abundantly.

Isaiah 6:1–8 (C) (L)

Isaiah 6:1–2a, 3–8 (RC)

See also Trinity Sunday, (E).

Isaiah's call starts with a mixture of history and mystery. "In the year that King Uzziah died" anchors the reader in the historical record of Middle Eastern kings: King Uzziah's death has been placed at 742 B.C.E., so Isaiah's active period as a prophet probably extended until the turn of the next century, approximately 700 B.C.E. Uzziah's reign was the end of a period when Judah was independent; for most of Isaiah's adult life Judah fought off Assyrian invasions. In the midst of all this Isaiah articulated a vision that has fascinated Jewish and Christian writers ever since, a vision that wove together the hope of comfort and joy and the darkness of judgment.

The first verses of Isaiah 6 offer a portrait of a young man overwhelmed by the sensations of being inside the holy temple: the smoke of the incense, the choirs singing to one another, the sculpted angels, the throne of Yahweh, and the vision of the Lord sitting on that very throne. All of this could easily undo a young and eager worshiper. Isaiah allows his readers to see him as frightened as well as impressed with what he finds. Two crucial actions come after this initial vision: (1) Isaiah is struck by his unworthiness, and that of his people; and (2) Isaiah is purified by a coal from the altar, applied to his mouth so that he can speak with purity to others. Mouth purification was a ritual done first to royalty in Middle Eastern nations and later applied to priests as well. As with other passages in the Bible (see the comments above concerning Luke 5:1–11), these verses offer a personal example of the process of seeing the holy, feeling one's own unholiness, and being given a gift of cleansing so that one's words can go forth to bear fruit.

Verse 8 brings the deity into the transaction, but not at first in an assertion of almighty power. Yahweh is shown in consultation with the angels, a monotheistic equivalent of the council of gods, asking "Who will go for us?" While the entire passage is technically a call account, the fact that Isaiah is in the position of volunteering rather than being conscripted is theologically and psychologically important. "Here am I! Send me." Isaiah responds quickly and gratefully to the purification rite; he is now a prophet waiting for the message to send.

Some lectionaries omit vs. 9–13, because the message is highly negative and somewhat difficult to interpret. The words seem to say that people will choose to turn away from God for a long time, until there has been widespread desolation. Then only a small remnant, a tenth, will return to God. The text for v. 13 has been pieced together out of problematic Hebrew phrases: the Hebrew word for "stump" has to do with the word substance, not with the root or trunk of a tree, and the use of "holy seed" for the obscure Hebrew word in the last clause was probably a postexilic editorial addition. Even with its difficulties, this section of chapter 6 still conveys clearly that Isaiah has been given a daunting message to carry to the people, and that he is empathic with his audience (v. 11) while being committed to carrying out his task. But questions remain about the attitude to be attributed to the God who asks Isaiah to speak desolation to the people. Does God care what are the results of this oracle of reproach? Does God intend that human beings fail to respond? Does God have Isaiah identify the major forms of resistance so that the truth will set the remnant free? Whatever the interpretation of vs. 9–13, it is clear that Isaiah is being challenged to convey the truth with integrity, not to attempt to be persuasive at all cost. One is reminded of the statement made at various times by Jesus as he preached in parables: "Let anyone with ears to hear listen!" Jesus did not expect to control the responses of his audience; in fact, he seems to have expected to divide them, much as God told Isaiah to expect that his audience would be divided.

Preaching from this call passage in its shorter form allows the preacher to contrast the awe people feel in the presence of the holy with the smallness they feel in terms of their own gifts and confidence. The pulpit is a good place from which to offer reassurance that God's word can be sent forth from mouths that need purifying and from bodies that are less than imposing. As for the longer passage, preaching can help to identify the points of human resistance that make people choose not to understand and not to perceive. Those choices are costly, and as Yahweh reveals, it may take years of pain and desolation before a small remnant of the people see and hear the truth and act on it. Isaiah's insight, difficult as it is to hear, can have a bracing effect on a community that has avoided its difficult choices in the past.

Judges 6:11–24a (E)

This passage offers another call text, this one less well known but in some respects more accessible than the call narrative of Isaiah. Gideon, or Jerubaal, was from the clan of Abiezer in the tribal area of Manasseh. He probably followed Deborah as judge in Ephraim, though the dating and sources of the present story of his call are not agreed upon. What seems clear is that the Israelites were facing attacks from the outside and poverty due to looting by the invaders. Gideon's appointed task is not to prophesy, but to defeat the outside enemy. Gideon is commissioned by a divine messenger or angel, and he replies (like many biblical figures to whom God has given large jobs to do) with doubt because of his own and his family's limited strength. Unlike some of the prophets, however, Gideon follows his expression of hesitation with an assertive arrangement to verify the truth of the angel's mission. He uses the cultic framework of offerings or presents to test the angel's claim. He brings the angel a present, and when the meat and cakes are consumed by the angel's touch of fire, Gideon affirms that he knows this to be a true angel of God. Although Gideon expresses both doubt in his adequacy and fear at seeing an angel of God face to face, Gideon seems so resourceful in this narrative that God's reassurances appear almost unnecessary. Gideon, like Jacob, is a man able to take care of his own interests, even when those interests diverge from the claims of the deity.

A **preacher** might develop the initiative of Gideon as a vivid personal response to God's initiatives taken toward human beings.

1 Corinthians 15:1–11 (C) (RC) (E)

See also Easter Day, (L).

In the beginning of chapter 15 Paul reminds his readers in Corinth of the basic terms of their belief in the resurrection of Jesus Christ. Paul's role in this section of the letter is to bring to the forefront the truth claims that he considers definite and beyond doubt for those who believe in the Christian message. The beginning of the chapter shows its dependence on what has come before: "Now I would remind you, brethren, in what terms I preached to you the gospel." The function of this phrase is to nail back on the wall a frame for the picture which has become cloudy. The chapter preceding includes material about which there was strong dissent, for example, the role of women in church, whether to speak or be silent. Recent scholars have said that Paul was questioning those who sought to keep women silent in church, as indicated by his transitional "What! Did the word of God originate with you?" (14:36). Paul's conclusion of the earlier section reiterates earlier points about the use of gifts in the church. Now, in starting chapter 15, Paul moves to reclaim the central facts about the life, death, and resurrection of Jesus Christ.

Paul presents himself as a messenger, a prophet of the past and of the future. He recounts the essential facts in the history of Jesus on earth: he died for our sins, was buried, was raised on the third day—these forming the triad of first-level events. Then come the series of appearances: to Cephas, to the Twelve, to five hundred people at once, to James, and then to all the apostles, and then to Paul himself—these six forming the accepted set of appearance stories. Paul is said to be untimely born, for he would wish to have been one of the original twelve; also, at the earlier time he was engaged in persecuting the very Savior that he would later claim as his own. Paul is likely to be aware of the irony when he says, "I worked harder than any of them" because it can refer both to his missionary zeal as a Christian and to his earlier zeal in opposing Christians.

Paul omits the appearance of the risen Christ to Mary Magdalene and other women in his account of postresurrection visits by Christ, for reasons that are not altogether clear. For a **summary of the issues** related to Paul's omission of the appearance of the risen Christ to women at the empty tomb and their report of this appearance to the male disciples, see Evelyn and Frank Stagg, *Woman in the World of Jesus,* and Rachel Conrad Wahlberg, *Jesus According to a Woman* (New York: Paulist Press, 1975). One plausible explanation is that in the Jewish legal tradition of Paul's background, the testimony of a woman was not honored in a court. Despite Paul's egalitarian treatment of women religious leaders, as reported in the Book of Acts, he may have decided on an expedient adaptation to the culture of his surroundings. The Synoptic Gospels, written later than Paul's letter, insert the witness of the women, though not in a consistent manner.

1 Corinthians 14:12b–20 (L)

Comments on this passage are included in the material for Epiphany 4. In the present context, it can be mentioned that Paul is working to raise up an active and thoughtful church. Any gift, as with any preaching, should be considered in the light of its effect as well as its form or aesthetic merits. Paul was concerned to see how tongues or any other gift would be able to empower people in the church. There is the implication in this passage that some uses of tongues may have evil effects, particularly in producing division in the church.

Theological Reflection

Central in all of this week's readings is the idea that God calls people to undertake God's work in the world. While individual responses vary, the major threads are the awareness of being in the presence of the holy, the knowledge of the gap between God and human, the willingness to follow where God may lead, and God's reassurance that the one called will not be alone. Dialogue in various forms is essential to the process, for God does not enlist human assistance by force. The Isaiah passage makes this dialogical element the most obvious by having Yahweh ask a council of angels (in a way that may be rhetorical display more than serious debate) who will be sent, allowing the young Isaiah to stand up and affirm his decision to take on the prophet's mantle. Peter questions briefly Jesus' request to go back for more fish, and Gideon sets up a self-made experiment to verify the angel's veracity. In both of these cases the forthrightness of the human agents adds to the power of the transaction, for God does not pick passive followers with no ideas of their own. Paul was a powerful witness precisely because he had been so insistently against the new band of Christians, before being called to preach and teach their message himself. The stronger the human agent, the more likely that the message will have the ability to withstand opposition, an opposition that God knows will come to the prophets and witnesses of the Word.

Children's Message

Sometimes children are asked to do things that seem to be impossible to do. I recall times when I've been asked to go apologize to someone that I had hurt, and I thought that I would die before I did it. (As you can see, it didn't kill me, it just made me embarrassed to have to admit that I was wrong.) I know of other people who have been asked to do something they thought was impossible to do too—to ride a bicycle or walk farther than they had ever gone, while they were at Scout camp, or to memorize a Bible passage when they had never even remembered their phone number correctly! How do you feel when someone asks you to do something very hard, something that may even sound impossible to you? (Wait.)

The writer Luke tells of a time when Jesus was asking some men to do something they thought was impossible. Simon Peter, James, and John fished for a living, and when Jesus met them they had just had a terrible day of fishing, but Jesus said to them, "Get on out there, and here is where you should put your nets." They were not at all sure about this, but they listened, and after a short while they took in more fish than they had ever seen. There were so many fish that the nets were breaking, and the load was so heavy it almost sank their boats. Jesus had great confidence in the three men, more than they had in themselves. In fact Simon (whom we know as Simon Peter) was amazed and frightened at Jesus' power to locate the fish, and he said, "Depart from me, for I am a sinful man." Do you suppose he thought he wasn't good enough to follow this amazing Jesus? (Wait.) I can imagine feeling that way. Sometimes I look at a person I admire and think, Oh, that person is so wonderful, but I just can't live up to that person. He or she is just beyond me! But Jesus encouraged Simon and said "Do not be afraid." He seemed to understand what it is like to think you're not good enough to do something. Jesus knew at the same time that he would be there to help Peter and James and John.

Through Jesus, God reminds us that we may be asked to do things that seem impossible; but we will never be alone, so we don't need to be afraid. The next time something really tough comes along, you can say, "OK, Jesus, help me find my fish. Thank you!"

Hymns for Epiphany 5

Immortal Love, Forever Full; Lord, Speak to Me, That I May Speak; Jesus Calls Us; Called by Christ to Love Each Other (*A Singing Faith*).

Epiphany 6

Ordinary Time 6

Proper 1

Psalm 1 (C)

Jeremiah 17:5–10 (C) (E)
Jeremiah 17:5–8 (L) (RC)

1 Corinthians 15:12–20 (C) (E)
1 Corinthians 15:12, 16–20 (L) (RC)

Luke 6:17–26 (C) (L) (E)
Luke 6:17, 20–26 (RC)

Meditation on the Texts

God of all fruitfulness, we come to you in the knowledge that you alone are living water. You alone are the one in whom the faithful flourish. Those who trust in you are like trees planted by the water; like trees with deep roots are those who place their faith in you. When we receive our life from you, O God, we are like green trees in winter. We praise you for life that has no end, that shines forth and bears fruit wherever we are found and whatever circumstances surround us. In this season of Epiphany, when the world does not surround us with greenness and ripe fruit, we need your presence to remind us of what makes for life and true fruitfulness. We need your presence to remind us of the clear and immediate difference between living by faith and living by self-absorption. We need your presence to remind us that the resurrection is beyond debate, that the new creation embodied in Christ is our own new life, in you.

Spirit of God, guide my words this week so that the word from you will flow forth from my lips like water from a stone. Aid me in recognizing in my own life the mixture of laughter and weeping, poverty and riches, hunger and satisfaction. Help me to hear your word for my own ministry, so that I will seek not to be popular but to have that poverty of spirit that simplifies and directs my life toward you. Help me to hear the pain of those people with whom I worship, and to see in their struggles the battle against the power of death and in behalf of the power of your resurrection. Give me insight so that I may speak of the resurrection as a lived truth in my life, and thereby lift it up as the living water for the community around me. Finally, keep me in your presence so that I, like others, might bear fruit in this season. Amen.*

Commentary on the Texts

Luke 6:17–26 (C) (L) (E)

Luke 6:17, 20–26 (RC)

This passage is the beginning of Luke's version of the Sermon on the Mount. It is usually called the Sermon on the Plain because Luke states that Jesus came down and "stood on a level place" (v. 17). The audience is the apostles, who have just been chosen (according to vs. 12–16), a "great crowd of his disciples," and a multitude of people who have come varying distances in order to hear Jesus speak. Jesus is portrayed by Luke as preaching both to a circle of insiders and to people not directly familiar with him and his teachings. Both Jews and Gentiles were likely to have been present, since Judea and Jerusalem are paired with Tyre and Sidon in the north. Whereas Matthew has Jesus sitting down to speak to the crowd, Jesus in this account stands up and looks at the disciples—

*Portions of this meditation have been adapted from Ruth C. Duck and Maren C. Tirabassi, eds., *Touch Holiness: Resources for Worship* (New York: Pilgrim Press, 1990).

presumably a group of followers who are in addition to the chosen apostles. The reason for Jesus' standing may have had nothing to do with synagogue practice (which was alluded to regarding Luke 4:21–32 for Epiphany 4). The constraint of level ground and large numbers of people would require that the people sit and Jesus stand.

Jesus' words of blessing and woe, traditionally called the Beatitudes, are placed by Luke within an explicit framework of healing. Many people had heard of Jesus' healings, Luke reports, and they hoped to touch him because "power came forth from him and healed them all" (v. 19). This phrasing may remind readers of the process described in the story of the woman with a flow of blood (Luke 8:42b–48; Mark 5:21–43; Matt. 9:18–26), for when she touches Jesus' robe he is aware that power has gone from him to heal her. In the present passage the prominence given to healing is also applicable to the healing power of Jesus' words in the sermon that follows. His words were uttered in a culture in which there was a strong belief in the efficacy of the word. For one to name principalities and powers, for example, was to find the capacity to deal with them.

The blessings Jesus offers the large crowd of listeners are intended to heal the spirit and attitude of the hearers. To an extent they are also words directed to the speaker himself, for Luke's Jesus already knew what it was to be excluded, reviled, and even hated in his hometown of Nazareth. The blessings are both private and public, for they involve individual responses to the struggles of life as well as shared events of conflict and celebration. In essence these words revolve around the issue of perspective on life—how one sees the events that pass and what one considers important or unimportant in general.

Several commentators have noted that the pronoun "you" is found in each statement of blessing and woe. This contrasts with the word "they" and noun phrases such as "the peacemakers" which are found in Matthew's version of the Beatitudes. Matthew begins his account by saying that Jesus "taught them," while Luke's Jesus simply "said" his words. Whatever the original intent, it is clear that Luke's version is more immediate for the hearer, and harder to place at a distance from one's own behavior. Luke sets up a more confrontational tone by the use of a repetitive second-person pronoun.

Luke goes further than pronoun use in setting this sermon in a rhetorical framework that requires some personal response on the part of its hearers. Luke's set of blessings is briefer than Matthew's, and Luke has added material in vs. 24–26 that provides a woe or curse to parallel each of the blessings in vs. 20–22. This is the outline of a structure found much earlier in Deuteronomy 11:26–28, where the audience is reminded that following the commandments of God brings blessing, and disobeying the commandments of God brings a curse on the whole people of Israel. The passage in Luke echoes the moral framework of the Hebrew passage, but there is a parallel closer in time and eminently familiar to Luke. The Magnificat of Mary is full of social reversals and divinely sanctioned revolution. As discussed in the material for Advent 4, this song is personal in context, but in language and form it has more similarity to songs of triumph and social justice than any private song of individual fulfillment. Echoing the social justice theme of the Magnificat in the Sermon on the Plain, Luke has set forth a socioeconomic-political world in bold relief, telling his community that the Jesus they heard or heard of is not only a healer but a prophet.

An eschatological consciousness hovers over the sermon, even though the time frame is not always the future. The poor are told theirs *is* the kingdom of God; the hungry and weeping are told they *shall* experience the opposite; and the persecuted are told that their reward *is great* in heaven because hatred and exclusion *did* happen to the prophets. The residual message is one of cosmic logic; Jesus tells how the blessings and curses come naturally according to the behavior and situation of the various people. God's time frame rules here: to believe in the kingdom of God is to believe that good and bad fruits come from their appropriate roots, and that this was, is, and will remain true.

Luke probably imagined Jesus' large audience as including extremes of behavior and situation, from the extremely privileged to the extremely poor and discouraged. For present-day preachers, it is less than likely to have one congregation with such a mixture of circumstances. Thus, it would be wise for a preacher to find a way to absorb and understand the situations of people very different from his or her own immediate group of parishioners. One way is to wander into a social situation that may be unfamiliar—a homeless shelter, a country club, a fitness spa, a downtown grocery store—and simply to listen to what people are talking about. Another means for widening awareness about the groups to which Luke's Jesus was preaching is to read about unfamiliar groups and settings. For example, reflecting on childhood memories of growing up around a young Zapotec girl named Esperanza, Mark Kline Taylor has written a contemporary theology that deals with the personal as well as the cultural complications embedded in trying to understand the statement "Blessed are the poor." See his *Remembering Esperanza: A Cultural-Political Theology for North American Praxis* (Maryknoll, N.Y.: Orbis Books, 1990).

In general it is better to avoid placing oneself or one's listeners in polar positions with regard to the blessings and curses. Instead, **preachers** have a chance by an inductive approach (story or testimony first, then venturing possible meanings) to dislodge unexamined categories in people's thinking that hinder them (us) from owning terms like "rich" or empathizing with others who are in fact "excluded." The heart of the Beatitudes is finally what is in the human heart.

Jeremiah 17:5–10 (C) (E)

Jeremiah 17:5–8 (L) (RC)

Essential in this passage is the structural contrast between the righteous life and the life of the wicked or selfish. Here, as in the Lucan passage just discussed, the heart of the matter is human consciousness. The very word "heart" in v. 5 appears in v. 1 and twice more in vs. 9 and 10. The section vs. 5–13 is a series of wisdom sayings which have been inserted into a longer section of Jeremiah's complaints to Yahweh about his adversaries and the nation's fate. Some think that this small section of wisdom poems has been placed there to offer some justification for the negative fate of the nation. Chapter 17 as a whole may be a literary gathering of traditions about Jeremiah and his work that had reason to be preserved.

The grammatical structure of this passage is somewhat awkward, for it begins with the traditional prophetic phrase "Thus says the LORD" but then goes on to use the appellation "the LORD" several times in a way that suggests the Lord is the object of focus but not the speaker. This fact is one reason for referring to this pericope as a psalm rather than a prophecy.

Seen as a psalm, this section of Jeremiah is a delight of sensory imagery and memorable parallels and contrasts. The self-absorbed person is described first, as a shrub in the desert with no neighbors, no sustenance, and no fruits. In vivid contrast to this portrait, the righteous one is like a tree planted by water, nourished in all seasons and ceaselessly bearing fruit. The power of this contrast lies in its skillful language and structure, but even more in its use of an organic image to lift up the life of faith. In the Middle East in particular, a tree planted by water is not a taken-for-granted part of every habitation. Further, the implied features of naturalness, of growth, and of helpfulness to its environment all enrich the tree image so that those hearing it could expand its connotations on their own. Within these lines is the truth of the proverbial statement, "Virtue is its own reward," but the idea is taken to greater depth in this psalm. To be righteous is to be as one was created to be, and to improve the whole creation through one's fruitfulness as a believer. To fight off God's sustenance is to set oneself apart from God's created world of water, food, and fruits. **For further study** of this contrast, see the analysis of Psalm 1 in Patrick D. Miller, Jr., *Interpreting the Psalms* (Philadelphia: Fortress Press, 1986).

In the Common and Episcopal lectionaries vs. 9 and 10 are included in this week's pericope. The tone shifts in these verses; in v. 9 the heart is said to be untrustworthy, but then in 10 the Lord speaks of testing the heart so as to repay each person according to that one's behavior and basic nature. One writer has suggested that vs. 9 and 10 are a fitting introduction to vs. 14–18, with v. 9 being Jeremiah's complaint about his persecution, v. 10 Yahweh's response to that complaint, and vs. 14–18 Jeremiah's prayer. If vs. 9 and 10 are part of the pericope, it can be said that the sentiments are fitting for Jeremiah, both in the frustration at human duplicity and the conviction that God alone can examine the human heart for truth or falsehood.

For preaching, this passage is wonderfully suited to tying the idea of faith to the experiences of the daily fabric of life. Stories are rampant of people who pushed and rushed to find success in the workplace, only to look around and find no one nearby to share in the spoils. Stories are also available of people who somehow have the strength to outdo their cancer, give to others despite having little money themselves, and act honestly when there is no earthly reward for them to do so. The reasons for these actions are not accessible to computer or questionnaire; they come from the heart. Jeremiah's knowledge of that inner truth is a gift to the modern world.

1 Corinthians 15:12–20 (C) (E)

1 Corinthians 15:12, 16–20 (L) (RC)

The death and resurrection of Christ are the center pole on which Paul constructs the tent of Christian belief. Therefore in this letter to Corinth, Paul needs to affirm the truths that he has already reviewed for his readers (as discussed for Epiphany 5) and to deal with the disagreements that he has experienced elsewhere and had reported to him as occurring in Corinth as well. Scholars assume that Paul had sent at least one previous letter to Corinth, and had received a response indicating to him that he had been misunderstood. Thus the present letter seeks to clarify points of importance to that community, and the present passage is clearly a pivotal point.

Paul indicates that "some" in the new church at Corinth are arguing that there is no resurrection from the dead (v. 12). The next seven verses are a rhetorical tour de force in which Paul uses "if-then" statements, a key form of syllogistic reasoning in the Greek schools, to make the negative argument unsupportable. He appears to address all the necessary issues, including the possible misrepresenting of God, the vanity of Christian preaching, and the resulting futility of faith. In fact, however, Paul's argument begs the basic question: Was Christ raised from the dead? Having asked the question in v. 14, he simply asserts in v. 20 "in fact Christ has been raised from the dead." For "some" who doubted that truth claim, Paul's prior propositions would not change their opinion. For those who wished to be able to state their beliefs with more confidence, these statements might bolster that confidence. For those who believed in the primary value of Paul's personal witness, Paul's own experience could be more important than his rhetorical syllogisms.

The center of gravity of this passage seems to be the writer's own certainty of the truth of the resurrection, based on his first-person encounter with Christ on the road to Damascus. The structure of the series of appearances in 15:1–11 makes Paul's encounter the culmination of them all, thus undergirding his credibility as the witness par excellence of the resurrection he preaches. It is that credibility that makes the present verses work; Paul himself has centered his life on the resurrected Christ, so he "knows" the truth of the resurrection claim as few others can know it. Truth outweighs Fact. **For further discussion** of both the concepts of witness and the center of gravity in a passage, see Thomas G. Long, *The Witness of Preaching* (Louisville, Ky.: Westminster/John Knox Press, 1989).

From the standpoint of **preaching,** the evangelical element of this passage should be noted. Paul is first "I," then one of the "we" who are preachers and evangelists, and also one speaking to "you" whose faith would be in vain if the truth of the resurrection were denied. The movement is from personal testimony to preaching to (implicitly) empowerment of future evangelists. One other element to consider in relation to preaching: the phrase "in vain" begins and ends chapter 15 of the letter, and it appears twice in the present passage. The fear to which Paul alludes is the terrible fear of believing in something that is not only factually inaccurate, but more important (for Paul) inefficacious. It is likely that a great many present-day church members wonder if their faith, in whatever state they find themselves, is without impact, and without usefulness to themselves or the world. Paul's personal situation, and his engagement with the complex and demanding Corinthian community, provide counterevidence to despair.

Theological Reflection

The season of Epiphany focuses on the revelation of God in the manifestation of Jesus the Christ. All the readings for this day do not immediately appear to fit that pattern, except for Paul's First Letter to the Corinthians. Yet all of them bear on the theme of the inner life of the believer, specifically that of the Christian in the light of the death and resurrection of Christ. The portraits of the righteous and the wicked in Jeremiah center on the consciousness of each, on what is thought and felt and wanted by the faithful or faithless person. What begins within emerges naturally in good fruits or in dry bones. For Paul, a conviction of the death and resurrection of Christ form the heart of his message to the Corinthians and to every other mission community. To believe in the resurrection is to believe in God's rule over creation and God's love for humanity. So Paul presses this point out of personal conviction, and also out of the confidence that others will gain from sharing the solid faith he brings to them through his letters. Thus the inner life necessarily becomes expressed in a social environment; faith is intended to be shared. In Luke's Sermon on the Plain, the inner life again becomes a social phenomenon; what one centers one's life upon is either self-destructive or life-enhancing. The life-enhancing options are God's power brought to fruitfulness. The destructive ones are subject to reversal and revolution. Luke specifically brings the privileged under scrutiny in this passage, making clear prophetically that the haves will become the have-nots in God's system of justice.

Children's Message

Has any one of you ever lived on or near a desert—a very dry area with sand and hot sun and few plants? (Wait—probably no one.) Has anyone here ever lived next to water, especially a river or stream or flowing creek, where there are many plants? (Wait. Perhaps a yes.) In at least two places in the Bible there is a brief story about two kinds of people who were like these two kinds of places: the very first psalm, Psalm 1, and the writings of the prophet Jeremiah. I'll tell you especially about Jeremiah, because he wrote about both kinds of people. The one person, he said, was like a shrub in the desert, depending only on itself and on its own powers, and turning away from God. Now I've lived for short periods in New Mexico, where there are a few shrubs and not many trees. The shrubs are bumped around by the wind, and they don't get very green because there is so little rain and so much hot sun. What kind of life do you think Jeremiah is saying that would be? (Wait.)

Jeremiah also describes another kind of life—life like that of a tree planted by a stream. In this case the tree can be green all the time because it has plenty of rain and good soil—God's word—and it bears good fruit. The last phrase is one that comes up over and over again in the Bible—bearing good fruit. What do you imagine it means for a person to bear good fruit? (Wait for answers, and look for ideas related to good actions, bearing and caring for children, ways of treating other people, telling God's story, Jeremiah even says that in a year when there is not much rain, this tree won't worry, because it will still be able to bear good fruit. It will still have in it the nourishment it needs to produce God's fruit. What do you think Jeremiah is saying about the life of a person who is like a tree planted by a stream? (Wait.)

You and I are not exactly trees and shrubs, but in a way we are like plants. We are put on this earth to grow, to be part of the world, and to produce good results from our being a part of things. The Bible writers knew that people can choose their way of life, whether to be isolated and selfish, or to be open and caring and connected to other people. You may have "shrub moments" when you want to get away from other people, but you can be sure that God will help you be a tall, strong tree with good fruit if you allow God to help you grow. So this week, your theme can be, "Be a tree for God!"

Hymns for Epiphany 6

Christ Has Called Us to New Visions (*A Singing Faith*); He Arose (*Songs of Zion*); Be Still, My Soul; My Hope Is Built on Nothing Less.

Epiphany 7

Ordinary Time 7

Proper 2

Psalm 37:1–11 (C)

Genesis 45:3–11, 15 (C)
Genesis 45:3–8a, 15 (L)
Genesis 45:3–11, 21–28 (E)
1 Samuel 26:2, 7–9, 12–13, 22–23 (RC)

1 Corinthians 15:35–38, 42–50 (C) (E)
1 Corinthians 15:35–38a, 42–50 (L)
1 Corinthians 15:45–49 (RC)

Luke 6:27–38

Meditation on the Texts

God of grace and glory, you meet us this day in a world full of conflict. Nations are in conflict with other nations over material goods such as land and petroleum and computer products, and over symbols like sovereignty and human rights. Parts of our own nation have conflict with each other over where to put dangerous waste materials and how to fund the activities of government. Communities are in conflict over taxes and schools and land use. Households are in conflict over money and children and the varying images people hold of a loving relationship. Individual people are in conflict within themselves, often caught between a drive to have the perfect life in this world and the uncertainty that they can look for anything of importance beyond the immediate present. In all of this, dear God, a great many of us are in pain and in confusion about what to do with ourselves, what to believe, and what to say to you.

Whatever our circumstances, you continually come to your people with a word of grace. You continue to remind us that the ancient stories, of David and Saul, of Joseph and his brothers, of Hannah and Peninnah and Samuel, are truthful in our own day and fruitful for our response to the times of conflict. These stories are powerful; they can move us beyond a narrow logic of action and reaction and into the realm of grace and freedom. You also move us through the affirmative writings of Paul to see resurrection as distinct from our present lives, but connected to life as we know it in a natural way. In all these scriptures we can begin to discern the working of your providence in the working out of our difficulties with each other. Your constant love is full of paradox and surprise; it asks that we in response honor the paradox and surprise in our own lives.

May my studies in preparation to preach in the midst of this Epiphany season be open to paradox and surprise in my own experience. May I be honest with you, God, about my conflicts within myself and my struggles with other people, so that I can bring integrity, and wholeness into the event of preaching and leading worship. May I submit myself to the grace that goes beyond human logic, and to the resurrection that is life-giving to all who accept it. May I have one foot in the dust of human struggle and one foot in the heaven that claims my life. To the glory and honor of the resurrected Christ. Amen.

Commentary on the Texts

Luke 6:27–38

The material in this passage is widely thought to be part of a compilation of sayings attributed to Jesus by the early church. Within that context, the present passage is the most coherent of the five sections of the Sermon on the Plain (vs. 20–26, 27–36, 37–42, 43–46, and 47–49). It begins with a version of the rhetorical cue often attributed to Jesus when he was speaking to a varied audience. ''I say to you that hear'' is a kind of code language, a reminder to initiates that not everyone is equipped to absorb and act on Jesus' words, since hearing and doing were considered a unified response. Jesus is speaking out of a view of the world that some already know and others are open to discovering. Some, however, may be so inflexible in their own perspectives that no real "hearing" will occur on this day.

Verses 27–30 offer a group of admonitions to love one's enemies and respond to other people without regard to their prior treatment of oneself. These verses are followed by Luke's version of the Golden Rule, a principle familiar from writers outside as well as inside the biblical canon. Guiding both the specific advice and the general rule is the principle of initiating rather than reacting. If one waits to see whether another person will act fairly or kindly toward the self, one is choosing to be in a reactive position. The alternative is to be certain about one's governing principle in the first place, and always to act on that basis. For the Christian, behind the idea of acting rather than reacting is the notion of behaving toward others without tying the behavior to the worth or recent actions of the recipient. This is an alternative to the philosophy of having contractual relationships, a principle popular in the modern United States wherein positive action on the part of one person is expected to be reciprocated by another person, thus producing a kind of tit-for-tat arrangement. As Luke's Jesus asks, "If you love those who love you, what credit is that to you?" (v. 32).

The modern writer Paul Watzlawick has studied in the context of close human relationships the ways people can at times make changes in behavior and thought that are not reciprocal but instead capable of moving the parties into an altogether different frame of reference. His work shows the validity in psychological terms of breaking through the bounds of reciprocity and operating according to a different logic, one that allows for paradox and surprise. **For further information** about these ideas, see Paul Watzlawick et al., *Change: Problem Formation and Problem Resolution* (New York: W. W. Norton & Co., 1974), and Paul Watzlawick, *The Language of Change: Elements of Therapeutic Communication* (New York: Basic Books, 1978).

While the present passage from Luke is effective in dislodging from our habitual thinking a strict adherence to reciprocity, the passage also contains some disturbing echoes of cause-effect reasoning about the rewards of human action. These hints lead receivers away from the main message of freeing human beings to take the initiative in love and forgiveness. The problematic phrases are "your reward will be great, and you will be sons of the Most High" (v. 35), the repeated phrase "what credit is that to you?" (vs. 32–34), and the final verse in the passage, "For the measure you give will be the measure you get back" (v. 38). Taken as a whole Luke's passage shows Jesus demonstrating for his listeners that cause-effect thinking is too narrow for those who believe in the Christian gospel. The few discordant notes act primarily as reminders that even would-be believers may retain in their thinking some vestiges of hierarchy and competition (being better than the sinners, striving to be sons of the Most High).

In terms of **preaching** from this passage, the first priority must be to give these words a new hearing. Both pastors and parishioners have heard these admonitions for a long time, in most cases, and that fact makes it difficult to apply the ideas to current situations. One option for preaching is to seek vivid redefinitions of words like "enemy" so that hearers may consider whether an uncommunicative neighbor, a president of a corporation making harmful products, or even a rebellious family member are enemies in terms of their behavior or the listener's own behavior toward them. Another option is to look at the positive reciprocity as a problem—business tit for tat or friendships that bypass real issues in favor of maintaining convenient arrangements. In this case as in others already mentioned, the preacher's willingness to look authentically at her or his difficulties with these admonitions will give significant help to parishioners in hearing the passage with new ears.

Genesis 45:3–11, 15 (C)

Genesis 45:3–8a, 15 (L)

Genesis 45:3–11, 21–28 (E)

This passage, excerpted from the story of Joseph and his brothers, is a tiny segment of a biblical saga which begins in Genesis 37 and ends at the conclusion of the Book of Genesis at the end of chapter 50. Despite its limited size—the longest lection is still only 17 verses—this passage is important as the pivot on which the entire saga turns. Joseph, who has been mistreated, sold into slavery, lied about, and forgotten, encounters his conniving brothers openly for the first time. His words to them are a shock to them, and presumably to many readers of the Genesis account. Joseph tells his brothers that he knows what they have done, but in effect their actions are irrelevant because he has come to preserve life and to provide for them and their children. God's plan for them all has no place for vengeance, so Joseph puts aside the issue of paying them back for their evil actions. No cause-effect relationship governs this resolution of the long problem of exile and survival. Instead the relationship is simply that of God relating to human beings—through Joseph—in gracious love.

Joseph's speech to his brothers redefines their relationship to him, the meaning of the past actions, and the future prospects for their family and community. Through these simple words the petty struggle of person with person evaporates, replaced by a theological truth that is embodied in Joseph's leadership. The parallel in a classical dramatic play would be the denouement, the moment in which all the twisted threads of plot and motivation are unwound and displayed in front of actors and viewers, with the result that all that has occurred suddenly makes sense. There is a difference in this case, however. The act of Joseph does not "make sense" in terms of the logic of action and equivalent response. Joseph responds, but he defines as irrelevant the motives and scheming of his ten brothers. As he speaks, they are no less venal than they were before, *except* that he has renamed them as part of God's providence and Joseph's own household. The center of grace in this narrative is the act of coming together without working out the expected tit for tat. Joseph's action is profoundly illogical in a world of reciprocity but profoundly right in a world of providential love.

Paradoxes and paradoxical logic are prominent in the Joseph saga. Joseph, sold into slavery and doubting at times that he will even survive, is enabled to become the second in command over all of Egypt. In contrast, when he confronts his family, he does not act in a self-important manner, and he deals with his wealth and power only in terms of his realistic chance to save the entire family from the effects of the long famine.

1 Samuel 26:2, 7–9, 12–13, 22–23 (RC)

This passage from 1 Samuel 26 is another instance of a person who has every right to seek retribution from another, but chooses not to do so. Saul has persecuted the young David for a long time, and at the start of this passage he has gathered three thousand men to try to find David in the wilderness. In a dramatic reversal, David instead sees Saul in a deep sleep amid his soldiers and decides to visit Saul's camp at night along with the volunteer Abishai. Abishai acts somewhat as a tempter in this case, offering to pin Saul to the ground while he sleeps, but David answers nobly that he is not willing to kill God's anointed. Despite the long conflict of the two men, David decides to honor Saul's position as king. Interestingly, the two take Saul's spear and his jar of water, symbols of his survival and his prowess in battle. Once these have been removed it is clear that Saul's end is not far away.

While David literally turns away from killing the sleeping Saul in his tent, there is not a central value in this passage given to the gracious providence of God. Saul is going to be destroyed later if not now, and David's second mention of his unwillingness to kill God's anointed sounds a bit self-serving. The militaristic perspective in general is maintained. Thus in terms of **preaching,** it is important to keep the larger context in mind with this 1 Samuel passage, lest it seem to promote a more gracious approach to resolving conflict than is actually supported by the text.

Elizabeth Achtemeier's *Preaching from the Old Testament* (Louisville, Ky.: Westminster/ John Knox Press, 1989) offers further assistance to **preachers** in responding to narratives such as these, giving particular attention to the elements of rhetoric and genre.

1 Corinthians 15:35–38, 42–50 (C) (E)

1 Corinthians 15:35–38a, 42–50 (L)

1 Corinthians 15:45–49 (RC)

The present passage from 1 Corinthians 15 continues Paul's discussion of his central theological tenet of the resurrection and its implications for believers in Corinth and elsewhere. He has already reaffirmed the truth of Christ's resurrection through his own testimony and the reports of appearances to others; he has already attempted to solidify the necessity of believing in the resurrection if the Christian faith is to be meaningful. He has already defended his efforts and suffering as being worthwhile only in the light of the resurrection (vs. 30–32, not included in the lectionaries at this point). Now Paul turns to a more analytical description of the resurrection body. First he flings an epithet at an imagined interlocutor who asks Paul a question that seems to him off the point. "You foolish man!" Paul writes, and then he moves immediately into a discussion of resurrection as related to organic life and to human history. One writer has referred to Paul's exclamation as diatribe, but to this writer it seems more accurate to view Paul as a teacher impatient with presenting over and over the same basic material to a group of students, not all of whom have met the prerequisites for the course. Paul wants them to understand, but he appears to be frustrated that some of the Corinthians lack both his conviction and his direct experience with the risen Christ. Nevertheless, Paul uses in this passage effective tools of logic and rhetoric to assist the Corinthian church in imagining the resurrected body in terms of everyday life. He brings them knowledge in usable form.

Contrast is central to the structure and the details of these verses, no matter which of the different lections is examined. The shortest passage, vs. 45–49 in the Roman Catholic lectionary, hinges on the distinction between the physical realm, represented by the original "man of dust" (Adam), and the spiritual realm, represented by Christ, the man of heaven. Paul in this section refutes the sequence posited by the first-century Jewish writer Philo, who contrasted the "first Adam" (Gen. 1:27), made in the image of God, with the "second Adam" (Gen. 2:7), who was of dust and given a "living soul." Elisabeth Schüssler Fiorenza discusses this and related points in analyzing 1 Corinthians in the *Harper Bible Commentary* (San Francisco: Harper & Row, 1988). The very fact that Paul introduces the verses about the physical and the spiritual with the phrase "Thus it is written" imparts to them the conventional authority of the scriptures.

The longer versions of this pericope include Paul's analogy of the seed as the physical body, which must "die" by being buried in the ground before it can come to life in its eventual fruit. The Lutheran lection omits the phrase that states that God gives "to each kind of seed its own body" (v. 38b). The three verses that follow this phrase also deal with different kinds of natural bodies, both terrestrial and celestial; none of the lectionaries has included this material, perhaps because it moves into the realm of the sciences and appears to leave behind theology. In fact, Paul's rhetoric is strong in this entire section because it uses the force of accessible parallels and contrasts to lead his receivers to accept the idea of difference in "kind" as opposed to difference in "degree" where physical and spiritual bodies are concerned.

The most overt contrasts in this entire section come in vs. 42–44. Paul holds in one hand the qualities of the earthly human body and in the other the qualities of the body as resurrected. In these verses the logical hinge is opposition, not just difference. Whereas the verses preceding and following these verses promote thinking about difference as range, development, and distinct genres of experience, this middle section promotes thinking that can easily slip into stereotype and lose the qualitative distinctions of the natural, organic material. Paul is trying in several ways to make the concept of the resurrection of the body available to a variety of people. Because people tend to respond in cognitively different ways to such material, Paul's choice of rhetorical strategy seems valid.

From the standpoint of **preaching,** the point just made would suggest that readers read larger segments of 1 Corinthian 15 than any of the lectionaries currently advise. While it may be easiest to talk about resurrection within only one frame of reference, there is a strong possibility that a single framework will not help the thinking of all within a congregation. One approach for preaching may be to read the entire section, vs. 35–50, and then to deal with the four subsections within the sermon as language choices to respond to a pluralistic situation. The section divisions would be vs. 35–38a, 38b–41, 42–44 with 50 as a coda, and 45–49. As an alternative, if only one section is the focus of the sermon, one can talk about the assumptions made in that section and encourage people to think about the degree to which they share or do not share in those assumptions.

Theological Reflection

Governing the diverse lections for this week is the issue of how humans and God respond to diversity and dissent. Both of the stories from the Hebrew Scriptures deal with situations in which a logic of retribution could be expected to apply. The returning Joseph knows that his brothers have sent him into ruin and falsified his fate to a loving father. The young David knows that he has the opportunity and even the right to kill his persecutor Saul. In both cases the people who are expected to seek vengeance instead turn away from it. There is no logical explanation for these actions; only the providence of God made vibrant in the lives of David and Joseph can give their actions meaning. In the passage from Luke's Sermon on the Plain, Jesus continues the theme with his insistent claim that reciprocity and contractual relationships are not the way of the Most High God. Loving one's enemy is an appropriate label for the actions of David and Joseph; expecting a reward for it is wrong, though Luke's Jesus does suggest that reward will come in the form of a lap overflowing with goodness. The passage from Paul's First Letter to the Corinthians takes a different direction from these other pericopes, dealing with the ways one can understand the existence of a resurrection body. Even here, however, the question of diversity emerges, for Paul is trying to reach a diverse audience with varied rhetorical materials that will make resurrection available to their imaginations. While conflict is not the center of that passage, it emerges in his brief invective to a "foolish" interlocutor, and it reminds us that Paul of all the apostles was always at least on the edge of conflict within and surrounding the first-century church.

Children's Message

The Bible talks about many people who have big hopes and a great deal of happiness in their faith, but the Bible also talks about people who have fights with each other. That is one reason it is the most widely read book on earth: it tells the truth about people, both the good and the bad side of things. Perhaps you have had a fight sometime with a brother or a sister. Perhaps you have gotten really mad at a parent and said things that you later wished you hadn't said. Maybe you've been so unhappy about something that you threw down a favorite toy, or even kicked the dog or cat that you love. Well, if any of those things has happened to you, you can be sure God understands, because God's people have been having those kinds of troubles all along.

One of the Bible stories for today is the story of Joseph and his brothers. The ten brothers were jealous of Joseph because they thought their father loved him the best. So they did things that are almost unbelievable now: they sold him into slavery in another country, and then they lied to their father and to other people, saying that he was dead, when they knew they themselves had sold him for money. Joseph survived hard times, and, because he was very clever, he worked his way out of slavery and into a position to lead other people. After a while Joseph met his brothers again. What do you think he did then? He could have punished the ten brothers for their terrible act of selling him into slavery; he could even have killed them. But he didn't! He forgave them! He decided to return a good act for a bad act. He promised them food and a better place to live. He asked only one thing of them, that they tell their father the truth about him and about what had happened. Do you think Joseph was silly to do these things? Some people might think he should not be kind to them. But Joseph was able to be truly happy this way. He had his whole family back, he was able to help them, and he knew what God wanted for him. That may just be more fun than punching someone in the nose.

Forgiving somebody may seem really hard when you are very angry at that person. But remember this week how happy Joseph was when he forgave his brothers and was able to help them instead of hurt them. Forgiving gives you the best kind of power—the power to love, as God loves us.

Hymns for Epiphany 7

God of Grace and God of Glory; (When the Storms of Life Are Raging) Stand by Me; Be Thou My Vision; By Contact with the Crucified (*Praising a Mystery*).

Epiphany 8
Ordinary Time 8
Proper 3

Psalm 92:1–4, 12–15 (C)

Ecclesiasticus (Sirach) 27:4–7 (C) (RC)
Isaiah 55:10–13 (alt. C)
Jeremiah 7:1–7 (8–15) (L) (E)

1 Corinthians 15:51–58 (C) (L)
1 Corinthians 15:54–58 (RC)
1 Corinthians 15:50–58 (E)

Luke 6:39–49 (C) (L) (E)
Luke 6:39–45 (RC)

Meditation on the Texts

O God of Word and Silence, we are ready this day to listen to you. We know that we are surrounded with words that are trivial and false and destructive. We know that in our less happy moments we ourselves use words that hurt. At times we simply get tired of all the words that confront us, and we long for a silence that will allow us to rediscover what we really think. We can identify with Jeremiah, hearing the false views of the people of Judah and trying to hold on to a solid vision of the truth. We can appreciate the words of both Sirach and Jesus on the Plain, reminding us that character does come forth in the way that one talks.

Preparing to preach, I can feel some apprehension about how fully and honestly my character will emerge as I try to preach your word. I know I do not want to preach myself, to have my own concerns get in the way of the gospel, but at the same time I realize that my journey in faith is one of the real journeys in the community to which I preach. You have not asked me to be an angel, but a human disciple. Be with me, dear God, as I try to tell the truth in an enlivened way and in an empowering way. Help me to come to the scriptures as a child, viewing each of them as an adventure instead of hearing them repeated as if in a sleep. Help me to feel the lift of the resurrection, and to know in the depths of my being that death has been swallowed up in God's victory in Jesus Christ. Amen.

Commentary on the Texts

Luke 6:39–49 (C) (L) (E)

Luke 6:39–45 (RC)

This passage is from the latter section of Luke's Sermon on the Plain. It is similar in form to wisdom literature like Sirach or Ecclesiasticus (discussed below), in that it includes pithy statements of observation and advice. This material may well have been gathered by listeners to Jesus in several different times and settings. This pericope contains both single statements and longer units of thought. The three longer units are vs. 41–42, concerning the idea of looking for improvement in the self before trying to correct another, vs. 43–45, concerning the relation of character to its fruits, and vs. 46–49, contrasting houses (and human beings) built with and without solid foundations. The proverbial nature of these verses makes them accessible on a first reading, but they do not bear significantly on the ministry of Jesus. As v. 40 suggests, they may be most useful as a reminder that Jesus was a teacher as well as a healer, a doer of miracles, and a prophet. Mary of Magdala called him "Rabboni!" or teacher when she encountered him in the garden after he was raised from the dead. Much of the teaching done by Jesus of Nazareth was in the form of longer parables, more cryptic in style and more challenging to the imagination than

the present proverbial statements. Yet the material in this pericope has had strong mne-
monic power for believers, for it uses effectively the rhetorical tools of contrast, imagery
from nature, and narrative details. The passage also echoes other scriptures both canonical and apocryphal. The section on fruits echoes the Ecclesiasticus 27 passage discussed below, and the material on the two houses links to the passages about true and
false words that are found in Isaiah and Jeremiah.

To preach from this passage, one could do well to choose one of the sections described above, and let it resonate in the imagination concerning the present-day experiences that test or confirm its truth. For a longer sermon one might try to move in and out
of the whole pericope, with the context being the relationship between outer behavior and
inner belief.

Ecclesiasticus (Sirach) 27:4–7 (C) (RC)

Today's passage from the wisdom writer called Sirach or Ecclesiasticus is part of a
longer section of an apocryphal book that combines advice for wise thinking, analysis of
the qualities of good and bad character, and indicators of what is needed for society to
function effectively. These proverbial statements are centered on the relationship between
a person's inner being and integrity of thought and the outward manifestations of that
individual's inner being which become known through behavior. The passage offers three
wonderfully concrete images to make its point: the sieve which holds the unwanted
remains of a solution, the kiln which determines whether an earthen vessel will hold form
or crack, and the fruit which shows how a tree has been cared for in the past. The fruit is
the image most familiar in biblical use; it differs from the other two images in being a
product rather than a container of a product. The writer is intent on showing the reader
that there is an unavoidable link between what materials lie in human thought and what
results from that thought.

The last line of the passage is the reason for the previous three verses. It is advice to
the person who deals with others, to test the quality of another's character by watching
and listening to that person reason (or discuss, in another translation). One may be
impressed by a person's appearance or by a brief formal presentation, but only in the
effort of addressing the comments or objections will one come to know whether the
individual has depth of intelligence or only its exterior.

For the season of Epiphany, this passage provides an appealingly different angle on the
concept of the appearance or manifestation of the glory of God. **Preachers** are in the
position of arguing in behalf of the truth and significance of the death and resurrection of
Jesus Christ and the power of the Holy Spirit in the church as well as in individual lives. If
the preacher is a mediator whose truthfulness is doubted, the work of God will be ham-
pered. This makes it doubly important that preachers seek to be in the pulpit a congruent
presence, as one who both sends the gospel message and knows that she or he fully
needs to hear that message at the same time. Only in the expression will the thought be
appropriately tested.

Isaiah 55:10–13 (alt. C)

This selection may be one of the most quoted passages in the Hebrew Scriptures. One
reason is that the poetic qualities of these verses make them memorable, and the notes of
optimism and celebration bring affirmation to present-day worshipers. These four verses
are actually part of a longer poem, Isaiah 55:1–11, which is a hymn of God's generosity
and sovereignty in relation to the redeemed bride, Zion. In an even larger sense, the four
verses for today are part of the whole section called Second Isaiah, which extends from
chapter 40 through chapter 55 and which is centrally concerned with the purpose of God
and the future of Israel beyond the exile.

Verses 10 and 11 are particularly pertinent to preaching, for they are God's speech
about the word of God. Verse 10 begins with the image of the rain and the snow, evoking
the ancient conviction in the Eastern nature religions that rain is the ultimate gift of the
gods, bringing with it fertility and life itself. This image is of course familiar throughout the
Hebrew and the Christian Bibles, for both literal water and the "living water" of John 4:10

100

flow throughout the scriptures. By treating the word that goes forth from the mouth of God as analogous to not only rainfall, but by extension to sprouted seeds and loaves of bread, the writer has already made a claim that the word is fruitful, even before stating that "it shall not return to me empty, but it shall accomplish that which I purpose, and prosper in the thing for which I sent it" (v. 11). The natural flow is from the purposeful mind of God through the chosen messenger and into the consciousness of the hearers. The process is unitary, coherent, and beyond question. Preachers may or may not be happy to realize that in this speech God does not attach any humanly based time frame to the efficacy of the Word, but neither does the speech include escape clauses. David Buttrick has written a theological statement about preaching which respects and extends Isaiah's notion of the word going forth and accomplishing the purpose of God. See the final chapter of Buttrick's book *Homiletic: Moves and Structures* (Fortress, 1987).

The second part of today's pericope moves into the realm of celebration. Scholars assume that in this second section the speaker is the prophet, since the allusion is made to "the Lord" having an everlasting memorial. Verses 12 and 13 have an imaginative freedom that suggests a liturgical dance of joy. The trees of the field symbolically clap their hands, and the new trees will be those of moist climates—the cypress and the myrtle—instead of the shrub that grows in the desert. The exiles will return to their homes, not lost or alone but being "led forth in peace" (v. 12). Whereas the Eastern kings had in the past constructed monuments to their victories in battle, in this case Yahweh's memorial will be the entire natural world in which the redeemed people find themselves. It will not be temporary, as in the battle monuments of later-defeated kings, but it will be everlasting, never to be cut off. In the light of the fact that there will be communication from every angle—even the mountains and hills will sing—the "memorial" can also be read as the Word, embodied in the joyful expressions of God's people.

Structurally, the Hebrew word "for" at the beginning of vs. 10 and 12 brings the reader or hearer back to the earlier assertion found in v. 6: "Seek the LORD while the Lord may be found." Second Isaiah is concerned to give an adequate rationale for bringing about a faithful response by the people. In the intervening verses the writer urges that those distant from the deity return to a merciful God and submit themselves to the truth that God is both different from and loving toward imperfect human beings. In this context, vs. 10 and 11 support the notion of a God whose words are naturally powerful for their hearers, and vs. 12 and 13 support the notion that people who follow God's way are enabled to know delight in God's everlasting presence.

One of the most useful approaches to **preaching** from this passage will be to analyze how you the preacher and those to whom you preach actually view the efficacy of the Word and words. What spoken or written words are treated as having high credibility? What words are assumed to be tainted or even worthless? In terms of the words spoken in the church, what do clergy or laypersons do that suggests we have a high respect for the preached word in its potential to accomplish God's purpose? What do we do (including avoiding discussion of preaching events that disturb or disappoint us) that suggests that God's word goes forth and returns without prospering or accomplishing its purpose?

A second useful approach to this passage is to consider the ways that "a memorial . . . which shall not be cut off" has existed in the history of the church generally and in the history and current practice of a particular church. To what extent do the answers to either question center on buildings? What is the short- and long-range impact of making God's memorial be an edifice with a steeple and a sanctuary space?

Jeremiah 7:1–7 (8–15) (L) (E)

The tone of this passage offers a vivid contrast to the Isaiah passage just discussed, but both are focused on the power of the word—God's word and the false words often uttered by human beings. Central in the present passage is God's house, the temple. It is a literal place, guarded at its gate by the prophet Jeremiah, and endangered by false prophets who violate the true word at the very threshold of the temple. The temple is not only a place; it is also a symbol of the holy, needing protection from the profane and the wicked. The ark of the covenant may have been destroyed by this time (Jeremiah referred to it only once, in 3:16), but the vestige of the holy residence for the deity remains as an echo in the present verses. The verses also look forward, to Jesus' attack on the commercial vendors in the Jerusalem temple (Mark 11:15–19).

Lies or deceptive words for Jeremiah represent more than statements of willing deviation from fact. They can refer to the claims of false prophets, with whom Jeremiah struggled for the ears of the people throughout his adulthood. They can refer to misguided beliefs about national security, leading the people of Judah into destructive choices. From a religious perspective, deceptive words mislead people into the worship of the gods, instead of affirming them in the belief in Yahweh and the right deeds that grow from that belief. Thus for Jeremiah, the contract for entry into the temple requires righteousness in daily life outside the temple: justice, nonviolence, and fairness to the alien, widow, and fatherless. The word of God is a word to guide the actions of individuals, not only a word to utter in the sanctuary of the house of the Lord.

To preach from this passage, it will be necessary to offer some context about Jeremiah's history of struggle with false prophets, and the ways Jeremiah perceived and responded to the people of Judah. Beyond that, it can be useful to examine the ways that modern churchgoers view the church as a sanctuary from the rest of the world—a place where no one is to argue, and a place where certain ethical prescriptions are to operate even though those same prescriptions are bypassed in the boardroom or living room. What if the door of the church opened to the world, allowing and even requiring dialogue between the two?

1 Corinthians 15:51–58 (C) (L)

1 Corinthians 15:54–58 (RC)

1 Corinthians 15:50–58 (E)

See also Pentecost 27.

This passage culminates Paul's long discussion of the resurrection. It is the most poetic of the materials, and the one that uses the Hebrew Scriptures in a way that is much more liturgical and celebrative than it is argumentative. The new tone is signaled by the first line in today's passage: "Lo! I tell you a mystery." The word "mystery" here joins the Jewish eschatological notion of God's secret plan with the Christian idea that the time is fulfilled and the mystery can now be shared with (if not fully comprehended by) those who believe. Paul uses the word often, in Romans 16:25–26; Colossians 1:26; 2:2; 4:3; Ephesians 1:9; 3:4; 3:9; 6:19; and 1 Corinthians 2:7. Paul appears to relish the task of revealing the Christian mystery to others for whom the meaning of God's work on earth can be liberating.

While the focus of this passage as a whole is not to debate fine points of theology, it is worth noting that Paul makes a distinction in v. 53 that would seem on the surface to contradict v. 50. (Interestingly, all the lectionaries except the Episcopal lectionary frame the present passage in such a way that the contradiction would not be apparent from an oral reading during worship.) The distinction has to do with the claim that the perishable (humanity) cannot "inherit the imperishable" (v. 50), whereas in v. 53 he says "this perishable nature must put on the imperishable." Commentators on this passage have not given much attention to this pair of verses. For the present writer, however, there is a contrast that seems to be theologically and psychologically sound. To inherit a nature is to be given it without any action on the receiver's part; to "put on" the imperishable is to take an action, an action that must involve responding to the gift of resurrection life made possible through Jesus Christ. While Paul as an evangelist is intent on communicating the truth and extent of Christ's gift, he is also a proponent of human beings' responding to that gift. It is unreasonable that the perishable can put on the imperishable, or that the mortal can put on the immortal, while turning away from the cross and the Christ of Epiphany. But when one can turn toward the resurrected Christ, one can become a new creation. **For further examination** of the idea of the resurrection as new creation and an analysis of the impact of this idea as applied to worship, see Wesley Carr, *The Pastor as Theologian: The Integration of Pastoral Ministry, Theology and Discipleship,* New Library of Pastoral Care (London: SPCK, 1989).

The work of Elisabeth Kübler-Ross has confirmed Paul's description of "putting on the imperishable" and of death being "swallowed up in victory." The autobiographical accounts of people who have been on the edge of physical death repeatedly include statements of seeing a radiant light and seeing hands reaching out to them from a beautiful realm in front of them. See, for example, Elisabeth Kübler-Ross, *Death: The Final Stage of Growth* (Englewood Cliffs, N.J.: Prentice-Hall, 1975) and *Living with Death and Dying* (New York: Macmillan Publishing Co., 1981).

The last half of this pericope is more a song of praise than a set of truth claims. Even here, however, Paul uses his training in rhetoric to set forth a chain of related concepts:

Sting of death = sin   and   power of sin = law.

The old training never entirely leaves the thought or the writings of Paul; trained to know the law, he also knows the power of the law to imprison the oppressed. This paean to the resurrection is not finally about law but about ultimate freedom. The last line in this resurrection chapter closes with an expression of great confidence that all the work done by Paul and his brothers and sisters is, like the word of God in Second Isaiah, not in vain. It will prosper.

Theological Reflection

The word, its powers, and its dangers take the center stage in the passages chosen for this week. The apocryphal passage from Ecclesiasticus is the most forthright in joining the inner qualities of the person to the outer expression of that person's mind. At a very different level, Second Isaiah offers a parallel claim about the God of history. The word of God is the natural fruit of the mind of a loving and faithful Yahweh, and that word is naturally as efficacious as the purpose of the God who sends it forth to humanity. Coming from a prophet, that claim raises the credibility of God's messengers, but more important, it raises the hopes of those hearing the word of God that it will sustain them and bring them home to God's realm in joy.

The word is problematic for Jeremiah because human beings so easily believe words that hurt and mislead; nevertheless this prophet tries to utter a word of warning that will be proved faithful both inside and outside the temple. The word of humans serves for Luke's Jesus as the means of conveying wisdom, and at its best it springs forth from the communicator like a fruit comes forth from a well-tended tree. Jesus in the Sermon on the Plain offers words as nuggets, reminders of the dangers in the world but at the same time images of the solid foundations on which a Christian faith can be built.

Paul, lover of the words of logic and disputation, moves very close to a mood of worship in his last section of his long chapter on the resurrection. It is as if he realizes that people are not finally convinced by the number of words one utters, but by the mystery that is felt in one's being and shared in humility and awe with other believers.

Children's Message

I don't know about you, but most of the children I know, and most of the grownups I know, find themselves sometimes getting into fights—fights with their brothers and sisters, fights on the playground, disagreements with their parents. Now you don't have to raise your hand, but you can just nod your head if you want to. Does that ever happen to you?

Would you guess that Jesus knew anything about fighting? (Wait.) He certainly did. People fought about him, about whether he was the true Messiah or not—a good guy or a bad guy, you might say—about who was to get closest to him—like deciding who is your *best* best friend—and about whether he should say and do what he did—whether he was breaking the big rules or the little rules. In the end, some of the leaders and many of the people fought with him because they didn't understand him.

Jesus understands you and me and what happens to us when we fight. One of the things we do, and I know I do this, is to make up a list in our heads of all the terrible things the other person does. (The preacher can use an example like the one that follows, either from personal experience or from the reports of people known to the preacher.) I used to think up some awful things to report about my younger brother, for example, "He took my book, he called me a name, he sat in my seat, he *sat* on me!" Then of course my brother would come back with his list—"She took my cap, she turned off the TV, she sat in *my* seat, she called me names." And on and on it went. Parents have to listen to a lot of this, and try to decide where the truth is.

The Gospel writer Luke says that Jesus knew what was going on when people made up these lists and complained to other people about the frustrating person. Jesus said to his followers, "You are trying to fix your sister or your brother, who has a tiny speck in one eye. What you're not looking at is the big log in your own eye—the bad habits in yourself that need to be worked on. If you worked on your own bad habits, you could be more fair to your brother or sister." I've noticed that Jesus' idea is true. If I am busy learning how to do something better—like keeping my room cleaner, or passing on messages more promptly, or talking about more positive things instead of complaining—I'll not have so much time to make my lists about my brother or someone else. Jesus is saying, "Work on the me problem first, not on the she or he problem first." Will you say that with me? "Work on the me problem first, not on the she or he problem first." Say that to yourself this week, and see if you don't have fewer fights.

Hymns for Epiphany 8

Lift High the Cross; Thine Is the Glory; Sing to Our God a Song of Cheer (*A Singing Faith*); Take Up Your Cross, the Savior Said.

Transfiguration of Our Lord
Last Sunday after Epiphany

Psalm 99 (C)

Exodus 34:29–35 (C) (E)
Deuteronomy 34:1–12 (L)

2 Corinthians 3:12–4:2 (C)
2 Corinthians 4:3–6 (L)
1 Corinthians 12:27–13:13 (E)

Luke 9:28–36 (C) (L) (E)

Meditation on the Texts

Holy One, you are the Alpha and the Omega. You are the Way, the Truth and the Life. You are the Beginning and the End, the Gate, the Vine, and the Bread of Life. You are the Light of the World, who was, who is, and who will be. You are the rays of the rising sun, and the whole canopy of stars. You are the One who sits with sorrow, and the One who feels our pain. You are the Hope of our tomorrow, and the One who is with us now. You are the Wisdom of the sage, and the refuge of all who weep. You are Living Water, for which we thirst beyond measure. You are the pillar of cloud, the mother eagle teaching her young, the fiery bush, and the movement of the wind. You are more than we can imagine. Your names are without end. We are in awe of your glory.

On this day when the church celebrates the Transfiguration of Our Lord, may I live within the holy place, where God visits the earth and asks me to listen to the Christ. May I listen to Peter as he tries, if awkwardly, to understand what happens to him on top of the mountain. May I see the face of Moses as it catches the glory of God, and may I identify with Moses' hope as he sees the new land that he himself will not be able to enter. May I share with both Paul and Ecclesiasticus the confidence that words uttered in honesty will bring forth the realm of truth. To the glory of the one God, now and forever. Amen.*

Commentary on the Texts

Luke 9:28–36 (C) (L) (E)

See also Lent 2, (RC).

All three of the Synoptic Gospels include this event. Jesus goes with three disciples to a mountain, either Mt. Horeb or the taller (9,200 feet) Mt. Hermon. The timing in Luke is eight days after the confession of Peter and the introduction of the necessity of the Passion; this timing compares to six days later in both Mark and Matthew. Jesus is joined on the mountaintop by Moses and Elijah, primary representatives for the first-century Jewish community of the Law and the Prophets. A cloud overshadows them and a voice announces Jesus to be "my Son, my Chosen; listen to him!" The three disciples then find Jesus alone and descend the mountain in silence.

Discussion continues among scholars and commentators as to how to characterize the account of the Transfiguration: (1) a historical event; (2) a mystical vision experienced by Jesus himself, and shared in some respect with the three disciples; (3) a later appropriation of a postresurrection appearance; or (4) a literary vehicle for conveying the glory and majesty of the Christ. These interpretations are not mutually exclusive; more than one of them can be valid. In any event, the narrative has been developed in the light of the first Easter. For the present writer, it makes sense to consider that a historical moment has

---

*The first section of the above meditation has been adapted from a liturgy in Miriam Therese Winter, *Woman-Prayer, WomanSong* (Oak Park, Ill.: Meyer Stone Books, 1987).

been recounted with the knowledge of both the Hebrew Scriptures as a background and the passion and resurrection of Christ as the foreground events of Christian faith.

The transfiguration is the moment in all three Synoptic Gospels when Jesus of Nazareth most clearly becomes the Christ of God. No one of the three accounts supplies all the details. Luke alone of the three says that Jesus went up the mountain to pray; Luke earlier had reported that Jesus was praying when he received the Holy Spirit (3:21–22). Luke alone of the three Gospel writers reports what Jesus, Moses, and Elijah talked about atop the mountain: it was "his departure, which he was to accomplish at Jerusalem" (v. 31). Mark 9:2–13 adds to Luke's account the statement that Peter did not know what to say, because they were all afraid, while Matthew 17:1–8 describes the three disciples as falling on their faces in awe and being roused by the touch of Jesus. Apart from these differences of detail, the three accounts are one in focusing on Jesus' radiant appearance and on the voice from the cloud which calls him "my Chosen (or Beloved)" and calls the disciples to listen to him.

The transfiguration passage includes many echoes from the Exodus account of Moses' encounter with God on Mt. Sinai (in Ex. 24:12–18). The mountain itself, the cloud covering it, the fact that Moses is accompanied (by his servant Joshua), the period of six days of waiting (a parallel to Mark and Matthew, but not to Luke), the voice to Moses coming from the cloud, and the amazing appearance of "the glory of the LORD" as seen by the people of Israel—all of these indicate the interweaving of the Old and New Covenants as experienced in the first-century church. Jesus' standing on the mountain with Moses and Elijah is a way of saying to believers that he is in continuity with the history of the people of Israel, and that he has transcended the older way of being in and with God. Moses and Elijah disappear, and Jesus remains.

Readers of the story of the transfiguration sometimes lose track of the fact that it is located in a natural as well as spiritual setting. In the Hebrew consciousness the surroundings of people are inevitably bound up with their experiences of the deity, while in the Greek consciousness there is more tendency to separate the concretely physical from the spiritual realm. The present passage is enriched by imagining its parallels as well as its contrasts with the Exodus theophany account in 24:12–18. **To further aid** one's thinking about modern treatments of the natural world in a theological context, see the essay by Carol P. Christ, "Rethinking Theology and Nature," in Judith Plaskow and Carol P. Christ, eds., *Weaving the Visions: New Patterns in Feminist Spirituality* (San Francisco: Harper & Row, 1989).

Peter's role in the transfiguration scene is more prominent than are the roles of James and John, who are not named after v. 28. As the one who had recently confessed Jesus to be "the Christ of God" (9:20) Peter may expect to continue in a leadership role in the mountain event, but Luke indicates that Peter's offer to make three booths, presumably for the upcoming Festival of Booths, is a ridiculous idea. Peter emerges as "not knowing what he said," attested to by his attempting to manage a vision that has broken open the boundaries of time, space, and everyday logic.

The contexts for the transfiguration passage are important. The transfiguration marks the later boundary of the Epiphany season that was begun by the account of the Wise Men coming to visit the newborn Son, led by the star in the East. This season has also brought us the story of Jesus' baptism and his appropriation of the Spirit of God. The transfiguration story itself comes in Luke's account immediately after Peter's rousing affirmation "You are the Christ of God" and Jesus' clarification that to be the Christ is to suffer rejection, be killed, and be raised on the third day. What is glorified on top of the mountain is a Christ with a story that can be seen in radiant light only if one absorbs all its facets. Jesus asks that the disciples try to absorb all these truths, but recognizing that they are difficult, he "charged and commanded them to tell this [Peter's confession of Jesus as the Christ] to no one" (9:21) even before leading the three up the mountain. The context for the passage also includes the fact that it is followed by Jesus' casting out of an unclean spirit from a young man and the twelve disciples disputing about their relative place in the eye of Jesus. Luke more than the other Synoptic Gospel writers has chosen to affirm that life as usual will continue, and that the knowledge of Christ's glory may not immediately alter the human tendency toward competition. The transfiguration is a precursor of the Passion and resurrection, but for Luke it cannot in any way supplant them.

In the present narrative and the verses that immediately precede it, one can hear the voice of God, not only on top of the mountain but also in telling the disciples how the saga of ministry, misunderstanding, passion, and resurrection must unfold. The Spirit of God is present in guiding the disciples into a drowsy state and then into the vision and hearing of God. In this event there are no firm boundaries between the supposed "persons" of the Trinity, but instead a transaction in which various relationships between divinity and humanity emerge as they are appropriate. For further study of trinitarian issues that bear on the transfiguration event, see the stimulating discussion on "the dance of God" by Brian Wren, in his book *What Language Shall I Borrow? God-Talk in Worship: A Male Response to Feminist Theology* (New York: Crossroad, 1989).

It can be frustrating to try to encompass all the meanings in the transfiguration passage, and it may not be necessary in any one sermon. **Preachers** can choose a single way to enter into the passage and to be faithful to that way for a given sermon. The present writer has heard seven different people in a seminary setting preach on this one passage, and each of the seven sermons was unique in its capacity to express that preacher's experience and to grasp an important theme in the passage. The radiance of Christ, Peter's response, the conversation of the three, the voice from the cloud—any of these can be a means to hear the message of the glory of God and God's active presence moving toward humanity.

Exodus 34:29–35 (C) (E)

Seeing the face of God is a complex phenomenon in the Book of Exodus. In the encounter at the burning bush Moses hides his face because he is afraid to look at God. In later parts of the Exodus saga, Moses is told by God that he cannot look on God's face, but only on the back of God as God's glory passes by (Ex. 33:21–23). This interaction suggests that one can see the presence and power of God only in retrospect, after God has acted in behalf of the people. In yet another part of the saga Moses and Yahweh-God are described as conversing face to face, as one would do with a friend, outside Moses' tent (Ex. 33:11).

The present passage is placed beside the transfiguration passage in the lectionary because it brings out another perspective of God's glory as it is experienced in a human context. The key elements in this case are that Moses takes on the glory of God through the shining of his own face after he has met with God to receive the second set of tablets, and that this shining is so bright that the Israelites are afraid to come near him. Moses does speak to the people directly after he has first come down from the mountain, but after that he covers his face with a veil until returning again to talk with God. The shining face is God's glory conveyed to God's messenger. The veil connotes the adaptation of Moses' experience of God, allowing him to function on an everyday basis with his people.

The fact that the veil was a traditional facial covering for women in the Israelite community seems not to have been a detriment to Moses' decision. Instead he carried out an act of ministry, recognizing that the glory of God could not be borne by everyone who had not had a firsthand encounter with the deity. As noted below regarding Paul's interpretation of this event, the veil has had varying moral and intellectual interpretations since the time of Moses.

Preachers employing this passage have available the natural connection between the radiance shown by Moses and examples of radiant countenance that are found in people who experience phenomenal events—seeing an infant child for the first time, being told one is loved, receiving news of the safety of a loved one in a time of danger, coming to a peaceful state of mind through prayer, and realizing the working of God in a significant event. By looking at both Moses' encounter with God and his choice to adapt to those who lack that privilege, it may become possible to comprehend more fully the movement of people between the poles of individual spirituality and communal expressions of faith.

Deuteronomy 34:1–12 (L)

Deuteronomy is an eighth-century book of the law as mediated by Moses to the people of Israel. The book is a mixture of guides to social and liturgical practice and exhortations said to have come from the mouth of Moses. After offering a utopian blessing of Moses that goes beyond legalism to a vision of Israel's life under God, the writer ends the book with the bittersweet report that Moses saw the Promised Land but never entered it. Moses is described in the terms of a eulogy: he died at the age of one hundred and twenty, with an eye not yet dim and natural force not abated. He was also unique as a prophet because he knew the Lord "face to face" (v. 10) and brought many signs and wonders from the Lord to the people of Israel. As an Epiphany text this is a renewal of the refrain throughout Exodus, one that is later recalled by the New Testament evangelists—the theme that the glory of God was shown upon the face of Moses and through him was made manifest to the people of Israel.

Preaching from this passage, one might develop the two sides of the passage at once: the elegaic note that Moses was not able to experience personally the fulfillment of his dream, and the happier note that Moses' efforts brought God's people into a new land, new leadership, and new possibilities for a loving covenant with their God. Because so many people worry about not achieving all that they have worked for in their own lives, this story can have an affirmative impact.

2 Corinthians 3:12–4:2 (C)

In this passage the apostle Paul appropriates the image of the veil from the Book of Exodus, turns it into a metaphor, and makes it a rhetorical tool for reminding his readers of the dangers of losing their courage or clear thinking. Paul in fact bases his use of the veil image on an apparent misreading of the Exodus text. Paul's phrase "so that the Israelites might not see the end of the fading splendor" does not find a warrant in the original Exodus account. A closer parallel to the function of the veil may be Matthew's or Luke's transfiguration accounts, each of which involves a means whereby the three overwhelmed disciples are enabled to experience the glory of God and still live. Luke has the three become drowsy, as in a twilight sleep, and Matthew has them face down on the ground, in awe. Paul's purpose is clearly to distinguish between the old and the new dispensations, and to build up the faithful in their courage to speak openly about the gospel of Jesus Christ. In doing so, he depends on contrasts, between the new and the old, between the veiled mind and freedom of thinking, between the others who still read the old covenant and Paul's audience who behold the glory of God the Spirit in Jesus Christ.

Historical circumstances are relevant to this passage. Paul in dealing with the Jews who did not believe in Christ would have experienced frustration with their dependence on the older scriptures and their unwillingness to address the story of Jesus Christ in relation to the presence of God. So Paul, trained in debate and accustomed to conflict, places the old covenant people on one side and the new covenant people on the other. As a tactic for building up believers, this can be effective, but in modern times tactics such as this one by Paul and others of his followers have contributed to placing a wedge between Christians and Jews that has just recently begun to be dislodged.

2 Corinthians 4:3–6 (L)

Paul's comments on sight and blindness in this passage share with other passages for this Sunday the dual meanings of sight and blindness. Literal sight allows believers such as Peter, James, and John to see Jesus surrounded by radiant light; symbolic vision allows them—more after the resurrection than during the journey to Jerusalem—to see the world as it is seen by the redeeming Christ. In the present pericope Paul chooses to charge the unbelievers with veiling their minds intentionally so that they will be unable to see the open and honest gospel Paul communicates. This is another instance in which the Hebrew use of the veil in the exodus is being shifted into an application that loses its liturgical weight and takes on a negative moral connotation as personal resistance against the truth. Paul goes on in v. 6 to use the metaphor of light that is familiar in Matthew's and John's Gospels and additionally in many religions and cultures other than Christianity. The metaphor is reciprocal for the light has come to human followers of the Light of the World, and the light can be either spread or blocked by the words and actions of human beings.

See Epiphany 4, (L).

Theological Reflection

The idea and experience of perspective is central to the lections for the Transfiguration of Our Lord. What one sees in Jesus of Nazareth is a matter of what one is permitted to see (only three of the original twelve went up the mountain), what one is ready to see (Peter imagined a festival more than an epiphany), and what one is capable of seeing (Moses and Paul both find many people unable to see all that is presented to them). The Gospel of Luke itself carries a perspective, on events in history, on the identity of the believers who would come to see and know God in Jesus Christ, and on the power and glory of God.

The relationship between Epiphany and transfiguration is at least in part the relationship between manifestations of God's glory and the *potential* appropriation of those experiences by the original apostles, by the wider group of first-century followers, and by the modern members of the Christian community—all of whom can discover the word of God through scripture, preaching, prayer, and celebration. The word ''potential'' is of particular importance here, because the transfiguration event is in no way a show of force to back up the request from the cloud to ''listen to him.'' The vision is placed before the three, just as the narratives of Jesus' teaching and healing and prophesying are placed before the modern church, but no one is obligated in absolute terms to see, to hear, or to walk along a new path. Through the Epiphany season and culminating with the event of the transfiguration, we see evidence of *kairos* (God's moment) intervening in *chronos* (the flow of time). Whoever wishes to move the veil aside and see the glory of God, even for an instant, has that choice. The choice involves the freedom of the imagination, the freedom to take for oneself a perspective, as a precursor to taking up a cross.

Children's Message

I'd like you to close your eyes now and imagine that you're home where you live, and it's raining outside very hard and you are trying to look outside. Can you picture that? OK, then what do you see? (Wait.) Sometimes when it rains, it rains so hard that you can't even see the house across the street from you. Have you ever thought that the house or building across the street just floated down the street and disappeared? Well, it probably didn't, except for those very rare times when a big flood occurs. But for a while nothing outside looks the way you are used to. Sometimes that can be frightening, to have nothing look the way you expect it to look.

Now close your eyes again and imagine that the rainstorm is over and the sun is coming out now, shining bright. Can you picture what that looks like? (Wait.) What happens when the sun comes out? Yes, the leaves and the grass and the streets all look shiny and clean. It seems as if the rain has washed the world, given it a bath, so that we can see what is around us much more clearly than before.

In the reading from Luke for today there is a special story about Jesus. He went up to the top of a mountain with several of his followers, and suddenly his face and clothing appeared dazzling white. I think it must have been something like the way the sunshine appears after a rainstorm. There he was, surrounded with dazzling white light, and even talking with the Old Testament heroes Moses and Elijah. As if that weren't enough, a voice came from a cloud above the mountain, telling the followers to listen to Jesus. As you can guess, the followers were dazed: they didn't know what to say or think because they were so amazed at what they had seen. There was Jesus in dazzling light, the Jesus they had known as a leader and friend.

Now Jesus is more in our lives than a bit of sunshine after a rainstorm, but it's not a bad idea to think of how you feel when the sun comes after the rain. Jesus often brings new hope, new courage, new ideas for dealing with difficult things, and those can be just like a wonderful bright light after a dark and stormy time. So the next time a storm comes, and then the bright sunshine makes everything clear and shiny, remember the way Jesus can clear things up if you let him.

Hymns for Transfiguration

God of Many Names; Immortal, Invisible; Holy, Holy, Holy; Glory Be to Our God on High (*Songs of Zion*).

The Seasons of Lent and Easter/Pentecost

The focus of this part of the Christian year is on the heart of the Christian faith: the life, suffering, death, resurrection, and ascension of Jesus and the gift of the Holy Spirit. The Lent and Easter/Pentecost cycle and the previous one of Advent and Christmas/Epiphany, which centered on the incarnation, are the two festival cycles of the Christian church's calendar. The incarnation celebrates the act of God by which "the Word became flesh and dwelt among us" (John 1:14). Now in this season we are reflecting on the meaning of the atonement, the act by which God in Christ made us at one with God by grace through faith. God sent forth the Son in the fullness of time (incarnation) to suffer and die and be raised (atonement) for our salvation. The risen Christ ascended into heaven, from which we expect his return in power and glory, a major theme of the Advent season. Thus we see that the festival season of the church year is especially intertwined with common themes. The gift of the Holy Spirit is the gift of the living Christ, bringing the power of Christ's death and resurrection to human lives.

Since the very beginnings of Christian worship the celebration of Easter has been the highlight of the Christian year. Easter, along with Jesus' passion and death, shaped the life and worship of Christians for each week. The celebration of these saving events of God in Christ shaped the life of community and individuals. We can rightly observe the seasons of Lent, Easter, and Pentecost only as we reflect on their relationship to one another and to the mystery of salvation in Christ. Lent and Easter/Pentecost are formed by the pattern of Jesus' death, resurrection, and the gift of the Spirit which offer eternal life to all who believe.

The Season of Lent

Color: Purple.

The word "lent" is related to the words "long" and "lengthen." It came into use in reference to the lengthening of the hours of sunlight in the springtime. This season has been referred to as "the Easter penitential period" in order to keep the focus on *Easter* rather than on Lent itself. During this season the joyous Gloria and Alleluia are omitted from worship.

Note carefully that the Sundays during the Lenten season are *not* considered an integral part of Lent because Sundays are a celebration of the resurrection. Therefore we speak of Sunday *in* Lent, not *of* Lent. The beginning of Lent is determined by the date of Easter. Lent begins on Ash Wednesday, which comes forty-six days before Easter, and the season itself lasts forty days.

The intention of the season of Lent is to imitate Jesus, who following his baptism, fasted for forty days, but the church also recalls in this fast the forty days Moses fasted on Mt. Sinai (Ex. 34:28), Israel's forty years of wandering in the wilderness, and Elijah's forty days on his journey to Mt. Horeb (Sinai) (1 Kings 19:8). By the second century, Christians were already observing a two-day grief-inspired fast as they prepared for celebrating Easter. The first Ecumenical Council of Nicaea (323 C.E.) refers to a forty-day period of preparation for Easter that was familiar to all churches by that time.

The fast of Lent was first observed by the eating of only a single meal each day, in the evening. Later the fast included abstinence from meat and wine, and then even later dairy products and eggs. The practice continued until the Middle Ages and later. Recall that fasting for medical reasons was not uncommon for the Greeks and the Romans of the ancient world. For Christians of the early church fasting was a source of fervor in prayer. The prayer of a person fasting was compared to the soaring of a young eagle, in sharp contrast to the prayer of one who did not fast.

The central purpose of observing Lent was to *prepare for receiving the Spirit*. The Spirit was a powerful ally in the fight against evil spirits. Fasting was also preparation of candidates for baptism and the Eucharist. Denying oneself food during Lent was a way of freeing up money to give to the poor. But the church was always aware of the danger that fasting could become a mere external formality. It recalled Jesus' warnings in the Sermon on the Mount regarding fasting for fasting's sake and public show of piety.

The Roman Catholic Church's Vatican II Council gave directions for observing Lent which put special emphasis on the recalling of baptism or preparation for it and on penance. The purpose of Lent continues to be the preparation of the faithful for Easter. To do this the Christian is called to repent and turn from sin, with hatred for it because it is an offense against God. The Vatican II statement indicates that penance should be not only internal and individual but also external and social and should be adapted for different regions and individual circumstances.

Ash Wednesday, the beginning of Lent, is so named because on this day penitents put on penitential clothes and had ashes sprinkled on them, both of which were familiar Old Testament practices. In about the twelfth century the rule developed that the ashes used either to sprinkle on the heads of men or to mark a sign of the cross on the foreheads of women should come from the burning of palm branches left from the previous year's Palm Sunday celebration. In many communities of faith Ash Wednesday is still observed as a day of fasting on which ashes are distributed. But Vatican II relaxed some of the strictness of traditional Lenten observances, and now Catholics are allowed to eat meat on Fridays and to eat breakfast before a Communion.

Many congregations observe Lent with special services, such as a noonday luncheon followed by worship once a week. As people better understand the meaning of Lent and its purpose they can find in its discipline a means of self-discipline and self-denial in preparation for celebrating Eastertide and Pentecost. Lent is a period during which many Christians examine their spiritual development and give more time to devotional reading, to service in the programs of the church and community, and to special worship services. Thus it is a time of growth in service both to God and to others.

As pastor and people join in planning and carrying out Lenten programs of worship the time can be one of spiritual journey of the congregation as they engage in "the work of the people," the literal meaning of the word "liturgy."

Holy Week

Holy Week is also called Passion Week to indicate Jesus' suffering and death and is observed in Protestant as well as Roman Catholic churches. Some hold special midday or evening services each day of this week following the themes of Jesus' movement each day. Tradition tells us these are the themes:

Monday	Cleansing of the temple
Tuesday	Jesus' verbal conflict with opponents
Wednesday	Day of silence and retreat to Bethany
Thursday	Jesus' final conversations with the disciples
Friday	The crucifixion
Saturday	Jesus' body in the tomb

Maundy Thursday is so called because the word "maundy" is derived from the new "mandate" or "commandment" Jesus gave the disciples to love one another and his commandment to celebrate the Lord's Supper until he returns. The occasion is usually observed with a candlelight service of worship in which the Lord's Supper is celebrated.

Good Friday is another occasion for special services, often a three-hour service of worship from noon until 3 P.M. The practice began in the Roman Catholic tradition in the seventeenth century and is now often observed in Protestant congregations as a way of remembering Jesus' suffering on the cross during that time. Often congregations in a community join together for a union Good Friday service in which different speakers present brief meditations on Jesus' seven last words from the cross or on another theme. In strict liturgical observance of Good Friday the altar is stripped, candles are left unlit, and the cross is veiled in black to remind all of Jesus' death on this day.

The official end of Lent is at noon on Saturday before Easter. The period from sunset on Maundy Thursday until sunset on Easter Day has come to be known as Triduum, a time in which the early church, following a long rigorous fast, celebrated the saving work of Christ on Easter Eve and on into Easter Day in one unified service.

The themes of exodus, deliverance from death, liberation from slavery—all themes that come to a focus during the passover-Easter period—have special appeal to black congregations. Other ethnic groups have special traditions that enrich not only their worship but the worship of the church worldwide as they are shared.

Easter

Color: White or gold. Gold expresses the prominence of this peak of the Christian year.

The first purpose of Easter preaching is proclamation of the resurrection of Jesus from the dead and its meaning for faith and life. Faith in Jesus' resurrection was universal in the Christian community from the beginning. Through the ages the celebration of Easter in worship has been the high point of the whole Christian year. The church declares in word and sacrament that the Christ who was crucified, dead, and buried has been raised from the dead and exalted to the Godhead. We celebrate the presence of the living Christ in our midst by the power of the Holy Spirit. The first day of the Christian week is the Lord's Day, celebrating Christ's resurrection on the first day of the week. Therefore Easter may be thought of as a ''big Sunday'' rather than Sunday thought of as a ''little Easter.''

The dominant mood is joy. Jesus' death and resurrection are the central focus of the Easter celebration.

Notice that although Easter is the *climax* of the church's worship and is concentrated on one day, the celebration of the resurrection continues throughout Eastertide, which continues until Pentecost.

Be aware of the contrast between Lent and Easter/Pentecost. Lent is penitential, with a mood that is sober, reflective, and watchful. Standing in dramatic contrast is Easter/Pentecost, whose mood is exuberant. The joyful mood of this season should be expressed in all aspects of worship, including music, visual images, and the sermon itself.

We should be aware of the tension involved between Christ's death and resurrection and the gift of the Holy Spirit. Easter has been referred to as the ''Eighth Day,'' which ushers in the End time and brings promise of the light of eternal life. The risen Christ is the New Adam whose resurrection is the beginning of the new humanity and new creation. Worship and preaching during this season should keep in focus the tension between the death/resurrection of Jesus and the gift of the Holy Spirit.

Pentecost

Color: Flame red; other bright colors, such as gold.

Pentecost celebrates the outpouring of the Holy Spirit on the day of Pentecost when the church was no longer desolate, since the living Christ had returned by the Spirit to the disciples. Thus Pentecost, in a sense, is a reliving of the meaning of Eastertide, which runs from Easter until Pentecost. One of the major church festivals, Pentecost ranked second only to Easter until greater emphasis was placed on Christmas. Pentecost includes three festivals of the church: Ascension, Pentecost, and Trinity Sunday. It is the great climax of the Easter/Pentecost season. It is particularly fitting to celebrate the Lord's Supper with great joy on this day and to join in special gatherings and a festive common meal. It is also a time for dramatizing the first Pentecost experience by having several people read different texts simultaneously in several languages, and then experience the unity of speech heard in the preaching of the gospel.

Ascension Day comes forty days after Easter and is not completely separate from the celebration of Pentecost. In fact, until the end of the fourth century the ascension of Christ and the descent of the Spirit were celebrated on the *same* Lord's Day. Thus the exaltation of the risen Christ is linked in an integral fashion with his giving of the Holy Spirit. The color for Ascension Day is white.

Lent 1

Psalm 91:9–16 (C)

Deuteronomy 26:1–11 (C)
Deuteronomy 26:5–10 (L)
Deuteronomy 26:4–10 (RC)
Deuteronomy 26:5–11 (E)

Romans 10:8b–13 (C) (L) (E)
Romans 10:8–13 (RC)

Luke 4:1–13

Meditation on the Texts

Eternal God, we acknowledge that you have created all of life. We pause to express our thankfulness for the great gift of life and the opportunity to praise your good name. Open our eyes and ears to see and hear your presence all around us—in the heavens above, the flowers, grass, and trees around us, in the streams, lakes and rivers, in the birds of the air and the fish in the water; and most especially in the lives of the persons we meet daily. May your presence be so strong that we will be fortified to meet whatever difficulties or temptations we encounter. Amen.

Commentary on the Texts

Luke 4:1–13

The story of the temptations of Jesus is recorded in both Matthew (Matt. 4:1–11) and Luke. Mark devotes only two verses to Jesus' temptations (Mark 1:12–13). The order of the temptations in Luke differs from Matthew's account. They both begin with the temptation to change stones into bread, but the temptation which Luke relates as second was the last one in Matthew's presentation. Luke's reason for this interchange is unclear. He may have placed it last to show Jesus' final rejection of the devil, or because Jerusalem was the place Jesus finished his earthly ministry by his death on the cross.

Under difficult conditions and on numerous occasions, Jesus faced "the dark night of the soul." His temptations were not limited to forty days in the desert but were an ongoing struggle throughout his ministry. At his baptism, Jesus had received confirmation that he was the Messiah, and he had experienced the presence of God's Spirit. Following this experience, he was immediately (according to Matt. 4:1 and Mark 1:12) plunged into a period of testing.

Although Luke has placed the genealogy of Jesus between his baptism and the temptations, this was not an attempt to separate these two experiences. At his baptism, Jesus had committed himself to the ministry to which his Father had called him. Following this exalted experience, he went into the wilderness to reflect and pray about this commitment. Luke's phrase "was led" (v. 1) affirms the continuous presence of the Spirit during Jesus' forty days in the wilderness. The verb used in Mark 1:12 is even stronger—"drove." The costly nature of Jesus' commitment required him to examine thoroughly in solitude and by fasting the decision he had made. Baptism had been a high moment for him, but his time of testing came immediately to see whether he would be obedient to his mission.

There were no mountains in Palestine or anyplace that would be high enough for anyone to see all the kingdoms of the world. The reference is obviously not meant to be taken literally but as an "inner" symbolic experience. This would be true also for the reference to Jesus' being taken to the top of the temple in Jerusalem. Tradition has attempted to locate the place of the temptation on a mountain above Jericho. But the direction Jesus was traveling as he returned to Galilee probably carried him farther north in the desert hill region west of the Jordan Valley. Others have tried to place it in the wilderness between the Dead Sea and Judea in a place called "The Devastation."

Wherever it was—in some isolated, barren, harsh, rugged place—alone, exhausted, and hungry, Jesus met the devil. In Mark 1:13 the evil one is called Satan and in Matthew 4:3, he is designated "the tempter." One does not have to assume that the devil took a visible form. Nowhere else in scripture does Satan appear visibly. Likely the wilderness experience symbolizes the continual struggle that Jesus had with the real and personal power of the forces of evil. His struggle in the wilderness and through his life was between the kingdom of God (the kingdom of light) and the kingdom of evil (the kingdom of darkness).

The reference to forty days in the wilderness (v. 2) may also have more a symbolic than a literal meaning. Moses and Elijah both fasted forty days (Deut. 9:9; 1 Kings 19:8). Moses was seen as the greatest lawgiver of Israel and Elijah was the greatest of the prophets. As one who was greater than the greatest lawgiver or prophet, Jesus likewise spent a similar time in fasting and prayer. Forty has also been a number identified with suffering in the scriptures. The rain that caused the flood that covered the earth fell for forty days and nights (Gen. 7:4, 12, 17). The children of Israel wandered in the wilderness for forty years (Num. 14:33).

The story of Jesus' temptations has the appearance of a dramatic dialogue. The Gospel writer likely used this literary method as a means of showing the continuous struggle Jesus had with temptations throughout his ministry, and it also served as a model for the early Christians in the way they might combat temptations as well.

The first temptation that Jesus had was an appeal to satisfy the appetites and physical needs of his body. The tempter began by referring to the divine voice which Jesus heard at his baptism: "If you are the Son of God" (v. 3). "If you are" suggests a subtle doubt about his Messiahship which was planted in the mind of Jesus. The devil suggested that Jesus perform a miracle to prove who he really was. Some other scholars suggest that the correct translation is "since you are the Son of God." Satan acknowledges that he and Jesus know who he is, but the temptation is to use his Sonship in some way other than by being a suffering redeemer.

Many sections of the wilderness areas in Palestine are covered with fragments of limestone rocks. Many of these pieces of rocks resemble loaves of bread. Singling out one of the stones, the tempter said, "Command this stone to become bread" (v. 3). Jesus answered with words from Deuteronomy 8:3 (NRSV), "One does not live by bread alone."

The first temptation was to try to get Jesus to fulfill the popular messianic view and be a messiah who would satisfy the material needs of people. A banquet feast was one of the most familiar pictures of the messianic age (Isa. 25:6–8). He could be like Moses, who fed the children of Israel in the wilderness (Ex. 16:4), and they would respond to him as the Messiah.

Jesus rejected the attempt to win the people by material means. He would not abandon his spiritual mission. Jesus was not unconcerned about the physical needs of people. He had seen famine and poverty, but he knew that bread could not satisfy the deepest needs of men and women.

The second temptation focused on another popular Jewish concept of the Messiah— one who would liberate Israel from their enemies and establish a political reign like King David had enjoyed. Many Jews prayed for God to send a deliverer to liberate them. Zealots had armed themselves in hope of overthrowing Roman rule. These persons looked for a messiah to establish his reign with force and violence.

Looking across the vast wilderness in silent meditation, Jesus suddenly had a vision within his mind of world domination. The appeal to worship Satan was an attempt to get Jesus to acknowledge that the world was under diabolic control and not under God. Jesus was tempted to doubt the power of God's way of winning the world and to compromise by worshiping the devil.

This temptation sought to get Jesus to complete his mission by fulfilling the Jewish people's expectation for a political messiah. The Gospels note on several occasions that the disciples urged Jesus to seize power and become a king. Jesus rejected Satan's proposal to use force and coercion to accomplish God's purpose, by quoting from Deuteronomy 6:13. With unswerving commitment, Jesus affirmed his intent to serve only God.

The third temptation relates another vision where Jesus sees himself on the pinnacle of the southeast corner of the Royal Cloister of the temple which overlooked the Kidron Valley. If Jesus would jump from this high place, all the people would see him, and Satan promised to bring him down safely. The spectacular method was another temptation to respond to the popular expectations of the Messiah. Some of the prophets had written that the Messiah would "suddenly come to his temple" (Mal. 3:1).

Again the devil taunted Jesus with doubts, "If you are the Son of God" (v. 9), give a sign. Test God. God has said he would protect you from all harm. Throughout his ministry, Jesus often faced the demand for a sign (11:16).

The devil supported his argument by quoting a proof text from Psalm 91:11-12. Satan and others often distort scripture by citing isolated texts and using them for their own purposes. Jesus again drew on the scriptures as he responded to this temptation (Deut. 6:16). Jesus declared that testing God was the opposite of trust. Faith did not require signs. Jesus refused to try to bring in God's kingdom by sensational means.

Jesus' dramatic experience in the wilderness concluded with Luke noting that the devil "left him for a while" (v. 13, TEV). This wilderness encounter was symbolic of the larger lifetime struggle Jesus had throughout his ministry. Jesus' battle with his recurring temptations to compromise his messianic vision and be a popular messiah continued all the way to the Garden of Gethsemane and to the cross. These temptations often came through the demands and hopes of others, especially his disciples. Remember Jesus' rebuff to Peter at Caesarea Philippi (Matt. 16:21-23).

The sermon may focus on the temptation of Jesus to accomplish his goal as the messiah by compromising his commitment to God through using questionable methods or sensational appeals. Preachers still struggle with these same appeals today to accomplish a good goal by using unchristian methods. The sermon may also focus on the resources which Jesus used to combat these temptations—prayer, scripture, personal commitment to God, and the inner struggle of God's Spirit. These same resources are available to all Christians. Some guidelines for ways in which the Christian might draw upon them can be developed.

Deuteronomy 26:1-11 (C)

Deuteronomy 26:5-10 (L)

Deuteronomy 26:4-10 (RC)

Deuteronomy 26:5-11 (E)

The writer reminds his readers of the time that the children of Israel were looking forward to possessing the Promised Land and harvesting their first crop and how they should offer their firstfruits from this crop to God.

This passage focuses on two basic points: (1) The basket of firstfruits, which may be the same as the tithe mentioned in 14:22-27 or may have been another offering, had to be presented at the central sanctuary each year. (2) At the time of this offering, a confession was to be made to God.

The offering of the firstfruits may have been presented at the sanctuary in Jerusalem, most likely during the harvest festival, or Feast of Weeks. This offering acknowledged that they possessed the land as God had promised them and was symbolic of their gratitude to the true God for their first crop of the season. The repetition of the name Yahweh, the Lord, underscored the fact that Yahweh alone was God. By directing the worshipers to take their offering to the sanctuary in Jerusalem, the writer was calling them to proper worship.

A part of the liturgy in their worship in Jerusalem was recitation of a creed or a confession. This passage gives us a page from the oldest "prayerbook" of ancient Israel. It reflects Israel's response to God's mighty acts in history. This statement of faith contains four affirmations.

This creed begins with a confession of a humble beginning as a nation in the wandering of "a Syrian" (an Aramean). This was most likely a reference to Jacob (Gen. 24:4ff.). The second article in this creed tells about the journey of a few nomadic people into Egypt and how they settled there and became a great nation. The third article of faith focuses on the hardships Israel experienced in their slavery in Egypt and the wonderful way God delivered them from their bondage.

It is interesting that this confession does not mention the years of the wilderness wanderings or the giving of the law at Mt. Sinai. This has led some scholars to conclude that these experiences were not a part of the knowledge of these worshipers. Others have suggested that the law may have been handed down through a completely different festival tradition. The reason for its omission here can probably never be known.

The last article in this confession focuses on the land of Canaan which was God's gift to Israel. It was depicted as "a land flowing with milk and honey," which most likely meant that it was fertile and rich in resources.

After repeating this confession of faith, the worshiper would then offer before the priest in the sanctuary the firstfruits of the harvest to God as recognition of God's blessings. Harvest festivals were common in the ancient world. But Israel carefully bound their harvest worship to their historical faith and made it an occasion to remember and celebrate what God had done in their nation's history.

The sermon might develop the thought that underlying our thankfulness for our material blessings is a deeper call to remember, as Israel did, what God has done in creation and in history. In acknowledging our indebtedness to God, we affirm that the chief end of all persons is to adore God, not for what we can receive from this relationship, but simply so we can enjoy God forever. Genuine worship is rooted in thanksgiving. The sermon might move in another direction and focus on the value of the confession of Israel's faith in aiding the Israelites to worship and the role confessions or creeds have in the proper worship of God in the Christian church today. The Apostles' Creed might be used as an example of the church's liturgy to perpetuate the historic message of the Christian faith.

Romans 10:8b–13 (C) (L) (E)

Romans 10:8–13 (RC)

The pericope from Romans is set within a larger context where Paul was trying to convince the Jews to reject the way of legalism and accept the grace of God as revealed in Christ. Earlier Paul had contrasted the righteousness of the law with the righteousness of faith (vs. 5–6). He argued forcefully against the idea that people could by their own efforts through keeping the law bring Christ into the world ("who will ascend into heaven?" v. 6) or raise him from the dead ("bring Christ up from the dead," v. 7).

Paul proclaimed that the word of faith had replaced the law. God had come near to God's people through Christ as God had brought the commandments near to them at Mt. Sinai. Quoting from Deuteronomy 30:11–14, Paul interpreted the response people needed to make to the central event of God's salvation in the death and resurrection of Christ. The incarnation could not be made possible by any human efforts. The incarnation had already been accomplished for humanity by God. The important thing for people to do was to respond and accept God's act.

Some scholars feel that Paul has allegorized this scripture and taken it out of context. But he uses it to drive home a point. Moses was declaring in the Deuteronomy passage that God's law was not distant, inaccessible, and impossible but present in a person's mouth, life, and heart. Christ is the fulfillment and end of the law. The word of faith has superseded the law. The word of faith Paul is talking about here is the death and resurrection of Christ. The content of faith points not to some abstract theories about God but to an objective, historical event. The life, death, and resurrection of Christ was the way God fulfilled the law. This was God's righteous act.

The Jews thought that salvation came about by keeping the law through their own efforts. Paul challenged them to see that salvation was closer to them than they had ever realized and had been proclaimed in their hearing. Paul argued that the law which Moses had described was fulfilled in Christ. The law was no longer the avenue to God. The

118 essence of the law had been incarnated in Christ. This was the message which Paul said had been preached to them. They had heard the message preached and now was the time to respond.

Verses 9 and 10 are probably the earliest Christian creed. This creed seems to be composed of two basic thoughts and a call to confession. This is the only place where Paul relates faith to a belief in certain propositional expressions. Faith, for Paul, usually focused not on intellectual statements but on trusting God. Note his earlier statement in Romans 1:16 (NEB): "I am not ashamed of the Gospel. It is the saving power of God for everyone who has faith."

First, the shortest form of the early Christian creed was the declaration that "Jesus is Lord." Some scholars argue that Paul may have drawn on the imperial Roman emphasis of speaking of the emperor as Lord, or the Lord as master of his slaves, or on a reference to the Greek gods; but most commentators believed that Paul drew on the familiar Old Testament reference to the Lord as Jehovah. No one could make the confession that Jesus is Lord, Paul wrote in another letter, "except by the Holy Spirit" (1 Cor. 12:3). God had conferred on Christ the "name above all names" (Phil. 2:9–11, NEB).

Some scholars believe that this confession, "Jesus is Lord," was an early baptismal confession. Sometimes a candidate was baptized "in the name of the Lord Jesus" (Acts 8:16; 19:5). It seems unlikely, however, that this early confession was confined to the time of baptism. If a person confessed that Jesus was Lord, that individual was declaring that he or she had seen a unique revelation of God through Christ. This confession entailed that converts who belonged to the community were exclusively Jesus worshipers, were committed to the Christlike way, and were devoted to the One who was not only head of the church but the universe as well (Phil. 2:11; Eph. 1:10, 22; 1 Cor. 15:25). To the Jews Paul writes, "The same Lord is Lord of all," but in this passage the Lord about whom Paul writes is Christ.

The second part of this early creed stated that a person had to believe that God raised Jesus from the dead. The resurrection is the foundation stone of the Christian church. If Christ had not been raised from the grave, there would not have been a church. In another place Paul wrote, "If Christ has not been raised, then our preaching is in vain and your faith is in vain" (1 Cor. 15:14).

The resurrection of Christ brought the church into existence. It was essential for every convert to believe in the risen Christ. He or she needed to believe that Jesus had not only once lived but that he was alive today. Paul's emphasis on the resurrection of Christ stressed how absolutely paramount was this belief.

Third, a person not only had to have an experience in his or her heart (the inner place of feeling, thought, and will), but each believer had to confess verbally that belief. A person who really believed in Christ needed to be willing to share that commitment in a public way. Paul had been willing to share his faith with others, aware that often it brought him ridicule, rejection, hostility, and sometimes threats and personal danger. Belief is always personal but cannot remain private. The Christian wants to share his or her experience with others. Witness is an essential part of real belief.

Paul concludes his argument by declaring the universal dimensions of this belief. (1) There will be complete acceptance. He quotes from Isaiah 28:16: "No one who believes in him will be put to shame" (v. 11). (2) There will be no distinctions: "For there is no distinction between Jew and Greek; the same Lord is Lord of all" (v. 12). (3) There will not be any exceptions. He quotes from Joel 2:32: "For, 'every one who calls upon the name of the Lord will be saved' " (v. 13). Faith in Christ removes all barriers and opens belief to persons of every race, class, or sex.

Do a word study of Lord. Examine Deuteronomy 30:11–14.

The sermon may be developed around the three articles in the early Christian creed in vs. 9 and 10: (1) Jesus is Lord; (2) the belief that God raised Jesus from the dead; (3) public confession of one's faith. This sermon may interpret the meaning of the simple declaration "Jesus is Lord," expound the importance of the resurrection of Christ for the church and the individual Christian, and state how one can witness to the faith in modern society. Or the sermon may focus on the universality of God's salvation. The emphasis would be on the inclusiveness of God. All persons are not only accepted but welcomed and loved by Christ. Distinctions, restrictions, and legalism are removed in the person and work of Christ.

Theological Reflection

The Christian confession Paul proclaims in Romans reminds us of the earlier and much older confession of the Jewish people in Deuteronomy. The gratitude the Jews felt for God's blessings in the firstfruits of their crops reminded them to recall and declare again the story of God's guidance and deliverance of God's people through the centuries. The passage in Romans serves as a grand conclusion to God's activity through the ages for God's chosen people. Christ is the fulfillment of God's promise of blessing. Christ is the goal God had in mind by which God would redeem humanity.

In the light of Lent, these passages remind us that our reason for confession of our sins and self-examination is our gratitude to God for God's undeserved love. The story of the temptations of Jesus reminds us in the Lenten season that our Lord was tempted to turn away from his call to be God's Suffering Servant and to fulfill his ministry through appropriate means. Paul has reminded us that the appropriate response of the Christian to God's gift of salvation in Christ is acceptance and gratitude. God's forgiveness of our sins is not due to our own efforts but the response of the universal love and grace that is characteristic of God's nature. As we trust God's grace, we pause to thank God for such unbelievable love.

Children's Message

The message might begin by asking the children to mention some things for which they are thankful. After their response, tell them the story of the harvest feast as recorded in Deuteronomy. Help them to envision the Jews taking their baskets of food to the sanctuary to offer them to God. Continue the story by letting them know that this offering reminded the Israelites of God's special care of them. It might be helpful to have a basket of fruit and vegetables to symbolize the offering. Remind them that Lent is a special time of remembering God's great love for us through the death of God's Son.

Hymns for Lent 1

Now Thank We All Our God; Who Throughout These Forty Days; Join All the Glorious Names; Today I Live (*Choirbook for Saints and Singers*).

Lent 2

Psalm 127 (C)   Philippians 3:17–4:1

Genesis 15:1–12, 17–18 (C) (E)   Luke 13:31–35 (C) (L) (E)
Genesis 15:5–12, 17–18 (RC)   Luke 9:28b–36 (RC)
Jeremiah 26:8–15 (L)

Meditation on the Texts

Lord God, we, like the inner circle of Jesus' disciples, long for a mountaintop experience with you. But we confess that too often our worship is routine, casual, and free from surprises. We confess that, like Abraham, our faith is often clouded with doubts and fears. We, too, want signs and certainties of your presence. Give us inner assurance with the power of your presence to live our lives for you with courage and confidence. Surprise us with your presence in unlikely and unexpected places as we open our hearts to meet you. May that encounter strengthen us to meet the challenges and difficulties that lie before us with faith and hope, as we follow Christ, who trusted you all the way to the cross. Amen.

Commentary on the Texts

Luke 13:31–35 (C) (L) (E)

There is no way to know whether the Pharisees in this passage came as friends to warn Jesus about Herod's threats or were tools of Herod to try to convince Jesus to leave Herod's realm. Pharisees like Nicodemus and Joseph of Arimathea had been friendly with Jesus, and there may have been others. Like John the Baptist, Jesus had become a popular figure with the common people and this caused Herod to fear him and want to eliminate him without angering the people.

Jesus, however, would not be intimidated by Herod's threats. The term "fox" as applied by Jesus to Herod was a term of contempt. The use of the feminine gender of the Greek word for "fox" likely refers to the immorality and inferiority of Herod's character. Jesus' reply reflects courage on his part. He knew that Herod had already beheaded John the Baptist. Nevertheless, Jesus declared that his future direction was clear. He would not be distracted from his course by Herod. He would finish what God had sent him to do.

Like Abraham, Jesus avowed his absolute trust in the providence of God. Indignantly, Jesus told the Pharisees to return and say to the crafty king that he does not have the power to alter God's plan. The precise meaning of Jesus' reply is not completely clear, but the central thrust is. The mighty messianic acts of casting out demons, performing cures, and consummating God's plan of salvation were at hand. The reference to the "third day" likely pointed to the resurrection for the early Christians. The word "finish" seems to underscore that emphasis. There seems to be a reference in the word "finish" to the consecration of a priest. Jesus' death and resurrection were seen by the writer of Hebrews as his high priestly work (Heb. 2:10; 5:10).

Jesus indicated that he was driven by a divine imperative to go to Jerusalem. Some scholars believe that Luke's use of the phrase, "today, tomorrow, and day following," was not just a reference to an indefinite period of time but to the three stages of the ministry of Jesus: Galilee, the journey, and Jerusalem. Jesus was going to leave Galilee but not because he was afraid of Herod. To die in some obscure village in Galilee would not fulfill his destiny. Jesus acknowledges that his fate is to be like that of other prophets and die in Jerusalem.

The reference to the holy city of Jerusalem led Jesus to lament over the fate of the city he loved. The sad truth was that the city of Jerusalem had often before met her prophets with hatred, rejection, violence, and death. Now he sensed that the same destiny lay before him in this sacred city. The city he so loved would be unloving to him. The words "how often" imply that Jesus had tried to minister to Jerusalem on other occasions, but his message had been rejected.

The lament over Jerusalem is filled with Old Testament images. The gathering of the scattered children like a hen her brood was a popular messianic theme (Isa. 60:4; Zech. 10:6-10). The reference to the "desolate house" may be describing either Jerusalem or the temple (Ezek. 8:1ff.; Jer. 12:7). The last phrase, "Blessed is he who comes in the name of the Lord!" is a quotation from Psalm 118 which pilgrims chanted as they entered Jerusalem at one of her great festivals.

Jesus yearned to bring deliverance to Jerusalem, but he wept because he knew his love would be rejected. It is one of the sad facts of life that a person may pour out his or her heart in love for others only to be rejected and scorned by them. Jesus knew that this would be his reception by Jerusalem. In sending God's love through Christ, God gave humanity the freedom to accept or reject that love. The deep compassion of Jesus for his people broke his heart when he realized that they were going to reject him as they had other prophets. The last verse (v. 35) is a warning of judgment, but it also contains an urgent appeal to respond to him.

Do a **word study** of "fox," the third day, finish, and desolate house.

The sermon might focus on the love and tenderness which Jesus had for the city of Jerusalem and his urgent appeal for her to respond positively and not spurn his love as she had that of the prophets before him. The sermon might then move toward the present congregation and expound the costly dimension of Jesus' love and the freedom he gives us today to accept or reject that love. Suggest how our own casual attitude toward Christ and his church affects our Lord. Ask if we do not often cause our Lord to weep by our actions or apathy. Or the sermon might develop the divine imperative which Jesus indicated he felt to go to Jerusalem to "finish" his work. Note the providence of God in guiding Jesus' path toward the cross. Or the sermon may raise the question: What is the contemporary Jerusalem that causes Jesus to weep today? Is it the city where you live? How are we to respond to his laments today?

Luke 9:28b-36 (RC)

See also Transfiguration of Our Lord, (C).

The account of the transfiguration of Jesus is recorded also in Mark 9:2-8 and Matthew 17:1-8. In Mark's account, the experience takes place six days after Peter's confession at Caesarea Philippi. Luke states that a period of eight days had passed. In each case the reference is to a week. In both accounts the Gospel writers link Jesus' transfiguration with his passion statements. Suffering and death are a part of his exaltation.

Jesus took three of his disciples, Peter, James, and John, and went up a mountain to pray. This mountain was most likely Mt. Hermon, which is 9,200 feet high and only about fourteen miles from Caesarea Philippi. Jesus and his disciples climbed to one of the slopes or to the top. The hard climb and the lateness of the hour, as it probably was dark, caused the disciples to fall asleep while Jesus was praying. They awoke suddenly to see Jesus in a "glorified" state. The word translated "transfigured" is more literally "metamorphosed," indicating a radical change in the whiteness of his garments and the brightness and aura of his presence. The disciples saw Moses and Elijah with Jesus in this transfiguration. All of this terrified the disciples.

What is the significance of this story? Let us begin first by looking at its significance for Jesus. The transfiguration was a confirmation of his ministry. It was God's stamp of approval on Jesus' understanding of his ministry. It was God's signature across his life and work. Moses, the great and first lawgiver of Israel, and Elijah, the greatest of the prophets, appeared with Jesus. In this scene Jesus is called God's Son. The voice of God from the cloud declares, "This is my beloved Son" (v. 35, KJV). Moses and Elijah were servants but Jesus is called "my beloved Son." The message to Jewish people was clear. Here was One who was greater than the lawgiver Moses, and greater than Elijah, the greatest of the prophets.

Out of a cloud, God spoke to the disciples. A cloud had often symbolized for Israel the presence of God. In their wilderness journeys, God had appeared to Israel as a cloud that went before them by day. Here the presence of God in a cloud announced God's approval of Jesus.

Luke says that Moses and Elijah discussed the "departure" of Jesus. The Greek word translated as "departure" can be rendered "exodus." What they were discussing was the exodus of Jesus. Moses had led Israel in an exodus, now Jesus Christ was soon to begin a new exodus—a new covenant, a new relationship with God. This mystical vision of the transfiguration was a confirmation of Jesus and his ministry.

The transfiguration was also a witness and encouragement to Jesus' disciples. At first they were terrified. They did not know what to make of this vision with these two historic figures and Jesus in a glorified state. This strange voice from a cloud also left them stunned. Later the disciples would reflect on what they had seen, and write about it. In John's Gospel we read: "So the Word became flesh; he came to dwell among us, and we saw his glory, such glory as befits the Father's only Son, full of grace and truth" (John 1:14, NEB). Then in the Second Letter of Peter we read these words: "It was not on tales artfully spun that we relied when we told you of the power of our Lord Jesus Christ and his coming; we saw him with our own eyes in majesty, when at the hands of God the Father he was invested with honour and glory, and there came to him from the sublime Presence a voice which said: 'This is my Son, my Beloved, on whom my favour rests.' This voice from heaven we ourselves heard; when it came, we were with him on the sacred mountain" (2 Peter 1:16–18, NEB).

The disciples saw the glory of Christ manifested in that moment on the mountain and on many other occasions. This mountaintop experience was to them an affirmation of who Jesus was. Here God affirmed in their minds that Jesus was engaged in the work and ministry which God planned for him. This vision helped them understand God's plan for Jesus.

Simon Peter wanted to prolong that experience by building three tabernacles. He wanted to hold on to that experience and capture it, but Jesus reminded Peter and the other disciples that they could not remain isolated from the rest of the world, as wonderful as that experience was. Hurting humanity waited in the valley below to be helped. We worship to serve in the world.

Do a **word study** of transfigured, departure, and tabernacles.

The sermon may develop the central focus of the exalted Christ to which this passage attests. Note that after the disciples heard the voice from the cloud, which proclaimed Jesus as God's Son, they looked up and saw "Jesus only." Develop this thought to show how Jesus has revealed what God is like. Affirm why Christ is at the center of the church's proclamation. Or the sermon may deal with the importance of high moments of worship but the equal importance of ministering in the name of Christ in the world.

Genesis 15:1–12, 17–18 (C) (E)

Genesis 15:5–12, 17–18 (RC)

See also Pentecost 12, (L) (E).

Our pericope focuses on the impatience of Abraham as he waits for God to fulfill God's promise. Abraham's faith has reached a low point, and he seems disillusioned and uncertain about God's covenant with him. Abraham had been promised by God that he would have an heir to perpetuate his line, but Abraham and Sarah experienced only barrenness. This continued barrenness led to doubt. Yahweh's delay in fulfilling this promise led to Abraham's distrust of God. How could Abraham continue to trust God when there was no evidence to justify this trust?

In a vision, which may have come in a dream, God told Abraham not to be afraid. God assured him that the divine Presence would be a "shield" to protect him. The word "shield" was a military term and had cultic usage, especially in the psalms. God reassured him that he would be greatly rewarded. The Hebrew word for "reward" focuses on an economic settlement, like a person's payment for a job. But the emphasis is not on wages that have been earned by one's own efforts but rather on something given in recognition for faithful and courageous service a servant may have rendered to his or her master. The figurative image of the shield of protection and the promised reward in the future are reminders by God of the divine destiny that awaited Abraham.

These words from God, however, are not reassuring enough to Abraham. His faith is not the timid kind. He boldly confronts God and, with what sounds like sarcasm, he asks God: "How can there possibly be any kind of meaningful reward if I have no son?" Abraham noted that his only heir at this point was a slave named Eliezer. Records have been discovered in excavations at Nuzi in Mesopotamia, which revealed that, when a couple was childless, a friend or a slave could be named their heir to make certain that they received care in their old age and would be properly buried. It seems that Abraham had made such a contract with his slave Eliezer.

What his arrangement reveals, however, is a real reflection on Abraham's lack of faith in God's promise to him. Rather than trusting God to provide him a son by marriage, he chooses a slave to be his heir. This was not the first time that this "pioneer of faith" had shown a lack of confidence in God. When he was in Egypt and feared for his life, rather than trusting God, he pretended that Sarah was his sister and not his wife (12:10–16).

To reassure Abraham again, God, in the same vision, invites him to go outside his tent and look up into the heavens. God instructs Abraham to look at the vast number of stars in the heavens and promises him that his descendants will be numberless. This time the words from God are sufficient; he is reassured and "he believed the LORD."

The words, "he believed," are a potent response. A few moments before, Abraham had been lamenting his lack of a son as an heir, and after this brief exchange, he believed. Why such a radical change? In this vision Abraham has such a powerful personal experience with the divine Presence that he now opens his life to that Presence, so that God's promise is not merely a wishful dream but an assured reality.

The narrator makes a theological assertion about Abraham's faith at this point: "He reckoned it to him as righteousness" (v. 6). This statement is one of the high watermarks in the Old Testament. This sentence defines the meaning of faith. Faith is depicted as absolute trust in God's promise, even if there is no evidence to verify that trust. This kind of faith is based on an internal confidence in God that is revealed by the very presence of God. Abraham's faith is now based not on the physical evidence of a son brought about by his own action, but on the word of promise from God. That word was sufficient.

In some ways Abraham's confession of faith is similar to the one made by Simon Peter, "You are the Christ, the Son of the living God" (Matt. 16:16). Like Abraham's abrupt declaration, Peter's confession seems to be too great an insight for one who continued to struggle with his own doubts. Jesus' reaction to Peter's confession reveals how such faith is possible: "Blessed are you, Simon Bar-Jona! For flesh and blood has not revealed this to you, but my Father who is in heaven" (Matt. 16:17). Here, then, is the key to understanding Abraham's change from doubt to faith. His confession did not rest on what he and Sarah had accomplished—flesh and blood—but on the power of God working within his own heart.

Abraham's faith put him in a right relationship with God. That right relationship is what is meant by "righteousness." What is affirmed here about Abraham is not what he has accomplished but what his trust in God realizes. The emphasis is not on the contrast between faith and works but on trust and the lack of trust. Abraham had demonstrated his lack of faith in God by selecting a slave as his heir and taking his future into his own hands and away from God. Following this vision, he obviously rescinded that agreement and put his trust in God's word. He moved from unbelief to belief. He was assured by God's word. He no longer needed proof before he would believe.

Some scholars have seen this passage as the Old Testament version of the doctrine of justification by faith which Paul writes about in the New Testament. The apostle Paul drew on this text in his argument in Romans 4:3f. and Galatians 3:6f. Faith is in response to God's grace and is not based on the works of anyone. James also quotes this verse in his brief epistle (James 2:23). The favorable assessment of God on Abraham was not based on what Abraham had done but on his faith alone.

The strange and uncertain ceremony described in vs. 7–11 was like some ancient form of a blood oath to assure Abraham of God's promise. He is instructed how to cut the animals, and he even has to drive off the vultures that came to feed off the carcasses. A covenant was usually "cut" and not "made" in ancient times. This is likely one of the reasons for including this ancient ritual. Jeremiah speaks about cutting a covenant and the people passing between the pieces (Jer. 34:18–19). Some scholars think that this action might symbolize that the persons who pass between these slain animals are now united, but if the covenant is broken, their fate will be similar to what has happened to these animals.

Abraham then falls into a deep trance. In this trance he hears a promise about the land that will be given to his descendants and about their future period of slavery and exodus and the vast extent of Israel's boundaries. One sees the narrator most likely speaking to his present hearers to explain to them what happened between the time of Abraham and Israel's entrance into Canaan.

While still in his trance, Abraham sees a smoking firepot and a flaming torch pass between the severed animals. These two fiery objects probably symbolized the presence of God who passed between the carcasses. Abraham saw this act as a sign of God's covenant with him. God had assured him in images he could understand and in a ritual he knew, that God's word was now given in a solemn agreement. Abraham could now wait confidently in faith.

It would be helpful to **do a word study** of righteousness.

The sermon may draw upon the paradigm of Abraham's struggle with doubt and faith to address the continuous battle that most believers have with their trust in the promise of God's presence, especially in times of illness, grief, or difficulties. Or the sermon may focus on the believer's constant demand, like Abraham, for some sign or assurance of God's guidance. Or the sermon may show the parallel between the statement about Abraham's faith, "He reckoned it to him as righteousness" (v. 6), with Paul's doctrine of justification by faith as recorded in Romans 4:3f. and Galatians 3:6f.

Jeremiah 26:8–15 (L)

This passage presents the reaction to Jeremiah's sermon. A longer account of his sermon is given in 7:1–15. Jeremiah warned the people that unless they turned from their evil ways, God would destroy the temple like he did Shiloh, and the destruction of Jerusalem would be an example of God's curse upon them. The priests, prophets, and other cultic personnel of the temple were indignant and accused Jeremiah of being a false prophet. They declared that his words were blasphemous for two reasons: (1) They were proclaimed in the temple itself in the name of Yahweh. (2) He said that the temple and the Holy City, which they believed were indestructible, would be annihilated.

The priest and other cultic leaders condemned Jeremiah and were on the verge of "lynching" him. But someone either sent word for help or all the commotion caught the ears of the princes of Judah—the state officials—and they came to the temple, stopped what the priests were about to do, and convened a court at the entrance to the new gate of the temple. At this trial, Jeremiah makes a quiet defense based on the fact that he had only prophesied what God had told him to do. Without fear or desire for vengeance, Jeremiah declared that he was innocent because he had been true to the message God had commanded him to preach. He told them again that the people still had time to repent and turn back to God. In v. 16 the princes rejected the judgment of the priests and declared that Jeremiah was indeed a prophet of God.

The sermon might compare Jeremiah's defense before the court with the "defense" of Jesus before the Sanhedrin and Pilate. Note the different responses. Or the sermon might explore the negative reaction the word of God often brings when it challenges our preconceived beliefs or prejudices, like the religious leaders who thought Jerusalem was invincible.

Philippians 3:17–4:1

Paul was addressing a problem that had arisen in the Philippian church because of the life-style of some of its members. Scholars are uncertain who these "enemies of the cross'' were. Some have suggested that the reference was to Judaizers, who wanted the Gentile converts to obey the Jewish law. Others believe they may have been Gnostics, who claimed that because the body was evil it did not matter what a person did. Sexual immorality, physical indulgence, and drunkenness were unimportant because they were a part of evil matter.

Although the identity of these persons may not be certain, Paul was challenging a libertine life-style that distorted freedom in Christ to mean that a Christian could indulge in any manner of sexual behavior, engage in any overeating and drinking customs that he or she desired. Paul argued strongly against the Christian's being dominated by physical appetites. Paul encouraged the church at Philippi to do what might sound egotistical to us, imitate his example (v. 17). But this was a practice common with teachers and their students or disciples in Paul's day. By word and example, Paul had showed them how Christians were to regard their bodies.

Paul drew on an image of a colony, which would have been very familiar to the patriotic Philippians since they were a Roman colony. As the Philippians never forgot they were Roman citizens, so Christians must never forget that they are citizens of heaven. Their conduct should reflect their heavenly citizenship. Paul expressed his warm affection for them and encouraged them to ''stand firm,'' as a soldier had to remain firm in the heat of battle.

Do **a word study** of colony, imitate, and example.

The sermon may develop Paul's admonition to follow his example. Paul's words can also be tied to Jesus' words to his disciples after he had washed their feet: ''I have given you an example, that you also should do as I have done to you'' (John 13:15). This thought might be advanced further by examining the instruction to the early church: ''For to this you have been called, because Christ also suffered for you, leaving you an example, that you should follow in his steps'' (1 Peter 2:21).

Theological Reflection

In this Lenten season, the church is reminded that salvation is not based on our actions but on the righteousness of God. Our behavior is modeled after Christ and in response to our complete commitment to him in faith. Although our faith can never be free from all doubts and fears, ultimately our righteousness is realized only in confidence in God as we have experienced God's presence in Christ. The personal assurance of God's presence enables the Christian to live with courage and hope. But this mountaintop experience with God compels the Christian to live out that trust by responding to the human needs along the journey.

Children's Message

The message might deal with Jesus' lament over Jerusalem. Begin by asking the children if they have ever cried. Ask them to tell you some of the things that caused them to cry. Tell them the story of Jesus crying about Jerusalem and the people's rejection of his love. Remind them that Jesus loves all people, in cities or wherever they live, and that he is sad when people reject his love.

Hymns for Lent 2

O God, Our Help in Ages Past; Now Let Us All with One Accord; Now Quit Your Care; Out of Our Night of Day (*Choirbook for Saints and Singers*).

Lent 3

Psalm 103:1–13 (C)   1 Corinthians 10:1–13 (C) (L) (E)
    1 Corinthians 10:1–6, 10–12 (RC)

Exodus 3:1–15 (C) (E)
Exodus 3:1–8b, 10–15 (L)   Luke 13:1–9
Exodus 3:1–8a, 13–15 (RC)   Luke 13:10–17 (alt. C)

Meditation on the Texts

We praise you, O God, for the assurance of your love and presence on the darkest day. Thank you for hearing our aches and joys, our fears and hopes, our sorrows and pleasure, our remorse and our confidence. Thank you for your loving concern for those in need, as you revealed your eternal presence to Moses centuries ago. Open our eyes to see your presence in burning bushes all around us today. As we experience the loving and forgiving power of your presence through your Son, Jesus Christ, empower us to minister to those in need around us. Teach us, through the example of Christ, how to live lovingly, generously, faithfully, joyfully, and sacrificially. Amen.

Commentary on the Texts

Luke 13:1–9

This pericope begins with a horror story about a report of some Galileans killed by Pilate, who poured their blood on their own altars. This story may refer to an ugly incident, which Josephus, the Jewish historian, reported, that occurred when some Jews were working on an aqueduct into Jerusalem. In order to finance this project, Pilate appropriated funds from the temple treasury. Many of the Jews protested strongly and gathered to insist that Pilate stop this action. Pilate called out the Roman soldiers and had each man conceal a dagger under his cloak. When the Jews refused to disperse, he gave the order to the soldiers to attack the Jews. Caught unprepared and unarmed, many of the Jews were killed.

The telling of such a tale served as a vehicle to try to provoke the Jews emotionally to respond violently against the government in power. Those who told this story to Jesus and asked him what appeared to be a theological question may have had other motives in mind. They may have been Zealots trying to provoke Jesus to condemn the Roman government for such violence against the Jews, hoping that he might support a rebellion against Roman rule. Such open condemnation would have branded Jesus as a revolutionary and made him an enemy of the state.

Rather than responding to this atrocity story with a denunciation of the Roman rulers, Jesus takes a surprising turn and looks at the dilemma of sin and suffering as an opportunity to call his Jewish hearers to repentance. Instead of accepting the glib answer that these Galileans were supersinners, Jesus tells his listeners that unless they repent, they will likewise perish. He then adds his own headline horror story: "Siloam Tower Collapses and Kills Eighteen." That this unforeseeable accident took the lives of eighteen workers, who may have been part of the construction crew building the temple, the city wall, or a tower at the Pool of Siloam, did not mean that these persons were unusually sinful.

Like Job's friends, these questioners engaged freely in discussions about the unfathomable mystery of sin and suffering, but they were unwilling to look within their own souls and repent of their own evil. In a stunning refrain that Jesus repeats twice, he calls for his listeners to repent, lest they also perish (vs. 3, 5).

The urgent call to repentance Jesus sounded in vs. 1–5 is carried forward in the parable told in vs. 6–9. This parable reminds those who hear it that God's judgment is concerned not only with individuals but with nations as well. To find a fig tree in a vineyard was not unusual. Jesus may have called attention to the fig tree because the fig usually bears fruit ten months of the year, and the owner can almost always find fruit on the tree. The fig tree and vine are closely related in the Old Testament and are often identified in the same way as symbols for Israel. The vine and fig were both symbols of peace as well as representing the nation Israel. Hosea links them together as images of Israel (Hos. 9:10).

Israel was often depicted as a vineyard (Isa. 5:1–7; Micah 7:1; Jer. 8:13). As the people of the covenant with God, Israel was "planted" for a special reason—to serve God. Their reason for living was to tell others about God. Their privilege as God's chosen people carried responsibility. Just as a fig tree had the purpose of producing figs, Israel had the obligation of producing fruits which demonstrated its special relationship with Jehovah.

The owner (God) had waited patiently (nine years) for the tree to produce fruit (vs. 6–7), but it had produced none. Fig trees were given three years to grow after planting. The next three years the fruit was considered unclean and forbidden to eat (Lev. 19:23–24). Each year for three years after the fruit could be eaten, the owner had come to get fruit from the tree and had been disappointed. The purpose of a fig tree was to bear figs. If it bore no fruit, it was a hindrance to the vineyard because it took up space and robbed other plants of necessary water.

The uselessness of the fig tree threatens its own destruction (v. 7), but the vinedresser (a reference Jesus likely used of himself and his call to repentance) pleads for another chance for the tree (vs. 8–9). The vinedresser's request for another year to work with the tree is a plea for a period of grace to see if it will respond. Some scholars believe that the reference to the use of manure in the parable is probably a humorous dig directed at the religious leaders.

There is a limit to God's patience (v. 9), "If it bears no fruit in the future, dig it up." God offers opportunity for repentance in response to God's mercy, but there is a limited time to respond. This parable speaks of both God's grace and judgment. The parable ends without telling what happened. It ends like a story "to be continued." Only the listener can really determine the ending of the story.

Consult a Bible dictionary for the image of Israel as a vineyard.

The sermon may develop the theme that the mystery of sin and suffering should not prevent persons from repenting of their own known sins. It may help persons to reject easy theological solutions to the dilemma of undeserved suffering while they respond to God's grace in the midst of their own personal struggles. Or the sermon may focus on God's expectation that Christian disciples are expected to produce fruits as evidence of their commitment. It may note that not only are Christians expected to produce fruit in God's vineyard but failure to do so not only harms but hinders the work of God's kingdom. The sermon may be a reminder of God's mercy and the opportunity to experience renewal through repentance, but it may note that this parable is not only about grace but also about judgment.

Luke 13:10–17 (alt. C)

The setting for this story about Jesus' healing a crippled woman on the Sabbath took place in one of the synagogues, likely in Galilee. This is the last reference to Jesus teaching in a synagogue. It is interesting to note that here, as on other occasions when he taught in synagogues, Jesus aroused the anger of the religious leaders. When he preached at his hometown in Nazareth, Jesus' words made his listeners so angry that they tried to throw him off a cliff (Luke 4:16–30). The message Jesus brought was often disturbing, not comforting.

Some scholars feel that the teaching of this episode is closely related to the stories found in Mark 3:1–6 and Luke 14:1–6. The early church was engaged in a controversy with its Jewish members over the observance of the Sabbath. Some see this and other miracle stories that took place in the synagogue as the church's attempt to respond to that issue. Others believe that the conflict over proper Sabbath observances originated with Jesus' challenge to the religious leaders of his day.

The story of the woman's infirmity reveals the compassion of Jesus. For eighteen years this woman had suffered from an ailment which kept her bent over, unable to straighten up completely. Some have interpreted the phrase "spirit of infirmity" (v. 11) to refer to the power of demons, so that in some sense they see this cure as an exorcism. Jesus addressed the woman personally and assured her that she was freed from her illness. He then touched her—"laid his hands upon her" (v. 13)—which might have been a type of exorcism. Luke stresses that Jesus healed a woman and that he physically touched her in public. Other scholars have argued that this healing by Jesus with laying on of hands was a sign of forgiveness and blessing. The woman was made whole immediately and glorified God.

The ruler of the synagogue accused Jesus of breaking the law by healing the woman on the Sabbath. It is interesting that the ruler of the synagogue did not direct his criticism directly to Jesus but to the people. They tried to turn an act of beauty into something ugly to maintain their rigid regulations. Luke deals with this same controversy about Sabbath observances in two other places, 6:6–11 and 14:1–6. Healing, according to the Sabbath laws, was considered work.

Jesus gave three reasons to justify his action on the Sabbath. (1) He stated that this reaction to his act of healing was hypocritical since the Jewish law allowed an owner ways he could water his animals on the Sabbath. (2) A fellow human being is more important than an animal. It is incongruous to be more merciful to an animal than to a person in need. (3) The references in v. 16 to Satan, the covenant with Abraham, and the power to "set free" or loose the woman who was bound are signs of the messianic age.

The controversy here focuses not merely on a literal or a free interpretation of Sabbath laws. The concern is a larger one—the radical nature of the kingdom which Jesus came to initiate. In Christ's kingdom there would be "neither male nor female" (Gal. 3:28); there would be a new covenant based on God's victory over the power of the evil one; and there was also the note that the Lord of the Sabbath was at hand.

Jesus claimed that "it was necessary" that this woman be set free on the Sabbath. The word "necessary" is the same word which was used to express Jesus' "necessity" about his death on the cross (9:22). The kingdom of God was imminent, and the ministry of delivering those who were bound by the power of Satan was at hand. It was necessary for this work to continue seven days a week. The Sabbath, as the day set aside for release from the bondage of physical labor, was a sign of the greater release from the bondage of sin which awaited God's people with the coming of the kingdom of God.

Compare this episode to the one in Mark 3:1–6 and Luke 14:1–6.

The sermon might focus on the constant danger of the church's being more concerned with making people conform to certain traditional beliefs than with showing compassion for the physical or emotional needs of these people. Develop the theme that Jesus—the Lord of the Sabbath—has founded his kingdom on grace and not on human achievements. Note examples of the kingdom of Satan against which the kingdom of God continues to contend in modern society, such as racism, war, hunger, disease, and bigotry.

Exodus 3:1–15 (C) (E)

Exodus 3:1–8b, 10–15 (L)

Exodus 3:1–8a, 13–15 (RC)

Chapter 3 is probably one of the most important sections in the Book of Exodus. In this chapter, Moses is commissioned to lead Israel out of bondage in Egypt, and God reveals the name "Yahweh" to Moses. Moses towers over other figures in the Old Testament as the ancient Egyptian pyramids tower over the desert. He was the first and probably the greatest of the Hebrew prophets. Moses was also the great lawgiver as evidenced in the Ten Commandments.

The call of Moses into God's service on Mt. Horeb is a strange but well-known story. Moses led his sheep up the mountain of Horeb, or Sinai, where he had gone numerous times before. He called this place "the mountain of God." While he was on Mt. Horeb one day, a day probably like any other day, Moses saw a bush that was burning but was not consumed by the flames. He knew that a shrub like that should have burned quickly and turned to ashes, but for some reason the bush was not consumed. "How is this possible?" he must have asked.

How is one to interpret this story? Scholars have had all kinds of difficulty trying to explain the burning bush that was not consumed. Some have said that this shrub was really like the "burning bushes" that some persons have growing in their yards today. In the fall of the year, the leaves on the burning bush turn bright red like fire. It is difficult to believe that this is the answer, however. Moses saw those bushes all the time. Why would their fall glow have captured his eye and made him think they were aflame?

Other scholars feel strongly that this account should be taken literally and was evidence of the supernatural power of God. Still others believe that this was an inner experience of Moses. These persons have suggested that if someone else had been present with Moses he or she would not have seen the burning bush. What happened was visible only within Moses' own consciousness. This vision addressed his mind alone in the same way that Jesus heard the voice of his Father say, "This is my beloved Son in whom I am well pleased." Others around Jesus did not hear the voice but only thought it thundered. Paul experienced a blinding light on the Damascus road and saw and heard the risen Christ, but others on that same road did not see the light.

Whatever happened on that mountainside at Horeb was real to Moses. It was so vivid to him that it changed his life forever. The how is not important. The burning bush was the means of communicating God's presence to Moses. Moses saw within the bush that was not consumed the very presence of God. When the Exodus writer says that "the angel of the LORD appeared to him," this is a reference to the presence of God. Here in a thornbush, on a mountainside of Sinai, God appears to Moses. The experience of God is vivid and real in the sights and sounds Moses perceives within his own consciousness.

Moses turns aside and responds to God. Moses sees and hears God and responds in awe and reverence. As he approaches the great mystery of the presence of God in the burning bush, he hears the voice say to him, "Take off your shoes, because you are on holy ground." He kneels in wonder, worship, and awe before God who says, "I am the God of your father, the God of Abraham, the God of Isaac, and the God of Jacob."

God reveals that at the center of the divine Presence is concern. God declares that God has "seen," "heard," and "knows" the misery, suffering, and plight of "my people," "and I have come down to deliver them." This is anthropomorphic language, but it indicates in clear imagery that God is not detached or indifferent to human sufferings. God is a God who is so concerned that God comes near. God tells Moses that God has come down to deliver the enslaved people.

Following his experience with God, Moses is commissioned. God informs him that he has been selected as God's prophet to speak to Pharaoh, but Moses immediately protests, "O God, who am I?" Here is a reluctant prophet. "Who am I, God, to undertake such a task? I am a nobody. Who am I?" But God insists that Moses has been God's prophet. "I will be with you," God promises him.

Next Moses asks, "Who are you, God? Who am I supposed to say is sending me?" The words of response have kept scholars wrestling for ages to determine their precise meaning. The divine name in Hebrew is "Yahweh." The Hebrew phrase is usually translated, "I AM WHO I AM." Moses hears welling up in that phrase the explanation of the name of God. "Tell them that the One who has no beginning or end, whose existence is in the now is the God who is sending you. Tell them that the God before whom you kneel in mystery and awe, the God of your forebears, the God who is not confined to this mountain, but the God who will lead God's people out of slavery into the Promised Land, the God who is offended by injustice is the One who will send prophets to speak out against this oppression and set God's people free. I AM WHO I AM," says God.

People define their existence by stating that they are the children of their parents. We are the product of our parents and our environment. We are derived from what has gone before us. But God is "I AM WHO I AM." God is the eternal One without beginning or end. God is original, primary, absolute, and underived.

Some scholars have stated that they believe that God's reply is an attempt to be evasive. God is the *deus absconditus.* Although God's reply is clouded in the mystery of the divine Presence, God did, nevertheless, reveal the divine name to Moses. A literal translation of Yahweh might be, "I am the one who am." It is likely that the meaning of God's name is to affirm God's existence as the only real deity over all other gods.

Do a word study of the word "Yahweh."

The sermon may focus on Moses' response to God as he said, "I will turn aside and see this great sight." Note Moses' openness and sense of expectancy as he is drawn to this strange phenomenon. Compare the way many persons today allow their senses to become dulled and unresponsive to God's presence. Or develop the meaning of the name of God which was revealed to Moses, "I AM WHO I AM." What difference should God's name make in the way a person comprehends God's nature? Or develop a different theme and show God's concern for the enslaved persons in our world. This sermon may address the concern God has for black people in South Africa or brown-skinned persons in America or persons anywhere, male or female, who suffer under the bondage of racism, prejudice, or national political tyranny.

1 Corinthians 10:1–13 (C) (L) (E)

1 Corinthians 10:1–6, 10–12 (RC)

On the first reading of this pericope, it appears that Paul has moved away from addressing the issue of eating meat which had been used in the worship of idols. But that is not the case. Earlier in chapter 9, Paul has used his own behavior as an example of proper response to the eating of this meat. Now he draws upon several episodes from the desert wanderings of the Israelites to make his point.

Paul refers to Israel's being guided by the cloud and passing through the Red Sea (Ex. 14:19–31) as uniting the people to Moses in such a bond of unity that it is a type of "baptism into Moses" for them. For contemporary Christians, this may seem like a strange passage to use as a reference to being baptized into Christ, but Paul likely saw Moses as a type of Christ to his people.

God sustained Israel by spiritual food—manna (Ex. 16:13ff.)—and spiritual drink which was supplied by a rock that followed Israel in their wilderness travels. There is a reference in the Old Testament to a rock where Moses drew water for his people (Num. 20:1–11), but the story of a rock that followed the Israelites is based on rabbinic legend. Some scholars feel that references to such a rock are found in Psalms 78:20; 105:41; and Isaiah 48:21. Paul sees the rock as a symbol of the presence of Christ (v. 4).

Even with God's special blessing and guiding presence, Paul reminds his readers that the Israelites committed several blatant sins on numerous occasions. He notes that, because of their sins, twenty-three thousand of them died in the desert from serpent bites. Paul was probably quoting from memory, because the correct figure was twenty-four thousand (Num. 25:9). He draws on these stories to point out four temptations the Corinthians will have to confront, just as the ancient Israelites did. Their struggle will be with the following sins: (1) idolatry, (2) fornication, (3) presuming on or testing God's patience, (4) grumbling and complaining.

Paul issues a call to vigilance on the part of the Corinthian Christians. He uses the desert stories as a "warning" to remind the Corinthians that even those who think they are spiritually strong may still fail in times of testing. He notes three things about the tests or temptations: (1) temptations are a part of life; (2) everyone will face similar temptations; (3) a way of escape is also provided with all temptations. The image here is like an army surrounded in the mountains by its enemy but which is able to find a mountain pass, permitting escape from what seemed an impossible situation.

Study the accounts in Exodus 14:19–31 and 16:13ff.

The sermon may focus on the Christian's ongoing struggle with temptations. Draw on Paul's example of the temptations of the Israelites in the desert as images which not only address the struggles of the Corinthian Christians but speak to contemporary Christians as well. Develop the Christian's need for vigilance by building on Paul's three assurances about temptations (vs. 12–13). Stress the faithfulness of God and the danger of self-assurance.

Theological Reflection

All the texts focus on God's concern for the sufferings of men and women, whether it is the bondage of slavery, accidental calamity, the physical pain of a suffering individual, or the burden of personal temptations. God is not aloof and unconcerned about the pain and struggles of humanity. The exodus and the cross of Christ are supreme revelations of God's involvement in the suffering of humanity and the deliverance which God brings to those who bear the weight of the burden of sin and suffering. Moses' experience on Mt. Horeb and the compassion of Jesus to persons in need reveal a God of love and concern.

Children's Message

The message might deal with the story of Moses' encounter with God on Mt. Horeb. Tell the story about Moses meeting God in a burning bush on the mountainside of Horeb as he took his sheep to graze one day. Be vivid in your retelling of the tale and focus on the bush that was not consumed, God's words to Moses, the removal of Moses' sandals, the meaning of God's name, and God's concern for the Israelites. Help the children to understand how they might be able to sense God's presence in worship, in Communion, and in nature around them.

Hymns for Lent 3

Guide Me, O Thou Great Jehovah; From Deepest Woe, I Cry to Thee; The God of Abraham Praise.

Lent 4

Psalm 34:1–8 (C)

Joshua 5:9–12 (C) (E)
Joshua 5:9a, 10–12 (RC)
Isaiah 12:1–6 (L)

2 Corinthians 5:16–21 (C)
2 Corinthians 5:17–21 (RC) (E)
1 Corinthians 1:18–31 (L)

Luke 15:1–3, 11–32 (C) (L) (RC)
Luke 15:11–32 (E)

Meditation on the Texts

We remember, O God, the power of your hand that delivered Israel from their bondage in Egypt. We pause to reflect on the great sacrifice that your Son made on the cross for our redemption. We marvel at such suffering, caring love that would go to such an extent to show the depths of your compassion for all peoples. We pause to express our gratitude for such undeserved love. Forgive us when we exclude by our words or actions others whom you have included in your family of grace. Thank you for accepting us. Teach us how to accept your acceptance of us and how to accept others as you have accepted us. Amen.

Commentary on the Texts

Luke 15:1–3, 11–32 (C) (L) (RC)

Luke 15:11–32 (E)

The parable of the prodigal son has been called the greatest short story ever told. Some have described it as the parable of all parables. Others have called it the gospel within the gospel. When properly understood, this parable seems to be more about the gracious love of the father than the waywardness of one of his sons. The father's behavior toward both of his sons is unexpected. The parable really begins and ends with the focus on the father.

Jesus began the parable, "A certain man had two sons" (v. 11, KJV). Women should not feel excluded from this story. Jesus held this parable up like a mirror so all of his listeners could see themselves in the reflected image. At some time or another, this parable is every person's story—male or female.

The first scene depicts the younger son imploring his father for his portion of the estate. At the death of the father, an elder son legally received two thirds of the estate, and a younger son got one third. This younger son's request is a grave insult to the father. What he is saying to his father in essence is: "I wish you were already dead so I could have now what is rightfully mine." It was a shocking request. The father would have been hurt and humiliated.

Jesus stated that the younger son left home alone. This indicates that he was most likely still single. He was probably no older than seventeen because a Jewish man in ancient times usually married between eighteen and twenty. His request for his share of his father's wealth was a demand that he be set free from the authority of his father. He naively assumed that if he had money, he would have freedom.

This kind of request by the younger son would have outraged the whole Jewish community in that day. They would be shocked by such a harsh request and would have turned against him. We do not know what their family life was like. Nothing was said of that. The son simply wanted to leave. He longed to have freedom and be his own man. He wanted liberty. "Give me . . . , give me freedom," he cried. "Set me free. Let me have my way." In his heart he was already in the far country.

One of the amazing features of this story is that although fathers were all-powerful then, the father granted his son's request. He sold some of his property and gave the money to his son.

The second scene shifts to the far country where the son began to be in want. There is no indication where the far country was. Maybe it was Nineveh or Babylon. There simply is no way to know. It is left to the imagination of the hearer. The far country for every age is different. "The far country," Augustine wrote, "is forgetfulness of God."

The son went to the far country and soon found that he had spent all. Then a famine came in the land, and he was in want. Desperate for work, he got a job with a local farmer feeding pigs! One could almost hear the shock that would go through the crowd of Israelites as they heard that. A Jewish man feeding pigs! Unheard of! The fact that he was tending pigs indicated that he was not keeping the traditions and laws of his religion.

In the third scene, the picture changes some. The young lad "came to himself." The word that is used here in Greek is really a medical term. Luke, the physician, describes the response of a person who has "awakened" from a fainting spell. When he came to himself, he recognized his sin: "I have sinned against God and my father. I will arise and go home and ask to be made a hired servant." He took responsibility for his own actions. "*I* have sinned." He offered no excuses, but repented. The son acknowledged that his sin hurt not only himself but also his father. His sin not only affected his father, his family and himself, but he had also sinned against God. "I have sinned against heaven," he said. Then he said, "I will arise." He didn't say, "I will stay in my sin and keep on doing whatever I have been doing." Instead he declared, "I will arise and go home." He left the far country and went toward home.

The next scene shows the father receiving his son back home again. The father embraced his son, and the Greek words indicate "continually kissed him." The kiss demonstrated that father and son were reconciled again. The "best robe" had to be the father's own robe. By putting his own robe on his son, the father telegraphed a message to the community that the prodigal was accepted as a son again. The ring was a sign of his authority in the family. "Put shoes on his feet." Only slaves went barefooted. He was a son, not a slave. The instruction to "kill the fatted calf" was an invitation for the whole community to come to a feast. A fatted calf was too much for a family to eat. This feast was for the community. The community had seen the father's disgrace, and now they were all invited to rejoice in the return of the son.

If this story had only ended at the return of the younger son, everyone would feel better, but there is a fifth and final scene in this drama. In this scene the elder brother enters the story. When he discovered what the festivities were all about, he refused to go in the house and remained outside. This is another insult to his father. It was customary for the elder son to mingle with the guests and entertain them. He was supposed to be responsible for making sure that the party went well. He, like the younger son, had now insulted his father.

The father went outside to talk with his elder son. The son revealed that he was ungrateful to his father. He had only worked out of a sense of duty. He did not express any real love for his father and for what he had at home. He was also unwilling to forgive his brother and accept him back into the family. He was self-righteous. "I have served you like a servant and never disobeyed your commands." The elder son most likely represents the scribes and Pharisees who have made religion primarily the keeping of certain rules and traditions, devoid of joy. Self-righteousness can be the sin of those who remain at home.

This wonderful parable proclaims that, whether one is a sinner in the far country or at home, he or she can experience the forgiving grace of God, who waits longingly for all to respond to this divine joyful love.

The sermon may develop the theme of the amazing love of God which is open to all persons. The sermon might be presented by examining the five scenes in the parable. Key words may be lifted out of each scene of the text and developed: "Give me," "the far country," "he came to himself," "let us rejoice," and finally, "Child, you are always with me.'' Or the sermon might focus on two types of sin, one represented by the son in the far country and the other by the self-righteous son who stayed at home.

Joshua 5:9–12 (C) (E)

Joshua 5:9a, 10–12 (RC)

As the Israelites prepared to enter the Promised Land, with their enemies the Canaanites and Amorites before them, they paused and observed two important rites. The first was the rite of circumcision, which had not been practiced since the Israelites left Egypt forty years before. Yet, as slaves in Egypt, they had been faithful in their observance of this custom. Circumcision was essential before one could be a member of the covenant community.

The words in v. 9, where God states, ''This day I have rolled away the reproach of Egypt from you,'' have traditionally been seen as referring to the Israelites resuming the rite of circumcision. Scholars are uncertain if this reference means that their uncircumcision was due to their plight as slaves in Egypt, or was a reference to the uncleanliness of the foreign land they were about to enter, or referred to their long period of wandering in the desert. This text ends in a pun as it states that the name Gilgal means in Hebrew ''to roll.'' Circumcision was a sign that ''the reproach of Egypt,'' which had extended into forty years of desert wandering, had been ''rolled away.'' Circumcision was a sign that the Israelites had renewed their covenant with God.

The second rite which the Israelites celebrated was the Passover. The Passover had not been observed since they left Egypt. It was restored right before they entered the Promised Land. Circumcision had to be initiated first, because only the circumcised could share in the Passover. It is interesting to note that there is no mention of Egypt or the sacrifice of a lamb in this version of the Passover. The hand of a later Priestly editor may be seen in the way the Feast of Unleavened Bread and the Passover are joined at Gilgal.

The day the Israelites ate the parched grain cakes, derived from the new land, the manna ceased. Here the editor combines two significant events in the life of Israel by referring to the Passover and the eating of the unleavened cakes—at the exodus from Egypt and the entrance into the Promised Land. This combination symbolized the transition of Israel from existing on manna to eating the bounty of Canaan. God provided Israel with another source of food when the manna ceased.

The traditions of circumcision and the Passover, which the Israelites reinstated prior to entering the land God had promised them, were signs of their recommitment to God. This celebration might be similar to Christian soldiers observing the sacrament of the Lord's Supper before they go into battle in time of war.

Study the traditions of Passover and circumcision.

The sermon may focus on the importance of religious traditions like the Passover in Jewish worship and the celebration of the sacrament of the Lord's Supper in the Christian church. Or the sermon might take v. 12 as a text and show how God always provides another door of opportunity for his servants when one closes.

Isaiah 12:1–6 (L)

Chapter 12 concludes the first main division to the prophecies of Isaiah. The disciples of Isaiah, who collected his prophecies and preaching, highlighted the end of this first section by two songs which could be sung when the remnant of Israel returned to Jerusalem from their exile in Assyria. Scholars are uncertain whether this lyrical epilogue is from the hand of Isaiah or one of his disciples, or was a common psalm of praise and thanksgiving used in Israel's worship.

This psalm points back to the time when the Israelites left Egypt and God made a pathway through the Red Sea so they could cross over to the other side. Safely there, the Israelites paused to sing a song of thanksgiving for God's salvation (Isa. 11:11–16; Ex. 15:1–18). The two hymns in this chapter draw on similar themes to those in Moses' song of deliverance.

The opening verse of the first hymn is shocking. It can be translated literally, ''I thank you, O God, because you were angry with me." This hymn begins with a personal expression of one who had experienced the anger of God as delivering him (and other Israelites) into exile. God's anger has been requited, and the period of discipline in exile is now over. Deliverance—salvation—is at hand. God has become his salvation. This is the first time the word "salvation" is used in the Book of Isaiah, except for the references in the name Isaiah, which means "The Lord is salvation."

In the first song, the writer expresses gratitude to God for forgiveness, deliverance, comfort, release from fear, strength, and joy. He has experienced both God's judgment and redemption. Verse 2 echoes Psalm 118:14 where God is called "my strength and my song." Thanksgiving and trust vibrate throughout this psalm. The psalmist bursts forth with jubilant praise about the salvation of God.

The second hymn uses the metaphor, "with joy you will draw water from the wells of salvation" (v. 3). This image conveys the poet's assurance of the abundance and life-saving supply of God's grace. The "wells of salvation" may also be a reference to the water that flowed out of "the rock" in the wilderness and "the cup of salvation" mentioned in Psalms 114:8 and 116:13. This reminds the Christians of the reference of Jesus to "a spring of water welling up to eternal life" (John 4:14).

The psalmist calls for the proclamation of God's praise not just by an individual or a congregation; this praise should resound so loudly that it invites all nations to join this joyful song. This hymn reflects the unshakable faith of the prophet in the darkest of times—during exile in a foreign land—that God ultimately would deliver Israel. It is a song of absolute trust in the sovereignty of God.

Compare this hymn to Jesus' promise in John 4:10, 14.

The sermon may focus on "The Song of the Redeemed." The movements of this sermon might be: God is my salvation, God is my strength, and God is my song. Or the sermon might develop the text, "The Wells of Salvation" (v. 3), noting the abundance of God's provision, the availability of salvation for all who will call upon God's name, and the exultant joy for all who drink from the well. Show the relationship of Jesus as the "living water" (John 4:10) and as "a spring of water welling up to eternal life" (v. 14) to the well of salvation in Isaiah.

2 Corinthians 5:16–21 (C)

2 Corinthians 5:17–21 (RC) (E)

Reconciliation is one of Paul's great words to expound the message of God's love and grace. Reconciliation in Paul's mind is a word that encompasses all that is involved in redemption—forgiveness, the costly nature of grace, and the restoration of personal friendship with God. Paul's phrase "In Christ God was reconciling the world to himself" (5:19) encompasses the saving work of Christ. The word "therefore" in the beginning of v. 16 points to the results of the work of Christ on the cross. People are no longer the same after their conversion to Christ. They are valued not by race, wealth, power, position, national origin, or sex, but by the change which Christ brings about in his act of "new creation."

Paul's reference that he knew Christ "according to the flesh," or translated differently "from a human point of view," has left scholars puzzled. It is likely a reference to Paul's view of Jesus before he was converted. Did he mean that he knew Jesus whom some were projecting as an earthly Messiah? Did he understand Jesus to be a heretic, as many of the religious leaders then believed him to be? Had he seen or heard Jesus teach in Jerusalem? Had he actually seen the physical Jesus?

Paul's use of this phrase is unclear, but we do know that he experienced a new understanding of Christ on the Damascus road and that experience changed his life forever. He knew that his earlier image of Jesus was wrong. He now saw everything from a new vantage point. He had become "a new creation." The old things had passed away and he now lived a completely new way of life. He had received a new motive. His old motive was to live according to the law. His new motive was to live life in the name of Christ. His old way was self-centered; his new way was Christ-centered.

"In Christ God was reconciling the world to himself" (v. 19). Paul stresses God's involvement in the cross. The cross discloses the heart of God, who has always been a loving, suffering, caring God. The identification of Jesus with the Suffering Servant points to God's way of redeeming men and women. Jesus did not have to persuade God to love men and women and be reconciled to them; instead he revealed that his death was to persuade us to be reconciled to God who already loved us. In the cross of Christ, God gives us not what we deserve to receive, but grace.

The cross also reveals the costly nature of human sin and the humility and willing suffering of Jesus. The cross shows One who was willing to lay down his life for others. The extent of Jesus' sacrifice is seen in the One who became "a sin offering" for humanity (Rom. 8:3). This image is likely based on the Suffering Servant figure in Isaiah 53:6–10. Christ's death atoned for the sins of humanity.

In this passage, Paul also reminds his readers that those who have been reconciled have been called to a ministry of reconciliation. Paul had a new perspective—the love of Christ constrained him. Christ the pleader and God the beseecher entreated him to walk a new path. Having responded to the imploring love of God, he in turn beseeches others to come to Christ. He is an ambassador for Christ, one sent to carry the message of the love for Christ to others. But he declares that all Christians are to be representatives, ambassadors, for the Lord who has redeemed them.

The sermon may develop Paul's theme, "In Christ," and all that figure entails regarding reconciliation and discipleship. Explore how God was in Christ on the cross, and the costly nature of human sin which Christ had to bear. Then go a step further and note Paul's challenge to those who have experienced God's grace to accept their call to a ministry of sharing this message with others. Or the sermon might be built on a word study of key phrases from the text such as "new creation," "God was in Christ," "made him [Jesus] to be sin," and "the ministry of reconciliation."

1 Corinthians 1:18–31 (L)

Paul asserts that the cross is paradoxically both foolishness and wisdom. He notes that to the Jewish mind the cross was a scandal. No Jew expected the Messiah to hang on a cross. The Jewish law stated, "A hanged man is accused by God" (Deut. 21:23). To be crucified was to be accursed. The crucifixion was clear evidence to them that Jesus was not the Messiah. They were looking for a political Messiah, someone who would come with military might and strength of arms to overthrow the Roman rulers. This talk about the crucified Christ as the Messiah was to them a stumbling block. The words in Greek for stumbling block literally mean a trap or snare. To the Jewish mind, the thought of a crucified Messiah was a trap that was simply unacceptable. Paul had persecuted the early Christians because he could not accept this teaching.

To the Greeks, the concept of a crucified God was considered just plain foolishness. The Greeks took pride in their rational knowledge and logical understanding of life. The word "foolishness" is derived from a Greek word which is the root for our word "moron." The Greeks ridiculed anyone who believed that a crucified carpenter could bring salvation. To them a crucified Messiah was totally absurd.

Paul is bold to declare that what seems a scandal and foolishness to others is, when understood properly, the power and wisdom of God. The cross is the power of God because it is an expression of God's sacrificial love. Although it sounds foolish, Paul affirms: "To us who are being saved it is the power of God." Paul preaches that God's strength is made perfect in Paul's weakness. The cross event reveals God's power in a unique way. God does not try to coerce or force people to love, but God draws people by love.

The cross is not only the "power of God," according to Paul, but it is the "wisdom of God" as well. Unlike many itinerant Greek teachers of wisdom who emphasized rhetoric and eloquence, Paul declared that he proclaimed an unadorned gospel (see 2:1–3). The Jews wanted something that would satisfy the mind, but the image of God on a cross was unacceptable to them. The wisdom of God which Paul is describing could never be reduced to some system of beliefs about God or to a set of propositions, but it is the wisdom which was personally revealed through Christ's death within history.

The word "mystery" or "secret," which Paul uses in 2:7 to describe God's "wisdom," is not a reference to something that remains unknown or a puzzle, but refers to that which was previously unknown. The reference is to the redemptive work of God in Christ. Something that was previously unknown about God's nature has been revealed through the death of Christ. In a unique way Christ has revealed the power and wisdom of God's love. This love is available to all who will believe. The Christian bears witness to a person, not to a philosophy or a system of theological thought. We preach Christ crucified. He is not just an example, or teacher, or martyr. We preach Christ crucified—God's Suffering Servant who laid down his life for us.

An examination of the root meaning of the words "foolishness," "wisdom," and "stumbling block" might be helpful.

The sermon may develop Paul's concept of the cross as both "the wisdom and foolishness" of God.

Theological Reflection

The theme of God's deliverance or salvation is central to all our texts. The note of joy and gratitude is affirmed in them as well. God's love for the sinner is clear in the parable of the loving father. The celebration of the two rites before the Israelites entered the Promised Land testified to their assurance of God's sovereignty. The cross of Christ is the supreme revelation of the suffering love of God and the salvation that is accomplished through the passion of Christ.

Children's Message

The talk with the children might center on the parable of the prodigal son. Tell the story in a dramatic fashion. It might be helpful to role-play the parts of the father, the younger son, and the elder son. Help the children to see how God loves and accepts each of us no matter what we might do, just like the father in the parable.

Hymns for Lent 4

O Come, O Come, Emmanuel; Come, Ye Disconsolate; Just as I Am, Without One Plea; Christ Is Crucified Today (*Choirbook for Saints and Singers*).

Lent 5

Psalm 126 (C)   **Philippians 3:8–14**

Isaiah 43:16–21   **John 12:1–8 (C)**
                             John 8:1–11 (RC)
                             Luke 20:9–19 (L) (E)

Meditation on the Texts

We praise you, O God, for the assurance of your unfailing love which we have seen in your Son Jesus Christ. Your providential care has been extolled in the exodus of the Israelites from Egypt and their deliverance from their bondage in exile. The prize of the upward call of Christ Jesus presses us to reach for the maturity we can possess in your grace. We thank you for the relationship we can have with you through faith in Christ. As we continue on this pilgrimage to grow to be more like Christ, give us the strength and courage to follow that path, even if it leads through the fellowship of suffering. Amen.

Commentary on the Texts

John 12:1–8 (C)

This narrative is clearly related to the similar stories that are given in the Synoptics (Mark 14:3–9; Matt. 26:6–13; Luke 7:36–50; see Pentecost 4), but there are notable differences as well as similarities. For example, while John names the woman as Mary of Bethany, none of the other Gospel writers gives the woman a name. Mark's account, on which Matthew's version is based, gives the setting in the home of Simon, who has been cured of leprosy. Mark's and John's accounts set the story in Bethany, while Luke's is set in Galilee. John and Luke present the woman anointing Jesus' feet, while Mark shows her pouring perfume on his head. There is no way to clear up all these slight differences unless one is willing to say they represent two different incidents, but this seems highly unlikely. Most probably John has received material that incorporated both the traditions of Mark and Luke, which came to him independently of them.

Jesus returned to Jerusalem to celebrate the Passover, but first he paused at the home of his good friends Mary, Martha, and Lazarus, who lived in Bethany, a small village near Jerusalem. Some scholars suggest that they arranged a supper for Jesus in the house of Simon, the former leper, rather than having the meal in their own house. This helps to reconcile one of the differences. Martha was depicted as serving the tables. Lazarus, whom Jesus had raised from the dead, reclined at the Lord's table. His presence likely attests to the significance of this story as a testimony to the burial and resurrection theme. This meal, eaten six days before the Passover, probably took place on a Saturday night at the conclusion of the Sabbath.

Jesus and the others present for the meal were reclining around a low table on benches, or possibly on the floor. Mary enters the room bearing a very expensive flask of alabaster. She pours the ointment on Jesus' feet. The aroma fills the room. Down through the centuries the fragrance of that act has continued to touch the lives of those who hear or read about it.

"She has done a beautiful thing to me," Jesus said, according to Mark. Her motive for this act was one of love and gratitude for Jesus. If this is Mary, the sister of Lazarus, as the Gospel of John states, then this act was an expression of her gratitude to Jesus for bringing her brother back from the dead. Lazarus, who had recently been dead, was sitting with the other guests. Mary was compelled to express her gratitude.

Immediately her motive was misunderstood and her act condemned. Judas led the whispers of discontent. "Why wasn't this ointment sold for three hundred denarii and the money given to the poor?" Judas and the others saw nothing to praise in Mary's act. They only condemned. They saw this as a foolish waste of money. Imagine a year's wages, which was the estimate of the value of this perfume, invested in something that produces an odor for a moment. Jesus observed that kindness to the poor was always possible. This opportunity would not always be there.

Mary's action was one of extravagant love. Jesus was at a critical moment in his life. He knew that he was going toward Jerusalem and that his death was imminent. It was important for him to know if there was anyone among his disciples or other followers who had really heard him and understood what his ministry was all about. Was there anyone? This woman stepped forward and anointed him, and Jesus realized that someone had understood his message. He had come to win the love of people, and here in this act, where Mary poured her ointment upon Jesus to express her love and gratitude, he realized that he had won a place in the heart of at least one person.

Mary likely used the bottle of ointment which she had been saving for her own burial. She shared one of her most valuable and significant possessions with Jesus. Usually the only way to use ointment of this kind was to break the neck of the flask. Once it was broken open, all of the contents poured out. Mark indicates that the flask was broken. Some of the wording in John leaves that point unclear. Some scholars have translated v. 7 to read "in order that she may keep." Another rendering might avoid that difficulty, "she has kept."

This moves us to the real meaning of the story. Jesus said, "She has anointed my body beforehand for burying." It is not certain that Mary understood all that she was doing when she broke that bottle and anointed Jesus. Did she realize what she was doing? The Gospel writers seem to indicate that Mary recognized Jesus as the Messiah before the male disciples came to that insight. This woman, who sat at Jesus' feet, perceived through his teachings and messages that he was the Messiah, the Anointed One, which is what the word "Messiah" means.

This was her way of acknowledging him as the Anointed One. Her action was a prophetic word, an anticipatory act about the One who would suffer and die for our redemption. She anointed him in advance of his death. Her anointing his feet with the ointment, her tears of devotion, and her wiping off the perfume with her hair were all signs of her love and gratitude. John, some scholars suggest, may have placed this story here in his Gospel to announce Jesus' entry into Jerusalem as the anointed king.

Compare this account to the story in Mark 14:3–9.

The sermon may focus on the symbolism of Mary's anointing of Jesus' feet as anticipation of his burial. It might be helpful to compare the other Gospel accounts of this story and note the similarities and differences. The sermon might also note the sacrificial and uncalculating manner that Mary expresses in this act of devotion and its example of the costly nature of Christian discipleship.

John 8:1–11 (RC)

The manuscript and internal evidence has convinced most scholars that this pericope was not a part of the original Johannine Gospel. The 1946 edition of the RSV placed this passage in a footnote, but the 1971 edition and the New Revised Standard Version (1989) put it back in the text. Textual scholars have noted that it comes as an interruption to the story being told in 7:52 and 8:23, and the Greek vocabulary, style, and emphasis are different from the rest of the Gospel. Some consider this pericope a spurious text and feel that it should not be used as a basis for a sermon. Others believe that it may be a misplaced fragment from the Synoptic tradition, probably Luke, and did not get a place in the canon until late because the account was an offense to the early church. This story has been accepted as canonical in the Vulgate, which is recognized by the Roman Catholic Church, and has been a part of the text for the Byzantine Church.

Many who think that the episode is not Johannine consider the story, nevertheless, to be a genuine account, in keeping with the character of Jesus. On looking at the story, one has to wonder why the scribes and Pharisees brought this woman to Jesus in the first place. It may have been an attempt to put Jesus in a no-win situation. If he decided to release the woman, he would violate the written law of Moses. If he said she should be stoned, this would put him in conflict with the Roman government, which alone could decide on capital punishment.

There has been endless debate about what Jesus may have written in the sand. It is unlikely that he was writing anything. He was probably sitting, as was the custom for a teacher, and scratching in the sand in front of him with his finger or a stick in a thoughtful, preoccupied way. But the accusers were persistent in their demand for an answer.

The reference that a woman caught in adultery should be stoned is noted in Leviticus 20:10 and Deuteronomy 22:21. Jesus, however, refused to be put in the judgment seat and judge the guilt of this woman on their terms. As a spiritual teacher concerned with searching the motives in every heart, Jesus turns the mirror inward and instructs, ''The man without sin, let him cast the first stone'' (see v. 7). This first man would be the witness to the act of adultery called for in Deuteronomy 17:7. Then Jesus turned away from the accusers and wrote in the sand again. The matter was resolved for him. ''Being convicted by their conscience'' (v. 9, KJV), the accusers left, one by one.

After standing up, Jesus asks the woman if anyone has condemned her. The accusers have now left, and she replies that no one has condemned her. Although Jesus does not condemn the woman, he does condemn her sin in his words, ''Go, and sin no more'' (v. 11, KJV). The response of Jesus is consistent with his behavior as seen in the Gospels, where he always places more value on persons than on religious laws. The story does not indicate whether the woman was repentant or not. It does demonstrate Jesus' priority for persons.

It might be helpful for the preacher and the congregation to **explore the textual problems** in 7:53–8:11. This might serve as an occasion to teach the church about the way the canon was formed.

The sermon might focus on the hypocrisy of condemning the sins of other people, especially sexual sins, without examining the way that we often exploit other people ourselves in business or recreational pursuits.

Luke 20:9–19 (L) (E)

This pericope is set at the beginning of the final week in the life of Jesus. Jesus has already made his dramatic entry into Jerusalem on the back of a colt. In Mark's Gospel the cleansing of the temple occurred on the day after the triumphal entry and was the final incident that ignited the hostility of the religious leaders. Luke notes that the Jewish religious leaders had questioned the authority of Jesus (20:2) while he was teaching in the temple and had tried to trap him by asking him a question about the authority of John the Baptist; but Jesus turned the tables on them and caught them in their own trap. Then Jesus told a parable about a man who planted a vineyard and rented it to tenants and stayed in another country for a long time. Since foreigners often owned large portions of the land in occupied territories like Palestine, this practice would be familiar to Jesus' listeners.

Some scholars believe that this parable is an allegory. Few of Jesus' parables are allegories, but it is hard not to see the obvious equivalents in this story. The owner of the vineyard is God. The vineyard represents the nation Israel. The tenants in the vineyard represent the Pharisees and scribes—the religious leaders. The servants who were stoned or killed represent the prophets, and the son represents Jesus. Some have pressed the images further and stated that the tower stood for the temple, the hedges for the law and traditions, and the winepress for the altar. The truth of the parable may be pressed too far if one tries to make every detail have an allegorical meaning. When Jesus told this parable, the religious leaders understood that it was directed against them.

The vineyard is clearly a picture of God's dealings with Israel. The vineyard was planted and hedged about; a winepress was dug and a tower was built. The vineyard had been readied for the tenants, and they were privileged to run it. The nation Israel was a people chosen by God. They were a privileged people, who had been specially selected by God.

They were God's select vineyard, and they had known the special care and blessing of God.

The parable also denotes that the tenants had freedom. The owner went off to another country and left the tenants in charge. The parable does not relate any rigid rules or restrictions imposed on the vinedressers. They obviously had to pay the owner either a certain rental fee or a percent of their produce. According to this parable, the owner did not place any rigid regulations on how they were to care for the vineyard. The work was allocated to them, and then they were entrusted with it. They had freedom to run the vineyard as they wanted. If they cultivated the vineyard, it would abound in produce. If they neglected it, then weeds would grow up in it, and soon the vineyard would grow wild and be useless and unfruitful.

God gave the nation Israel the privilege of being God's chosen people and God also gave them freedom. They were free to follow God's leadership or reject it. Unfortunately, Israel did not always remain loyal to God but chose instead to become a wild vine.

God chose the nation Israel not just for their own edification, but so they would be a blessing to others. They were chosen as God's special people not merely to be the recipients of God's wonders and blessings but to share God's love with other nations. Instead of sharing God's grace with others, they built a "hedge" around God's laws and began to say that they alone were God's people. Rather than sharing the good news, they kept it to themselves. They forgot that the greater the privilege, the more significant the responsibility. The Old Testament is clear that Israel would lose their place as God's chosen people if they were not faithful to their covenant with God. Again and again they violated the covenant. Israel was the vine that had gone bad (Jer. 2:21).

This parable shows the persistence of the vineyard owner. He continued to send one messenger after another, hoping to awaken the right response from the tenants. God persistently pursues God's children, just as the father and mother continually love their child even when he or she rebels. Like "the hound of heaven," God continues on the path in pursuit of wandering children. God's unfailing love is the subject of this parable. God persistently seeks to express love and concern to humanity, even when men and women are unlovable.

This parable also speaks about judgment. When the tenants rejected the owner's servants and finally killed his son, judgment was certain. "What will the owner do now?" "The owner will come and take the vineyard away from them and will give it to someone else." When people continue to reject God, it ensures their own judgment. By rejecting the Son, Israel brought their own judgment. The increasing violence of unworthy religious leaders assured the destruction of Jerusalem.

Some scholars feel that vs. 13–16 were likely added by the early church as they reflected back on the destruction of the temple and the city of Jerusalem by the Romans. Other scholars see this declaration as an ultimatum by Jesus to Israel to repent or face destruction. The quote from Psalm 118:22–23, "The stone which the builders rejected has become the chief cornerstone," is a reference to Jesus' rejection and crucifixion by the religious leaders, which became the foundation stone on which the New Israel—the church—was built (Gal. 6:15–16). To fall or trip on that stone was a reference to those who found the crucifixion of Christ an offense—a cause for stumbling, literally a snare. The picture of the stone falling on a person is an image of judgment (Dan. 2:34–35).

Do a word study on the meaning of the vine and vineyard as symbols for Israel, and Jesus' statement that he was the true vine (John 15:1–11).

The sermon may focus on the unfailing love of God which continues to reach out to men and women, even when they continue to reject God's grace. The sermon may be built on Israel's rejection of Jesus—his death on the cross, and the New Israel, the church, which arose out of that rejection. The sermon may stress the freedom God gives to respond to divine love, and the judgment which is certain if there is ultimate rejection of God's love.

Isaiah 43:16–21

In this passage Isaiah presents an oracle of promise for Israel's deliverance from exile in Babylon. He pictures this liberation as a new exodus. He reminds the captive Israelites that in God's first exodus for Israel from their bondage in Egypt God made a path through the sea for them (v. 16) and destroyed the Egyptian army which was pursuing them (v. 17).

This same God, who delivered Israel in such a mighty way in the past, was about to deliver them again. The anticipation of the new thing God was going to do was so wonderful that it would eclipse that first exodus. He exhorted them not to assume that God was only the God of the past. In the new exodus, God would provide, first, a highway through the desert (v. 19). The road or way motif is a familiar image in Isaiah. Second, water would be provided in the desert along their road (v. 20). This image reminds that in the first exodus God provided Israel with water from the rock and manna in their journey through the desert. But in the new exodus the promise is that the desert will be transformed with rivers of water, and the wild animals as well as men and women will rejoice in this transformation. The beast and birds will have lost their wildness and will join humanity in a song of praise. The new exodus, like the first, will cause the liberated men and women, along with the desert animals, to break into joyous song (v. 21; Ex. 15:1–18).

The images in this oracle are obviously poetic and were not literally fulfilled. The desert was not transformed into an oasis, but Israel was delivered from its bondage and a joyous way was provided for its restoration.

The sermon might draw on the image of "the new exodus" and develop the theme of the providence of God. The sermon might show God's providential care of Israel through the exodus from Egypt, the new exodus from Babylon, and God's working in the church and in the lives of men and women today.

Philippians 3:8–14

This pericope begins right after Paul has completed the listing of his credentials as a Jew. Paul shows how he had carefully kept the Jewish law since he was a child and had been circumcised when he was only eight days old. The Judaizing preachers at Philippi, who were trying to discredit Paul, could not equal his compliance with the Jewish laws and traditions. Paul stresses his zeal and loyalty to the law. His pursuit of fulfilling the Jewish law had been all-consuming. As worthy as that may have been, when compared to what Christ has done for him, he now considers that pursuit as refuse. What he is rejecting had been the central priority and value in his life. What he had cherished and valued he now counts as refuse. Refuse comes from a Greek word which literally means "garbage, table scraps, street sweepings, or excrement." What Paul is now declaring worthless was not his wicked or evil ways but the highest and best he had known.

A key word in this passage is righteousness. For Paul, righteousness meant "a right relationship with God." Paul had tried to get into a right relationship with God by a strict observance of the Jewish law, but he learned that he could not earn his relationship to God through the law but only by faith in Jesus Christ.

Pushing his argument further, Paul draws on an image of a runner in an Olympic contest. Although his figure sounds a little contradictory to what he has just said, Paul states that faith for him is like a runner eagerly moving forward and filled with anticipation of victory. Like a runner, his faith involves running, straining, and reaching for the prize before him. This is not accomplished by his efforts, however, but by the work of Christ.

The prize—the goal of his journey—is "the upward call of God in Christ Jesus." Although it is not clear what Paul means by this phrase, it likely refers to his own personal experience with Christ.

As he is striving for that prize, Paul mentions three factors in the struggle: (1) He is "forgetting what lies behind" (v. 13). This may be a reference to the Judaizers who wanted to cling to the Jewish law, or it may be an indication that Paul refuses to rest on his past achievements or defeats in his service for Christ. (2) The Greek word sometimes rendered "perfect" (v. 12) would be better translated "mature" or "full grown" (v. 15). (3) Paul knows he has not reached the goal to be like Christ, but he continues to press on toward that goal. Although he knows he will never measure up to the standard of Christ, he steadfastly pursues that goal. Paul affirms that his faith in Christ has set him on a pilgrimage, and that he will always be in process of becoming, continuously reaching toward the example of his Lord.

It may be helpful to **do a root word study** of certain key words: righteousness, refuse, to know, perfect or mature, and the prize. It would also be helpful to examine several groups of persons about whom Paul was speaking, such as the antinomians and the Judaizers.

The sermon may develop Paul's image of a runner in a race who is pressing toward the prize ahead.

Theological Reflection

As Holy Week grows closer, our texts allow us to focus on different facets of our Lord's sacrifice. The passage from John 12 recounts the story of Mary's extravagant expression of gratitude as she anointed Jesus' feet. Her act was a prophetic sign of the One who would suffer and die for the salvation of the world. John 8 reflects the limitless dimension of Jesus' forgiving spirit. The parable in Luke again emphasizes the unfailing love of God, even when that love is rejected, but the parable also reminds us that ultimate rejection brings judgment. Isaiah assures us that the providential care of God will bring a surprising and joyous occasion of deliverance. Paul points not to his own accomplishments but to the work of Christ and the righteousness of God as experienced in him.

Children's Message

The talk with the children might develop the theme of God's love toward people even when they reject God's love. Drawing on the parable from Luke, tell this story in a contemporary setting. The owner of a large farm leased it to some farmers in America, while he lived in England. Help them to see how the farmers' rejection of the owner's representatives and son symbolizes the response of many to God's love.

Hymns for Lent 5

Eternal Lord of Love, Behold Your Church; O Worship the King, All Glorious Above; There's a Wideness in God's Mercy.

Lent 6

Palm Sunday/Passion Sunday

Psalm 118:19–29 (C)

Isaiah 50:4–9a (C)
Isaiah 50:4–7 (RC)
Isaiah 45:21–25 (E)
Deuteronomy 32:36–39 (L)

Philippians 2:5–11 (C) (L) (E)
Philippians 2:6–11 (RC)

Luke 19:28–40 (C)
Luke 22:1–23:56 (L)
Luke 22:14–23:56 (RC)
Luke 23:1–49 (E)

Meditation on the Texts

O Holy God, as we reflect on the events from Palm Sunday to Jesus' death on Golgotha, we are overwhelmed at humanity's rejection of your Suffering Servant. His agony in the Garden of Gethsemane, his ridicule and scourging by the soldiers, his unjust trials, and the unspeakable burden of the sin and guilt which he had to bear on that cross force us to our knees in shame and remorse. We cannot fathom such sacrificial love and obedience. We pause and kneel in the presence of such grace. We confess that we cannot grasp the mystery of the incarnation, but, in quiet faith, we confess that Christ is Lord. We recommit our lives to his service. Amen.

Commentary on the Texts

Luke 19:28–40 (C)

The final week of the life of Jesus opens with his dramatic entry into Jerusalem. It did not make any difference from what direction a person came, a traveler always referred to "going up to Jerusalem." Bethany was a small village outside Jerusalem where Mary, Martha, and Lazarus lived. The exact location of Bethphage is unknown, but it is assumed to have been near Bethany on the slopes of the Mount of Olives.

Although some like to assume that Jesus' instructions to his disciples about the colt were an example of his clairvoyant power, it was more likely a prearranged signal, "The Lord needs it," which he had arranged with some friends in Jerusalem (vs. 29–34). Luke, for some reason, does not quote the passage from Zechariah 9:9 as do Matthew and Mark; but this image had that prophecy in mind. A colt that had not been used as a beast of burden was the only animal considered appropriate for sacred emphases (Num. 19:2).

Jesus chose to enter Jerusalem riding not on a horse, which would have been the sign of a military conqueror, but riding instead on an ass—a colt—which symbolized peace. He deliberately offered himself to the people as their king. But all the details of the entry—the borrowed colt of peace, the garments placed on the beast by the disciples, the garments thrown in the pathway before him and the waving banners of palm branches, and the joyous loud cry of the coronation psalm, "Blessed is the King who comes in the name of the Lord!" (Ps. 118:26; Luke 19:38)—were clear signs of the kind of messianic kingdom Jesus had envisioned. This dramatic appeal was not to call the people to follow a nationalistic reign of an earthly, courtly king, but a kingdom of peace, which all these borrowed, nonmilitary symbols depicted. His procession announced the inauguration of the messianic reign of peace about which the angelic choir sang at his birth (2:14). In using Psalm 118:26, the normal blessing which the priest pronounced on pilgrims as they came to the temple for a festival, Luke inserted the word "king" to demonstrate that the people were declaring Jesus as the Messiah.

Luke is the only Gospel to note the protests of the Pharisees to the people calling Jesus "king." Their rebuke may have been a fear that the Romans would consider this demonstration an act of sedition and punish the whole nation as well as Jesus who had precipitated it. But Jesus responded to their objection by declaring that if the people, who had so lovingly anticipated this moment in their history, did not respond, the stones along the pathway of the pilgrims would announce his arrival (Ps. 107:2).

The sermon may focus on Jesus' triumphal entry into Jerusalem as a sign of his messianic reign as the Prince of Peace. The sermon might contrast the nationalistic desire for a military king with Jesus' concept of his intention to establish a reign of peace. Or the sermon might focus on the text, "the stones would cry out," and the necessity for followers of Christ to proclaim the salvation which his death provides.

Luke 22:1–23:56 (L)

Luke 22:14–23:56 (RC)

Luke 23:1–49 (E)

Since the passages in this section cover so much material from the two long chapters in Luke 22:1–23:56, the focus will have to be limited to an overall outline and the notations of a few key passages. The pericope includes the following events:

1. The plot by Judas to betray Jesus (22:1–6)
2. The preparation for and observance of the Lord's Supper (22:7–23)
3. The discussion about who is the greatest in Christ's kingdom (22:24–30)
4. The prediction of Jesus that Peter will deny him (22:31–34)
5. Instructions to the disciples (22:35–38)
6. Jesus' prayer of agony on the Mount of Olives (22:39–46)
7. The arrest of Jesus (22:47–53)
8. Peter's denial of Jesus (22:54–62)
9. Jesus' appearance before the Jewish Council, Pilate, and Herod (22:63–23:12)
10. The sentence of death (23:13–25)
11. The crucifixion and death of Jesus (23:26–49; see also Christ the King (L) (RC) (E).)
12. The burial of Jesus (23:50–56)

The reference to the "feast of Unleavened Bread" or the Passover (22:1) is a pictorial way for Luke to introduce the account of the passion of Christ. In a word, he is alerting his readers to the fact that the blood of Christ is a greater sacrifice than the one marked by the exodus from Egypt. Jesus was God's chosen instrument for salvation, while Judas was Satan's agent to accomplish his dark deed. Why Judas betrayed Jesus has caused a storm of debate. Was it for money? Was he a Zealot who wanted to force Jesus' hand, or a disappointed idealist? The fact that the early church saw Judas as being under the power of Satan places the conflict on a cosmic level.

In Luke's description of the Supper (22:14–19), there is a reversal of the order of the elements, the cup first and then the bread. In 1 Corinthians 11:23–26, Paul states that the loaf precedes the cup, but in 1 Corinthians 10:16, the cup is mentioned prior to the bread. Most probably the early church did not have a set practice for the order of the elements. The disciples all drank from Jesus' cup. This may have symbolized not only their unity but their willingness "to drink the cup of which he drank."

There is a textual problem with vs. 19b–20. These verses are not found in the Western text and several others. Some scholars believe that Luke may have taken the words directly from Paul in 1 Corinthians 11:24–25. Other scholars support the longer text as being Lukan.

Jesus predicted that Peter would deny him three times (22:31–34). He then went out to the Garden of Gethsemane on the slope of the Mount of Olives and struggled in prayerful agony with his own commitment to the sacrifice that lay before him. The agony Jesus experienced in Gethsemane was not only a reflection of his real humanity but an awareness of the "cup" he was going to have to drink. The Greek word for agony depicts one who is fighting a battle with great fear. The costly nature of what he had to endure as the

Lamb of God "to give his life as a ransom for many" gripped him bitterly in these moments. Was there another way to atone for the sins of humanity? Could he avoid the cross? Did doubts fill his mind?

Finally, in quiet confidence, Jesus voiced his unfaltering faith, "Nevertheless not my will, but thine" (22:42). The warning by Jesus to his disciples about the dangers of temptation pointed to the powers of evil that he had to confront. They, too, would have to battle these cosmic forces (22:46).

Jesus had to endure four trials before he was finally condemned. First, Jesus was brought before the Sanhedrin, which is similar to our Supreme Court. The Sanhedrin was composed of seventy-one members and had to have at least twenty-three present for a quorum. Scholars have noted many illegal procedures in their trial. (1) A person could not be tried at night for a capital offense. (2) It was illegal to meet on the Sabbath or a feast day or the day before or after either one of these. They were conducting the trial on the Passover and the day before the Sabbath. (3) A trial could not begin and conclude with a guilty conviction in one day. (4) They tried to get Jesus to incriminate himself. (5) They unanimously condemned Jesus. A unanimous decision by the Sanhedrin was illegal. This was thought to indicate that there were no advocates for the accused, that he had not had a friend or defender in the court. A trial with a unanimous vote was considered "mob rule."

The Sanhedrin found Jesus guilty of blasphemy (22:70–71), but sent him to Pilate because only the Roman government could administer the death sentence. When Pilate heard that Jesus was from Galilee, he sent him to see King Herod, who was ruler over that territory and happened to be in Jerusalem at that time. Herod mocked Jesus but was met only with silence. According to Luke, it was Herod's soldiers who dressed Jesus in the royal robe and treated this whole event with mockery (23:8–12). In a short time, Herod sent Jesus back to Pilate and told him to decide Jesus' fate. Pilate did not want any more problems with the Jews. When the priests told him that if he did not kill Jesus he was not Caesar's friend, he knew that they were threatening his political security.

Pilate offered the people a choice between Barabbas and Jesus (23:16–21). Tradition has it that the choice Pilate offered was between Jesus Barabbas, a political insurrectionist, or Jesus the Christ. The people cried, "Give us Barabbas." And in response to Pilate's question, "What would you have me do with one called Jesus the Christ?" they yelled: "Crucify him, crucify him." Pilate then washed his hands of the matter and told the crowd that Jesus' blood was on their hands. (See Matt. 27:21–24.)

It seems that Pilate had genuinely tried to get the charges against Jesus dismissed. Three times he had declared Jesus innocent. He had tried to sidestep making a decision by sending Jesus to Herod. When that didn't work, he had tried to get the people to set Jesus free. Failing that final effort, he had washed his hands of the episode and granted the wishes of the priests that Jesus be sentenced to death.

After Jesus was scourged by the Roman soldiers, he was forced to carry the beam of the cross to which his arms would be nailed when he was crucified. From the several scourgings he had endured, Jesus fell exhausted under the weight of his cross as he was forced to carry it through the streets to his place of crucifixion. A soldier compelled Simon from Cyrene, the capital of North Africa, to carry the cross of Jesus (23:26). Simon is identified as the father of two well-known first-century Christians (Mark 15:21; Rom. 16:13). The experience of bearing Jesus' cross and seeing him crucified seems to have led to Simon's conversion.

Luke alone tells about the women who wailed like they were part of a funeral procession for Jesus before he was dead. The words of Jesus to them were a prophetic warning about the suffering and weeping at the destruction of Jerusalem. Verse 31 is a proverb that warns the people about what will happen to the guilty in the light of what is done to an innocent person.

Luke does not give any vivid details of the crucifixion itself, knowing that his readers were very familiar with the ugly scene. He notes that two "thieves," who were crucified "one on the right and one on the left," were placed beside Jesus, probably to add to Jesus' disgrace. The place of "The Skull" stood outside the city walls beside a busy road where travelers to Jerusalem could easily see what happened to criminals under Roman justice.

The Gospels record seven words that Jesus spoke in his six hours on the cross. Luke records three. The first word was, "Father, forgive them; for they know not what they do"

(23:34). The outcries of those who were executed were usually curses, jeers, and profanity, but Jesus' utterance was a prayer of forgiveness. About whom was Jesus speaking? Was it the soldiers who crucified him, the priests and Pharisees and the other members of the Sanhedrin who condemned him, Pilate who sentenced him, Judas who betrayed him, Peter who denied him, his disciples who fled in terror, the crowd who yelled, "Crucify him"? Likely all of these and more. These words were so disturbing to the early church that some of the earliest manuscripts such as Codex Vaticanus or Codex Bezae do not contain them. The early Christians did not know how to pray and ask forgiveness for the Jews and Romans for what they had done.

The second word on the cross was a promise to a penitent thief that life goes on after death. This incident of Jesus' responding to a criminal, a sinner, in his final moments of life is at the core of what Luke's Gospel is all about. The thief symbolizes the type of people Jesus came to save. Throughout Luke's Gospel Jesus has reached out to sinners of all kinds. This thief's plight indicates that no person can be so far from God that he or she is not acceptable. Jesus promised the penitent thief, "Today you will be with me in Paradise" (23:43). Jesus assured this thief that he was important to God and would not be forgotten but would share his personal companionship "with me in Paradise." Paradise is a Persian word for a place of Blessedness, like Abraham's bosom—where God is.

The death of Jesus was of such significance that it was followed by two dramatic signs, symbolically true if not actual occurrences: An eclipse of the sun from noon until three P.M. (the ninth hour), and the curtain in the Holy of Holies in the temple torn in two (23:44–45). The tearing of the curtain symbolized that direct access to God was possible now for all people. The seventh word, "Father, into thy hands I commit my spirit!" (v. 46), was the ultimate prayer of trust and surrender. Having witnessed his death, the centurion joins Pilate and the penitent thief in declaring that Jesus was innocent (v. 47).

The body of Jesus was given to Joseph of Arimathea by Pilate. Joseph was identified as a member of the Jewish council, but he must not have been present when Jesus was condemned, because Luke states that he had not agreed with the action of the others (23:51). Joseph's "rock-hewn tomb" (v. 53) indicates that he was rich, which is verified in Matthew (27:57). The certainty of Jesus' death was affirmed by the witness of the Roman soldiers, the Jewish religious leaders, the crowd, and by the family and disciples of Jesus. Some women from Galilee saw Jesus' body wrapped in a linen shroud and laid in Joseph's tomb. They went to get burial spices and ointments to anoint his body after the Sabbath was over.

Do a word study of cup (22:42), agony (22:44), and the Skull (23:33).

The sermon might focus on a particular section of this passage such as the sacrament of the Lord's Supper, Jesus' agony in Gethsemane, the trial, the crucifixion, or one or more of Jesus' words from the cross. The intent of the sermon is to show the costly sacrifice which Jesus made for the sins of humanity.

Isaiah 50:4–9a (C)

Isaiah 50:4–7 (RC)

This pericope is usually referred to as the third Servant Song. The first two songs, Isaiah 42:1–9 (see Baptism of Our Lord, (L) (E), and Isaiah 49:1–7), focus on the servant's mission. The fourth, found in Isaiah 52:13–53:12 (see Pentecost 27), is the familiar Old Testament passage that portrays the suffering of the servant for others. This third song speaks of obedience during persecution. For the first time the element of suffering is noted in the life of the servant. Some scholars have called this passage the Gethsemane experience of the Suffering Servant.

The servant, speaking in the first person, testified to three things: (1) He notes his personal communion with God (vs. 4–5). His relationship to God has been described as that between a pupil and a teacher. He has had to discipline himself to rise early each morning to respond to God. Through this rigorous discipline, he has acquired both the ear—the ability to understand the message, and the tongue—the ability to teach others what he has learned. He now communes with and for God. The purpose of his living has been to comfort the weary Israelites in exile with the word of consolation (v. 4). (2) He has been utterly loyal to God in the face of vigorous persecution (v. 6). He has been the object of insults (shame and spitting) and physical abuse (blows to his back and pulling of his beard), but he has maintained his fidelity to God and suffered this humiliation. (3) He has continued in his confidence in God in the midst of all his difficulties (vs. 7–9). He has set his "face like a flint" to carry out his mission from God and will not be distracted by violent treatment. He uses the image of a law court and depicts God as his advocate and vindicator (v. 8). He does not fear the trials because God will contend for him while his accusers will be ruined like a moth-eaten piece of clothing (v. 9).

Look up the meaning of adversary (v. 8) in a Bible dictionary.

The sermon may treat this passage as an anticipatory picture of the suffering, mockery, and humiliation of Jesus before his accusers at his trials. This theme may also be extended to the sufferings that all Christians must sometimes experience in their witness for God.

Isaiah 45:21–25 (E)

This passage depicts a courtroom scene where God calls together all the nations who have survived the judgments Isaiah spoke about in the earlier chapters. God charges the nations with worshiping false, worthless gods. The Lord declares, "There is no other god besides me," and proclaims the evidence for this is the prediction and control of history (v. 21).

Instead of pronouncing judgment, God unexpectedly offers the remnant nations an opportunity to be saved (v. 22). Cyrus is not to be God's instrument to destroy the nations but a vehicle to bring them to salvation (see 44:28). What God wants from defeated enemies is not to make them slaves and treat them harshly; God requires acknowledgment and worship. This is a wonderful declaration of the universal love of God. Persons of all races and nations who will worship Yahweh are acceptable to God.

Idolatry is destroyed by the integrity of God's own being ("By myself I have sworn") and the unalterable word from God's own mouth (v. 23). "Every knee shall bow, every tongue shall swear" (v. 23) denotes the absolute sovereignty of God. This passage parallels directly Philippians 2:11 where "every tongue shall confess that Jesus Christ is Lord."

The sermon might focus on God's invitation for persons of all races and nations to worship God. This text can be joined with Philippians 2:11, noting how the Isaiah passage is fulfilled in the call to confess the redemptive work of Christ.

Deuteronomy 32:36–39 (L)

When a nation has been crushed by war, pressed into slavery, and taken into exile by another nation, it is easy to want revenge. In this Song of Moses, which has been dated variously from the eleventh to the seventh century B.C.E., God is pictured as speaking to the Israelites in their exile and assuring them that they have not been abandoned. In v. 36, God promises the nation that they will be delivered. This promise was fulfilled later under Cyrus when he led the Persians to victory over the Babylonians.

The image of a "rock" is used six times in this poem, in vs. 4, 15, 18, 30, 31, and 37. The emphasis is on God's stability and Israel's inconsistent attitude toward God. Israel is assured that they can trust the Lord to deliver them from their bondage. "Vengeance is mine," says the Lord (v. 35). God will not ignore Israel's suffering, but the remedy will be of the Lord's own choosing.

Do a word study of rock and vengeance.

The sermon may focus on our need to "wait upon" the Lord in confidence in times of suffering and difficulty, assured that the Lord knows about our need and is providentially bringing about a resolution to our struggle.

Philippians 2:5–11 (C) (L) (E)

Philippians 2:6–11 (RC)

This passage is one of the most powerful statements on the incarnation and death of Jesus in the New Testament. Here Paul has expressed some of his most profound thinking, with lofty eloquence. This hymn, however, has also been a storm center of theological debate. Scholars have struggled with almost every line. **The careful reading of several modern commentaries is advised.** Paul describes Christ as being in the "form of God," which likely refers to what Christ was in his "inner essence." This would refer to his preexistence, as in John 1:1. Other New Testament passages that note the preexistence of Christ include Colossians 1:15; 2 Corinthians 8:9; Hebrews 1:1–4.

One of the central emphases of Paul in this hymn is the self-emptying (*kenosis*) of Christ. This Greek word for "emptied" pictures something being poured out of a container. Of what did Christ empty himself? He obviously did not divest himself of his divinity. He poured out his life in humiliation and obedience in sacrificial service. Paul may have had in mind the vision from Isaiah 53 where the Suffering Servant takes upon himself our stripes and sins. Christ was obedient even to his death on the cross.

But the crucified Christ becomes the exalted Servant (v. 9). The servant is now Lord (2 Cor. 8:9). The doxology in vs. 10–11 affirms the earliest Christian creed—Jesus is Lord: "Every knee should bow . . . to the glory of God the Father." Paul wrote this hymn to address the problem of disunity in the Philippian church and to remind the people that humility, obedience, and service are at the heart of the Christian faith.

The sermon may deal with Paul's concept of Christ emptying himself in obedience and becoming a servant. It would be helpful to **do a word study** of certain phrases such as "*being* in the *form* of God," "Christ *emptied* himself," "servant," and "equality with God."

Theological Reflection

All our texts speak about the redemptive work of God. The Gospels trace our Lord's journey from the Last Supper to his death on the cross and his burial in a borrowed tomb. The Old Testament passages assure God's people of the Lord's providential care and their ultimate deliverance from bondage. Paul's hymn calls all nations to bow before Christ in worship to glorify God.

Children's Message

The message might picture Jesus' triumphal entry into Jerusalem. Palm branches and some pieces of clothing might be laid in a path to describe the ride Jesus took and the reaction of the people. Help the children to understand that Jesus was not announcing that he was an earthly king but rather the Prince of Peace, who would shortly be rejected and crucified.

Hymns for Lent 6

At the Name of Jesus; Go to Dark Gethsemane; O Sacred Head Now Wounded: I Am Meat and I Am Drink (*Choirbook for Saints and Singers*).

Easter Day

Psalm 118:14–24 (C)

Acts 10:34–43 (C) (E)
Acts 10:34a, 37–43 (RC)
Isaiah 65:17–25 (alt. C)
Exodus 15:1–11 (L)

1 Corinthians 15:19–26 (C)
1 Corinthians 15:1–11 (L)
Colossians 3:1–4 (RC) (E)

John 20:1–18 (C)
John 20:1–9 (RC)
Luke 24:1–11 (L)
Luke 24:1–10 (E)

Meditation on the Texts

Eternal God, who raised Jesus Christ from the dead, we praise your grace and love. The wonder of the living presence of Christ thrills our hearts. Thank you for the assurance we have of life and eternal life through his resurrection. We rejoice in your inclusive grace which reaches out to persons regardless of race or sex. Like Mary Magdalene, John, Paul, and others who were witnesses to the risen Lord, open our eyes and ears to sense, feel, see, and hear Christ's living presence with us today. May the new life we experience in Christ affect everything we do and say. Amen.

Commentary on the Texts

John 20:1–18 (C)

John 20:1–9 (RC)

Mary Magdalene, who had not previously had a significant role in John's Gospel, other than being listed along with other women at the cross (19:25), is thrust to the forefront as the first witness to the empty tomb (v. 1) and the first person to see the risen Christ (v. 16). The Synoptic Gospels indicate that Mary came to the tomb with other women (Matt. 28:1; Mark 16:1; Luke 23:55–24:1, 10). The use of "we" in the verse, "*we* do not know where they have laid him" (v. 2b, italics added), might indicate that Mary had been with other women and was not alone when she first came to the tomb.

Mary may have arrived before the other women. John notes that she arrived very early on Sunday morning "while it was still dark." Mary had come to anoint the body with spices and ointments, unaware that this had already been done. When she saw the empty tomb, she immediately concluded that Jesus' body was gone and that it had been stolen by someone, by either his enemies or grave robbers. Unfortunately, the practice of robbing tombs was common in Palestine.

She rushed to inform Peter, who, in spite of his denial, was still the leader of the disciples. He, along with John, ran to the tomb to see what had happened. John, being younger, arrived first, but paused at the entrance to the tomb and looked in. Impulsive Peter rushed inside to see what had happened. They found that the burial wrappings were not disheveled but were lying as though still wound around Jesus' body and that the napkin which had been about his head still retained its shape. When Peter and John went into the tomb, they did not find that the spices weighing down the body had been hastily dislodged as if someone had tried to remove the body quickly. The words in Greek have been interpreted to describe the grave cloths as if the body inside them had evaporated or undergone a metamorphosis. Some scholars believe that the cloths around Jesus' body retained their shape after the body "passed through" or "evaporated out," because the aromatic oils and spices on the body caused the cloth to remain firm.

Although the appearance of the grave cloths likely convinced Peter that robbers or enemies had not stolen the body, since they would have taken the body in its linen wrappings, he did not grasp the deeper truth. But this evidence of the shape and appearance of the burial cloths was enough for John, and the beloved disciple "saw and believed" (v. 8). The wrappings were a "sign" to him. This verse notes that the disciple "whom Jesus loved" was the first to believe in the resurrection of Christ, even before he had seen the risen Lord himself.

Some scholars believe that the apologetic witness of John's belief in the risen Lord was essential to first-century readers since the testimony of women, especially a woman such as Mary, who had a wicked reputation and had also been demon-possessed (Luke 8:2), was unacceptable to Jewish minds. The sight of the cloth burial wrappings of Jesus was a sufficient sign for John to believe in the resurrection. Although this passage does not affirm or deny Peter's belief in the resurrection at this point, many scholars argue that Peter as well as John believed because of the sight of the grave wrappings. Peter is depicted as the representative of Jewish Christianity and John of Gentile Christianity.

John and Peter returned home but Mary remained at the tomb weeping. Mary's lack of surprise or sense of awe at the appearance of the angels in the tomb is puzzling (vs. 12–13). Perhaps her mind was so overwhelmed with grief that she failed to comprehend the significance of their presence. Then she mistakes the presence of a figure near her for the caretaker of the graves. She suddenly thinks there might be another option to account for the missing body of Jesus. Since the grave was a new one, perhaps the caretaker has removed it somewhere else. Through her tears, Mary asks, "Sir, if you have carried him away, tell me where you have laid him, and I will take him away" (v. 15).

Mary, like the couple on the road to Emmaus (Luke 24:16–31), did not recognize Jesus at first; but when Jesus called her name, "Mary," she recognized him. Her love and faith welled up in her response, "Teacher." Falling down in adoration before him, she began to cling to his feet. Much debate has centered around v. 17. Jesus' request that Mary stop clinging to him was a warning against trying to hold on to the physical presence when his spiritual presence was soon to be available. His physical presence would be withdrawn in his ascension, but a more universal presence would then be available.

Some scholars have found v. 17 perplexing because Jesus commands Mary not to declare that he is risen but "I am ascending to my Father." This declaration likely notes the indissoluble connections between the resurrection and the ascension. Jesus had completed his earthly work, and was in process of going to God the Father. Jesus' kingly reign was beginning. Mary immediately rushed to the disciples and declared: "I have seen the Lord." This woman, a forgiven sinner, was the first message bearer of the resurrection.

Compare John's account with the Synoptic Gospels.

The sermon may focus on Mary's initial failure to recognize the risen Christ and our own failure to see his presence with us today because of our grief, difficulties, or spiritual blindness and deafness. Or the sermon may be based on the sign which John saw in the burial wrappings of Jesus where "he saw and believed." Develop the thought that our belief, like John's, in the resurrection of Jesus is based not on physical sight but on faith. The written testimony of the early believers is a sign for us today.

Luke 24:1–11 (L)

Luke 24:1–10 (E)

Many explanations have been given to try to explain the empty tomb of Jesus. The Jewish religious leaders alleged that the disciples of Jesus took his body out of the tomb. Others declared that enemies stole his body. Still others have tried to state that Jesus did not really die on the cross but only fainted or swooned and was not really dead when placed in the tomb. But the Gospels are emphatic in noting his death. If his enemies had taken his body, why did they not produce it and put an end to all the talk about resurrection? The disciples would not have been willing to suffer and die for a lie. Something radical happened that changed the lives of the disciples.

Luke's account relates the reason for the radical change in the lives of the disciples, from persons filled with fear and doubts to individuals empowered with courage and faith. The difference was brought about by the presence of the risen Lord. The empty tomb itself did not produce this belief. In John's Gospel the empty tomb provoked a fear that Jesus' body had been stolen (John 20:2). In Luke's Gospel the absence of Jesus' body produced perplexity (v. 4). The empty tomb by itself was not evidence of the resurrection.

When a group of women came to anoint Jesus' body on Sunday morning, they found that the stone in front of the tomb had been rolled away. In the East, tombs were often carved like caves in sides of rock mountains. A heavy circular stone, shaped like a large cartwheel, was rolled in a groove in front of the entrance to close the grave. On arriving at Jesus' tomb, the women found that the stone had been rolled back. Going inside the tomb, they found it empty. "While they were perplexed about this" (v. 4), they saw two men in dazzling apparel. It is interesting to note the slight variations in the Gospel accounts. Mark speaks about a young man in a long white robe (Mark 16:5). Matthew says that he is the angel of the Lord (Matt. 28:2). John states that there were two angels (John 20:12).

Who could have remembered such an extraordinary happening with clarity? The women all had slightly different recollections of that wonderful moment. All of these accounts point to the empty tomb and the angelic declaration: "Why do you seek the living among the dead? He is not here, but has risen" (vs. 5–6, margin). This statement affirms the foundation stone of the Christian faith. The messengers remind the women that Jesus had told them that he would be crucified and on the third day rise again (v. 7).

When the women told the disciples, who seemed to be together in one place where they were probably in hiding, they rejected the account as an idle tale and did not believe them. Many of the enemies of Christianity in the first century attempted to reject the resurrection stories on the same basis, as fanciful tales by foolish women. The disciples did not believe until they had their own personal experience with the risen Lord. If one draws from all the Gospels the women named in this group, the list would include: Mary Magdalene, Joanna, Mary the mother of James (v. 10), Joses, and Salome (Mark 15:40).

The sermon may focus on the words of the two messengers to the women who came into the empty tomb and found the body of Jesus missing. The basic text might be: "Why do you seek the living among the dead? He is not here, but has risen" (vs. 5–6, margin). It would be helpful to develop the thought that the empty tomb only provoked perplexity until the reality of the resurrection was affirmed, first by the angels, then by the women, and then the disciples' own experience.

Acts 10:34–43 (C) (E)

Acts 10:34a, 37–43 (RC)

See also the Baptism of Our Lord, (L) (E).

The visit by Peter to the house of Cornelius produced a remarkable sermon. What is contained in this passage is probably only a summary of the sermon that was actually delivered. The sermon began with a shocking statement from a Jew: "I perceive that God shows no partiality" (v. 34). Peter had been slow to reach that conclusion, but Peter came to a new revelation.

This sermon shows one of the best examples of early Christian preaching. Its basic content includes: The tie that connected Jesus to John the Baptist, the anointing of Jesus with the Spirit and power, the power of Jesus' healing ministry, his death by crucifixion and his resurrection, the apostles' witnessing of the resurrection appearances, the call to preach God's judgment on sin, the witness of the prophets to Jesus, the invitation to anyone, regardless of race, to receive forgiveness of sins through belief in Jesus' name.

Evidently Cornelius was already familiar with the Gospel message (v. 36). Someone else had planted the seeds of the good news of God's salvation before Peter arrived. It may have been another one of the disciples or some unknown Christian who shared his knowledge about Jesus with him, a Gentile. The Greek word translated "partiality" literally means "receiving to the face." God did not have favorites. Cornelius had been eager to receive the gospel, but Peter, until his rooftop vision at Joppa (10:23–33), had been reluctant to share the gospel with Gentiles. On the day Cornelius became a believer in Christ, there were in reality two conversions—that of Cornelius to Christ and that of Peter to the awareness that the gospel of Christ is for the larger world outside Judaism.

It would be helpful to **do a word study** of the word "partiality" to clarify the inclusive message of the gospel.

The sermon may deal with the good news which the power of the risen Christ offers to all persons of every race and nation who will confess their sins, accept his forgiveness, and believe in the name of Christ. The joy of the Easter faith and the power of God's forgiving grace are available to all who will believe.

Isaiah 65:17–25 (alt. C)

Isaiah's oracle depicts a glorious new world for God's people. Although the writer of the Book of Revelation drew on images from this passage to describe God's final triumph (Rev. 22:5; 21:1–4), Isaiah had this world in mind for Israel. He offers five promises for the servants of God: (1) Sorrow and distress will be replaced by joy and gladness (vs. 18–19). (2) They will not die prematurely, but will live to an advanced age (v. 20). (3) They will enjoy the fruit of their own labors (vs. 21–23). (4) Their prayers will be answered before they pray (v. 24). (5) Peace will reign even in the animal kingdom (v. 25). The picture seems to depict a return to paradise for Israel.

The sermon may show that the prophet's image for humanity will be fulfilled ultimately only in God's final reign which is depicted in Revelation 22:5; 21:1–4.

Exodus 15:1–11 (L)

This passage has been extolled as one of the finest poems in the Pentateuch. It has been called the Song of Moses, Song of the Sea, Victory Hymn of Moses, among others. This poem or hymn, which was likely used in Israel's worship and Passover observances, celebrates the overthrow of the Egyptian armies in the sea as Israel follows Yahweh to the Promised Land.

Some scholars have suggested that "thank" (v. 2), in translations like Moffatt, is a poor rendering for the Hebrew word. The words "praise" or "bless" are a better rendering of the Hebrew word than "thank." Praise elevated and exalted God in response to the Lord's goodness. This hymn gives praise for the Lord's mighty deeds. "Man of war" in v. 3 means warrior. The right hand or arm of God (v. 6) is an image of God's power. There are various anthropomorphic pictures of God, as in v. 8 which calls the strong wind "the blast of your [God's] nostrils." Israel's rejoicing at the drowning of the Egyptians in the Red Sea reflects their hatred toward their slavemasters and their primitive concept of God, but it also points to the awareness that both good and evil come ultimately from the hand of God.

Do a word study of the word "thank" or "praise."

The sermon might deal with the mystery of God's majesty in permitting both good and evil which culminates in the cross of Christ.

1 Corinthians 15:19–26 (C)

1 Corinthians 15:1–11 (L)

See also Epiphany 5, (C).

Paul begins this passage with a ringing declaration: "I am not giving you Corinthians something which is just my words. This message is not original with me, I am telling you what you have already received." Received from where? Paul's teaching was a part of the early Christian tradition which taught that Christ was crucified, died, was raised from the dead, and continues to live. At the time of Paul's writing to the Corinthian church, the people could not pick up a New Testament and read the Gospel accounts of Jesus' death and resurrection.

The Gospels did not yet exist. Paul's Corinthian letter, written between 50 and 60 C.E., with its references to the appearances of the risen Christ, was likely the earliest written testimony to the resurrection. The Gospels and the Acts of the Apostles were written between 60 and 75 C.E. John's Gospel was written much later. Paul's letter was the first written reference about those who had seen the risen Lord, but it was based on the oral tradition which went back to the disciples. Paul did not originate the tradition but handed on what was considered the early creed of the church—Christ crucified, dead, buried, and risen again.

Paul also noted that what he proclaimed to them was "in accordance with the scriptures" (v. 4). The early church believed that Jesus was raised on the third day according to the scriptures. Although it is difficult for us to know exactly which scriptures the early church used as predictions that Jesus would rise again, several contain references. In the Suffering Servant passage in Isaiah 53, the writer foretells the triumph of the Messiah. Various psalms are quoted in the New Testament to show the fulfillment of prophecy, such as Psalm 2:1, quoted in Acts 4:25–26; Psalm 16:8–11, quoted in Acts 2:25–28; Psalm 110:1, quoted in Acts 2:34–35, and Psalm 118:22, quoted in Acts 4:11.

Paul then summed up the content of the gospel in three short affirmations: Jesus died, was buried, and was raised on the third day (vs. 3–4). He was nailed to a cross, a spear thrust through his side to make certain he was dead. He was then buried in a borrowed tomb. The tomb was sealed by Roman soldiers. He was indeed dead and buried.

Paul claims that the church is not a memorial society but is built on the resurrection of Christ. The resurrection is the solid foundation of the Christian church. Note Paul's declaration concerning the appearances of the risen Christ. In this letter he lists six resurrection appearances. There are only ten or eleven recorded in the Gospels, the Acts of the Apostles, and Paul's letters. Paul affirms that Jesus first appeared to Peter, then to the Twelve, to more than five hundred persons at one time, to James, to all the apostles with Thomas present, and finally Jesus appeared to him.

The Gospels state that Jesus first appeared to three women, among them Mary (Mark 16:9; Matt. 28:1–10; John 20:11–18). Why didn't Paul include women on his list? The Gospel writers record that women were the first to see the risen Lord. Women did not count as witnesses in that day. Paul didn't want people to think that the church's faith was based on a tale told by women. He wanted to use what he thought would be the strongest appeal possible.

The second recorded appearance of Christ occurred on Easter afternoon as two disciples of Jesus were on their way to Emmaus (Mark 16:12–13; Luke 24:13–35). He appeared also to the disciples by the Sea of Tiberias (John 21:7–14), on a mountain in Galilee (Matt. 28:16–20), and on Mt. Olivet just before his ascension (Luke 24:50). Were the last two appearances Paul's reference to Jesus' appearing to more than five hundred at once? In the Book of Acts, Luke states that Jesus "presented himself alive after his passion by many proofs, appearing to them during forty days, and speaking of the kingdom of God" (Acts 1:3). In one of his sermons, Peter stated that Jesus was crucified and killed, "but God raised him up, having loosed the pangs of death, because it was not possible for him to be held by it" (Acts 2:24).

Paul then draws upon some images very familiar to his Jewish readers (vs. 20–28). The image of "the first fruits of those who have fallen asleep" refers to the great harvest festival and the sheaf of the firstfruits which they were to bring to the celebration. The firstfruits were a sign of the full crops yet to be harvested. The resurrection of Christ was a sign of the life after death.

The Jews had a strong concept of racial solidarity. They literally believed that all persons sinned and fell in Adam's fall. Adam was seen as a historical person whose sin brought upon humanity the sentence of death (Gen. 2:17), but Christ, the new Adam, brought about a radical change. The first Adam gave us sin and death. Christ, the second Adam, gave us forgiveness and victory over death. Just as all sinned in Adam, all are made alive in Christ. The resurrection of Christ destroyed the power of death (v. 26). Christ had a mission to save humanity, and being the "first fruits" demonstrated his assurance of our own resurrection. Death is seen as an enemy because it ends human life, but Christ's resurrection has defeated death and assured us of resurrected life as well.

Do a study of the harvest festival and the meaning of "first fruits."

The sermon may develop the theme of the resurrection as the foundation stone of the Christian church. Draw on Paul's example of the resurrection appearances of Christ and note the radical change these appearances produced in the lives of the disciples. Help the listeners to affirm and testify to the grand miracle of the resurrection on which our religion is based as the risen Lord becomes more real to us.

Colossians 3:1–4 (RC) (E)

See also Pentecost 11, (C) (L) (RC).

In this pericope Paul uses Christian baptism as a picture of the radical change that occurs in a new Christian's life when he or she is buried in death under the waters and then is raised to live differently in Christ. It is a radical change from death to life. The Christian now has a different perspective and values which are not based on material, worldly ends but are set against eternal standards.

The destiny of the believer is now interpreted in the destiny of Christ. Paul calls Christ "our life" (v. 4). Jesus said, "I am the resurrection and the life" (John 11:25), and "I am . . . the life" (John 14:6). Paul's theological image denotes that one in Christ has died to sin and has been raised to walk in newness of life. In another letter he wrote: "It is no longer I who live, but Christ who lives in me" (Gal. 2:20).

Examine Paul's meaning of Christ as "our life."

The sermon may focus on what it means to call Christ "our life." Note how his living presence should determine a Christian's values, goals, and behavior.

Theological Reflection

The resurrection of Christ is the foundation of the Christian faith. Our New Testament texts affirm that the Christian religion was not founded on a delusion but on the miracle of God raising Jesus from the dead. A large number of witnesses to his resurrection are noted in these texts. These eyewitnesses filled their preaching and their lives with the personal experiences they had with the risen Lord. The presence of the living Lord turned a defeated, despairing group of disciples into crusading evangelists with a message of good news for all persons regardless of race or sex.

Children's Message

The children's talk might focus on the first Easter when Mary Magdalene came weeping to the tomb and thought Jesus was the caretaker until he called her name. In retelling this lovely story, help the children to sense the wonder, mystery, and miracle of the resurrection and the difference the living Lord can make in their daily living.

Hymns for Easter Day

Christ the Lord Is Risen Today!; Good Christians All, Rejoice and Sing!; Jesus Christ Is Risen Today; A Carol for Two Seasons (*Choirbook for Saints and Singers*).

Easter 2

Psalm 2 (C)

Acts 5:27–32 (C)
Acts 5:12, 17–32 (L)
Acts 5:12–16 (RC)
Acts 5:12a, 17–22, 25–29 (E)

Revelation 1:4–8 (C)
Revelation 1:4–18 (L)
Revelation 1:9–11b, 12–13, 17–19 (RC)
Revelation 1:9–19 (E)

John 20:19–31

Meditation on the Texts

Almighty God, the Alpha and the Omega, the One who is, and who was, and who is to come, we praise you for your redeeming grace. Strengthen us by your living presence to rise from doubt to faith, skepticism to conviction, defeat to victory, and fear to peace. Gird us, O Living One, with the strength of your strong right hand to face the difficulties of life and the terrors of death with the assurance of Jesus Christ, your faithful witness. Amen.

Commentary on the Texts

John 20:19–31

See also the Day of Pentecost, (E).

Our pericope shows the disciples of Jesus gathered together, most likely in the same room where they had partaken of the Last Supper with Jesus before he was arrested. They were filled with despondency, defeat, hopelessness, uncertainty, and fear. They had not anticipated that Jesus would rise from the grave. The stories by the women and the accounts of the empty tomb by Peter and John were not sufficient.

The door to the upper room was bolted shut. They may have thought that the Roman and Jewish authorities, who had put Jesus to death, would soon come and arrest them. The disappearance of Jesus' body may have added to their fear and confusion.

Suddenly, even with the door bolted shut, Jesus appeared in their midst. How do we explain his appearance? There is no simple explanation. Whatever else one may want to say to describe the resurrection of Christ, the Gospel writers depict it as an objective historical event. But their descriptions of this event say more than that. It was also wrapped in mystery and awe. The resurrected body of Jesus was obviously different in some way than it was before. In his risen body, Jesus was not limited by space or time. He appeared and disappeared at will. He somehow entered a room when the door was bolted shut. Earlier he had appeared to two disciples on the road to Emmaus and they had not recognized him. Later he appeared to the disciples by the seashore. Although his body was different in some ways, they knew that it was Jesus, their Master.

As Jesus appeared in their midst, his first word to the disciples was the typical Jewish greeting, "Shalom," "Peace be with you." To the Jews of that day, this greeting was almost as common as "Good morning" is today. Yet "Shalom" meant much more to the disciples on this occasion. The arrest, the death of Jesus, and their abandonment of him had left them terrified and without peace. Suddenly the Christ, whom they had forsaken and rejected, appeared among them. He calmed their fears with the familiar word, "peace." He had told them earlier, "Peace I leave with you; my peace I give to you; not as the world gives do I give to you."

Some scholars see this event as the first infusion of the Spirit for the disciples. Breath and the Spirit of God are often identified in the scriptures. In the creation story, God breathed into a human being and that one became a living person (Gen. 2:7). Jesus breathed into his disciples the breath of peace, inspiration, power, and presence. To carry his message, the disciples needed to be empowered by Christ.

Other scholars have identified the forgiving of sins with the experience of baptism. John likely identified this act as a gift within the community of faith. Each Christian forgave others as he or she had experienced forgiveness from Christ in that community, the church, which had received the Holy Spirit.

When the disciples had first met and had seen the risen Lord, Thomas was not present. There is no reason given for his absence. Thomas, however, would not accept a second-hand faith. He was a skeptic and demanded proof. A week later, Thomas was with the disciples. Thomas set up high requirements before he would believe the resurrection. He said, "Unless I touch and see the nailprints, I won't believe." When Jesus stood in their midst, he repeated almost Thomas' very words. "Touch and see these nailprints," Jesus said to Thomas. There is no evidence that Thomas actually touched Jesus. He stopped short of what he had said he would require.

Thomas then fell at Jesus' feet and made a remarkable confession. His confession was bolder than the one Peter had made at Caesarea Philippi. "My Lord and my God!" he exclaimed. This confession was the goal toward which John's Gospel was moving. In the Prologue to the Gospel, John had written: "In the beginning was the Word, and the Word was with God, and the Word was God" (1:1). The resurrection appearance of Jesus produced in Thomas, the man with all the doubt, fears, and questions, this extraordinary exclamation: "My Lord and my God!" The great doubter became the great believer. For John, Thomas was representative of the doubters among the followers of Jesus.

The beatitude which Jesus pronounced was directed not simply to Thomas but to all present and future persons who had not seen his appearance: "Blessed are those who have not seen and yet believe" (v. 29). The early disciples had tangible signs of the risen Christ, but future Christians would not be limited to seeing Jesus with the physical senses. Faith would draw not only on the testimony of the disciples but also on the inward eye, a perception within, a "sense of the presence" of Christ in our conscious and subconscious mind.

John's original Gospel likely ended with v. 31. John presented his story about Jesus through various signs (seven in particular). The central sign was the resurrection. He indicated that his Gospel contained only a few of the known signs about the work of Christ. But he states boldly that his purpose in writing was that the reader might believe that Jesus was the Messiah, the Son of God, and thereby the believer would have life. This life was the redeemed, abundant, eternal life that only Christ could give.

Compare the giving of the Spirit in John's account with Acts 2.

The sermon may focus on the skepticism of Thomas, who would not settle for a secondhand report about the resurrection of Christ but demanded tangible proof. Thomas may represent many who have questions and doubts about the faith. Those who are bold to question and struggle with the whys of life can identify with the doubter who became the great believer.

Acts 5:27–32 (C)

Acts 5:12, 17–32 (L)

Acts 5:12–16 (RC)

Acts 5:12a, 17–22, 25–29 (E)

Our passage in the Book of Acts presents a brief description of what the early Christian church was like. The Christians gathered daily in a conspicuous place in Solomon's colonnade in the temple (vs. 13 and 14 seem contradictory). Scholars have struggled to know the meaning of "none of the rest." Did the death of Ananias and Sapphira (5:1–11) frighten the people away? It is likely that "none of the rest" refers to the religious leaders who did not dare join the church, while the common people responded favorably to the Gospel message. Believers were increasing and the church was growing.

158

The signs and wonders in the early church seemed to account for some of the greater numbers who were drawn to the church. Peter's healing reputation had grown so much that some of the people became superstitious and believed that his shadow had healing power (v. 15). Paul had a similar problem in Ephesus, where some of the people took handkerchiefs and aprons which Paul had used to heal the sick (19:12). Luke probably told this to show the veneration the people had for Peter.

The account in vs. 17–26 is similar to the first account of Peter and John being arrested (4:1–31). Some scholars have felt that this might simply be another account of the same story, but there are enough differences to convince others that this is a separate record. Since the disciples had continued to preach and heal in the temple area when they had been forbidden to do so, it is easy to understand why a second arrest might be probable. Boldly these disciples had gone straight back and were preaching again. Their audacity and increasing influence on the Jewish people filled the high priest and Sadducees with jealousy. They had all of the disciples arrested and put them in the city jail.

Before a council of the Sanhedrin could be called the next day, temple guards came to the prison and discovered that the prisoners were not in the jail. The doors were still locked and the guards at the doors, but the prisoners were gone. During the night "an angel of the Lord" (v. 19) opened the door. The word "angel" is the ordinary word for messenger, and one does not have to assume that they escaped by supernatural means. The messenger could have been a friend, a member of the temple guard, but Luke most likely is implying a miraculous intervention.

The angel told the disciples that they were liberated to go back and communicate to the people the words of life. Life was a word the Gospel of John had constantly on the lips of Jesus: "I am the way, and the truth, and the life" (John 14:6). Paul had spoken about the life in Christ as a "new creation; the old has passed away, behold, the new has come" (2 Cor. 5:17). The word "life" is used thirty-six times in the New Testament, and stands for the gift of salvation which is found in Christ.

The officers found the disciples teaching in the temple, but they arrested the disciples peacefully. The officers knew that if they used force, the crowd would be upset and might turn against them. When the disciples were brought before the council, the high priest told them that they had been "strictly charged" not to teach in Jesus' name (v. 28) or to accuse the religious authorities of his death.

Peter, as the spokesperson for the disciples, declared that there are limits to human authority: "We must obey God rather than men" (v. 29). This was an imperative by which the disciples said they must live. Religious traditions or state laws were subordinate to it. The central message of apostolic preaching is found in this sermon: The crucifixion of Jesus, his resurrection from the dead, his exaltation to the right hand of power as Lord and Savior, and his invitation to repentance and assurance of the forgiveness of sins (vs. 30–31). Peter asserts that not only are they witnesses for Christ, but so is the Holy Spirit. It was impossible for them not to declare what they had seen and heard personally.

Consult several commentaries to discern the possible meaning of the reference to "none of the rest" (v. 13).

The sermon might deal with the imperative of obeying God and the conflict this sometimes brings for the Christian with the civil laws of one's own country. Following Christ's imperative can sometimes create tension within one's own family. The sermon should invite the hearers to search their conscience to see if civil disobedience is not sometimes one of the Christian's most powerful forms of witness.

Revelation 1:4–8 (C)

Revelation 1:4–18 (L)

Revelation 1:9–11b, 12–13, 17–19 (RC)

Revelation 1:9–19 (E)

The word "Revelation" comes from the Greek word *apokalypsis,* which means "an uncovering, a revelation, or a disclosure." This type of apocalyptic literature developed during the postexilic period. Apocalyptic literature is filled with dualism between a good God and an evil one (for example, Jehovah and Satan), with visions, the figure of the Son of Man instead of the Messiah, symbols, numbers, and other dramatic images. Apocalyptic literature is a special kind of literature and should be read symbolically and not literally. John wrote in a ''code'' to smuggle his letter out of prison. His captors would not have understood his message, but the church to whom he wrote had the key to decipher its meaning. Unfortunately, many today are unacquainted with the strange images from another era and this writing has never been fully grasped. It continues to be the subject of varied interpretations.

The Book of Revelation is really a letter that was written to seven churches in the Roman province of Asia. The seven churches, mentioned in v. 11, were representative of all the churches in Asia. These churches were real churches that once existed. The doctrine of the Trinity is set forth at the beginning of the letter in an ascription of praise. ''The seven spirits who are before his throne'' is likely a reference to the Holy Spirit (v. 4). The number seven, which is often mentioned in the book, is a symbol for perfection or completeness. The Holy Spirit is thought of as the perfect Spirit.

God the Father is represented in this passage as the One ''who is and who was and who is to come.'' God is the Eternal One. Jesus is also spoken of as the One who will come ''with the clouds'' (v. 7) and those who pierced him ''will see him.'' Could this be in some way John's way of writing about the unity of the Son and the Father?

Three images of Christ are presented: (1) Jesus was the witness (martyr). His death was his ultimate testimony. (2) He is ''the first-born of the dead'' which implies that his victory over death prepared the way for others. (3) Jesus is sovereign Lord because he is ''the ruler of kings on earth.'' In one breath, John speaks of the sacrificial death of Christ, his resurrection, and his exalted reign of power. John continues in his praise of Christ by extolling him in a threefold way: He loves us, his death has freed us from our sins, and he has made us a kingdom of priests. Then John breaks out into a doxology (v. 6).

With this ascription of praise, the writer warns his readers about the judgment that will be ''coming with the clouds.'' For John, and a church under persecution, this apocalyptic vision assures them of the triumphant return of Christ to rescue his suffering people. The first word of warning is to those who crucified the Lord.

The reference to God as ''the Alpha and the Omega'' denotes the Lord's completeness. These are the first and last letters in the Greek alphabet, similar to our A to Z and ''the beginning and the end.'' He is saying in essence that God is the Lord of the beginning of history, the end of history, and all that falls between. God is absolute sovereign, eternal, and almighty.

John identifies himself (v. 9) as a brother (a Christian) and one who had also experienced tribulation as his readers had. He indicates that he had been exiled, because of preaching the Christian faith, to the Isle of Patmos, a small island in the Aegean Sea about sixty miles southwest of Ephesus. While on this small island, only five miles wide by eight miles long, John had his vision. He experienced a call, a trumpet voice, that directed him to speak to the seven churches in Asia.

In his vision John sees a seven-branched golden lampstand representing the churches in Asia which are to receive his message. This image is likely drawn from Exodus 25:31–37 and Zechariah 4:2. Using images of the churches as lamps, he is quick to observe that the lampstand is not the light, but the setting for the Light. The churches reflect the light they receive from the Light (vs. 12, 20).

In the midst of the lampstands, John sees a strange man. His vision is filled with Old Testament apocalyptic images drawn from Daniel, Ezekiel, and others. The figure of ''one like a son of man'' is dressed in a long robe, expressing dignity, and he is adorned with a golden girdle at his breast, a sign of a priest. His hair, white as wool or snow, symbolizes his purity and wisdom. His blazing eyes represent judgment while his feet, like burnished bronze, symbolize his mighty strength. His voice, sounding like a great waterfall, denotes power.

The work of the Son of Man is to bring judgment, pictured in the two-edged sword protruding out of his mouth, which is the power of his word. The Gospel of John calls Christ the Word of God (John 1:1). He also holds ''the seven stars,'' the pastors (messengers) of the seven churches, in his hand. Even while holding ''the seven stars,'' Christ reaches out to John, calms his fears, and assures him of his authority over life and death: "I am the first and the last, and the living one; I died, and behold I am alive for evermore, and I have the keys of Death and Hades" (vs. 17–18). The risen Lord has power over death and the grave.

Read an introductory section in several commentaries on apocalyptic literature and the Apocalypse.

The sermon may focus on Christ as "the first and the last." It would be helpful to do a word study of this phrase. The fear of death will be lessened as the Christian grasps more clearly the promise of Christ and his victory over death.

Theological Reflection

Common themes running through the readings for today are the assurance of the presence of the risen Christ, belief over skepticism, the giving of the Holy Spirit, the conflict of Christ's imperative to witness with religious or secular opposition, and the triumphant power of the risen Christ. The sight of the risen Christ transformed the doubts of Thomas into profound faith. The presence of the Holy Spirit empowers the disciples to preach boldly in Christ's name. The courage and faith of the early disciples to teach and preach the Gospel in the face of opposing religious and political powers serve as a model for Christians through the ages. The assurance of the presence of the exalted, risen Christ strengthens Christians to face whatever tribulation or difficulties they meet in life.

Children's Message

The children might grasp something about the story from the Book of Revelation if you dress dramatically for the part. Wear a long robe, put a yellow sash around your chest, wear a white wig, and put on heavy boots. Stand beside some kind of lampstand or a replica of one someone might make for you out of wood. Describe the vision John had and the meaning of the symbols in the color code of the Son of Man. Then have all the children read together the words of praise: "To him who loves us and freed us from our sins with his life's blood, who made of us a royal house, to serve as the priests of his God and Father—to him be glory and dominion for ever and ever! Amen" (Rev. 1:6, NEB).

Hymns for Easter 2

Praise Him! Praise Him!; Rejoice, the Lord Is King; We Walk by Faith and Not by Sight.

Psalm 30:4–12 (C)

Revelation 5:11–14 (C) (L) (RC)
Revelation 5:6–14 (E)

Acts 9:1–20 (C) (L)
Acts 5:27b–32, 40b–41 (RC)
Acts 9:1–19a (E)

John 21:1–19 (C) (RC)
John 21:1–14 (L) (E)

Meditation on the Texts

Eternal Lamb of God, who conquers the hearts of men and women by the power of love, we praise you for your sacrificial death. We thank you for your converting grace that continues to forgive our sins and does not give up on us. As we remember the denial of Simon Peter and your forgiving, restoring love, motivate us to reach out with the assurance of your welcoming love to those who have turned from your way. O Lamb of God, who takes away our sins, inspire us to respond to others as we have been loved by you. Amen.

Commentary on the Texts

John 21:1–19 (C) (RC)

John 21:1–14 (L) (E)

This whole chapter is considered by most scholars to be an appendix or an epilogue to the Gospel. It is believed that John's original Gospel ended with the twentieth chapter. The material in this chapter is different but is considered a part of the text of sacred scripture. Some commentators believe that John included this addendum himself for some purpose he felt important, while others think a Johannine disciple wrote this chapter. Still others think it may have been written by one of the followers of the beloved disciple who was dismayed at his master's death. Others argue that one of Simon Peter's disciples may have penned the section to show Peter's rehabilitation and his pastoral role in the church. Many scholars see two separate sections here; vs. 1–14 are one unit and vs. 15–19 are another.

For many, it is difficult to understand why the disciples would return to fishing right after receiving knowledge of the resurrection. Some have seen this as a sign of apostasy on the part of the disciples, but it may have been only their desire to get food in their traditional way. The setting is beside the Sea of Tiberias. The angels at the tomb had told Jesus' disciples that he had gone ahead of them into Galilee. Although John states this is the third appearance of Jesus to the disciples, some scholars attribute that to the editor, and suggest instead that this may be the first appearance to the disciples as a group. Although it is difficult to determine the time sequence of many of the resurrection stories, it seems unlikely that this appearance was the first.

Seven disciples, including Peter, Thomas, Nathanael, Andrew, and John, had fished all night and caught nothing. Jesus, who was unrecognized by them, instructed them to cast their net on the right side of the boat. When they did, their net was so full it almost broke. Suddenly they remembered a similar experience when Jesus had first called them to follow him (Mark 1:17), and this catch became a "sign" to them of the resurrected Lord. John was the first to recognize Jesus. When Peter realized that it was Jesus, he jumped into the water and swam to the shore.

When they all arrived at the shore, Jesus invited the disciples to share a meal of fish and bread. Much debate has centered around whether this was a eucharistic meal. John's Gospel records only two such meals, the feeding of the multitude (6:11–13), with the declaration following that Jesus is the Bread of Life, and this meal by the sea. In both meals, fish and bread are mentioned. Most scholars agree that chapter 6 reports a eucharistic meal. This meal beside the shore has much similarity to that other meal and likely bears the same kind of emphasis. The Lord was made known to the disciples on the road to Emmaus "in the breaking of the bread," but here they recognized the Lord first, and then shared in the meal.

Probably few catches of fish have been discussed as much as this netfull on the Sea of Tiberias. All kinds of theories have been suggested for the significance of the number of fish they caught. Since John was noted for his signs, some have suggested that the hundred and fifty-three fish caught represent the total number of the variety of fish which were known in that time. This would represent further the universal nature of the Gospel. The disciples as "fishers of men" were to be witnesses for Christ to all the races of the world. Christ's net was inclusive. It would reach out to the point of breaking to include all who would believe.

In the "sign" of the fish, Jesus directed the disciples to their mission outside the church. In his conversation with Peter, Jesus noted the ministry to those within the church. Jesus addressed Peter in a very formal way: "Simon, son of John, do you love me more than these?" What was the reference of "more than these"? Some have thought that it referred to the fisherman's possessions like his boats and nets. "Is your love greater than these things?" More likely, however, Jesus was asking Peter if he still claimed to love the Lord more than did any of the other disciples. Peter could not make any claim that he loved Jesus more than the others did.

Peter previously had denied Jesus three times, and here three times Jesus confronted him with the question, "Do you love me?" Three times Peter is called to penitence and responds, and then he is challenged to feed the flock. Peter's love for Jesus will be revealed in his care for the people.

Some scholars believe that it is improbable that the repeated question of Jesus to Peter and the differences in the terms for love which Jesus used were deliberate. These scholars see this variation only as John's use of synonyms for the word "love." Other scholars believe that Jesus did use a Greek word for love which acknowledges a higher spiritual commitment than the responding word which Peter uses. The diminishing scale might be expressed: "Do you love me more than these?" "Do you love me?" "Do you love me even as a friend?"

Deeply grieved at the declining emphasis and the painful repetition of the question, Peter affirmed that the Lord knew all things and so had to know the depth of his love, even though he had denied him. Jesus was aware of this love, and each time after Peter responded to his question of loyalty, Jesus challenged him to be a pastor to his people. This story affirms one of the great truths about the forgiving grace of Christ. Peter, who had denied his Lord before, was now commissioned and restored as a disciple. He was commissioned to "feed my lambs," "tend my sheep," and "feed my sheep."

Much debate has centered around the meaning of the commissioning of Peter by Jesus. Some have seen this commissioning as giving Peter exclusive pastoral authority over the other disciples, while others have recognized Peter as a *primus inter pares,* a first among equals. This chapter needs to be studied along with Matthew 16:18–19 and Luke 22:32. Space does not allow a lengthy discussion here. His commission to be shepherd was a call to minister in Jesus' name. He was challenged to assist the young in the church (lambs) to grow toward maturity. To "tend and feed my sheep" carries the responsibility of ministering to the spiritual welfare of the mature members of the church. Peter's encounter with Jesus issued in a concrete assignment—feed and care for the flock, both new and older members.

Compare Matthew 16:18–19 with Peter's commission in vs. 15–19. Do a study of the various words for love which both Jesus and Peter used. Examine the word "shepherd" and compare it with the word for "bishop" as used in 1 Peter 2:25; 5:1–3; Acts 20:28; and other places.

The sermon might focus on the method Jesus used to call forth love and loyalty from

Peter. Faithfulness cannot arise out of those who do not yet love the Lord. Drawing on Jesus' example of forgiving grace, the church seeks to equip those who feel loved by Christ and who in turn minister lovingly to others.

Acts 9:1–20 (C) (L)

Acts 9:1–19a (E)

When the apostle Paul spoke about his faith, he often began with his experience with Christ. The Book of Acts records three occasions where Paul spoke about his experience of meeting Christ on the Damascus road. He had witnessed earlier the death of Stephen. He was so outraged at the Christians that he secured special papers from the high priest to go to the synagogue in Damascus to see if he could find any Christians there and put them to death. After getting the necessary papers, he began the journey from Jerusalem to Damascus, which was a trip of about a hundred and forty miles. It took six days by caravan to travel that distance in biblical times.

What went through the mind of Saul as he was walking or riding by camel along that road? He was a Pharisee, so he would not have much to do with the guards who were from the Sanhedrin. He was very devout, and his piety would separate him even from them. He probably walked alone. This gave him a lot of time to think and reflect. He may have asked himself, "Why would someone like Stephen die for this Christ? Who was this Jesus, who had turned people to a new religious way, that they were willing to die for him?"

As Saul approached the end of his journey, the road climbed Mt. Hermon, then down below lay the city of Damascus. It is at this place that tradition says Saul had his experience with Christ. Suddenly there was a blinding light and a voice like thunder addressed him. Others on the road did not see Jesus, but they heard a voice. Out of that experience, Saul became Paul. His life was transformed. Others had not shared the same experience which Paul had, but this encounter left Paul blind for three days.

Note the two questions Paul raised in his encounter with Christ. The first was, "Who are you, Lord?" The word "Lord" does not mean that Paul recognized Jesus. The word "lord" was the Jewish way of simply saying, "sir." "Who are you, sir?" "I am Jesus." Jesus' response must have terrified him. Paul likely responded with disbelief, fear, and great anxiety. Here on the road where he was traveling to put Christians to death, he met the One who had inspired these people to live and die for him. Out of this experience, which he had neither planned nor anticipated, he met Christ, and his life was forever changed.

Whenever people would talk to Paul after that, his basic arguments were not philosophical, theological, or propositional, but experiential. A person might be able to disagree with some of his theological arguments, but one could not discount his experience with Christ. His experience with the living Christ was a life-changing encounter. "Last of all . . . ," Paul said, "he appeared also to me" (1 Cor. 15:8). This experience could not be set aside.

"Who are you, Lord?" Paul asked. "I am Jesus, whom you are persecuting." Now wait a minute, Paul may have thought to himself, I'm not persecuting you. I am persecuting your followers. But soon Paul would learn from Jesus, "As you did it to one of the least of these my brethren, you did it to me" (Matt. 25:40). Jesus identified himself with his persecuted church. Here on the Damascus road, Paul began to understand that the church was "the body of Christ."

Saul's conversion underscores God's power to reach people who seem to be unreachable. God changed a man who had been an enemy of the church. Ananias was afraid when he was told that Saul had a conversion experience and had become a Christian. He did not want to talk to him at first. He was frightened. "That man has been putting Christians to death," he declared. We say it frequently: "Don't waste your time with him." "She is hopeless." "An old dog can't learn new tricks." "Forget them, go on your way." Though we may give up on people and quit, God does not. God keeps coming into our lives.

Ananias is one of the great heroes of the early church. He went to the street called Straight in Damascus, likely a street which ran from the east to the west side of the city.

Rather than meeting Paul with hostility or suspicion, Ananias trusted the power of God's grace and greeted him with the words, "Brother Saul." This was a marvelous example of trust and forgiveness. It is interesting to note that Ananias, who was not one of the original apostles, laid his hands upon Paul before he was baptized. Ananias took God at his word and believed that Paul was God's chosen instrument to convey God's name before people and kings.

Notice the second question Saul raised to Jesus on the Damascus road: "What shall I do, Lord?" (Acts 22:10). Saul learned that his life was not to be controlled by his own ambitions but by obedience to Christ. Paul would later refer to his relationship to the Lord with the phrase "in Christ." Christ now dominated, directed, and guided his life. Christ gave him a new agenda and a new responsibility.

Do a word study on the meaning of "goods" (v. 5) and "chosen vessel" (v. 15).

The sermon might arise out of Saul's two questions to Jesus on the Damascus road: "Who are you, Lord?" (v. 5) and "What do you want me to do, Lord?" (v. 6). The sermon might show how essential these two questions are to genuine conversion.

Acts 5:27b–32, 40b–41 (RC)

See Easter 2, (C) (L) (E).

Revelation 5:11–14 (C) (L) (RC)

Revelation 5:6–14 (E)

Chapters 4 and 5 contain five hymns of praise to God. The first (4:8) focuses on the holiness of God. The second (4:11) depicts the twenty-four elders praising the creative power of God. The third hymn (5:9–10) is a response by the elders in honor of the Lamb. Worship is depicted in instrumental praise, "each holding a harp" (v. 8), and the prayers of all believers symbolized in the "golden bowls full of incense." Believers are assured that their worship and prayers are never lost but preserved. The only one who could open the scroll of destiny (v. 1), which was sealed with seven seals, was one who possessed both worthiness and power.

Ironically, the one who was the Lamb possessed such traits. This is John's first use of his definitive image for Christ. The reference to Jesus Christ as the Lamb occurs twenty-nine times in the Revelation to John. The seven horns on the Lamb symbolize complete power and honor—omnipotence. Remember that the number seven denotes perfection, and the seven eyes symbolize perfect vision or insight—omniscience. The vulnerable Lamb has become Redeemer because he was willing to sacrifice his life for humanity. The Lion of the tribe of Judah (strength) has conquered by the impossible power of a Lamb that depicts weakness and victimization. But this Passover Lamb, "standing, as though it had been slain" (v. 6) had conquered (v. 5).

John's use of the word "conquer" occurs twenty-three times in his book. As M. Eugene Boring notes in his *Revelation,* Interpretation series (p. 111; Atlanta: John Knox Press, 1989), conquering does not mean destructive judgment on the enemies of Christ; in the case of Christ and Christians it means nothing more nor less than dying. This word "conquer," like his use of "Lamb" and many others, were given new definitions and meanings by John.

The slain Lamb was ironically the One worthy enough and powerful enough to open the scroll. The redeeming Lamb gave his life for everyone, "every tribe and tongue and people and nation" (v. 9), and binds all believers into a priesthood (v. 10). The sacrifice of the Lamb destroys all barriers, national, racial, or sexual, and provides his followers a kingdom, a priesthood, and an earthly reign.

The song the elders sang was a "new" song (v. 9). The psalmist often spoke about the desire to "sing to the LORD" a new song (Ps. 98:1; 144:9; 33:3). The word "new" is one of John's favorite words. He writes about a "new name" (2:17; 3:12), a "new Jerusalem" (3:12; 21:2), a "new heaven and a new earth" (21:1), and that all things will be made "new" (21:5). Jesus Christ has indeed brought something radically new into existence, and the believer can share in this "new creation."

The fourth hymn (v. 12), which later inspired Handel to write the oratorio *The Messiah*, praises the worthiness of the Lamb. Thousands of angels sing of the Lamb's worthiness because he "was slain." Repeatedly John uses the image "was slain" to refer to the Lamb. The death of Christ on the cross was the perfect sacrifice and the fulfillment of all Jewish expectations for the Messiah. The Lamb is worthy to receive the gifts any world ruler would desire—power, wealth, wisdom, and might—but these gifts will be used by Christ to carry out his spiritual reign. Because the Lamb has completed God's sacrificial purpose, he is worthy to receive our worship, which is denoted in the honor, glory, and blessing we ascribe to him.

In the fifth and final hymn (v. 13), the angelic choir of thousands breaks forth into jubilant praise to the Lamb. They are then joined by every creature in heaven, on earth, under the earth, and in the sea, all creation, in universal adoration of the Lamb. "Every creature in heaven" may refer to the singing of birds, the stars, suns, and other heavenly bodies, or the angels. The creatures under the earth may refer to the dead in Hades. The picture is inclusive of all creation—humanity and all the rest of creation. "The throne" of God represents the unseen presence of God. This throne conveys the image of God's majesty, mercy, and judgment.

The scene concludes with the four living creatures crying, "Amen." So be it! And the elders fall down and worship the perfect redeemer.

A **special study** of Lamb, conquer, Lion of God, and throne of God would be useful.

The sermon might focus on the image "Worthy is the Lamb" (v. 12). The costly nature of Christ's sacrifice can be noted and the necessity of devoting our earthly resources of power, wealth, wisdom, and might to his will, if we are going to bring honor, glory, and blessing to him.

Theological Reflection

The central thrust of these texts focuses on the forgiving, transforming, redeeming power of the living presence of Christ. John presents this theme in the call and recommissioning of Peter. Paul's radical conversion attests to the power of the resurrected Lord. The account from the Apocalypse proclaims the risen Lord as the Lamb of God, who was slain for our sins, and is worthy of our praise and adoration. The assurance of the living Lord continues to be the foundation of the Christian church.

Children's Message

The children's story might draw upon the image of the Lamb of God from Revelation. A picture of a lamb or a small stuffed lamb might be shown, if they are available. Help the children to envision the sacrifice and suffering that Jesus bore as the Lamb of God. Remind them that Jesus' death on the cross was a costly sacrifice for all people. Focus your major attention on God's sacrificial love through Christ.

Hymns for Easter 3

Alleluia! Sing to Jesus; All My Sins Have Been Forgiven; The Day of Resurrection; Christ Is Made the Sure Foundation.

Easter 4

Psalm 23 (C)

Acts 13:15–16, 26–33 (C) (E)
Acts 13:15–16a, 26–33 (L)
Acts 13:14, 43–52 (RC)

Revelation 7:9–17 (C) (L) (E)
Revelation 7:9, 14b–17 (RC)

John 10:22–30 (C) (L) (E)
John 10:27–30 (RC)

Meditation on the Texts

Eternal Lamb of God, we praise you for your suffering love which cleanses us from all our sins and washes us white as snow. Thank you for your shepherding love which assures us of your presence, grace, forgiveness, guidance, and the security that no one can separate us from that love. We praise you for your inclusive grace which overcomes all barriers of race, country, or sex. Give us the courage to share the good news of Christ's redemption with all who will listen. May the joy of serving eternally before your throne inspire us to worship and love you more faithfully every day. Amen.

Commentary on the Texts

John 10:22–30 (C) (L) (E)

John 10:27–30 (RC)

In discussing this instance in the life of Jesus, John notes both the date and the place. He dates it at the Festival of the Dedication, which commemorated the purification of the temple by Judas Maccabeus and his brothers after the altar was polluted by Antiochus Epiphanes in 170 B.C.E. This same celebration is sometimes called the Festival of Lights, or Hanukkah, still observed by Jews today.

John's date would indicate that it was winter. That may have been the reason Jesus was walking on Solomon's Porch, which was one of the covered sections of colonnades off from the Court of the Gentiles. This would shield him from the cold winds and damp weather. Some scholars believe, however, that, with John's love for symbolism, the reference to winter might be an indication of the frozen spirits and cold reception Jesus received from the Jewish leaders rather than merely a notation about the weather.

While Jesus was walking under the shelter of Solomon's Porch teaching his disciples, he was confronted by some of the Jewish leaders who asked him to tell them plainly whether or not he was the Messiah. The way they asked Jesus the question did not indicate a genuine desire to know, but rather was an attempt to trap him so they could accuse him of blasphemy. Some scholars have translated v. 24, "How long will you keep us in suspense?" as "How long do you intend to annoy or provoke us?" Their desire to know was colored by hostility and impatience. This inquiry is similar to the ones recorded in Mark 14:55–65 and Luke 22:67.

Jesus' answer "I told you" (v. 25) sounds strange in that John has given no clear public statements by Jesus to the Jewish authorities about his messiahship. John noted that Jesus had told the woman at the well in Samaria (4:26) and the man who was born blind (9:37) that he was the awaited Messiah. Most likely, Jesus was stating that both his teachings and works clearly revealed who he was. This had been the same message he sent to John the Baptist when he inquired from prison whether Jesus was really the Christ (Matt. 11:2–6).

Jesus told them that the works he did in his Father's name bore witness for him, but they did not understand, because they did not belong to his flock. Jesus knew that he was not the Christ of these Jewish leaders' expectation. His words and deeds testified to a suffering Messiah which only his followers (sheep) could understand. He boldly declared that "the Son of man must suffer" (Mark 8:31). A simple answer to their question was impossible. Jesus was indeed the Messiah but not the messianic figure they anticipated. They did not hear his words because Jesus was a "stranger" to them—not the shepherd of their flock.

Then Jesus notes four ingredients in discipleship (vs. 27–28): (1) His disciples receive his message, because his sheep hear the voice of the shepherd. (2) They are aware of his personal, caring knowledge of them. (3) Because they trust him, they "follow" him. (4) As the Good Shepherd, Jesus gives his "sheep" eternal life which no one can take away from them. The elements of discipleship reveal a hearing and response on the part of the disciples and a knowledge of his disciples and the gift of eternal life from the shepherd.

The word "snatch" in v. 28 is the same one that was used to describe the wolf who attacks the flock (v. 12). Christ reminds his followers that they do not have to rely on their own strength because God will provide the resources to protect them. Paul summed up this same truth in response to his own question, "Who shall separate us from the love of Christ?" "Neither death, nor life, nor angels, nor principalities, nor things present, nor things to come, nor powers, nor height, nor depth, nor anything else in all creation, will be able to separate us from the love of God in Christ Jesus our Lord" (Rom. 8:35, 38–39).

Jesus stated that no one could snatch, tear away, his disciples from his hands. Jesus declares that the assurance of his ability to "guard" his sheep is based on his unity with God his Father: "I and the Father are one" (v. 30). God had given him the sheep and God's hand will give safety to the sheep.

The sentence "I and the Father are one" (v. 30) has been at the center of controversy since the early church began. Scholars have debated whether this statement was an ontic claim about the essence of divine being, a mystical expression of unity, a unity of will, or a statement about a unity of function and purpose. Some scholars have observed that the word for "one" refers to a unity "in action and not in person," but others believe that the accusation of blasphemy which the Jews directed against Jesus (vs. 32–33) is evidence that John did present Jesus as having made some metaphysical statement about his relationship to God. Still other scholars feel that the doctrine of the Logos set forth in the Prologue is now placed on the lips of Jesus.

A real hint at the kind of unity about which Jesus is speaking may be discovered in his discourse on the unity he prays will exist in his church (17:11). Jesus prays that his disciples (sheep) will be in unity with the shepherd as he is one with God.

The declaration in v. 30 is filled with the mystery of the divine nature of Christ. The christological meaning of this stupendous claim is best understood in the light of the image of Jesus as the Shepherd who lays down his life for the sheep. The Son has demonstrated his unity with the Father through his loving obedience to the will of his Father. In love and obedience, Jesus is united with the Father's love for God's children. Through his intimate relationship to God, Jesus has revealed the nature of God the Father—redemptive, suffering love. Is that not what Jesus means when he declares elsewhere: "He who has seen me has seen the Father" (John 14:9)?

Study v. 24, "How long will you keep us in suspense?" in several translations or in the Greek. Note the tone. Do a word study of "suspense" (v. 24), "plainly" (v. 24), and "snatch" (v. 29). Note the textual problem in v. 29. A review of several interpretations of v. 30, "I and the Father are one," would be very helpful.

The sermon might focus on the way Jesus has revealed his claim to be Messiah through his words and deeds. Examples from his teachings to the Samaritan woman and the man born blind and others may be noted. Or the sermon might examine the great christological claim, "I and the Father are one." You might want to note some of the ways this verse has been interpreted by others and then share your own perspective.

Acts 13:15-16, 26-33 (C) (E)

Acts 13:15-16a, 26-33 (L)

Acts 13:14, 43-52 (RC)

Acts 13 contains Paul's first recorded sermon and the longest sample in the New Testament of his preaching. Luke has most probably given the basic thrust of Paul's thought in a digested version and not his actual words. The words appear more Lukan than Pauline. This sermon, which Paul delivered at Pisidian Antioch, brought a reaction from two groups of listeners, the Jews and the God-fearing Gentiles. Their reaction (vs. 42-52) set the course for Paul's future missionary journeys.

By the time Paul and Barnabas reached Antioch, Paul had become the leader of the missionary group. John Mark had decided to return to Jerusalem. They entered the synagogue on the Sabbath day. After the recitation of the Shema, prayer and readings from the Law and the Prophets, the leaders of the synagogue, according to their custom when a distinguished guest was present, asked Paul and Barnabas if they would like to speak. Paul took advantage of this opportunity and shared the good news about Christ with them.

Paul's sermon is similar to the one Luke records in Acts 2 which was preached by Simon Peter. It has basically three divisions: (1) God's preparations for the coming Messiah (vs. 17-25), (2) the Gospel message of the death and resurrection of Christ (vs. 26-37), (3) the challenge to the hearers to respond (vs. 38-41).

The first part of the sermon lays the historical base for the preparation of the coming of the Messiah through the judges, prophets, and John the Baptist. The second part of the sermon (vs. 26-37) presents the basic pattern for apostolic preaching: how prophecy has been fulfilled, the innocent nature of the crucified Christ, how the death of Jesus was part of God's divine plan, how God raised Jesus from the dead in vindication of his obedient sacrifice, and how the risen Christ was witnessed by a number of people.

Paul declares that the Jewish rulers did not understand the real nature of what they had done to Jesus, because they did not recognize that he was God's Anointed One. Paul stresses that Jesus was truly dead and laid in a tomb. The resurrection of Christ was proof that God's promises could not be defeated. God's raising of Jesus from the dead demonstrates the undefeatable power of God.

The resurrection was seen as the final proof that Jesus was God's chosen Messiah. Paul then quotes from Psalm 2:7 to prove that Jesus was God's chosen one and from Isaiah 55:3 and Psalm 16:10 to prove he was raised from the dead. In the witnesses to the resurrection, it is interesting that Paul does not list himself, as he did in 1 Corinthians 9:1 and 15:8, as a witness to the risen Lord.

After the service, many of the worshipers followed Paul and Barnabas out of the synagogue and urged the missionaries to tell them more. Paul was asked to speak again the next week. The next Sabbath the synagogue was packed with people who came to hear Paul. The Jews recognized the radical nature of Paul's messages and began to interrupt his sermon and challenge his interpretation of the scriptures. They began to call Paul and Barnabas names and tried to turn the people against them.

Many of the Jewish people rejected the gospel. Paul noted that he first made his appeal to the Jews, but, "since you thrust it from you, and judge yourselves unworthy of eternal life, behold, we turn to the Gentiles" (v. 46). In response to the antagonistic behavior of the Jews at Antioch, Paul and Barnabas declared that they would turn away from the Jews who refused to hear the good news about God's salvation through Christ and turn instead to the Gentiles. They based their authority for such a decision on a passage from Isaiah 49:6. More than a proof text, this quote was noted to point to Jesus as the one who had fulfilled God's servant role for his people.

This was a momentous point in the ministry of Paul and Barnabas. Recognizing that the Jews were not going to accept the Gospel message, they turned to the Gentiles. Until this moment, the gospel had been preached to the Jews in the synagogues. The Gentiles who had been converted to Christ had come through the synagogues, but Paul and Barnabas realized that this was not true for many of the Gentiles who responded that day to Christ.

Paul's announcement that they were going to take their message to the Gentiles was received with great hostility from the Jews. The Jews stirred up the "devout women of high standing and the leading men of the city" (v. 50), probably Gentiles of the upper class who became allies with them against Paul and Barnabas. They then drove Paul and Barnabas out of Antioch, but before they did, Paul and Barnabas saw the joyful response of the Gentiles to the gospel (v. 48). The word of God spread throughout Pisidia because of the response of the Gentiles.

The two apostles left Antioch, after shaking the dust off their feet, demonstrating their release from responsibility for the decision the Jews had made there. They had proclaimed the good news of Christ to the Jewish community, and the Jews there had rejected the message. The blame for the Jews' action was their own and not the burden of Paul and Barnabas. (Note Luke 10:19–21.)

After they were ejected from the town by the Jews, Luke makes a strange observation: "And the disciples were filled with joy" (v. 52). Even after experiencing anger, scorn, denunciation, persecution, and ejection from the city, the disciples rejoiced, because they had seen God's salvation come into the lives of new believers. They had witnessed the great power of God's salvation.

Compare Paul's preaching to Simon Peter's sermon in Acts 2. Study the messianic references in Isaiah 49:6; Isaiah 55:3; Psalm 2:7 and 16:10.

The sermon might focus on the inclusive nature of the saving grace of God which is available for all persons who believe. Note how all persons—Jew or Gentile, male or female—have the privilege of responding to God's grace. Like the Jews at Antioch, no one is forced to respond, but the good news of God's saving love is available for all who will accept it.

Revelation 7:9–17 (C) (L) (E)

Revelation 7:9, 14b–17 (RC)

John has just finished describing the church militant in vs. 1–8. The number 144,000 in his discussion is a whole number which stands for all true believers. The seal on the forehead of all the believers is drawn from the Passover images of the blood of the lamb which the Israelites placed on the doorpost of their houses to protect them from the death angel. This seal does not protect the Christian from suffering or death but from the judgment of God.

From the church militant, John then turns to the church triumphant. Here John gives his readers a glance into the heavenly state of the believers which he expounds more completely in chapters 21 and 22. Many scholars have identified the "great multitude" with the early Christian martyrs. Rather than focusing merely on those who died for their faith, John is more likely writing to encourage the whole church to remain faithful to Christ in the midst of their "tribulation." All those who remain faithful to Christ under persecution are included in this number and not just the martyrs.

Several interesting features about this "great multitude" are noted by John: (1) The multitude was countless. The promise by God to Abraham that his seed would be countless as the stars is fulfilled in the church. (2) The multitude is universal and inclusive. All tribes, peoples, and tongues from all nations are represented. (3) The multitude stands in God's presence, "before the throne and before the Lamb." (4) The white robes of the multitude are a sign of victory and the cleansing which they received from the Lamb. (5) The palm branches which the multitude holds are another symbol for victory and triumph. (6) They praise God and the Lamb for their salvation or victory. In these last three images, John is drawing upon the common practices which were seen in the Roman military victory celebrations to depict symbols of triumph for the church.

Encircling the throne of God were angels, the elders, and the four living creatures who joined the praise of the multitude. In their praise, they ascribed blessing, glory, wisdom, honor, power, thanksgiving, and strength to God. They have given a litany of praise to God which could serve as a directive for all Christians in worship.

The elder asked for the identity of the multitude. John describes them as the persons who have come out of the great tribulation. John is trying to give his readers a vision to see beyond their present suffering and persecution, "great tribulation," to the promised glory which awaits them with God. It is a great misunderstanding of John's purpose in writing his letter to see it as a vision about some future suffering and not to see it as a positive word of comfort and encouragement to his present readers.

In some powerful theological images and beautiful poetry, John depicts the redeemed Christians, who come out of the tribulation, as wearing white robes which have been cleansed by the blood of the Lamb. Although the image of dirty clothes being washed white in blood sounds strange to us, John was drawing his symbolism from Old Testament images of dirty clothing as an image of an unclean life, sins that are red as crimson, made white as wool (Isa. 1:18; 64:6; Ex. 19:10; Zech. 3:4). The blood of the Lamb symbolizes the powerful cleansing effectiveness of the redeeming death of Christ on the cross.

The phrase "before the throne of God" (v. 15) indicates that the multitude has now realized their desire to be in the presence of God. They are sheltered by God's presence and their spiritual and physical needs are now satisfied, "they shall hunger no more, neither thirst any more" (v. 16). They will no longer be victims of the blazing desert sun. They will no longer be uncomfortable and suffer. Their hunger, thirst, pain, and sorrow have come to an end. The Lamb will guide them to springs of living water (Ps. 23:2) to satisfy their spiritual quests. The tender care of the Lamb is seen in the phrase "wipe away every tear from their eyes" (v. 17).

John uses a paradoxical figure when he declares that "the Lamb . . . will be their shepherd" (v. 17). The sacrificial Lamb has become the Shepherd to guide his flock, the church. Another paradoxical image is used in the "Lamb in the midst of the throne." Here the humble lamb has become a ruling king. The divine Shepherd (John 10:11, 14) has the power to give his sheep, his church, real life.

John does not depict the redeemed as living eternally in idleness in heaven. He pictures the great multitude continuing their service for God. The redeemed "serve him [God] day and night" (v. 15). The Lamb of God has cleansed us from our sins to serve him.

Examine some of the Old Testament passages about dirty clothes as an image about purifying one's life and one's sins though red as crimson being washed white as wool (check Isa. 1:18; 64:6; Ex. 19:10; Zech. 3:4).

The sermon might focus on the image "the Lamb . . . will be their Shepherd." The paradoxical nature of this figure should be noted. It would be helpful to include a discussion of the redeeming, guiding and ruling nature of Christ as the Lamb and Shepherd in the midst of the throne. Or the sermon might focus on "the church triumphant." Here the vision of the future victory and glory of the redeemed can be expounded.

Theological Reflection

One of the common theological themes in all these passages is the redemptive suffering of Christ. In John's Gospel the focus is on the misunderstanding of the Jewish people in their concept of the Messiah. Jesus had told them through his words and deeds that the Messiah would have to suffer and die. The image of the suffering Messiah is more applied than stated. Paul's sermon in the Book of Acts relates the picture of the suffering Christ and the impact it has on the decision to share the gospel with the Gentiles. In the Book of Revelation the vision of the robes washed in the blood of the Lamb symbolizes the suffering of Christ in a beautiful, paradoxical figure.

Children's Message

The children's talk might develop the theme of Christ as the Good Shepherd. Tell the children about the care, guidance, and protection that a shepherd gives his sheep. You might want to tell about the shepherd's personal knowledge of the sheep and how they follow him because they trust him and know his voice. Help them to see how the characteristics of the shepherd are applied to Christ as the Good Shepherd in the way he loves, guides, and cares for us.

Hymns for Easter 4

In Christ There Is No East or West; Ten Thousand Times Ten Thousand; Behold the Lamb of God.

Psalm 145:13b–21 (C)   Revelation 21:1–6 (C)
                          Revelation 21:1–5 (L)
Acts 14:8–18 (C)   Revelation 21:1–5a (RC)
Acts 13:44–52 (L) (E)   Revelation 19:1, 4–9 (E)
Acts 14:21b–27 (RC)

                          John 13:31–35 (C) (L) (E)
                          John 13:31–33a, 34–35 (RC)

Meditation on the Texts

O God of love and grace, you have commanded us to love one another. Forgive us for our unwillingness to love others and accept them as you have loved and accepted us. Your creative world speaks volumes to us about your design and order. Thank you for such grace and guidance. May your church respond to your directive for us to strengthen our fellowship with gifted leaders and dedicated servants. We open ourselves to the new creation which you bring to us individually and to your church. Transform us into your image by your redeeming grace. We lift our praises to you and rejoice that we have the assurance that in the new order of your eternal kingdom, we will be free of tears, pain, suffering, and death. We live and die with confidence in your eternal reign. Amen.

Commentary on the Texts

John 13:31–35 (C) (L) (E)

John 13:31–33a, 34–35 (RC)

This pericope begins with the departure of Judas from the upper room where Jesus had gathered with his disciples to observe the Passover. Judas had not been rejected by Jesus but left by his own free choice. He left to betray Jesus. The course was now certain; the crucifixion was inevitable. Jesus' "hour" had now come. The Son of Man would be glorified in his death on the cross. Jesus had not sought personal glory for himself but was obedient to God's will which led to the cross.

The glory of Jesus was in his sacrifice when he was "lifted up" on the cross. Jesus glorified God by emptying himself, and in glorifying God, Jesus participated in that glory. The humiliating betrayal by Judas set the wheels in motion that led to Jesus' death and ironically his glorification (17:4–5). God is glorified in the sacrificial death of Jesus, because it is a revelation of God's love for humanity. This glorification is both a past event (the Son of Man has been glorified) and a future event (God will glorify him).

After Judas leaves, Jesus speaks to the disciples about his own leaving and they are perplexed. In the discourse that follows, he assures them that they will be in the Father's house forever (14:2–3). His time was at hand and he had to walk a path of suffering that no one else could walk for him. His entrance into God's glory would separate him from the disciples for a while.

The atmosphere in the upper room was charged with tenderness, love, affection, and sadness. Jesus, knowing that this would be his last discourse with his disciples before his crucifixion, gives a special word. "I give you a new commandment," Jesus said (v. 34, NEB). What was the purpose of this new commandment? Jesus stated its purpose very clearly: His disciples are to love one another.

What is new about that? Was not love for other persons taught in the Old Testament? When Jesus summarized the law, he declared that the essence of the law was to love God with all of your heart, soul, mind, strength, and the second commandment was similar to the first, "Love your neighbor as yourself." There are powerful teachings about love in the Old Testament. This teaching did not deny or reject those teachings. Communities like the one in Qumran taught their followers, "Love all the children."

What is new about this commandment? Some scholars have suggested that this was the first time Jesus taught this view to his disciples—perhaps, but this seems unlikely. Maybe the newness is realized in conjunction with the whole meaning of what happened that night at the Last Supper. This commandment is new as a part of the new covenant which was established at that meal. The Last Supper depicted a new relationship which was being established with God. There was a freshness surrounding this commandment.

The extent of this love is depicted in the words "one another." "You disciples are to love one another." This is a love that is different from the love for a neighbor or an enemy. The scope of this love is the love of Christian followers for each other. Here is a part of the newness. Jesus' disciples are to love each other in a way that is different from the world's understanding of love.

This love is founded on the oneness we have experienced within our relationship to Christ. When we stand at the foot of the cross, all barriers are down. All Christians are brothers and sisters in Christ. Paul would describe this relationship by saying: "There is neither Jew nor Greek, there is neither slave nor free, there is neither male nor female; for you are all one in Christ Jesus" (Gal. 3:28). Jesus Christ binds us into a new unity. Christians are brothers and sisters in one family, whether we are Americans, Germans, French, black, white, men, or women. We are bound together in a fellowship of brotherhood and sisterhood by the blood of Christ. His sacrificial death has drawn us into a community built on love. Christ's death establishes a community of grace. We have first experienced love through Christ's love, and love each other as we have been loved.

Jesus has called his followers not to a philosophy but to a way of life. Our creeds are reflected in our deeds. Love is expressed more in actions than words. We cannot separate faith and works. James says, "Show me your faith apart from your works, and I by my works will show you my faith" (James 2:18). The real evidence that we are Christians is demonstrated in our love for others, especially those within the fellowship of faith. This is the test. If we do not love one another, we are not Christians. Jesus is clear on the matter. Doctrines, creeds, laws, ideas are not the test. We pass or fail as his disciples in the way we love our fellow Christians. Love is the fulfilling of the law.

Do a word study of glorification, my children, and new commandment.

The sermon might develop the words of Jesus, "I give you a new commandment." Note the newness of this commandment compared to the commandments taught in the Old Testament. Stress the radical difference that should exist in the love Christians have for one another within the Christian church. The sacrificial death of Christ has founded a community built on inclusive love.

Acts 14:8–18 (C)

Luke relates an interesting experience Paul and Barnabas had in Lystra. A man who had been lame since birth gave some evidence of faith to Paul, and Paul healed him. The crowd was stirred by the man's healing and began to exclaim in their native Lycaonian dialect that they believed that Paul and Barnabas were gods come to earth in human form. They thought Barnabas was Zeus and Paul, because he was the chief speaker, was Hermes. The crowds summoned the local priest who brought oxen and garlands to the gates. The priests were making preparations to offer sacrifices to Paul and Barnabas as gods.

Paul and Barnabas had watched all the reaction of the excited people but were unable to understand what they were saying because of the unfamiliar Lycaonian language. When they finally heard someone speaking in Greek and realized what a mistake was being made, they immediately protested by tearing their garments in typical Eastern fashion. They shouted with a loud voice: "Men, why are you doing this? We also are men, of like nature with you" (v. 15).

Then Paul delivered a brief sermon, which shows his approach to preaching the gospel to pagans who had no knowledge of the Old Testament. He started with the pagan knowledge of nature and God as the Creator of all things. He urged them to turn away from their idols. He states that they were not without witness and that God had been known by his goodness in the past. Even the pagans had revelation of God.

At this point, Luke does not present Paul completing his sermon. He was likely going to witness to Jesus as the one through whom God was made known. The crowd may have interrupted the sermon and Paul was not able to finish it, or Luke simply did not relate the rest of the sermon for some reason. The sermon Paul delivered at Areopagus in Athens (17:22–31) is another example of Paul's preaching to pagans.

The Lystrans were so stirred up by the healing of this crippled man that they never got an opportunity to hear the good news of the gospel. Like others today, they tried to identify the good news with old familiar concepts or forms. They also tried to glorify the message bearers rather than the Lord they were proclaiming, but Paul and Barnabas had too much integrity to allow the misunderstanding that they were gods to go unchallenged.

A brief study of the Greek gods Zeus and Hermes might provide helpful background.

The sermon might focus on the tendency of many people to try to press the good news into old categories which are familiar and acceptable to them. The radical nature of the good news needs to be heralded with clarity and assurance.

Acts 13:44–52 (L) (E)

See Easter 4, (RC).

Acts 14:21b–27 (RC)

Paul and Barnabas had to leave Lystra because of the persecution of some Jews who arrived there from Antioch and Iconium. They stirred the crowds and got them to stone Paul and drag him outside the city thinking he was dead (14:19), but Paul was not dead, and shortly he and Barnabas returned again to Lystra, Iconium, and Antioch. It is uncertain why they were allowed to return. They may have come in secret or new leaders may have been in charge of the cities, but it does show the courage and determination of these missionaries to share the gospel of Christ with others.

Four things were accomplished by this missionary journey to these three cities: (1) Paul and Barnabas strengthened the small group of Christians to face the persecutions that would inevitably come to them. They helped them to see that the way of Christ was the way of the cross and suffering (v. 22). (2) They appointed leaders, elders, to guide the new Christians in these churches. The word "appointed" literally means "choosing by a show of hands." Some scholars are not certain if this was the actual meaning of the Greek word in Luke's day. Others feel that Paul and Barnabas likely selected the elders. In a service of prayer and fasting, the elders were set apart. Whatever the process was, elders were chosen to guide the young church. From the beginning, the community was a vital factor in the role of the church. (3) In all of their travels they stressed the work of God through them and others and did not focus on their sufferings or difficulties. They saw themselves as working with God. (4) They emphasized that God had opened "a door of faith to the Gentiles" (v. 27). Gentiles could already become Jewish proselytes through the rite of circumcision and keeping of the law, but Paul saw a new door that was opened to the Gentiles by faith in Jesus Christ. This was too radical for the Jews, and consequently they made every effort to stop Paul's work. Chapter 15 shows how acute this problem became in the church.

Examine the root meanings of the words "appointed" and "elders."

The sermon might focus on the "open door of faith to the Gentiles" and stress the opportunity for all persons to respond to God's salvation through Christ. Or the sermon might stress the suffering Christians often have to encounter in their journey of following the Lord. The cross cannot be removed from genuine discipleship.

Revelation 21:1–5a (RC)

In this section of the Apocalypse, John turns to his vision of the new heaven and earth. What he envisions is not merely a reformation of what has been but something completely new in quality. Isaiah had spoken about such a new creation (Isa. 65:17). The former "had passed away." In a remarkably beautiful and brief passage of only about a hundred words, John presents his vision of the new order. In this vision John reaches a climax not only to the message of his book but to the quest of the human soul.

The phrase "and the sea was no more" (v. 1) expressed several things for John. In a sense, it was autobiographical since John's imprisonment on the Isle of Patmos had separated him from his Christian friends. But more than that, the sea represented chaos and destruction in the ancient world. Drawing on mythological images of the dragon arising out of the sea (13:1), John depicts the sea as symbolizing evil and the enemy. The sea was the place where the forces of evil lived. The end of the sea meant the end to the forces that were hostile to God and humanity.

John envisions not only a new heaven but a new earth. Out of this new creation comes a new city. In the midst of persecution and suffering, John comforts his readers with his vision of a new and holy city—the New Jerusalem. This new city is not the result of human restoration of the old city but is a completely new city which comes "down out of heaven." The New Jerusalem is personified as a bride who is adorned for Christ. The New Jerusalem is a lovely bride which stands in vivid contrast to the harlot, city of Babylon (Rome), which he had described earlier in chapters 17 and 18.

"A loud voice from the throne" proclaims the joyful news: "See, the home of God is among mortals" (v. 3, NRSV). Here in the New Jerusalem the Shekinah glory of God was fulfilled. This is a declaration that the fellowship which man/woman had with God in the Garden of Eden has been restored (Gen. 2:15–22). Heaven is a place where Christians enjoy the presence of God directly. "He will dwell with them, and they shall be his people, and God himself will be with them" (v. 3). The word "dwelling-place" literally means "tent" or "tabernacle." The One who "pitched his tent" among us in the incarnation has now established his eternal Tabernacle where we will see his glory forever (Jer. 31:33; Ezek. 37:12).

The presence of God does not bring judgment but concern and comfort. A litany of things that will be no more are announced: Sorrow will be ended—"he will wipe away every tear from their eyes," death is vanquished—"death shall be no more," grief and suffering will not exist—"neither shall there be mourning nor crying nor pain any more." God gives life which cannot be touched by pain, suffering, or death. Here is the fulfillment of Isaiah's dream when he wrote centuries ago: "I will rejoice in Jerusalem, and be glad in my people; no more shall be heard in it the sound of weeping and the cry of distress" (Isa. 65:19). With the coming of the new creation—the New Jerusalem, the old order—the former things have passed away.

For the first time in the Apocalypse, God speaks from the throne. "Behold, I make all things new" (v. 5). In the first creation, God said: "Let there be. . . . And it was so" (Gen. 1:3, 7). Here the angel of God instructs John to record that the message from God that all things would be new was "trustworthy and true" (v. 5). This newness of God has been manifested in the risen Christ and guaranteed by the faithfulness of God. The words "I make" denote the future activity of God, but this action is based on the redeeming work of Christ. The apostle Paul expressed this same truth in his words: "If any person is in Christ, he or she is a new creature" (see 2 Cor. 5:17).

The words "It is done!" (v. 6) echo the triumphant words of Jesus on the cross when he exclaimed: "It is finished" (John 19:30). From the throne in heaven, God declares that the work of redemption is complete and the new order has fully come. The goal of history has finally been realized. The concluding curtain has fallen on the last act which reveals that the new creation has become a reality.

At this point John repeats the claim Christ made in 1:8, "I am the Alpha and the Omega, the beginning and the end'' (v. 6). Alpha is the first letter of the Greek alphabet and omega is the last. The phrase, "the beginning and the end" states the same truth in a slightly different way. God is the source or origin of all things. There is no existence apart from God. John is stressing that God, as the Omega or end, is the goal or consummation of all things. The beginning, the intermediary process, and the ultimate goal are all under the guiding presence of God.

Do a word study of dwelling of God, new creation, the sea, New Jerusalem, and Alpha and Omega.

The sermon might describe the vision of "the new Jerusalem" where there will be no tears, pain, suffering, or death. Show how the presence of God is depicted in this passage as the One who dwells within this new city. Or the sermon might develop the theme about the redeeming grace of God expressed in the figure of "the Alpha and the Omega."

Revelation 19:1, 4–9 (E)

In this passage the scene opens with a limitless host singing a song of jubilation over the destruction of the great harlot—Babylon (Rome). This victory song is raised because the arrogant early empire which has persecuted the church has been defeated and judged. This host, consisting of thousands of angels, the twenty-four elders, and the four living creatures around the throne of God, break forth with the cry: "Hallelujah!" "Te deum laudamus." We praise thee, O God.

The word "hallelujah" literally means "praise God." Hallelujah is frequently rendered in a translated form in the psalms (for example, Ps. 146–150), but this chapter is the only place in the New Testament where it is found. Handel's great oratorio, *The Messiah,* has expressed some of the spirit of this passage. This doxology makes four affirmations about God: (1) God is praised because the Lord's salvation, glory, and power have been recognized and acknowledged. (2) The multitude praises God's true and just judgments. (3) They praise God's judgment on the great harlot—Rome. (4) The servants, who have been faithful unto death, praise God because the faithful have been avenged by God's judgment against Rome.

In the second outpouring of praise, the servants (the prophets, see 10:7) and martyrs (19:2) and the small and great—all Christians—join in the hallelujah to God (v. 5). Then the whole host of the redeemed break into a shout of praise that God's reign is clearly seen. They rejoice that the marriage of the Lamb to his bride, the church, is now at hand. The metaphor of marriage was often employed in the Old Testament as a figure of God's love for Israel. The figure of the church as the bride of Christ is a familiar New Testament image (see Matt. 22:1–11; John 3:29; Eph. 5:22–27).

The Lamb's bride, the church, stands in contrast to the great harlot (ch. 17). The harlot had been clothed in garments of purple, gold, and scarlet, while the church is clothed in "fine linen, bright and pure," the righteous deeds of the saints (v. 8). The faithful service of the redeemed is the "clothing" which symbolizes the wedding gown of the Lamb's bride. Their works have revealed their faith (James 2:17–26).

This pericope concludes with a beatitude, "Blessed are those who are invited to the marriage supper of the Lamb" (v. 9). John implies that the anticipated Jewish messianic banquet is realized in the marriage feast of the Lamb and his bride. This picture affirms that the kingdom of God has truly come.

Do a word study of hallelujah and the messianic banquet.

The sermon might focus on the church's call to praise God during all the circumstances of life. Praise can always be offered to God because the Christian is assured of God's faithfulness and triumphant reign.

Theological Reflection

The new commandment, "Love one another," which Jesus gave to his disciples in the upper room continues to be the major imperative for Christians in the church today. Love for one another is the genuine test of our allegiance to our Lord. The story in Acts reminds us of the constant temptation to clothe the gospel in contemporary images which reduce it to our own familiar views and cause us not to understand the radically new creation

God's salvation brings. The reading from Acts 14:21b–27 reminds us of the importance of securing effective leadership and direction for new and established churches. The vision from the Apocalypse assures us of the new creation that God will establish, which will be free of pain, suffering, grief, and death. At the throne of God Christians will offer praise for God's glory, power, and salvation and rejoice because God's reign has finally come.

Children's Message

The talk with the children might deal with Jesus' new commandment to his disciples, "Love one another." Emphasis can be placed on the necessity of those within the Christian community to express the kind of love for each other which Christ showed to them through his sacrificial love. An example that might be familiar to the children is forgiving someone who has said something to hurt their feelings. Help them to see Christ as our model for love.

Hymns for Easter 5

Holy God, We Praise Your Name; Rejoice, Ye Pure in Heart!; Jerusalem the Golden; They'll Know We Are Christians by Our Love (*Hymns for the Family of God*).

Psalm 67 (C)

Revelation 21:10, 22–27 (C)
Revelation 21:10–14, 22–23 (L) (RC)

Acts 15:1–2, 22–29 (C) (RC)
Acts 14:8–18 (L) (E)

Revelation 21:22–22:5 (E)

John 14:23–29

Meditation on the Texts

Eternal Spirit of God, guide us into deeper insights in the teachings of our Lord. May your presence be so real to us that your way will be clear for us to follow. We praise you that our redemption is based not on our own efforts or the result of fulfilling traditional rules but on your love and grace which we see manifested in the death of your Son on the cross. May the vision of your heavenly city which John described in the Apocalypse be so vivid to us that we will long to kneel before your throne in the glorious city and behold your face. Help us to live lives that will reveal our longing to drink from the river of the water of life and to eat from the fruit of the tree of life and praise you forever. Amen.

Commentary on the Texts

John 14:23–29

See also the Day of Pentecost, (C).

Love is one of the key words throughout John's Gospel and he returns to that theme in this pericope. Jesus links love and obedience. In v. 23 Jesus reasserts what he has said earlier in v. 15, "If you love me, you will keep my commandments." It is essential to keep the word of Jesus if one wants to experience the love of God. "We will come" (v. 23) notes that God the Father is also present in the coming of the Son. The word "home" or "abode" calls to mind the Old Testament concept of God dwelling with humanity (Ex. 29:45). John has returned to his emphasis on the unity and intimacy of God the Father and Jesus. The two are so united that the love for one is an expression of love for the other.

In v. 24 the reverse is noted. Not to obey Jesus is disobedience of God and is the rejection of God's presence. Jesus is bold to claim, "The word which you hear is not mine but the Father's who sent me" (v. 24). Just as Jesus had lived his life in obedience to God, he stated that it was essential for his disciples to live their lives in obedience to his word if they were to have the divine presence of God lodge within them. Obedient love opens the respondent to a deeper experience of the presence of God. The more one obeys God, the more God is revealed to that person.

Jesus indicated that his personal ministry in the flesh was about to come to an end: "These things I have spoken to you, while I am still with you" (v. 25). At the same moment, Jesus proclaims the coming of the Paraclete (Counselor, RSV). In v. 16 the first of five references to the Paraclete is mentioned (see also 14:26; 15:26; 16:7–11, 12–15). The Greek word means "one called alongside." This word cannot be translated precisely into English. In secular society the term "paraclete" was used in the court system for one who was called to help another plead a difficult case, but it never became an official term for a professional legal adviser. "Comforter" (KJV) is not a good modern translation for Paraclete. Originally the word "comforter" came from a Latin word which meant "strong" or "brave." Comforter today has a different meaning, one who comforts a person in sorrow. This is inadequate for the rich meaning of Paraclete. Neither is the RSV use of "Counselor" really adequate. This word as well comes from a Latin root meaning "to give advice." The work of the Holy Spirit is much more comprehensive than that.

Another note from v. 16 is helpful here. Jesus said that the Father would give "another Paraclete." The implication is that Jesus himself was a Paraclete and that at his departure God would send another Paraclete to continue his ministry with the disciples. Jesus' earthly mission was soon coming to an end, John notes, and the ministry of the Paraclete was not to be "for ever" (v. 16). The words of v. 18, "I will not leave you desolate; I will come to you," have led some scholars to conclude that the Paraclete whom God will send (v. 26) is really the ascended Christ.

In v. 26 God "will send" the Spirit in "my [Jesus'] name." Here the work of the Spirit and of Jesus are allied. John has noted earlier that Jesus was "sent" by God (for example, 6:38–40; 12:44–49). The Spirit is also sent by God. Jesus declared that he had come "in the name" of the Father (5:43) and the Spirit is sent "in the name" of Jesus. The reference in v. 26 (italics added), "*he* will teach you all things," indicates the personal nature of the Spirit. Verses 16–31 have been the focus of much creedal debate over whether the Spirit "proceeds from the Father" or "proceeds from the Father and the Son." Space does not permit a discussion of this theological debate, but it would be helpful to **read the discussion** which Gerard S. Sloyan in *John,* Interpretation series (Atlanta: John Knox Press, 1987), George R. Beasley-Murray in the *Word Biblical Commentary on John* (Irving, Tex.: Word Books, 1987), and others have to say on these passages dealing with the Paraclete.

The task of the Paraclete, Jesus said, is twofold: (1) "to teach you all things and (2) "to bring to your remembrance all that I have said to you." The Christian disciple will always be a learner, eager to grow more deeply in the knowledge of Christ and his way. As Jesus had taught his disciples while he was on earth, God's Spirit would continue to guide them in the knowledge of his words.

The coming Paraclete, Jesus noted secondly, would reawaken his disciples to the revelation he had already taught them. This is still being done in a special way as God's Spirit has used the scriptures through the ages to enable new disciples to recall the teachings of Jesus. The Gospel of John is itself an inspired product of a disciple, remembering what Jesus taught and how he lived and died, and then this instrument of remembering becomes a means through which God's Spirit continues to work to reach others with the good news.

The special gift or legacy Jesus promised his disciples was peace. The word "peace" which Jesus used was the familiar greeting "shalom." This was commonly used when people met or departed. At this time the Roman world claimed that its mighty military power had brought about peace. This was called the Pax Romana. Roman peace was controlled by force and many people were enslaved under Roman dominance, but the kind of peace which Jesus gave did not depend on external conditions. The reign of Christ does not offer a peace that provides an escape from the difficulties and problems of life, but an inner security that rests on God's saving grace (Phil. 4:7; Rom. 5:1).

Jesus affirmed: "Peace I leave with you; my peace I give to you; not as the world gives do I give to you. Let not your hearts be troubled, neither let them be afraid" (v. 27). Calmly, Jesus urged his disciples not to be disquieted because he would soon be leaving. This was only *au revoir* because God the Father was sending the Spirit. Jesus' absence would be filled by the Spirit, who would continue his work. Jesus was telling them again about his approaching death and his return in a victorious presence following the resurrection.

If the disciples really understood what was going to happen, they would rejoice (v. 28). Jesus would return to his Father who would send the Spirit to guide them always. The peace that Jesus gives provides inner strength and joy because it is based on the assurance that God is in control of all things. Nothing separates us from that love (Rom. 8:38–39).

Throughout this chapter and in other places in John's Gospel, Jesus' unity with God the Father is affirmed (1:1–18; 10:30; 20:28). The words in v. 28b, "the Father is greater than I," have been debated since the Arian controversy. Some scholars have concluded that this reference reflects the obedience of the Son to the Father which the incarnation entailed. Others see it as a reflection of the Father sending, supporting, and asking obedience of the Son. Others see this as a reference to the Son's destination with the Father in glory, where he is released from his earthly limitations.

Still other scholars see this verse as an indication that the Son is once more absorbed into the Divine Oneness of God which overshadows his earthly manifestation of divinity. The mystery of the Trinity is apparent. Jesus declared elsewhere that the Father and the Son are "one" (10:30). He also said (in 13:16) that the One who sent him is greater than he and again (in 14:28), "I go to the Father; for the Father is greater than I." This brief discussion indicates that the preacher will have to labor long over these verses to grasp the profound theological mystery here.

Do a word study of abode, Paraclete, peace, teach, and "bring to your remembrance." A special study, using a Bible and theological dictionary, such as *The Interpreter's Dictionary of the Bible* edited by George A. Buttrick, would also be helpful.

The sermon might explore the nature and work of the Paraclete, the Holy Spirit. It might be helpful to speak about the difficulty of translating Paraclete into English to retain its original meaning. The twofold ministry of the Paraclete, of teaching and of reminding the disciples of the sayings of Jesus should be stressed.

Acts 15:1–2, 22–29 (C) (RC)

Many modern preachers might want to avoid Acts 15 because it deals with a church quarrel. "There's enough quarreling in the church. Why read about these first-century church fights today?" someone might argue. As strange as it may seem to many of us, this early church's debate became a crucial turning point in the life of the church. A group of Judaizers from Judea (likely Jerusalem) came down to the churches of Antioch, Syria, and Cilicia and began to insist that the Gentile Christians had to keep the law of Moses by being circumcised or they would not be saved.

Many Gentiles were becoming Christians by accepting Jesus as the Messiah by faith. Some Jewish members of these churches believed that these Gentiles had to become Jews before they could become Christians. Paul and Barnabas entered into a heated debate over this issue. The Judaizers said that circumcision was a tangible proof of a person's conversion and evidence of his desire to keep the law. If the Judaizers had been successful, Christianity would have become merely a sect of Judaism and soon might have disappeared.

The argument reached a high peak in the church at Antioch as Paul and Barnabas challenged the views of the Judaizers. These Pharisees demanded that the Gentiles had to keep the Jewish law, the Torah, and be circumcised. The church at Antioch was so torn apart by this debate that the church decided to appoint Paul and Barnabas to go to Jerusalem, which was the base for apostolic authority, to see if the apostles and elders there could settle this divisive issue. The issue was paramount. Was salvation the gift of God by grace or was it the result of works?

A council was held with representatives from the Jerusalem and Antioch churches. Luke indicates that much debate transpired. But in a few verses, Luke explains to Theophilus how the matter was resolved. Simon Peter spoke first, pointing to his experience with Cornelius, and argued that the law would be a yoke too heavy for converts to bear. He concluded by declaring that salvation for the Jew or Gentile was by God's gift of grace and not by their keeping of the law (15:6–11).

Paul and Barnabas presented their argument by pointing to the signs and wonders that had been seen in God's blessing on the Gentiles (15:12). James, the brother of our Lord, was the head of the church in Jerusalem. James quoted the Septuagint version of Amos 9:11–12 to show that this ancient prophet had predicted the conversion of the Gentiles. James offered a compromise. He agreed with the Christians at Antioch that circumcision was unnecessary for the Gentile converts, but he did offer four abstentions for the Gentile. These demands would be pleasing to the Jewish Christians and also help the Gentile Christians to live moral lives. These restrictions were: (1) not to eat meat that had been offered to idols; (2) to be faithful in marriage and refrain from other sexual practices; (3) not to eat the meat of animals killed by strangulation; (4) to refrain from eating blood (15:20).

The big issue of circumcision was removed, but minimum requirements for certain ethical practices were deemed necessary to keep the Christians distinct from the rest of the pagan world. Gentiles did not have to become Jews, but they did have to live by moral values which reflected the high standards of the church's Lord.

The position of James seemed good to the Jerusalem church and they decided to follow his compromise (v. 22). The Jerusalem church in turn decided to send a delegation to Antioch with their decision. The church assembly chose Judas Barsabbas, possibly a relative of the Joseph who had been considered to fill Judas Iscariot's place as an apostle (1:23), and Silas, who later would travel with Paul on some of his missionary journeys. These men were preachers in the Jerusalem church and obviously noted for their character and dedication.

These two men carried the letter outlining the decision from the church in Jerusalem, and they were accompanied by Paul and Barnabas. If Paul and Barnabas had returned alone with the Jerusalem letter, it might not have been so warmly received. Since Judas and Silas were official emissaries of the Jerusalem church, they could explain the meaning of the letter and answer any questions the Antioch Christians might have.

When the Gentile Christians in Antioch, Syria, and Cilicia received the letter, they ''rejoiced at the exhortation'' (15:31). The legal restraints of Judaism would not be imposed on the Gentiles. Gentiles did not first have to become Jews before they could be Christians. This was more than a battle between conservatives and liberals in the young church. It was a pivotal decision about salvation. Paul and Barnabas were commended to the mission church as ''men who have risked their lives for the sake of the Lord Jesus Christ'' (v. 26), and this they would do on numerous other occasions.

The sermon might stress the importance of grace over works, drawing upon the attempt of the Judaizers to force Gentile converts to observe the Torah, and also noting the necessity for Christians of maintaining moral standards demonstrating that they had not adopted the values of the pagan society around them.

Acts 14:8–18 (L) (E)

See Easter 5, (C).

Revelation 21:10, 22–27 (C)

Revelation 21:10–14, 22–23 (L) (RC)

Revelation 21:22–22:5 (E)

Drawing on images that are similar to the vision in Ezekiel 40:2, John has a vision of being carried to a high mountain where he sees the city of God descending upon that mountain (v. 10). Some scholars believe that John's vision combines images that fulfill two traditions: the Old Testament prophecy and pagan Babylonian beliefs that viewed the mountain as the house where God lived (Ezek. 28:13–14). The Seer of Patmos saw this Holy City as meeting the deepest needs of all persons of all races. The messenger of God told John to write to the church at Philadelphia that the New Jerusalem would come down from God (3:12). This vision which unites heaven and earth shows that God's work of redemption is now complete.

The vision depicts the holy city of Jerusalem as radiating with the glory of God. The figure of ''a most rare jewel'' and ''jasper, clear as crystal,'' are images to stress the glory of God's presence in the city. The New Jerusalem is the Holy of Holies where God will ''tabernacle'' with humanity (21:3). God has been described as ''light'' (1 John 1:5), and the radiance of God's presence is the first impact the city makes. ''The city has no need of sun or moon . . . , for the glory of God is its light, and its lamp is the Lamb'' (v. 23).

After John's eyes adjust to the glittering light of the radiant heavenly city, he begins to see some of its other features. The city has a ''great, high wall'' around it. In Zechariah's version of the newly constructed Jerusalem, God declared: ''I will be to her a wall of fire round about'' (Zech. 2:5). The wall seems to be a symbol for the security of the saints within its bulwark.

Access to the city is made possible by twelve gates with the names of the twelve tribes of Israel written over them. Again John's vision is parallel to that of Ezekiel (48:30–35). There are three gates on each of the four sides of the heavenly city with an angel guarding each of the gates. Can these twelve gates not represent the completeness, variety, and catholicity of the church? The twelve tribes tie the New Jerusalem with the old covenant, but the twelve foundations of the city have inscribed on them "the twelve names of the twelve apostles," which denote the new covenant. The city is uniquely built upon the apostles and upon Israel's patriarchs.

The number twelve which appears throughout this section stands for wholeness or completeness. When John is told to measure the city (vs. 15–17), he measures 12,000 stadia by 12,000 by 12,000, which is a cube. The literalism of the measurement is not the chief emphasis. John is declaring that the city of God is large enough for all believers.

Few statements could have been more shocking to John's Jewish readers than his statement, "I saw no temple in the city" (v. 22). John's vision of the New Jerusalem without the temple was a reflection of the teachings of Jesus. Jesus had predicted the destruction of the temple in Jerusalem (Mark 13:2) and that another temple would be built without human hands (Mark 14:58). Some scholars have suggested that the risen Christ, the Lamb, is the symbol for the temple of God in the Holy City (John 2:21). The cube shape of the city (vs. 15–17) is another way that John may be describing the New Jerusalem as the Holy of Holies. It needs no temple because the whole city contains the presence of God. The temple had symbolized God's presence with Israel in the past, but in the Holy City God's presence would be with the believers in a unique way.

The glory of God and Christ as the light of the world (v. 23) are so powerful in their radiance that the sun and moon are absent. The Lamb is the lamp. There is "no night" (v. 25). Drawing on Isaiah 60:19–20, John tells his readers that night, which was held in great dread by ancient people because of its association with fear, danger, and evil, would be overcome by the glory of the Lord and the Lamb as the lamp.

The gates of the city are never shut and all nations and kings of the earth will worship God. This fulfills the hope of ancient prophets that the Gentiles will respond to God's grace (Zech. 2:11; 14:9; Isa. 2:2–4; 66:18–19; Dan. 7:14). It declares that the kings of earth, including Rome, will one day exclaim that Christ is "Lord of lords and King of kings" (17:14; cf. 19:16). This chapter ends with a warning that only those who are clean, who do not practice abominable things or use falsehoods and whose names are written in the Lamb's Book of Life will enter the city. The Holy City is pure and those who want to cling to their sins are excluded. Those whose names have been written in the Lamb's Book of Life have been forgiven of their sins and reflect the nature of the Lamb in their behavior.

The seventh and final vision of the Holy City is given in 22:1–5. In this vision John combines two images—"the river of the water of life" and "the tree of life." The image of "the river of the water of life" is reminiscent of the river in the Garden of Eden (Gen. 2:10–14) and in Ezekiel 47:1–7 where a river flowed from the temple. John's vision of the river flowing from the throne of God likely symbolizes the abundant life that God gives to the believer.

The symbol of the "tree of life" is also drawn from the story of the Garden of Eden (Gen. 3:6) and the image in Ezekiel 47:12. The twelve kinds of fruit and the healing qualities of the tree's leaves denote the complete and inexhaustible quality of God's grace to the saints in the holy city. The sufferings, grief, and pain of the believers will be healed. The tree of life is also a sign of eternal life. Both the tree and the river of water represent the abundant life that Christians will enjoy in the New Jerusalem. Nothing that could harm the Christian will be in the city (v. 3).

In the center of the city will be the throne of God and the Lamb where the Christians will worship their redeeming God. The mark on the foreheads of the worshipers indicates that they belong completely to God. In the Holy City the saints will see God's face as Jesus had promised to the pure in heart (Matt. 5:8). Cleansed of their sins, the forgiven sinners can look into the face of God free of shame and guilt. Standing in the presence of God, Christians will worship and reign endlessly with the God they love and adore.

Do a word study of the glory of God, the number twelve, the New Jerusalem, the river of the water of life, and the tree of life.

The sermon might be built on the theme of the foundations of belief. Draw on the images of the twelve gates, the patriarchs or the old covenant and the twelve foundation stones, the disciples or the new covenant. Or the sermon may expound the meaning of the river of the water of life and the tree of life as symbols of eternal life.

Theological Reflection

Jesus promised his disciples that the ministry of the church and guidance into deeper spiritual knowledge would come from the Paraclete he would send. Jesus assured his disciples of an inward peace that would strengthen them to withstand the conflicts of life. Luke has reminded his readers in Acts 15 that salvation is not realized by keeping the Jewish Torah but is the result of God's grace. Our relationship with Christ does demand, however, a moral standard modeled after our Lord's example. John's vision in Revelation describes the heavenly city of God as one where the glory of God is the light of the city and one that needs no temple because the city itself is the place where God dwells with the believers. The river of the water of life and the tree of life assure the faithful of the abundant life in the Holy City.

Children's Message

The children's talk might describe John's picture of the heavenly city in Revelation. The symbols of the walls, gates, river of the water of life, and the tree of life can be explained to help them grasp some image of eternal life. Help them to see the heavenly city as a place of joy, peace, awe, and worship.

Hymns for Easter 6

Jesus Shall Reign Where'er the Sun; All Hail the Power of Jesus' Name; In Heaven Above; A Minimal Hymn (*Choirbook for Saints and Singers*).

Psalm 97 (C)

Revelation 22:12–14, 16–17, 20 (C) (RC) (E)
Revelation 22:12–17, 20 (L)

Acts 16:16–34 (C) (E)
Acts 16:6–10 (L)   **John 17:20–26**
Acts 7:55–60 (RC)

Meditation on the Texts

Eternal Shepherd of our souls, we praise you for your love which unifies your church and strengthens us to meet the struggles and difficulties of life as we serve you. Fortify us to glorify your name through our love and witness for you. Open our hearts to sense the leadership of your Spirit while we are awake or asleep. May we be willing to follow wherever your Spirit leads to service near or far. Help us, Lord, to glorify you when others ridicule, misunderstand, or reject your grace. May the assurance of the consummation of your kingdom empower us to live daily for you. *Maranatha,* "Come, Lord Jesus." Amen.

Commentary on the Texts

John 17:20–26

Jesus' prayer given in John 17 began with a personal plea that he might glorify his Father in the ultimate sacrifice on the cross (17:1–5) which lay before him. Next he prayed for his disciples, that they might be consecrated to God's truth in order to serve Christ as he sends them into the world (17:9–19). Jesus then offers his prayer for those who will believe in him in the future. All believers who read these verses (vs. 20–26) overhear the Lord's prayer for them.

Even as Jesus faced the most difficult experience in his earthly life, his prayer reveals a quiet trust in God's presence and guidance. With the certainty of the cross before him, rejection by the crowds around him, and desertion by the disciples who were closest to him, Jesus maintained his faith in what God would do in the future.

Jesus' prayer not only reflects his certainty about God but also affirms his confidence in the disciples. Even knowing the disciples' fears, ambitions, struggles, and weaknesses, Jesus did not lose trust in them. He had chosen them after long hours of prayer and he was convinced that God would use them as instruments to spread the good news throughout the world.

Jesus prayed for the unity of the future church. He prayed that the future growth of the church would not inhibit its unity. He prayed that the future disciples in the church would be united as he and God the Father were united: "That they may all be one. As you, Father, are in me and I am in you" (v. 21, NRSV). Jesus' unity with his Father was based on a unique personal communion of the Son with the Father. The church's unity is a reflection of the unity within the triune God.

The unity for his church for which Jesus prays extends beyond organizational or ecclesiastical uniformity. The basis of the church's unity, as it is modeled after our Lord's unity with his Father, is rooted in the nature of God and Jesus' obedient love. God was "in" Jesus, and Jesus was "in" God. As God the Father has "sent" the Son, so Jesus "sends" his disciples into the world (v. 21). Jesus mediated the presence of God through the temple of his body (2:17–19), and the flock was united under Jesus, the one "Shepherd" of his church (10:16). The unity of the church in the contemporary ecumenical movement needs not to be a unity void of all diversity of theology or administrative form. Instead, it is a unity based on the triune nature of God, characterized by the diversity within the unity of the Father, Son, and Holy Spirit.

If Christians loved one another as Jesus loved his Father and the Father loved the Son, this same expression of love would be evident in the life and work of the church. The motivating power of God's love which guided the ministry of Jesus would be then the dominating expression of the church's mission. The way Jesus mediated the Father to his disciples convinced them of his Father's love. In a similar way, the unity of the church, which rests on the redemptive love of God manifested through the incarnate Christ, will convince the world that its mission is really from God (v. 21). The disunity of the church continues to be a compelling argument to the world that the church has lost sight of its redemptive mission to share God's love as it claims to have experienced it in Christ.

The reason Jesus prays for the unity of the church is so that the world might know the true nature of God as one. Note the three stages through which God manifests God's glory: (1) Jesus received glory from God. What was this glory? This glory was revealed through Jesus' incarnate life, words, and ministry. This glory may have been a reflection of Jesus' obedient love of his Father. Glory may have been a reference to Jesus' death on the cross. When Jesus spoke about his death, he usually spoke of being "glorified" (11:4; 12:23). (2) Jesus transmits this glory to his disciples (vs. 22–23). As Jesus had reflected the light from God, the disciples were to be lights to show others the way to God. Sometimes the disciples would suffer as the Lord had suffered. The ministry of the church is not to call attention to itself but to lead people to God. (3) Ultimately Christ's glory will not be realized in this world but in the eternal glory which he has gone to prepare for his disciples. During times of tribulation, the disciples can take hope in the love and promise of God (see Rom. 8:18–25; 2 Tim. 2:11–12).

It would be helpful to **do a study** of Jesus' use of the terms "glory" and "glorified."

The sermon might focus on Jesus' prayer for the unity of the church. Show how this unity will need to be based on a theological premise, the triune nature of God, and not constructed around organizational approaches.

Acts 16:16–34 (C) (E)

Chapter 16 lists a strange variety of converts to the Christian faith in Philippi. Lydia, mentioned in vs. 14–15, came from the upper class. In this passage a slave girl becomes the next convert. On one of their visits, which took place on a day other than the Sabbath, Paul and Silas were followed for days by a young slave girl who continually shouted, "These men are servants of the Most High God, who proclaim to you the way of salvation" (v. 17). The slave girl had "a spirit of divination" (v. 16), which would be better rendered "a spirit of Python." This was a reference to Phythian Apollo, who was said to dwell in the snake-god at Delphi. The slave girl was called a Pytho, a person who gave oracles about the future. She either had a natural gift or was trained also as a ventriloquist. Her owners exploited her "illness" and gifts for their own financial gain.

After several days of her shouting, Paul became annoyed and exorcised the unclean spirit from her. He charged the spirit "in the name of Jesus Christ to come out of her." Immediately she was cured and sane.

Rather than rejoicing at this young woman's cure, her owners were furious because a source of financial revenue was cut off. Unfortunately, too many people determine their concern for others on the basis of exploitation and not human need. The owners brought charges against Paul and Silas not for curing their soothsayer, for they knew that would be a strange and unacceptable accusation. They played on the prejudices of the citizens of Philippi against Jews and accused Paul and Silas of advocating customs that were illegal for Romans. This charge was probably proselytism. "What they are doing is not lawful for 'us Romans,'" the owners cried, appealing to nationalism. Soon a mob had surrounded the two missionaries and, without a trial, the magistrates stripped the clothing off the two men and had them beaten with rods. Paul and Silas were then put in the maximum security section of the jail with their feet in the stocks.

Although Paul and Silas had been placed in the innermost part of the prison, they did not despair and give up hope but began to pray and sing hymns. About midnight an earthquake shook the ground, the doors of the prison opened, and the chains and stocks on all the prisoners snapped loose. The jailer, who under Roman law was responsible with his life for the security of the prisoners, awakened to see what had happened and was about to kill himself with his sword, because he thought the prisoners had escaped.

Paul shouted to the jailer and told him not to harm himself because they were all still there. The jailer rushed in with a light to see if this were really true. Seeing that it was, he fell down trembling at the feet of Paul and asked: "Men, what must I do to be saved?" Luke does not give enough details to know whether the jailer had heard the Gospel message before or overheard it through Paul's and Silas' singing and prayers that night. Out of fear turned to amazement, this pagan jailer reached out for salvation.

Paul informs him that the one thing necessary is: "Believe in the Lord Jesus, and you will be saved, you and your household" (v. 31). Here is one of the shortest summaries of the message of salvation in the New Testament. For a pagan man without background in the Old Testament tradition and for thousands through the ages to come, this same message is the basis for salvation: "Believe in the Lord Jesus." Surely Paul or others taught this man and his family more later about the meaning of this statement, but for his present need this word was sufficient as Paul and Silas "spoke the word of the Lord to him and to all that were in his house" (v. 32).

The words by Paul "Believe in the Lord Jesus, and you will be saved" were first spoken following an earthquake. But these same words have been adequate through upheavals of all kinds, whether personal such as illness, grief, or death, or national or international such as war, revolution, famine, poverty, disease, economic deprivation, or social or political changes. The Lord Jesus is our salvation in any disturbance.

After his conversion, the jailer took Paul and Silas into his own home and washed their wounds from their beating. He and his family were baptized that night. The jailer, who was not a Jew, then invited Paul and Silas to eat at his own table. Eating at the table then and now is an expression of acceptance and fellowship. Paul and Silas sat at the jailer's table and included this Gentile convert and his family in the community of Christians. The joy of salvation had been confirmed in baptism and in a fellowship meal (vs. 33–34).

Examine the meaning of the following words or expressions: "a spirit of divination," "to be saved," and "your household."

The sermon might use vs. 30–31 as the text. Paul's response to the jailer, "Believe in the Lord Jesus, and you will be saved," is still the essential message of the good news today.

Acts 16:6–10 (L)

For some time Paul had wanted to go to Asia and preach the gospel, but Luke notes that the Holy Spirit prevented Paul's journey in this direction. The Greek in v. 6 is difficult to translate and scholars have not been clear where Paul went on this detour. While he was in the Galatian-Phrygian region, Paul came to Troas and received guidance from the Holy Spirit regarding his travels.

There is no clear way to know how Paul received the message of the Holy Spirit. Some scholars have suggested that it was a direct vision. Others have thought that it was more likely an inner experience, while others have stated that God may have spoken through another person who communicated directly with Paul.

One of the most interesting possibilities is that God's Spirit may have spoken through Luke, the author of the Book of Acts. In v. 10 there is the first appearance of the "we" passage. The story up to this point is presented in the third person, but now it unfolds in the first person. Maybe Paul had been ill with his "thorn in the flesh" and Luke, a medical doctor from Macedonia, came to treat Paul's physical needs. Could Luke have been pleading with Paul to come to Macedonia with the gospel rather than go to Asia? Later when Paul fell asleep, was Luke the man Paul saw in his dream begging him to come to Macedonia with the gospel? However it happened, Luke stresses that the Holy Spirit is the source behind the decision.

Some scholars have suggested that Paul's going to Macedonia constitutes the introduction of the gospel to Europe. If Paul had gone to Asia instead, they suggest that Japanese and Indians might be trying to convert Europe and America instead of our missionaries preaching to them. However, Suetonius and Paul's Letter to the Romans indicate that Christians were in Rome almost from the beginning of Christianity. Luke's intent here was not basically geographical but rather with extending the gospel into the Gentile world which at this point happened to be Macedonia. The Roman province of Asia was not the same as the continent of Asia. Lines were not drawn as sharply then as they are now.

The sermon might focus on Paul's vision to preach the gospel in Macedonia and how the Holy Spirit continues to communicate to persons today to share the gospel with others. It might be helpful to address God's call to both lay people and clergy to share in the preaching and teaching ministry.

Acts 7:55–60 (RC)

When the early church appointed seven to a ministry "to serve tables" (6:1–7), Stephen was among those selected. He was a man "full of grace and power and did great wonders and signs among the people" (6:8). Members of several Jerusalem synagogues accused Stephen of blasphemy. He came to speak before a council which they convened with the charge that he "never ceases to speak words against this holy place and the law" (6:13). Stephen's speech before the council is a lesson in the history of God's activity with Israel and the conclusion that God's presence has never been restricted to any one country (piece of land) or place, a reference to the temple.

The sudden departure from Stephen's speech and strong verbal attack on his accusers as being stubbornly blind and violators of the law they claimed to defend may have been caused by his reaction to a heckler in the council. Like his Lord, Stephen accuses the religious leaders of rejecting God's prophets and killing them.

Stephen's speech so enraged the council that they "ground their teeth" and hissed at him. At that very moment Stephen had a vision of Jesus and told his listeners that he saw "the Son of man standing at the right hand of God" (v. 56). This is the only place in the New Testament where the reference "Son of man" is used of our Lord by anyone other than Jesus himself. Drawing on the image from Daniel, Jesus had shown his identification with humanity to the point of laying down his life on the cross as the Suffering Servant. Stephen's vision denoted that Jesus was beside his Father in authority and bore witness to what was happening on earth (see Luke 12:8).

Although it was customary in Jewish law to stone someone accused of blasphemy, the reaction of the council does not appear to be a legal formal execution but rather a mob action. The loud shouting, the covering of their ears, and the violent move to take Stephen by force indicates the reaction of a lynching crowd (v. 57). He was taken outside the city, so it would not be tainted by this act. The execution by stoning was in keeping with Jewish law (Lev. 24:10–16; Deut. 13:6–11).

As the stones were being hurled at him and he knew death was near, Stephen prayed, "Lord Jesus, receive my spirit," and then he knelt down and prayed for his executioners in words similar to those of our Lord on the cross, "Lord, do not hold this sin against them" (v. 60). Compare these words with Jesus' words in Luke 23:34. Stephen's strong faith in Jesus gave him the courage to face death with confidence.

Some semblance of legality is given to Stephen's stoning in the reference to the witnesses against him, who would be the first ones to cast stones at him (v. 58). In words that read almost like an aside, Luke observes that the witnesses laid their outer garments, which they had removed for the stoning, at the feet of a man named Saul. The courageous death of Stephen must have made a lasting impression on this young Pharisee, because only he could have related these particular details later (Acts 22:20). The prayer and heroic stance of Stephen planted the seed for Paul's conversion.

Compare the last words of Stephen with the last words of Jesus as recorded in Luke 23:34 and 23:46.

The sermon might focus on the actions of the hostile crowd in covering their ears and refusing to listen to Stephen's interpretation of the gospel. Too many listeners close their ears and refuse to hear the gospel when it challenges their preconceived notions or prejudices. Note how the preacher is often rejected along with the message. In Stephen's case he was stoned to death, but in more polite society the preacher might be ostracized, ignored, or fired.

Revelation 22:12–17, 20 (L)

John concludes his writing with a promise and a warning. The words "I am coming soon" have been noted earlier by John in 3:11 and 22:7, but this time the words reflect Isaiah 40:10, where each person will be rewarded according to his or her work. The time for Christ's return is near. Christ proclaims that he is "the Alpha and the Omega, the first and the last, the beginning and the end." The intent of John is to affirm the complete, authoritative, and eternal power of Christ to execute judgment at his coming. The Lamb and the Father speak as one. John had made earlier references to "the Alpha and the Omega" in 1:8 and 21:6.

The last beatitude of Revelation, "Blessed are those who wash their robes" (v. 14), draws upon an image John used earlier about the cleansing of dirty clothes (7:14). Those who have been made pure by the atoning work of Christ enter the new "paradise" where the tree of life is in the city of God. The image of washing one's robe in Christ's blood denotes a decision and action on the part of the believer. Purity by Christ's atonement is essential before one enters eternal life.

The unclean remain outside the city gates. They are described as "dogs" (v. 15). In ancient times dogs were not household pets but ran wild as scavengers. The use of dog to describe a person was a term of absolute contempt. The term seems to apply to all the godless who have not been washed in the blood of the Lamb. "Sorcerers and fornicators and murderers and idolators" represent those who follow the immoral teachings of the Antichrist (13:12–18) and "every one who loves and practices falsehood" are those who have identified their character with the lie of the Antichrist. To be outside the city is to be outside of God's grace. This image is similar to the picture of those cast into the lake of fire (21:8).

In v. 16 Jesus affirms that what John has reported in his revelation is true. Although mediated by angels, John's revelation has its source in Jesus. Jesus authenticates his claim by declaring, "I am the root [source] and the offspring of David" (see Isa. 11:1), God's king, and "the bright morning star" (see Num. 24:17).

The Spirit and the bride cry to the exalted Christ, "Come." The Spirit is the Paraclete, who intercedes for us in our prayers (Rom. 8:38–39). The bride is the church. The word from the Spirit and the church are an invitation to those who have not experienced God's grace: "Come." They are invited to drink from the river that flows from the throne and find redemption. This echoes the words of Jesus, "Let anyone who is thirsty come to me, and let the one who believes in me drink" (John 7:37–38, NRSV). Although the Apocalypse reads like a drama, it is a letter, and John concludes with the words of Jesus, "Surely I am coming soon" and the response of an early Christian confession, *Maranatha*, "Come, Lord Jesus!" With this coming, the church anticipates the reward and judgment of the Lord (1 Cor. 16:22).

Do a **word study** of dogs, root and offspring of David, the bright and morning star, and *Maranatha*.

The sermon might be drawn from the text, "Come, Lord Jesus!" (22:20). Note the church's prayer that the Lord come soon, bless those washed in the blood of the Lamb, and pronounce judgment on those devoted to evil.

Theological Reflection

Jesus prays for his future disciples as they carry his message into a hostile world. He prays for them to be united and to glorify God through their lives. Luke notes the presence of God's Spirit with two new disciples, Paul and Silas, as they are imprisoned because of their preaching. Even while they are in prison God's Spirit uses them to bring the message of salvation to their jailer. In a dream, God's Spirit leads Paul away from Asia and into Macedonia with the gospel. The presence of God's Spirit sustained Stephen as he was stoned to death because he proclaimed God's salvation in Jesus Christ. Those persons who have been washed in the blood of the Lamb pray for the Lord to come soon with his reward and judgment.

Children's Message

The children might be asked if they remember a dream they had while they were sleeping. Tell them about Paul's dream and God's call to Paul through that dream to go to Macedonia and preach. Remind them that God can sometimes "speak" to us through our dreams.

Hymns for Easter 7

Love Divine, So Great and Wondrous; The Church's One Foundation; Christ Is Coming.

Psalm 104:24–34 (C)   Romans 8:14–17 (C)
                             Romans 8:8–17 (RC)
Acts 2:1–21 (C) (L)   1 Corinthians 12:4–13 (E)
Acts 2:1–11 (RC) (E)
Genesis 11:1–9 (L) (alt. C) John 14:8–17, 25–27 (C)
                             John 14:15–16, 23b–26 (RC)
                             John 15:26–27; 16:4b–11 (L)
                             John 20:19–23 (E)

Meditation on the Texts

Holy Spirit of God, who has inspired and purified our hearts by your cleansing power, continue to guide us to live as Christ has taught us. Forgive our prideful ways and unwillingness to listen to you and each other. We praise you, O Counselor, who will guide us into deeper knowledge of Christ's way and will motivate and strengthen us to witness for him. As we remember the outpouring of your Spirit at Pentecost, we open our souls to you to be set on fire anew by the power of your presence. We dedicate our gifts to you and acknowledge their origin from your Spirit. Anoint our words, thoughts, gifts, and service that they all might glorify your name. Amen.

Commentary on the Texts

John 14:8–17, 25–27 (C)

John 14:15–16, 23b–26 (RC)

See also Easter 6.

Philip's request to Jesus "Lord, show us the Father, and we shall be satisfied" (v. 8) is an expression of every person who longs to worship God. Moses had expressed this same desire to God on Mt. Sinai: "Show me thy glory" (Ex. 33:18). In many of the mystery religions of the ancient world, the initiation of the worshiper ended in a supposed "vision" of their god. Some scholars believe that Jesus is contrasting the desire to "see" God with one's physical eyes with the higher response "to see" or "believe" with inner spiritual sight. In words that are voiced in a mild rebuke, Jesus tells Philip, "He who has seen me has seen the Father." The purpose of Jesus was to reveal God. What Jesus said and did was to lead people to God. Jesus was not claiming that God was limited to his (Jesus') presence but that the Father was uniquely present in him.

John has written earlier about Jesus' claim of unity with God, "I and the Father are one" (10:30, 37–38). Here is the highest Christology. To see Jesus is to see God, because he is the incarnation of God the Father. The One who was sent by the Father has fellowship with the Father and fully represents the Father who sent him. John has reached a high point in his Gospel. He is insisting that the major manifestation of God's presence in Jesus is known most clearly not by his "signs," his teachings, or even his death but in the incarnated person of Jesus himself: "And the Word became flesh and dwelt among us, full of grace and truth; we have beheld his glory, glory as of the only Son from the Father" (1:14).

Jesus moves a step further with Philip and his other disciples. If his past companionship and "words" have not been sufficient to affirm his claim to reveal the Father, Jesus then tells his disciples, "Believe me for the sake of the works themselves" (v. 11). His first claim was based on his personhood and what he said. The second claim was his "works." John's Gospel has focused on seven signs which attest to the saving presence of God in Jesus. If Jesus' word is not enough, then his miracles, "signs," or works should be sufficient proof. His ability to heal the sick and cure other diseases and afflictions affirms Jesus' claim. As Nicodemus said, "No one can do these signs that you do, unless God is with him" (3:2).

Jesus further claims that those who believe in him will do "greater works" (v. 12). Some scholars believe that Jesus is not referring here to greater miracles than his own. These greater works will be realized in the presence and power of the risen Lord who would not be restricted by the limitations of the incarnation. He states that it is necessary for him to depart if "another Counselor" is to come. Some scholars believe that v. 18, "I will not leave you desolate; I will come to you," is an assertion that the Counselor is the risen Lord.

Some have misunderstood Jesus' statement "If you ask me anything in my name, I will do it" (v. 14). They think these words guarantee that any prayer they ask will be granted, but the key is "in my name." Any prayer "in Jesus' name" will not be voiced with selfish or dishonest motives. We will want to do the will of our Lord. The use of Christ's name is not a magical formula.

The proof of love, according to John, is obedience. Jesus said, "If you love me, you will keep my commandments" (v. 15). Real love for Christ is never limited to conversation or speeches but is to be lived out daily in following Christ's teachings. To follow Christ's way is not easy. Our Lord knew that the Christian way would demand that we have special help. He assures his disciples that he will send another helper or counselor to sustain them. Jesus' return to the Father makes available a different presence, yet like the one they had known in his human life. "Yet a little while, and the world will see me no more, but you will see me; because I live, you will live also" (v. 19).

See Easter 6 for the discussion on the Paraclete (vs. 16–17, 23–27).

Do a word study of the various ways Paraclete has been translated: Counselor, Comforter, Helper, and Advocate, among others, and determine which you believe to be the best rendering of the Greek word.

The sermon might focus on the way Christ has revealed God's presence through his words and deeds. Develop this thought to include the church's response to this message and its responsibility to share that word of redeeming grace with those who have not heard the good news.

John 15:26–27; 16:4b–11 (L)

In the midst of warning that he and the disciples would be persecuted, Jesus consoles them with a description of the work of the Holy Spirit. The disciples had probably voiced their fear of witnessing to the gospel message which Jesus was teaching. Jesus assured his disciples that he was going to "send" the Counselor, the Paraclete, but the Spirit would also proceed from the Father. In contrast to the lies which the Jewish religious leaders had told about Jesus, the Paraclete is the Spirit of truth. The Spirit would bear witness within the human heart to the redeeming work of Jesus. The disciples are likewise charged to be witnesses to Jesus because of their personal knowledge of him. The Paraclete's primary purpose was not to defend the disciples but to witness to Jesus.

Fear and grief began to fill the hearts of Jesus' disciples at the thought of his departure, but his return to the Father by his death on the cross and his ascension would result in the sending of the Paraclete. Since the Spirit would not come while Jesus was still present in the flesh, the earthly body of Jesus limited his ministry. Jesus' departure, which the disciples did not yet understand, was necessary for the Spirit to come in fullness.

The Spirit's work, which is described in this discussion, focuses on the world and not on the church. Some scholars feel that the work of the Spirit mentioned here is to "convince the world." This would be seen primarily as an evangelistic purpose. Others think the word in v. 8 should be translated "convict the world." The word "convict" is drawn from a courtroom setting. The Spirit will "convict" the world which had previously rejected Jesus.

The Spirit will convict the world of three things: (1) The Spirit will show that the world's sin is a result of refusing to believe in Jesus. (2) Humanity will be assured that the death of Jesus was the righteousness of God. The Paraclete will show people the righteousness of

Jesus through his resurrection and ascension to the Father. (3) The Paraclete will convict people of God's judgment. Those who judged Jesus will be judged. The Spirit will show that God's purpose was realized through the crucifixion. The Holy Spirit will be the interpreter of Jesus to the world, convicting and converting the people in the world that his death was not defeat but victory, not the end but the beginning. The Paraclete will enable the world to see that judgment is not reserved for the end of history but is a present reality. "The ruler of this world is judged." The writer of the Fourth Gospel knew that it was essential for the early church to know that the death of Jesus was not the result of official execution of a criminal by the Roman rulers, but was instead the work of the Holy Spirit in completing God's act of redemption.

Do a word study of "Spirit of truth" (15:26), "convince" or "convict," "righteousness" (16:8).

The sermon might expound the threefold responsibility of the Paraclete in the world as set forth in 16:8–11. The alternate translations of the Greek word in 16:8 for "convince" or "convict," and the image of it which arises from the cross-examination of a witness in a courtroom setting may be used to clarify the meaning of v. 8.

John 20:19–23 (E)

See Easter 2 for the emphasis on the appearance of the risen Lord. Note briefly this further word for Pentecost. In this passage, as in other biblical references, breath is associated with the Holy Spirit. In the Genesis account of creation breath is mentioned, "And the LORD God formed man of dust from the ground, and *breathed* into his nostrils the *breath* of life; and man became a living being" (Gen. 2:7, italics added). Ezekiel saw the valley of dry bones and heard God say, "Come from the four winds, O breath, and breathe upon these slain, that they may live" (Ezek. 37:9). In Acts 2 the Holy Spirit came "like the rush of a mighty wind." God's Spirit comes with creative and renewing power.

Acknowledging again that he had been sent by God, Jesus instructs his disciples, "As the Father has sent me, even so I send you" (v. 21). Following these words, he breathed on them and declared: "Receive the Holy Spirit." Some scholars have stated that this was only a partial giving of the Spirit to his disciples which was fully given at Pentecost. More likely John is presenting a different tradition of the coming of the Holy Spirit than the one presented by Luke in Acts 2. In John's discussion the death, resurrection, and ascension of Jesus are bound together. Unlike Luke, who sets the day of Pentecost after the ascension which came forty days after the resurrection, John, according to some scholars, sees the ascension of Jesus at the occasion of his last resurrection appearance.

"Receive the Holy Spirit." The Holy Spirit is given as a divine gift, but it has to be received. When the body of believers has received the Holy Spirit, they extend the forgiving grace of God through their pronouncement of God's act. The church has authority and power to render this ministry upon the condition that it has first received the Holy Spirit. The church was established to share the ministry of Christ. The Holy Spirit empowers the church to fulfill that function.

Examine the various references to the word "breath" and the Holy Spirit.

The sermon might focus on the Johannine Pentecost and the meaning of "receiving" the Holy Spirit and the promise of power and responsibility that are linked with the Spirit's anointing.

Acts 2:1–21 (C) (L)

Acts 2:1–11 (RC) (E)

In the life and faith of the early church, the Spirit was a commanding force. The story about Pentecost has fascinated Christians and others through the ages. The nation Israel celebrated three basic feast days: Tabernacles, Passover, and Pentecost. Pentecost, the feast day which furnished the setting for the story about the coming of the tongues of fire, was the festival that came fifty days after Passover. It was a week of weeks or the fiftieth day after Passover. Pentecost was celebrated as a remembrance of the time God gave the commandments to the children of Israel. It was also a harvest celebration. Harvest had already been gathered in, and Israel expressed its thanks for God's bounty. Two loaves of bread from the community were offered on the altar to express thanksgiving to God.

The disciples were gathered in an upper room. Perhaps it was the same room where they had met following the crucifixion of Christ. The disciples had assembled in one accord, waiting for the promised Spirit which Jesus said would come to anoint them. In the upper room they experienced the power and presence of God. God's presence came through two symbols in this story.

One of the symbols of the Holy Spirit is wind. Notice that it says "like wind." It is not wind, but it seems like wind. The Spirit made an audible sound as it came rushing upon them. As it has been noted in other discussions, the Spirit is often depicted as breath. The word "Spirit" is derived from the word which means "breath."

Unfortunately, some people describe Pentecost as the occasion for the coming of the Holy Spirit as though the Spirit had not existed before this time. God has eternally been Father, Son, and Holy Spirit. The Hebrew Scriptures as well as the New Testament have numerous references to the work of the Spirit: "The Spirit of the LORD took possession of Gideon" (Judg. 6:34); "The Spirit of the LORD began to stir Samson"; "And the Spirit of the LORD came mightily upon him" (Judg. 14:6; see 13:25); "The Spirit of the LORD came mightily upon David" (1 Sam. 16:13). The Spirit descended upon Jesus at his baptism (Luke 3:21–22). Jesus stood up in the synagogue and said: "The Spirit of the Lord is upon me, because he has anointed me to preach" (Luke 4:18–19). The Spirit has always been active, but at Pentecost the Spirit anointed the disciples in a special way.

In our text, there is also a visible symbol. The Spirit appeared as tongues of fire. Luke did not say that it was fire, but it looked like fire. The symbol of God as fire is an ancient one for Israel. God appeared to Moses in a burning bush. Elijah saw the fire of God's presence come down from heaven and consume his sacrifice when he was in competition with the gods of Baal. Elijah was carried into heaven in a chariot of fire. God is sometimes depicted as a consuming fire. Fire, in the scriptures, is a sign of the vital presence of God among God's people.

The tongues of fire also symbolize the purifying nature of God's presence. Just as fire can remove all the dross from the metal which is cast in its heat, the redeeming grace of the fire of God's presence purifies our lives. In the temple, Isaiah had an experience with God and was so moved by his encounter that he envisioned an angel touching his lips with a hot coal to purge him from his sins. Whenever a person enters God's presence, that person is made aware of his or her sinfulness.

On the day of Pentecost, the tongues of fire also came as a transforming force. The disciples were gathered together waiting to be filled by God. Now they would learn more of God's way. They would open themselves again and again to a growing experience with God. This coming of the Spirit was not the final expression of all that they would receive. They had to remain open to the Spirit's continuous presence, so that God might fill them again and again.

The tongues of fire in this story also denote the praise and proclamation that resulted from the Spirit's impact. One can get distracted by lengthy debates about whether the disciples spoke in "unknown" tongues, glossolalia, or in other "foreign" languages, since the multitude seemed to hear the message in their various languages. Some scholars have suggested that the reference to people hearing the gospel in their own language is an indication that the confusion of language which resulted from the construction of the Tower of Babel (Gen. 11:1–9) was healed by the Spirit. But the focus is not on speaking but hearing. "Each one heard them speaking in the native language of each" (v. 6, NRSV). The real emphasis is on the "use" of the tongues. The tongues were used to praise God and proclaim God's mighty works. The disciples' praise was misunderstood by some of their listeners, and they were accused of being drunk.

The first Christian sermon is recorded in vs. 14–36. This first example of apostolic preaching was directed to Jews (v. 14). Peter draws upon the prophecy of Joel to prove that the messianic age has arrived. Although all the things Peter cited from Joel had not occurred, the outpouring of the Spirit was a sign that the "last days" had begun. Peter's use of the apocalyptic image from Joel was to announce the "last days" in which Jesus had ushered in the kingdom of God. God has acted uniquely through the death of Jesus to bring salvation to all persons. In v. 21 an evangelistic appeal is made: "And it shall be that whoever calls on the name of the Lord shall be saved."

Do a word study of Pentecost, tongues of fire, and "speak in other tongues."

The sermon might focus on the image of the tongues of fire. It may be helpful to stress the symbolism of fire as a sign of God's presence, the purifying and transforming power, and the stimulus for praise and proclamation.

Genesis 11:1–9 (L) (alt. C)

The ancient story of the Tower of Babel may have been an attempt to explain the diversity of human language. The legend shows human pride and the arrogance of assuming that one could possess the throne of God. Humanity's pride in its own achievements caused the people to attempt to build a ziggurat, a multistoried tower, into heaven itself.

The author uses a play on words with the word "Babel." Babel was the Hebrew equivalent of a Babylonian word that meant "gate of God." The writer then uses a word very similar to the other Hebrew word which is translated "confusion." The irony is that in attempting to reach the gate of God, humanity's foolish pride results in confusion.

Some scholars are convinced that the real thrust of this story is the people's failure "to listen" to each other (v. 7) rather than a failure "to understand" each other. The inability to listen to each other reflects the divisions within the world. The Tower of Babel has replaced Eden, where humanity lived in harmony with one another and God. The story of Pentecost in Acts 2 depicts "a new community" where humanity can hear, "listen" to one another again.

Do a word study of Babel.

The sermon might contrast the confusion which resulted from the Tower of Babel with the new capacity to hear which came at Pentecost.

Romans 8:14–17 (C)

Romans 8:8–17 (RC)

The pericope stresses that the Christian lives by the guidance of the Spirit (v. 9). The Christian is so possessed by the Spirit that everything one does is dominated by this Presence. The "fleshly" desires are no longer first in a Christian's life, but the Spirit enables the Christian to be fully alive (vs. 10–11).

In vs. 14–17, Paul writes about the Christian being adopted into the family of God. Among the possible meanings of this image are the following: (1) an adopted child is one chosen by God, (2) this relationship is a gift, (3) past sins (slavery) are forgiven, (4) membership in God's family is vital and intimate, (5) the child is expected to carry on the work of the Father. We suffer not apart from Christ but with Christ, which sanctifies and provides hope in our suffering.

Do a word study of flesh, Spirit, adoption, children of God, and heirs of God.

The sermon might examine the phrase where Christians are depicted as having been adopted as children of God.

1 Corinthians 12:4–13 (E)

See also Epiphany 2.

The church as the body of Christ has a variety of spiritual gifts, but all of these gifts come from the same Spirit and therefore some are not better than others. Paul was probably confronting the problem in the church of those who spoke in tongues thinking that their gift was a superior one. He acknowledges that gift but notes many others, all inspired by God's Spirit.

The emphasis of this passage is stated in a series of parallel statements that convey the Trinity:

There are varieties of gifts, but the same Spirit;
There are varieties of service, but the same Lord;
There are varieties of work, but the same God.''
(See vs. 4–6.)

The sermon might show the variety of gifts God's Spirit uses in the ministry of the church.

Theological Reflection

All our texts share a common theme on the work of the Holy Spirit. The Spirit has always been at work in the world, but the ascension of Jesus began the interpretative ministry of the Spirit to reveal Christ's words and deeds to humanity. The arrogance and confusion symbolized by the Tower of Babel have been surmounted by the new community created at Pentecost.

Children's Message

The minister could tell the story of the building of the Tower of Babel. Emphasis might be placed on the confusion which usually results when people refuse to listen to God or each other and continue to try to control everything without concern for others or for God.

Hymns for the Day of Pentecost

Come, Holy Spirit, Heavenly Dove; Spirit of God, Descend Upon My Heart; Breathe on Me, Breath of God; We Are the Church (*Choirbook for Saints and Singers*).

The Sundays After Pentecost

Color: Green. But other colors or combination of colors may be used, such as red, purple, and white. Red, symbolizing the fire of the Holy Spirit, might be used for evangelistic services. White is used on Trinity Sunday and Christ the King Sunday, the first and last Sundays of this season.

Trinity Sunday is observed on the Sunday immediately after Pentecost. It celebrates the mystery of the Godhead: Creator, Son, and Holy Spirit, one God in three persons. Use of the Nicene Creed is appropriate in worship this Sunday, since it has special emphasis on the nature of Jesus Christ as well as setting forth the Trinity. This can be a challenging day to preach as you seek to declare the scriptural understanding of the Godhead.

The nonfestival half of the Christian year has been called a variety of names: Season After Pentecost, Kingdomtide, Ordinary Time, and others. (The other nonfestival portion of the Christian year comes between Epiphany and Lent.) Each Sunday stands on its own, and you have some freedom in selecting the passages on which to base your sermon. One suggestion is to follow a nine-year cycle, preaching on the Gospel one cycle, on the Epistles another, and on the Old Testament lesson the third cycle.

Or you may choose from among the three readings in selecting the text for the sermon, using the Gospel one Sunday, the Epistle another, or the Old Testament lesson. Another choice is to follow a semicontinuous reading, using either Old Testament, Epistle, or Gospel readings for the sermon for a period of time. By following one reading from a narrative of the Bible, such as the life of David, the congregation may build interest in a kind of miniseries of sermons on a person or theme of the Bible. Another choice is to depart from the lectionary (after preaching through years A, B, and C) during some or all of Ordinary Time in order to address specific issues or books of the Bible that are omitted from the readings of the Common Lectionary. For example, you might preach a series on one or more of the minor prophets, or on the Book of Esther (not included in the lectionary), or on the psalms. Or the series might be on the basics of the Christian faith, dealing with topics such as the Lord's Prayer, the Apostles' Creed, the Sermon on the Mount, or the Ten Commandments. A series might deal with some current social issues. You may want to use subjects requested by the congregation, such as death, why the innocent suffer, or life after death.

The lectionary readings are determined by the days within which a Sunday falls on the calendar. For instance, the readings for a particular Sunday will be designated for the Sunday between two dates (e.g., ''August 14–20'') regardless of the date of Pentecost.

Because this half of the church year is less structured, congregations may be creative in celebrating each Sunday. Point out that the color green symbolizes life and growth in nature and thus can symbolize the growth of Christians and congregations.

There are possibilities for preaching ''occasional sermons'' which respond to particular civic occasions or to the congregation's life, such as a church anniversary, July 4, Labor Day, or Thanksgiving. When this is done, an appropriate scripture reading is selected and substituted for the Gospel, Epistle, or Old Testament reading from the lectionary that Sunday. When Communion is celebrated, you may want to select an appropriate passage of scripture if those of the lectionary are not fitting.

By way of overview, it should be pointed out that the Christian year is *not* a sequential following of the life of Jesus from cradle to grave and beyond. Rather, the pattern of the Christian year is *a theological ordering of the church's commemoration of God's saving action.* The reforms that have occurred in recent years since Vatican II have been directed to returning the Roman Catholic Church to earlier practices rather than introducing innovations. Thus, what may seem new is usually the restoration of an ancient practice of the Christian church that had been dropped during the centuries.

Trinity Sunday

Psalm 8 (C)

Romans 5:1–5 (C) (L) (RC)

Revelation 4:1–11 (E)

Proverbs 8:22–31 (C) (L) (RC)

Isaiah 6:1–8 (E)

John 16:12–15

Meditation on the Texts

O God, you created the world and all that is in it, you redeem us from our sins, you empower us to live as your people. We thank you for the revelation you have given us of yourself in the three persons of the Trinity. We pray that the mystery of this revelation may keep us humble and that we may be continually moved to awe and wonder at your majesty, your love, and your constant guidance. In the name of the Father, the Son, and the Holy Spirit. Amen.

Commentary on the Texts

John 16:12–15

This passage is one of the Paraclete sayings in which John sets forth the work of the Holy Spirit. In the previous part of this chapter, John has been pointing out that the world has sinned by refusing to believe in Jesus, and that judgment will come for "the ruler of this world" after Jesus has departed. However, although the Spirit has a role in condemning the world's sin, it has other functions as well. In this passage, John is pointing to the Spirit's role as an instrument of revelation. He has moved away from the work of the Spirit in the world to the work of the Spirit in the life of the believer.

The disciples were still growing in faith and they were still struggling to understand many of Jesus' teachings. Jesus' words show his awareness that there are things they are not yet ready to hear (v. 12).

In v. 13, Jesus refers to the "Spirit of truth." In the other sayings the word "Paraclete" or "Counselor" is used, but John's understanding seems to be that "Spirit of truth" is another name for the Holy Spirit. It is the "truth" that will keep the disciples firm in a sinful world. The Spirit will teach the disciples those things they were too immature to understand under Jesus' tutelage. In this way the Spirit glorifies Jesus by helping the disciples to a clearer understanding of his teaching. The Spirit is not teaching "new" truth, but rather elucidating the teachings of Jesus. We must be careful not to interpret this to mean that every voice we hear is the voice of the Spirit. The test is whether that voice is telling us things consistent with the teachings of Christ.

Scholars differ as to exactly what the phrase "things that are to come" (v. 13) means. Does this refer to the end times of Jewish apocalypticism, or simply to the fact that Jesus is the fulfillment of the Old Testament prophecies? Does it mean that it is the Spirit who reminds us constantly of that hope we have of God's final, complete victory over sin and death, of the Lamb on the throne? Or does it refer to the trials the disciples will face in their own lives as they struggle to be faithful? There will always be new situations for Christians to face, and the Holy Spirit will teach us what to speak in those new situations, will interpret Jesus' teachings to us in new structures.

The Spirit will speak with the same authority Jesus had, which comes from God. This consistency is integral to the Trinity. There is no competition between the Spirit and Jesus. The Spirit's role is to make Jesus known (v. 14).

Further word study on glory and authority would be very beneficial in interpreting this passage. See any good Bible dictionary or theological wordbook.

The sermon might introduce the doctrine of the Trinity by beginning with Jesus' acknowledgment of the role of the Spirit as one who will continue to interpret the truth he has been teaching. This will not be "new truth" but a revelation of what Jesus would have taught in new situations. Thus, the Spirit interprets to us the truth Jesus received from the One he called Father. This collaborative work, mutuality, and cooperation is integral to an understanding of the Trinity and the way the Trinity relates to us.

Proverbs 8:22–31 (C) (L) (RC)

In this passage, Wisdom is described as being present at the moment of creation; indeed, as being God's firstborn or the first of God's creative acts. The personification of wisdom in this passage is foundational to the understanding of the "logos" which was "in the beginning with God" in the Prologue to the Gospel of John and for Paul's description in Colossians 1:15–16 of the Son as the "first-born of all creation."

The use of personification was a common literary device in wisdom literature and often used in the Psalms. It is not meant to be taken literally. Wisdom represented to the Hebrews not rational thought but rather a right attitude toward God: "the fear of the Lord."

In v. 22, the verb translated "created" can also be translated "begot" or "gave birth to." Poetic language is difficult to analyze, but this passage seems to be saying that the right attitude about God comes from God; therefore it is God's creation or even God's child. The birth image is reinforced in vs. 24 and 25, where the same verb is used ("was brought forth," RSV).

Verse 23 uses a rare verb translated "set up." It can also mean "was fashioned" or "became a reality," which reinforces the idea of wisdom as the child of God, the first of God's created works, becoming a reality as a result of God's giving birth. In the Old Testament, distinctions between the concepts of birth and creation are blurred. Birth is creation; creation is birth.

Verse 30 describes the role of wisdom by a noun which can be understood in two ways: as a "master workman" or as "a little child." If we accept the translation of "gave birth to" in v. 22, the "little child" translation seems logical. The child is pictured as growing up at God's side, bringing pleasure to God and then making the world her playground, finding pleasure in God's handiwork and in human beings.

In vs. 30 and 31, the word "rejoice" can also mean "making sport" or "laughing." This reinforces the picture of a happy child. Thomas Merton describes wisdom as a "feminine child, playing in the world, obvious and unseen, playing at all times before the Creator" (*A Thomas Merton Reader,* ed. T. P. McDonnell, p. 509; New York: Image Books, 1974). This is a delightful understanding of a right attitude toward God: it is a perspective that enables one to see the order and beauty in the world and to enjoy it in a fresh and childlike way.

If, on the other hand, we accept the translation of "master workman" or "architect," we have a different picture of Wisdom. She then becomes the agent or instrument of creation; the one who gives order and meaning to the universe. This understanding of Wisdom makes a direct connection with John's Prologue, for the *logos* of Greek thought also meant structure and meaning. John saw Christ as the one who provides that meaning in its clearest definition.

It is entirely possible that the writer of this passage intended for both metaphors to stand side by side. Poetry is like that. One metaphor enhances and illuminates another. Colossians 1 blends both images, for it is the "first-born of all creation" who is the one in whom "all things were created," and in whom "all things hold together." It is the Christ who has finally given definition to the order and meaning of the world, who has provided the ultimate personification of a right attitude toward God.

For further helpful reading on the relation between Wisdom and the Word, see those headings in a Bible dictionary.

The sermon could begin with the picture of wisdom as God's child, rejoicing in the whole order of creation, exemplifying a right attitude toward God. This image could then be related to the Prologue to John's Gospel which connects wisdom or *logos* to Christ.

Wisdom for us means having the right attitude toward God, an attitude exemplified by Jesus Christ and revealed to us by the Holy Spirit.

Isaiah 6:1–8 (E)

See also Epiphany 5, (C) (L).

This familiar story of Isaiah's call is an account of an extraordinary vision of God. Its imagery is powerful and unforgettable. Its language is apocalyptic: thrones, mysterious beasts, trembling foundations, burning coals, and the thundering of the voice of the Lord all remind us of other apocalyptic visions (notably Ezekiel 1 and Revelation 4). The attributes of God which appear in this passage, God's majesty, holiness, and righteousness, are of central importance to Isaiah's theology.

No description is given of the Lord, but the height of the throne and the fact that the hem of God's garment or train filled the temple gives some idea of God's awesomeness (v. 1). This picture of a long, sweeping robe is a reminder of the long robes worn by kings which symbolized their authority. The "throne" was also a symbol of authority and majesty. John 12:41 says that Isaiah saw the glory of Christ.

The "seraphim" (v. 2) were winged celestial beings of uncertain identity. Some authorities describe these as griffinlike creatures, others as winged serpents. The word "seraph" means "burn" and was used to describe the fiery serpents that attacked the Israelites in the wilderness (Num. 21:6–8). However, even if these seraphim did have serpent forms, they also had three pairs of wings. Their function here seems to be to guard the throne and sing God's praises.

The threefold repetition of "Holy, holy, holy" in v. 3 is to emphasize the infinite holiness of God. Three is the symbol of completeness. God is all holy and the only holy one. The holiness of God calls the whole of the earth to become holy. The seraphim showed in their attitudes and words enormous reverence for God. Even if they were heavenly beings, there still was a distance between them and the Lord. They were still God's creatures. The name used for God is "the LORD of hosts" or Lord Sabbath. This name represents the unlimited power of God over all authorities on heaven and earth. The first line of this praise song celebrates God's holiness and majesty which stands far above all of creation. The second part celebrates God's presence in the world. The earth being full of God's glory reminds us of Romans 1, where Paul describes God's power being revealed in everything that has been made. In Revelation 4, this song of the seraphim is sung by the Christian community. (See the commentary on Revelation 4 for today.)

The shaking of the foundations in v. 4 suggests the "fear of the Lord" inspired by the song of the seraphim. To be in the presence of God is a breathtaking, terrifying experience, and even the physical environment demonstrated awe and stress. The smoke concealed the Lord from view, thus enabling the prophet to live. Both smoke and earthquakes usually accompany theophanies.

Verse 5 shows the terror of the prophet. Being in the presence of the Almighty has made him intensely aware of his guilt. God's holiness brings his unholiness into stark relief. He also believes that it is not possible to face God and not be struck dead, and that strikes terror into his heart. "People of unclean lips" may be a reference to the fact that the great king Uzziah had been stricken with leprosy as punishment for usurping priestly prerogatives. On the other hand, it may refer to the sins of speech among the people generally. But Isaiah admits that he, too, is unworthy to stand in God's presence. Unlike the seraphim, he is unable to sing praises from a pure heart.

The meaning of "LORD of hosts" is not clear. It may mean Lord of the Israelite armies, or it may mean Lord of all gods. The best way to understand it, however, seems to be the Lord, the ruler of all or the Lord of the powers. It is an expression of God's absolute sovereignty.

In spite of Isaiah's guilt, God has chosen him and has provided a coal, the symbol of purification because it comes from the consecrated altar, to remove his guilt (v. 6). The Hebrew words for sin and guilt signify "departing from the norm." The word "forgiven" can be translated "covered." "To cover" is a cultic, sacral word, literally meaning "to atone." We cannot cover or remove our own sins; only God can do it, just as God covered Isaiah's sins. He is now free to do the will of God.

The question "Who will go for us?" (v. 8) reminds us that the scene is the heavenly court; God is asking this of the heavenly beings in the court. Although there are many call narratives in the Old Testament, we find that this one is distinctive because Isaiah does not follow the pattern of demurring that we see in the cases of Moses and Jeremiah. Isaiah does not beg off, nor does he ask about the consequences. He accepts the call and declares his readiness to serve without hesitation. He recognizes the call as a sign of God's unmerited grace, and he is willing to be faithful to it.

The sermon might develop the concept of the Trinity as a way to express the completeness of the nature of God. These verses give a symbolic picture of the three persons of the Trinity: God as the Creator whose glory fills the earth, Christ the Redeemer who purifies and forgives us, and the Holy Spirit as the dynamic force who sends us forth in mission.

Romans 5:1–5 (C) (L) (RC)

The passage that begins with Romans 5 and continues through chapter 8 has been described by some scholars as the most important section of this letter, and perhaps of all of Paul's letters. Paul has been setting forth the doctrine of justification by faith and now begins to show what the results of that justification are in the life of the believer. The justified one, the one made righteous by faith, is at peace with God. As Paul uses the terms, justification and reconciliation are not identical. They are different metaphors for God's act in Christ. Justification can be impersonal, as when justice is meted out by an impartial judge; but God's act for us is highly personal, and involves an overcoming of alienation between those who once were friends. This is reconciliation: becoming friends of God once more. It is the result of justification. Paul wants us to understand just what the blessings are which that reconciliation will bring.

This brief passage contains a richly packed description of the Christian life: its demands and its rewards. It is a life based upon hope: hope of sharing the divine glory. Paul wants to show how that hope is appropriate.

In v. 1 Paul speaks of a peace which is not a serene, "floating on clouds" experience, but peace in the sense of not being enemies. It has the same meaning here as "reconciliation." Because we are justified, we have peace, a sense of harmony with the universe, of having our house in order.

The phrase "we have obtained access" (v. 2) was commonly used to denote access to a royal person's chambers. It would have been almost impossible to achieve this without someone to act as a go-between. Christ is the one who introduces us to the grace "in which we stand." We do not have to work to receive it. This is the condition of those who enjoy divine favor. "We rejoice" can also be translated "boast" or "exult." There is a sense of elation in the prospect of sharing in God's glory. The juxtaposition of joy and peace is a reminder of the old saying: "Peace is joy resting; joy is peace dancing."

Paul says we will share in "the glory of God." In the rabbinical tradition, Adam's face shone with brightness before the fall, and that brightness will be restored in the messianic kingdom. Afflictions are a cause for joy because God teaches us through them. We rejoice in our hope of glory, in our sufferings and in God.

"Endurance produces character." The NEB translates this "proof that we have stood the test" and the TEV calls it "God's approval." It is the assurance that we can meet the test that gives us hope. This hope is grounded in God's love which comes to us through the Holy Spirit. This anticipates a fuller discussion of the work of the Spirit in chapter 8. Note that although it was Christ who brought about the reconciliation with God, it is the Holy Spirit who fills us with the knowledge of God's love. This is the wonder and mystery of the way the Trinity works.

The sermon might show how the doctrine of the Trinity is a source of hope. In spite of our waywardness, the God who brought us into being loves us, and through grace, has provided a way to bring us back into harmony. It is through our faith in Jesus Christ that we can be restored to peace with God, a reconciliation that gives us the hope of sharing in the glory of God and enables us to endure suffering. It is the Holy Spirit who sustains us by assuring us constantly of God's love, and thus keeps our hope alive.

Chapter 4 begins a major new section of the book. The letters to the churches are finished, and this chapter opens with a vision of God as Sovereign Creator and Redeemer. This vision leads into the account of the events preceding Christ's final triumph.

There is an abrupt change of scene with this chapter. The earth (represented by the seven churches) has been left behind, and the writer has been lifted up into the middle of the heavenly council before the very throne of God. Being caught up into heavenly spheres is a common feature of apocalyptic writing. There is a definite resemblance to Isaiah 6, the Old Testament lectionary passage for today.

The voice referred to in v. 1 is that of the risen Lord, the One who is both sovereign Lord and suffering lamb. The "open door" is the door of revelation. John is told that he will be given a glimpse of what lies ahead. This will include terrible conflict with the forces of evil. Before that, however, John is given a vision of God on the throne, in control of the universe, no matter how threatening the forces of evil.

The phrase "in the Spirit" refers to having an ecstatic experience. "Throne" is a symbol of the absolute sovereignty of God. John used this symbol ten more times in the book. Being "seated on the throne" indicates the double role of king and universal judge. This image was undoubtedly influenced by Ezekiel's vision of God's throne-chariot, which also included creatures, rainbow, thunder and lightning, and a figure on a throne (see Ezekiel 1). John has used familiar images from the apocalyptic literature to convey the truth that God is in charge; the universe is not ruled by blind chance. Just as in our Isaiah passage for today, there is no description of God, but it is clear that to John, God has been defined in Jesus Christ.

Verse 3 is rich in highly symbolic images. Jasper (jade) and sardis (carnelian) were stones found in the breastplate of the high priests. Jasper represented the translucence and brightness of the holiness of God. Carnelian represented the wrath of God. The rainbow is a reminder of the covenant promise to Noah.

There are various ways to interpret the "twenty-four elders" in v. 4: they could represent the church in its totality, a combination of the twelve patriarchs and the twelve apostles; the image might come from 1 Chronicles 24, where twenty-four divisions of priests were each headed by a chief or elder, thus representing the people of God; or they might be a group of heavenly beings performing the mediating function of expediting prayers. Their white garments represented purity, and the golden crowns, royal dignity.

The lightning and thunder (v. 5) remind us of God's appearance on Mt. Sinai. The lightning is a symbol of God's majesty and power. The seven torches or seven spirits represent the Holy Spirit, God's active presence in the world.

The "sea of glass" (v. 6) is a symbol of separateness. It is not really a sea but looks like one. It heightens God's holiness by putting distance between God and God's creatures. The "living creatures" remind us of the seraphim in Isaiah 6; here they represent all living creatures. The creatures celebrate God's holiness and power in the past, present, and future.

The elders join in the praise in v. 10. Falling down denotes an attitude of reverent prostration before a ruler or a deity, but their praise differs from the creatures in that it is addressed directly to God. All that exists is under God's rule. When we see the brokenness of creation, and of our own lives, we need to be reminded that God is in control.

The sermon could show John's understanding of the Trinitarian nature of God. It is the voice of Christ who opens the door to heaven and calls John. Through the power of the Spirit, John is able to experience the presence of God. John sees all of creation giving honor and glory to the Lord God Almighty, who made all things, who was and is and is to come. In the same way, through the invitation of Christ, and by the power of the Spirit, we too are able to be brought into God's presence and reminded that everything is under God's control.

Theological Reflection

Since this is Trinity Sunday, it is not surprising that these texts provide help in understanding the relationship between the three persons of the Godhead. All of them reflect the glory and authority of God (both translations of the Hebrew word *kābōd* and the Greek word *doxa*). All except the John passage contain the element of rejoicing, particularly rejoicing in God. All the passages recognize God's sovereignty. The Proverbs passage shows the intimate relationship between God and wisdom at creation, later adopted by Paul to describe the relationship between Christ and creation. The passages from John and Romans underline the role of the Holy Spirit in giving hope and teaching the truth about Christ given by God. The Isaiah and Revelation passages glorify God's sovereignty over all the earth but also indicate the redemptive and empowering aspects of God's nature revealed in the person of Jesus Christ and the Holy Spirit.

Children's Message

One way to discuss the Trinity with children is to talk about the different roles persons play. You might ask the children to tell some of the things their mother or father does (cook, go to the office, teach, mow grass). Then ask, "Can a cook and a teacher and a gardener be the same person?" Go on to explain how when we talk about God, sometimes we talk about God as the One who made the world, or as Jesus Christ, who died for us, or as the Holy Spirit who gives us power to do the right things. All three are the same, even though they do different things. That is why we sing "Holy, holy, holy, God in three Persons, blessed Trinity."

Hymns for Trinity Sunday

Holy, Holy, Holy!; Ancient of Days; Come, Thou Almighty King.

Pentecost 2

Ordinary Time 9

Proper 4

Psalm 100 (C)

1 Kings 8:22–23, 41–43 (C)
1 Kings 8:41–43 (L) (RC)
1 Kings 8:22–23, 27–30, 41–43 (E)

Galatians 1:1–10 (C) (L) (E)
Galatians 1:1–2, 6–10 (RC)

Luke 7:1–10

Meditation on the Texts

God of all peoples, we praise you for your great compassion which knows no geographical limits or racial boundaries. We praise you for your listening ear which hears the prayers of all those who call on your name in faith. We praise you for your abundant grace which sets us free from the constraints of having to earn our salvation by our works. May our faith be as great as that of the centurion who, without seeing you, believed in your power to make all things well. In the name of our Lord Jesus Christ. Amen.

Commentary on the Texts

Luke 7:1–10

This account of the healing of the centurion's servant begins a series of stories that highlight how Jesus was received by various people, including those outside the Jewish faith, such as the centurion. This story is similar to that of the raising of Jairus' daughter in Luke 8, the official's son in John 4, and the Syrophoenician woman's daughter in Mark 7.

This story is also found in Matthew 8:5–13. Matthew and Luke agree essentially in their telling of the story, especially in the dialogue, but differ in the details. For instance, Matthew has the centurion coming directly to Jesus, while in Luke he goes through intermediaries. We shall discuss Luke's reason for this change as we examine the text.

This is a paradigmatic story of the coming of the Gentiles to Christ. It illustrates the readiness of the Gentiles to accept Jesus which Luke develops as a main theme in Acts.

Further light on the purpose of the story is shed when we look at its place in Luke's narrative. Luke follows this story and the story of the healing of the widow's son with the question brought to Jesus by the followers of John the Baptist, "Are you he who is to come?" It is possible that Luke is illustrating with these two healings the answer Jesus will give to that question, namely, "Go and tell John what you have seen."

Note also that it follows a long discourse similar to the Sermon on the Mount in Matthew. Unlike Matthew, Luke divides Jesus' teaching into smaller units with particular themes. The first unit in this discourse, which begins at 6:20, is that of the persecution and poverty of the disciples. The second, beginning at 6:39, is about the peril of blind leaders. It ends with the importance of doing good. He then introduces the story of the centurion, an account of a man whose life is characterized by good deeds.

The centurion was worried about one of his servants who was "dear to him" (v. 2). The Greek word used here can be translated "precious" or "valuable." The centurion's concern, however, does not appear to be about losing valuable property, but rather, about losing someone precious to him. It seems to be a humane rather than a mercenary concern. A centurion was an officer in command of one hundred men; this one was probably in the service of Herod Antipas. He may have been in charge of mercenary troops or soldiers who had customs duties. A centurion corresponds to a noncommissioned officer in our army.

In Matthew's account of this story the centurion came himself, but Luke seems to want to stress the man's humility. For a Gentile to come directly to a rabbi would have been too bold. Since this was the first account of a Gentile approaching Jesus, it is likely that Luke wanted to enlist his readers' sympathy.

The "elders" were not "old men," but a special group of Jewish community leaders in Capernaum. Their high respect for the centurion is indicated by their willingness to intercede on his behalf, and the complimentary language they used about him. The phrase "he loves our nation" is similar to the words the Jewish historian, Josephus, used of Alexander the Great: "He honored our nation."

The leaders' statement, "he built us our synagogue" indicates that the centurion was both wealthy and generous. Although he was clearly a Gentile, he seemed to have been attracted to Judaism, possibly because of its high moral standards. The centurion's words about himself, in v. 6, "I am not worthy," stand in contrast to the flattery of the elders, and are an indication of his humility. He is also aware of and sensitive to Jewish scruples about entering a Gentile home.

The centurion asks Jesus to simply "say the word" (v. 7). He recognizes the power of a word spoken with authority. From his army experience he knew how a word of command could produce results. With this statement he acknowledged Jesus' special authority and his belief that it could produce healing.

The climax of the story is in Jesus' words of praise found in v 9. Nowhere in the Gospels does he utter higher praise of a person, and this particular person is not a Jew, but a Gentile. Jesus was not praising the centurion's good works, his personal piety, or even his humility. Instead he was praising the faith that recognized Jesus' authority, even without seeing him.

The story closes in a characteristic manner with the healing accomplished. This healing is unusual because it is accomplished at a distance. The only other story in which this is true is that of the Syrophoenician woman.

It would be helpful to **do additional study** of the Greek word *exousia,* translated "authority," using a Bible dictionary or theological wordbook.

The sermon might center on the meaning of true worth. The centurion was worthy by worldly standards: wealthy, benevolent, generous, humanitarian, concerned for his servant, respected by the leaders of the community, influential. This could be contrasted with the ways in which he considered himself unworthy: not a religious man by Jewish standards; not worthy to have Jesus enter his home because he was an outsider, a Gentile; of limited authority (could not heal the sick servant). What made this man worthy in Jesus' sight? It was his faith in a higher authority, and his recognition of that authority in Jesus. He is a vivid contrast to the "blind leading the blind" in the previous discourse. Likewise, it is our faith in God's grace that makes us worthy. We are "justified by faith," not by our works. God in Jesus Christ has the authority to make us whole.

1 Kings 8:22–23, 41–43 (C)

1 Kings 8:41–43 (L) (RC)

1 Kings 8:22–23, 27–30, 41–43 (E)

The dedication of the temple by Solomon has been called the central point of the Book of Kings by means of which we understand all the rest. The occasion was a gathering of the people in the seventh month for the Feast of Tabernacles and a ceremonial covenant renewal. During this celebration, Solomon brought the Ark from the city of David into the temple as a focal point of the temple dedication. This was symbolic of God's taking possession of a new dwelling: a house built for God by Solomon in accordance with David's dream. Solomon has reminded them of the past and how God had fulfilled the promise to David by allowing him, Solomon, to finish the temple. The eternity of the Davidic dynasty and the temple are also emphasized.

The goal of the whole chapter is to evoke admiration for the king, the temple, and God. This chapter reveals a God who is trustworthy, who will hold to the covenant and keep promises. This is also a God like no other, who is steadfastly loving, who expects obedience, who is a God of "all the peoples on earth."

In v. 22, Solomon offers a prayer for the Davidic dynasty. This is a hymnlike invocation of God as one without equal, who keeps covenant loyalty. Note that Solomon did not kneel but stood before the altar for this prayer. This is the customary attitude before a deity, which can be seen in carvings from many neighboring cultures of Solomon's day. Kneeling to show reverence came much later. The king had priestly prerogatives and served as a vital link between God and the community. This verse contains the first mention of the altar in the description of the temple.

The phrase "no God like thee" in v. 23 expresses the incomparable nature of God, but still allows for the existence of other gods. However, this marks a major step toward true monotheism.

To "walk before thee" means to keep the law. God's steadfast love (hesed) is the foundation for the covenant and demands a response. God's grace takes the initiative but we are to show loyal obedience to the covenant.

Verses 27–30 express the tension that always exists in holding together the idea of the transcendence of God with the sense of God's presence in the temple. Solomon wants the people to understand that God is not restricted to the temple, but does promise to hear the earnest prayers offered up there. The temple, like the tabernacle, is a symbol of God's presence.

In vs. 41–43 we find an expression of God's concern for all people. The foreigners spoken of here are not just the groups of protected aliens now living in Israel, but are those who have been attracted to the Jewish faith and have begun to worship God. The story of Naaman the Syrian in 2 Kings 5 is the story of one such "foreigner."

The phrases "mighty hand" and "outstretched arm" in v. 42 suggest that it is the stories of the exodus which have attracted the foreigners to the worship of the God of Israel. The phrase "great name" is more than the title by which God is called, but represents God's presence and fame.

The prayer in v. 43 represents a broadened understanding of God as more than just the God of Israel. God is also concerned about other peoples, and rejoices when they come in faith to worship. The good news of God's love is for the whole world.

For further study, the preacher might explore the richness of the Hebrew word hesed, variously translated "steadfast love, loyalty, mercy, or loving-kindness."

The sermon might develop the ways in which our God is like no other: a covenant God who shows love but expects obedience; a faithful God who always keeps promises; and a God of all people who answers the prayers of faithful seekers.

Galatians 1:1–10 (C) (L) (E)

Galatians 1:1–2, 6–10 (RC)

Martin Luther loved the Letter to the Galatians, and based the foundation principles of the Reformation on it. It is truly a book that underscores grace.

Unlike Paul's other letters, however, it is not a letter of praise, but begins with a tone of sharp reprimand born out of Paul's disappointment in his converts at Galatia. To understand why he is so angry, we must know the context of the letter.

Twenty years after Pentecost, the Apostolic Council of Jerusalem reached an agreement between Paul and Barnabas on one hand and James, Cephas, and John on the other, which gave the missionary movement momentum by endorsing Paul's work. Paul refers to this in 2:7–9 where he relates how the council gave him "the right hand of fellowship," or, in another translation, "accord between equals." Paul then began his mission to the Gentiles, establishing churches and using the literary epistle as a tool to address church policy. He used many associates in his work and conducted a well-organized operation, which, nevertheless, ran into many obstacles. One of the key issues was whether Gentiles ought to live like Jews and participate in all the Jewish religious customs, notably circumcision. It is this issue which the Letter to the Galatians addresses.

Paul wrote this letter to the churches he had founded in the province of Galatia in central Asia Minor. We do not know exactly where these churches were located: whether in northern or southern Galatia.

It is also not clear when he wrote the letter, but he leaves no doubt as to *why* he wrote it. Shortly after Paul left Galatia, a group of people who insisted that all converts should scrupulously observe the Jewish law, infiltrated the church.

Who were they? It is not easy to identify them because we have little information about them, and most of that comes from Paul, their opponent. Charles Cousar suggests the following possibilities for their identity (of which he prefers no. 2):

1. Jewish Christians from Jerusalem
2. Jewish Christians with no support from Jerusalem
3. Jewish Christians of gnostic persuasion
4. Not Jews but Gentile Christians
5. A mixture of two groups: Judaizing activists who urged submission to the law and radicals who felt exempt from moral issues

See Charles Cousar, *Galatians,* Interpretation series, p. 5 (Atlanta: John Knox Press, 1986), for details of his argument.

Paul was obviously shocked by the impact of this legalistic influence on the Galatian Christians. He saw it as undermining the freedom given by the gospel and undercutting grace. Paul felt that to insist on circumcision and other observances of the law was a return to salvation by works. It was a crucial issue for early Christians. Paul felt that it was an attack on him and his whole ministry. He felt that he was being accused of "incompleteness," by de-emphasizing the Old Testament understanding of piety—obedience to the law. The result was this letter which is both personal and emotional.

Paul wanted no compromise with the freedom offered by grace. He wanted the message of justification by faith alone to be clear and definite. He felt that Old Testament legalism was as dangerous to the Christian faith as the pagan ideologies with which the Galatians were surrounded. In this letter, Paul brings to the Galatians, and to all of us who are endangered by contemporary versions of works righteousness a declaration of faith in God's forgiving love readily available to us.

Letters in ancient Greece customarily opened with a simple salutation that usually took the form of "A to B, Greetings." Paul expands this salutation to make affirmations that will set the stage for the central message of the letter. In v. 1 he uses a double negative to identify himself. He is probably quoting what the opposition has been saying about him. In this very first verse, he establishes his authority by stating the source of his authority: Jesus Christ and God the Father. Paul is probably referring to his commissioning by Jesus Christ on the Damascus road, the basis of his claim to apostleship.

The term "the brethren" (v. 2) could well be "the Christians." He may be referring to his traveling companions who went with him on his trip to Jerusalem at the end of the third century to take the collection gathered for the poor.

In v. 3 we find a standard Pauline greeting. These words stand like bookends for the letter with the opposing set of bookends being the words "peace and mercy" in 6:16. Grace is basic and peace is the result of grace. Peace, as it is used here, is the equivalent of shalom, the condition of well-being when God is our friend and all is well with us. This greeting is important, for in it Paul sets forth his theology and summarizes in this one verse the message of the next four chapters: there is no salvation except in the crucified Christ.

In v. 4 Paul speaks of Christ's voluntary action as giving himself to deliver us from "the present evil age." This is language borrowed from Jewish eschatology to describe the domination of evil in contrast to the age of freedom and hope which is yet to come in its fullness. This cycle has been broken, Paul says, and we are already delivered from the bondage of the evil age. The will of God has been revealed in the saving work of Christ. To suggest that Christ's death and resurrection was not enough for salvation is to fail to understand God's will.

The doxology in v. 5 may have come from early Christian worship. Doxology is the only proper response to the gift of God in Jesus Christ. This is not normally a part of a salutation. Instead of praising the readers, Paul praises God.

In his other letters, after the salutation Paul usually includes warm words of praise. This is not true here. Instead there is an abrupt transition. Paul expresses his shock, hurt, pain, and anger at the Galatians' defection. Paul accuses them of "deserting." This is a strong word, indicating a shameful change of mind. It was an expression commonly used for changing philosophic schools or religions.

"The gospel of Christ" (v. 7) is that which comes from Christ and is about Christ. It is basically grace initiated by God. We are called into it through preaching. To leave this gospel is to leave Christ.

In vs. 8–9 we find Paul using very strong words about the evil of preaching a perverted gospel that is not based on grace. The word "accursed" indicates being declared anathema, put out of the community, and committed to destruction. For Paul there is no middle ground.

The questions in v. 10 reveal the charges that had been leveled against Paul. He wants to make the point that if he had compromised in order to make the gospel more marketable to the Gentiles, he would not have been a faithful servant of Christ.

The word "servant" can also be translated "slave." Paul uses it also in Romans 1:1 and Philippians 1:1. It connotes absolute obedience which knows no will but that of the Master. It is interesting to parallel this with the idea expressed in Galatians 5:1 of being freed from "a yoke of slavery." It is one of Paul's ironies: we are freed from slavery by becoming slaves.

The sermon might develop the importance of justification by faith by recognizing how the Galatians' difficulty in accepting grace led them to return to a doctrine of salvation by works. A comparison could be made to Christians today who are tempted to rely on works righteousness. Paul calls us to a clearer understanding of the implications of justification by faith for our lives: our works are the response to our justification not the reason for it.

Theological Reflection

All these passages stress the fact that God will hear the prayers of those who come in faith. God's grace is not limited to certain persons, as indicated by Solomon's prayer and the centurion story, but is available for all the peoples of the earth. The Galatians passage reminds us that it is important to remember that a response of faith means we are not to let ourselves be trapped by the seductive patterns of works righteousness. Instead, we must trust in the authority of God's grace even as the centurion believed in Jesus' authority to heal his servant.

Children's Message

Tell the story of the centurion, who was an important soldier, but who believed that Jesus was even more important than he was and could do things he could not do. Explain how this important man was willing to ask Jesus for help for someone he cared about. Remind the children that Jesus is ready to help them too. All they have to do is ask him for help and have faith in him like the centurion did.

Hymns for Pentecost 2

Christ Is the World's True Light; O Zion, Haste, Thy Mission High Fulfilling; Christ for the World We Sing.

Pentecost 3

Ordinary Time 10

Proper 5

Psalm 113 (C)   Galatians 1:11–24 (C) (L) (E)

                  Galatians 1:11–19 (RC)

1 Kings 17:17–24

                  Luke 7:11–17

Meditation on the Texts

O God, we are grateful that you have called us and set us apart by your grace. We pray that our faithfulness to this call may cause others to recognize your power and glorify your name. May we constantly remember that our authority is from you; that all we say or do for your kingdom is rooted and grounded in your grace and empowerment of us. Make our lives witnesses of your love, so that all those we meet will acknowledge your power and give you glory. Amen.

Commentary on the Texts

Luke 7:11–17

This story of the raising of the widow's son at Nain, not found in the other Gospels, continues one of Luke's favorite themes of how Jesus was received by different groups of people, especially Gentiles. Along with the story of the healing of the centurion's servant in last Sunday's Gospel reading, this story, too, prefaces the answer given to the disciples of John the Baptist. Not only is Jesus healing the sick, they say, but the dead are being raised to life. The raising of the widow's son is a story that illustrates just that. Luke describes two other resuscitations in his narrative: that of Jesus raising Jairus' daughter in Luke 8 and of Peter raising Dorcas in Acts 9. All of them illustrate the power of God to overcome death.

This is a typical miracle story, its purpose being to identify Jesus as a miracle worker, thereby linking him with the Old Testament prophets. Luke emphasizes Jesus' similarity to Elijah by including in this account many similarities to the raising of the widow's son by Elijah which is the subject of today's Old Testament text, 1 Kings 17:17–24. Both Elijah and Jesus arrive at a town; in both stories a widow is met at the gate; and in both a widow's son is revived. The phrase found in 7:15 "gave him to his mother" even uses almost the same wording as 1 Kings 17:23. In the affirmation of the crowd, "A great prophet has arisen among us!" (7:16), there is a very marked similarity to the words of the widow in the Elijah story who, after her son is revived, proclaims her certainty that he is a man of God through whom God speaks.

One difference in this story and in that of the centurion's servant is that there is no mention of faith here. The mother does not request Jesus' help, but he gives it out of his tremendous compassion for her in her grief (v. 13).

Jesus had left Capernaum with his followers and had journeyed about twenty-five miles southwest to the village of Nain at the foot of a mountain called Little Hermon. This story introduces us to some of the Jewish funeral customs. It was customary for the Jews to bury their dead outside the cities since tombs were considered a defilement, and to have the funeral on the evening of the day of death. It was probable that the procession included professional mourners whose wailing or music would precede them.

Note that there are two "large crowds" mentioned in this story. One, accompanying Jesus, is approaching the gate of the town of Nain, quite possibly in a mood of exultation and excitement after the successful healing of the centurion's servant (v. 11). The other, accompanying the bereaved widow, is filled with grief, sorrow, and helplessness in the face of death (v. 12). The fact that the dead man was the widow's only son lends a particular poignancy to the story, since the inference is that now she has no means of support.

Jesus sees both her grief and her helplessness and takes pity on her. Luke speaks of him here as "the Lord" which is appropriate in view of the confrontation with death which is about to take place. The body was being carried on an open bier, or coffin. It was Jewish custom not to use closed coffins but to wrap the body in a shroud and place it on an open bier for burial.

Jesus stopped the procession by simply touching the open coffin, in spite of knowing that he would incur ritual uncleanness (v. 14). This highly symbolic act was a defiance of legalistic custom in order to carry out an act of compassion. Jesus speaks with authority as the Lord of life and death. His command, literally, "Be raised up," is obeyed and the young man sits up and begins to speak (v. 15).

The result is that the crowd is filled with a mixture of fear and praise, and Jesus is acclaimed as "a great prophet" through whom God has visited the people (v. 16), words bearing a similarity to the words of Zacharias in 1:68. It is worth noting, however, that this expression of acclaim does not refer to Jesus' messianic role, but rather to his role in serving others. Through this service, God's compassionate concern can be seen. The Greek word for fear, *phobos,* is frequently used by Luke to express the reaction of the crowds to heavenly interventions or miraculous happenings, as in the healing of the paralytic (5:26), and is nearly always followed by ascriptions of praise to God from the crowd. This is, indeed, an appropriate response to the healing touch of God's compassionate love.

The sermon might begin with the contrasting moods of the crowds, symbolic of the times when celebration and affirmation are confronted by the pain and tragedy ever present in this life. The compassion of Christ is made very real in this story, and the power of his healing touch transforms tragedy into great joy; grief into awe and praise of God. The people recognize Christ's authority as one who acts by the power of God. Life comes through an encounter with the living Lord. The only appropriate response to this is awe and praise.

1 Kings 17:17–24

The story of the raising of the son of the widow at the village of Zarephath is one of the miracle stories told to enhance the reputation of the prophet Elijah and establish the authority of his word (see v. 24).

This particular passage is the sequel to a story that turns upside down the natural order of things: a widow, normally expected to be the recipient of charity, becomes its provider. This story of caring for another out of meager resources reminds us of the widow in Mark 12:41–44 who gave "everything she had."

This parable of caring takes a tragic turn, however. The widow's son dies and the widow interprets his death as punishment for her sins, an attitude that persists in New Testament times (see John 9:2). Her question of Elijah, "What have you against me?" means, literally, "What have you and I [in common]?" which is an idiom for "Why do you interfere in my affairs?" This expression occurs several times in the New Testament, notably in John 2:4 where Jesus asks the same question of his mother at the wedding in Cana. The woman's anger toward Elijah suggests that she felt that it was his presence in her home which has drawn attention to her "sin," or as the NEB says "You came here to bring my sins to light." As a "man of God," he represented God's holy presence, and her response was not unlike Isaiah's, "Woe is me! . . . for I am a man of unclean lips." A sense of God's holiness evokes a consciousness of sin. And, in her mind, since sin merits punishment, she was being punished by the death of her son.

Elijah's response to her accusation is not defensive. Instead he shows his authority and compassion by taking control of the situation. He takes the child up to his room, probably a temporary shelter on the flat roof. Guests were typically housed in this way in peasant homes, permitting even unattached women to offer traditional Semitic hospitality without infringing on decorum. He stretched out upon the boy three times. There is a similarity here to "contactual magic" whereby the health of one is transferred to the other. There are many references to similar practices in Babylonian texts. Paul does the same thing in Acts 20:9–10. The emphasis here is not on the magical act, however, but on Elijah's prayer. It is God who heals the boy, not Elijah's magic.

Was the boy actually dead? The text does not make it clear. The Hebrew word used for "death" may actually signify a temporary suspension of animation. Elijah's prayer for the return of the nephesh (soul) in v. 21 does not necessarily mean the boy had been dead. The word means primarily "breath" or "animation." Hebrew, more than English, talks of "reviving" without implying that the person had been physically dead. However, even though the boy's death is not confirmed by the writer, the widow believes him dead. The question of whether he was dead or just near death would not have mattered to the original audience. Richard Nelson points out that there was "no sharp line between life and death in the Old Testament" (Richard D. Nelson, *First and Second Kings,* Interpretation series, p. 111; Atlanta: John Knox Press, 1987). Even after the soul had left the body, it was thought that the soul and body could be reunited, provided the soul had not descended to Sheol.

In v. 24, the mother's response is entirely natural. Elijah was already a man of God, but now she knows in her heart that he is one. His authority has been proved to her by the miracle that has taken place—the movement from death to life.

The sermon might focus on God's power to turn the normal order of things upside down: death is transformed to life; anger is changed to gratitude; grief becomes joy; doubt becomes faith. Elijah's faith makes him an agent of God's power to turn things upside down, and it is this divine authorization the widow recognizes and affirms. God can use us also to be agents of the power that turns things upside down, rights wrongs, and brings wholeness and healing.

Galatians 1:11–24 (C) (L) (E)

Galatians 1:11–19 (RC)

Paul begins this pericope with his "disclosure" formula, which is variously translated: "I would have you know" (RSV); "I must make it clear to you" (NEB); and "Let me tell you" (TEV); all of which indicate there is something important to come. He uses a similar expression in 1 Corinthians 15:3.

The "something important" is Paul's vehement defense of the authority of the apostleship in vs. 11 and 12. It is derived from the gospel, he says, which is not of human origin. It is an authority that is not dependent on any congregation or church council but comes directly from Jesus Christ. In both the Corinthians and Galatians passage, Paul speaks of having "received" and "passed on" the good news. What is this gospel he preaches? It is basically that salvation is possible for all through faith in Christ.

In v. 13, Paul refers to his former life in Judaism, in which his dedication to upholding the law and the tradition resulted in his persecuting the Christian churches. (NOTE: the expression he uses to refer to the Christian churches is the Old Testament expression "assembly of the LORD," as in Deuteronomy 23:2). The tense of the verbs indicates repeated, habitual action. He was a diligent Pharisee, and he does not apologize for it. The "tradition" for which he was so zealous consisted of the six hundred thirteen commandments the rabbis had added to interpret the Torah. Paul's zeal stemmed from his devotion to and admiration for this tradition. He follows this admission of violent persecution with a clear statement of his feeling that he had been chosen by God before birth (1:15) to be an apostle, an echo of Jeremiah 1:4, "before you were born I consecrated you; I appointed you a prophet to the nations." Paul was claimed by God's grace; it was God's decision and action that changed his life. It was not a "conversion," however, so much as a commissioning or call, since he did not repudiate his former life, but rather saw the church as the fulfillment of God's promises to Israel.

In vs. 17 and 18, Paul describes the details of his call in order to make clear that his commissioning was not done by the leaders of the church but by Christ himself. Although he is not specific about the reason for his going to Arabia (the area south and east of

Syria) and to Damascus, his primary purpose in including this material seems to be to stress the fact that during this time period he had no close connection to the apostles in Jerusalem. Therefore, his call did not come from them. The Greek word *historeō* in v. 18, which is behind the translation "to visit Cephas" in the RSV, has several meanings. Perhaps a better translation would be "to get information from Cephas." Cephas is the Aramaic term for Peter. It would be only logical that Paul would go to Peter to learn more about Jesus. However, this was not a visit to get the Jerusalem church's approval for his ministry. He underscores this assertion with a sacred oath in v. 20.

Paul then went to his hometown of Tarsus in Cilicia on the southeast coast of Asia Minor (see Acts 9:30), where he centered his ministry for a number of years. This is why the people in the churches of Judea did not know him "by sight" but only by reputation (v. 22). The reason they glorified God when they heard of his zeal for the gospel was that they recognized that only God could have brought about such a dramatic change.

The sermon might focus on the revolutionary change that is possible through the grace of God in Jesus Christ. Paul, who had been a deeply religious man, and as such, a persecutor of the church, tells the story of his discovery that he had been set apart and called through grace to preach the good news to the Gentiles. This claim of God on his life not only enabled him to change but was the source of his authority. The change in his life was a testimony to God's power and caused the people who knew him to glorify God. The sermon might remind all who have been "set apart" by God of the testimony their lives can make to the power and grace of God.

Theological Reflection

All three of the lectionary passages are stories about the authority that comes as a result of faithful response to God's grace. In each case, the exercise of that authority results in praise to God as its source. Elijah healed the widow's son, and she acknowledged him as a "man of God" who spoke God's word. Jesus healed the son of the widow of Nain and the people acclaimed him as a great prophet and glorified God. Paul goes to great lengths to explain that his authority was not from other men but from the God who had set him apart and changed his life. The resulting change caused people to praise God as its author. Our only real authority comes from being chosen by God and redeemed through grace, not from our accomplishments or by human decree.

Children's Message

Tell the story of Jesus bringing the widow's son back to life. Emphasize the compassion and sympathy Jesus had for the widow when he saw how sad she was. Describe how the people praised God when the boy was healed. Remind the children that Jesus feels sorry for us, too, when we are hurt or sad, and he can make things all right for us again. Our response to Jesus' healing love should be one of joy and praise. You might close by asking the children to sing with you, "Jesus Loves Me!"

Hymns for Pentecost 3

O God, Our Faithful God; Christ of the Upward Way; Amazing Grace.

Ordinary Time 11
Proper 6

Psalm 42 (C)

1 Kings 19:1–8 (C)
2 Samuel 11:26–12:10, 13–15 (L) (E)
2 Samuel 12:7–10, 13 (RC)

Galatians 2:15–21 (C)
Galatians 2:11–21 (L) (E)
Galatians 2:16, 19–21 (RC)

Luke 7:36–8:3 (C) (RC)
Luke 7:36–50 (L) (E)

Meditation on the Texts

God of compassion and grace, you look at our lives and see our frailty. Our good intentions are puffs of dandelion; our obedience falters on feet of clay; our sinful desires clamor to be heard. Help us to remember that you came to Elijah in his despair and discouragement and gave him strength; that you came to David in his pain and remorse and forgave him; that you pardoned the woman of the city and accepted her extravagant gift of love with praise; that you reminded the Galatians through Paul of your abundant grace which we do not have to earn with works. With these assurances of your forgiving love in mind, we ask that you accept our repentance for our frailty and wash us white as snow, that we might live with the assurance and joy of resurrected people. Amen.

Commentary on the Texts

Luke 7:36–8:3 (C) (RC)

Luke 7:36–50 (L) (E)

In the previous passage, Jesus is accused of being a friend of sinners. In this pericope, we see an illustration of that in the story of the anointing of Jesus by a sinful "woman of the city." It is a complicated story because it combines a pronouncement story, whose purpose is to show Jesus as Messiah, with a parable (vs. 41–43). It is similar to anointing stories found in Matthew 26:6–13, Mark 14:3–9, and John 12:1–8 (see Lent 5, (C)), but differs in significant details from all of them. It is possible that Luke may have heard this story from his own sources, and combined it with details from Mark's similar story. In the early days of the church before the tradition was written down, it was extremely likely that details from one story became incorporated into other similar stories.

In spite of these complications, the point of this story is easy to discern. It describes the repentance of one of Israel's outcasts, the forgiveness offered her by Jesus, and her emotional demonstration of love and gratitude in response to that forgiveness.

The setting of the story is the home of one of the Pharisees who had invited Jesus to dinner (v. 36). This was courageous of the Pharisee, but it was not the only time Jesus received such invitations. Two other times Luke tells of Jesus' being hosted by a Pharisee (11:37; 14:1). While in some cases their motives may have been genuine interest or curiosity to know more about Jesus, in others, often it was in simple obedience to the hospitality laws, which required that the key persons in the synagogue invite the visiting rabbi home for a meal. It is possible that this incident followed just such an occasion of Jesus' preaching. Since Simon seems to think of Jesus as a prophet (v. 39), he may simply want to honor him, but the breach of etiquette indicated in vs. 44–46 argues against that.

The expression "and behold" is an indication that something surprising is about to happen. Although it was not uncommon for passersby to enter homes where banquets were being held, the appearance of a woman who was very likely a prostitute at a gathering such as this would have been scandalous. Although tradition has often linked this woman with Mary Magdalene, because of the mention of her in the next chapter (8:2), there is absolutely no evidence of that. Neither is there any reason to link her with Mary of Bethany. It is not unreasonable to infer that she came because she had heard Jesus preach and was deeply moved by his message.

In v. 38, the woman bent over Jesus to anoint his feet with myrrh, a gesture of honor usually accorded distinguished guests. She began weeping and her tears fell on the feet of Jesus, since he was reclining at the table with his feet behind him. Her wiping the tears away with her hair may have been from embarrassment, but her kissing his feet was a gesture of deeply felt gratitude and respect.

The Pharisee's words, "If this man were a prophet" may be a reference to the acclaim of the crowd in v. 16, "a great prophet has arisen." The Pharisee's ironic remark is answered by Jesus' ironic parable which accurately reads the mind of Simon (v. 40).

The point of the parable in vs. 41–43 is that the response of grateful love is proportionate to the amount one has been forgiven.

In vs. 44–46 note the description of the obligations of Semitic hospitality, all of which were ignored by Simon, in what was perhaps a deliberate affront. The contrast in "oil," which was cheap olive oil, and "ointment" (v. 46), which was the expensive myrrh, is further evidence of the woman's unstinting generosity, contrasted with Simon's lack of love.

The phrase "for she loved much" in v. 47 is ambiguous, but taken in context, it seems to indicate that she loved much because she was forgiven, rather than the interpretation frequently given that she was forgiven because she loved much. She came to Jesus as one already forgiven by God, and poured out her gratitude in tears, kisses, and perfume. This explanation fits with the point of the parable.

Jesus sees her response of love toward him as confirmation that her sins have been forgiven by God (v. 48). It is her faith that has saved her (v. 50). This is the statement that usually accompanies the miracles of healing, but this time it is healing of the soul, not of the body, that has taken place. The expression "go in peace" (v. 50) is, literally, "go into peace," and is a common dismissal formula, echoing the Old Testament (as in 1 Sam. 1:17). It also is descriptive of the kind of life that is now possible for her.

Further exploration of differences and similarities in the Old Testament and New Testament concepts of forgiveness would be fruitful for the preacher.

The sermon might follow the movement of the passage from the woman's repentance for her sin to her overwhelming joy and gratitude which cause her to offer Jesus her tears, kisses, and precious ointment. Jesus praises her response to God's forgiveness and contrasts it to the Pharisee's indifference. The sermon might then suggest that since God has forgiven us in Christ for our many sins, our response should be a similar one of unstinting devotion and adoration.

1 Kings 19:1–8 (C)

This story follows Elijah's great victory over the priests of Baal on Mt. Carmel. There is some doubt as to whether the two events actually followed each other chronologically. There are some puzzling ambiguities in the story. Why would the Elijah who is so fearless in chapter 18 become so afraid of Jezebel in this pericope? Why would he flee for his life, and then beg God to take his life?

It has many similarities to the story of Moses in the Sinai wilderness. Elijah is running for his life into the desert, much as Moses did after killing the Egyptian overseer (Exodus 3). An angel appeared to Moses at the burning bush to encourage him. An angel appears to Elijah under the broom tree to give him comfort and strength. Both instances lead to a later more immediate encounter with God, known as a theophany.

In the previous two chapters Elijah and Ahab were the main figures, but now Jezebel comes to the fore as the one to be feared. Jezebel sends "a messenger to Elijah" with a threat (v. 2). She would probably not have warned him if she had seriously wanted to kill him; she was probably telling him to get out of the kingdom. In any case, Elijah takes the threat seriously.

He goes to Beer-sheba, in the far south, the end of the settled areas (v. 3). Since Beer-sheba was the final frontier, it may be symbolic of a flight to a lonely, faraway place. It was about one hundred and thirty miles south of Jezreel. "From Dan to Beer-sheba" was an expression used to describe the limits of the inhabited area of the country. Note that Elijah leaves his servant here, and goes on into the wilderness (perhaps symbolic of bleak despair) alone.

Elijah begs God, "Take away my life" (v. 4). Once again there is a similarity to Moses in the desert, who became discouraged over the enormous task of leading the people and begged God, "The burden is too heavy for me. . . . Kill me at once" (Num. 11:14–15). Elijah may be referring to this incident when he says "I am no better than my fathers." He asks God to take his life, for in the Semitic tradition, suicide was forbidden.

An "angel," literally, a messenger or a divine intermediary, comes to Elijah's aid (v. 5). For the second time, Elijah receives food in an unusual way. The food is similar to that in 17:4–6. The "cake" was a round, flat cake of bread (like pita bread) which was customarily baked on hot stones.

Instead of just a day's journey to Beer-sheba, the idea of a "journey" is introduced in the words of the angel (v. 7). This provides a transition to the account of Elijah's visit to Mt. Horeb. The distance to Horeb, or Sinai, was about three hundred miles, so it would have been possible for him to walk it in less than forty days easily. This number may have been used to connect the story to Moses' forty days and nights on Mt. Sinai, or it may have been used as a conventional round number.

The sermon might begin with a description of Elijah's fear, panic, and depression. Even the "great prophets" were not immune to these very human emotions, especially when under an overload of stress and fatigue. In the midst of all this distress, however, God sustains Elijah with loving care for all his needs. This sermon could provide a strong reminder of God's providential care, even when things are at their worst, and we feel most alone and depressed.

2 Samuel 11:26–12:10, 13–15 (L) (E)

2 Samuel 12:7–10, 13 (RC)

Verses 26 and 27 of chapter 11 set the stage for the parable that follows in chapter 12. David had had Uriah killed so that he might marry Bathsheba. Even in the midst of her mourning, he marries her and eventually she bears him a son. But, the writer says, God was not happy.

Second Samuel 12:1–6 tells the parable of the ewe lamb. The prophet Nathan proved himself to be a man of courage by calling David's attention by means of this simple and beautiful parable to the wrong which he had done, violating the accepted moral codes of the time and displeasing God.

Verse 7 begins with Nathan's direct confrontation of David: "You are the man." Nathan wanted to be sure David got the point of the parable. Nathan speaks of David's anointing, of his deliverance from Saul, and of all he had been given by God. David had apparently even inherited Saul's harem but wanted still more (v. 8).

David's lust and greed for Uriah's wife had led him to murder. David's real sin, however, was not living up to his anointed role. As a result, Nathan sees dire things ahead. His prediction "The sword shall never depart from your house" (v. 10) came true in a tragic manner in the stories of David's sons, Amnon and Absalom. Some scholars feel that Nathan's prediction in v. 11 is so explicit it may well have been added by a later editor. The "neighbor" is presumed to be Absalom.

In vs. 13–14, David confesses his sin in a frank and open way. In the Old Testament, this kind of confession was a necessary prerequisite for God's forgiveness. When David confesses, Nathan pronounces God's forgiveness. According to the law of the times (the law of exact retaliation—an eye for an eye), David should have been put to death, but it was the child who died instead. This was interpreted as a mark of divine favor to David. However, the verb "put away" literally means "has caused to pass over," implying that the effect of the evil David had done would continue.

The sermon might explore what happens when we rationalize our sinful desires and allow them to overpower us. It could move from the parable of the greedy rich man to Nathan's confrontation with David, and his predictions of the dreadful fallout from David's sin. David's moving confession of sin and Nathan's pronouncement of God's forgiveness bring in the good news of the gospel. Through Jesus Christ, God has shown us abundant love and compassion and has been willing to put our sins away from us just as God did with David. The sad thing is that our sin results in pain and suffering in the lives of others even when we have repented.

Galatians 2:15–21 (C)

Galatians 2:11–21 (L) (E)

Galatians 2:16, 19–21 (RC)

The importance of this pericope is indicated by the fact that Martin Luther devoted eighty pages to it in his commentary on Galatians. It contains a very important discussion of the relationship of law and gospel. Paul's keynote of freedom is strongly sounded here.

The incident described in the beginning of this pericope took place in Antioch, where Gentiles had been welcomed into the church, even sharing meals with Jewish Christians. Peter had entered into this table fellowship until "certain men came from James," and he stopped eating with the Gentiles, apparently out of fear of the Jerusalem church.

Verses 11–14 tell how Paul forced Peter to face up to his inconsistencies with regard to the Gentiles. It took courage for Paul to do this, for he obviously regarded Peter as his superior. The problem was not circumcision, which had been settled at the council, but observance of the Jewish dietary laws. The issue at stake, however, was more than table manners; it was the unity of the church. Peter's changing his mind and refusing to eat with the Gentile Christians implied that only those Christians who complied with the Jewish laws were truly faithful. Table fellowship in Semitic culture carried connotations of bonding and acceptance. For the Jews it was an act of worship, framed by prayer. To eat with the Gentiles, therefore, meant accepting them as kin, and affirming Gentile Christianity as valid. The gospel provides the basis for Christian unity.

In v. 13 "the rest of the Jews" refers to Jewish Christians who went along with Peter, thereby disrupting the harmony of the fellowship between the Jewish and the Gentile Christians. Paul is reminding the Galatians of this incident at Antioch because they, too, are having problems about whether salvation is dependent on following the law or comes from following Christ.

Paul understood the "truth of the gospel" (v. 14) to lie in the freedom we have in Christ (2:4), which included freedom from legalistic requirements.

Verses 15–21 contain a succinct résumé of Paul's gospel, a condensation of much of the doctrine found in Romans and Galatians. This section introduces for the first time in Galatians the theme of justification by faith. Paul uses the word "justify" four times in these verses. It is a passage that highly influenced the sixteenth-century Protestant Reformers, especially Luther. Paul's understanding of justification by faith grew out of his concern for the Gentiles and his desire to bring the gospel to the whole world.

In v. 15 "we" refers primarily to Peter and Paul. Paul is arguing that since they, who were Jews, do not insist on obedience to the law in its totality, why should it be expected of Gentiles who had never been under the law. He points out that justification comes not by "works of the law" (v. 16), but by faith in Christ.

Verse 17 is a typical Pauline literary device: a dialogue with a rhetorical question followed by the strong negative, *Mē genoito!* (by no means). The KJV translation is even stronger: "God forbid!" The question being asked is that, since the law is from God and disobeying it is sinful, would not Christ be the agent of sin? The answer to this question is found in v. 19, "I . . . died to the law, that I might live to God." No one is capable of observing the law, so therefore the law is self-destructive. Trying to obtain salvation by means of it can only make us sinners because we can never observe it perfectly. Any hint of trying to build up again a merit system of salvation by works is abhorrent to Paul. In Paul's understanding, it was bondage to the law which led to the crucifixion of Christ.

Being crucified with Christ means being set free from the law. It is Jesus' sacrificial death, not our attempts to live by the law, which brings salvation.

Paul uses the phrase in v. 20, "in the flesh," to mean limited by his own sinful condition. The expression "I live by faith" implies that complete surrender and commitment are necessary if one is to be truly free. This is one of the beautiful ironies of the life of faith. We are free only when we have put up the white flag and become prisoners! This verse has been referred to as the heart of the gospel. It is one of the most dramatic statements about change that Paul makes. It underscores the new life power released at baptism, the sense of "Christ in me" that changes everything. Charles Cousar comments that to Paul living "by faith" meant "taking the leap, rejecting all false offers of security, risking the confession that life can be found in death, and trusting the one 'who loved me and gave himself for me.' Being crucified with Christ is not a temporary stage to be quickly passed through in the journey toward a blissful life without pain, anguish, and struggle. It remains the daily experience of the community, justified and ordered by the power of God" (Cousar, *Galatians,* p. 61).

The word "nullify" in v. 21 is a legal term for setting aside a will, the law, or a commandment. There is an irony in Paul's words: he is willing to nullify the law, but not grace. The two are mutually exclusive. It is an either-or situation.

The sermon could deal with the inconsistencies in the lives of those followers of Christ who claim to be justified by faith but continue to fall back on the false security of works. From Paul's denunciation of Peter's inconsistency about eating with Gentiles, the passage moves to a glowing statement of what it means to surrender wholly to God's grace, to "live by faith in the Son of God." Letting go of the dependency of works means a true surrender, a different kind of life-style that relaxes in God's grace.

Theological Reflection

All the passages for today deal with our human frailty and God's willingness to stand by us and deliver us through grace. God cared for Elijah in his time of utter despair and panic. Jesus praised the woman who poured out her love and gratitude because she had been forgiven. God "put away" even David's enormous sin when he repented in humility. Paul reminded the Galatians that God's grace is all-sufficient; we do not have to rely on our works to be justified. We have freedom in Christ when we surrender in faith to him.

Children's Message

The talk with the children might center on God's daily loving care for us when we are tired or sad as Elijah was in the desert. Just as God came to Elijah when he was afraid and hungry and gave him food and took care of him, so God will take care of every one of us.

Hymns for Pentecost 4

God Will Take Care of You; God Is Our Sure Foundation; When I Survey the Wondrous Cross.

Pentecost 5

Ordinary Time 12
Proper 7

Psalm 43 (C)

1 Kings 19:9–14 (C)
Zechariah 12:7–10 (L)
Zechariah 12:10–11; 13:1 (RC)
Zechariah 12:8–10; 13:1 (E)

Galatians 3:23–29 (C) (L) (E)
Galatians 3:26–29 (RC)

Luke 9:18–24

Meditation on the Texts

O Lord of compassion, we thank you that you stand by us in our times of despair and confusion, even as you did the prophet of Elijah. We are grateful that you do not leave us to wallow in self-pity but faithfully redirect us to our calling as your people. We ask that in our times of pain and suffering you strengthen us by reminding us of the repentance that can come to others by the testimony of the hope that is within us. Help us to have the courage to take up our cross and bear it faithfully and well, remembering that it is only as we lose our lives for you that we truly gain them. Amen.

Commentary on the Texts

Luke 9:18–24

The first part of the ninth chapter has told of the commissioning of the disciples, the perplexity of Herod about Jesus' identity, and the feeding of the multitudes.

Luke does not tell us where the incident in vs. 18–24 took place, but the Matthew and Mark versions of this story locate it near Caesarea Philippi, near Mt. Hermon. Jesus had withdrawn from the region ruled by Herod and from the eager crowds.

Luke uses a characteristic expression to describe Jesus' withdrawal, "praying alone" (v. 18). This is a phrase he has used at other significant moments, such as at the baptism of Jesus (3:21) and at the calling of the Twelve (6:12).

Since this pericope follows the account of the feeding of the multitudes, Jesus' question, "Who do the people [or the crowds] say that I am?" seems to have been triggered by the reaction of the crowds to the miracle. We hear in it a tone of loneliness and frustration. The answer the disciples give is the same as the answer given to Herod when he asked about Jesus in v. 9 of this chapter. The rumor among the people was that Jesus was either John or Elijah or one of the prophets of old returned from the dead. Therefore, this pericope with Peter's confession forms a climax to the preceding passage with Herod's question.

Jesus then turns to the disciples to ask what they were saying about him (v. 20). This personal question results in Peter's confession, which is a crucial turning point in Mark, but here serves primarily as an answer to Herod. Peter's answer is given with his characteristic impulsiveness. The phrase "Christ of God" in this verse is a title used to describe the Messiah in the Old Testament sense as the representative of the one God. It is similar to the expression used regarding Simeon in 2:26. Peter, therefore, is not making an admission of full Christian faith which could come only with the resurrection, but sees Jesus as the fulfillment of the messianic promises.

After Peter's confession, Jesus charged the disciples with secrecy, or as the NEB says, "gave them strict orders not to tell this to anyone." Jesus does not want the crowd to misunderstand and acclaim him as Messiah for political or nationalistic reasons. Jesus does not refer to himself as Messiah here, but uses the Old Testament phrase, "Son of man'' when he speaks of his impending suffering. The word "must" as used by Luke in v. 22 is very strong. It denotes a divine necessity, an obligation imposed by God's plan of salvation; it is not speaking of a possibility or an option. In the Book of Daniel, there is also a reference to the Son of Man (7:13) and to the suffering of the saints (7:21). This is the opposite of the common understanding of the messianic rule as a time of victory under the leadership of a dazzling king of earthly power and glory who would lead them to victory against the Romans.

Jesus speaks of being "rejected" by the elders, chief priests, and scribes. The word "rejected" is probably a technical term denoting rejection of a candidate for legal office after careful scrutiny. The leaders of organized religion would consider him and then reject him. However, even though this rejection would result in death, Jesus reminded his followers that God was still in control. The phrase "be raised" emphasizes that the resurrection was God's act. "On the third day" probably means "in a short time." This is the way it is used in Hosea 6:2 in a reference to Israel's passing through death and "on the third day" being raised up. Perhaps Jesus was thinking of this passage, and saying to his disciples that even though the New Israel would pass through suffering and death, it too would be vindicated and restored or raised up.

This grim announcement of suffering and death is followed by one equally as depressing: Jesus' followers, also, would have to suffer (v. 23). Taking up the cross meant the utmost in self-denial. And, says Jesus, it must be done day after day—a daily dying to self. See Paul in 1 Corinthians 15:31: "I die every day." This is the opposite of a life that is lived purely for itself and its own glory. Jesus' followers must be willing to lose their lives for his sake (v. 24). The apostles exemplify this way of life, as Luke makes plain in Acts 15:26 when Paul speaks of those who "have risked their lives for the sake of our Lord Jesus Christ."

The sermon might move from posing the same question Jesus asked the disciples, "Who do you say that I am?" to a consideration of the cost of confessing Jesus as Savior and Lord. If we are truly to be disciples, we must be willing to give up everything for Christ, even our lives. The sermon might focus on the seductiveness of trying to "gain the whole world" and the terrible price that is paid when that becomes one's goal in life. In contrast, the sermon might paint a picture of the life that is "saved" by being "lost" or surrendered to Christ.

1 Kings 19:9–14 (C)

In 19:1–8 for Pentecost 4, Elijah has begun his pilgrimage to Horeb. This passage continues that narrative with his arrival and taking shelter in a cave. This echoes the story of Moses hiding in a cleft rock where he saw the back of Yahweh (Ex. 33:22). The scene is set for one of the most dramatic of the Old Testament theophanies (appearances of God).

"The word of the LORD" (v. 9) may have originally read "the voice of the LORD" since it is followed by "and he said." God asks Elijah to explain his presence, whereupon he lays out his complaints in an aggrieved and self-justifying fashion. The word "jealous" means literally "to have great zeal and devotion." The fact that it is the people of Israel and not Ahab or Jezebel who are now the offenders suggests that this may be a later insertion. The complaint that he alone is left is a typical case of the Semitic use of hyperbole for emphasis. A similar usage of this phrase is found in Job 1:16–17, 19.

In v. 11 Elijah is told to go out on the mountain. Then, in an extraordinary passage, God "passed by," followed by the wind, the earthquake, and fire, the three traditional elements of Old Testament theophany. (See the one found in Ex. 19:9ff.) God was not "in" these elements, since the Old Testament is careful to distinguish God's presence from any outward manifestations. However, we must note that God is associated with these manifestations in the phrase "passed by."

The assumption is usually made that God's presence is made known in the "still small voice." This is translated in various ways: "a low murmuring sound" (NEB); "a gentle whisper" (NIV); "soft whisper of a voice" (TEV). The Hebrew literally means "a voice (or sound) of fine (or thin) silence (or quietness)." Many writers have asserted that what this text seems to be saying is that the place to expect God's presence is not in some unusual or supernatural occurrence but in the quiet, ordinary course of daily life.

Richard Nelson takes a different view. He maintains that the contrast is between the "fireworks of God's theophany and the quiet calm that followed, not between God's presence and absence" (Nelson, *First and Second Kings*, p. 124). The point of this passage, Nelson asserts, is to show that even the theophany with its earthquake, wind, and fire could not arouse Elijah from his depression and burnout. When it was all over, signaled by the silence or quiet murmur, he came out of his cave unchanged, with the same complaints and self-pity as before. He had not responded with a renewed commitment to his prophetic office.

Elijah wraps his face in a mantle, in a way that suggests Moses hiding his face so he would not see God (Ex. 33:20–22). This again confirms the link between the two theophanies and suggests that Elijah is being presented as a second Moses, but as a "Moses" who is reluctant to accept the prophetic role. Once again Elijah hears the question that is both rebuke and comfort: "What are you doing here?" And once again he tries to justify himself. Breaking off the story here lends a certain "To be continued" quality to the story, since the conclusion is in next week's lectionary reading. If you do not intend to use the 1 Kings passage next week for Pentecost 6, you might combine the two pericopes into one sermon.

This dramatic story certainly lends itself to a **sermon** about the down times of life. The text leaves no doubt about Elijah's depression and despair. It is also clear that Elijah was filled with self-pity. The dominant note of the story, however, is that God did not abandon or give up on him but was present with him and continued, relentlessly, to stir his devotion by challenging his apathy and resentment. Our God will not let us go, even when we are ready to give up! This relentlessness is a message of hope.

Zechariah 12:7–10 (L)

Zechariah 12:10–11; 13:1 (RC)

Zechariah 12:8–10; 13:1 (E)

The first eight chapters of the Book of Zechariah were written in the early years of the return from Babylonian exile. Zechariah's concern was twofold: (1) that the temple be rebuilt and (2) that the people not be so caught up in their religiosity that they ignore justice and mercy (see ch. 7). He uses the traditional style of apocalyptic literature to encourage the people with visions of the future.

Most scholars agree that the passage chosen for our text today was a part of a later addition to Zechariah's work, written by a different author or authors, judging from its literary style and content. It makes no reference to the Persian period, but rather speaks of the Greeks (9:13) and was therefore probably written between 300 and 200 B.C.E. There is no mention of rebuilding the temple, but rather of universal war and the siege of Jerusalem. The writer, or writers, connect with the first part of Zechariah by the use of eschatological and messianic themes.

This later addition (9:1–14:21) is referred to or quoted thirty-nine times in the New Testament, especially in the passion story, where we find quotes from Zechariah which have become very familiar to us, such as "the blood of my covenant" (9:11) and "your king comes . . . humble and riding on an ass" (9:9). There are two sections in this addition, each introduced as a "burden" or "oracle."

The second of these oracles begins with chapter 12. It speaks of a time of sorrow and dejection, out of which will come purification and hope, in preparation for the day of the Lord.

Verses 7–10 tell of the promise of victory to the Davidic house and the beginning of the great lament. In v. 10 there is the promise that the Lord will pour out his spirit of compassion and supplication. In other words, God will provide the kind of grace we need, the grace that makes it possible for us to please God and to obtain favors from God. It is this compassionate grace which will make the people sensitive to "him whom they have pierced" (v. 10). It is possible that this is a reference to the rejection and death of the good shepherd "doomed to slaughter" mentioned in 11:4. Some scholars associate this shepherd with Josiah, slain at Megiddo in 609 B.C.E. There is also a similarity to the concept of the Suffering Servant in Isaiah 53 and to Matthew 23:37, when Jesus laments over Jerusalem who had so often killed the prophets and stoned those who were sent to her by God. The main idea is that the repentance of the people is evoked by the suffering of an individual, whether real or symbolic as in the Suffering Servant passage. It is clear that the New Testament sees in these lines a messianic significance (see John 19:37).

Verse 1 of chapter 13 contains an image of the messianic kingdom being cleansed of wickedness, especially in those holding sacred offices.

For further study, refer to apocalyptic literature and Suffering Servant in a Bible dictionary.

The sermon might deal with the suffering that comes to those who are God's appointed messengers, because of their rejection at the hands of God's chosen people. This text could be correlated to the Gospel passage which speaks of the necessity of Jesus' followers taking up the cross. The central message is the poignant truth that repentance is often evoked by the willingness of the faithful to suffer and even die for God. Examples could be given of the impact of faithful lives, such as the influence of Stephen on Paul and the powerful impact of the life and death of Dietrich Bonhoeffer on all of Christendom. Out of the pain and sorrow experienced by God's servants, hope comes to countless others.

Galatians 3:23–29 (C) (L) (E)

Galatians 3:26–29 (RC)

See also Christmas 1, (E).

Paul continues to discuss the role of the law. In this pericope he explains that the law is important because it witnesses to the salvation that comes in Christ. By "law" Paul means the Mosaic law given at Sinai. He says it serves to keep Israel pointed in the right direction, toward the coming of the new age and its fulfillment. The law instructs the Christian community in what it means to live in love.

All through chapter 3, Paul has been showing how Jews and Gentiles belong together as a community based on God's promises. In v. 26, he reaches the climax of his argument for unity. Because the people of God are no longer enslaved to the law, it is no longer the symbol of their identity. Instead they are defined by being "in Christ," a phrase Paul uses more than sixty times in his letters.

Paul uses two metaphors in this pericope to describe the role of the law. The first, found in v. 23, is the image of a jailer who guards the people of God by placing them in rigid confinement. This was necessary only until Christ came. Faith in Christ provides a new kind of protection but also grants a new kind of freedom.

The second image in vs. 24–25 is that of the *paidagōgos*, or attendant, the Greek slave who was assigned supervision and responsibility for a son in a Greek family. He was not a teacher but had responsibility for the boy's conduct. The law's function was similar, to provide some authority and discipline, even though that authority was transitory. The termination of that discipline came with uprightness through faith in Christ.

The phrase "sons of God" (v. 26) is a description normally reserved for Jews, and it is exceptional and extraordinary that Paul attributes this status to Gentiles. It is possible because they have been "adopted" through the ritual of baptism. Being "baptized into Christ" gives them a new identity. The preposition "into" means "in union with."

Once again Paul resorts to metaphor to get across his meaning. The expression "put on Christ" pictures Christ as a heavenly garment with which the Christian is enwrapped and transformed into a new being. A new status brings new dignity. This metaphor may be borrowed from the Old Testament expression for the adoption of someone's moral dispositions and outlook.

This new being is characterized by oneness: "neither Jew nor Greek, . . . slave nor free, . . . male nor female" (v. 28). The differences in the groups remain, but the barriers of hostility and prejudice that divide them disappear. Although these words did not cause an immediate end to slavery or the subservience of women, this verse has been a watershed theological statement in the ongoing struggle for the achievement of true human equality. It is also the climax of Paul's letter.

In v. 29, Paul goes on to explain that before Christ, it was the law that set God's people apart; after Christ, all that changed. God's promise to Abraham has come to fulfillment in the Gentiles, who have now become, through baptism, Abraham's offspring and heirs.

The sermon might follow the movement of the passage by beginning with a definition of the role of the law as guard (jailer) and guide (pedagogue). The next move is to a picture of the new person in Christ who has a new dignity and freedom, and no longer needs the protective custody of the law. All people, regardless of race, nationality, or status are made equal, because they have been clothed with the new dignity that comes from being children of God through Christ. Our oneness comes from our relationship to Christ which makes us heirs of the promises of God.

Theological Reflection

Several of the passages for today have the theme of the transforming effect of suffering. In the Elijah narrative from 1 Kings, God is present with Elijah in his pain and despair, his hurt and confusion, recalling him to his true vocation. The Zechariah passage shows how God will bring the people to repentance through the suffering of one of God's chosen servants. In the Luke passage, Jesus is describing the pain that will be his lot and the lot of those who are his faithful followers, but reminds them that cross bearing is the way to life that is real. In the Galatians text, Paul is pointing joyously to the new dignity and freedom possessed by those who are freed from the law and are now heirs of the promise.

Children's Message

This might be a good opportunity to make the point that God loves all kinds and colors of people. God loves everyone equally, whether short or tall, rich or poor, American or Chinese. The message might include having the children sing "Jesus Loves the Little Children."

Hymns for Pentecost 5

If You Will Only Let God Guide You; In Christ There Is No East or West; Be Still, My Soul. *Contemporary alternatives*: Lift Every Voice and Sing; By Gracious Powers.

Ordinary Time 13

Proper 8

Psalm 44:1–8 (C)

1 Kings 19:15–21 (C)
1 Kings 19:14–21 (L)
1 Kings 19:16b, 19–21 (RC)
1 Kings 19:15–16, 19–21 (E)

Galatians 5:1, 13–25 (C) (L) (E)
Galatians 5:1, 13–18 (RC)

Luke 9:51–62

Meditation on the Texts

We are grateful, O God, that you have called us to be your disciples. May we put your call to us before everything else as Elisha did. May we not make excuses to hide our laziness, our halfheartedness, our cowardice, and our selfishness. May we put our hands to the plow with eagerness and excitement and the full commitment of our hearts. Enable us to give ourselves so completely to the new freedom to which you have called us that our lives will glow with the fruit of the Spirit. Amen.

Commentary on the Texts

Luke 9:51–62

This is part of a larger section usually called the journey narrative (9:51–19:28). The first verses do not have an exact parallel in the other Gospels but can be linked to Mark 10 and Matthew 19. Although Jesus has been on the road before, what is new here is his destination, Jerusalem. Up until now most of Jesus' ministry has been in Galilee, now he heads for Jerusalem in an intentional way through the land of the Samaritans. This is not so much a geographical journey as an indication of Jesus' willingness to go all the way to the cross. It is also an important part of Jesus' training of his disciples. As they accompany him to Jerusalem, they will become witnesses of his death and resurrection and will be ready for the mission of proclaiming him to all parts of the earth. The teaching that he does along the way is more important to Luke than an exact travelogue.

Our pericope deals with the seriousness of the call to discipleship. From the cold reception by the Samaritans in the opening verses to the words of Jesus in v. 62, the tone is one of warning to those who are not prepared to accept rejection, loneliness, and even death.

Verse 51 acts as a title for what follows. It concentrates on what Jesus does. The fulfillment of the time appointed by God is emphasized. The Greek word *analēmpsis*, translated "received up," has connotations of both death and ascension. It is used only this once in the New Testament. It carries a strong reminder of Elijah's ascension, but Luke is probably thinking rather of the events that lie ahead: crucifixion, resurrection, and ascension. Jesus "set his face to go to Jerusalem." In biblical usage, "to set one's face" is an indication of determination, or a conscious act of will, as in Isaiah 50:6–7, "I have set my face like a flint." It literally means "he stiffened his face." Ultimate security comes from rock-hard devotion to God. The TEV translates this "he made up his mind," but that does not seem to capture the strength of his quiet determination.

The opening incident describes the rejection of Jesus and his disciples by the Samaritans (vs. 51–56). This episode is not found in any of the other Gospels. It is the first time Luke mentions the Samaritans. Luke's interest in them comes from his belief in the universality of salvation, although in this incident they were not open to Jesus' message. Who were the Samaritans? Although their origin is not clear, they may have been descendants of the alien tribes brought in by the Assyrians who intermarried with the people of the land. They lived in the area between Judea and Galilee, west of the Jordan, and were traditionally enemies of Israel. The Samaritans were not accepted as true believers by the Jews; rather, they were viewed as secessionists who did not observe the Mosaic traditions and ritual laws. (Leopold Sabourin, *The Gospel According to Luke*, p. 225; Allahabad, India: St. Paul Publications, 1984.) It is not surprising, therefore, that Jews were not accepted with open arms.

Since it was a small village, it was necessary for Jesus to send messengers (probably some of the Twelve) ahead to make arrangements for them to stay in. However, hospitality was refused them and in v. 53 we are told that the Samaritans would not receive Jesus on this occasion because of his destination, Jerusalem. The verb literally means "his face was proceeding to Jerusalem." The symbols of the hostility between the Jews and the Samaritans were their rival places of worship: Jerusalem and Mt. Gerazim, each claiming to be the one true sanctuary of the Deuteronomic law (see G. B. Caird, *The Gospel of St. Luke*, p. 140). They were not willing to help anyone go to Jerusalem to worship.

James and John react impetuously. Their suggestion in v. 54 recalls 2 Kings 1:10–12 where Elijah caused fire to strike down the men from Ahaziah's army. Jesus rebukes James and John sharply. His way was not Elijah's way. In his way, calling down God's curse on enemies has given way to loving enemies and even dying for them. It does not consist in punishing those who reject Jesus and his mission.

Verses 57–62 are partly found in Matthew 8:19–22. They contain three different responses to the challenge of discipleship. The first potential disciple is very eager (v. 57) so Jesus utters words of caution, indicating that the man had not thought through the demands of discipleship. The second (v. 59) hesitates but Jesus refuses to compromise, implying that once a person has been called, the proclamation of the kingdom takes priority over everything else. This is particularly stringent here because proper burial was very important to the Jews, taking precedence over everything else, even study of the law. The third (v. 61) begins eagerly but also wants a compromise, perhaps an excuse to delay, eliciting Jesus' stern rejection of lukewarmness. Note that the excuse of the third potential disciple is similar to that offered by Elisha. Jesus knew that his only security was in God, and that only a person who is open and vulnerable can truly proclaim the kingdom. The kingdom has no room for those who look back.

The sermon might move from the complete dedication of Jesus as he "set his face" toward Jerusalem, knowing what would be in store for him, to the meaning of discipleship for us today. The three types of potential disciples offer possibilities for modern-day counterparts. The sermon might end with a clear challenge to commitment in following Jesus.

1 Kings 19:15–21 (C)

1 Kings 19:14–21 (L)

1 Kings 19:16b, 19–21 (RC)

1 Kings 19:15–16, 19–21 (E)

Verse 14 begins with a repetition of Elijah's complaint in v. 10, which shows that he has been totally unchanged by the theophany he has witnessed (or, perhaps, failed to witness since he was hiding in the cave the whole time). But God will not let Elijah give up on his call. In vs. 15–16, God gives him a new task, which involves the anointing of two kings and a successor. Although he does not literally carry out all of these commands, since he does not directly anoint Jehu and Elisha, Elijah receives new energy and a new sense of purpose. He and those he anoints will be the instruments through which God will bring about the overthrow of Jezebel. The explicit nature of these predictions is to bring courage to Israel in a later period suffering from the Syrian wars and the influence of foreign cults. This passage reminds them that the crisis is God's punishment on Israel, and that this judgment was set in motion by Elijah and carried out by Hazael, Jehu, and Elisha. Elijah's authority had been validated by the many comparisons of him with Moses.

Elijah also receives the comforting news that he is not, as he had been saying, the only one left who does not worship Baal (v. 18). Kissing an image was a common practice; it is found also in Hosea 13:2: "Sacrifice to these, they say. Men kiss calves!" This verse serves as a reminder to Israel that no matter how severe God's judgment, there is always a remnant which is spared because of its faithfulness, the true Israel. The text says that there are seven thousand who have not bowed to Baal, but it must be noted that seven thousand is a symbolic number in Jewish thinking. It is a multiple of seven, the perfect number. This is the first suggestion of the remnant idea in the Old Testament.

Elijah accepts the commission. Without further complaint, he departs (v. 19) for the wilderness of Damascus and forthwith finds his new helper Elisha, whose name means "God is salvation."

The primary focus of our text for today is the commissioning of Elisha, which calls him to a total commitment, leaving all other loyalties behind, including the dearest family ties. It is very similar to the story of the man in today's Luke passage, who responded to Jesus' call by saying that he wanted to say goodbye to his family.

Elisha was plowing with not one but twelve yokes of oxen (v. 19), which probably indicates that he was extremely wealthy. Elijah's throwing his mantle over Elisha was a highly symbolic act. The mantle represented the personality and authority of its owner. The official dress of the prophets was a hair shirt (see 2 Kings 1:8 in which Ahaziah recognized Elijah's description by the mention of the garment of haircloth). Placing this official garment around Elisha's shoulders was a clear and unmistakable sign of his initiation ("anointing") as a helper to Elijah.

In v. 20, Elisha makes a normal request, to which Elijah responds enigmatically. Is he affronted? Is his response a rebuke? Does it simply mean "Go on. I'm not stopping you"? Or is Elijah simply telling him to go but not to forget what had been done to him? The emphasis seems to be on the uncompromising nature of the call. Elisha's response is clear enough; he indicates his wholehearted commitment by sacrificing all twelve of his oxen and hosting a meal to which all of his friends and neighbors are invited. He has even destroyed the yokes along with the oxen to indicate his renunciation of his former life. The meal was a symbolic thank offering for the call he had been given. He goes with Elijah as an attendant in much the same way that Joshua attended Moses (Ex. 24:13). And, eventually, in the same way that Joshua became Moses' successor, Elisha became Elijah's successor.

The sermon might concentrate on the wholehearted commitment God requires. The text begins with God's expectation that Elijah make a renewed commitment to being God's instrument in the destiny of Israel. It acknowledges God's compassion on the seven thousand who remained faithful instead of turning to Baal, thereby demonstrating their commitment in times of great danger. Then the story of Elisha's call is a clear illustration of the necessity of leaving everything to follow God in obedience and love. Every effort should be made to challenge listeners to examine their lives and renew their commitment to God, even at the risk of personal sacrifice.

Galatians 5:1, 13–25 (C) (L) (E)

Galatians 5:1, 13–18 (RC)

Chapter 5, v. 1 is seen by some scholars as being a logical continuation of chapter 4, and this is why the NRSV prints it as part of chapter 4. Chapter 4 ends with a description of Sarah as a "free woman" and this verse goes on to discuss the freedom to which Christ has set us free. The language of freedom is a reminder that when Israel was set free from bondage in Egypt, Israel became "God's own people." Likewise, as we are set free from the bondage of sin, we, too, become God's own people with new allegiances. Paul wants the Galatians to maintain that freedom and not submit again to "a yoke of slavery." He illustrates what that means with a passage devoted to circumcision (vs. 2–12).

In v. 13, Paul begins a new section discussing the characteristics of the life of freedom to which we are called and how to use that freedom responsibly. The keynote of the passage is found in this verse: "through love be servants of one another," or literally "be slaves of one another." Edgar Krentz says, "Love without the service is an abstraction or narcissistic self-congratulation; service without love is bondage. Freedom is not something an individual possesses; it is an activity that benefits others" (Edgar Krentz, *Galatians*, Augsburg Commentary on the New Testament, p. 76; Minneapolis: Augsburg Publishing House, 1985). Paul wants the Galatians to understand that love is not another burdensome law but an expression of freedom. Christian freedom is the foundation of Christian ethics, not the law. We do not know what specific problem in the Galatian church Paul was addressing here. It is possible that the fighting was over circumcision. Another theory suggests that some of these early Christians who possessed the Spirit in an ecstatic way had failed to recognize the ethical dimensions of the Spirit's work and had to be reminded about love, joy, peace, and patience.

The word translated "flesh" can be interpreted in different ways as "lower nature," "human nature," "sinful nature," "self-indulgence." It can mean the body, humanity as a whole, or all that is material. It is not always used in the New Testament in a negative sense. Here, though, it means that which stands against God, which pretends to offer meaning and purpose in itself, materialism and secularity that are not open to God's presence.

Verse 14 tells why the Galatians should be loving servants. Paul quotes Leviticus 19:18 to show how this is a fulfillment of the law. Verse 15 gives a picture of the Galatians' behavior that sounds more like a den of wild animals than a church.

In vs. 16–26, Paul describes Christian ethical behavior, and the role of the Spirit in relation to ethics. The RSV is not as clear as the NEB in v. 16. Paul is saying, "Walk by the Spirit and then you will never gratify the desires of the flesh." Living by the Spirit is the key to acting ethically. In v. 18 the Spirit and the law are set in opposition again.

Verse 19 begins a list of "the works of the flesh." This could as easily be translated "effects" or "products." Eight suggest visible conduct: "plain" to the eye. The list of works can be divided into four groups: (1) sexual vices: fornication, impurity, licentiousness; (2) religion: idolatry and sorcery; (3) argumentative or divisive attitudes: enmity, strife, jealousy, anger, selfishness, dissension, party spirit, and envy; (4) excesses in drinking and celebrating (a term often used of religious celebration). This list as well as the list of virtues is probably from the *didachē* (teaching) of the early church.

In v. 22 there is a contrasting list of the fruit of the Spirit in straightforward, clear terms. Note how Paul speaks of "works" of the flesh, but "fruit" of the Spirit. He never speaks of the "works" of the Spirit. Although this is the only time he uses the term "fruit of the Spirit," elsewhere he uses "gifts" to express much the same idea (1 Cor. 12:4). It is the infilling of the Spirit that produces this fruit, not our own efforts.

How do we know when the Spirit is leading us? Paul's answer is clear. The fruit of the Spirit is recognized by the marks of love, joy, and peace. If there is strife and division, the Spirit is not present. These three virtues serve as a foundation to the other six. Patience, kindness, and goodness are the ways in which peace is expressed. The final three are virtues also found in Greek ethical lists. Faithfulness meant reliability; gentleness meant being not-proud; self-control meant mastery over desires and pleasure in the Greek philosophic tradition.

In v. 23 Paul ends the list with a bit of irony: "against such there is no law." The Christian has died, not only to the law but to the "flesh," the earthbound, selfish, degraded tendencies (v. 24).

Living by the Spirit in v. 25 implies being open to God's redemptive power. "Walk" is a military term implying "be in step" or "walk a straight line." It is the Spirit who gives order and direction to our lives and is thereby the standard for our lives.

For further study, look up freedom, flesh (*sarx*).

The sermon might follow the movement of the text from the freedom we have found in Christ to the relationship of that freedom to love, which is expressed in our ethical behavior. Care should be given to clarify that Paul is not laying down a new set of laws of ethical behavior, but rather is listing those attributes which are the natural outgrowth of love. The sermon might draw a contrast between the works of the flesh and the fruit of the Spirit. It is the latter for which we are freed in Christ.

Theological Reflection

A common theme in these passages is the seriousness of discipleship. The story of Elijah shows how God does not leave Elijah cowering in the cave but calls him to a new commitment. This is followed with Elisha's leaving everything to become Elijah's successor. The Gospel lesson describes the varying reactions of those who are called by Jesus, and Jesus' commendation of the one who "does not look back." Paul's words to the Galatians are a reminder of the serious challenge of faithful living, when our newfound freedom is expressed, not in license, but in love.

Children's Message

The story about James and John wanting to call down fire from heaven on the Samaritans provides a good opportunity for dealing with a difficult issue for children: wanting to get even. Tell the story simply, describing the long-standing friction between the Jews and the Samaritans, their refusal to let Jesus and his disciples go through their village since they were going to Jerusalem to worship, and the angry reaction of James and John. Show how Jesus' answer suggests that his way is not to get revenge, but treat people with understanding and peaceful attitudes.

Hymns for Pentecost 6

O Master, Let Me Walk with Thee; Jesus Calls Us; Take Thou Our Minds, Dear Lord.

Pentecost 7

Ordinary Time 14
Proper 9

Psalm 5:1–8 (C)	**Galatians 6:7–18 (C)**
	Galatians 6:1–10, 14–16 (L)
1 Kings 21:1–3, 17–21 (C)	**Galatians 6:14–18 (RC) (E)**
Isaiah 66:10–14 (L)	
Isaiah 66:10–14c (RC)	**Luke 10:1–12, 17–20 (C) (RC)**
Isaiah 66:10–16 (E)	**Luke 10:1–12, 16 (L)**
	Luke 10:1–12, 16–20 (E)

Meditation on the Texts

O God, we are grateful that you have chosen to give us the message of salvation. As we spread the good news of how you have loved us as a mother loves her children, may we constantly remember that your invitation to life demands a serious decision. May we take our commitment to our inheritance as seriously as did Naboth. May we see your hand at work as did the seventy as they went about Galilee. And may we constantly strive to express our faith in our lives, not growing weary in well-doing. Amen.

Commentary on the Texts

Luke 10:1–12, 17–20 (C) (RC)

Luke 10:1–12, 16 (L)

Luke 10:1–12, 16–20 (E)

This pericope could be called "the mission of the seventy." Only Luke tells of the sending out of this large group, although the account is somewhat similar to Matthew's account of the sending out of the Twelve.

Jesus sends messengers ahead to announce his coming (v. 1). They are his representatives. The number seventy might be a symbolic reference to the seventy Israelites who went to Egypt (Ex. 1:5), or the seventy elders of Israel (Ex. 24:1; Num. 11:16). Jesus' instructions in v. 2 are similar to those given on other occasions. In John 4:35 he also speaks of the fields being "white for harvest."

While "lambs in the midst of wolves" (v. 3) is obviously a reference to the dangerous situations they would find themselves in, there is an interesting similarity to the description of the peaceable kingdom where "the wolf [not the lion] shall dwell with the lamb" (Isa. 11:6) in the coming of peace (*shālōm*). Like that Isaiah passage, this pericope deals with the coming of the kingdom.

Purse, bag, and extra sandals were excess baggage; whatever is not absolutely necessary gets in the way (see Matt. 10:10). In Luke there is an added urgency: they are not even to greet anyone on the road. This probably means that their mission was so important that they were not to reduce it to polite chatter with passersby (v. 4).

In Semitic thought, words like "peace" and "blessing" were considered very concretely, illustrated here by the idea that peace could literally rest upon a house or, if refused, return to the disciples like a homing pigeon. The expression "son of peace" is used only here in the New Testament. It is an Arabic expression that means someone whose life is characterized by shalom.

In v. 7, the seventy are cautioned not to flit from house to house seeking either more luxurious quarters or more congenial social gatherings. Their work is urgent and they must keep at it.

The oft-quoted "eat what is set before you" in v. 8 has nothing to do with children who do not like spinach, but rather, is a reminder that they are not to worry about food that is ritually unclean. The disciples were being prepared to go into non-Jewish towns. Eating with Gentiles later became an important symbol of unity in the Christian community (see Gal. 2:12).

Verse 9 demonstrates Jesus' concern for the healing of the body as well as the spirit. The kingdom has been brought near in the coming of Jesus, and would be brought even nearer through the mission of the disciples.

In vs. 10–11 we see that the invitation to salvation is serious business. Shaking the dust off the feet was a symbolic act. There was a rabbinic idea that the dust of Gentile lands carried defilement and strict Jews are said to have removed it from their shoes when they returned to Palestine from abroad. For the disciples to do this declared in symbol that Israelites who rejected the kingdom were no better than Gentiles (Leon Morris, *The Gospel According to St. Luke*, p. 164; Grand Rapids: Wm. B. Eerdmans Publishing Co., 1974).

The commissioning of the disciples ends with a warning of judgment on the towns in Galilee that have rejected Jesus' message, once more underlining the seriousness of the invitation to salvation. The implication is that the rejection of the message is a rejection of Jesus.

The group returned "with joy," a typical Lukan expression (v. 17). They report their success in exorcising demons but nothing is said about preaching or healing. The "name" of Jesus is important to Luke. Jesus' power is present when it is called on. Acting in someone's name means representing that person. In Luke's thinking, miracles and teaching go together and result in faith and praise.

Jesus tells the disciples that Satan has already fallen (v. 18). God has won the victory over darkness through Jesus Christ. The perfect tense of the verb indicates that Jesus has already conquered Satan, a victory that will be realized through the church. "From heaven" can mean "from power" and does not necessarily refer to the fall of the angels. It is a symbolic way of telling the disciples of the success of their mission. The signs of this victory are found in the experience of believers (v. 19). However, v. 20 warns against putting too much value on experience as it is always ambiguous. Jesus wants us to see the reality of God at work behind events.

The sermon might have as its central message the seriousness of preaching the good news of salvation. The urgency is suggested by the instructions given to Jesus to the seventy—to take no excess baggage, not to reduce their message to polite chatter with passersby, not to flit from house to house, and not be deterred by getting caught up in legalisms. Shaking the dust off their feet and the warning of judgment on the towns showed that both the Jews and the Gentiles who reject the word brought by the disciples are rejecting Jesus.

The Common, Roman Catholic, and Episcopal readings go further than the Lutheran to describe the triumphant return of the disciples. The sermon might include the reminder that although the sign of the success is indicated in the experience of the believers, it is God, not the disciples, who has brought the victory. Although we must take seriously the task of bringing the good news of salvation to all the world, we must remember that the results are in the hands of God.

1 Kings 21:1–3, 17–21 (C)

The story of Naboth's vineyard is a story in the literary sense of the word. The scene is set and the dilemma stated in the opening verses with Ahab's offer to trade a "better vineyard" for Naboth's plot, which happened to be located next door to the king's palace. Conflict arises in vs. 3–7 when Naboth refuses to trade. The suspense builds when Jezebel enters the story and assumes command of the situation by acting "in Ahab's name." Tragedy ensues with the death of Naboth. The climax of the story comes in Elijah's condemnation of Ahab and Jezebel. The rest of the story, which is not in our reading for today, tells of Ahab's remorse and the reprieve his remorse brings.

A closer look at the story reveals the fascinating details that are the mark of a good storyteller. Ahab's request opens the negotiations for purchase. On the surface, this does not seem to be an unjust takeover by a monarch. Ahab seems to be making a reasonable offer for land adjoining the palace. He offers either money or a "better vineyard." Why did Naboth refuse? Most scholars feel that his refusal was based on his attitude toward the land, an attitude markedly different from that of the king.

First of all, his anger may have been triggered by Ahab's desire to turn his vineyard into a "vegetable garden." There may be here an ironic reference to Deuteronomy 11:10 which contrasts the "garden of vegetables" of Egypt to the Promised Land which was often referred to as a "vineyard." Naboth does not want to see his inheritance, a vineyard that was the fruit of long and careful nurturing, turned into an Egyptianlike "vegetable garden"—here today, gone tomorrow (v. 3).

Second, Naboth has a religious conviction that God as proprietor of the land had given it to him as an inheritance. It was very important in Israel for one to continue holding one's own land since it was a gift from God. This custom was protected by law and not even a king could force a person to sell family property. Ahab's offer was an attempt to assert his power by denying that the land was a gift from God. It was consistent with the way in which he had violated other long-standing traditions to assert his own power and authority.

In vs. 17–19 Elijah gives voice to God's condemnation of Ahab. These words contain both accusation and threat. The graphic description of the dogs licking Naboth's blood adds to the solemn tone. Ahab is told that because he has done evil God will bring evil on him. Richard Nelson points out that this story is a reminder that offenses against the heritage of the defenseless are offenses against God (Nelson, *First and Second Kings*, p. 144).

In vs. 20–21 Ahab is accused of breaking two of the Ten Commandments: against murder and coveting property. Even though Jezebel was behind the wrongdoing, Ahab is being held responsible. Because he had sold himself to evil (v. 20), not only will the dogs lick his blood as they did Naboth's but his male line will be destroyed. This condemnation of Elijah's is one of the sharpest criticisms of any of the kings of Israel.

The sermon might follow the progression of the story in the text, beginning with the contrast in the attitudes of the king and Naboth toward the land: one wanting to "possess" more and more land; the other seeing himself as a steward of the "inheritance" God had given him. The next move would show how the greed of the king was the spur for even more evil at the hands of the conniving Jezebel, who did not hesitate to use murder to acquire Naboth's land. The final move would spell out God's anger against all who use their positions of power against the defenseless because of their own greed, and God's willingness to forgive those who truly repent. It is important that this sermon not be limited to issues of nation against nation, but to the injustice and greed which creep even into the lives of well-meaning Christians.

Isaiah 66:10–14 (L)

Isaiah 66:10–14c (RC)

Isaiah 66:10–16 (E)

In vs. 7–9 the image is given of the birth of a nation, "in one moment," from the remnant of Jews who have returned from exile. George Knight suggests that the pains of exile were the pains of labor, and that now that Mother Israel is back home she has brought forth a new nation. Verses 10–11 are addressed to the children of Mother Israel, or Zion, and the inhabitants of Jerusalem. They are called to rejoice in her, and to stop mourning that she is dead. (George Knight, *Isaiah 56–66: The New Israel*; Grand Rapids: Wm. B. Eerdmans Publishing Co., 1985.)

Verse 11 contains a beautiful image of Zion as a nursing mother. The word translated "abundance" in the RSV probably means "nipple," and *kābōd* which is translated "glory" can also mean "riches" or "abundance." The phrase probably means "from her rich supply of milk."

Verses 12–14 contain a mosaic of quotations and seem to be a commentary on vs. 7–11 rather than a continuation of thought. The word "prosperity" in v. 12 is actually the

Hebrew *shālōm*, which includes the ideas of peace, harmony, wholeness, perfection, and fullness of life. This is probably a reference to 48:18. The promise is that the *shālōm* which had been forfeited because of sin is now to become a reality. "An overflowing stream" is used here as an expression of blessing. In the Near East, the wadi is a dry riverbed, but when the rains come it becomes an overflowing stream.

The image of Zion as a loving mother is picked up again in the latter part of v. 12 in a beautiful, tender image of kindliness and care. In v. 13, however, the metaphor shifts, and it is God who becomes the loving mother. Here again is a picture of love, comfort, and trust.

The phrase in v. 14 "bones shall flourish" is an image of rejuvenation and health.

Verses 15–16 interpret the last phrase of v. 14, "his indignation is against his enemies," with a picture of judgment, using the traditional elements of the theophany: wind and fire. This is a picture of God coming to help the people and punish their enemies. Note that in the Old Testament, "fire" represents the nature of God (see Deut. 4:24, "The LORD your God is a devouring fire"). It also represents judgment (see 9:5). When God sends fire, it is God's own self which is coming in judgment and wrath (Amos 1:4). Fire is a symbol of God's war against evil. It is also a picture of God's love, since it burns in order to refine (48:10). It represents the passionate, saving love of God.

The central theme of **the sermon** might be the loving care of God, who has provided a home for the exiled, the lost, and the lonely, a home that will be like a mother offering comfort and nurture. This provision demonstrates the mother love that God has for the people and is the occasion of great joy.

The Episcopal text includes the other side of the coin: the love of God is not without its stern demands; the presence of God is a cleansing and chastising fire. The love of God for the people of God is balanced by God's burning anger against the enemies of God. As in the Gospel text, we see here that salvation is serious business.

Galatians 6:7–18 (C)

Galatians 6:1–10, 14–16 (L)

Galatians 6:14–18 (RC) (E)

Verse 1 is connected to 5:25–26 and is addressed to those who "live by the Spirit" or who are "spiritual." Paul is telling the mature Christians in the community who have experienced the life-giving presence of the Spirit to take that presence seriously and restore those who have fallen away. He is addressing a specific situation that might arise in a Christian community. The words "if a man is overtaken in any trespass" are in the standard literary form for presenting laws in the Old Testament (see Ex. 21:1–22:16). Although freed from the Mosaic law, Christians nevertheless have a responsibility to the "law of Christ" (v. 2), which is an injunction to love others, expressed in mutual burden bearing. The "law of Christ" is also referred to in 1 Corinthians 9:21. Paul is not talking about excommunication or punishment of the sinner here, but is rather concerned that the attitude of the community be one of gentleness, one of the fruits of the Spirit in 5:23.

Because the task of helping others, particularly those who have fallen, so easily leads to self-satisfaction or even a sense of superiority, Paul issues a stern caution in v. 3, for those who are "spiritual" not to think they are "something." One interpretation of this is "know your limitations." Verse 4 continues this idea with the demand, also common in Greek philosophy, for rigorous self-examination, for example, Socrates' "Know thyself." Note that it is our works that are to be tested, not our words. The proof is in the doing. The question is not how we compare to others, but how we measure up to our own responsibilities. In other words, we are not to boost ourselves up by putting others down.

In v. 5, the "load" is not the same thing as "burdens" in v. 2, but probably refers to accountability for one's own life in the final judgment. J. B. Phillips in *The New Testament in Modern English* translates this, "For every man [sic] must shoulder his own pack." It is not clear what Paul means in v. 6 by "all good things," but the most likely interpretation is that the phrase refers to the financial support of the teacher or catechist, and not spiritual communion. There is a similar reference in 1 Corinthians 9:14. It does not seem to fit neatly into this section, but may have been triggered in Paul's mind as a down-to-earth illustration of bearing one another's burdens.

Verses 7–10 deal with the necessity of perseverance in "well-doing" (v. 9). The sowing and reaping metaphors are reminders of the punishment and rewards that come as a result of God's justice, and are meted out according to our zeal or lack of zeal in living as God wishes us to live. Charles Cousar puts it succinctly: "This sobering word written to the Galatians reminds them that they cannot presume upon God's grace, as from time to time Israel of old had done. They cannot grow lax and take God for granted. They cannot let faith degenerate into mere credence or the cultivation of warm feelings" (Cousar, *Galatians*, p. 147).

Verses 11–18 constitute a concluding postscript, which includes Paul's signature and a résumé of what has gone before. The letter has been dictated to a scribe up to this point. Now Paul adds a postscript in his own handwriting. These concluding remarks are the longest of any letter. They include almost none of the usual elements of conclusions: personal greetings, requests for intercessions, and so forth. Instead he summarizes the major themes of the letter: circumcision, flesh, law, the cross of Christ, boasting, and persecution.

Paul begins by making two accusations about the selfish motives of the agitators: that they advocated circumcision to "make a good showing," and that they only required it to avoid persecution themselves. The persecution probably came from those Jewish Christians who were adamant about circumcision and who made life difficult for those who were not. Even they, however, do not try to observe the whole law, which makes them somewhat hypocritical in Paul's eyes. The word translated "glory" (RSV) in vs. 13 and 14 may also be translated "boast." Paul's boast is not in the pride of proselytizing, but in dependence on God's grace demonstrated in the cross of Christ (v. 14). The word for world, *kosmos*, means here all that is in opposition to God, the "present evil age" mentioned in 1:4. Paul uses a perfect tense here so the implication is that this world is not completely over and done with. He is expressing the condition in which he finds himself as he lives in the world and struggles to live a life of faith. "Not that I have already obtained," he writes in Philippians 3:12, "but I press on."

The phrase "a new creation" in v. 15 suggests that through the cross has come a profound reshaping of identity. This is a phrase Paul has not used before in this letter, but it does appear in 2 Corinthians 5:17. The possibility hinted at in the prophets of "a new thing" (Jer. 31:22) or "new heavens and a new earth" (Isa. 65:17) has been realized. Through Jesus Christ, there is the possibility of transformation, of a "new humanity" (Eph. 2:15, NEB). This means a life directed not by the law, but by the crucified and risen Christ. The result is a life ordered by new priorities, disregarding the old divisions and prejudices, a community of love, bearing one another's burdens.

"The Israel of God" (v. 16) means that Christians are the new offspring of Abraham. This benediction is an adaptation of the one in Psalm 125:5 (NEB), "Peace be upon Israel!"

"Let no one make trouble for me" (v. 17, NEB) indicates that Paul feels that this letter has resolved the crisis in the church. His reference to the "marks" of slavery indicates that he thinks of his suffering as the mark of his being a slave to Christ.

In v. 18 he reminds the Galatians to base their lives on grace, not on the law. The word "brethren," used here for the only time in a Pauline benediction, may indicate a parting spirit of reconciliation in contrast to the harsh words that began the letter.

For extra study, look up *kosmos* (world), *kauchaomai* (boasting), *ktisis* (creation).

The sermon might center on the meaning of living "by the Spirit." Following the movement of the text, the first step would be a discussion of the change of attitude which is implied by responsibility to the law of Christ. This involves a sense of community and mutual burden bearing. The next move is a warning of the subtle dangers of pride that accompany doing good for others. The third move is to the necessity for perseverance in well-doing, not to grow weary and give up. The next move is a reminder that what we do have to boast about is the cross of Christ. Finally, the sermon could close with a description of the new creation which we are called to be with new priorities, new values, and a new allegiance.

Theological Reflection

Two common threads in these texts are that God is at work behind the events of history, and that the message of salvation is serious business, indeed. The seventy go out to bring stern warnings to the villages of Galilee, and as they return rejoicing are cautioned not to assume credit for God's works. God's displeasure with Ahab and Jezebel demonstrates the seriousness of God's expectations for human behavior. The punishment that befalls Ahab's family evidences God's intervention in history. The Isaiah passage underscores the seriousness of God's love and justice; and the Galatians passage, the seriousness of the Spirit's presence in our lives, and the necessity to live out our faith in our actions.

Children's Message

This might be a good opportunity to talk about mothers and the comfort and care they provide, and then use Isaiah 66:13 to talk about how God is like a mother.

Hymns for Pentecost 7

Eternal God, Whose Power Upholds; What Does the Lord Require; God of Our Life.

Pentecost 8

Ordinary Time 15
Proper 10

Psalm 139:1–12 (C)

Colossians 1:1–14 (C) (L) (E)
Colossians 1:15–20 (RC)

2 Kings 2:1, 6–14 (C)
Deuteronomy 30:9–14 (L) (E)   Luke 10:25–37
Deuteronomy 30:10–14 (RC)

Meditation on the Texts

You have set us apart, O God, to be your people. Help us to take up our roles as your servants with the wholehearted commitment of Elisha. Grant that we may learn how to live lives of simple compassion like the good Samaritan. Teach us what it means to walk in your ways, and to live lives worthy of the price Jesus paid in reconciling us to you. We are humbled when we recall how the Lord of the universe became flesh and lived among us so that we might share in the inheritance of the saints in light. Grant us strength, endurance, patience, and joy as we learn to live as your people. Amen.

Commentary on the Texts

Luke 10:25–37

This pericope contains the well-known and well-loved parable of the Good Samaritan, which is found only in Luke. It follows Jesus' words about the privileges of discipleship. When a question is put to Jesus by a lawyer about salvation, Jesus answers with a description of true discipleship.

The Gospels differ as to who it is that asks Jesus the question. Luke says it is a lawyer (v. 25); Matthew, a Pharisee; Mark, a scribe. In Matthew and Mark, he asks about the great commandment in the law, but Luke is writing to a Gentile audience, so instead of the law, the question is about "eternal life."

The lawyer "stood up" (v. 25). This indicates that people had been sitting down, probably because Jesus was teaching. A lawyer was a person educated in Jewish law, an expert in the Torah. Lawyers also served as judges in courts and trained young men in discipleship. His question, which was in essence asking what "works" are necessary for salvation, was a way of putting Jesus to the test by seeing how well he knew the details of the Torah requirements. Answering a question with a question, Jesus refers him to his own area of expertise, the law (v. 26).

The lawyer's answer is a combination of Deuteronomy 6:5, "You shall love the Lord your God with all yourt heart, and with all your soul, and with all your might," and Leviticus 19:18, "You shall love your neighbor as yourself." The word used for neighbor is broader than just those who live nearby; it contains the sense of living in community with others, although to the Jews the "others" were other Jews, not Gentiles.

The lawyer knows all the right words to say; the challenge from Jesus is that he live out the spirit of those words. If we really love God "with our whole selves" in response to God's love for us, then our love for others is a part of that response, not the cause of God's loving us (v. 28).

The lawyer's question in v. 29 is a good one, but it is asked from the wrong motive. He wants boundaries drawn, so that he will know when he has done enough. He wants the "neighbor" defined, so that he can be sure he has loved the right people in order that he might inherit eternal life. The rabbis held endless debates about who was included and who excluded from the term "neighbors." Jesus refuses to enter this debate but answers the question, "Who is my neighbor?" by telling a story that in effect shows that the lawyer is asking the wrong question.

The distance from Jerusalem to Jericho is about seventeen miles and the road descends precipitously more than three thousand feet. It was not uncommon for travelers to be set upon by thieves and robbers as they made their way cautiously down the steep descent. The word for "robbers" (v. 30) is the same used of Barabbas and the thieves crucified with Jesus.

Why would the priest and Levite refuse to help the wounded man? Touching blood or a corpse made a person unclean according to Jewish law. Luke makes a point that the man was left "half dead" and so the priest could not be certain he was not already completely dead without touching him. He did not want to risk defilement by doing that, so he deliberately avoided all possibility of contact by crossing to the other side of the road. The Levites were assistants in the temple, giving instructions in the law and tradition and performing administrative tasks. The same possibility of ceremonial defilement perhaps affected the Levite's decision not to help the wounded man.

The Samaritan was a symbol of everything the Jews despised. Samaritans were already ceremonially unclean, so there was no risk of defilement. The point of Jesus' story is that it is not necessarily those who are schooled in the law and devoted to the practice of "religion" who truly have the secret of eternal life. The Samaritan showed compassion where the priest and Levite had not. He used wine to disinfect and cleanse the wounds and oil to soften them and ease the pain, set the man on his own beast (which meant he would have had to walk) and took him to an inn, where he continued to take care of him. When the Samaritan had to leave, his mercy went the second mile. He left money to assure continued help for the man. Then he went about his life without undue heroics. The Samaritan was simply a compassionate person who saw a need and responded to it.

Jesus did not answer the lawyer's question specifically. Instead he implied that the real question is "To whom am I neighbor?" It was evident that the lawyer would have had a difficult time being neighbor either to the half-dead man or to the Samaritan himself. By choosing an unlikely hero for the story, Jesus scored a double point. Both religious legalism and religious superiority get in the way of love. The definition of a true neighbor is defined in the lawyer's answer: "The one who showed mercy" (v. 37). It is ironic that even as he makes this admission, the lawyer cannot bring himself to speak the hated name, "the Samaritan." This story is intended to shock its hearers out of their complacency as God's elect people.

The Good Samaritan story lends itself to a **sermon** that considers the nature of true compassion. The story might be retold with some interpretation added, and illustrations might be given of real-life persons who go about compassionate living without undue heroics. The stories should encourage the hearers to examine their prejudices and their lack of compassion and make a new commitment to lives that are willing to cross all barriers to minister to people's needs in the name of Jesus Christ.

2 Kings 2:1, 6–14 (C)

These verses concern the succession of Elijah by Elisha. The Elisha cycle runs from 2:1 to 13:21. The writer is not attempting to write a biography of Elisha but wants to establish the authority of the prophets and to show the fulfillment of their prophecies. He is not particularly concerned about the chronology or the plausibility of the stories, but rather chooses stories that serve his purpose.

The story begins as Elijah and Elisha make their way from Gilgal to Bethel, the site of one of the colonies of prophets. A statement of what is to come is provided in v. 1. Verses 2–5, omitted in our reading, tell how the prophets at Bethel and later at Jericho come out to meet them and tell Elisha that Elijah is about to be taken away. Finally, in v. 7, the two prophets are left alone by these "sons of the prophets," as the members of the prophetic guild were called. In the previous verses, Elisha swears three times that he will not leave Elijah. The mood of anticipation is building. Something significant is about to happen. All Elisha can do is watch and wait.

Once again, Elijah's acts remind us of Moses. He strikes the water and it parts in much the same way that the Red Sea did for Moses and the Jordan for Joshua (v. 8).

Elisha asks for a "double share" of Elijah's spirit (v. 9). It was customary in Hebrew families for the oldest son to receive a double share of the inheritance. Elijah is asking that he be recognized as the "heir" to Elijah.

Elijah's response is a curious one. "If you see me as I am being taken from you" probably refers to whether Elisha has the ability to hear and understand the spiritual world (v. 10). In the middle of their conversation, Elijah is taken up in a theophany. Note that the passage says the chariot of fire and horses of fire separated the two prophets, but it does not say that Elijah actually went up to heaven in the chariot. He went up rather by a whirlwind. We are not given many details about this marvelous incident, but the fact that Elisha saw the fire, the symbol of God's presence, meant that he had met the requirements laid out in v. 10.

Elisha makes a confession of faith, declaring that Elijah is more powerful than chariots and horsemen and then ritually tears his clothes as a sign of sorrow and mourning for his lost mentor (v. 12). As proof of his authority to be Elijah's successor, he takes Elijah's mantle, the symbol of his prophetic office, and duplicates the previous action of Elijah by striking the water so that it parts and he may pass over.

The theme of **the sermon** might be how God calls us to take up the roles of service which others have handed on to us, and how we pass those roles on to others. Themes from the Elijah-Elisha story which might be used are Elisha's faithfulness and loyalty, Elisha's request to be a "spiritual son" of Elijah inheriting his spirit and prophetic insight, and Elijah's careful concern that Elisha have the gift of spiritual discernment necessary for the prophetic ministry. The call of God to service includes more than just our willingness; we also need to have the qualifications for ministry.

Deuteronomy 30:9–14 (L) (E)

Deuteronomy 30:10–14 (RC)

This text is part of a larger passage (30:1–20) which addresses the exilic community. Punishment has already been carried out, but the assumption is that Israel has repented and is turning back to God. The passage is not written as an exhortation but in the style of prophetic predictions. For example, in v. 9, God's delight in prospering Israel is found also in Jeremiah 32:41. As in Jeremiah, the speaker is more interested in the prospect of a blessed future when the people turn to the Lord "with all your heart and with all your soul" (v. 10) than in pronouncing judgment upon disobedience. These words connect this passage with the Gospel lesson for today from Luke, as they also promise salvation as the result of a wholehearted response to God's love.

Verses 11–14 are especially powerful from an oratorical perspective and are perfectly balanced in structure. With beautiful poetic imagery, they assure the listeners that the law is not difficult to understand; mystical experiences are not necessary to interpret it; it just needs to be internalized and meditated upon. When the law is in our hearts and mouths, it is easy to obey. The spirit of this passage is echoed in Psalm 119, especially in v. 97: "Oh, how I love thy law! It is my meditation all the day."

The theme of **the sermon** might be the necessity of a wholehearted response to God by living lives of love and obedience to God's law. Even today, for many worshipers, there is a sense in which the word of God is very remote and the commands of scripture are very obscure. This passage speaks to those who feel that God's word is somehow "lost in the clouds" and needs a special envoy to bring it down.

Colossians 1:1–14 (C) (L) (E)

Paul's letter to the Colossians was written to counteract the influence of false teachers who were teaching a form of gnosticism. They believed that "elementary spirits" were controlling the universe and the destinies of people. The letter consists of a doctrinal section (1:1–3:4) and practical exhortations (3:5–4:18).

Verses 1 and 2 contain the greeting to the "saints and faithful brethren in Christ at

Colossae." In the Old Testament, Israel was called "holy," meaning "belonging to God"; Paul uses it here as "saints."

Verses 3–8 comprise the thanksgiving which was a customary part of Greek letters. Paul used the thanksgiving to proclaim what God had done. This thanksgiving includes the triad—faith, hope, and love—which is familiar to us from 1 Corinthians 13:13. Faith produces love, and hope is the final outcome of both.

In v. 6, a central theme of the letter is set forth: the gospel in "the whole world" is a sign of the universal power of Christ. The two verbs that describe the spread of this gospel, "bearing fruit and growing" are found only here and in Mark 4:8. Paul repeats "bearing fruit" in v. 10.

Verse 9 begins a new section, a prayer for the church at Colossae. "Knowledge" is one of the key words of this letter, since gnosticism was based on a "secret knowledge." Another key word is "wisdom," since as Paul says, the false teachings have the "appearance of wisdom" but true wisdom is only to be found in Christ (2:3). A third key word is "understanding." All three of these, as Paul points out, are not speculative and theoretical for Christians, but down to earth and practical, related to concrete instances in life. The purpose is to show the Christian how to live. In the Old Testament, true wisdom meant understanding God's will. This is also the way Paul uses the term.

How we are to live is further spelled out in v. 10. Christians are to live "a life worthy of the Lord," one of Paul's favorite expressions. "Fully pleasing to him" is a phrase found only here in the New Testament and means "having every kind of pleasing attitude." Finally, Paul links together two characteristics of growth toward maturity: "bearing fruit" and "increasing in the knowledge of God."

In v. 11 Paul mentions specifically two examples of the Spirit's fruit which they are to bear, patience and joy, both of which will be needed in the face of persecution and opposition.

God has qualified us to share in a unique "inheritance" (v. 12). In the Old Testament, the inheritance was the Promised Land. The priestly tribe of the Levites, however, received no land. Since Christians are also "priests," our inheritance is a spiritual one: the presence of the Lord. "The saints in light" may refer to the angels who live in the presence of God. He is assuring the Christians that they will share in this presence on an equal footing with the angels, thereby combatting the worship of angelic powers which was a part of the gnostic teaching.

Verses 13–14 speak of our deliverance from the "dominion of darkness" to the "kingdom" through the redemption and forgiveness offered through Christ. Some writers feel that this is a way to counteract the gnostic belief of immediate entry into the kingdom through baptism, without having to repent or make any moral changes. Paul is stressing here that between deliverance from "darkness" and entry into the kingdom is the middle ground of repentance and forgiveness. **For further study,** look up gnosticism, *stoicheia* (elementary spirits), knowledge, wisdom, understanding.

The key idea for **the sermon** in this passage is how we are to live as Christians. Following the text, one might begin with Paul's description of knowledge, wisdom, and understanding as being related concretely to life. With this understanding as foundational, one might move to a description of the life pleasing to God as one that bears fruit and increases in the knowledge of God. The next move might be to describe those fruits, and finally, to speak of our moving from darkness to light by means of repentance.

Colossians 1:15–20 (RC)

In this beautiful passage, called a Christ hymn, Paul is emphasizing both the cosmic and the reconciling role of the church's Lord. There are the two sides of his office: the cosmic agent in creation and the church's reconciler through whom harmony is restored between God and God's creation.

The Colossians were caught in the bondage of bad religion. They had fallen into the trap of fatalism and legalism, both of which breed despair. This passage is a reminder that what gives life meaning is not observance of human tradition and rules, but the death and resurrection experience in which the old nature dies to self and sin and the new nature is received as a gift from God.

236

There were two main errors in the gnostic philosophy: first, they demoted Jesus to just another angel intermediary. Second, they believed there was no final salvation, no clear redemption, just the vague possibility that by placating the elemental spirits who ruled human destiny one could enter the heavenly realm.

This hymn sets forth a very different picture of the role of Jesus Christ. He is the image of God: the one who represents God's active power and goodness (v. 15). He is the visible expression of God in human life. As such, he is both the bearer of the might and majesty of God and the revealer and mediator of the creative and sustaining power of God in the world. He is not just one of the *stoicheia*, the "elemental spirits" (see 2:8), but the one who accomplishes the will of God by allowing God to become known as the one who is active, who enters the world and has an effect on it.

Verse 16 points to Christ as the cosmic Christ who is Lord over the whole of the created order. "All things" repudiates the dualism of gnosticism which divided the material from the spiritual, and implies that all spiritual beings were created in Christ; there is to be no worship of angels. Verse 17 reminds us that since Christ is the one in whom God's creative activity has taken place, he is the one who holds the world together and gives it meaning.

Although Christ is head over the universe, only the church is his body (v. 18). The church is the place where we acknowledge Christ's Lordship and demonstrate what that means in our lives.

The poem concludes with the affirmation of the reconciling work of Christ (v. 20). It is when this reconciling work of Christ becomes real in our lives that peace occurs.

The theme of **the sermon** might be the Lordship of Christ, who is both cosmic Lord and reconciler. Acknowledging Christ's Lordship means letting our lives reflect his reconciling work.

Theological Reflection

Most of these passages reflect the theme of how our faith is reflected in our lives. The Good Samaritan story is a clear and simple statement of what it really means to obey the laws of God by living lives of simple compassion. Elisha's faith was reflected in his willingness to take up Elijah's mantle and live a life of service to God. The Deuteronomy passage challenges us to "walk in God's ways." The Colossians hymn inspires us by reminding us that the Lord of the universe is the same Lord who loved us and reconciled us to God, asking for our wholehearted commitment.

Children's Message

Tell the parable of the Good Samaritan to the children. To apply the story to the children's lives, suggest ways of being good Samaritans. This might include not only ways to help others but ways to reach out to persons who are looked down upon, as the Samaritan himself was.

Hymns for Pentecost 8

More Love to Thee, O Christ; We Love Your Kingdom, Lord. *Contemporary alternative*: Jesu, Jesu, Fill Us with Your Love.

Ordinary Time 16
Proper 11

Psalm 139:13–18 (C)

2 Kings 4:8–17 (C)
Genesis 18:1–10a (L) (RC) (E)

Colossians 1:21–29 (C) (E)
Colossians 1:21–28 (L)
Colossians 1:24–28 (RC)

Luke 10:38–42

Meditation on the Texts

Creator God, we are grateful that you break through the limits of our ordinary expectations, and do impossible things. We praise you for your grace which is poured out upon us in ways we never dared dream. We thank you for hope that shatters our hopelessness. Help us to remember how important it is to turn daily to your word for renewal and sustenance, and release us from the treadmill of "much doing." Inspire us with your energy so that we might take the good news of your reconciling love to all the earth. Amen.

Commentary on the Texts

Luke 10:38–42

The story of Mary and Martha is found only in Luke. Luke may have placed it right after the Good Samaritan parable as a warning to overzealous do-gooders who see in the parable an encouragement to "salvation by works" and take pride in their much doing. G. B. Caird states it well, "[Martha] has not yet learned that unselfishness, service, and even sacrifice can be spoiled by self-concern and self-pity, that good works which are not self forgetful can become a misery to the doer and a tyranny to others" (Caird, *The Gospel of St. Luke*, p. 150).

Although the village is not named, we know from other passages that Mary and Martha lived in Bethany (see John 11:1), which is about two miles from Jerusalem. In this story the house is said to be Martha's. It was Martha who had welcomed Jesus into her home (v. 38). Perhaps it was because she was the hostess that she felt responsible for carrying out the duties of hospitality.

Mary, on the other hand, took advantage of her opportunity to sit at the Lord's feet and listen to his teaching (v. 39). This action tells us something about the acceptance Jesus gave women. No other rabbi would have permitted women to sit at his feet. Mary's behavior did not meet with Martha's approval. Verse 40 says that she was "distracted," literally, "pulled in many directions." This is understandable if Jesus is still accompanied by the seventy (10:17), plus the Twelve, and Martha had to feed them all! Perhaps Martha wanted to join Mary at Jesus' feet but had become preoccupied with preparations for the meal. At any rate, it is clear in the story that her resentment at her sister grew in proportion to her fatigue and frustration.

Finally, it gets the best of her and she explodes and addresses her anger not at Mary but at Jesus. There is more than just a touch of reproach in her words, "Do you not care?" (v. 40). Jesus answers her demand by repeating her name, "Martha, Martha," which implies a gentle chiding. He understands her anxiety (v. 41) but tells her that her priorities are wrong.

The point of the story is in v. 42. In the process of exhausting herself to serve Jesus, Martha had neglected the most important thing—attention to his teaching. Some scholars

238

have interpreted the "one thing" to be "one dish," but it seems clear that he is stressing the importance of the choice Mary had made. Martha's doing good was preventing her from being good. Jesus was not anxious that she be the perfect hostess, but he did want her to be a devoted disciple. This was the "good portion" that Mary had chosen, and for which he praised her. Hearing Christ's word is also *diakonia*, a lasting service that will never be taken away and one that is necessary if good works are to have the proper undergirding and not become something we do to salve our egos. This text is a good one for all Christians who are prone to works righteousness and forget the importance of serving Jesus by listening to his word.

The sermon might follow the movement of the story by contrasting the two sisters and the ways they chose to serve their Lord. The sermon should point out the dangers in the kind of attitude Martha had when she allowed her self-pity to undermine the lovingness of her service. Jesus' praise of Mary gives us a glimpse into the kind of followers he wants us to be: faithfully dependent on his word like Mary and not anxiously seeking approval for all the good things we do for others like Martha.

2 Kings 4:8–17 (C)

This story is one of several that deal with the impact of Elisha's ministry. The story framed in our pericope for today is a particularly engaging one, the story of Elisha and the Shunammite woman. Its theme is the possibility for newness breaking into a seemingly impossible situation, framed in a folktalelike fashion in the story of the birth of a child to a barren woman. The story centers around one of the most remarkable women in the Old Testament, the wealthy woman (whose name is not given) who lived at Shunem. Her story is strongly reminiscent of Hannah's.

Shunem (v. 8) was a village at the foot of the southwest slopes of the Hill of Moreh. Elisha often went to Carmel which was only fifteen miles away, so it was not unusual for him to be offered hospitality by the leading citizens of the towns through which he passed.

A separate room (v. 10) was built for him by the Shunammite because, as a man of God, he was ritually sacrosanct. The word "holy" indicates an aura of power about him, which might even make it dangerous for others to come in close contact with him. For this reason, it was not appropriate for him to stay in the family quarters as other guests might have done. The use of the word "walls" indicates that it was a permanent room, not a temporary shelter like those often built out of boughs for travelers.

Elisha wanted to reward her for this hospitality and offered to secure protection for her, or possibly a reduction of taxes, since her husband was old and could not provide it (v. 13). Elisha, who was a person of influence with the king and the army, could make this promise. Her answer was full of quiet dignity as she assured Elisha's servant, Gehazi, that she had all she needed. She knew that she could rely on nearby kinfolk.

This first conversation (vs. 13–15) was held indirectly through Gehazi, since it would have been inappropriate for the woman to visit the prophet in his quarters. When Gehazi reports her answer to Elisha, Elisha is perplexed as to what can be done to reward her, but Gehazi, who seems to have a keener perception of her situation than his master, supplies a solution. The second time she is called (v. 15) she appears before Elisha, but stands discreetly in the doorway.

Elisha makes a promise to her which seems impossible: that she will have a son, "when the time comes round" (v. 16). This phrase can mean "this time next year" or "according to the time of pregnancy." This was the one thing for which she did not dare to hope, and she cannot help protesting to Elisha that he not raise her hopes by lying to her. Her reaction reminds us of Sarah's laughter and Zechariah's disbelief at similar announcements. In all of these cases, the power of God to shatter hopelessness is clearly revealed.

Look up holiness, hospitality, barrenness.

The sermon might follow the movement of the passage to describe the Shunammite woman as one who had everything: wealth, prestige, a home and a husband, good character, kindness and consideration of others but whose life contained an empty void. She was a barren woman, and, as such, felt incomplete. Into this seemingly hopeless situation, God brings new life and hope. Her story speaks to us in our times of quiet desperation as a reminder of the newness that is always possible with God.

Genesis 18:1–10a (L) (RC) (E)

The story of the promise of a son to Abraham and Sarah is a description of the miraculous breaking into the ordinary routine of daily life. The scene is vividly described and gives us the fullest description of desert hospitality in the Old Testament. According to the accepted tradition of the "guest meal," the visitors to the tent of Abraham were greeted by Abraham with a gesture of respect (v. 2). He referred to the guests with traditional Oriental deference as "My Lord." There has been much textual debate about why the three were referred to in this singular fashion. The Orthodox Church has long revered this passage as indicating a reference to the Trinity, a belief which is reflected in the most treasured icon of their tradition, Rublev's *The Holy Trinity*. It is not very helpful to debate the issue; the most important thing is to recognize the sense of God's presence that Abraham felt in the visitors and his feeling that their revelation was from God.

Abraham's deferential manner and the haste of his preparations build suspense that something important is about to happen (vs. 6–7). He invited the guests to join him under the oak trees for rest, refreshment, and foot washing without asking any questions, as was the Oriental tradition. Sarah was told to bake bread while Abraham and his servant prepared a calf and brought curds and milk to the guests.

The emphasis shifts to the guests in v. 9 and the point of the story comes to focus with the question about Sarah. Note that they knew her name and that she was childless. This is followed by the incredible promise of a son to Sarah, who was not only barren but well past childbearing years. The promise is given, not by the three men, but by "the Lord." It was the fulfillment of the covenant promise which had been reiterated five times to Abraham.

Sarah's response was to laugh, but not in amusement (v. 12). The Hebrew word used for "laugh" here indicates "superior knowledge expressed with scorn." She knew the facts: her age, her lifelong barrenness.

The dramatic climax is reached with the question put to Abraham (and to Sarah listening in the tent) by the Lord: "Is anything too hard for the Lord?" (v. 14) which is similar to the statement made by the angel to Mary in Luke 1:37. This question points to the power of God to move past the laws of logic and reason into the unimaginable, beyond the limits of the ordinary, average existence. It is a clear word of grace that goes beyond anything we can ask or think.

The sermon might follow the story from the point of view of Sarah, despairing and bitter in her barrenness, resigned to the impossibility of ever seeing the fulfillment of her dreams and of the covenant promise. The turning point comes as she is confronted by the grace of God with its incredible good news. In the same way, God breaks through our cool, ordered logic with the possibility of miracle, and we are confronted with the question in v. 14: "Is anything too hard for the Lord?"

Colossians 1:21–29 (C) (E)

Colossians 1:21–28 (L)

Colossians 1:24–28 (RC)

This passage serves as a commentary on the Christ hymn and stresses the reconciling work of Christ, so that believers are moved from darkness to light (echoing vs. 12–14).

Sacrificial terminology is used to describe Christ's act of reconciliation (vs. 21–22). Note that in the New Testament it is always the individual person, not God who has to be reconciled. Reconciliation is not a matter of soothing or paying off an angry God, but of bringing the estranged one back into relationship with a loving God. The verb "to present" is used in a sacrificial sense, as in "Present your bodies as a living sacrifice" (Rom. 12:1).

In words that echo the cosmic language of the Christ hymn, "to every creature under heaven" (v. 23), Paul is proclaiming that the gospel has now been preached everywhere. This reminds us of Jesus' words in Mark 16:15: "Go into all the world and preach the gospel to the whole creation." Paul's reference to the part he had in fulfilling that mission leads into the missionary charge found in vs. 24–29.

In these verses Paul explains how world mission is to be seen as a revelation of the "mystery" of the gospel. He begins by describing his own suffering for the sake of bringing the gospel to places where it has not been preached. The expression "I complete what is lacking in Christ's afflictions" (v. 24) has been the cause of much discussion. It is obvious that Paul is not speaking about Christ's work as redeemer which is complete. Rather, he is saying that Christ could not undergo all the suffering that is necessary for the spread of the gospel. Those who are his followers, including Paul himself, must also undergo suffering if they are to carry out Christ's work. In this way, Paul sees himself as an extension of Christ. The term "mystery" which is used in v. 26 is found in the Greek Old Testament (see Dan. 2:19, 28–29) and in the Greek mystery cults, but for Paul, it refers to the great secret that had been hidden with God for ages, namely, the fact that the Gentiles are also heirs of the promise. He goes on, in v. 27, to exclaim that it was God's purpose to make this mystery known. This mystery is a glorious thing, says Paul, which reaches the peak of its glory in Christ Jesus. Christ's presence among believers serves as a "guarantee" of glory to come. The Greek word *pas*, "all" or "every," is used four times in v. 28, which emphasizes the inclusive nature of the gospel. There are no limits to its power. This is the missionary task: to proclaim Christ by warning "everyone and teaching everyone in all wisdom, so that we may present everyone mature in Christ" (NRSV). This "wisdom" is the same as that mentioned in v. 9, which is not human knowledge or religious theory, but that wisdom which comes from above whose aim is spiritual maturity. The Greek word *teleios*, which is translated "mature" in the RSV, has the same root as *telos* (goal) and literally means "fulfilling the promise" or "being what God has in mind for you to be." This maturity is not measured by secular definitions of moral or ethical perfection, but by Christ.

Verse 29 returns to the theme of v. 24 and emphasizes once more that all of Paul's activity for the gospel, which demanded hard work and deliberate effort, was due to the power of Christ working in him.

For further study, look up reconciliation, mystery, the body of Christ.

The sermon might have a strong mission emphasis. Follow the moves of the text from the reconciling work of Christ, bringing us into a right relationship with God, to the challenge to steadfast commitment in the faith. The result of this commitment will be a desire to "make the word of God fully known" as Paul did, proclaiming, warning, and teaching to help people grow in Christian maturity. The final emphasis is that the energy for this missionary activity comes from Christ.

Theological Reflection

Three of the stories for today are about women who learned something new about God while they were engaged in extending hospitality to God's representatives. Martha learned that the desire to serve Christ must be based on a willingness to listen to and learn from his word, and not on a heavy, exhausting agenda of do-goodism which leaves us in a mire of self-pity and resentment. The Shunammite woman and Sarah learned that God's power can break through the most hopeless situations and bring new life. The Colossians passage is also a reminder of the new life which is possible through the reconciling work of Christ, and that this life is for "every creature under heaven."

Children's Message

The story of Mary and Martha might be told, emphasizing that Martha got cross even with Jesus because she was trying to do so much and was not taking time to sit at Jesus' feet. The talk might remind the children of how easy it is to get cross when we get tired. Suggest that it is important to have quiet times to hear the stories of Jesus and to think about the kinds of boys and girls Jesus wants them to be. You might ask the children how they think Jesus wants them to act. Remind the children that Jesus loved Martha even when she was cross, but wanted her to spend more time with him as Mary did, instead of always being so busy.

Hymns for Pentecost 9

Great Is Thy Faithfulness; Hope of the World; Open My Eyes That I May See. *Contemporary alternative*: We Meet You, O Christ.

Ordinary Time 17
Proper 12

Psalm 21:1–7 (C)   **Colossians 2:6–15 (C) (L) (E)**
Colossians 2:12–14 (RC)

2 Kings 5:1–15ab (C)
Genesis 18:20–32 (L) (RC)   **Luke 11:1–13**
Genesis 18:20–33 (E)

Meditation on the Texts

Compassionate God, we are grateful that our Lord Jesus taught us that we can approach you as little children approach their loving father, full of trust and confidence, as we learn in the Gospel of Luke. We are grateful that your love extends to all peoples, regardless of race or nation, as we learn in the story of Naaman the Syrian. We are grateful that you are a God of righteousness and justice, willing to hear the cries of suffering people as we learn in the story of Abraham. We are grateful that you have forgiven us for all our sins through Jesus Christ and have freed us to experience the fullness of life as described in the Letter to the Colossians. For all of this we give you thanks in the name of Jesus Christ. Amen.

Commentary on the Texts

Luke 11:1–13

The pericope begins with a description of Jesus at prayer, followed by a question from one of his disciples who wants instruction in prayer (v. 1). To have someone ask Jesus a question to which he responds with instruction is typical of Luke's style. He wants to emphasize that Jesus' teachings were practical and down-to-earth, related to specific situations and not abstract theorizing.

In vs. 2–3 we find Luke's version of the Lord's Prayer. It is sufficiently different from Matthew's for some scholars to conclude that it came from a different liturgical tradition. Others believe that since it is shorter than Matthew's, it is earlier, but that Matthew's version has retained more of the Aramaic flavor. Some recent interpretations have suggested that the prayer is strongly eschatological, and that "thy kingdom come" is the key theme. Note that while this prayer can be prayed privately, it is essentially a corporate prayer, since all the pronouns are plural.

Luke's version begins simply "Father" rather than the longer "Our Father in heaven" as Matthew puts it (v. 2). The longer phrase was common in Jewish prayers, and Matthew uses it several times in his Gospel. The actual Aramaic word that Jesus used was the personal *abba,* which corresponds to our use of "daddy." It indicated the unique and intimate quality of his relationship to God. "Thy name be hallowed" is another phrase commonly used in Jewish prayers. The name of a person carried special significance in the Old Testament. It represented a person's character and status. To "hallow" God's name is to give reverence to it and thereby to all that has been revealed to us of God. Instead of "thy kingdom come" some manuscripts read "thy Holy Spirit come upon us and cleanse us." This would be consistent with Luke's theology, but most translations prefer "thy kingdom come." This echoes Jesus' many teachings about the kingdom, which is already among us in the hearts and lives of the redeemed, but which has yet to be realized in its completeness.

The phrase "daily bread" in v. 3 has caused a great deal of discussion. Does it mean "bread for every day" in the sense of rations, or "bread for tomorrow" in an eschatological sense, or, simply, "the food we need"? The RSV uses "daily bread," and that is perhaps the best translation. The basic affirmation behind all these translations is our need to depend on God constantly.

It is interesting to note that the first three petitions, in reverse order, address the issues raised in the three temptations of Jesus in the desert (4:1–12).

In v. 4 Luke uses "sins" where Matthew uses "debts." This is the only petition based on human action. It does not imply that God's forgiveness is contingent on our own, but rather, that if we sinful humans can forgive, how much more will God be able to forgive.

The second part of the text contains some instructions about prayer, the first in the form of a parable in vs. 5–8, which shows why importunity, or "shameless asking" in prayer is not only good but necessary. The story is about a man whose journeying friend arrives in the night seeking food. Semitic hospitality required him to meet his friend's needs, but since his cupboard was bare, he went to borrow bread from another friend. The friend's reluctance to get up was overridden by the first man's relentless persistence. The implication is that God responds to those who ask in confident expectation and persistence, who do not "play at prayer."

Verses 9–13 enlarge upon the point of the parable by the three imperatives: ask, seek, knock. Again, Jesus is urging persistence. He is not teaching what to pray for but how to pray. God will answer our prayers in the way that is best for us, that is, with good gifts. These verses are similar to Matthew 7:7–11 except that Luke limits the concern to prayer, while Matthew enlarges his text to include almsgiving and fasting and other admonitions, including the Golden Rule. Luke's citing the Holy Spirit is consistent with his understanding that all good gifts come through the Holy Spirit.

For **further study,** look up *abba,* hallow.

The sermon might follow the text in outlining the pattern for prayer as laid out by Jesus. Although many familiar elements from Jewish prayers were used by Jesus, it is obvious that one difference is his insistence on the intimate, personal relationship to God as *abba,* or "daddy." This pattern points to the need for daily prayer, for prayer based on and claiming God's forgiveness which moves us to be willing to forgive others, and for relentless persistence in prayer with the confident expectation that it will be answered.

2 Kings 5:1–15ab (C)

This pericope is in the style of a wonder narrative because it tells the story of Elisha's cure of Naaman's leprosy and of Naaman's subsequent statement of faith. More important, it is a story of God's concern for all peoples, even the enemies of Israel, the Syrians.

The narrative begins by describing the virtues of Naaman, whose name actually means "charm or pleasantness" (v. 1). He was a commander in the army of the king of Syria, probably Ben-hadad. He was a "great man," "in high favor" whom God had rewarded with a major victory. He was also a leper. There were many forms of leprosy, some of which were not quarantined. Apparently, Naaman's was of this type.

The storyteller creates sympathy for Naaman, not only by the generous words of praise in v. 1 but by the reaction of the little maid, an Israelite, who waited on Naaman's wife. She had been captured in one of Syria's raids on Israel. Her concern about Naaman brings Elisha into the picture.

The little maid tells her mistress about "the prophet who is in Samaria" who could cure Naaman's leprosy (v. 3). Elisha is not called "man of God" as he is in other places, but "prophet," and is not even identified by name at first.

Naaman tells the king, and the king agrees to write on his behalf to the king of Israel (v. 5). Similar letters from one king to another concerning healing have been recorded in the Amarna Tablets. Naaman goes to the king of Israel, well equipped with gifts. The amount of silver and gold described would have been worth about eighty thousand dollars. This may be an exaggeration, but it is an indication of the extent to which Naaman was willing to go to be cured. Naaman's status was indicated in that he was sent directly from one king to another (v. 6).

The story of the reaction of the king of Israel to Naaman's request is a humorous one. There is a wordplay in the words "read" and "rent" which sound alike in the Hebrew (v.

7). The king's distress is caused by the fact that the king of Syria forgot to mention in his letter that the cure was to be done by the "prophet in Samaria," not by the king himself. He assumes it is some kind of trap set for him by the king of Syria.

Elisha makes his entrance in v. 8. In a tone of mild reproof, he suggests that the king send Naaman to him. Naaman arrives at Elisha's door "with his horses and chariots" (v. 9). Despite all the impressive pomp, Elisha does not come out to greet him, but sends a servant instead. This may have been a test of Naaman's faith. Naaman was to wash seven times since seven was the number that symbolized wholeness, or completeness (v. 10).

Naaman is outraged by the treatment he received. He felt that he had been insulted by being asked to bathe in inferior waters, the waters of Israel. It is his more pragmatic servants who save the day, by convincing him to obey the strange command.

In vs. 14–15 there is another wordplay with the repetition of the Hebrew word, *shub,* which is translated "restored" in v. 14 and "returned" in v. 15. Verse 15 contains Naaman's surprising reversal. The proud commander describes himself humbly as a "servant," and makes a confession of faith in the one God.

The sermon might develop the theme of God's love for all people by telling the story as it unfolds in this pericope. God uses an unlikely messenger, a servant girl taken in captivity, to bring the news of the possibility of healing to one of Israel's enemies. This "great man" must learn humility before he can become as a little child and be "clean." Restored or "returned" to wholeness, he "returned" to his men and made his confession of faith in the God who is God of all the earth. The sermon should stress God's love for all people, regardless of nation or race, and our role in telling all people about the possibility of healing for them through Jesus Christ.

Genesis 18:20–32 (L) (RC)

Genesis 18:20–33 (E)

The story of Abraham interceding for Sodom is a theological reflection on a difficult issue: the relationship between the way we live and the things that happen to us. The question is the same one that dominates the Book of Job: Must the righteous suffer along with the unrighteous? Because collective responsibility was an accepted theme in Israel, the question in this narrative concerns what standards God will use to decide whether or not to punish the city and all its inhabitants, both righteous and unrighteous. If the sin of a few can bring punishment on a whole community, can the righteousness of a few save the community?

This incident follows the visit of the three strangers to the tent of Abraham. In keeping with the rules of Oriental hospitality, Abraham sets out with the visitors to see them safely on their way toward Sodom. As they are walking, God begins a soliloquy about Abraham. In this soliloquy, God decides to confide in Abraham about the fate awaiting Sodom. In this way, God indicates that the covenant promise has put Abraham on such a level that he is worthy of God's confidence. Also, by understanding the justice of what God is about to do, Abraham will be better able to instruct future generations about what is right and just (v.19).

In v. 20 the dialogue between Abraham and God begins. God announces to Abraham that he has heard terrible "outcries" against Sodom and Gomorrah, and that their "sin is very grave." The Hebrew word for "outcry" has many nuances, recalling Abel's blood crying out (Gen. 4:10) and the cries of the Hebrews in Egypt (Ex. 2:23). This cry, then, is a cry of the helpless victims of corruption. God was sensitive to their oppression, as God always is. This is reinforced by the words "I will go down to see" (v. 21). God does not remain aloof, nor does God allow Abraham to be. On the heels of a great personal joy (the promise of Isaac), Abraham is thrust into a concern for the pain of others.

As the visitors move on toward Sodom, Abraham is left facing the one who is now referred to as Yahweh (v. 22). While most translations say "Abraham still stood before the LORD," the original text probably read "Yahweh paused before Abraham." This gives a better picture of God waiting for Abraham's response. This response comes in the form of a theological question human beings have been asking ever since: Why must the righteous suffer? Would a just judge permit that?

The word used in v. 25, which is translated "right" in the RSV and "justly" in the TEV, comes from the same stem as the word "judge." For Abraham the "Judge of all the earth" must of necessity do the "just" or "right" thing.

Verses 26–32 contain a rhythmic repetition, not unlike a children's story, which serves to build suspense. In Abraham's insistent petitioning, we catch a glimpse of his character. His humility before God is apparent (he calls himself "dust and ashes"), but he does not give up seeking a confirmation that God is a God who practices righteousness and justice. It was essential that Abraham be assured of this if he were to pass on to his descendants the importance of keeping the way of the Lord by "doing righteousness and justice" (v. 19).

Why did Abraham stop at ten (v. 32)? One possible answer is that the number ten represented the smallest possible number that could be defined as a group. If there were fewer than that, they would be saved as individuals, as in the case of Lot's family. Abraham had received his answer: the collective power of ten righteous individuals could save the city. His importunity had affirmed God's ultimate righteousness.

For further study, look up righteousness.

The sermon could deal with the difficult issue of the suffering of the innocent and the righteous. Tell the story in the pericope by making the following moves: God hears the cries of innocent sufferers and is not aloof from their pain; God is a God who practices righteousness and justice; God hears the persistent intercessory prayers of the righteous.

Colossians 2:6–15 (C) (L) (E)

Colossians 2:12–14 (RC)

This pericope contains Paul's words of advice and warning to the Colossian church, particularly about the dangers of gnostic philosophy.

The verb "received" used in v. 6 comes from rabbinic Judaism and has to do with transmitting and safeguarding a tradition. The tradition in this case concerns the person and place of Jesus Christ.

In v. 7 Paul uses three metaphors to make his point: "rooted" which is horticultural; "built up" which is architectural; and "established" which is legal, suggesting a binding contract. In the phrase "as you were taught" Paul is referring to his own teaching in the early days of the church. Paul's use of the word "live" is practical, having to do with the way Christians are to conduct their lives.

In v. 8 the expression "makes a prey of you" means literally "kidnap, capture, or carry off as a captive in war." The term "philosophy" represents not the intellectual discipline as we know it, but the gnostic teachings which Paul sees as hollow and "empty." "Human tradition," as opposed to the tradition they had received from him, includes the heretical teachings to which they had been exposed, such as the place given to the *stoicheia,* the elemental spirits of the universe who rivaled Christ in authority.

The Gnostics believed that the fullness (*plērōma*) of God (v. 9) was spread through the universe in the form of the elemental spirits. The intent of v. 9 is to show that the "fulness" of God came to its expression in Christ, not in the cosmic powers. Those spirits cannot act as intermediaries between God and humanity, as the Gnostics claimed; it is only Christ who can do that, since it is in him that the "fulness" of God is revealed. The word that is translated "of God" is *theotēs* which means the "essence of God," as contrasted with the similar *theiotēs,* which means the "divine characteristics." Christ is not "like God" but *is* God. The meaning of "bodily" is not clear. It could mean "corporately," "incarnate" or having a bodily form only in appearance. It probably is intended to indicate the fully human life which Christ lived, even though he possessed the fullness of God.

The result for us is "fulness of life" (v. 10). We partake in the fullness of God through our oneness with Christ. We need nothing else, no other rites or powers. Christ is announced as the one who has subjugated all other powers, "the head of all rule and authority."

Verses 11–15 elaborate the theme of "fulness of life in him." The key phrase is in v. 11: "putting off the body of flesh." It is a reminder of the baptism process wherein the believers took off their clothes for baptism and put on new ones afterward. It is not the first time Paul makes the suggestion that baptism replaces circumcision, becoming a circumcision of the heart, not of the hands, that is, wholly the work of God. The "circumcision of Christ," therefore, means baptism.

Paul then moves to a death and resurrection metaphor of baptism (v. 12). We are resurrected with Christ through faith in the *energeia* of God. The TEV translation of *energeia* as "active power" is stronger than the RSV "working."

In vs. 13–15 we see a clear picture of God at work: forgiving trespasses, canceling debts, and disarming the principalities and powers. Christ shows them up for what they are: petty tyrants. The final image is of public officials being divested of their honor.

Look up the significance of Paul's use of the term "fulness."

The thrust of **the sermon** might be the new fullness of life that is possible for us in Christ. Just as Christ died and was resurrected, so we have died to our sins and been made alive by God. It is the energy of God which has brought us to life. Our baptism is a symbolic act of our death and resurrection. God's willingness to forgive all our sins has set us free and given us a new sense of the richness and fullness of life. We do not need any other philosophies, rites, or supernatural powers to give our lives meaning.

Theological Reflection

Each of today's texts tells of the compassionate, forgiving nature of God. The Naaman story is a reminder that God's love goes out to all people, regardless of nationality. The Abraham story affirms that God hears the outcries of innocent sufferers and is a God of justice and love. Jesus' teachings on prayer are predicated on belief in a loving *abba* who stands ready to forgive us our sins and who wants us to ask for what we need. The Colossians passage reminds us of what God has done for us in Jesus Christ out of abundant grace and love.

Children's Message

This might be a good opportunity to discuss with the children the meaning of some of the phrases in the Lord's Prayer, such as *abba,* "daily bread," and "forgive us our sins." The talk could be closed by asking the children to join the congregation in reciting the prayer.

Hymns for Pentecost 10

All Hail the Power of Jesus' Name!; O for a Thousand Tongues to Sing; Breathe on Me, Breath of God. *Contemporary alternative:* Christ, You Are the Fullness.

Pentecost 11

Ordinary Time 18
Proper 13

Psalm 28 (C)

2 Kings 13:14–20a (C)
Ecclesiastes 1:2; 2:18–26 (L)
Ecclesiastes 1:2; 2:21–23 (RC)
Ecclesiastes 1:12–14; 2:18–23 (E)

Colossians 3:1–11 (C) (L)
Colossians 3:1–5, 9–11 (RC)
Colossians 3:12–17 (E)

Luke 12:13–21

Meditation on the Texts

O God, we thank you that you have raised us with Christ to a new life. We rejoice that the word of Christ dwells in us. We are grateful for the peace of Christ in our hearts. We confess, however, that sometimes we become absorbed in our pursuit of things that are on earth, and in the process of building bigger barns are lukewarm about our commitment to the things that are above. Help us to keep our priorities straight and to live lives that reflect that we have been chosen by you, set apart by you and loved by you. May all our actions be guided by that love which binds everything together in harmony. Amen.

Commentary on the Texts

Luke 12:13–21

This pericope contains the parable of the rich fool which is found only in Luke. It begins with a question relating to the inheritance laws from a man in the crowd. Since, according to Deuteronomy 21:17, the elder brother received a double share of the inheritance, the question is probably being asked by a younger brother, who is questioning the division. Since the Jewish law contained a section to help rabbis settle family disputes, the man apparently came to Jesus for that sort of intervention. However, Jesus refused to enter into the family wrangle and disclaimed any authority to make that kind of legal decision. His disclaimer begins with the word "man," which indicates a decided lack of warmth toward the issue. Instead, he used the quarrel to make a point about the value of earthly riches. Not only are material possessions impermanent, but placing too much value on them is a form of egotism which has no place in the kingdom of God.

In v. 15, he begins this teaching with a note of solemn warning against covetousness: "Take heed, and beware." The TEV is stronger and is closer to the real intent of the words: "Watch out and guard yourselves." The implication is that covetousness can sneak up on a person like a thief in the night, taking otherwise well-meaning folk by surprise.

The parable begins with v. 16, telling the story of a rich man whose land was so productive that he needed bigger barns. It is interesting to note that this rich man was not the worst offender one could imagine. There is no hint that he was storing up his goods to drive the market price up; nor was he trapped in a compulsion to maximize his profits by continuing to produce. Instead, he simply wanted to put aside something for tomorrow, so that he could enjoy life without having to worry about where the next meal was to come from. His whole orientation was toward himself; there is no suggestion that he gave any thought to helping others by sharing his accumulated wealth.

It was not a criminal offense that God accused him of in v. 20 but stupidity. His stupidity consisted of believing that he could control his destiny, that ultimate meaning resided in the possession of things, and that he could keep those possessions indefinitely. By living this way, he was missing real life. In v. 21 the point is broadened to include anyone who thinks only of himself or herself and is "not rich toward God." Being rich toward God indicates having a different orientation toward possessions. This phrase has also been translated "a pauper in the sight of God" (NEB), which says something about how God views those individuals who fail to recognize God's ultimate Lordship. This is further amplified by 12:34: "Where your treasure is, there will your heart be also."

The sermon might deal with the insidious power of greed over human lives. The story of the rich man who needed bigger and better barns bears a tragic resemblance to many persons in the world today who have bought the upward mobility dream. The parable is a stern warning about the importance of having the right priorities. Jesus bluntly attacks the prevalent notion that the mark of the good life is to have an abundance of possessions. Instead, true spirituality, being "rich toward God" is the only kind of richness that really matters. The sermon should point to ways in which we might reexamine our attitude toward our possessions to make sure our first loyalty is to God.

2 Kings 13:14–20a (C)

This passage tells the story of the death of Elisha at the end of his prophetic career. The story begins with a description of King Joash's grief over Elisha's impending death (v. 14). As he weeps, Joash calls out, "My father, my father! The chariots of Israel and its horsemen!" His use of the word "Father" expresses a teacher-student relationship. These are the same words used by Elisha of Elijah.

Elisha gives the king a strange command: Shoot an arrow eastward from the window (vs. 15–17). Elisha covered the king's hands with his own as he aimed the arrow. This signified the transfer of divine power which Elisha had received from Elijah. The belief was that touching someone who possessed this power would cause some of that blessing to spill over in a kind of anointing. A dying person was also supposed to possess unusual power.

The arrow flying east symbolized the victory Joash, who was the grandson of Jehu, would have over Syria which lay in that general direction. Next, the dying prophet commanded the king to strike the arrows on the ground. The king struck only three times, and Elisha angrily denounced him, saying that if he had continued for six times, he would have been able to strike down Syria completely (vs. 18–19). Was the prophet testing the king by the ritual of the arrows? It was not uncommon in that period to consider symbolic acts powerful enough to change future events. There is also the possibility that the prophets used these kinds of symbolic acts to make a vivid point. Elisha's shout "the LORD's arrow of victory" (v. 17) seemed to give added power and significance to the incident. Was the king simply humoring the dying man by striking halfheartedly? Was that the reason for Elisha's impatience with him? Or does this story symbolically indicate that in the death of Elisha, the dynamic power which he brought to Israel was gone, to be replaced by the halfheartedness and lack of determination of a series of weak kings?

In v. 20a we learn of Elisha's death, but the story does not end there. Subsequent verses (not in our text for today) tell that Elisha's bones still had enough power in them to bring a dead man to life again.

The sermon might center on the contrast between the God-given energy and power of the prophet Elisha and the halfheartedness of King Joash. God needs our wholehearted commitment, not our lukewarmness. Unlike Joash, we need to follow God's commands with enthusiasm and obedience.

Ecclesiastes 1:2; 2:18–26 (L)

Ecclesiastes 1:2; 2:21–23 (RC)

Ecclesiastes 1:12–14; 2:18–23 (E)

The name Ecclesiastes is a Greek word meaning "a member or speaker of an assembly." It might be used here as a name given to the author as the personification of wisdom, or as one who collects or gathers wisdom teachings, or as one who is a speaker or preacher at an assembly. Perhaps the best translation is Teacher. The book has been attributed to Solomon, but most scholars feel that the use of Solomon's name was simply a literary device.

The book is a difficult one. It struggles with the question: How can life be best lived? It was written by someone who had found that the traditional answers no longer satisfied him. He has tried everything and has found it all "vanity." He looks at life's anomalies and because he cannot explain them, he finds life meaningless. He never loses his faith in God, but thinks of God as a distant Sovereign rather than close friend and redeemer. His final conclusion is to enjoy life and have reverence for God and not worry about the future.

However, there are many things about the book that give it value. Martin Luther wrote, "The design of the book is to teach us to use with grateful hearts the things present and the creatures which are bountifully bestowed upon us by God, without anxiety about future temporal blessings" (in Robert Davidson, *Ecclesiastes and The Song of Solomon,* Daily Study Bible, p. 3; Philadelphia, Westminster Press, 1986). The book is a realistic appraisal of the hypocrisy, injustice, and oppression that are the hard realities of life. It is also an acknowledgment that a purely secular approach to life, stressing the acquisition of possessions is futile and empty, an echo of the parable of the rich fool in today's Gospel lesson.

"Vanity" (v. 2) translates a Hebrew word meaning "breath or vapor" which implies futility or transitoriness. The author has looked at life "from both sides now" and found it futile. He enjoys life, but he confesses he does not know what it is all about.

In vs. 12–14, he describes his search for satisfaction. In these verses, he assumes the identity of Solomon to present the viewpoint of someone who had access to everything wealth could buy. In this role he searches for meaning and finds nothing. Even the pursuit of wisdom can drive one to despair.

In 2:18–23, he discusses another area of futility; he hates the fact that although he has worked hard all his life, using all his wisdom, knowledge, and skill, someone else will enjoy the fruits of his labor. The issue for him is that he has no control over whether his successor will be wise or foolish. There is no certainty in life. The reality to which he points is indisputable. However, the reality for us is that as long as God is the center of our lives, we do not need to think only in terms of *this* life. Disillusion and despair set in only when we think that this life is all there is.

Verses 24–26 point to the one way the Teacher has found to be happy. He says in spite of its anomalies, life can be enjoyed on the practical level. This is a gift from God. He decides that there is nothing better than to eat and drink. God wants us to enjoy them. Verse 26 ends on the note that the person who has the right attitude has the promise from God of wisdom, knowledge, and happiness. However, some people fail to please God and end up losing everything. Their labor then has become "a vanity and a striving after wind."

For further study, look up vanity and wisdom.

The sermon might deal with the frustration and despair everyone feels with the anomalies of life. Some of these might be cited, paralleling them with examples from the text. It is important to point out that the writer of Ecclesiastes is not affirming the basic theological values of the Old Testament, but is raising critical questions about the meaning of life, and in the process, even questioning the traditions of the faith. A comparison might be made to those in our world today who see life as basically meaningless, and are asking hard questions of the church. A challenge should be made to the hearers to acknowledge that while there are many big questions we cannot answer, the meaning of life is found for us in our confidence in a sovereign God who is the source of all true wisdom and knowledge.

Colossians 3:1–11 (C) (L)

Colossians 3:1–5, 9–11 (RC)

See also Easter Day, (RC) (E).

The theme of this pericope is a new pattern of life. The first four verses form a transition from theology to the practical daily living out of our faith. We are to have a new aim in life, to see things from a different perspective.

Instead of playing with the gnostic notions of heavenly "realities," Paul is calling the Colossians to concentrate on "things that are above, where Christ is" (v. 1). True knowledge is found in him, not in astrological speculation. "The right hand of God" is an expression that denotes a position of power, holiness, and victory. This may be a quote from Psalm 110:1, which is frequently quoted in the New Testament. It is a reference here to Christ's Lordship.

Although the verb "seek" actually means "think" or "judge," the intent is not to describe a mental exercise so much as a change in one's whole orientation, in the motives which guide one's conduct. It is here that we can see a relationship to the parable in Luke, with its warning about where we should place our priorities.

The word "hid" is a difficult word to interpret; it is possible that there is a continuation of the metaphor of dying in baptism by making a play on the Greek idiom which says that in death a person is "hidden in the earth." It is also possible that it means that the world is not able to see the new life of the believer, but since we are one with Christ, on the day when he appears, our true life will also be revealed. "Appear with him in glory" may be a reference to the resurrection of the body. This seems to be a definite reference to the Parousia.

The next section contains a series of verses some scholars hold to be baptismal instructions. Certainly the phrase "put to death" is baptismal language. The "therefore" in v. 5 points to what has gone before. The implication is that if we have died, then we must take action and "put to death" those unworthy traits which were characteristic of our previous life. "What is earthly" refers back to v. 2 and begins a list of five physical vices, all the result of loss of self-control. "Fornication," "impurity," "passion," and "evil desire" all denote moral impurity. Although "covetousness" could have sexual connotations, it actually means "greed." The Greek word literally means "to have more." It is well illustrated by the parable of the rich fool in the Gospel lesson for today. Greed for possessions is a form of idolatry.

It is not uncommon for lists of vices in the New Testament to end with a note of solemn warning (v. 6; see 1 Thess. 4:3–6).

"Walk" is a metaphor Paul especially likes (v. 7). Here he is contrasting walking in sin with walking in Christ (see 2:6).

Verse 8 begins a new list that contains the sins of speech. The quality of the new Christian life is indicated by the quality of communication between its members. All the vices listed can wreck the harmony of a community. Perhaps all of them existed in one form or another in the Colossian church.

Verse 9 adds lying to the list of vices to be abandoned. This verse goes on to pick up the baptismal metaphor again with a verb that suggests disrobing. Paul seems to be urging the Colossians to act upon their baptismal confession by being true to it and to become what they were declared to be in their baptism. The old goals no longer apply; they are now part of a new humanity alive unto God. Because of our baptism we have a new ability to understand and obey God's will and command (v. 10).

This new humanity can now live together without divisions (v. 11). This is an amplification of Galatians 3:28. Our baptism brings us together, breaking down walls of race, nationality, social status, and even religious observances. "Barbarian" refers to those who did not speak Greek. "Scythian" was a term applied to tribes around the Black Sea, which were not held in very high repute. The final glorious summary is that "Christ is all" we need to be a part of this new community. Christ has dissolved all barriers between human beings in whom he dwells, and created a new life for them.

The sermon might follow the movement of the passage from the reorientation of values through our baptismal death from those sins that "so easily beset us" to being part of the new community in Christ, who has created new life for us.

Colossians 3:12–17 (E)

In this passage, Paul moves from the list of vices to be "put away" to a list of virtues to be "put on." This is how we are to live as God's people. The three adjectives, "chosen, holy, beloved" are the terms used of Israel in the Old Testament. It is in keeping with Paul's references to the church as the New Israel.

250

Paul lists five moral qualities Christians are to wear. "Compassion," "kindness," and "lowliness" show how the Christian is to relate to others. Paul stresses throughout his letters God's kindness toward the needy and the necessity for Christians to demonstrate the same kind of kindness. "Lowliness" does not mean self-depreciation, but neither does it mean self-love. "Meekness" contains elements of consideration of others and willingness to give up one's rights. "Patience" is the opposite of resentment or revenge; it promotes tolerance and forgiveness. All five are ways Christians should relate to others.

Verse 13 emphasizes the importance of forgiveness, because we have been forgiven. In v. 14 love becomes the overcoat that goes on top of all the other virtues. It holds the others together and gives them motive and meaning. Love is the bond that produces perfect harmony in the Christian's life.

"The peace of Christ" (v. 15) must enter the lives of the community and set their priorities in order. "Heart" in biblical language is the center of the religious life which determines moral conduct. The call to "be thankful" is a reminder to the community of their need to be grateful for their freedom and deliverance into a new life.

"The word of Christ" is to be an antidote to false wisdom (v. 16). The singing of the community was to be done in a spirit of thanksgiving for the mission and accomplishment and exalted place of Jesus Christ. The life of the community finds its truest expression in giving thanks to God. This leads to the challenge to do everything in the name of Christ, not just acts of worship, but in the whole of life (v. 17).

The sermon might follow the progression of the passage from the fact that as the chosen ones of God who are set apart and loved by God, we must live our lives in keeping with that high calling. A discussion of the virtues could then be presented, ending with the challenge to peace, harmonious praise of God, and thanksgiving for all we have received in Jesus Christ.

Theological Reflection

All the passages reflect the urgent necessity of a total commitment and a reorientation of values if we are truly to be the people of God. The story of Elisha and King Joash underscores the need for wholehearted commitment. The parable of the rich fool and the verses from Ecclesiastes point out the vanity of putting one's faith in one's possessions. The Colossians passages point clearly to the need to let go the false values of the world and choose the values that are from above, especially putting on love which binds all the other virtues together.

Children's Message

Tell the parable of the rich fool and talk with the children about how easy it is to let our greediness for things make us selfish and unkind.

Hymns for Pentecost 11

In the Cross of Christ I Glory; So Let Our Lips and Lives Express; O Jesus, I Have Promised.

Ordinary Time 19
Proper 14

Psalm 14 (C)	**Hebrews 11:1–3, 8–19 (C)**
	Hebrews 11:1–3, 8–16 (L) (E)
Jeremiah 18:1–11 (C)	**Hebrews 11:1–2, 8–19 (RC)**
Wisdom 18:6–9 (RC)	
Genesis 15:1–6 (L) (E)	**Luke 12:32–40 (C) (L) (E)**
	Luke 12:32–48 (RC)

Meditation on the Texts

Creator God, we stand in awe before your majesty. As we reflect on the wonders and mysteries of the universe you have brought into being, our hearts are humbled, remembering our frailty. We are like faulty clay pots, yet you choose to accept our repentance and redeem our brokenness. As we reflect on the lives of the heroes and heroines of faith who have gone before us, our hesitancy and lack of faith become glaringly obvious. We continue to ask for cognitive "proof" instead of taking the leap of faith. We do not move with assurance of things hoped for, but creep along in fear and apprehension of things dreaded. Teach us how to rely fully and completely on your grace that we, too, might please you by our faith. Amen.

Commentary on the Texts

Luke 12:32–40 (C) (L) (E)

Luke 12:32–48 (RC)

In this pericope Jesus returns to the theme of earthly and heavenly riches. He begins with a reminder of the precious gift God has given them. Note that this is the only time the expression "little flock" is used in the New Testament (v. 32). It gives an image of a shepherd's care, exemplified in the promise of the kingdom.

Because his followers have this real treasure, the kingdom, they do not need earthly treasure. Therefore, it is possible for them to unburden themselves of their possessions and give the money away (v. 33). Jesus is not denouncing private ownership entirely, but is returning to the theme of the parable in vs. 13–21 of not being dominated by treasures that are temporal and nonlasting. The kind of renunciation of enslavement to worldly goods is a way of showing total devotion to God (v. 34).

In v. 35, Jesus introduces a parable, the theme of which is the unexpected coming of the Son of Man. The phrase "Let your loins be girded" is reminiscent of the preparations for the first Passover. The TEV translates it "Be ready for whatever comes, dressed for action." Literally, it refers to gathering up one's long ankle-length robe into one's belt for a speedy departure. The phrase "lamps burning" has overtones of the parable of the ten virgins. A lighted lamp is a symbol of watchfulness. The metaphor is that of a bridegroom returning home after a wedding feast, greeting those who are waiting for him. Then, in an unexpected shift, the bridegroom not only invites those who are awake to a banquet but serves them himself (v. 37). They are truly blessed, for this is an unusual honor. The Romans divided the night into four watches, but the Jews only three. For the servants to be awake during the second and third watches, therefore, means that they stayed awake all night long. The point is that although the coming of the Son of Man is certain, the time of that coming is vastly uncertain. All we can know is that it will be at an unexpected hour, so we must be ready at all times.

Continuing with the theme of surprise visits, v. 39 begins another mini-parable of the thief in the night, who was unanticipated by the master of the house. Unlike the first parable, this one has the sense of impending catastrophe.

In v. 41, Peter asks Jesus if these parables refer only to the Twelve. Jesus answers with a third parable which stresses the importance of loyalty and readiness. A steward was a slave who had responsibility for running the household. A diligent steward continued to carry out his duties responsibly and well, even if the master were away, whereas an unworthy steward took advantage of his absence to abuse the privileges of his rank. The master's return then would result in punishment.

Verses 47–48 are found only in Luke. This passage points out in a graphic way the greater responsibility and therefore the greater accountability of the leaders in the Christian church. The idea behind this saying is that those who have been entrusted with tasks have also been given the ability to carry them out.

The sermon might follow the movement of the passage beginning with the reminder that what we treasure most in life determines our allegiance. If we are preoccupied with acquiring material possessions, we may miss the spiritual inbreakings of God. We must keep ourselves mentally, spiritually, and morally prepared for the unexpected revelations God makes. This includes the final Parousia for which we must be constantly ready, with loins girded and lamps burning.

Jeremiah 18:1–11 (C)

This story of the visit to the potter's house is an example of how Jeremiah used the experiences of everyday life to make a theological point about Israel's sinfulness. The prophet interprets this visit as a sign or vision from God.

The idea of God as a potter was a familiar one in Hebrew thought. Genesis 2:7 describes God making human beings out of clay. Isaiah used the metaphor three times (29:16; 45:9; 64:8). In this case, however, the potter is not satisfied with the end result and reworks it into something brand-new. Jeremiah sees this as an illustration of how the destruction of Jerusalem can also be the work of the Lord, and how God's providence can rework the fallen nation into something new and beautiful. It is a message of hope.

Verses 7–11 contain a call to repentance. Destruction can be turned aside if there is true repentance and returning to God. God demands and expects such a response, and has promised that it can change the future. In other words, the responsibility for the destruction that was about to befall Judah was her own, not that of a capricious God. If she continued in her stubborn willfulness, turning away from God, disaster and punishment were sure to follow. If, however, she repented, then divine grace would be willing to permit a new beginning, to create a new vessel from the shattered clay.

The sermon might move from a consideration of our imperfectness to the message of hope that God can rework us to produce something beautiful. The necessary ingredient, of course, is our repentance. If that is not present, our disobedience will result in disaster; but if we repent, God's grace will make us into new vessels.

Wisdom 18:6–9 (RC)

This passage is part of a hymn praising the Lord as a righteous and merciful judge. Verses 6–7 point out the difficulty in penetrating the wonders of the Lord. The confusion that results because of this human inadequacy to understand God is further proof to the writer, Ben Sirach, of the majesty of God's glory. No matter how long we contemplate the wonders of the Lord, when we think we have finished, we have just begun. No scientific investigation can penetrate God's mind. When we give up our inquiries, we are still bewildered. Verse 8 is similar to Psalm 8:5 in exclaiming over human insignificance compared with God: "What is a human being, of what worth is he? the good, the evil in him, what are these?" Even our good and evil deeds pale into insignificance beside God's transcendent glory. Verse 9 with its echo of Psalm 90:10 continues that thought by stressing how short our lives are. The author exaggerates the limits of a life span to make his point, perhaps drawing the number one hundred from the Egyptian measurement of a life span, rather than the Hebrew seventy or eighty years, used in the psalm.

The sermon may begin, as the writer of the text does, with a description of the wonders of the universe that the human mind cannot grasp. Even all our scientific knowledge cannot explain the mysteries of creation. Our human achievements shrink into insignificance. When we contemplate the glory and majesty of God and of God's creation, our response should be that of awe, praise, and adoration.

Genesis 15:1–6 (L) (E)

Walter Brueggemann calls Genesis 15 "pivotal," adding that "theologically, it is probably the most important chapter of this entire collection." This is because it offers crucial resources for "faith" and "covenant." (For further discussion of this, see Walter Brueggemann, *Genesis,* Interpretation series, p. 140; Atlanta: John Knox Press, 1982.)

Our pericope for today describes the prophetic vision in which Abraham is promised as many descendants as the stars. Remember that at this point he had no children, for the birth of Isaac had not yet occurred. In the face of this, how was it possible for Abraham to believe the promise God was making? This passage shows Abraham's struggle as he argues with God in vs. 2–3. Yet, after God makes the incredible promise of a multitude of descendants, he did believe, and it was this affirmation of belief in the unbelievable promise that justified God's faith in him and demonstrated the depth of his faith in God.

The phrase "The word of the LORD came" (v. 1) is a phrase associated with God's revelations to the prophets, and indeed Abraham is called a prophet in 20:7. "Fear not" is a word of greeting that was addressed to Abraham's fear that the promise given by God in 13:15–16 was never to be realized. God promises a reward to Abraham which was the land. In v. 2 Abraham responds to this offer with a question, How could he inherit the land without descendants? There is an allusion here to the custom whereby an adopted slave could become an heir.

Once more the Lord affirms the promise in clear and specific words: "Your own son shall be your heir" (v. 4). Abraham does not ask how this impossible thing is to happen; he simply believes. The movement from disbelief to belief has been accomplished by the power of God. The words "Look toward heaven" in v. 5 are a reminder of Psalm 8:3, "When I look at thy heavens" which leads the psalmist to a realization of the mighty power of God with whom "nothing is impossible." Perhaps it is a recognition of this truth which leads to Abraham's belief.

In v. 6, Abraham is described as one whose belief in God caused him to be considered righteous in God's sight. This implies that now he has come to rely utterly on God by responding to the gift of grace. His faith has made him whole. Paul based Romans 4 on this passage, and summarized it beautifully in Romans 4:18, 20: "In hope he believed against hope" and "he grew strong in his faith as he gave glory to God." Faith is clearly not so much a matter of cognitive understanding, but of implicit trust.

Look up faith and covenant.

The sermon might have as a central theme struggling with doubt. A connection might be made between Abraham's doubts about the fulfillment of the covenant promise and faith questions that arrive in our own lives. Follow the movement of the text to a consideration of the mighty power of God as we "look toward heaven," and the final assertion of faith made by Abraham affirming that nothing is impossible with God. Faith does not overcome doubt by cognitive reasoning but by what Søren Kierkegaard referred to as the "leap of faith" which believes the impossible. As our Hebrews text for today puts it, it is "the conviction of things not seen" (Heb. 11:1).

Hebrews 11:1–3, 8–19 (C)

Hebrews 11:1–3, 8–16 (L) (E)

Hebrews 11:1–2, 8–19 (RC)

This passage in Hebrews has been described by various writers as a roll call, a picture gallery, a catalog, and a list of heroes and heroines of faith. It is a description of men and women who have been examples of the kind of faith pictured in 10:39: "those who have faith and keep their souls."

In v. 1 there is a limited definition of faith. Faith is not personal commitment as it is to Paul, but rather, trust or confidence. The two key words in this definition, "assurance" and "conviction," need a closer examination. Assurance is the Greek word *hypostasis,* which has to do with that which is still in the future but expectantly awaited, while conviction has to do with the proof of the reality of that which can only be understood by faith. In other words, "things not seen" describes all that is beyond our normal knowledge or comprehension. This is a good description of the "already but not yet" aspects of the Christian life. We have faith in ("hope for") that which has not yet happened: the complete fulfillment of God's promises; we also have faith in that which is "not seen," the assumption of the saving power of the death and resurrection of Jesus Christ.

Verse 2 reminds us of the Genesis text for today, when Abraham's faith merited God's approval, and v. 3 reflects the thought of the Wisdom passage in its reminder that the creation of the world is a matter of faith not scientific proof. The world was created by the word of God as we find not only in Genesis 1 but in Psalm 33:6, 9 and in 2 Peter 3:5. The word translated "created" here means "set in order," "put to rights," "furnished completely," or "equipped." In other words, through the eyes of faith, we see the work of God not just in initiating but in establishing and keeping in motion the whole created order.

Verse 4 begins the list or honor roll of faith. The first person cited is Abel. Abel's act of faith was apparently having the right attitude toward God which resulted in his making the right kind of sacrifice. We are not told in Genesis just how God signified acceptance of the sacrifice, but the implication is clear that Abel was approved of by God (see Gen. 4:4, "The LORD had regard for Abel"), and the author of Hebrews says this approval affirmed his righteousness.

The basis for the assertion in vs. 5–6 that Enoch pleased God apparently comes from the Septuagint, where Genesis 5:24 is translated to read that Enoch "was well-pleasing to God." Since the author believes that without faith it is impossible to please God, then, he reasons, Enoch must have had faith, and it must have been because of his faith that he was "taken up."

The ark was a visible evidence of Noah's faith (v. 7). As he went about obeying God's command, his faithfulness became a condemnation to the disbelieving scoffers who were subsequently punished by the flood.

Verses 8–12 recount the story of that giant of faith, Abraham. The proof of his faith was that he "went out, not knowing where he was to go." His faith was demonstrated in his obedience. The word "sojourned" (v. 9) meant to dwell as a stranger in a certain locality. Abraham had no property until he bought a cave for the family burial ground. His faith made Isaac and Jacob "heirs with him of the same promise" (v. 9). "The city which has foundations" (v. 10) is the heavenly city which is permanent in contrast to the nomadic tents.

Sarah's faith is praised (v. 11), but for surprising reasons: it implies that her power to conceive was a result of her faith. This presents a difficulty when compared with the Genesis account, where her response was one of mocking disbelief, or lack of faith. One explanation is that the verb "conceive" refers to Abraham and not Sarah. This is supported by the perplexing fact that the verb which is used literally means "depositing seed," which could only be an action of Abraham. Another possible way to translate the verb, however, is "for the founding of a race." With this translation the sense of the verse is that Sarah's faith enabled her to receive power from God to found a race. It is, of course, possible for Sarah's initial disbelief to have been transformed by an attitude of trust in the faithfulness of the One who had made a covenant promise to them and had led them into the "land of promise."

In vs. 13–16, although the wording seems to apply especially to Abraham, the writer seems to be thinking of all the patriarchs. A "homeland" (v. 14) was not just a place of habitation, but a place to put down roots. The phrase "a better country, that is, a heavenly one" (v. 16) is characteristic of the epistle because of the emphasis on a spiritual rather than a national inheritance. The greatest praise that can be given is found in the phrase "God is not ashamed to be called their God."

In vs. 17–19, the author cites one more example of Abraham's faith: the faith that enabled him to be willing to sacrifice his son, Isaac. The author adds something to the Genesis text, which is that Abraham believed that God had the power to resurrect Isaac. The author may be using this incident as a symbol of the resurrection of Christ.

For further understanding, look up the meaning and use of faith, assurance, and hope.

The sermon might follow the text in moving from a description of how faith is expressed in individual lives by giving specific examples. Some of these might be from the lives of living heroes and heroines of the faith. The sermon might emphasize that faith is believing in the complete fulfillment of God's promises, and, therefore, is an attitude of trust and confidence.

Theological Reflection

A central theme in today's texts is the meaning of true faith. In the Luke passage, those with true faith recognize the power of God to break into life unexpectedly and so they try to be ready by being more attuned to spiritual than to material pursuits. In the Jeremiah text, the life of faith is characterized by true repentance and a willingness to be remodeled into new creations. The text from Wisdom reminds us that true faith means recognizing that our human achievements pale into insignificance beside God's glory. The Genesis passage is a reminder that Abraham's faith did not depend on his understanding how God could fulfill the covenant promises, and the catalog of heroes and heroines in Hebrews is eloquent testimony to faith that is the "conviction of things not seen."

Children's Message

This would be a good opportunity to talk with the children about the wonders of God's creation. A few nature objects (some seashells, a few flowers, several leaves) might be used as you discuss the marvelous variety in the world God has made. The point to make is that when we see all the wonderful things God has made, we are reminded of how great God is and how little we are, and we are grateful that this great God loves us and takes care of us.

Hymns for Pentecost 12

How Great Thou Art; Have Thine Own Way, Lord; For All the Saints. *Contemporary alternative:* Earth and All Stars.

Pentecost 13

Ordinary Time 20
Proper 15

Psalm 10:12–18 (C)

Jeremiah 20:7–13 (C)
Jeremiah 23:23–29 (L) (E)
Jeremiah 38:4–6, 8–10 (RC)

Hebrews 12:1–2, 12–17 (C)
Hebrews 12:1–13 (L)
Hebrews 12:1–4 (RC)
Hebrews 12:1–7, 11–14 (E)

Luke 12:49–56 (C) (E)
Luke 12:49–53 (L) (RC)

Meditation on the Texts

O God, your word is a fire burning in our hearts. You have called us to preach it faithfully, even when it brings conflict and division. Forgive us for the cowardice that makes us want to tone down the rigorous demands of the gospel so that it will not be ''offensive'' to anyone. Let us, like Jesus, endure the cross and despise the shame as we run with courage and patience the race you have set before us. Amen.

Commentary on the Texts

Luke 12:49–56 (C) (E)

Luke 12:49–53 (L) (RC)

This is a collection of loosely organized sayings that deal with Jesus' sense of his own mission. Verses 49–50 are found only in Luke. The passage begins with the strange statement by Jesus that he has come to ''cast fire upon the earth'' (v. 49). The meaning of ''fire'' in this passage is a cause for debate. Fire is usually a symbol of judgment, or the presence of God, but here it may indicate the purifying of those who will be a part of the kingdom. This purifying idea of fire is found in Zechariah 13:9 and Malachi 3:2–3. God's plan of salvation involves judgment, and Jesus seems to be saying that he has come, not to inflict judgment but to bear that judgment for others. The expression ''would that it were already kindled'' is a difficult one. It seems to indicate Jesus' anxiety about the coming events. He is anxious for the final consummation of his work, but he understands that it will bring suffering for him and his followers.

This thought is continued in v. 50 where ''baptism'' is used as a metaphor for the cross, as in Mark 10:38. Jesus is thinking of the inevitable suffering that awaits him. He then goes on to make a statement that seems a direct contradiction to his words in John 14:27, ''Peace I leave with you.'' We must recognize that although there is a sense in which Jesus did bring peace, the reality expressed here is that the message of the cross is divisive, because it forces hard choices and demands a total change of loyalties. Even families will be divided. Luke has already given us a hint of this in the birth narrative with the words of Simeon, that Jesus was a child ''set for the fall and rising of many in Israel'' (2:34). The peace that Jesus brings is not superficial harmony.

In vs. 54–56, Jesus is rebuking the crowds for their density, saying that although they have been able to develop skills in predicting the weather, they are blind to the signs of the coming kingdom, which have been present in his teaching and works. This passage is similar to Matthew 16:2–3, but there Jesus is answering the Pharisees and Sadducees instead of addressing the crowds. The word translated ''interpret'' literally means ''determine the character of.'' They did not even pay enough attention to determine the character of events around them. The words have a tone of judgment. It is not enough to have prolific information about what is happening in the world, if one is blind to the spiritual truths that are being unfolded.

For further study, look up fire and baptism.

The sermon might begin with an emphasis on the serious demands of the Gospel. The reality of Christ's life, death, and resurrection is that it forces us to make choices which may even result in suffering. Christ did not come to bring superficial harmony. We are called to be alert to the signs of the inbreaking of the kingdom in our world, wherever love and justice and compassion rule. These are the true "signs of the times."

Jeremiah 20:7–13 (C)

In the previous chapters, Jeremiah has spoken an unflinching word of judgment, which has brought great hostility upon him. It is also very painful for him to speak out so harshly against the city he loved. We see the result in today's passage: he has plunged into despair and depression reminiscent of Elijah hiding in the cave. Verses 7–18 are a poem in which he eloquently puts his case before God. It is not total despair; it is broken in the middle by a doxology of praise and optimism, after which his mood becomes grim again. These verses remind us of a lament psalm, but are typical of Jeremiah's pathos.

In v. 7 the word "deceived" also means "harassed," "abused," "taken advantage of," "seduced," or even "raped." It is the same word used of a virgin being seduced in Exodus 22:16. The word "prevailed" is also used in accounts of seduction. The *Jerusalem Bible* translation makes use of this sexual imagery: "You have seduced me, Yahweh, and I have let myself be seduced; you have overpowered me: you were the stronger." With this strong language, Jeremiah is saying that he feels helpless before the power of God and yet betrayed because God had not stood beside him. Jeremiah has already recounted how the Lord sent him to both destroy and build up. In v. 8 he is complaining that all he has been allowed to do is destroy, not build.

In v. 9 Jeremiah is in a no-win situation. If he speaks out boldly, he makes enemies; if he keeps quiet, the word burns like fire in his heart. His passionate words "I am weary with holding it in" are echoed in Jesus' words in the Luke passage for today when he also speaks of fire and exclaims, "Would that it were already kindled!"

In v. 3, Jeremiah had called his enemy "Terror on every side" and now in v. 10 that phrase is being turned against him in derision. He turns to God with an affirmation of faith (v. 11), even though he has accused God of not standing by him in previous verses. This affirmation leads to a prayer for vengeance against his enemies.

The first part of the poem culminates in a doxology of praise in v. 13, which is characteristic of the lament psalms. After all is said and done, Jeremiah has turned in faith once again to the God who has called him. Although this verse is problematic and may not belong in the original poem, there are strong arguments for its being a fitting climax to what has gone before. Jeremiah is driven back to God as the source of meaning for his life, not as a God who betrays, but as one who is utterly reliable.

The sermon may follow the movement in the passage beginning with Jeremiah's sense of betrayal and discouragement. His faithfulness in speaking the word of God boldly has caused him to become a laughingstock and an object of derision. He feels that God has seduced him into speaking an unpopular message and then abandoned him to the mockery and rejection of the people. In his hurt and anger at this betrayal, he decides that he will not speak for God anymore, but then he finds that there is a fire burning in his heart that he cannot hold in. He turns again in faith to God and reaffirms his commitment. This reaffirmation of faith causes him to sing praise to the God who is not a betrayer, but who stands by to deliver the needy from evil. This sermon should provide encouragement to continue speaking for God and living in obedience to God, even when persecution and suffering are the result. Even though we become disheartened and discouraged, the word of God burning like fire in our hearts calls us again and again to renewed commitment.

Jeremiah 23:23–29 (L) (E)

In the first part of chapter 23, Jeremiah has been denouncing the false prophets, those religious leaders who have betrayed their calling by taking part in the corruption and evildoings of the people, who have appealed to the popular imagination by raising false hopes of peace, and by communicating "the will of God" by dreams. Those dreams are false because they make the people forget the true nature of God. The poetic words in vs. 23–24 are a reminder to these prophets that God is not captive to the temple cult. God is not "near" in the sense of being available only in the temple, but is free to fill heaven and earth. The prophets wanted to tame God by refusing to speak the word of God faithfully and truthfully—that word which Jeremiah understood to be both "fire" and "hammer" (v. 29).

This passage also reminds us of the Gospel lesson for today, in which Jesus points out that the fiery word of God brings judgment, not a false sense of peace and security. Jeremiah's words in v. 29, "Is not my word like fire, says the LORD, and like a hammer which breaks the rock in pieces?" may have been in Jesus' mind when he spoke of the fire which he had come to bring to earth.

The thrust of **the sermon** might be the danger of wanting false peace or cheap grace and ignoring the deadly serious demands of the gospel. It is important to remember that the word of God, while infinitely comforting in one sense, has disturbing dimensions as well. When it is truly preached, it may bring fear as well as peace. It has the capacity to set the world on fire, and to break evil systems and loyalties like a hammer.

Jeremiah 38:4–6, 8–10 (RC)

This passage provides an example of what happens when the word of God is truly preached. King Zedekiah had modified Jeremiah's imprisonment from dungeon to house arrest in the court of the guard (37:21). While Jeremiah was there he continued to shout out to anyone who would listen his opinion that the best course for Zedekiah would be to surrender to the Babylonians under King Nebuchadnezzar. He saw this as the best way to save as many lives as possible, but it was a dangerous and controversial stance to take. Some of the Judean nobles saw this as a threat to the alliance with Egypt which they favored, so they persuaded the king to let them put Jeremiah to death (v. 4). To accomplish this, they lowered him into a deep cistern where he sank into the muck at the bottom (v. 6). He would have died there of starvation or suffocation had it not been for an Ethiopian court official named Ebed-melech. Although described as a eunuch, this does not necessarily mean a physical eunuch; the term could have simply meant "palace official." Ebed-melech interceded with the king to save Jeremiah's life and then rescued him.

The accusation against Jeremiah that he was "weakening the hands of the soldiers who are left in this city, and the hands of all the people" meant that he was weakening morale. He was being portrayed as a traitor, when his real aim was to preach faithfully the will of God. In a word, he was being divisive. This is another sharp reminder that the word of God can cause controversy when it is faithfully preached, especially when that word seems directed at what are perceived to be national interests.

The sermon might recount the story of Jeremiah's faithfulness under fire. Even from the dungeon he continued to preach the word he had been given from God. The challenge of this text to us is to be faithful to God's word, even when what we have to say is unpopular.

Hebrews 12:1–2, 12–17 (C)

Hebrews 12:1–13 (L)

Hebrews 12:1–4 (RC)

Hebrews 12:1–7, 11–14 (E)

Note that the first two verses are a continuation of the preceding chapter, but the emphasis is now, not on the past with its heroes of faith, but on the present and the necessity to keep a focus on Jesus. The metaphor is that of a footrace. The past heroes of faith are now "witnesses" or spectators (v. 1) who are there to encourage and cheer on those now running the race of faith. It is fairly obvious that the "weight" refers to anything that becomes a hindrance. The word translated "clings" is found only this once in the New Testament and is difficult to translate, but because of the context it obviously refers to anything that prevents the athlete from maximum achievement, whether it is a distraction, a danger, or simply something that is overwhelming or engulfing, like a long robe that could be the cause of stumbling. In the writer's mind this hindrance or impediment is sin. The phrase "let us run with perseverance" implies endurance and courage, staying with the race until the finish. The word for "race" itself is *agōna,* whose English derivative "agony" suggests that this will not be an easy sprint, but a grueling test of strength.

The course has been set, not by ourselves, but by God. The goal is clear: it is Jesus himself, and it is only by keeping firmly focused on the goal that we will be able to stay the course. This is the sentiment expressed in the words of the well-known song of the civil rights movement, "Keep your eyes on the prize." The word translated "pioneer" can also be translated "founder" or as the NEB puts it, the one "on whom faith depends from start to finish." The word translated "perfecter" has the same root as *telos* or goal. Although it is found only here in the New Testament, the word itself is a very rich one. It means the one who brings about completeness or wholeness, the one who enables faith to be what it should be, to reach its goal. The RSV adds a personal pronoun, "our," which is not in the Greek. Jesus is the founder and perfecter of "the faith," the whole of Christian experience. Joy and suffering are linked in this verse. Jesus' joy was the work of redemption in spite of the suffering which he knew lay before him. However, the cross is not an end in itself. This verse ends with a description of Jesus' being seated victoriously at the right hand of God.

There is an allusion in vs. 3–4 to the passion story, and the hostility Jesus experienced, as an encouragement to those followers who might be growing "weary or fainthearted."

Verses 5–6 quote Proverbs 3:11–12, a text about parental discipline. This is followed by a homily on discipline in vs. 7–11. It was accepted in biblical times for a father's word to be seen as law within the family. Discipline and punishment were a normal part of bringing up children. The quote shows two ways children might respond to strict discipline: by rebelling or by being crushed. Neither is good; the right course is to accept discipline in its truest sense, with the understanding that it is for your own good. The word "discipline" is the Greek *paideia* which means "upbringing, training, or instruction," and when it is seen in this way, it can be very beneficial. God's discipline of us grows out of God's love for us as true children.

In v. 12, the author goes back to the image of the race. "Drooping hands" and "weak knees" are the signs of exhaustion. This is a quote from Isaiah 35:3 which is a passage designed to instill hope in the exiles by reminding them of the goal ahead: the restoration of Zion. Isaiah exhorts them, "Strengthen the weak hands, and make firm the feeble knees" and goes on to add, "Say to those who are of a fearful heart, 'Be strong, fear not! Behold, your God will come with vengeance, with the recompense of God. He will come and save you.'" The writer of Hebrews is reminding the discouraged saints that the promises of God are the source of our hope and energy. Although most translations see this as encouragement to the runners who are flagging, the Greek does not use the word "your," so it could also be a message to the runners to speak words of hope to others who are "drooping."

"Make straight paths" is another Old Testament quote. It is part of a passage in Proverbs which speaks about being focused: "Let your eyes look directly forward, and your gaze be straight before you. Take heed to the path of your feet, then all your ways will be sure" (Prov. 4:25–26). The phrase suggests moving all obstacles out of the way and keeping directly toward the goal. This is especially important for runners who are already limping, and do not need extra obstacles which might dislocate an already weakened joint. The image is a reminder that not everyone running the Christian race is in top-notch shape. There are many who are struggling with severe weaknesses. Inherent in this passage is the implication that part of the Christian runner's responsibility is to exercise care and loving concern for those who might be struggling with extraordinary difficulties. We do not run the race alone, but in company with the community of faith.

In vs. 14–17 the author leaves behind the athletic metaphor and begins a series of admonitions, although some have suggested that these are examples of the "straight paths."

First, there is striving for peace, a phrase that suggests energetic effort (v. 14). Second, there is striving for holiness so that we might be ready to see God. This does not mean to see physically, but rather has the Old Testament understanding of worshiping acceptably.

In v. 15, the phrase "see to it" introduces a series of commands laid on the community. They are urged not to fail to appropriate the benefits which grace has supplied. The "root of bitterness" is an expression from Deuteronomy 29:18 which refers to the way the root of a plant affects its fruits. The writer is warning of the kind of bitterness that corrupts and spoils. The next warning is against immorality, citing the example of Esau. It is a reminder of the tragedy of those who fail to appropriate the benefits of grace.

Look up the way in which races and games were conducted in the world of the New Testament.

The sermon might center on the image of the footrace as a metaphor for life. Attention could be given to the fact that the word for "race" implies stress, struggle, and agony. Following the movement of the text, the sermon could describe the heroes and heroines of the faith who make up the "cloud of witnesses" whose memory encourages us as we run our race. The sermon might then move to a consideration of the preparations necessary for running a good race: stripping away the encumbrances that hold us back and getting ready to give it everything we have. The most important point, however, is to keep focused on the prize: becoming like Christ. All of this takes discipline and steadfastness remembering that God will provide the strength we need.

Theological Reflection

A theme common to all of the texts is the necessity for endurance if we are to be faithful. We may have to endure suffering if we are to speak the truth and not settle for false assurances of peace. We may even feel abandoned or betrayed by God when everyone turns against us, but we must remember that God is unfailingly faithful. Even though the life of faith can at times be an "agony," we must continue to run faithfully keeping our eyes on Jesus, the One who gives us the strength to run the race.

Children's Message

You might begin the talk by asking the children if they have ever seen or been in a footrace. Then ask them what a person has to do to win a race. Tell them that the Bible says life is like a race, and read from the TEV Hebrews 12:1b–2a. Explain that this passage means that if we are to live as God wants us to live, we must learn to be like Jesus. The goal of our race is to be like him.

Hymns for Pentecost 13

Be Thou My Vision; Take My Life and Let It Be; Awake, My Soul, Stretch Every Nerve. *Contemporary alternative:* Guide My Feet.

Ordinary Time 21
Proper 16

Psalm 84 (C)	**Hebrews 12:18–29 (C)**
	Hebrews 12:18–24 (L)
Jeremiah 28:1–9 (C)	**Hebrews 12:5–7, 11–13 (RC)**
Isaiah 66:18–23 (L)	**Hebrews 12:18–19, 22–29 (E)**
Isaiah 66:18–21 (RC)	
Isaiah 28:14–22 (E)	**Luke 13:22–30**

Meditation on the Texts

O God of all the universe, we celebrate the surprising nature of your love that knows no limitations and includes those we would rather forget. Forgive us for our prejudices and arrogance.

We celebrate the surprising nature of your truth which will never yield to expediency for the sake of false peace. Forgive us for our cowardice that sends us scurrying for shelter when people reject our preaching.

We celebrate the surprising nature of your providence that provides security for us on firm foundations. Forgive us for being willing to covenant with death out of fear and lack of faith.

We celebrate the surprising nature of your awe-ful self, the great God who welcomes angels and members of the New Jerusalem in heavenly joy. Forgive us for being so caught up in our "dailyness" that we fail to offer you acceptable worship, with reverence and awe. In the name of Jesus Christ. Amen.

Commentary on the Texts

Luke 13:22–30

This passage marks the beginning of the second part of Jesus' journey to Jerusalem. The problem addressed in this pericope is the question put to Jesus by an anonymous person: How many will be saved? This was a question much debated by the Jewish scholars of the time, especially in the Sanhedrin. Although there were many different viewpoints, the generally held belief was that all Jews would be saved, but virtually no one else. These verses are also found in Matthew but are scattered in various places.

Jesus' answer (v. 24) does not offer wholesale reassurance, but instead a word of caution that there may be some surprises in store in the last days. There is a note of urgency in the word "strive" which is the Greek word *agōnizomai* from which we get our words "agony" and "agonize." It means a strenuous exercise of muscle and willpower. (NOTE: This verb has the same root as the word for "race" in Hebrews 12:1 and was used as the technical term for competing in the Olympic Games.) The tense denotes continued present action. Jesus is urging the necessity of ongoing wholehearted commitment to the faith, especially in terms of true repentance and ethical conduct. This is not works salvation, but rather a reminder of the necessity for a passionate, not a halfhearted commitment. We are not sure what the "narrow door" means, except it is obviously the door to salvation. A similar expression is found in Matthew 7:13–14 where he speaks of the narrow gate that leads to life. However, in Matthew the antithesis is a broad door, whereas in Luke it is a closed door, which is much more emphatic, and underlines the urgency of making choices while there is still time.

This leads into a parable about the end of the age, where the householder (the Lord) has closed the door and says to those who come too late (like the ten virgins in Matthew 25), "I do not know where you come from." Note how these words are used of Jesus by the Jews in John 9:29. Jesus is probably using the Old Testament idea of the chosen people as those "known by God" (see Jer. 1:5). These protesters seem to be the Jews who heard Jesus' teaching but failed to accept him as the Messiah. They can only claim that they were in his presence, but they give no indication that they understood what he taught in the streets (v. 26).

Total rejection is expressed in vs. 27–28. Those who have closed their eyes and ears to Jesus' message are called "workers of iniquity" and told by the master of the house to depart. The culmination of their rejection will be when they find themselves shut out from the presence of the patriarchs and the prophets in the coming kingdom. The verb "thrust out" is a strong one, possibly indicating the active opposition of God.

This pericope closes with a surprising answer to the question raised in v. 23. The four directions represent the four corners of the earth, which means that Gentiles as well as Jews will be included in salvation. "Sit at table" refers to the joyous messianic banquet, a symbol of the end times frequently used in the Old Testament. Eating together implied becoming kin, being bonded together as one family. The implications of including Gentiles in this promise of salvation would have been a real shock to the Jews, especially when they heard that they themselves were excluded. The joy of the banquet is a strong contrast to the weeping and gnashing of teeth.

Verse 30 is an often-quoted proverb, found also in Mark 10:31 and in Matthew 20:16 where it is used in different contexts. The meaning is clear here, however. All the usual expectations have been turned upside down. The picture of salvation in this pericope contains a warning against pride and smugness, an exhortation to true repentance and wholehearted commitment, and the recognition that only God knows the final answer to the question.

Look up the use of the term "kingdom of God."

The central theme of **the sermon** might be the unpredictability of the Gospel. The text begins with a favorite topic for intellectual debate in Jewish religious circles. Instead of the usual lines of argument, Jesus turns the question upside down with a parable that implies that the questioners themselves, the strongly respectable religious element of Jewish society, may find themselves excluded from the messianic banquet. In their places will be the Gentiles, actually sitting at table instead of watching while others feasted. All reasonable expectations can be turned upside down by God. Any time we give way to religious smugness, we are in for surprises. Our categories may become meaningless, our personal prejudices turned inside out, and our preconceived notions about who is in and who is out totally irrelevant. Our God is a God who does surprising things—just when we think we have everything figured out.

Jeremiah 28:1–9 (C)

The incident contained in this chapter dates back to the fourth year of King Zedekiah's reign. Jeremiah had urged the king not to rebel against Babylon, and had put around his neck a wooden yoke symbolizing that it was God's will that the people bear the yoke of servitude to Babylon a while longer. However, another prophet named Hananiah began proclaiming a different message. He did this in the style of true prophets, invoking the name of the Lord of hosts, the God of Israel. His prediction was that the yoke of Babylon would be broken within two years and that even the temple vessels taken by Nebuchadnezzar in 598 B.C.E. would be returned.

Jeremiah's answer in vs. 5–9 begins by expressing a wish that the prophet's predictions were indeed true. Hananiah had expressed the deepest longings not only of the king and the people but of Jeremiah himself. His prophecy fit with the patriotic sentiments of the people, whereas the gloom and doom of Jeremiah was not what people wanted to hear. How did Jeremiah know he was right in interpreting the word of God? Ronald E. Clements suggests that the word of God can only be grasped "through a process of responsive and critical discernment." It is not fatalism, nor is it an escape from wrestling with issues; instead, it is a call for informed and responsible decision making. (See Ronald E. Clements, *Jeremiah*, Interpretation series, p. 167; Atlanta: John Knox Press, 1989.)

Jeremiah does not denounce Hananiah directly, but tries once more to make a distinction between true and false prophets. He implies that what Hananiah is saying is not in the tradition of the great prophets who did not promise peace but fearlessly proclaimed the judgment of God against countries and even "great kingdoms." In v. 9, Jeremiah states the final test of whether a prophet is true or false: the fulfillment of the prophecy. The one who preaches the true word of the Lord will be vindicated. God's truth will stand the test of time. This is still an important criterion for the church today in interpreting the word of God, but it must be accompanied by discernment and courage.

The climax of the story comes in the verses following our assigned passage, when Hananiah symbolically breaks Jeremiah's yoke. Jeremiah replaces it with one of iron, and Hananiah dies with no one to mourn or bury him. Everyone who read the story knew the final ending: that Jeremiah's word would be confirmed. All the confusion caused by the false prophets and their rebellion against the Babylonians led to the final fall of Jerusalem in 587 B.C.E. and the resulting captivity.

The sermon might begin with the dangers of twisting the word of God to make it more comfortable and palatable to its hearers. Hananiah had figured out just how to do that. The next move might be to explore the characteristics of the true prophet as exemplified by Jeremiah and the prophets who preceded him. First, they were unafraid to speak fearlessly and boldly the messages God had given them in spite of the fact that the people wanted to hear messages of false assurance. Second, they used their powers of critical discernment to distinguish truth from subtle falsehood. The sermon should challenge the hearers to speak the word of God fearlessly without regard for the consequences, to realize that the temptation to subvert the word of God is very real and that it takes responsive and critical discernment to be attuned to what God is trying to say. Finally, the sermon should remind the hearers that the standard by which "truth" is to be measured is found in the person of Jesus Christ.

Isaiah 66:18–23 (L)

Isaiah 66:18–21 (RC)

This final section of Isaiah has an eschatological character. It is a stirring picture of the gathering of the nations in the last days so that they might see God's glory. Verse 18 is a difficult one because it does not include the word "know" in the Hebrew, although some ancient translations add the word. The verse begins with an emphatic phrase best translated "As for me," then continues with "their works and their thoughts." There is a sudden breaking off of the thought here, but the implication seems to be that God's thoughts are not ours, an idea already expressed in 55:8. The second difficulty is in the next clause. The first verb is third person singular, and can read "he is coming" or "it is coming" although some ancient translations have used "I" as do most contemporary translations. This fits better with the rest of the pericope which proclaims God's act in bringing people from all corners of the globe to join in worship on the "holy mountain." Isaiah has already given us pictures of all the nations coming to Zion in 2:2 and 25:6. This is an expression of the truly universal nature of salvation. The nations are to gather to see God's glory, which could mean here the proof of his sovereignty.

In v. 19, the "sign" is the same as that mentioned in 55:13, an "everlasting sign," a reminder of God's presence and activity. It may be that the sign will be the "survivors" who will be witnesses to the nations. These survivors have already been mentioned in 45:20–25 and invited to accept salvation. In this passage, those who have turned to the Lord are now being commissioned as missionaries. This understanding of mission is very similar to the apostolic commissioning in the New Testament.

As these survivors return to Mt. Zion, they will bring with them the Israelites who have been dispersed to the far corners of the earth (v. 20). These Israelites will be brought as offerings to the Lord. Those who bring them are compared to the "clean vessels" in which the Israelites brought their cereal offerings to the house of the Lord. The mention of their modes of transportation (horses, chariots, litters, mules, and dromedaries) is a picturesque way of illustrating both the diversity of the nations and the distances from which they will come.

There are differences of opinion among scholars about the interpretation of v. 21. "Some of them" could refer either to the nations or to the Israelites they are bringing back with them. It is probably a reference to the nations, and a further indication of the radical reversal of the accepted order of things. Not only are the Gentile nations to be given salvation, but they will also be admitted into the priesthood.

The literary form changes from prose to poetry in v. 22. There is also a change to the second person, and it is not clear which group is being addressed: the nations or the returning Israelites. Is the promise one to the Jews that they will retain their national and cultic identity, or is it a broadened understanding of the New Israel which will be a part of the "new heavens and the new earth"? In either case, it is a beautiful picture of the permanence and stability of the people of God, as they join in worship "from new moon to new moon [every month at the time of the new moon], and from sabbath to sabbath [every week on the Sabbath day]."

The central thought of **the sermon** might be the universal love of God. The text moves from the announcement of God's intention to bring all nations together to be witnesses of God's glory. These representatives will then be sent as missionaries to all nations. Finally, there will be a glorious gathering on Mt. Zion, where all people will join in worship and praise to God.

Isaiah 28:14–22 (E)

This passage could be entitled "a covenant with death." The background for the oracle contained in the pericope seems to be the negotiations for an alliance with Egypt against Assyria during the time of Sennacherib. The prophet is warning that this alliance offers a false security which would end in destruction. The "covenant with death" in v. 15 is perhaps an allusion to Osiris or Seth, the Egyptian gods of death who ruled over the underworld. Instead of trusting in God, the people are putting their trust in lifeless idols to escape the "overwhelming scourge" of Assyria.

In v. 16 the "cornerstone" represents the salvation guaranteed to the Davidic dynasty. It is this salvation in which the people should put their trust. It is a secure building built with God's plumb line of justice (v. 17). God will annul the covenant with death. Because the people had failed to put their trust in the cornerstone, the "overwhelming scourge," acting as God's instruments, will bring sheer terror and destruction on the people.

The central thrust of **the sermon** might be the importance of putting our trust in God and resting on the sure foundations which God has laid. God's building is secure and altogether trustworthy, in contrast to pacts based on lies and falsehoods, which in the end are covenants with death and can only lead to destruction. The cornerstone of the house built by God is named in 1 Peter as the Lord Jesus Christ. In him is our true security.

Hebrews 12:18–29 (C)

Hebrews 12:18–24 (L)

Hebrews 12:5–7, 11–13 (RC)

Hebrews 12:18–19, 22–29 (E)

See also Pentecost 13, (C) (L) (E).

In this pericope, the author is contrasting the giving of the law at Mt. Sinai with the gathering of the redeemed on Mt. Zion. The former, with its accompanying theophany of fire, darkness, storm, trumpet sounds, and the thundering voice of God, struck awe and fear into the hearts of the hearers. Even Moses was terrified (v. 21). This description is drawn from Exodus 19–20 and Deuteronomy 4–5. Note that the trumpet sound which became louder as the sense of the presence of God increased (Exodus 19) became an apocalyptic symbol for authoritative command.

The gathering in the city of the living God (vs. 22–23) is described in very different terms: the festal gathering of angels, the judge who is "God of all," the assemblage of "just men made perfect," and above all, the gracious presence of the divine mediator,

Jesus Christ. This passage is written in a poetic style, using no articles except in v. 24, which gives it a liturgical sound. The picture of the New Jerusalem given here foreshadows the fuller picture which will be given in the Book of Revelation.

Verse 22 mentions innumerable angels surrounding God. This is a stark contrast to the unapproachable God on Mt. Sinai, and gives a picture of constant celebration and worship. Along with the angels, there is a gathering of those who are the officially accepted members of the New Jerusalem (v. 23). This idea of being "enrolled" is also found in Luke 10:20 and in Revelation 21:27.

The blood of the mediator is contrasted with the blood of Abel that cried out for revenge. "Sprinkled" (v. 24) is a term that suggests the sacrifices of the Old Testament, which have been replaced by the blood of Christ.

Verse 25 begins in a different tone, with a warning. There is a contrast made between the voice on earth and the warning from heaven. Although it is not stated, we can assume both warnings are from God. The shaking of the earth in v. 26 is another reminder of Mt. Sinai, and is also connected to the earthquake imagery of apocalypticism. Haggai had written of an earthquake which would accompany the final revelation of God (Hag. 2:6). The author goes on to say that now a stability has been established in the form of a kingdom that is unshakable. The response to this gift of stability is gratitude, reverence, and awe (v. 28). Awe is inevitable before a God who is a "consuming fire," a description found also in Deuteronomy 4:24. Even though God is merciful, compassionate, and gracious, God is still the god of Sinai and is to be treated with respect.

The sermon might follow the text by beginning with a contrast between the giving of the law at Mt. Sinai and the gathering of the redeemed on Mt. Zion. Instead of fear and terror there is joy and celebration. Instead of earthquake there is stability in the form of an unshakable kingdom. The next move might be to describe the appropriate response to the God of Sinai and Zion, a response that is based on an awareness of the two aspects of God's nature suggested by these places.

Theological Reflection

A thread that runs through all of today's texts is surprise: how God turns upside down the usual expectations of how things should be. In the Luke passage, Jesus surprises the Jews by announcing that Gentiles will be present at the messianic banquet. Jeremiah surprises the king, the people, and the prophet Hananiah by refusing to go along with the kind of prophetic teaching that tells people what they want to hear rather than speaking the surprising truth God has given. One Isaiah passage gives the surprising news of God's love for all nations, while in the other the prophet, like Jeremiah, surprises the people by refusing to go along with political expediency by endorsing the "covenant of death." Finally, in the Hebrews text, the picture of the New Jerusalem offers a surprising glimpse of the God of Sinai who is no longer the unapproachable God of the mountain, but is a God who is surrounded by a gathering of angels and the members of the New Jerusalem in a festal atmosphere of worship and celebration, rejoicing in a kingdom that cannot be shaken.

Children's Message

The talk might center on God's love for all people, from north, south, east, and west. God wants all people to live together in love and harmony as brothers and sisters. In God's kingdom people from all nations will sit down and eat together. In God's kingdom there will be no war.

Hymns for Pentecost 14

Before Jehovah's Awful Throne; Glorious Things of Thee Are Spoken; God of Grace and God of Glory.

Pentecost 15

Ordinary Time 22
Proper 17

Psalm 15 (C)

Ezekiel 18:1–9, 25–29 (C)
Proverbs 25:6–7 (L)
Sirach 3:19–21, 30–31 (RC)
Sirach 10:12–18 (E)

Hebrews 13:1–8 (C) (L) (E)
Hebrews 12:18–19, 22–24a (RC)

Luke 14:1, 7–14

Meditation on the Texts

O God, you rule in mercy and justice to redeem your creation and desire the death of none, but yearn for repentance in the most wicked and careless of us, your children. We confess that we, like the exiles of old, have not wanted to shoulder responsibility. We have preferred to blame those who have gone before. We have been less concerned with repentance than with rewards. Turn our hearts away from status seeking and vain thoughts of rewards. Teach us the mind of Christ, who was meek and lowly of heart. Let us learn from him who humbled himself even unto death, that we may receive your blessing. May we find happiness in those duties which you have been pleased to teach us—love for others, hospitality to strangers, fidelity in marriage. We pray in Jesus' name. Amen.

Luke 14:1, 7–14

According to commentators, vs. 7–14 contain two separate hortatory counsels of Jesus, which are connected by a wisdom saying: "All who exalt themselves will be humbled, and those who humble themselves will be exalted" (v. 11, NRSV). Because they are based on similar metaphors, the two teachings have been linked together.

The first counsel, vs. 7–10, is that disciples should avoid status seeking. The parable that makes this point is one about guests at a wedding feast, who are well advised not to make a grab for the best seats. The second, vs. 12–14, is a warning against seeking recompense for every good deed. The illustration is again that of feasting: When disciples give a feast, they are to invite those who cannot repay the favor—the poor, the disabled.

On one level both counsels are typical rabbinical wisdom. They are the observations of a shrewd observer of human behavior. Warnings against status seeking and reward seeking would not be out of place in the Book of Proverbs or the Wisdom of Ben Sira.

However, in the literary setting in which Luke places them, both counsels point beyond humane, courteous human behavior to the behavior of God. God will exalt the humble; God will bless those who give with no thought of reward. The text says "those who humble themselves will be exalted" (v. 11, NRSV), and "you will be blessed" (v. 14). This is the theological passive voice. It is God who exalts and God who blesses.

Why should this be so? Why should God lift up the humble and reward those who are unselfishly kind to the poor and disabled? Is this a reflection of God's preference for the lowly, the meek, the outcast, the disadvantaged?

Look again at the literary setting of these counsels. Both are set in the context of a Sabbath dinner party given for Jesus by a well-placed Pharisee. The Pharisee and his other guests are carefully watching Jesus to see if he will violate some Sabbath observance, but Jesus turns the dinner table on them, so to speak. He makes some shrewd observations about *their* behavior. He notes that they have scrambled for the best seats—and that they are well favored and well fed. Is this the way to keep God's Sabbath? he asks in effect. Does not God rather favor humility and unselfishness? Such behavior does not honor God; it reflects failure to know God.

Jesus' quarrels with the Pharisees were usually theological. Status seeking and reward seeking reflect a failure to know God, who lifts up the lowly and rewards those who seek no reward. It belongs to fallen human nature to seek status and rewards; it belongs to the nature of God to be concerned with just the opposite.

Use your concordance to locate a variety of New Testament passages that show Jesus in confrontations with the Pharisees. Note how they want to dispute about observances; Jesus prefers to focus on the proper knowledge of God.

The movement of a sermon on Luke 14:7–14 might follow Jesus' line of thought. He begins by observing the actions of his fellow human beings. He compares and contrasts these with the actions of God. He then counsels a life-style that is consonant with God's actions.

The sermon might begin with reflections on the behavior of the Pharisee host and of his guests. How typical they are of other human beings! The movement is then to contrast their behavior with that of God. God is merciful, which means that God cares for those who need a helper, who stand a little outside the normal range of benefits and entitlements.

Then attention might be focused once more on our behavior. We are to avoid status seeking and reward seeking, not because it is wrong in and of itself, but because it is not an appropriate response to the way God acts.

Ezekiel 18:1–9, 25–29 (C)

This passage from Ezekiel is usually interpreted as setting forth a doctrine of individual responsibility. Ezekiel was, you will remember, a prophet to the exiles in Babylon. The exiles may have felt that they were suffering for the sins of their forebears, and such self-pity may have been eating away any sense of personal responsibility. Therefore it was necessary for the prophet to strike the note of individual responsibility for one's life and actions.

Indeed, that is one of the themes of the passage. The prophet repudiates the wisdom contained in a proverb, "The fathers have eaten sour grapes, and the children's teeth are set on edge." Rather, he says, each shall bear the consequences of his own behavior. If he obeys the statutes of Yahweh and seeks a righteous path, he shall live; but if he sins, he shall die. If the righteous turn away and commit wickedness, they shall die; their record of former probity will not save them. But if a wicked man turns from his wickedness and lives a godly life, he shall live.

However, that brief résumé of the passage clearly reveals two other themes, which in biblical thought are inseparably joined to the theme of individual responsibility: One is righteousness, the other is repentance. Not only are we human beings responsible for our choices, but we are to choose the way that is pleasing to God—we are to follow the path of righteousness. And even when we fail in our quest for righteousness—or deliberately flaunt God's way—we may be restored to God's favor if we turn to God in contrition.

This threefold teaching of responsibility, righteousness, and repentance is typical of the prophets of Israel. It bears testimony to Israel's understanding of Yahweh as one who is both just and merciful, whose justice is never compromised by mercy, and whose mercy is never substituted for justice.

As Ezekiel observes, some find this teaching hard to accept: "Yet you say, 'The way of the Lord is not just' " (v. 25a). How can God be just if God does not credit the former good deeds of one who turns to wickedness, if God does not count as debits the wicked needs of one who turns to righteousness? But the prophet will not have any of that kind of argument. It is Israel that is not just, he says; it is Israel that needs to take responsibility for her wickedness and turn to God in repentance.

Do some biblical study of the concept of righteousness. One theologian has pointed out that God's righteousness—as revealed in the law—has a threefold intent or purpose: justice, mercy, and the knowledge of God. This comes to expression in Micah 6:8 "[God] has showed you . . . what is good . . . to do justice, and to love kindness, and to walk humbly with your God."

The sermon might be built on the contrasting metaphors of the clean record and the clean heart. The metaphor of the clean record suggests a copybook that has never been blotted, a life absolutely free of any stain of evil or disobedience. But a clean heart suggests a turnabout, a change in direction, a new beginning. How hopeless to think that we can come to God with a clean record! What an impossible standard to set before ourselves or others! The list of virtues in vs. 6–9 makes that clear enough. Even a wicked man, who has broken all the commandments, can turn to God in repentance and have a clean heart.

Proverbs 25:6–7 (L)

This proverb was undoubtedly chosen for the lectionary because of its correspondence to Jesus' parable in Luke 14:8–11. Perhaps Jesus had this proverb in mind when he told his fellow guests not to grab the best seats.

If one chooses to **preach** on this text rather than on Luke 14:1, 7–14, one could nevertheless draw the Lukan passage into the sermon. One might begin with the commonsense wisdom of not rashly putting oneself forward in social situations. There are all sorts of circumstances in life in which that is excellent advice. Then, as the climax of the sermon, one might show how Jesus turned that wisdom about human behavior into a commentary on God's behavior.

Sirach 3:19–21, 30–31 (RC)

Verses 19–21 are taken from a poem (vs. 17–24) in which the author praises the virtues of humility. The Hebrew word that is rendered as "humility" may also be rendered as "modesty" or "meekness." One commentator describes it as a combination of attitudes that includes patience, docility, awareness of one's limitations, and utter dependence on God. The reward of such a spiritual condition is favor with God.

Jesus makes a similar claim for meekness in his Sermon on the Mount, "Blessed are the meek, for they shall inherit the earth" (Matt. 5:5). Micah summed up God's requirements as doing justice, loving kindness, and walking humbly with God (Micah 6:8). The opposite of humility is the pride that is condemned in Sirach 10:12–18 (see below).

Those who choose to **preach** on this passage will do well to follow the lead of that commentator who described humility as a cluster of attitudes. This is closer to the biblical notion than is that popular notion of humility that stresses self-abnegation.

Sirach 10:12–18 (E)

One commentator describes these verses as an essay on the roots and fruits of pride. The roots are in a deliberate turning away from one's Maker, an act of both intelligence and will by which one refuses to fear God. The one who does this then becomes shameless; and that is the beginning of pride. Pride, says the author of Sirach, leads to the most terrible punishment imaginable to the Israelite: God will blot out "their memory from the earth" (v. 21, JB).

One who chooses to **preach** on this passage will do well to set pride in contrast to the humility described in Sirach 3:19–21 (see above). The metaphors of roots and fruits will prove irresistible to some preacher!

Hebrews 13:1–8 (C) (L) (E)

Hebrews 12:18–19, 22–24a (RC)

See Pentecost 14, (E).

Hebrews 13 is a compilation of general exhortations appended to the elaborate theological exposition of the first twelve chapters. Commentators seem to agree that vs. 1–6 are a literary unit, describing what might be called social duties. The subsequent unit, vs. 7–16, is what one commentator calls a list of religious duties and what another calls a mixture of doctrine and ethics. In linking vs. 1–6 with the two verses that follow, those who developed the lectionary evidently wanted to provide some spiritual foundation for the list of social duties.

That list is an interesting reflection of what we know of the social context of early Christianity. The urge to "let brotherly love continue" suggests a sect that practiced the sharing of material goods among its members. The "strangers" to which one is to show hospitality were likely Christians from other communities, who depended in their travels for board and room provided by the local fellowship. (The author of Hebrews reminds his readers that Abraham and Sarah unwittingly provided hospitality to angels when they opened their home to unknown visitors. See Genesis 18.) And "those who are in prison" could well have been Christians imprisoned by the Roman authorities as social deviants. There is plenty of evidence in the letters of Paul that missionaries of the church were "ill-treated." The readers of Hebrews are reminded that all are of one body, so that if one suffers, all suffer.

The exhortation to fidelity in marriage should come as no surprise to Christians with strong ties of Judaism. And it may have been especially necessary to exhort Gentiles to shun adultery. Recall the anarchy in sexual ethics that Paul addressed in his First Letter to the Corinthians.

Some commentators attribute the exhortation to "keep your life free from love of money" as an indication that the readers of Hebrews were well-to-do. From what we read in other New Testament epistles, we know that the early Christians were drawn mostly from the poorer classes. No matter. Both rich and poor need to avoid the love of money, which Paul called "the root of all evils" (1 Tim. 6:10). To reinforce that teaching, the author of Hebrews cites two Old Testament assurances of the providence of God, Deuteronomy 31:6 and Psalm 118:6.

Although vs. 7–8 are not properly part of the list of social duties, they provide spiritual underpinnings for that list: Remember and imitate those who are your leaders. Jesus Christ remains faithful to himself; let that fixed star be your guide.

Those who choose to **preach** on this passage have several options: One might emphasize the social dimensions of Christian discipleship as an antidote to the individualism of so much of Americana Christianity (Read Robert Bellah's *Habits of the Heart* for illustrative material); or one might choose to develop a "table" of commandments for the twentieth century comparable to the list given by the author of Hebrews for his century.

Theological Reflection

Each text for this Sunday teaches the following lesson: A godly life-style is one grounded in the knowledge of God's way. Jesus' parable teaches that. So does the prophecy of Ezekiel. The beginning of right living, as well as of wisdom, is the fear of God. Human ethical speculation, divorced from devout theological reflection, will always bring one to the conclusion drawn by Ezekiel's audience, "God is not just." But those who learn the way of God will never say that!

Reflect on this statement from Vaclav Havel, made in his speech to the U.S. Congress in February 1990: "The salvation of this human world lies nowhere else than in the human heart, in the human power to reflect, in human meekness, and in human responsibility. . . . We are still incapable of understanding that the only genuine backbone of all our actions—if they are to be moral—is responsibility. Responsibility to something higher than my family, my country, my firm, my success."

Children's Message

Children like stories with a twist, with a surprise, so tell them the story of Jesus' Sabbath dinner at the home of the Pharisee. Set the stage by describing in some detail how all the guests were watching Jesus, hoping to catch him in some mistake, some violation of the Sabbath rules. Then tell that all the while Jesus had been watching them. Tell what he saw and how his observations led him to reflect on how God behaves. Don't moralize about humility. Children will not understand what you are talking about. Just report what Jesus said about God's response to those who go for the cheap seats.

Hymns for Pentecost 15

He Is King of Kings; Jesus Calls Us, O'er the Tumult; Immortal Love, Forever Full.

Pentecost 16

Ordinary Time 23
Proper 18

Psalm 94:12–22 (C)

Ezekiel 33:1–11 (C)
Proverbs 9:8–12 (L)
Wisdom 9:13–19 (RC)
Deuteronomy 30:15–20 (E)

Philemon 1–20 (C) (E)
Philemon 1, 10–21 (L)
Philemon 9b–10, 12–17 (RC)

Luke 14:25–33

Meditation on the Texts

If you, O God, were not our help, our souls would soon dwell in the land of silence, even as Israel languished in captivity. If you did not give us Wisdom, we would dwell in the land of ignorance. Blessed are you, O God, whose Spirit has invaded our darkness, showing us to choose good and life and turning from death and evil. Continue, we pray, to be our Mentor and Guide, as you were for the prophets and apostles before us. Keep us from selling out for cheap grace, easy answers, and no-fault discipleship. Help us to count the cost, even when that may mean financial loss. We pray in the name of Jesus Christ, who did not shrink from hard choices. Amen.

Commentary on the Texts

Luke 14:25–33

The theme of this passage is weighing the cost of discipleship. The text may remind us of Matthew 16:24–28, where Jesus tells the disciples, "If any want to become my followers, let them deny themselves and take up their cross and follow me" (v. 24, NRSV) (A similar passage is Mark 8:34–38). But the setting of the Matthean and Markan sayings is different—and so is the emphasis. Those teachings are set in the context of Peter's confession, and the emphasis is on the high cost of discipleship. Luke 14:25–33 is set in the context of Jesus' confrontation of the crowd that follows him on his journey to Jerusalem. While the high cost of discipleship is dramatically assayed, the emphasis is on weighing that cost.

The scene is a dramatic one. A large crowd is trailing after Jesus as he heads for Jerusalem and his showdown with the religious authorities. Presumably many in the crowd have either seen the signs and miracles that Jesus has done or are being swept along in a popular demonstration of support. Luke says that Jesus "turned and said to them . . . ," but the force of his teachings almost suggests that he turned *on* them, as though he would confront them, bring them up short, drive them back.

Jesus lays out for them in unmistakable language three radical demands of discipleship: (1) Disciples must be willing to break family ties. (2) Disciples must be willing to risk their lives. (3) Disciples must be willing to give up material possessions. One translator renders v. 33 to connote that a disciple must be ready to say goodbye to all that he owns.

While the three conditions are radical, they should not come to the reader as great surprises. The call to rupture family ties points back to the incident in Jesus' boyhood when he stayed behind at the temple at Jerusalem. When his mother scolded him, he responded, "Did you not know that I must be in my Father's house?" (Luke 2:49b). The call to take up the cross points forward to Jesus' crucifixion. The warning about material possessions anticipates the story of Ananias and Sapphira in Acts 5:1–11, who could not cope with the church's practice of holding goods in common.

Nevertheless, these teachings of Jesus are radical in the extreme. Compare and contrast "Whoever comes to me and does not hate father and mother" (v. 26a, NRSV) with "Honor your father and your mother, that your days may be long in the land which the LORD your God gives you" (Ex. 20:12). Contrast the injunction against killing in the Sixth Commandment with the evident disregard for one's own life in the call to bear one's cross—and the disregard for material possessions in v. 25 with the careful guarding of property rights in the Eighth and Tenth Commandments! This is the radical Jesus of Matthew's Sermon on the Mount, who takes up the ancient teaching and gives it fresh, deeper meanings.

However, the main thrust of the passage is not in the direction of the high cost of obedience; rather, it is directed to *weighing* the cost before vowing obedience. To that end Jesus offers twin, succinct parables—one about a person building a tower, the other about a king going out to repel an invasion. Each parable makes the same point: Before any large undertaking, one is advised to take counsel with himself or herself to see if what is undertaken can be carried through; otherwise, the consequences will be most unwelcome. The person building a tower needs to look to the sufficiency of resources; the king looking to deal with invaders needs to look to the size of his army.

The point made in the twin parables would seem to be this: Those who are so joyfully and noisily following Jesus on his journey to Jerusalem should carefully consider whether or not they want to be followers of his Way. To come to Jesus as his follower and disciple is a costly affair. Every disciple may not literally follow Jesus in leaving home, suffering crucifixion, and having no place to lay one's head. But those are costs that might well be assessed; and they stand as representative of the demands of discipleship.

Before writing a sermon on counting the cost, **read or reread chapter 1,** "Costly Grace," in Dietrich Bonhoeffer's *The Cost of Discipleship.* He wrote the book some years before his own imprisonment and execution for acts of defiance against Adolf Hitler. Surely he did not know that he himself would suffer martyrdom when he inveighed against "cheap grace" and solemnly proclaimed that when Christ called a man, he bade him come and die. Bonhoeffer's own death, however, makes us listen very, very carefully to what he said.

Bonhoeffer is but one of a number of *Martyrs of Our Time* described in a book of that name written by William Purcell. There were Betty and John Stam of the China Inland Mission, beheaded by looting Communist troops in 1934. The stories of Steve Biko, Martin Luther King, Jr., and Oscar Romero need no retelling. But who knows the names of the "Boy Martyrs" of Uganda, burned alive in 1886? And in that same country, in 1977, the Anglican Archbishop, Janani Luwum, died at the hands of followers of Idi Amin.

Stories of Christian martyrs are so dramatic that one is tempted to focus a sermon from Luke 14:25–33 on Jesus' warning about the cross that awaits the disciple. But that would not be faithful to the structure of the passage, which has as its main point the careful calculation of cost, rather than the cost itself.

The sermon might therefore be developed on this passage as follows. Begin by taking advantage of the dramatic contrast between the probable mood of the crowd and the severe conditions that Jesus lays down for discipleship. The "following" of the multitude would seem to have been something less than serious discipleship. Otherwise why would Jesus turn to them with such severity? Some may have come along out of curiosity; some may have come along because they had seen miracles and hoped to see more; some may simply have been pilgrims and holiday folk, already on their way to Jerusalem for the feast. The preacher can ring the changes on the mixed and sometimes trivial motives of people for wanting to be with Jesus.

Once the human motives for "going along with the Jesus crowd" have been explored, the sermon may then take a sober turn: Even as Jesus turned on the crowd, so the preacher can turn the attention of hearers to the high cost of following Jesus. This cost may be developed in terms of Jesus' own life and ministry, in terms of the experiences of the apostolic church as described in Acts, or in terms of the lives of modern martyrs and witnesses.

Care needs to be taken not to lay on the congregation more than they can bear. The call to "hate father and mother," for example, may be softened to mean not loving father and mother more than Jesus. There is little to be gained by recounting in great detail the bloody deaths of martyrs.

The main thrust of the sermon—the appeal to heart, mind, and will—should be saved for the question: Have you considered the cost? It may well be that no one ever put that question seriously to some of those in the congregation. It is time they had it put to them—not to shame them, or to frighten them, or to scold them, but to open their minds and hearts to hear once more about the high price that God paid for their redemption. There can be no serious talk about the cost of our following Jesus that does not lead to what it cost God to open that possibility for us. Surely that is the significance of this pericope in Luke being set in the context of Jesus' journey to Jerusalem.

The passages in Matthew and Mark that also deal with taking up one's cross are much more clearly linked to Jesus' foresight about his own crucifixion. But the absence of that direct reference in Luke should not keep the preacher from drawing out that connection.

Ezekiel 33:1–11 (C)

The theme of this passage is the role of the prophet as sentry or watchman. A sentry is set to watch for the approach of enemy forces. If he sees them approaching and blows the warning trumpet, those who fail to heed have only themselves to blame; but if he fails to blow the trumpet, he is in some way responsible for their death. By analogy with the sentry, the prophet bears a heavy responsibility. If Yahweh gives the prophet a warning for the people and he fails to pass it on, Yahweh will hold the prophet as bloodguilty; but if the prophet gives the warning and the wicked fail to repent, the prophet is innocent of their punishment.

This is a teaching about individual responsibility that is related to—but different from—the teaching in Ezekiel 18 (see the commentary for Pentecost 15). There the emphasis was on the responsibility of each person to know and obey Yahweh's statutes. Here the emphasis is on the responsibility of the prophet to speak Yahweh's word to the people, no matter how dreadful it may seem.

The story of Jonah suggests itself as an illustration of this responsibility of the prophet. Jonah at first did not want to go to Nineveh and "cry against it," presumably because he did not want to be the bearer of awful tidings. Even when Jonah does go and deliver Yahweh's warning, he is not happy with his role; for the people take responsibility for their sins and repent!

Investigate the role of the watchman in the culture of ancient Israel. Use a Bible dictionary or another reference book on Old Testament times. You may gain some insights into the role of the prophet. Most of us need new metaphors to explain prophecy to the people.

One way to **build a sermon** on this passage is to work with the metaphor of the watchman. It is the sole duty of the watchman to report what he sees or hears. If he keeps silent, the people may presume that nothing is amiss. One of the roles of the church in the world is to serve as a watchman for the culture. The church is not the critic of culture, devising its own canons of what is right and proper. Rather it delivers to the culture the divine word that has been given to it. And like the word that Jonah delivered to Ninevah, the prophetic message has the power to affect dramatic change.

Some who choose to **preach** on Ezekiel 33:1–11 may want to draw upon Luke 14:25–33 as an illustration of Jesus' prophetic ministry. Congregations may be able to bear the weight of Jesus' words about the cost of discipleship if they are heard as a watchman's cry of warning rather than some kind of impossible ethical standard. Or the preacher may wish to cite Jesus' "difficult" teachings in Luke 14:25–33 as evidence that sometimes an unsettling, disturbing word from God simply must be uttered and heard.

Proverbs 9:8–12 (L)

This passage is notable for the inclusion of v. 10: "The fear of the LORD is the beginning of wisdom, and the knowledge of the Holy One is insight." Otherwise it is typical of the wisdom literature, so well represented in Wisdom 9:13–19, which is another of the texts for this Sunday.

In his Anchor Bible commentary, R. B. Y. Scott provides this translation of v. 10: "The beginning of wisdom is to hold the Lord in awe, And knowledge of the Holy one is understanding.''

One way to **preach** on this text is to focus all attention on the phrase ''the beginning of wisdom''—and to draw out the idea that knowledge, understanding, insight are all anchorless without the knowledge of God that is also fear and awe.

Wisdom 9:13–19 (RC)

These verses provide the conclusion—and summary—of four chapters devoted to the praise of heavenly wisdom. In several pungent phrases the author reminds his readers of the limits of human intelligence: ''The reasoning of men is feeble'' (v. 14, NEB); ''With difficulty we guess even at things on earth'' (v. 16, NEB). Then he plaintively asks, ''Who ever learnt to know thy purposes?'' (v. 17, NEB), and supplies the answer, ''Thou hadst given him wisdom and sent thy holy spirit down from heaven on high'' (v. 17, NEB).

The easy and obvious tack to take in **preaching** on this passage is to trash reason and intelligence as adequate guides to human welfare. There is a sufficient anti-intellectualism in the American ethos to tempt the preacher to do just that. Few will fault him or her for doing it. But the more profitable course to take would be one of praise to God for the gracious disclosure of the divine will and purpose in Jesus Christ. As Paul reminds us in 1 Corinthians 1:30 (NEB), ''God has made [Jesus] our wisdom.''

A challenging piece of American intellectual history, which would make wonderful **background reading** for a sermon on this text, is James Turner, *Without God, Without Creed: The Origins of Unbelief in America* (Baltimore: Johns Hopkins University Press, 1985). Turner shows how religious leaders of the nineteenth century tried to adapt the knowledge of God to modern science—and opened the gates to atheism as a viable alternative to belief.

Deuteronomy 30:15–20 (E)

This is one of those passages which could well furnish the text of a sermon for one Sunday every year. It is a pivotal passage. In Deuteronomy it serves as the climactic conclusion to Moses' long speech of farewell. It stands at the end of the Deuteronomic exposition of the law and sets forth the essence of the Deuteronomic theology, which is a dominant in so much of the Old Testament literature.

The text says, in summary, that life and prosperity and possession of the land rest upon obedience to God's will, as set forth in God's law, and loss of life and land follow if the choice is to worship other gods. *There are no other possibilities.* It is either ''life and good'' or ''death and evil'' (v. 15). The responsibility so clearly set down in Ezekiel 18 (see the commentary for Pentecost 15) carries with it the awful consequences of wrong choice!

What is the Christian **preacher** to do with this passage, which seems so tightly bonded to Jewish law, the land of Israel, and the Jews as God's chosen people? The theological issue presented here—and unavoidable for Christian and Jew—is God's action in history. The Deuteronomic view is that God most certainly acts in history: God chose and blessed Abraham; God delivered Israel from Egypt; God gave Israel the good land; God punished Israel for idolatry and wickedness. When preaching on this text, it would be important to give a quick summary of this history.

The bottom line for Christians is that the God and Father of our Lord Jesus Christ is the Holy One of Israel. God's activity in human history, human responsibility for choice, the consequences of idolatrous living—all are still to be reckoned with, and wrestled with.

Philemon 1–20 (C) (E)

Philemon 1, 10–21 (L)

Philemon 9b–10, 12–17 (RC)

The Letter of Paul to Philemon has two special contributions to make to our appreciation of the life of the apostolic church. One is the richness of the metaphors that Paul uses to describe the relationships possible among Christians: "brother," "sister," "fellow worker," "fellow soldier," "father," "child," "partner," "fellow prisoner." The other is the necessity of restoration for the maintenance of healthy relationships.

These two aspects of the letter make it a useful case study in congregational life. We are moved by the richness of Paul's metaphors to ask: Where there is conflict in a congregation, is it possible that relationships have been frozen into one-dimensional patterns? Have we demanded that fellow soldiers act always like brothers? Or have we insisted on a father-child relationship with persons when a brother-sister relationship might prove more fruitful? Also, have we failed to seek proper restoration of ruptured relationships? Have we hidden from formal duties and obligations in a cloud of pious talk about brotherhood, friendship, shared difficulties?

Some congregations would profit from **a sermon** on Philemon that was based on those two aspects of the letter. The hearers could be drawn into the text if it were treated as a case study: Describe the apparent situation, in which the apostle is pleading for the restoration of a runaway slave. Give a brief sketch of the apostle as an imprisoned missionary, Philemon as his beloved co-worker in the Christian movement, and Onesimus as the runaway slave, whom Paul has befriended and who has been so useful to Paul in his imprisonment. Use the variety of metaphors from the letter itself to describe the relationships among these three persons. Then ask the hearers to weigh the merits of several resolutions of the situation. You might suggest renunciation (in which Philemon gave up all claim to Onesimus), repayment (in which Philemon was fully recompensed for what he had lost in services), or restoration (in which Onesimus returned to Philemon, but with improved status). Which is most likely to strengthen the church and its witness?

Theological Reflection

Consider how large a role *choice* plays in scripture. If there is a dominant theme in the passages for this Sunday, it is the responsibility of humans to make choices. Ezekiel says that the watchman must make the right decision or suffer the consequences; Moses bids the Hebrews to choose life and good or death and evil in the Deuteronomy passage; Jesus bids the disciples choose his way even if it means a break with family ties; and Paul pleads with Philemon to decide in favor of Onesimus. All of this is grounded on a belief that God chooses—God acts. We are not captive to blind fate; we live out our lives before the living God. Therefore life inevitably presents us with choices.

Children's Message

Don't miss the opportunity to tell the story of Paul, Onesimus, and Philemon. Children love stories about people who get a second chance. Onesimus is such a person. Tell the story from his point of view, how he ran away, how he was befriended by Paul and was useful to him, and how Paul persuaded him to go back to his master. Tell how Paul tried to clear the way for Onesimus' safe return. (There is no need to dwell on Onesimus' status as a slave or on Paul's status as a prisoner. Sociology can wait until children are older.)

Hymns for Pentecost 16

Once to Every Man and Nation; Who Is on the Lord's Side?; God of Our Fathers.

Ordinary Time 24
Proper 19

Psalm 77:11–20 (C)

1 Timothy 1:12–17

Hosea 4:1–3; 5:15–6:6 (C)
Exodus 32:7–14 (L)
Exodus 32:7–11, 13–14 (RC)
Exodus 32:1, 7–14 (E)

Luke 15:1–10 (C) (L) (E)
Luke 15:1–32 (RC)

Meditation on the Texts

O God, your going forth is as sure as the dawn and you come like morning showers to refresh and revive us. We acknowledge that in our goings and comings we are as inconstant as the dew that quickly vanishes in the heat and pressure of daily existence. If you at times seem withdrawn, it is because we have been drawn away from you! But even as you forgive those who act in ignorance and unbelief, so forgive us, who have known you and have promised true allegiance. Restore us to our former status of peace and joy, and we shall be your faithful agents of rescue and restoration. For we pray in the name and for the sake of Jesus Christ, whose perfect patience has been shown to us. Amen.

Commentary on the Texts

Luke 15:1–10 (C) (L) (E)

Luke 15:1–32 (RC)

The two texts prescribed for this Sunday contain three of the best-loved parables of Jesus: the lost sheep, the lost coin, and the prodigal son. All three proclaim what one commentator calls the favorite theme of Luke, which is the good news of God's love for the penitent sinner. Most preachers will use the third parable—the prodigal son—as illustration when preaching on the first two; most preachers will use the first two as illustrations when preaching on the third! So it makes some sense to consider all three together.

The setting of these parables is a confrontation between Jesus and certain scribes and Pharisees. They murmur against him because he consorts with what one commentator rightly calls "the outcasts of first-century Palestinian society." Luke designates them as "tax collectors and sinners." They are what "lost" points to in the parables of the sheep and the coin—the immoral, antisocial, irreligious, unregenerate members of society.

Each of the preacher's hearers will have his or her own list of such people; and the lists will not be at all the same. In a British television program on AIDS, one Scotsman advocated creating special reservations for sequestering homosexuals and persons with AIDS. Someone else might have on his or her list: rednecks, Ku Klux Klansmen, drug dealers, bigots, mafiosi, and child abusers, while someone else might want to include abortionists, fornicators, adulterers, thieves, layabouts, and drunkards. Who does not have a list of undesirables—those without whom society might be much better off?

Persons who were regarded by the scribes and Pharisees in that way were flocking to Jesus as he made his way to Jerusalem; and Jesus' social acceptance of them made the scribes and Pharisees question Jesus' sanctity. A people who worship a holy God cannot help being concerned with holy living. It seemed to these pious folks that Jesus was a strange sort of holy man if he did not perceive with what sort of human garbage he was in company.

In that context Jesus tells his confronters three parables: the story of the shepherd, who leaves ninety-nine sheep to go searching for one who has strayed; the story of the poor woman, who loses one of her ten coins and turns the house upside down looking for it; and the story of the father who "loses" his younger son to rebellion and profligacy but waits and yearns for his return.

In interpreting Jesus' parables, we should follow three rules: (1) Avoid allegory. (2) Look for the stress at the end. (3) Assume a single point or message. If we apply those rules to these three parables, the truth of each is the same: God greatly rejoices in the repentance and return of "lost" persons. In the climactic phrases at the end of each of the three parables we hear echoes of Ezekiel 33:11 (NRSV): "I have no pleasure in the death of the wicked, but that the wicked turn from their ways and live."

There are some dramatic **sermon possibilities** in Luke 15:1–32. One can invite each of the hearers to compile his or her own list of "lost" or socially disposable persons. A couple of case studies ought to get the imaginations to work. Suggest the list that might be compiled by a Presbyterian banker living in a small town in Missouri, a Roman Catholic nun working in an inner-city school in Chicago, a black Baptist deacon employed as a prison guard in Atlanta.

Compare and contrast the imagery in the parables of the lost sheep and the lost coin. The shepherd who loses one of his sheep is moderately wealthy, to judge by the size of his flock; but the woman is relatively poor. Ten drachmas—possibly her dower money— did not amount to much. The sheep owner seems almost careless in leaving his flock untended to go after the stray; while the woman, in a frenzy of ownership, turns her house upside down to find one little coin!

We are warned not to convert the parables into allegories, insisting that each detail points beyond itself to some essential truth. Nevertheless, it is worth noting in one's sermon that Jesus chose not only a rich person and a poor person but also both a male and a female to represent God's avid quest for the lost one. It underscores the "how much more" thrust of the parables. If rich and poor, man and woman, will search for lost animals and lost coins with such intensity of purpose, how much more will God seek after lost persons?

There is sermonic material to be found by a **study** of the customs of Israel in regard to the division and bequeathing of property. What was the significance, for example, of the younger son in Jesus' parable getting his share so early in life?

The **preacher** will, of course, not want to miss the dramatic possibilities in the confrontation between Jesus and his critics. This is serious business. How can a holy God be served by people who show no care for holiness? What is to be done with people who flout God's laws and even—as in the case of tax collectors—prey upon God's own? These parables are not "nice" stories about a "nice" God's dealings with "nice" people. They are about life and death, sin and redemption, wickedness and repentance.

Whatever dramatic devices the preacher elects, the main point of the sermon must be that of the parables themselves: God's holy glee at the repentance and return of seemingly lost persons. Why such joy in heaven? Because the end and goal of God's purpose, as revealed in Jesus Christ, is redemption. God's holiness is not some kind of moral purity, raised to the tenth power; rather, it is God's steadfast love for God's "fallen" creation. As the prophet Hosea so wonderfully perceived, God is forever the heartbroken husband, seeking reconciliation with his erring wife. God cannot and will not rest until the lost have been restored: God is like the seeking shepherd; God is like the restless housewife; God is like the waiting father.

Hosea 4:1–3; 5:15–6:6 (C)

The setting of these prophetic oracles is the Northern Kingdom of Israel in the decades preceding the fall of that nation in 721 B.C.E. It is a period of what one commentator calls "political, social, and spiritual anarchy."

That lawless situation is clearly reflected in the prophet's sweeping indictment of Israel's ethical lapses. The commandments of God have been flouted, specifically those proscribing swearing (3), lying (9), murder (6), stealing (8), and adultery (7).

As a consequence, "the land mourns." The ethical anarchy is reflected in ecological disasters. Even the fish of the sea are not spared.

The prophet calls for repentance, to a return to an earlier purity and piety. To this a promise is attached: If Israel turns to God, God will turn in mercy to Israel. There will be a time of renewing and refreshment. As seasonal showers refresh the land, so God will come and renew Israel—whose loyalty to Yahweh has been as inconstant as the morning dew.

It is to jar Israel out of this state of inconstancy that the prophetic word is spoken; for as the prophet declares in words taken up and used by Jesus: "Loyalty is my desire, not sacrifice, not whole-offerings but the knowledge of God" (6:6, NEB).

The thoughtful interpreter will want to **investigate** the aim or purpose of God's law. Lawlessness was more than just breaking rules. It involved disloyalty.

The sermon on this passage might be structured as a series of vivid metaphors for God: the judge (the passage begins in a court of law, where Yahweh calls Israel to answer for breaching the Decalogue); the bringer of punishment (tearing and lashing and hewing); the reviver and refresher (who is like the seasonal showers that bring new life to the parched ground). These do not add up to any kind of coherent picture. Rather, they are various roles that God takes up in order to work out the divine purpose, which is then expressed in the climactic verse, "I desire steadfast love and not sacrifice, the knowledge of God, rather than burnt offerings." That becomes the bottom line, as it were, toward which the metaphors lead us.

The sermon might well conclude with two brief case studies in which Hosea 6:6 is a critical element: Jesus' confrontation with the Pharisees, in Matthew 9:10–13, where the discussion takes place around supposed violation of food laws; and Matthew 12:1–8, where the confrontation with the Pharisees is over Sabbath observance. In both cases the matter at issue is knowledge of God's purposes.

Exodus 32:7–14 (L)

Exodus 32:7–11, 13–14 (RC)

Exodus 32:1, 7–14 (E)

It is easy to see why some groups would choose the story of the golden calf as the companion passage to Luke 15 and 1 Timothy 1:12–17. The theme of the first is repentance; the theme of the second is God's mercy. In the story of the golden calf is the extraordinary claim that God repented of evil that God intended to Israel and chose mercy instead!

However, the preacher-expositor does well to avoid getting entangled in a theological thicket by discussing whether or not God's mind changes. In a sermon on this passage one does better to emphasize several biblical themes that the story illuminates.

1. The story is illustrative of the human need for someone or something to worship. When Moses does not come down immediately from the mountain with some tangible evidence of God's presence, the people ask for other gods to worship. While idolatry is a sin—and a terrible sin—it has a kind of inevitability about it. Where there is no word from the true God, people will demand that gods of some kind be produced.

2. Idolatry brings wrath. If there is one clear lesson that the Old Testament teaches, it is that idolatry brings calamity upon the heads of idolaters. No good can come of it, said the prophets—over and over again.

3. God can be trusted to remember the covenant. It is true that in this passage Moses has to *remind* God of the covenant; God does not manage that act of memory alone. But the literary device of a dialogue between Moses and God should not deceive us into thinking that Moses persuaded God against God's will and purpose to have mercy on Israel. Rather, the external dialogue with Moses surely represents the choices that are open to God—to punish or to show mercy. And, in faithfulness to God's own covenant, God shows mercy. What else could we expect?

So **a three-point sermon** on this passage might have these points: (1) We need God more than God needs us. (2) When need drives us to idolatry, only trouble results. (3) God's mercy extends even to idolaters.

Just what one uses as contemporary examples of idolatry will depend on the preacher's imagination. The passage from Exodus suggests that idols are fashioned out of desperation, so that the preacher will avoid the obvious notion that golden calf = idol, therefore money (gold) = idol. Surely there are more telling examples of idolatry than the love of money.

If one wants to know about the idols of a people or a culture, ask about their highest values. To what do they ascribe supreme worth, so that they will sacrifice anything and everything for them? And then ask about the tangible symbols of those values. These symbols may be such things as material wealth, traditions, ideas, or family relationships.

1 Timothy 1:12–17

Scholars are not in agreement that the two epistles of Timothy were actually written by Paul to his protégé. It seems more probable that they were written in the decades following Paul's death by someone close to him, and were perhaps based on correspondence that came from Paul's own hand.

No matter. The central message of the passage does not depend on authorship. "Christ Jesus came into the world to save sinners," whether or not Paul wrote 1 Timothy! What the author says of himself is true, with some modifications, about every one of Christ's servants. Who of us, who call ourselves Christ's servants, could not claim, "I am the foremost of sinners" (v. 15)? If there is any justification for using our own experiences in the pulpit—and many of us were advised to shun "the vertical pronoun"—is it not that the preacher might be "an example to those who [are] to believe in [Christ] for eternal life" (v. 16)?

However, in a **sermon** on this passage, the preacher might do well to avoid either a discussion of Paul's experiences or an offering of his or her own Christian pilgrimage; for this passage offers a concept that cries out for exposition: *Christ's perfect patience.* The Greek word that is translated as "patience" also means "forbearance, long-suffering." In an age of the quick fix, of sudden turnovers, of rapid change, we need to hear that God's love is expressed as patience. We need to be reminded that God's mercy is expressed as forbearance, as long-suffering. The same patience that God showed the author of 1 Timothy is shown to the whole creation.

The interpreter will be rewarded by **investigation** of the Greek word *makrothymia,* which is translated as "patience" in the RSV. Look to see how it appears in other versions of the English Bible.

Richard Mouw, in an article in the *Christian Century,* tells how he was trying to explain the literalist-creationist perspective on Genesis. A Catholic scholar listened and then said in some agitation, "Don't these people realize that God likes to do things *slowly*?" If God seems to be slow to punish the world for its sins—racism, greed, oppression, sexual anarchy, idolatry—could it be that God is expressing love as *patience*? In offering Christ as offering for sin, does not God exhibit perfect forbearance, perfect long-suffering, perfect patience? Those are questions a sermon on 1 Timothy 1:12–17 might well explore.

Theological Reflection

In all the biblical narratives, the central character is God. In each narrative we ask: What does this story reveal about God? We are not so much interested in God's developing character—as we would be in a novel—but in the development of God's plan and intention. In all the passages studied for this Sunday, that intention and plan is quite clear: to have mercy upon us. That cannot be repeated too often or strongly: *God's eternal purpose is to have mercy on us.* God will be merciful, whether we deserve that mercy or not. Confronted with that revelation, we can only put our hands over our mouths in wonder.

Children's Message

Avoid the temptation to tell the story of the golden calf. It is not meant for children! Rather, tell both the parables of the lost sheep and the lost coin, with some embellishment of the details—such as how the one sheep might have wandered away from the flock;

such as how the woman moved furniture and bent to look into crannies for the lost coin. Boys and girls relish these details.

Rather than try to set the two parables in the Lukan context of Jesus' controversy with the scribes and Pharisees, in your comments on the two stories focus on *God's joy*. Like a farmer who found a lost sheep, like a woman who found a lost coin, God is joyful when things turn out right. It may come as a wonderful surprise to children to hear that God is capable of joy and happiness. (And here is a chance to bring in both a male and a female figure as proper models for God.)

Hymns for Pentecost 17

Immortal, Invisible; Savior, Like a Shepherd Lead Us; The Lord's My Shepherd, I'll Not Want.

Pentecost 18

Ordinary Time 25
Proper 20

Psalm 107:1–9 (C)

1 Timothy 2:1–7 (C)
1 Timothy 2:1–8 (L) (RC) (E)

Hosea 11:1–11 (C)
Amos 8:4–7 (L) (RC) (E)   Luke 16:1–13

Meditation on the Texts

You are God and not a human being, the Holy One in our midst. On your steadfast love and mercy rest all our hopes, for what have we to offer you, except a record of broken promises and a record of greed and exploitation? Have mercy on us, O God, who desire that all shall be saved and come to a knowledge of the truth. Hear our prayers and supplications for all people, especially for those who rule over us. Help us to live godly and sober lives, in quietness and peace, using all our possessions and all our days in your faithful service. For we pray in the name and for the sake of our Savior, Jesus Christ. Amen.

Luke 16:1–13

It takes a bold preacher to use this text as the basis for a sermon. Most Christians, hearing the parable of the unjust steward, will focus on his dishonesty; they may not be able to hear about anything else. It takes a skillful and patient preacher to draw attention away from the fraud and toward the point that Jesus wanted to make in his telling of the story.

It cannot be said often enough to expositors of the parables that one is spared much grief if one adheres to three rules: (1) The parables of Jesus are usually not allegories; every detail in the stories does not necessarily refer to an eternal verity. (2) Jesus used the parable to make one point, and that one point was theological. He did not draw morals from his stories, as did Aesop with his fables. (3) The rule of end stress is helpful in locating the point Jesus wanted to make. He would wait for the end to put his spin on the narrative.

If the above-mentioned rules are applied to the parable of the unjust steward, these insights follow: The steward does not represent the typical disciple or believer; he is not to be taken as a model for our behavior—nor does his master represent God. We are not to fret about the possibility that God condones fraudulent behavior. The sole reason Jesus chose the steward for his parable is that he wanted a vivid example of someone who used money to make friends—friends who could be enormously useful to him in the future. One supposes that Jesus might have chosen a beneficent rich man. But who would have been arrested by that kind of story?

The point of the story seems to be well stated by Jesus himself: "Make friends for yourselves by means of unrighteous mammon" (v. 9a). That seems quite in keeping with other teachings of Jesus about material possessions. They have the power to seduce, enslave, lead astray, corrupt. "You cannot serve God and mammon," Jesus warned his disciples (Matt. 6:24b). One way to turn the tables on mammon is to use it to make friends for oneself. And by "friends," Jesus seems to mean those whose friendship will count in your favor in the age to come. (Those who have read and taken to heart the Law and the Prophets will know that the poor, the orphan, the widow, and the stranger are high on the list of friends that deserve one's kindness.)

This interpretation of the parable is reinforced by the fact that the key verse comes at the end. It seems most likely that the end of the parable, as Jesus originally told it, came at

v. 9, and that vs. 10–13 were brought together with the parable when the Gospel was written. Those verses have their own point to make, and that point belongs in the sermon; but it is not central to the teaching of the parable. Those verses make a lovely conclusion to the sermon. When one comes to the end of the exposition and turns to the application of the biblical truth to life, one can use these verses. So what does it matter that one uses money in this way? Well, if you cannot be trusted to use money prudently, how do you expect God to entrust you with riches of a greater kind? If you wonder why God has not called you to greater responsibility, look to the way you take care of your money.

Use a Bible dictionary to be sure you know the full meaning of the biblical term "steward." Otherwise, the parable does not make full sense.

One of the opportunities that should not be missed is that of delineating the biblical meaning of steward and stewardship. Read Douglas Hall's book *The Steward: A Biblical Symbol Come of Age* (New York: Friendship Press, 1982). He points out that not only is stewardship one of the givens of church life in North America, but stewardship as we practice it is a pale copy of the biblical version. Hall makes two points about the steward as that role is understood in the New Testament: (1) the close identification of steward and master—with the steward being almost the vicar for the master; and (2) the insistence that the steward is not the owner, but is accountable to the master for all that the steward does.

However, in dealing with the stewardship concept, one should not be drawn away to discussing the proper stewardship of the land, or of the gospel, or of anything else but money; because that is what the parable is primarily about.

A strategy for **preaching** on this parable might be as follows: Begin with the point of maximum interest, which is the clever, rascally way in which the steward secures his future. That is what is going to capture interest, so don't fight it. Start there. Compare and contrast the steward with persons in our own day who thought to amass great wealth but who got caught in shady practices and ended up in prison and disgrace. (The junk-bond scandals, the savings and loan scandals—such current concerns offer plenty of illustrations of rascals who fiddled with other people's money and got caught at it.) In Jesus' parable the man did not get punished. In fact, his master is represented as praising him for his prudence and foresight!

Once you have captured the attention of the congregation, tell them openly and honestly that you began as you did because you knew that that part of the story would interest them most. Then point out that *Jesus did the same thing*. He hooked his hearers with a story about a clever, self-serving rascal in order to teach them something more important than honesty in business dealings.

Now that you have the attention of the congregation and have aroused their curiosity about what Jesus was up to, lay on them the point that Jesus made: You and I do well to use our riches to make friends for ourselves, friends whose good word for us will count in the age to come.

There is a danger, of course, that the congregation will understand you to mean that we can buy our way into heaven by doing good things for the poor and needy. Rather than deny that outright, why not raise the possibility that in the age to come our money will have no value, but what will bring us honor and praise will be our deeds of generosity. The robes we wear will be fashioned from the garments we gave to the naked; the shoes we wear will be cobbled from the shoes we gave to the homeless. One can go on like that for a bit without claiming some kind of saving virtue in acts of kindness.

Save the real firepower for the conclusion of the sermon. There are several ways in which to bring an exposition of a sermon on the unjust steward to a climax and conclusion. One is the happy notion that "unrighteous mammon" can be redeemed by using it to make friends. Instead of its being our slave driver and idol, we can turn it to our use by giving it to those who need it.

A better climax and conclusion can be fashioned from vs. 10–13, where Jesus asks the disciples: If you cannot be trusted to use money properly, who will make you stewards of the greater gifts? Paul speaks of the apostles as "stewards of the mysteries of God" (1 Cor. 4:1). One cannot hope to be entrusted with that kind of stewardship if one cannot manage money.

This is the time of the year when stewardship sermons are in order. What better way to tie the stewardship of money to the stewardship of the land and the stewardship of the gospel than with this parable?

Hosea 11:1–11 (C)

If you preached on only *one* Old Testament text in the course of a year, this could serve you well; for in this oracle the prophet rehearses the whole history of Israel in a series of vivid metaphors.

> When Israel was a child, I loved him,
> and out of Egypt I called my son.
> (V. 1)

There is the exodus—not imaged as in Cecil B. De Mille's movie, but as the rescue and nurturing of a helpless little boy! A foundling was delivered from the orphanage and brought to the home of the wealthy parent.

> The more I called them,
> the more they went from me.
> (V. 2)

There is the whole history of the kingdom and the prophets in one sentence! The more God pleaded with the people for righteousness and faithfulness, the more they—like willful children in defiance of the parent's voice—ran farther and farther away from home!

> Yet it was I who taught Ephraim to walk,
> I took them up in my arms;
> but they did not know that I healed them.
> (V. 3)

Forsaking the righteous Yahweh was not just the act of a willful child, who stubbornly refuses to obey the parent. It was a rejection of the One who had healed their wounds, who had rescued them from troubles.

> The sword shall rage against their cities,
> consume the bars of their gates,
> and devour them in their fortresses.
> (V. 6)

Rather than read these verses as predictions of the fall of Israel to the Assyrians in 722–721 B.C.E., they should be regarded as metaphors of God's judgment in history. They encompass all the perils and troubles of Israel, down to and including the exile in Babylon.

> How can I give you up, O Ephraim!
> How can I hand you over, O Israel!
> . . . .
> My heart recoils within me,
> my compassion grows warm and tender.
> I will not execute my fierce anger,
> . . . .
> for I am God and not man,
> the Holy One in your midst,
> And I will not come to destroy.
> (Vs. 8–9)

This is a poetic representation of the grand mystery of biblical faith, that God is at once just and merciful! Israel is punished, but not destroyed; God executes justice, but God is also merciful.

> They shall go after the LORD,
> he will roar like a lion;

> yea, he will roar,
> and his sons shall come trembling from the west;
>
> . . . .
>
> and I will return them to their homes, says the LORD.
>
> (Vs. 10–11)

There is the promise of restoration, following whatever disaster falls upon Israel. God's mercy is shown in rescue and restoration. It does not remain a promise only; it is fulfilled in history.

One Christian couple asked that this passage from Hosea not only be read as part of their wedding service, but that the preacher base his homily upon it.

Basic to the theology of Hosea is the concept of *hesed* (loyal love). In the RSV it is rendered as "steadfast love." **Skim the psalms** to see how often it is used.

A **sermon** on this passage could very well, as the prophet himself has done, rehearse the history of Yahweh and Israel. The sermon might consist of a series of flashbacks and flash-forwards—in the mind of the prophet in the tumultuous years preceding the fall of Israel in 721 B.C.E. Each can be built around one of Hosea's metaphors; each can focus on an event in Israel's history: exodus, wilderness, kingdom, exile, restoration.

The key verse, of course, and the one that the preacher wants to save for the climax, is 9b, "For I am God and not man, the Holy One in your midst, and I will not come to destroy." To have the holy God in our midst means to have to do with a Rescuer, not a Destroyer—no matter what the historical circumstances. That is the God and Father of our Lord Jesus Christ.

Amos 8:4–7 (L) (RC) (E)

Like Hosea, Amos prophesied in the Northern Kingdom in the decades preceding its demise and destruction. He probably predates Hosea by some years. Unlike Hosea he was not a native of the Northern Kingdom, nor was he a member of the prophetic guild. As he himself tells us, he was a countryman from the Southern Kingdom, who came north to warn Israel of the false security into which material wealth and political power had lulled them.

None of his bitter oracles against the rich and oppressive elite—and there are some pretty bitter oracles—are more telling than vs. 4–7. These words are directed against those who "grind the destitute and plunder the humble" (v. 4, NEB). In Amos' day, as in our own, there were those who valued everything in terms of the bottom line, that is, money. For these people the Sabbath was just a long intermission between business opportunities. Some of them were dishonest merchants, who fiddled the scales. One reads behind Amos' condemnation of crooked businessmen a contempt for their whole class, which used economic status as an excuse for oppression.

Before writing a sermon on Amos 8:4–7, you might want to **look into social and economic conditions** in Israel in the half century before its fall in 721 B.C.E. Evidently there were conditions prevalent that sound like chattel slavery—or at least indentured servitude.

Anyone who chooses to preach on this passage should not miss the "kicker" in v. 7. To those merchants who cannot forget for a holiday or Sabbath the money they might be making, Amos says, "The LORD has sworn . . . : 'Surely I will never forget any of their deeds'" (v. 7). The obsession of the merchants with their profits is exceeded by the single-mindedness of God, who will never forget a single one of their misdeeds—not the smallest, not the slightest!

1 Timothy 2:1–7 (C)

1 Timothy 2:1–8 (L) (RC) (E)

This is a fairly straightforward pastoral message, such as any older man might write to a younger protégé. It is best known for the appeal to the recipient to offer prayers "for sovereigns and all in high office" (v. 2, NEB). In many congregations the Sunday liturgy includes prayers for the welfare of the head of state.

However, it would be missing a grand opportunity if one were to concentrate on that particular verse and miss the chance to preach on this entire passage, for it offers a wonderful opportunity to preach a "centripetal" sermon. The model is a spiral, in which one begins with the periphery and moves to the center. One begins with the global and moves to the personal, one begins with the general and moves to the particular; for that is the movement of the passage.

The interpreter will want to **compare** 1 Timothy 2:1–2 with Romans 13:1–7. Do these passages sound similar? Are they both from the hand of Paul?

Here is how **the sermon** might be constructed. The preacher begins with a concern for the secular order, good government, wise rulers, peace and justice and order, and with the need of Christians to pray for such blessings. It is all motherhood and apple pie; who is not for such things?

Then one moves on to the consequences of good government and secular peace, which is our own peace and tranquillity. Again, this is what people need and want to hear—that God wants us to have quiet and peaceable lives.

But why? Because God desires that *all* be saved and come to true faith and knowledge. Our welfare is instrumental to God's larger purposes, and that purpose is not simply that humans live undisturbed, but that they may be saved from the consequences of their sin and folly and know the true God.

To that end God has provided a mediator, Jesus Christ, who sacrificed himself as a ransom for the world. Now the sermon has moved from general comments about the social order and God's saving purpose to God's great saving *act* in Jesus Christ.

To this saving work of God in Christ, the writer of the epistle—and, by inference, you and I—were made witnesses and witness bearers. Therefore, a sermon that began with some general concerns for the peace and welfare of the world ends with our vocation to be Christ's faithful witnesses.

Preaching on this passage is an opportunity to weave together into one unbroken cord various strands: concern for peace and tranquillity, the need to support rulers and sovereigns, God's saving purpose, God's saving acts, Christ's mediating death, and our personal responsibility to be Christ's witnesses. If one follows the flow of 1 Timothy 2:1–7, these concerns can be seen to flow out of and into one another with no need to weigh one against another.

Theological Reflection

There is no single theological theme common to all the texts for this Sunday. However, the matter of money and its use and abuse does feature prominently in the passages from Luke and from Amos. In Hosea's indictment of Israel considered in last Sunday's text, there was condemnation of lying and stealing. So some theological reflection on human economics and God's economy are in order. Remember that the Greek word from which we get "economics" has as its basis the concept of "household." Economics, then, has to do with welfare and well-being and food and shelter more than simply with profits and balance statements. Jesus and the prophets were together in trying to steer God's people away from economics as purely money-making.

Children's Message

One certainly does not want to tell children the parable of the unjust steward. There is no way to get that one past the concrete thinking of children without leaving the impression that the steward was pretty sharp and one whom we ought to emulate. Why not rather introduce them to Amos? Tell them about his upbringing as a country boy, about his visits to the cities of Israel and his outrage at what he saw. Tell them about his courage in attacking the ruling elites, who were oppressing the poor.

Hymns for Pentecost 18

O God of Earth and Altar; All Who Love and Serve Your City; The Light of God Is Falling.

Pentecost 19

(September 25–October 1)

Ordinary Time 26
Proper 21

Psalm 107:1, 33–43 (C)   1 Timothy 6:6–19 (C)
                          1 Timothy 6:6–16 (L)
Joel 2:23–30 (C)   1 Timothy 6:11–16 (RC)
Amos 6:1–7 (L) (E)   1 Timothy 6:11–19 (E)
Amos 6:1a, 4–7 (RC)
                          Luke 16:19–31

Meditation on the Texts

O God, who dwell in unapproachable light, whom no one has ever seen or can see, you have promised at the proper time to make manifest our Sovereign, Jesus Christ. Make us content to wait patiently and soberly for his appearing; content with that share of the world's goods that has fallen to us; mindful of the poor and needy; openhanded and generous with those less fortunate. Do not let us be poor in spirit, O God. Pour out your Spirit abundantly on all of us, your servants. Let our elderly dream dreams and our young have their visions. Let us be rich in the gifts of the Spirit—godliness, kindness, peaceableness, patience. For we pray in the name of Jesus Christ. Amen.

Commentary on the Texts

Luke 16:19–31

A successful teacher of creative writing says that her most frequent criticism of students' stories is that fledgling writers are uncertain as to what their stories are about. Before you set out to write a sermon on Jesus' parable of the rich man and Lazarus, be sure you are quite clear what the story is about. It is not about heaven and hell; it is not about life after death; and, in spite of its reference to one risen from the dead, it is not about resurrection. Rather, it is about the Word of God, delivered in the Law and the Prophets. The Word declares that God is not pleased with rich people who are blind to the plight of the poor.

There is no need to enter the debate here about God's preferential concern for the poor. That is not what Jesus was teaching about in this parable. What the parable was designed to do was to confront hearers with what they already knew, what the Law and the Prophets together make very plain: God will not stand by and watch the rich grind the faces of the poor in the dust—either by active oppression or callous neglect. The rich man who feasted while Lazarus starved, and who was more than amply clothed while Lazarus was covered with sores, was in grave spiritual danger.

For further study, check out Leviticus 19. Read Amos and Micah. Take a quick trip through the psalms and note how often the plight of the poor is brought before God's throne. Try Psalms 10, 12, 14, 35, 49, 53, 68, 70, and 72. Do some investigation into the justice system of Israel. In the story Lazarus is pictured as lying at the "gate." In the towns and cities of Israel, the gate was the traditional place where disputes were settled, where justice was administered. It may be significant for the story that the poor man lay in the place where he had some hopes of getting his due, his share.

How are you going to **preach** on this parable without raising a lot of questions in the minds of your hearers about the life to come—and most especially about highways—or the lack of them—between heaven and hell? It is often a useful rhetorical device to clear away the underbrush before laying the ax to the trunk of the tree. Why not begin by declaring to your hearers what this story is *not* about: It is not about the curse of riches; it is not about the fires of hell; it is not even about punishment. Then go on to state clearly—and early—what it *is* about: Jesus was calling the attention of his hearers to a dominant theme in scripture—the gulf between poor and rich is a terrible danger to the rich. Next ring the changes on "Moses and the prophets." Tell what the law says about helping the poor, the widow, the fatherless, the sojourner. Call as witnesses Amos and Micah. If you think your hearers will find this all a bit too much sociology and economics, let them overhear some of the psalmists at prayer!

You may say in conclusion that we prosperous Americans do not like to hear this sort of thing, being well-to-do persons, living in the richest nation on earth. But we don't want to be like the rich man in the parable, begging someone to go and warn his brothers of the danger they are in. Rather, let us listen to Moses and the prophets while we still have time for obedience.

Joel 2:23–30 (C)

Scholars place the writing of the Book of Joel sometime after the exile, somewhere between 500 and 350 B.C.E. The immediate circumstance of the prophecy—if one does not treat the plague of locusts as an allegory or metaphor—is the combination of a plague and drought. Some interpreters have thought Joel was actually describing an armed invasion, but it seems more likely he was describing an omnivorous swarm of insects.

If the locusts may be seen as some kind of army, it is God's avenging host, disciplining a disobedient people; and so Joel calls Judah to repentance. Grief and mourning at the natural disaster is not enough. "Rend your hearts and not your garments" is the word of God that Joel delivers (2:13).

Coupled with the call to national repentance is the promise of a better day to come, when God will send the rains that will make for a full harvest, and there will be a restoration of "the years which the swarming locust has eaten" (v. 25).

And then the prophet looks further into the future and sees a new day in which God's Spirit—like the abundant rains—is poured out on all, so that all shall prophesy. Material gifts shall be followed by spiritual gifts. It was, of course, this later promise of Joel that Peter quoted in his Pentecostal sermon.

Look into descriptions of the agriculture of ancient Israel. Work the details about such things as crops, rainfall, or plagues into your **sermon**.

The Book of Joel is noteworthy for the emphasis given to God's action in what one scholar calls "natural causes." We tend to think of the prophets as calling attention to God's mighty acts in history; but here it is a swarm of insects, not an Assyrian army, that is the rod of God's anger. Of course there is the story of the Flood in Genesis. For the most part the prophets were suspicious of identification of God with what we would call the "natural cycle of events." That was typical of Baalism, in which the divine got all mixed up with procreation and that sort of thing. We moderns would prefer Jesus' comment in the Sermon on the Mount, "Your Father who is in heaven . . . makes his sun rise on the evil and on the good, and sends rain on the just and on the unjust" (Matt. 5:45).

This passage from Joel is a considerable challenge to the preacher. The mind plays with these possibilities: (1) dwell on the locusts as divine punishment for disobedience; (2) dwell on the promise of restoration after the plague and drought; or (3) dwell on the refreshing rain as a foretaste of the pouring out of the Spirit on Pentecost. But to choose any one of those themes to the exclusion of the other is not to play fair with the text; it is to slice off a piece of the passage and leave the rest on the plate!

The dominant image of the passage is the refreshing rain following a period of drought and deprivation. That is the literary fact that ties the passage together. So why not make that the theme of the sermon? Fashion a sermon on the theme: God comes to us like rain after drought. For there do seem to be, in the lives of individuals, congregations, denominations, even nations, recurring periods of dryness followed by periods of growth and abundance. One can find illustrations of that in biography and history. The saints and mystics testify to periods of spiritual aridity; Israel wandered for forty years in the arid wilderness; the psalmist said, "My soul thirsts for God" (Ps. 42:2); Jesus on the cross cried out, "I thirst" (John 19:28).

The preacher can use the passage from Joel to describe the impact on a people of a time of plague and drought—a time of famine and thirst. Then the sermon can move to the idea of God as one who refreshes, and the climax of the sermon can be a doxology to the Spirit, who is the agent in our baptism (with water).

Amos 6:1-7 (L) (E)

Amos 6:1a, 4-7 (RC)

Remember that Amos prophesied in the Northern Kingdom beginning about 750 B.C.E. The land had fallen into semipaganism, says one scholar. Amos, who was himself from Judea, appeared to proclaim the judgment of God on the rich and powerful in Israel. It was a time, as one commentator has said, of "shallow optimism" and "false security," of commercial and political success, but of moral and social decay.

Amos 6:1-7 is an oracle directed against the ruling elites, who seem oblivious to the impending judgment of Yahweh. They are "at ease in Zion" (v. 1). They "lie upon beds of ivory" (v. 4). They "sing idle songs" (v. 5). They "drink wine in bowls" (v. 6). But they "are not grieved over the ruin of Joseph!" (v. 6).

Their punishment is this: "Therefore they shall now be the first of those to go into exile" (v. 7). The NEB translates v. 7 as follows: "You shall head the column of exiles; that will be the end of sprawling and revelry." There is no need to read into the reference to an exile a forecast of the Assyrian conquest of Israel in 722 B.C.E. or the Babylonian captivity of Judah a century and a half later. Both Northern and Southern Kingdoms lived always under the threat of captivity from more powerful nations to the south, north, and east. "Exile" here is a metaphor for God's judgment—not a prediction of a specific event. Amos points to other great cities that have fallen to invaders: Calneh, Hamath, Gath. Why not Bethel and Samaria?

What appeals to the preacher in Amos 6:1-7 is the vividness of the language: "At ease in Zion," "beds of ivory," "idle songs," "wine in bowls." Images come at once to mind of Nero playing his fiddle while Rome was in flames; the court of Louis XVI before the Revolution—that sort of thing. The ruling elites seem always the last to understand that their pleasures are masking the social ruin that invites disaster.

That's too easy! We have all had the changes rung on that sort of thing. Any one of us could climb into the pulpit and rail against the ruling elites of our own culture, nation, community, denomination, or congregation, using the metaphors of Amos 6. Some of us would especially like to have a whack at "idle songs" and "wine in bowls." Popular music and alcoholic beverages are favorite targets of reforming preachers. What kind of **sermon**, based on this passage, might dig a bit deeper than that kind of calamity howling?

One could do a comparison and contrast between Amos and Jesus—both "country boys" who come to the centers of power to challenge the values and life-styles of the rich and famous. Jesus' parable of the rich man and Lazarus is not that far removed, rhetorically speaking, from Amos 6:1-7. The woes pronounced by Amos find some echo in the woes pronounced by Jesus in Luke 11:42-52.

In his novel *The Spectator Bird,* Wallace Stegner has his seventy-year-old protagonist reflecting on the death of his only son, a California surfer. "What is that life style (that jargon term) except a substitute for life?" muses Joe. That might offer the preacher a way of musing about the life-styles of the rich and famous without seeming to be merely envious or censorious.

1 Timothy 6:6-19 (C)

1 Timothy 6:6-16 (L)

1 Timothy 6:11-16 (RC)

1 Timothy 6:11-19 (E)

Each of the four lectionaries slices up 1 Timothy 6 in a slightly different way! One supposes that some lectionary committees were concerned to locate some apostolic word about "riches" to go along with the prophetic oracles and with Jesus' story of the rich man and Lazarus. The Common Lectionary begins in the middle of a section, because that is where the author says, "There is great gain in godliness with contentment" (v. 6). That is a strong clue to us, the reader, what the members of that lectionary committee had in mind. Note that the Roman Catholic lectionary omits the comments on riches in vs. 6–10 and 17–19, except for the reference in v. 11 to "all this"—which seems to point back to "the love of money" in v. 10.

It seems difficult, however, to escape the impression that the entire sixth chapter of 1 Timothy *is* about the lure of greed, the great spiritual threat that riches pose for the Christian. "The good fight of the faith," which the author urges upon Timothy in v. 12, is offered as an alternative to seeking "gain." In other words, for the Christian the bottom line is never money but a life of faithfulness to Jesus Christ.

No two versions of the English Bible seem to have the same translation of the ancient proverb about the love of money and evil. **Compare and contrast** the translations in the versions you have.

If the bottom line for the Christian is *faithfulness, not making money,* then that should be the major emphasis of the **preacher** who chooses to preach on 1 Timothy 6. That does not imply a sermon on "Christian Economics" or an attack on the profit motive or the promotion of a particular life-style, but it does call for a clear order of priorities: faithfulness ahead of making money.

Once that clear line of argumentation is established, there are some subthemes that can be introduced: the profitability of contentment, the fact that "you can't take it with you," the God who richly blesses us with good things, the need for the wealthy to be rich in good deeds. These are the positive, healthy-minded aspects of the theme. One really ought not go on for twenty minutes on "the love of money is the root of all evils." There are other things to say about money than that—and the author of 1 Timothy provides them.

Who are the "rich"? Probably most of the people in most of our congregations! Don't let them think that when you talk about "the rich" you are talking about a few millionaires!

Don't miss the chance to relate this passage to Amos 6:1–7, which is a grand illustration of the truth that the love of money corrupts—even the people of God.

Theological Reflection

How seldom one hears sermons about money—except on Stewardship Sunday. Yet money was a dominant theme in the teaching of Jesus. It certainly comes up again and again in the preaching of the prophets. Money—or the lack of it—is also a dominant concern in the lives of most of us. Yet preachers tend to stay away from the theme of money, lest they be accused of being innocent of economics, of treading on ground where they are not sure of the path. Surely people want to hear—and need to hear—what the gospel says about money. One of the surest ways to "spiritualize" the gospel, to make it irrelevant to the lives of ordinary people, is to avoid any discussion of money from the pulpit.

Children's Message

What riches to choose from—the compelling parable of the rich man and Lazarus, the plague of locusts, Amos' fiery sermon! If you did not introduce children to Amos last Sunday, you might want to do that today. You could compare him with Jesus, who was also a young man from a small town who went to the city and condemned the life-styles of the rich and famous. Or you could do something with Joel's metaphor of God coming like rain after drought and plague. (The parable of the rich man and Lazarus might be a bit much for younger children.)

Hymns for Pentecost 19

Where Cross the Crowded Ways of Life; We Give Thee but Thine Own; We All Are One in Mission.

Ordinary Time 27

Proper 22

Psalm 101 (C)

Amos 5:6-7, 10-15 (C)
Habakkuk 1:1-3; 2:1-4 (L)
Habakkuk 1:2-3; 2:2-4 (RC)
Habakkuk 1:1-6, 12-13; 2:1-4 (E)

2 Timothy 1:1-14 (C)
2 Timothy 1:3-14 (L)
2 Timothy 1:6-8, 13-14 (RC)
2 Timothy 1:6-14 (E)

Luke 17:5-10 (C) (RC) (E)
Luke 17:1-10 (L)

Meditation on the Texts

Almighty God, you have not given us a spirit of timidity but a spirit of power and love and self-control, and have appointed us preachers and teachers of your gracious Word. As you spoke through the prophets and apostles of old, speak through us! Speak words of justice and righteousness in behalf of the poor and needy. Speak words of encouragement to the young and tender. Speak words of life and immortality to the dying. Speak words of faith to the doubting and fainthearted. And grant, when all our work is done, that we may hear from Jesus Christ, who became the Servant of all, "Well done, good and faithful servant." For we pray in his name. Amen.

Commentary on the Texts

Luke 17:5-10 (C) (RC) (E)

Luke 17:1-10 (L)

The first ten verses of Luke 17 constitute a collection of sayings of Jesus to the disciples. There does not seem to be a common thread, except that most general theme of discipleship. Verses 1–3a have to do with causing others to stumble; vs. 3b–4, with forgiving the offending brother; vs. 5–6, with quantifying faith; and vs. 7–10, with the dutiful role of the servant.

Besides being on a common theme, these sayings are represented as being given on the journey to Jerusalem; and they are directed to the disciples, who are traveling with Jesus.

For matters of interpretation, it would seem best not to try to tie these sayings tightly together, but to deal with them one by one. Otherwise a coherence is forced on them that is artificial.

Verses 1–3a have to do with occasions when the actions or attitude of one Christian causes another to fall away from the faith, to become apostate. The severity of the punishment for this, according to Jesus, is so dreadful that it would be better for the offender to be weighted with stone and drowned in the sea. "The little ones" does not refer to children so much as to any Christian disciple.

Verses 3b–4 envisages a circumstance when one Christian sins against another, is rebuked, and asks forgiveness. No matter how often this happens, forgiveness must be granted. "Seven times" points to the totality of the askings, not to a limited number. The teaching brings to mind Peter's question, "Lord, how often am I to forgive my brother if he goes on wronging me? As many as seven times?" and Jesus' response, "I do not say seven times: I say seventy times seven" (Matt. 18:21–22, NEB).

Verses 5–6 have to do with the qualitative aspects of faith. When the disciples ask Jesus to add to their faith, he responds with a vivid figure of speech: True faith the size of a mustard seed would be sufficient for them to replant a tree in the middle of the sea! The point of the figure of speech would seem to be that disciples with true faith can do extraordinary things.

Verses 7–10 consist of a parable (vs. 7–9) and its application. The parable describes the nature of servanthood: Even after the servant (slave) has done everything required of him, he still cannot claim special merit; he did only what was his duty. And the application to discipleship is this: If that is true of the relationship of the human slave and human master, *how much more* is it true of the servants of God that they cannot claim merit for their works? One commentator interprets this to mean (1) works do not guarantee salvation and (2) there is no room for human boasting.

One might want to **compare** this little table of discipline for disciples with other collections of similar sayings. The Sermon on the Mount in Matthew is one such, although of considerably greater length. In Mark 9:30–50 there is also a collection of discipleship sayings, which like Luke 17:1–10 were delivered as Jesus was on his way through Galilee, headed for Jerusalem.

The **preacher** has an initial choice to make: Shall I preach on only one of the four sayings in Luke 17:1–10, on two or three of them, or on all four? The advantages of selecting only one are obvious: You do not have the problem of finding a common thread tying several of the sayings together. If you preach on more than one, your audience will expect to be shown some relationship among the sayings and that will be difficult to furnish.

However, if you look at each of the sayings as texts for separate sermons, each offers its own difficulties: Do you really want to expound on the watery fate of those who cause apostasy in others? Do you want to belabor the need to forgive as often as one is asked for forgiveness? Do you want to explain how that mulberry tree got into the ocean? Do you want to explain why some people end up in life as masters, while others are slaves?

A better homiletical strategy might be to deal with several of the sayings under the rubric: ''Case Studies in Discipleship.'' Pick several of the sayings and present them as case studies. Follow each of the biblical sayings with a ''such as'' example. For instance, during the time of the Spanish Inquisition the church thought it was necessary to burn at the stake those who advocated heretical notions that might lead others into apostasy. In actual fact, it might have been better for those poor wretches to be drowned in the sea rather than burned alive.

Each of your case studies might be designed to demonstrate that discipleship is very difficult and demanding; it is a kind of servitude that is very heavy and burdensome. That will lead you to the conclusion stated in v. 10: ''When you have done all that is commanded you,'' you still have to confess to being unworthy servants. Then you may want to make use of these points made by one commentator on these verses: (1) Good works will not save us, only God's grace. (2) There are no grounds for human boasting.

If you can manage to make your case studies realistic and open-ended so that they confront your hearers with choices and decisions, those hearers will welcome the conclusion that works cannot save us, only grace.

Amos 5:6–7, 10–15 (C)

In this oracle there are five vivid images of social dis-ease:

1. ''They hate him who reproves in the gate, and they abhor him who speaks the truth'' (v. 10). The ruling elites cannot tolerate social criticism; they hate the prophets who preach judgment, who ''tell it like it is.''

2. ''You trample upon the poor and take from him exactions of wheat'' (v. 11a). ''You'' presumably has the same reference as ''they'' in the preceding verse; again the object of Amos' anger is the ruling class. In this instance, they are guilty of levying unjust taxes, ''exactions of wheat.'' It is ''the poor'' who have to pay.

3. ''You have built houses of hewn stone . . . ; you have planted pleasant vineyards'' (v. 11b). The ruling elites have indulged in conspicuous consumption; they have built stone houses in a land where most people live in clay (adobe) houses—stone houses that require extensive hand labor to build. They have indulged themselves in the cultivation of grapes for fine wines.

4. "You . . . take a bribe" (v. 12a). The justice system is perverted by bribery.

5. "[You] . . . turn aside the needy in the gate" (v. 12b). The village or city gate was not only the place where the elders dispensed justice; it was also the place where beggars—the disabled and disadvantaged—besought alms of the more fortunate. It was a kind of social welfare system. In this case, the well-advantaged ignored the pleas, the needs, of the wretched.

Using an Old Testament introduction or history, **do some research** into the justice system of ancient Israel—particularly the role of the "gate" as the place where disputes were settled.

The sole vocation of the prophets was not social criticism. Idolatry, apostasy, heresy, immorality, venality—these were also prophetic concerns. Hosea was apparently more concerned with apostasy than social problems, and Isaiah with international affairs. We do the prophets less than justice to represent them only as social critics.

Nevertheless, that was one of their important vocations—never so fully represented as in Amos. And the oracle in chapter 5 is one of his hotter blasts against the prevailing system. It is hard to read it and *not* think of our own Establishment: resentful of criticism, guilty of using the tax system to the advantage of the rich, conspicuous in its consumption, venal, callous to the plight of those clustered at the bottom rung of the social ladder.

How should one **preach** on Amos 5? Well, there isn't much mileage to be had by simply reading off the social sins of Israel and comparing them to our own. Hearers will simply shrug that off—once they have tired of the guilty thrill of being scolded one more time. The preacher will want to make use of the comparisons between Amos' time and our own; but in and of themselves, the similarities are not that useful.

The central message of Amos 5 is that God can come upon a society like a fire, to burn up the evil and iniquitous. Amos pleads with Israel to hate evil as God does, to seek goodness and to reform the social system to conform to God's righteousness. Then God *may* be "gracious to the remnant of Joseph" (v. 15b).

How does the preacher get from avenging fire to gracious preservation of a remnant? It is not easy. But then, it could not have been easy for Amos, either. Somehow the sermon has to take with utmost seriousness: the reality of social dis-ease as fatal sickness; the possibility of God's fiery judgment; the need for repentance and obedience; and the possibility of the gracious saving of a remnant! Death and life issues! There are no homiletical tricks that will get the preacher through this sermon.

Habakkuk 1:1–3; 2:1–4 (L)

Habakkuk 1:2–3; 2:2–4 (RC)

Habakkuk 1:1–6, 12–13; 2:1–4 (E)

The purpose of a lectionary is to allow the people to hear, over a period of time, from all sections of scripture. And in this season they are to listen to the minor prophets: Hosea, Joel, Amos, Habakkuk, Micah, Zephaniah, Haggai. One assumes that the lectionary builders sought in each of these small books a typical or key passage.

In the sections from Habakkuk presented for this Sunday, we have the prophetic call (1:1–6; 2:1–4). The prophet wonders out loud, "How long shall I cry for help?" (v. 2). He has seen the terrible threat posed by the Chaldeans, who threaten the whole world with conquest. He wonders if they have been "ordained" as God's judgment and chastisement. Then he sets himself as a watchman, to see what will happen and how God will respond to his concerns (2:1). And at that point comes God's call: *Wait for the vision.* The one who is faithful to God's covenant (v. 4) will see and understand and be able to make it plain to others (v. 2).

The setting of Habakkuk is probably in the decades before the exile—some date it during the reign of Jehoiakim (608–597 B.C.E.).

Verse 4b is one of the best known in all of scripture: "But the righteous shall live by his faith." Paul quotes it twice in support of his doctrine of justification by grace through faith. Sometimes it appears in Reformation Day sermons. But here faith means faithfulness to the covenant God—a ready and obedient response to God's steadfast love. A prophet who continues in that kind of relationship will one day see, one day understand, one day have fuller vision of what God is up to.

A **sermon** on this passage might well have these three points: (1) The righteous see calamities visited upon the world. (The Chaldeans may represent all sorts of plagues, invasions, catastrophes, crises.) (2) They mount their towers, which represent various attempts at reading the signs of the times, and look abroad and ask: How long, O God, before we see salvation? (3) The word from God is, Have faith and the vision will be forthcoming.

2 Timothy 1:1–14 (C)

2 Timothy 1:3–14 (L)

2 Timothy 1:6–8, 13–14 (RC)

2 Timothy 1:6–14 (E)

Although the two letters to Timothy and the letter to Titus—the pastoral epistles—have traditionally been assigned to Paul as author, there is considerable internal evidence that the apostle did not write the letters as they stand. More likely they are based on letters that Paul wrote, but dated to some time after his death.

Therefore the interpreter is warned away from adducing to the text all sort of biographical information about Paul. Rather, she or he will do well to stay with the text and look for meanings there.

Surely there can be no debate about these being letters of a pastoral nature from an older, more experienced Christian, to a younger colleague—perhaps even a protégé. Put together "my true child in the faith" of 1 Timothy 1:2 and "my beloved child" of 2 Timothy 1:2, and that is clear enough. It is the generational relationship that gives 2 Timothy 1:1–14 its dominant theme. We hear one generation of Christians talking to another.

Neil Postman has written a book called *Teaching as a Conserving Activity.* One important aspect of teaching is the preservation and handing on of the tradition. In this passage we see the older teacher wanting to make secure the "gospel" (v. 8), "the pattern of the sound words" (v. 13), and "the truth that has been entrusted to you" (v. 14).

You might do well to **read** Postman's *Teaching as a Conserving Activity,* or his *Amusing Ourselves to Death.* In both, but particularly the later work, Postman tries to show the difference between being entertained by television and learning in school. He is not happy about the way television "teaches" the young!

However, you do not want to **preach** a crabby sermon about how the young disregard the traditions of the elders and all that. Using 2 Timothy 1:1–14 you *can* point to some healthy and life-sustaining ways in which one generation hands on the tradition to another. The author mentions four:

1. *Legitimizing.* He reminds Timothy of "the laying on of my hands" (v. 6). What that signifies is the continuity of the gifts of God from one generation to another. Priests and pastors—and in some denominations, elders and deacons—are ordained by the laying on of hands of previously ordained persons. This makes it legitimate for such "ordained" persons to exercise certain offices in the church. Thus the one generation legitimizes another; it allows it to use the gifts given to the whole body. (Accreditation is a secular version of this. Doctors, lawyers, professors and the like are legitimized by those already occupying the profession.)

2. *Reminding.* While it may seem a bit tiresome to the young at times, one of the important teaching functions of the older generation is to remind the next about certain things. In vs. 3–7 the author calls a number of things to Timothy's remembrance—not the least of which is a reference to the author's own ancestors.

3. Then there is *patterning* or *modeling.* The author reminds Timothy of "the pattern of the sound words which you have heard from me" (v. 13a). Each generation sets a pattern of thought and behavior for the next. The pupil learns from the teacher a way of thinking, writing, speaking, and acting.

4. *Praying.* One of the services the older generation renders to the next is prayer. "I

remember you constantly in my prayers," writes the author (v. 3b). And why not? How in the world should the young know what to pray for or how to pray for themselves? They need the prayers of the former generation. Teachers should pray for their students, just as parents do for their children.

Second Timothy 1:1–14 could furnish an excellent text for a sermon on Christian Education Sunday; or for a Sunday when lay teachers in the congregation are being honored or installed in office; or for the service of installation of a minister of education.

Theological Reflection

In all four of the passages for this Sunday—Amos, Habakkuk, Luke, and 2 Timothy—the focus is on role responsibility; the responsibility for prophetic truth telling, the responsibility of the individual Christian in relationship to other individuals, the responsibility of the Christian teacher. While Robert Bellah's *Habits of the Heart* has warned us all about the dangers of individualism for American social life, nevertheless the word is often addressed to individuals, with peculiar opportunities, and with specific tasks. Faith is personal as well as corporate; so is responsibility.

Children's Message

Second Timothy 1:1–14 suggests that one ought, once in a while, to talk to children about the relationship of older persons to younger persons. Forget the scholarly doubts about Paul's authorship of the pastorals. Tell the children a bit about young Timothy and how he was Paul's protégé—and the object of Paul's affection and prayers. Then tell them about one older person—not a relative—who filled for you the role that Paul filled for Timothy. Every one of us has several such persons in our lives—if we will let ourselves remember them!

Hymns for Pentecost 20

Lord, Speak to Me; God of Our Life; Faith of Our Fathers!

Pentecost 21

Ordinary Time 28
Proper 23

Psalm 26 (C)	**2 Timothy 2:8–15 (C) (E)**
	2 Timothy 2:8–13 (L) (RC)
Micah 1:2; 2:1–10 (C)	
Ruth 1:1–19a (L)	**Luke 17:11–19**
Ruth 1:8–19a (E)	
2 Kings 5:14–17 (RC)	

Meditation on the Texts

O God, whose word is truth, whose word does good to those who walk uprightly, and whose word is healing and restoration, grant us ears to hear what you, the Lord our God, will say to us. Let us not be like those who could not bear the preachments of the prophet, or those who find joy in disputing about words. Let us rather be those who are faithful hearers of your word. And above all, O God, teach us the grace of thankful hearing! Let our response to your word always be one of grateful obedience. For we pray in the name of the Word made flesh, even Jesus Christ our Lord. Amen.

Commentary on the Texts

Luke 17:11–19

There is nothing very mysterious about this passage. It is a straightforward narrative of an incident that took place as Jesus was on his way to Jerusalem. Somewhere between Galilee and Samaria he entered a village, where he was confronted with a group of ten lepers. At their pleading, Jesus healed them. But only one of them—a Samaritan—turned back to thank his healer. Jesus praised the faith of this "foreigner," as he called the man.

And so this foreigner got himself written into the Gospels, along with other notable Samaritans: The woman at the well of John 4 and the good Samaritan of the parable. This Samaritan leper also joins another select company—those to whom Jesus said, "Your faith has made you well." The others are the woman with the issue of blood (Matt. 9:20–22; Mark 5:25–34; Luke 8:43–48) and blind Bartimaeus (Mark 10:46–52; Luke 18:35–43). One might add the Canaanite woman of Matthew 15:21–28, whose daughter Jesus healed and to whom he said, "O woman, great is your faith! Be it done for you as you desire."

If nothing else, this incident reminds the preacher and interpreter that faith is more than intellectual assent. From time to time we need to go to the lectionaries and commentaries to rediscover that. Faith, as it is used in the New Testament, has elements of belief, trust, confidence, and steadfastness.

How shall one **preach** on Luke 17:11–19? If one is given to thematic sermons, there are several obvious themes: The Role of Faith in Healing; The Importance of Gratitude; The Testimony of One Not of the Faithful; Jesus' Response to Need Wherever Found. But all of those themes are more springboards than they are platforms. How can one make a sermon out of the narrative itself?

The context of the healing might be a way to begin. Jesus is on the way from Galilee (his home base, where he feels safest and most secure) to Jerusalem (the capital city, where he faces conflict and possible execution). He comes to a village where a number of lepers—outcasts from society—are clustered at the edge of town. They represent, in one sense, the marginal people to whom Jesus has ministered and among whom he has found a reception. They call out for mercy, and Jesus calls back, telling them to go and show themselves to the priest. As they obey, they find themselves cleansed of their disease.

Up to that point, the story seems a piece with the rest of the Gospel narrative, but then the story takes a strange turn. One of the ten turns back and throws himself at Jesus' feet in gratitude. Now he happens to be a Samaritan—one of those with whom the Jews had no dealings if they could help it. Jesus is taken aback: Why this one "foreigner," as Jesus calls him? Why not the other nine? In a rare moment Jesus praises the man's faith. In a faithless and hostile world—one that even then was preparing Jesus' departure from it—appears this faithful foreigner.

Given the circumstances, it is a moment of extraordinary grace. It belongs alongside Jesus' healing of the daughter of the Syrophoenician woman and his healing of the woman with the issue of blood, who fought through the crowd to touch his garment. We are not permitted to know Jesus' thoughts, but as a dramatic moment in the Gospel narrative, it would seem to have provided him with a psychological lift.

The typical **sermon** on this text picks up on Jesus' question, "Where are the nine?" And then goes on to ring the changes on ingratitude. But that is the triumph of banality over imagination. What is remarkable about nine not coming back to give thanks? The nine were like most of us, most of the time; they were so preoccupied with their own problems and health that gratitude was something at the edges of their concerns. For how many of us, even the most faithful, is our *first* thought when something good happens, I must give God the praise?

No, the nine do not deserve our attention—not even as examples of bad manners. But that one who returned to give thanks, he is someone special. He earned himself a place in the Gospel story, along with a few special others—blind Bartimaeus, the woman with the issue of blood, the Syrophoenician woman. He is a witness, a messenger of the word. Let the sermon be in his praise. Let the congregation share, with Jesus, a gracious moment. And don't belabor ingratitude as sin or turn gratitude into one more duty.

Micah 1:2; 2:1–10 (C)

The Book of Micah contains material that seems to date from the middle of the eighth century B.C.E. to the end of the sixth century B.C.E. It seems likely that the first three chapters are from Micah himself; the rest of the book may have come from others who used some of his material. One commentator compares the Book of Micah to the Book of Isaiah; he points out that Micah is Isaiah in miniature. One thing you may want to do is to **compare and contrast** the books of Micah and Isaiah. Look for clues that would place both prophets at the same time in history. It seems likely that the oracle in Micah 2 was delivered by Micah in the reign of Hezekiah, shortly before the Assyrian invasion of 701 B.C.E. Compare Micah 4:1–4 and Isaiah 2:1–4; note the remarkable similarity.

In one aspect, however, Micah is quite different from Isaiah. Micah was a man from a small town who went to the cities, particularly to Jerusalem, while Isaiah was likely a native of Jerusalem. Micah was appalled at the social developments he observed in the city. A rich and powerful establishment was using its status and power to oppress the small landowners. The property of this lower class, if it is permissible to use such a term, was being expropriated. In Israel, once a family lost its ancestral lands, it was socially uprooted and dispossessed. Land was everything. This uprooting was not the work of an organized crime syndicate but the work of pious, religious, upright men! (That is the significance of vs. 6–7; they reflect the pious outrage of those against whom Micah directed his words. These rich and reputable men can find no theological basis for accepting Micah's words as true.)

So chapter 2 is really about *land*—the land of neighbors that is coveted in violation of the Tenth Commandment, land that will be taken away from all of Israel through captivity, land that will not be restored to the rich and powerful once the time of exile is over. That final conclusion is found in v. 4, where Micah warns the rich that in a time of restoration—after the return from captivity, when the lands are reassigned to families—*their families will get none.*

Micah 1:2; 2:1–10 is addressed to three audiences: As 1:2 makes clear, all the peoples of the world are summoned to hear the doom pronounced on Israel; other nations are to learn from the judgment that God will bring to that rebellious people. Then Israel herself is called to account, both Northern and Southern kingdoms. (Both Samaria and Jerusalem are mentioned in the first chapter.) But in 2:1–10 a special class within Judah is addressed—the prosperous ruling elite, which one commentator calls "the power structure."

The oracle in 2:1–10 is a considerable challenge to the preacher. There are several enticing themes. There is the theme of social injustice, the exploitation of the weak by the strong. One can always have a good time going after social Darwinism; it is one of the idolatries of modern Americans. And one can put into the mouths of the present-day power structure the words that Micah attributed to the powerful of his day: "One should not preach of such things" (v. 6).

Given the environmental crisis of this last decade of the twentieth century, one could pick up on the concept of land and how land will be taken away from those who abuse privilege. Americans, who have always been quick to take the lands of others on what seem to be very solid grounds, are threatened with the loss of the land as a fruitful, hospitable place. That is stretching the original meaning of the biblical passage; but a sermon could be constructed that would not do violence to the text.

A **sermon** could be built upon the religious circumstances reflected in Micah 2:1–10—how the rich and powerful were simply unable to listen to what the prophet was saying to them. They thought of themselves as good and righteous and civic-minded people—the very backbone of society. Their social status was proof, to them at any rate, of their propriety. (The preacher could have some fun with the play on words of "property" and "propriety.")

If you choose this later course, then follow the lead of several commentators, who see vs. 6 and 7 as the response of the rich to Micah's preachings.

If you do choose this third course of action, then there are some modern "prophets" who could be worked into the sermon. One such is John Muir, the small-town boy from Wisconsin, who fought against powerful business and governmental interests to preserve wilderness areas in California.

Ruth 1:1–19a (L)

Ruth 1:8–19a (E)

This passage from Ruth obviously made its way into the two lectionaries because of the theme of "return." This fits nicely with the Gospel story from Luke about the one leper in ten who returned to thank Jesus and to praise God. We are told that Naomi decided to *return* to Judah after the death of her husband and sons, that she pleaded with her Moabite daughters-in-law to *return* to their mothers' homes, that at first both women said they wanted to *return* with her to her people. Finally Ruth said to her, "Entreat me not to leave you or to return from following you" (Ruth 1:16a).

It was one of the themes of prophetic preaching that Israel should return to the state of obedience and purity that marked the early days of the nation. After the people had been carried to captivity in Babylon, return took on a different meaning: There would come a time when the people would be allowed to return to the land of Israel.

There is a contemporary situation that is related to this—the Law of Return in modern Israel. Any Jew in the world is entitled to come to Israel and settle and become a citizen. One of the aims of the founding of modern Israel was to make it possible for Jews to return to their ancestral homeland.

In **preaching** on this text from Ruth, you would do better to work with the larger aspects of return than to focus on the domestic problems of Naomi and Ruth. Let the return of Naomi to Judah be a type of larger events: the return of Israel to former states of obedience, the return from exile, and so forth. Begin with the story of Naomi's return in order to make a connection with the congregation's experiences and emotions, but then move beyond that to the larger themes.

If you can manage it, let the sermon climax with the second coming of Christ as his return to claim what is his own!

2 Kings 5:14–17 (RC)

This reading can only have made its way into the lectionary as a companion piece to Luke 17:11–19—the story of the Samaritan who returned to give thanks. These four verses from 2 Kings tell how the Syrian commander Naaman returned to reward the prophet Elisha, who had healed him of his leprosy.

There are some interesting parallels between the two stories: (1) Naaman, like the Samaritan, was a foreigner. (2) Both Naaman and the Samaritan praised God for their cures.

If you choose to **preach** on this text, why not yoke it with Luke 17:11–19 and preach on the two narratives together? Let Naaman become a "type" of those foreigners, and foreign nations, that testified to the acts of God in history. Let Elisha be a "type" or forerunner of Jesus Christ. And draw on the theme of "return" (See comments on Ruth 1:1–19a above).

2 Timothy 2:8–15 (C) (E)

2 Timothy 2:8–13 (L) (RC)

The pastoral epistles seem to be chiefly concerned with two matters: (1) the refutation of false teaching; (2) the promotion of sound Christian character. Both of these concerns come to the fore in 2 Timothy 2:8–15. It is part of a larger section, 2:1–13. The author employs several role models for the faithful minister and teacher: the disciplined athlete, the diligent farmer, and the faithful worker, as well as the single-minded soldier. The author also offers his own life as a testimony; for the sake of the gospel, he is enduring imprisonment.

Mingled with exhortations to faithful teaching are references to both the content of that teaching and to those who are not trustworthy teachers. In v. 8 it is possible that we have an early confession of faith: "Remember Jesus Christ, raised from the dead, a descendant of David" (NRSV). And in vs. 11–13 it is likely that we have part of an early hymn. In other words, we have an appeal by the author to the tradition.

In v. 14 we have a reference to those who are evidently *not* being faithful to the tradition. Rather than hold to what they have received, they enjoy "wrangling over words" (NRSV). In vs. 17–18 are explicit references to Hymenaeus and Philetus and the false teaching that they are spreading around—that the resurrection of the faithful has already taken place.

This passage has the two rather choice bits of tradition: the confession of faith and the hymn (if indeed they are such). In the confession, Jesus is identified in two ways—as raised from the dead and as a descendant of David. What is translated as "descendant" in the New RSV is variously translated in other places as "seed of David," "descended from David," and "sprung from the race of David." As one commentator points out, none of the creeds make anything of this messianic reference, although it was commonly held in the apostolic church that Jesus was indeed of the lineage of David. The interpreter might want to **do some additional study** into the significance of this reference to David's line.

The **preacher** has several initial choices to make. What deserves the greatest emphasis: the *content* of early Christian teaching? the need to teach the *true word* in the face of *false* teachers? or the *model* offered by the author, the faithful teacher?

The choice that would seem to exploit the most riches in the passage is the third. The other two emphases in the passage could be worked in as subthemes. The sermon might be called "The Teacher Unashamed" or "Approved by God." It could sketch the background of the letter, describing the relationship between the mentor and his protégé. Even if the entire letter was not written by Paul, certainly vs. 8–9 are consistent with what we know of his Roman imprisonment, and vs. 11–13 are consistent with his theology.

Two of the primary tasks of the faithful teacher could be described: (1) the handing on of the received truth and (2) contesting false doctrine. A third task is revealed in the relationship between the author and Timothy—that of finding, teaching, and encouraging new teachers!

Theological Reflection

A dominant theme in most of the passages is that of *return,* understood as an act of turning back, of not at once going on to something new—however enticing. What Micah hoped for was a return to the covenantal obedience of earlier years. He was not so much trying to turn back social development (''progress'') as to warn against progress at the cost of justice. Naomi wanted to return to Judah for economic reasons; she needed to go back home to be cared for. Naaman turned back from going home first to show appreciation for his healing. The man healed of leprosy did pretty much the same. And the author of 2 Timothy would at least turn the attention of his protégé to the fundamentals, the basics, the beginnings.

Turning back does not always mean turning back the clock. The Protestant Reformation, which set off tumultuous changes in the history of Western Europe, started out as an effort to get back to the Bible. There was Lot's wife, who turned back and was turned to a pillar of salt. But there is evidently a way of turning back, of returning to the true praise of God, that is vivifying and revitalizing. Ah, but which is which?

Children's Message

There is no question about what to talk about this Sunday: Jesus as descended from David! Tie together the story of Ruth (who was David's great-grandmother) with the reminder in 2 Timothy that Jesus was descended from David. See how many of the children have great-grandmothers who are still living. Go on from there to sketch in the story of Ruth, who is a reminder of Israel's greatest ruler, and finish off with a reminder that Jesus was descended from David.

Hymns for Pentecost 21

Turn Back, O Man; Christ Is Made the Sure Foundation; O Praise the Gracious Power.

Ordinary Time 29

Proper 24

Psalm 119:137–144 (C)

2 Timothy 3:14–4:5 (C) (L) (E)
2 Timothy 3:14–4:2 (RC)

Habakkuk 1:1–3; 2:1–4 (C)
Genesis 32:22–30 (L)   **Luke 18:1–8 (C) (RC)**
Genesis 32:3–8, 22–30 (E)   **Luke 18:1–8a (L) (E)**
Exodus 17:8–13 (RC)

Meditation on the Texts

O God, to whom a thousand years are but a day, we confess that our times hang heavy on us. We are impatient for the heavenly vision to be fulfilled, for the poor and needy to be vindicated, for all things to be put right, and for our work to be finished and our wrestling done! Grant us, O most gracious God, some measure of your own divine patience! Give us courage to be persistent in prayer, constant in faith, diligent in teaching, and hopeful in all our actions. You have given us the example of the patriarchs, the prophets, and apostles, as those who stayed the course and fought the good fight. Help us to follow in their example and not to grow weary with waiting and well-doing. For our prayer is in the name of our faithful Lord and Savior, Jesus Christ. Amen.

Commentary on the Texts

Luke 18:1–8 (C) (RC)

Luke 18:1–8a (L) (E)

The variations in the readings from several commentaries point to the editorial hand of the Gospel writer. The actual parable of the unrighteous judge is in Luke 18:2–5. The first verse discloses the thrust of the parable. Verses 6–8a are Jesus' commentary on the parable. Verse 8b is an isolated saying, added to give another point of view.

The ostensible reason for the telling of the parable is given in v. 1: The disciples (and after the disciples, the church) need to be encouraged to continual prayer. Even though God can be trusted to hold to the divine purpose to work justice and mercy, nevertheless the faithful are to continue to pray for the coming of the kingdom.

This is one of those "how much more" parables. If an unrighteous judge will grant justice to a widow because she is relentless in pestering him, how much more will God vindicate the cause of the poor and needy. Therefore the faithful are to be constant in prayer.

Apparently Jesus saw no contradiction between the notion that God would bring in the kingdom and the notion that the faithful ought to be ceaseless in their prayers for that kingdom. Biblical religion does not play off God's providence against human initiative, nor God's purposes against human striving and yearning. If one reads the Psalms—the prayer book of scripture—one discovers that the appeal throughout is to God's steadfast love. In other words, it is because God can be trusted to hold to promises and purposes that God's elect persist in appealing to that God for help.

The appeal of the parable, therefore, is straightforward: The people of God are to be constant in prayer, ceaselessly pleading for justice and vindication of the poor and needy. In the proposed Brief Statement of Faith of the Presbyterian Church (U.S.A.) is the affirmation: "We trust in God the Holy Spirit. . . . The Spirit gives us courage to pray without ceasing . . . and to work with others for justice, freedom, and peace."

Jesus assured the disciples that God would not delay unnecessarily, but would bring a speedy vindication. If the kingdom does not come as quickly as the faithful would wish, it is not because God is sluggish or slow or indifferent. Prayer is to continue, no matter what.

Before you attempt a sermon on Luke 18:1–8, **compare and contrast** the parable of the unrighteous judge with several other parables in which the central characters are less than admirable, such as the parable of the unjust steward in Luke 16:1–13 and the parable of the prodigal son in Luke 15:11–32. There Jesus uses the rhetorical device of "how much more . . ." to good advantage. For example, if the father in the parable will receive back his wayward son, how much more will a merciful God receive those who repent and turn to him.

If you decide to **preach** on Luke 18:1–8, "Prayer and Perseverance" or "Persistence in Prayer" would seem likely topics. The preacher may elect to preach on the parable only, or to add, as did Luke, Jesus' elaborative comments. It might be possible to work v. 8b into such a sermon, although it introduces another element that would seem a bit distracting. Remember the thrust of the parable: If an unprincipled judge can be driven by sheer persistence to vindicate a widow, *how much more* can God be trusted to bring the kingdom of justice. Therefore, let us be as persistent as the widow in our prayers.

Let that contrast and comparison carry the freight for the sermon. Don't attempt a rationale for praying for what God has already promised to do. Remind the hearers that in the Lord's Prayer we acknowledge both the coming of God's kingdom and our own need for daily bread! We do not pray ceaselessly for the vindication of the poor and needy because we have been persuaded by reason and common sense; we pray because God is just and because Jesus bids us so to pray!

Habakkuk 1:1–3; 2:1–4 (C)

See Pentecost 20, (L).

Genesis 32:22–30 (L)

Genesis 32:3–8, 22–30 (E)

The story of Jacob's wrestling with "a man" at the River Jabbok is as dense and difficult as any passage in scripture. Some early Jewish commentators suggest that this is another one of Jacob's dreams. Everyone agrees that it is a most mysterious story.

As one commentator observes, the narrative picks up the theme that is central to the Jacob-Esau stories, that of the blessing. Jacob is aggressive in his search for the blessing; God seems determined that Jacob—not Esau—shall have it. And both of those aspects of the blessing story come to the fore in the account of the night of wrestling.

With whom does Jacob wrestle on that murky night by the river? The Bible says simply "a man" (v. 24), but in Hosea it is said that Jacob "strove with the angel and prevailed" (Hos. 12:4).

Be that as it may, what is the story about? One interpreter offers us two choices: (1) The story is about how Jacob became a new man; he is no longer "The Deceiver," but is now "Israel." (2) God likes an aggressive partner; Jacob is given a new name as a sign of Yahweh's respect for persistence and courage.

Those who choose to **preach** on this passage will have to decide first of all what it is about. Is it about the struggle of two tribes—Edom (Esau) and Israel (Jacob)—for dominance? Is it about Jacob's "conversion" to a more mature manhood? Is it about God's demand for persistence and aggressiveness in covenant partners?

Read at least two commentaries on the story of Jacob at the Jabbok. Consider the evidence for the several views. Decide which you will accept.

One ought to give some credit to those who placed this narrative in conjunction with the parable of the unrighteous judge in Luke 18 and Paul's charge to Timothy to continue in faithful teaching, despite opposition. When the story is seen in that context, then the persistent, aggressive behavior of Jacob comes to the fore. The other themes may be mentioned in the sermon, but the emphasis falls on the long night of wrestling and Jacob's refusal to give up without getting something out of the struggle.

One has to suppose that this passage was chosen for this Sunday because it fits in with the themes of persistence and continuance, which are prominent in the Gospel and the epistle passages.

The context is the wilderness wandering of the people of Israel, between the Exodus from Egypt and the entrance into the Promised Land. The occasion is a skirmish with a tribesman named Amalek and his people. The Israelites prevail because of Moses' rod: When it is held high, the warriors of Israel—under the command of Joshua—prevail; when it is lowered, Amalek and his warriors prevail. With the help of Aaron and Hur, Moses holds the rod high until the enemy is vanquished.

This is the same rod that Moses was clutching when God appeared in the burning bush and called him to be the liberator of his people. When Moses protested that he was not up to the task, one of the things that Yahweh did was to command him to throw down his shepherd's staff. It was turned into a snake. This is the same rod with which Moses struck the Nile and turned it into a river of blood. With it he also struck the rock at Rephidim and brought forth water for the people. The rod is the continuing symbol of Yahweh's presence with Israel and Yahweh's willingness to intervene on Israel's behalf.

Before you begin sermon preparation on this narrative, look at some of those other incidents in which Moses' rod plays such a prominent part.

Those who elect to **preach** from this narrative have two rhetorical problems: How to keep the attention of the faithful from becoming fixed on holy warfare, and how to keep their attention from becoming fixed on Moses' wonderful rod! What both the warfare and the rod signify is the abiding presence of God with God's people. That is the message that ought to come through in the sermon. One might do well to establish that theme through the use of the Exodus narrative and then cite such New Testament passages as the parable of the unrighteous judge from Luke 18:1–8 and Paul's charge to Timothy in 2 Timothy 3:14–4:5, both of which have to do with the perseverance of the saints. The message of all of these passages is pretty much the same: Do not lose heart, but keep up the fight; God will not fail you, God will vindicate God's people.

2 Timothy 3:14–4:5 (C) (L) (E)

2 Timothy 3:14–4:2 (RC)

Although this passage contains a well-known statement about the inspiration of scripture, that is not its main theme. The passage is part of a larger section, 3:10–4:8, which is a charge from the writer to Timothy, his younger colleague in ministry. In urging Timothy to stick to the tradition he has received from his forebears and his mentor, the author includes scripture as that upon which he may rely in his teaching. But it does the passage a disservice to turn it into a debate about the authority of the Bible. The central themes are faithfulness to the tradition and persistence in the face of difficulty. The Christian preacher/teacher/evangelist is to hang tough in the face of opposition and suffering.

As the author warns Timothy, people have a tendency to drift away from sound teaching. *They find it boring.* They have "itching ears," meaning that they prefer teaching that is novel, that tickles their fancies, that entertains them. So while there is any opening to sound teaching, Timothy is not to waste that opportunity!

Anyone who has the remotest connections with the Old School/New School, Old Light/New Light, Fundamentalist/Modernist controversies in the church will feel himself or herself on familiar ground. In major controversies in the church, each side charges the other with failure to appreciate the tradition. Some will claim that the tradition must be preserved and handed on exactly as received, and that any attempt to alter it or translate it is accommodation to itching ears, that is, selling out to the desire to entertain and please people. Others will argue that they are carrying on the spirit of the tradition, while their opponents are stuck with the dead letter.

What ought to interest the expositor about this passage, however, is not so much the echo of ecclesiastical warfare as the penetrating insight of the author: "For the time is coming when people will not put up with sound doctrine, but having itching ears, they will accumulate for themselves teachers to suit their own desires'' (v. 3, NRSV). What a wonderfully accurate description of people as we know them in our culture! Neil Postman has written a book about them, *Amusing Ourselves to Death.* The book is about the impact of television on our culture; the point Postman makes is that television has greatly affected the way we learn. We expect learning to be entertaining. If it is not, we switch channels. We are folks with itching ears, for whom novelty is a right and a privilege.

You would do well to **dip into Postman's book** before you write a sermon on 2 Timothy 3:14–4:5. It will give you some new ideas; it will furnish you with some illustrative materials.

A **sermon** on this passage might well be entitled ''The Good News and the Evening News.'' Without getting into television bashing, the preacher can compare and contrast the task and the message of the Christian teacher with that of the network anchorman or anchorwoman. If the newscaster wants to hold his or her audience, he or she must give the news in snippets; it must contain elements of novelty and suspense; and the newscaster must not assume any great familiarity of hearers with history, sociology, science, or current events.

Contrast those assumptions with the charge given the Christian teacher-preacher by the author of 2 Timothy. Feed them with the tradition; rely on scripture; rebuke them if you must; persist even when no one seems to want to listen to you.

What is the *point* of such a sermon? Is it merely cultural commentary? No. Sound teaching is done ''in the presence of God and of Christ Jesus who is to judge the living and the dead, who is to appear and make manifest the kingdom'' (4:1). What does not and cannot appear on the television screen is the God who is revealed in Christ Jesus, the unseen Lord and Judge of all!

Theological Reflection

Time is a problem for the believer. Why does it seem that God delays the bringing of the kingdom? Why is the prophetic vision not immediately realized? Why are there the long nights of wrestling and doubt and fear? A recurring phrase in the psalms is ''How long, O Lord, how long?'' Sometimes the question is intensely personal: Why is my life prolonged when I yearn for rest and peace? Or, Why did my child die when she had lived so few years? Sometimes the question has a larger compass: Why do my people suffer oppression year after year? And the scriptural response seems to be: Persevere. Persevere in prayer, in struggle, in faithful teaching. Do not sit and wonder about the divine calendar or clock! Rather reread the lectionary passages with the call to persevere ringing in your ears.

Children's Message

Tell the parable of the unrighteous judge. Children will be taken with the image of the woman going every day to hammer on the judge's door or to shout outside his window. The story has a bit of the same lesson as ''The Little Engine Who Could,'' but that's OK. Be sure that the children understand that the story is about prayer, not about just any endeavor. (That would reduce the parable to a morality tale.)

Hymns for Pentecost 22

Through the Night of Doubt and Sorrow; If Thou But Suffer God to Guide Thee; Standing on the Promises.

Ordinary Time 30
Proper 25

Psalm 3 (C)   2 Timothy 4:6–8, 16–18

Zephaniah 3:1–9 (C)   Luke 18:9–14
Deuteronomy 10:12–22 (L)
Sirach 35:12b–14, 16–17 (RC)
Jeremiah 14:7–10, 19–22 (E)

Meditation on the Texts

O Holy One of Israel, in your presence we can only hang our heads and confess our sins and plead for mercy. Hear our prayers for forgiveness, O Lord, even as you most graciously hear the cries of the fatherless and the complaints of the oppressed, for we have been complicit in oppression and injustice. We have supported and profited from a system that grinds the faces of the poor and crushes the weak and helpless. And we have seen other nations destroyed because they would not seek justice—and we have secretly rejoiced in their misfortune and have not learned from what has befallen them! Teach us the ways of justice and peace, that by our example others may learn to do justly and to walk humbly with you. In Jesus' name we pray. Amen.

Commentary on the Texts

Luke 18:9–14

As one commentator points out, this passage makes a fitting finale to Luke's account of Jesus' discourse on the final journey to Jerusalem, for it sounds an important Lukan theme: God's mercy on sinners and other marginal people. The passage ends with a statement that occurs several times in the Gospels: "All who exalt themselves will be humbled, but all who humble themselves will be exalted" (v. 14b, NRSV). It was evidently one of Jesus' prominent teachings. It occurs also in connection with the parable of the wedding feast in Luke 14:7–14. It occurs in Matthew in the context of Jesus' denouncing the Pharisees and the scribes (Matthew 23:12). Note that all three of these occurrences involve the Pharisees. A similar statement is the one that occurs in Matthew 20:26–27, "Whoever would be great among you must be your servant, and whoever would be first among you must be your slave."

The saying is dialectical: Those who seek to elevate themselves will be brought low; those who abase themselves will be raised up!

The form critics see Luke 18:14b as a wisdom saying of Jesus that was originally independent, but was joined to the parable by Luke. Since the teaching of the parable does not depend on the saying, the interpreter can simply be grateful for the Gospel writer's perspecuity. The saying underscores what the parable clearly teaches: If one wants to "get right with God," the way of humble confession is more promising than the aggressive pursuit of obedience to the law. The tax collector in the parable got what the Pharisee clearly wanted: uprightness in God's eyes!

Again, note the dialectical structure of the parable, which neatly matches the dialectic of v. 14b. The Pharisee went to the temple in pursuit of righteousness (uprightness); he went away still a sinner. The tax collector went to confess his sin; he came away justified.

Compare this parable to the parable of the prodigal son. The elder son who stays home and tries to please the father never gets a party, but the younger son who flouts the father's love is feasted and feted.

Before you begin to write your sermon, **look up** Pharisees and tax collector in your Bible dictionary. Refresh your memory of these persons in Judaic society.

Preaching on the parable of the Pharisee and the tax collector is tricky. How can you present the parable without inviting the hearers to identify themselves with one of the persons in the narrative? If that happens, it is a lose-lose situation for the hearer. If he or she identifies with the Pharisee, by what psychic trick can all good deeds and striving be turned into sins like those of a typical tax collector? And if he or she identifies with the tax collector, how can that be anything but an occasion for self-congratulation—since Jesus clearly gives the nod to the tax collector as more likely to stand well with God?

So however you craft the sermon, stay away from the temptation to describe two types or classes of persons—those like the Pharisee, those like the penitent tax collector. That will inevitably lead to attempts on the part of hearers to compare themselves with others, and that leads in turn to the error of the Pharisee—comparing himself to one obviously less well-intentioned and decent and law-abiding than himself!

It is better to use the two characters in the parable as two tendencies present in each of us. (Which seems to be what Jesus had in mind in telling the parable.) There is within every person, however dim, an urge to uprightness, a desire to "get right with God," to have divine approval. In Jesus' parable both men went to the temple to pray. Presumably both were concerned with their standing with the Almighty.

However, there is in every person, strong or weak, a tendency to position himself or herself in relation to others—to seek out those with whom one can favorably compare himself or herself. If one can see one's self as better than another, that just might translate into being good. That leads to the situation to which Jesus addressed the parable. He told it to those who considered themselves righteous and despised others.

So the urge or inclination to be right with God can never find success by positioning oneselves in relation to others. The way of righteousness is the way of humble confession. "The sacrifice acceptable to God is a broken spirit; a broken and contrite heart, O God, thou wilt not despise" (Ps. 51:17).

The sermon might begin with the following invitation to go on a spiritual pilgrimage: Would you enter the City of the Righteous? Then let me tell you what will befall you on the way and how you will enter. You will be brought low; you will be driven to your knees; and only on your knees will you enter. This is what every spiritual pilgrim discovers.

Zephaniah 3:1–9 (C)

Zephaniah was a prophet in Judah during the reign of Josiah, before the reforms of 621 B.C.E. His was a time of social change and international upheaval; there was a threat from some unnamed peril from the north. Among some of the people in Judah there was optimism about the future: The day of Yahweh might be at hand, bringing peace and prosperity. Zephaniah's message is that the coming day of Yahweh will be catastrophic, not only for Israel but for all the nations. The day will bring salvation to a purified and humbled remnant, the peoples with "a pure speech" referred to in v. 9.

The Book of Zephaniah consists of several brief sections. One such is 3:1–7; it contains oracles against the city of Jerusalem. (Verses 8–9 seem to belong to a group of oracles about the remnant.)

One preaching value of the passage is its emphasis on social righteousness. The city of Jerusalem is condemned because of the oppressive actions of its ruling elite—the officials, the judges, the prophets, the priests. Nor do the people of the city escape judgment; they do not read in the destruction of neighboring kingdoms any lesson for themselves. They are "all the more . . . eager" in their misdeeds (v. 7). The wrath of Yahweh will descend upon whole nations and kingdoms. There will be, however, a saved and purified remnant, which is characterized in social terms; it will be a people having "a pure speech" and serving Yahweh "with one accord" (v. 9).

The point of contact with contemporary audiences may well be the indifference of the inhabitants of Jerusalem to the destruction of other nations. The Judeans read no warning in those affairs; they went right on with their disobedient ways. The officials, judges, prophets, and priests continued in their lawless paths; they were confident, one assumes, that Yahweh was preparing a better future for them.

History is full of examples of peoples and nations who fiddled and danced while the cities of other nations were in flames. Surely the resourceful **preacher** can find a few examples to display to the congregation.

A message based on Zephaniah 3:1–9 should not, however, be one of wrath and doom and hopelessness. Neither optimism nor pessimism is a choice for biblical faith. However, the message can and should be one of solemn *warning*—warning that God demands social justice and means to have it!

Deuteronomy 10:12–22 (L)

This passage is part of the second discourse of Moses, which begins with the Decalogue (Deut. 5:6–21). It follows the narration of how Moses was on the mountain forty days and forty nights and received the stone tablets and also the directions for building an ark to contain them. The "and now" in v. 12 introduces the inferences that follow from the events just related: Here is the appropriate response for the people of Israel. They are to be obedient to the Lord their God.

The knowledge and service of God are two sides of one coin. They are to be people with a "circumcised heart," that is, a willing and receptive heart for all that God has commanded. Circumcision was the sign of membership in God's chosen people; the notion of a circumcised heart points to the purpose of God's election—that God's people should do God's will and keep God's commandments.

Deuteronomy 10:12–13 is one of those great summary passages of scripture. Compare it to Micah 6:8a: "And what does the LORD require of you but to do justice, and to love kindness, and to walk humbly with your God?" And compare also Luke 10:25–28, where Jesus approves this summary of the law: "You shall love the Lord your God with all your heart, and with all your soul, and with all your strength, and with all your mind; and your neighbor as yourself" (v. 27).

Set down Deuteronomy 10:12–13, Micah 6:8a, and Luke 10:25–28 **in three columns**. Ask yourself: How does each passage by itself express God's intention for humanity? How do the three taken together express God's intention? See if you can write a statement of God's will that is a harmony of all three.

In preparing a **sermon** on this text, take advantage of the familiarity many people have with the summary statement from Micah and the one Jesus approved. People like to have things put in summary fashion, for example, "The Law of God in a Nutshell." Compare and contrast for them the summary statements from Micah and Luke with Deuteronomy 10:12–13. Also, take advantage of the specifics of the Deuteronomy passage, in which the mercy of God for the fatherless, the widow, and the sojourner is honored. To love God with heart, mind, and soul (to know God) is never separable from loving the neighbor in his or her concrete necessity (the widow, the fatherless, the stranger in need of food and clothing).

Sirach 35:12b–14, 16–17 (RC)

The book variously known as Sirach, The Wisdom of Ben Sira, and Ecclesiasticus belongs to the genre of wisdom literature. It was written in the opening years of the second century B.C.E., when Palestine had come under the rule of the Seleucids. The imitation of things Greek was a powerful force, particularly among the ruling elites, and against this modernization the author of Sirach sought to bring the force of the tradition.

Several versions and translations offer quite varied readings of vs. 12–17. Here is the translation by Patrick W. Skehan in the Anchor Bible:

> Give to the most High as he has given to you,
>   generously, according to your means.
> For he is God who always repays
>   and he will give you back seven times over.

> But offer no bribes; these he does not accept.
> Trust not in sacrifice of the fruits of extortion.
> For he is a God of justice
> who knows no favorites.
> He does not take sides against the weak,
>   but he hears the grievances of the oppressed;
> He does not reject the cry of the orphan,
> nor the widow when she pours out her complaint.*

The passage would seem to be addressed to the affluent of society, for it begins with an exhortation to generous giving to the temple. Ben Sira warns against exploiting the powerless, for whom God has a special concern. God is not like a corrupt judge, who can be bribed, the author says. Money is not to be offered as a sacrifice that has been squeezed out of widows and orphans.

An apt title for a **sermon** based on this passage would be ''God Cannot Be Bribed.'' At first the notion that God is susceptible to bribery seems ludicrous. Who would be so foolish as to suppose that? Begin the sermon with that disclaimer. Then follow the lead of Ben Sira, who pictures God as a judge, vindicating the cause of the weak and helpless—orphans and widows. Are those who make money from the oppression of such as these to buy off God with generous gifts to the temple? In effect, that is offering God a bribe—as though God were a corrupt judge, who could be bought off with money. In other words, generous giving is no substitute for just dealings.

Jeremiah 14:7–10, 19–22 (E)

Remember the historical situation of Jeremiah: The reforms under Josiah had not been enough to save Judah from becoming a vassal state of the Babylonians. Twice the armies of Nebuchadnezzar moved against Judah to quell rebellion. The second invasion ended in the deportation of many to Babylon and the destruction of Jerusalem (586 B.C.E.).

Jeremiah 14:7–9, 19–22 is an anguished prayer to Yahweh in which the prophet identifies himself with his people. The prayer is notable for its similes:

> Why shouldst thou be like a stranger in the land . . . ?
> Why shouldst thou be like a man confused,
>   like a mighty man who cannot save?
>
>   (Vs. 8a, 9)

These reveal the deep spiritual anguish of the prophet, as he contemplates the sins of his people and the evils that have befallen them. They amplify his complaint, ''We looked for peace, but no good came; for a time of healing, but behold, terror'' (v. 19b).

We think of the Psalms as the prayer book of the Bible. But in the Book of Jeremiah are a number of prayers, of which this is one. **Compare and contrast** this prayer with Psalms 23 and 88. Reflect on the wide range of spiritual confidence and spiritual confusion that the prayers of the faithful display.

In **preaching** from Jeremiah 14:7–10, 19–22, raise the question: What shall the faithful do when God's face seems turned away? (In reflecting on the meaning of the Holocaust, some modern Jews have concluded that for a time God turned away God's face from the Jews.) What are the faithful to do when God acts like a stranger in the land, like one confused, like a helpless giant?

The appeal of Jeremiah is to God's name, God's covenant, God's honor. How are these to be signs of hope and promise to us today?

2 Timothy 4:6–8, 16–18

This is one of those passages in the pastoral epistles that most certainly came from Paul himself. It seems to fit exactly with what we know of the apostle—that he ended his

---

The Wisdom of Ben Sira, New Translation and Notes by Patrick W. Skehan, Introduction and Commentary by Alexander A. DiLella. From the Anchor Bible (New York: Doubleday, 1987).

days in Rome, imprisoned, possibly executed. The mood in these verses is one of resignation. The end of Paul's life is near; he is ready for death.

Evidently he has successfully withstood some of the proceedings against him. At the preliminary hearing, "my first defense," he had no Christian to stand as his advocate; he had to face the imperial court alone. Somehow he impressed the court enough that the trial was delayed, "I was rescued from the lion's mouth." So he is confident that he can endure whatever lies ahead.

He has the satisfaction of knowing that his work as Christ's apostle is finished. Note the varied metaphors: the soldier ("I have fought the good fight"), the athlete ("I have finished the race"), the true believer ("I have kept the faith").

Make a study of the various metaphors Paul uses for his ministry: athlete, farmer, soldier, for example. Compare and contrast those with the metaphor that dominates *our* concept of ministry—shepherd (pastor). What can we learn from Paul?

Compare and contrast these statements from Paul, the ex-Pharisee, with the words that Jesus put into the mouth of the Pharisee in his parable in Luke 18:9–14: That Pharisee said, "God, I thank thee that I am not like other men, extortioners, unjust, adulterers, or even like this tax collector. I fast twice a week, I give tithes of all that I get" (vs. 11–12). Paul's statements about himself have nothing of the self-congratulatory tone of the fictional Pharisee. The issue with Paul is not self-justification, but grateful obedience to the One who has justified him through grace.

If you choose to **preach** on this passage rather than Luke 18:9–14, why not build the sermon around a comparison and contrast between Paul, the ex-Pharisee, and the fictional Pharisee of Jesus' parable? None of us wants to go through life beating our breasts and bewailing our sins, however much we recognize what Jesus was teaching in the parable about humility. Because we love Jesus Christ, we want to receive from him *our* crown. We want to be good Christian soldiers, disciplined Christian athletes, keepers of the tradition. And we do not want to be accused of trying to justify ourselves in the process of seeking to be obedient! See if you can draw a distinction between what Paul is saying about his life and what Jesus condemned in his Pharisee.

If you have no prejudices against the soldier metaphor, you may want to use in your sermon the concluding stanza of Vachel Lindsay's poem "General William Booth Enters Into Heaven." It reads like this:

> And when Booth halted by the curb for prayer
> He saw his Master thro' the flag-filled air.
> Christ came gently with a robe and crown
> For Booth the soldier, while the throng knelt down.
> He saw King Jesus. They were face to face,
> And he knelt a-weeping in that holy place.
> Are you washed in the blood of the Lamb?*

Theological Reflection

It is some procession that passes through our imaginations with the various readings for this Sunday: Moses, Jeremiah, Zephaniah, Ben Sira, Jesus of Nazareth, Paul, Timothy. Quite a lineup of faithful witnesses! Those of us who teach and preach are more than a little humble to know that we are part of that procession. Still the tradition is carried forward, still the message is taught and proclaimed, still the word is declared! Not because we, in some kind of exalted wisdom, have read the mind of God, but because God has spoken the word to us in Jesus Christ.

Children's Message

Go with Paul's metaphor of the life of obedience as a race to be run. Tell how the apostle, near the end of his life, in prison for his public witness to Jesus, is reflecting on what he has accomplished. Paul says, "I have finished the race." He does not say, "I

---

*From *Collected Poems* of Vachel Lindsay (New York: Macmillan, 1925).

have won''; he says only, ''I have finished.'' That is something every child can understand; that is something every child can do—keep on keeping on! There is courage in perseverance.

Hymns for Pentecost 23

For All the Saints; God Is Here!; Stand Up, Stand Up for Jesus.

Ordinary Time 31

Proper 26

Psalm 65:1–8 (C)	**2 Thessalonians 1:5–12 (C)**
	2 Thessalonians 1:1–5, 11–12 (L) (E)
Haggai 2:1–9 (C)	**2 Thessalonians 1:11–2:2 (RC)**
Exodus 34:5–9 (L)	
Wisdom 11:22–12:2 (RC)	**Luke 19:1–10**
Isaiah 1:10–20 (E)	

Meditation on the Texts

O God, you are kind and tender of heart, your mercy extends to the vilest of offenders, but you above all are faithful and steadfast in love for your people. We praise you for your steadfast love, which endures through all time and generations—through exile and return, through sin and repentance, through occupation and liberation, through times of building and times of destruction, through times of wandering and times of homecoming. There is none like you in heaven or on earth. And therefore with prophets and apostles we praise and thank you, with Moses and Isaiah, Haggai and the writer of Wisdom, Paul and Silvanus and Timothy—with all who have been steadfast in their faith and love. Grant us in our generation to make a good confession, to build wisely, to suffer affliction with patience and hope, and to be as merciful to others as you have been to us. For we pray in the name and for the sake of Jesus Christ our Savior. Amen.

Commentary on the Texts

Luke 19:1–10

This is one of those texts with which familiarity breeds contentment. The interpreter is inclined to gloss over the details of the passage, certain that he or she knows enough already to go at once to the task of crafting a sermon. But it is just our familiarity with the story of Zacchaeus that ought to make us pause and work through the details of the narrative once more before going to the sermon.

The setting of the story is what we have encountered in the previous passages from Luke: Jesus is on his way to Jerusalem for his passion. He passes through Jericho. His reputation—or the crowd—attracts the attention of Zacchaeus, a chief tax collector. Zacchaeus is not like the tax collector encountered in the parable of the Pharisee and the tax collector. He is a chief tax collector, one who successfully bid for the right to collect taxes for the Romans in an area. He then farmed out the work to employees, the more familiar tax collectors.

Zacchaeus' curiosity leads him to risk being ridiculed—he climbs a tree to get a look at Jesus. That brings him to Jesus' attention, and Jesus invites himself to Zacchaeus' house for a meal, although the onlookers murmur at Jesus' consorting with a man whom many would regard as an extortioner and traitor. Zacchaeus is so overjoyed at the presence of Jesus in his home that he repents of his ways and makes a lavish gesture. Although there was a limit on giving to prevent the abuse of charity—a fifth of one's wealth—Zacchaeus offers one half of his estate to the poor. Although an additional 20 percent was required in the restoration of money fraudulently taken, he offers 400 percent repayment to any he has defrauded.

No wonder Jesus pronounces salvation, not only on Zacchaeus but on his whole household! This is not as a reward for Zacchaeus' acts of penance, but because

Zacchaeus "also is a descendant of Abraham" (v. 9, TEV). God's grace is extended even to this man. Then the meaning of the event is plainly stated: "The Son of man came to seek and to save the lost" (v. 10).

The story illustrates a familiar Lukan theme: God's love for the sinner, the outcast, the marginalized, the lost. It is a companion piece to the parables of the lost sheep, the lost coin, the prodigal son, the Pharisee and the tax collector. In the mind of church people, the narrative has acquired the status of a parable. Zacchaeus—the little man who climbed the tree—has become a favorite character in church school stories, along with the prodigal son, the Good Samaritan, the woman who lost a coin, the shepherds who came to the stable, and the Three Wise Men.

Therefore the first task in **preaching** from this passage is somehow to demythologize the story, to diminish the role of Zacchaeus and to enlarge the role of God.

Somehow the scandalous features of the story need to be brought home. Zacchaeus was a *bad* man. By his own admission, he was one of those "extortioners" whom the Pharisee in Luke 18:9–14 ranked with adulterers. In the time of the Nazi occupation of Norway, the name Quisling came to be hated and feated; it was the surname of a man who had collaborated with the Nazis. The name was then applied to others who did the same. Zacchaeus was a quisling, who found a way to profit from the Roman occupation of Palestine. **Look up** tax collector in your Bible dictionary and concordance for more information about such persons.

Zacchaeus was possibly like one of the characters that Danny DeVito plays to such perfection in movies like *Romancing the Stone, Twins,* and *Ruthless People*: a small, furtive man, as immoral as an alley rat, who thinks altruism and honesty are for suckers.

If you want to find a contemporary occupation to demonstrate the kind of person Zacchaeus was, a drug dealer might serve the purpose—not the kind of person who hustles drugs on the street—but the one who hires others to do the pushing.

Does God love drug dealers? Are they also "descendants of Abraham," the object of God's redemptive activity in the world? The scandal of Jesus' going to have a meal with one such as Zacchaeus would seem to point to the scandalous message of the gospel: God seeks to save the "lost." It is the message of the Good Shepherd all over again. There is more rejoicing in heaven over the rescue of one "lost soul" than over ninety-nine who have not wandered far from the truth.

Haggai 2:1–9 (C)

Few passages in scripture can be dated as precisely as this one. It is an oracle delivered by the prophet Haggai to the leaders of Judah on or about October 17 in the year 520 B.C.E. Late in the summer of that year, with the encouragement of Haggai, the rebuilding of the temple had begun. Within a month of the beginning, the work had lagged, so Haggai was at the Jews again, encouraging their work and promising that it would be successful.

Haggai offers two inducements: (1) He promises that the latter glory of the temple will be greater than the first. (2) He sees the present shake-up in world affairs (rebellions during the early reign of the Persian monarch Darius) as omens of a day when all the nations will come to Jerusalem and acknowledge God's sovereignty. A messianic role is thus assigned to the temple. The "remnant" of which Haggai speaks in v. 2 are those who have survived not only the Babylonian exile but also the time of restoration. Some are evidently old enough to remember the glory of the former temple, in the time before the destruction of Jerusalem and the deportation of 586 B.C.E.

The interpreter needs to refresh his or her memory with the events of the sixth century B.C.E., and most especially with the rise of the Persian Empire under Cyrus, Artaxerxes, and Darius.

A **sermon** on this passage might well have for its theme "Encouragement in Kingdom Building." The church is not asked by God to build or rebuild the temple, but to work for the restoration of God's rightful dominion over the created order. Following the lead of Haggai, base encouragement on a correct apprehension of past, present, and future.

Bring to the attention of hearers that Haggai, in his message of encouragement, drew upon memory, awareness, and hope. He called the remnant to remember the former glory of the temple and also God's covenant promise. He urged them to be aware of the presence of God's Spirit with them. He painted a hopeful, almost fabulous picture of the future, of a time when the wealth of nations would flow to Jerusalem and the temple would be full of the glory of God.

Appeal to memories of God's past covenant faithfulness, to awareness of the presence of God's Spirit with the church, and to our hopes for the fullness of Christ's kingdom.

We Christians, like the remnant of the faithful in Judah, are being called by God to build in times of considerable international upheaval and unrest. The great temptation is to sit on our hands, to hedge our bets, to husband our energy and strength. If the prophet is to be believed, that is not what God wills. Now is the time to build, to restore, to glorify God through daily work and effort.

Exodus 34:5–9 (L)

The scene is Mt. Sinai; the occasion is the second inscription on tablets of stone of the Ten Commandments. The Lord shows to Moses the divine attributes: kindness, forgiveness, tenderness, but most especially "steadfast love and faithfulness." Moses is warned that while Yahweh is forgiving, iniquity will be requited unto the third and fourth generation! There will be no blinking at sin. Moses pleads for Yahweh's continued presence with Israel and for Yahweh's pardon.

A **sermon** on this passage might remind hearers that it is a terrible thing to fall into the hands of the living God. God's holiness is by no means compromised by the divine mercy. Despite God's declared intention to be gracious and kind to Israel, sin continues to have consequences.

Wisdom 11:22–12:2 (RC)

The introduction to the Book of Wisdom in the *Jerusalem Bible* reminds us that the author was probably a devout Jew, living in Alexandria, in the first century B.C.E. He is writing for Jews who may be fascinated with Hellenistic culture and drawn away from the worship and service of Yahweh. There are three sections: chapters 1–5, which define wisdom and contrast the destiny of the good and the bad; chapters 6–9, which deal with the origin and nature of wisdom; and chapters 10–19, which celebrate the part played by God and Wisdom in the history of Israel.

Our lectionary passage is drawn from this third section. It is preceded by a passage that describes the forbearance of God with the Egyptians. In the reading for our consideration, this forbearance is explained: God, who is all-powerful, loves everything that had been made. God is more interested in correcting those who offend than in destroying them.

Surely this passage was chosen to be read in tandem with the Lukan story of Jesus and Zacchaeus because it praises the forbearance of God and God's willingness to correct and forgive.

The sermon ought to remind the hearers of the forbearance that God has shown in history, with the Egyptians as the prime example. As the writer of Wisdom says, "Who can withstand the might of your arm? In your sight the whole world is like a grain of dust that tips the scales, like a drop of morning dew falling on the ground" (vs. 22–23. JB).

Isaiah 1:10–20 (E)

The time of this oracle would seem to be late in the eighth century B.C.E. The reference in v. 1:9 to the "few survivors" suggests that the invasion of Sennacherib and the reduction of the Southern Kingdom to the city-state of Jerusalem have already taken place. The occasion would seem to be a large assemblage of the people, with their ruling elites at their head. Very likely it was the harvest festival, with its obligatory sacrifices. The metaphor adopted by Isaiah for his speech is that of the court of law: Israel is called before the divine Judge to answer for her sins.

Verses 10–17 are part of Isaiah's speech before the "court," in which he contrasts the false and the true worship of God. While it might seem that Isaiah condemns the entire sacrificial system, such a conclusion is not required from the speech. Rather, the prophet is saying that sacrifices, prayers, services of worship, ritual, and the like are offensive to God *if* they are offered as a substitute for righteousness. God will not be bought off; God will have obedience.

The people are urged to repent of their ways, as a precondition of God's forgiveness. They are urged to purge themselves of their wickedness and to offer God the obedience God demands. Isaiah offers as an example of the obedience God requires the protection of the weakest members of society—the widows and orphans.

Verses 18–20 are a statement of reconciliation. God has the power and the will to forgive, to obliterate the worst guilt. If the assembly of God's people will become serious about doing God's will, it will receive God's forgiveness and escape the destruction that it merits. Just as Moses offered the people a choice of life and death in Deuteronomy 30:19, so the prophet urges his people to choose the way of obedience and life.

In a history of Israel or a commentary on Isaiah, **refresh your memory** of the historical situation at the time of Isaiah's ministry.

A **sermon** on this subject might well be titled "The True Worship of God." True worship is that which is offered to God in praise for divine grace and mercy. By contrast, false worship is offered as a substitute for obedience, as a way of buying God's favor, as a way of getting God to compromise the divine righteousness.

Lest the hearers think this is an academic exercise, point to the reference in Isaiah 1:10 to Sodom and Gomorrah. In addressing a solemn assembly of the "faithful" come to worship Yahweh, Isaiah compares their rulers to the rulers of Sodom and the people to the people of Gomorrah. And we all know what happened to those two cities! Social righteousness, worship, peace, and prosperity all are of a piece!

2 Thessalonians 1:5–12 (C)

2 Thessalonians 1:1–5, 11–12 (L) (E)

2 Thessalonians 1:11–2:2 (RC)

This second letter from Paul to the church in Thessalonica was probably written, like the first, from Corinth. The first letter is usually dated in 50 C.E. The second may have been written a few months or even a year after the first. The church at Thessalonica was one of several founded in Macedonia by Paul on his second missionary journey. Acts 17 describes the founding of the church and the active hostility of the local Jewish community to its members. Evidently that hostility continued. Paul writes in v. 4 of "your steadfastness and faith in all your persecutions and in the afflictions which you are enduring."

However, since the focal point of the letter is the coming of Christ, it seems likely that the occasion for the writing of the second letter had less to do with conflict with the Jews than it did with confusion about Christ's return. The first letter reflects belief that the return will be soon. It may be that the second letter was required to correct some wrongheaded activity that the first letter produced!

The passage for this Sunday, 1:5–12, has to do with a subtheme of the epistle, which is that God will render to each according to his or her deeds. Therefore the Thessalonians are to be patient under their afflictions, to see them as signs that they are counted worthy, and to hold fast to their calling.

As one scholar has pointed out, "Paul wrote for a tiny Church in the midst of a much larger Israel. . . . His concern was therefore centered on Israel's acceptance of this tiny gathering of Gentiles that he and few other Jews were trying to encourage" (from a speech by Paul van Buren to a Symposium at Princeton Theological Seminary on "The Church and Israel: Romans 9–11," 1989). The modern situation is quite reversed: A relatively small body of Jews is trying to maintain itself and its tradition in the midst of an enormous Gentile-Christian majority. Therefore the preacher—if not the interpreter—needs to tread very softly in representing the conflict in Thessalonica between traditional Jews and Jewish Christians. The "good Christian," "bad Jew" kind of stereotyping only contributes to anti-Semitism. If you decide to preach on this passage, **do some reading** in the literature of contemporary Jewish-Christian relations.

Second Thessalonians 1:5–12 makes three points, which could furnish the three points of a **sermon** on "Christians Respond to Persecution." Paul writes that (1) suffering for the sake of the gospel can be an assurance that those so afflicted are worthy of God's kingdom; (2) God will render to each his or her due; no one is going to go unpunished for making others suffer; and (3) Christians should strive to be worthy of God's call.

This sermon might present an opportunity for highlighting the conduct of Christian churches in Eastern Europe during the past decades. After all, it was the staunchness under persecution of a Reformed pastor in Romania that was the trigger for the overthrow of a tyrannical regime. Surely we have some things to learn from the churches in the Eastern European nations.

Theological Reflection

Writing in the *Christian Century*, May 9, 1990, about how his mind has changed in the past years, George A. Lindbeck looks at possibilities for the renewal of the church. One of these he calls "the development of an Israel-like understanding of the church." Christians, he says, need to see the Hebrew Scriptures as the basic ecclesiological textbook. "Christians see themselves within those texts, when read in the light of Christ, as God's people, chosen for service not preferment, and bound together in a historically and sociologically continuous community that God refuses to disown whether it is faithful or unfaithful, united or disunited, in the catacombs or on the throne" (p. 495). Those comments from Lindbeck would seem to apply to all the texts listed for this Sunday.

Children's Message

There isn't any choice for this Sunday: You must tell—or retell—the story of Zacchaeus. Children never get enough of it; neither do adults. Try to minimize the fact that Zacchaeus was *small*; that really has little to do with the point of the narrative. The point is that he was either a cruel or a thoughtless man, who put money above loyalty to his people or concern for the poor and defenseless. Yet Jesus befriended him and was the cause of Zacchaeus' amazing about-face and reformation. God can do wonderful things with some rather crude raw material.

Hymns for Pentecost 24

Amazing Grace; We Would Be Building; I Love to Tell the Story.

Pentecost 25

Ordinary Time 32
Proper 27

Psalm 9:11–20 (C)

2 Thessalonians 2:13–3:5 (C) (L) (E)
2 Thessalonians 2:16–3:5 (RC)

Zechariah 7:1–10 (C)
1 Chronicles 29:10–13 (L)
2 Maccabees 7:1–2, 9–14 (RC)
Job 19:23–27a (E)

Luke 20:27–38 (C) (L) (RC)
Luke 20:27, 34–38 (E)

Meditation on the Texts

O God, you raised our Lord Jesus from the dead and with his resurrection lit in our hearts the hope of eternal life. As you have chosen, sanctified, and called us to the service of the gospel, so continue us in faith and service. We confess that we buckle under pressure, that we have little stomach for conflict, that we would prefer not to suffer for our faith. And if we suffer, we would prefer it to be from prayer and fasting—not from public wrestling with the ungodly and their powers. But hearten us, O God, with remembrance of the prophets, apostles, saints, and martyrs—and above all, with the remembrance of the steadfastness of Christ. For we pray in his name. Amen.

Commentary on the Texts

Luke 20:27–38 (C) (L) (RC)

Luke 20:27, 34–38 (E)

This is one of several key passages for understanding the Christian doctrine of the resurrection of the body. (Another is 1 Corinthians 15.) It is the only such teaching that we have from Jesus himself. The passage in Luke has parallels in Matthew 22:23–33 and in Mark 12:18–27.

Jesus' teaching is given in a dialogue with several Sadducees, who represent one of the major divisions within Judaism. One of the features separating the Sadducees from a group like the Pharisees was that the Sadducees did not believe in the resurrection from the dead. They rejected the notion of the resurrection because they rejected as binding any doctrine not taught in the Pentateuch.

Their tactic in disputing with Jesus is to try to make him look foolish. Drawing upon the tradition or the law of levirate, which required a man to father children by his dead brother's wife, they pose an extreme scenario: What if seven brothers were all married, in succession, to the same woman? Whose wife would she be in the resurrection? (Of course in the law of levirate they saw a clear rejection of the notion of the resurrection of the dead, for the whole purpose of having a man marry his brother's widow was that the brother's name and line would not disappear from the earth.)

Jesus' response to their case study is two-pronged: (1) their interpretation of the Pentateuch is faulty and (2) they underestimate the power of God. They have based their case upon the provision for the levirate marriage in Deuteronomy 25:5–6 and Genesis 38. He counters with Exodus 3:6, where God says to Moses, "I am the God of your father, the God of Abraham, the God of Isaac, and the God of Jacob." God is the God of the living, who continues to define God's self in the present through the relationship to the patriarchs. Their death has not broken their covenant relationship to the living God.

Furthermore, says Jesus, they are wrong in supposing that the resurrection means simply the return of persons to their former earthly life. God is capable of something much greater than that. Those who are resurrected will be equal to the angels in their immortality. The children of this aeon marry and are given in marriage, but in that aeon, in the world to come, things will be different. (This is a teaching akin to Paul's notion of the resurrected having "spiritual bodies." See 1 Corinthians 15.)

The clear implication is that not all will experience the resurrection. It is not for everyone; it is the gift of God; it is for the just. (See Luke 14:14, where Jesus speaks of "the resurrection of the just.")

There are **two lines of inquiry** that the interpreter may want to follow before sitting down to write a sermon on Luke 20:27–38. One is to explore the phenomenon of the levirate marriage. *Levir* in Latin means "brother-in-law." The prescription for the levirate marriage is given in Deuteronomy 25:5–6. The notion that the husband's family owed his widow a chance to have children lies behind the story of Judah and Tamar in Genesis 38. In the story of Ruth, a critical role is played by the next of kin, who refuses to marry Ruth and thus redeem the land belonging to Naomi's husband. Either the story of Tamar or the story of Ruth might be used for illustrative purposes in a sermon on Luke 20:27–38.

The other line if inquiry would be an investigation into the differing views of the Pharisees and the Sadducees regarding the resurrection of the dead. A bible dictionary should be useful here.

A **sermon** on this Lukan passage needs to be carefully crafted, for as the Sadducees in the narrative learned, one can end up sounding ridiculous rather than profound. They thought to make Jesus look ridiculous; they were the ones who ended up looking less than brilliant. They asked a trick question; it backfired. How many times has every preacher been asked such questions as these: "Preacher, if a man loses a leg in an auto accident, will it be restored to him in the resurrection?" "Preacher, will I have my pet cat with me in heaven?"

Like the questions of the Sadducees, the question about the lost leg and the question about the pet cat are based on false assumptions. They ignore the teaching of scripture; they credit God with very little imagination. Any attempts to respond, in kind, to such questions in a sermon will lead the preacher into a quagmire.

Beware of the sermon on the resurrection that sets out to satisfy the curiosity of the hearers. It is better to begin the sermon by identifying yourself and your audience with the Sadducees—with those who have some vague, even bizarre notions about the resurrection. Confess that these notions are often not grounded in scripture and represent an immature notion of what God is like and what God's purposes are. Then go on to let Jesus instruct you on two counts: (1) what scripture teaches and (2) what our God is able to do. That opens the way to declare these Christian understandings of the resurrection: It is the gift of God; it does not rest upon the immortality of the soul. It is a work of God's power and imagination; it is not the extension of human potentiality.

Zechariah 7:1–10 (C)

This reading consists of parts of two separate oracles. The first is contained in vs. 1–7. The year is probably 518 or 517 B.C.E. The exiles have returned to Judah and are rebuilding the temple. Elders arrive in Jerusalem from the town of Bethel, with a question for the priests and prophets: Should the fast commemorating the fall of Jerusalem be continued as it had been during the years in captivity? The prophetic word given them by Zechariah is this: During all those years, the fasts in the fifth month (for the destruction of Jerusalem) and the fasts in the seventh month, commemorating the murder of Gedaliah (see Jer. 41:1ff.) were motivated by self-concern. Zechariah reminds the people that during the days before the fall the prophetic word had been the same: God is not concerned with fasts and feasts—but with other things.

No doubt the reference to "the words which the LORD proclaimed by the former prophets" (v. 7) are to such oracles as these:

> When you come to appear before me,
>   who requires of you this
>   trampling of my courts?
> . . . .

> Your new moons and your appointed feasts
> my soul hates.
>
> . . . .
>
> Cease to do evil,
> learn to do good;
> seek justice,
> correct oppression;
> defend the fatherless,
> plead for the widow.
>> (Isaiah 1:12, 14, 16–17)
>
> I hate, I despise your feasts,
> and I take no delight in your solemn assemblies.
>
> . . . .
>
> But let justice roll down like waters,
> and righteousness like an ever-flowing stream.
>> (Amos 5:21, 24)
>
> With what shall I come before the LORD . . . ?
>
> . . . .
>
> He has showed you, O man, what is good;
> and what does the LORD require of you
> but to do justice, and to love kindness,
> and to walk humbly with your God?
>> (Micah 6:6, 8)

On the strength of such passages the persons who selected the lectionary passage appended to the oracle in Zechariah 7:1–7 the beginning of the next oracle, which lists these requirements of God: "Render true judgments, show kindness and mercy each to his brother, do not oppress the widow, the fatherless, the sojournor, or the poor; and let none of you devise evil against his brother in your heart" (vs. 9–10).

Recall the warning of Jesus in the Sermon on the Mount about fasting as a means of winning the acclaim of others and Jesus' emphasis on the inclinations of the heart.

This is prophetic religion at its truest and purest: God wills righteousness, not ritual. If one has to ask about the propriety of some ritual, it is probably better to leave it alone.

In a history of Israel or a commentary on Zechariah, **refresh your memory** of the return of Israel from exile. What was the greatest challenge facing God's people at that time?

A good **sermon** topic for this passage might be "Ritual and Righteousness." Make a case study of the visit of the elders from Bethel, with what seems a legitimate question about the continuation of the fast commemorating the destruction of Jerusalem. Why shouldn't they be concerned to seek God's will in this matter? Why not inquire of the priests and prophets about what had been a holy fast? Should not *all* persons be concerned about keeping the feast days and fast days? Is not God concerned about correct liturgies, orderly worship services, properly decorous assemblies, good church music, the right seasonal colors, fine church architecture, and all that sort of thing?

To which the shocking answer must be: *Not very much!* Those are our concerns; those are the things that interest us; those are things we do "for ourselves," to use the prophet's words. What God cares about, what God cares passionately about, are matters of justice, mercy, kindness, love for the weak, brotherly affection.

1 Chronicles 29:10–13 (L)

This opening portion of David's prayer at the time of the presentation of the offerings for the building of the temple is one of the Bible's great doxologies. From time to time the preacher ought to deliver what can only be called a **doxological sermon**, whose sole purpose is to praise God for God's "greatness . . . power, splendor, length of days, glory" (1 Chron. 29:11, JB).

Those who chose this passage to be read on the same Sunday as Luke 20:27–38 had sound instincts. When contemplating the wonder and mystery of the resurrection, what can the believer do but praise God? Certainly it is not a time for metaphysical meanderings.

2 Maccabees 7:1–2, 9–14 (RC)

This lesson is part of a horrific story about the slaughter of a Jewish woman and her seven sons at the hands of Antiochus during the Syrian oppression of the Jews in the second century B.C.E. The eight Jews had refused to eat pork, and were tortured and killed, one by one. The second to die says before he expires: "Inhuman fiend, you may discharge us from this present life, but the King of the world will raise us up, since it is for his laws that we die, to live again for ever" (v. 9, JB). Before his death the fourth says to the king: "Ours is the better choice, to meet death at men's hands, yet relying on God's promise that we shall be raised up by him; whereas for you there can be no resurrection, no new life" (v. 14, JB).

The footnote in the *Jerusalem Bible* says that this is the first time in scripture that the resurrection of the body is asserted. That is undoubtedly why this reading was included in the lectionary.

Some commentators see this passage as referring to the resurrection of the just only. Others find a reference to a twofold resurrection: the resurrection of the just to eternal life; the resurrection of the wicked to judgment and eternal annihilation.

The story is not really about resurrection; it is about courage and steadfastness under extreme stress. So it would not seem proper to base a sermon about the resurrection on this passage. If you *must* **preach** on it, why not preach on it in tandem with Luke 20:27–38? You could use this story as an illustration of the kind of thinking about the resurrection that had developed in Judah prior to and including the time of Jesus.

Job 19:23–27a (E)

This passage is notable mostly for its inclusion in the text of Handel's *Messiah*. In the third part the soprano soloist sings:

> I know that my Redeemer liveth,
>   and that He shall stand at the latter day upon the earth;
> And though worms destroy this body,
>   yet in my flesh shall I see God.
> For now is Christ risen from the dead,
>   the first-fruits of them that sleep.

The probable meaning of v. 25 is as follows: "But as for me I know that my Redeemer lives [even when I am dead]; and at last upon the [grave] he will rise up [as my witness and vindicator]." The meaning of v. 26 is very uncertain. At this point the received text is notoriously corrupt. Who can know what it means?

The Hebrew word that is translated as "redeemer" or "vindicator" is *go el*. It is usually used to indicate that nearest of kin who is required to carry out vengeance, secure the inheritance, or—in the case of a widow—take her to wife and raise up children. (See Ruth 4.) In this passage from Job, does it really refer to Yahweh, who would appear to be Job's adversary?

This is a most difficult text from which to preach, simply because the meanings are so difficult to pin down. While it is traditionally used as a pre-Christian witness to the resurrection, it is a rather doubtful witness!

If you must **preach** on it, why not choose Handel's interpretation: I know that God is my vindicator, that God will raise me up at the last day, and that I shall see God face to face. You can say that the author of Job said in a veiled and cryptic way what Christians are able to say in a clear, unmistakable way!

2 Thessalonians 2:13–3:5 (C) (L) (E)

2 Thessalonians 2:16–3:5 (RC)

Paul is writing (from Corinth?) to the small, beleaguered house-church he has founded in Thessalonica. What he has to say is about what one would expect an apostle to write to a new, small, Jewish-Gentile Christian group that is facing strong opposition: Keep on keeping on. This passage includes both a prayer and a plea: a prayer for their continued steadfastness, a plea for them to stand firm, to hold to the tradition they have received.

Both Paul's prayer and plea for steadfastness are grounded in three indicatives: They have been chosen. They have been sanctified. They have been called. "God chose you from the beginning." God sanctified you "by the Spirit and belief in the truth." God "called you through our gospel." (Vs. 13–14.)

The doctrine of the perseverance of the saints does not get much attention these days, but that is what this passage is about. Those who have been sanctified (made to be saints) through word and Spirit are to stick it out despite the opposition of wicked persons.

As an incentive to perseverance, the apostle prays that the hearts of the Thessalonian Christians be directed to the steadfast love of God—that most characteristic attribute of God in the Hebrew Scriptures—and to the steadfastness of Christ. Presumably Paul had in mind the faithful behavior of Jesus in the face of deadly opposition.

See what you can **find in commentaries** or lexicons about the meaning of *hypomonē*, the Greek word that in v. 5 is translated as "steadfastness." It is an important concept in Paul's letters.

A **sermon** on this passage might well be entitled "Keep On Keeping On," "The Perseverance of the Saints," or "A Prayer and a Plea for Steadfastness." Let the believers be encouraged by God's faithfulness and the staunchness of Jesus under pressure to stand firm for what they have been taught. That is always harder than it sounds! The long haul is the tough haul. Christians need every reassurance they can get. They need to remember (1) their election, (2) their sanctification by the Spirit and the truth, and (3) their call.

Theological Reflection

Begin your reflection with the horrific story in 2 Maccabees 7 of the woman and her seven sons who were flayed alive—and then slaughtered—for refusing to eat pork. Now there is a kind of steadfastness that borders on folly. What is a mouthful of meat compared to eight human lives? we ask. Is that not carrying obedience to the law to extremes? Does God really want us to do that? Yet we remember with awe and gratitude the Christian martyrs who died rather than deny their Lord. We think of Paul as one such; we can imagine the church in Thessalonica being faced with thrashings and imprisonments, if not worse. Job, under the pressure of terrible suffering, did not give up his faith. That is why we speak of someone having "the perseverance of Job." What is it that makes people persevere? Is it the hope of being found faithful in the resurrection? Is it fear of *not* being found faithful in the resurrection?

Children's Message

By all means tell the story of the fellows who came to Jesus and tried to make him look foolish with their story of the seven brothers who all married the same woman! Children know that game. They have had it played on them; they have played it on others. The game usually begins with the expression, "Well, if you are so smart, then answer this for me." The question may be something like the old riddle, "Can God make a stone so big that even God can't jump over it?"

Point out what Jesus did when these fellows used a quotation from the Bible to make him look foolish: He showed them that he knew the Bible better than they did. We can learn from that; we can learn that we need to know a lot about the Bible, otherwise people will make ninnies out of us!

Hymns for Pentecost 25

He Who Would Valiant Be; Hope of the World; A Mighty Fortress Is Our God.

Ordinary Time 33
Proper 28

Psalm 82 (C)

2 Thessalonians 3:6–13 (C) (L) (E)
2 Thessalonians 3:7–12 (RC)

Malachi 4:1–6 (C)
Malachi 4:1–2a (L) (RC)   **Luke 21:5–19**
Malachi 3:13–4:2a, 5–6 (E)

Meditation on the Texts

Eternal God, you have promised to come and finish the good work you have begun, you have set us to our tasks and daily give us strength and sustenance to do them. Forgive us for poor and shoddy work, for the tired excuses we offer for jobs not completed, for the self-pity we lavish on ourselves when we are weary and worn down. Give us patience and strength to persevere in those things to which we have set our hands, to struggle and sweat and sacrifice until we have finished what we agreed to do. Bless with health, strength, and just rewards those who hew the wood and draw the water and do the hard and menial work of this world. In Jesus' name. Amen.

Commentary on the Texts

Luke 21:5–19

Luke 21:5–38 constitutes Jesus' teaching about the End time. It corresponds to Matthew 10:17–22; 24:1–25, 29–36 and Mark 13:1–32. Luke has the speech being delivered in the temple in Jerusalem—and not exclusively to the disciples, although some of the statements are addressed directly to them.

The message is about responsible behavior in the interim between Jesus' resurrection and the final acts of God that will consummate human history. As one commentator reminds us, those final acts bring to completion the goal envisioned by God in the creation; they are not concerned merely with the saving of a few souls. So Luke wants to exhort the church to responsible conduct in the interim, to avoid a flight into a fantasy world that refuses to take this world and life in this world seriously.

Presumably the Gospel was written after the destruction of Jerusalem (and the temple) in 70 C.E., so the author knows that what Jesus speaks of in v. 6 has already happened. That destruction is a sign of the passing away of the present age. However, the cosmic signs that portend the final acts of God have not yet taken place; so there is to be no false sense of certainty. Rather, the church is exhorted to show faithfulness under pressure, to endure in the confidence that the resurrection to eternal life is promised (the implication of v. 19).

Be sure that you are familiar with the events of 70 C.E.—the destruction of the temple and the fall of Jerusalem. You may want to **review the history** of the period so that you can use information about these events in your sermon.

Compare Luke's teaching about life in the interim with the other two statements about "interim ethics" that are included as readings for this Sunday: Malachi 4:1–6 and 2 Thessalonians 3:6–13. In both readings there is also an emphasis on behavior that is appropriate for the present in view of the future that has been promised. The prophet warns a careless, complacent people against the day of judgment; the apostle warns an overconfident people that they are to work for their living and not stand around in idleness, waiting for the coming of Christ!

For **preaching** to people in the pews today, probably the easiest access to Luke 21:5–19 is by way of the question of Jesus' contemporaries, "Teacher, when will this be, and what will be the sign when this is about to take place?" People in Jesus' day were curious about the signs and the timing of God's intervention in world affairs. They wanted to know about *what* and *when*. With the tumultuous changes that are presently taking place in our world, many of us want to know if these are in some way "signs" of God's intervention and what they portend for the future of humankind.

To such curiosity the Bible responds with a dual message: Yes, the upheavals of the present time *do* point to God's dissatisfaction with human affairs. But no, one cannot read in them any timetable for the consummation. A time of upheaval, therefore, is a time for faithful endurance, for responsible behavior, for obedience to the will of God as already revealed.

A sermon on Luke 21:5–19, therefore, might be entitled "Ethics for the Interim." It could begin with the Gospel writer addressing himself to a church that was living and witnessing in the years after the destruction of Jerusalem and the temple. Were Christians to regard these cataclysmic events as signs that the End was at hand? No. They were to regard them as signs that the present age was coming to an end, that it had no rosy future. But they were not to suppose that the End would come momentarily. Only cosmic signs could give assurance of that (see vs. 25–28).

In a comparable way, we are living in a time when great human constructs and institutions are being destroyed before our eyes: The end of communism has come with a rush and a roar. Is that a sign that the End is near? No. But it is a reminder that the present age is passing away, that our institutions are no more eternal than were the city of Jerusalem and the temple. Like the Christians of the first century, we are exhorted to faithful conduct, as befits those who know that the End is assured.

Malachi 4:1–6 (C)

Malachi 4:1–2a (L) (RC)

Malachi 3:13–4:2a, 5–6 (E)

Although the literary problems with these final verses of Malachi are formidable, it is a section of the Bible that has furnished Christian thought and piety with a host of images and metaphors! In the KJV, 3:17 contains the reference to "that day when I make up my jewels," the inspiration for the hymn "When He Cometh to Make Up His Jewels." In the KJV, 4:2 says that "the Sun of righteousness [shall] arise with healing in his wings." This was taken up by Charles Wesley in his Christian hymn, "Hark! The Herald Angels Sing" and applied to Jesus Christ:

> Hail the heaven-born Prince of Peace!
> Hail the sun of righteousness!
> Light and life to all He brings,
> Risen with healing in His wings.

The reference in 4:5 to the sending of Elijah before the coming of the day of the Lord is important for the New Testament. Some contemporaries thought Jesus to be the promised Elijah. Jesus himself identified John the Baptist as Elijah, "come first to restore all things" (Mark 9:12–13).

Many scholars, however, think that the final three verses of Malachi are not by the author of the rest of the book. The *Jerusalem Bible,* for example, separates those verses under the heading of "Appendices." Some scholars think these three verses were added by an editor or editors of the Book of the Twelve Prophets to serve as a summary statement for that entire portion of the Hebrew Scriptures. If indeed these three verses are not part of the original prophecy, then "the messenger" of which the prophet speaks may or may not be Elijah.

Some of the selections from Malachi for this Sunday reflect an awareness of these literary problems: The Lutheran and Roman Catholic selections do not include v. 3–6 of chapter 4.

Even if one decides that indeed 4:1-6 is from the hand of the same person who wrote the rest of the book, one has to deal with three rather separate themes: 4:1-3 is about the coming of the day of the Lord. Verse 4 is an exhortation to keep the law given to Moses. Verses 5-6 are about the coming of Elijah before the day of the Lord, to turn the hearts of God's people away from sin so that they may survive the judgment.

Except for the difficulties with the final three verses, scholars seem well agreed about the authorship and dating of the rest of the book. It is from the hand of a single person, whose name has been lost. Malachi means simply "my messenger." It was written in the middle of the fifth century B.C.E., very likely just prior to the reforms instituted by Nehemiah. It reflects the cultic and moral indifference that marked that period in postexilic Judah.

The theme of the book is clear enough: The people have grown weary with keeping the moral law and the ritual law; God is weary of their infidelities. They had better shape up; a day of reckoning is coming. God has written in his "book of remembrance" (3:16) those who have feared him; they will be spared, as a man spares a dutiful son. But the evil will be destroyed.

Before you write your sermon, **examine various references** in the Gospels to Elijah, for example, the transfiguration, and articles about Elijah in Bible dictionaries. What role did Elijah play in Jewish expectations of the future?

One way in which the **preacher** might deal with Malachi 4:1-6—plus 3:13-18, if one wants to include those verses—is to compare and contrast the interim ethics of Malachi with those of Luke 21:5-19 and 2 Thessalonians 3:6-13. All three of the passages listed for liturgical use for this Sunday deal with interim ethics, with how the faithful are to conduct themselves in the light of the impending End. Each deals with ethics in quite a different way: Malachi 4:4 directs the attention of the faithful to the law of God given at the mountain. In Luke 21:5-19, Jesus speaks of faithful witnessing under persecution. Paul writes to the Thessalonians to urge them not to stand around in idleness, waiting for the End, but to work for their living. These are all quite different ways of responding to the message that God has appointed an End, toward which the eyes of all should be directed. Each passage relates eschatology and ethics in a different way—yet none of the three relaxes the moral imperatives of the Bible one whit. All three give the lie to the Marxist notion that religion is the opiate of the people, designed to fix their attention on pie in the sky so that they will be oblivious to social evils here on earth.

2 Thessalonians 3:6-13 (C) (L) (E)

2 Thessalonians 3:7-12 (RC)

The point was made in the discussions of Malachi 4:1-6 and Luke 21:5-19 that in scripture interim ethics appear in a variety of contexts. In Malachi, hearers are enjoined to heed the commands of God because of the day of judgment that is coming. In Luke 21, the exhortation to remain faithful under extreme stress is given along with indications that believers are living in the End time. But in 2 Thessalonians, the context seems to be an expectation of the imminent appearing of Christ; believers are enjoined to work for a living, not to stand around in idleness as though the imminent return of the Lord made all normal activity irrelevant.

There is a sense in which all three of these passages reflect the urgency born of the imminence of God's intervention in history. In each situation the End is impending in the literal sense of the word; it hangs over current events. It casts a shadow, it forces a different way of looking at things, it is something always present at the margins of perception.

In the case of 2 Thessalonians 3, what that impending End impacts is attitudes about work. Evidently there were some in the Thessalonian community who, expecting the End to be any moment, had given up working. And what Paul has to say to them is this: (1) When he was among them, he voluntarily worked for his keep, so as not to be a burden to them and so as to give them a model for their own behavior. This was part of the tradition in which he himself stood—that God's people were to work and not stand around in idleness. (2) They are to follow his example; they are to work for their living and not stand around in idleness, waiting for Jesus to show up. (3) Anyone who is not willing to work

322

should not be fed. "We gave you a rule when we were with you: not to let anyone have food if he refused to do any work" (v. 10, JB). Some may read into that verse an indication that the Thessalonians were practicing the communal living described in Acts 2:43–47.

There is no systematic teaching about work in scripture. There are not even many satisfying treatments of the theme by contemporary writers. *God and the Day's Work* by Robert Calhoun, long out of print, is still a very provocative book. *Parables at Work* by John C. Purdy (Philadelphia: Westminster Press, 1985) is an attempt to formulate some Christian teachings about work, using Jesus' parables as source material.

Before you write your sermon, **look** at what is said about work in the wisdom literature—Ecclesiastes and Proverbs, for example.

Sermons on daily work are hard to prepare and even harder for congregations to hear with any receptivity. Everyone is an expert on work; we all do it; we all know about it; we do not need to be harangued about it! If there is a prevailing fault among Christians in mainline churches, it is that they are addicted to work.

However, this passage from Paul provides an opportunity to discuss faith and work in a fresh way, for it invites consideration of the question: Why does the imminent return of Christ not make any work ethic irrelevant? If indeed Christ is coming again, and if that coming might happen at any moment, why should any of us invest the major part of our lives and energies in work? Are we overachieving, workaholic people not denying in our actions a fundamental Christian truth?

A sermon on this passage might begin with questions such as those and move on to some interesting answers—answers based on the text of 2 Thessalonians 3:6–13. One "answer" is an appeal to tradition: Christians have always assumed that God expects from each person a full day's work. Another answer points to the example of Paul, who refused to live from the offerings of others but preferred to turn his hand to making his own living—at least while he was with the Thessalonians.

This passage will not carry you any further than that. You may want to formulate some answers of your own, based on other scriptures and other teachings. You may, however, limit yourself to the Thessalonian passage and use the very absence of a full-blown teaching about work as a warning: The imminent return of Christ does, in a sense, make a work ethic irrelevant. All our teachings about work, all our economic theories, all our work ethics, are limited, judged, relativized by God's reconciling and redeeming work in Christ.

As the plight of the Soviet social arrangements becomes more and more clear to us in the West, we are witness to some fascinating revelations about work. In an interview with people on a collective Russian farm, Hedrick Smith discovered that many of them did not want to own land and cattle. They shied away from the responsibility; the risks of private ownership frightened them; they were not confident that they could measure up. They were reluctant to let go of assured income, benefits, roles, and so forth. There is probably excellent illustrative material in the reports coming out of Eastern Europe for sermons on daily work.

Theological Reflection

As has been noted several times, the readings for this Sunday all deal with behavior that is appropriate for people who know that God intends to make an End of things. While biblical ethics do indeed look back to the revelation of God's commandments at Sinai, they also look forward to the better future that is also an expression of God's will. There can never be any question about going back to the good old days, as if there were once a golden age presided over by a good old God. How often have we thought—and preached—about ethics as though goodness meant a going back, a return to a better day. But is that biblical? Where is there justification for it?

Children's Message

Work is a four-letter word to children; to them it is something adults do and something adults want them to do more of. You are not going to get anywhere talking to children about work, but you can get their attention with this provocative question: Does God ever get tired? Then answer it by telling about Malachi and his preaching. "What a weariness this is,'' said the people of Judah, referring to the requirements God had laid on them. ''You have wearied the LORD with your words,'' is the prophet's answer. In other words, God gets sick and tired of hearing some of our lame excuses. Children might find that a rather refreshing idea. At least it would be couched in concepts they understand.

Hymns for Pentecost 26

Come, Labor On; Work, for the Night Is Coming; At the Name of Jesus.

Pentecost 27

(Lutheran only)

Isaiah 52:1–6
1 Corinthians 15:54–58
Luke 19:11–27

Meditation on the Texts

Almighty God, whose good pleasure it is to fight our battles for us, to defeat the powers of sin and death that hold us in thrall, we strain our ears to hear the distant shouts of victory, to hear the chorus of the saints in Zion praising the conquering Lamb. For we grow weary with the struggle against evil; we feel captive to the culture; we long for the end of night and would welcome the dawn of a new and better day. Grant us patience to exercise those gifts you have given us, in the place you have given us to work, with the sure and certain knowledge that you will multiply those gifts in ways that defy our dreams. We pray in Jesus' name. Amen.

Commentary on the Texts

Luke 19:11–27

What strikes the interpreter at once is the marked difference between this parable as narrated by Luke and what is apparently the same parable narrated by Matthew, in 25:14–30. In addition to some differences in details, there is the addition in Luke of an introduction to the parable in v. 11, which sets the parable in the context of Jesus' journey to Jerusalem. Then there is the addition of vs. 14 and 27, which tell of the hatred of the citizens for the nobleman and his revenge on them for attempting his overthrow.

These additions, as some commentators point out, suggest a historical situation for the editing of this parable in which the coming of the kingdom has been delayed and in which there are enemies of Christ who appear after he has gone away. One commentator suggests that the author of Luke's Gospel received the parable in this expanded form.

The interpreter has to make a choice: Shall I focus on the differences between what are apparently two forms of an original parable? Shall I focus on the similarities, and minimize the differences? Or shall I focus on the parable as told in Luke and see what message it has? This brief commentary will focus on the parable as told in Luke.

According to Luke 19:11, the parable of the pounds was told to clear away a misunderstanding on the part of some onlookers who thought, that because Jesus was proceeding triumphantly toward Jerusalem, the kingdom was near. These were people who thought that the kingdom would come with obvious signs and visible events. Whereas the parable makes clear that the kingdom will only be visible upon the return of Jesus. In the meantime it is invisible, just as investments are invisible riches.

Ten servants are mentioned as receiving *minas* (pounds), each of which amounts to three months' wages—not a huge amount of money. The service required of each servant is small—not at all commensurate with the huge rewards given to those whose service proves to be profitable. The final glory is in being a faithful servant and in doing the master's will—not in achieving some fixed goal or fixed measure of success. The differences in success seem to have more to do with the abilities of the servants than with anything else.

Once again we see the paradoxical judgment of Jesus: "To every one who has will more be given; but from him who has not, even what he has will be taken away" (v. 26). It is as paradoxical as Jesus' statements about the humble being exalted and the exalted humbled, and those who seek to save their lives losing them and those who lose their lives saving them.

One commentator points to the significance of the setting of the parable at the end of Jesus' journey to Jerusalem. Jesus does not capitalize on the messianic expectations of the crowds; the readers are turned from a visible kingdom to a discipleship that is content with faithful service, with risks, with hope for the Lord's return. At the Lord's return, there will be a time of judgment, when those who have been his enemies will be punished and those who have been faithful will be rewarded. And what of feckless servants like the one who hid his money away? What will happen to them? Unlike Matthew, Luke does not say what happens to the fearful servant—other than that he is scolded and his money is given to another.

The parable of the pounds presents the interpreter with two sets of problems. First, one has to decide which parable he or she will deal with: (1) the Lukan parable in its present form; (2) the apparently earlier form of the parable in Matthew; or (3) some kind of reconstruction of what may have been Jesus' original parable. And once having settled on the *form,* one is left with the task of reading out the *meaning.* As with other of Jesus' parables, the meaning is by no means obvious. Who are the servants? Who is the nobleman? What do the gifts of money represent? What is the one point that Jesus wanted to drive home? And what is the meaning of the cryptic phrase "To all those who have, more will be given; but from those who have nothing, even what they have will be taken away" (Luke 19:26, NRSV)? Did Jesus tell the parable to make the point that those with faith will be rewarded, but those with no faith will be punished?

The parables suffer from familiarity. **Do some fresh research** into the parables in books or articles, such as the works by Jeremias or C. H. Dodd.

As has been said earlier in this workbook, there are some helpful guidelines for the interpreter of parables. (1) There is the recognition that parables are not allegories, so that the interpreter is not obliged to find counterparts for each person or detail of the parable. In the case of the parable of the pounds in Luke 19, the nobleman does not necessarily have to represent Christ, or the servants those who believe in Christ, or the money entrusted to them the gospel, or the time between the nobleman's departure and return the time between Jesus' ascension and his second coming. (2) There is end stress. Jesus usually told a parable to make a single point, and that point usually comes at or near the end of the parable. In the case of the parable of the pounds, the approval of the faithful servants seems to be the point Jesus wanted to make. What matters is not the size of the task entrusted, nor the measurable success, nor the length of time the servant is employed—but only that the servant of God be faithful to his or her trust. Christ's servants are to hang in and hang on, not fretting about measurements but only about fidelity.

That would seem to be the message that the **preacher** would want to deliver, if he or she chose this text for this Sunday at the end of the long season from Pentecost to Advent. One could, in fact, make something out of how *long* it seems between Pentecost Sunday and the First Sunday of Advent. How long also it seems between the first Pentecost in the year 33 C.E. and Jesus' return. The interim gets longer with every passing decade.

Once one has taken the measure of the days and months and years, then one drops the parable on the congregation—and uses it to drive home the point that measurements are not what matter, but fidelity to the Master. Those who worry about measurements are apt to make the mistake of the servant who hid the money in a piece of cloth: Fear of the Master's measuring rod will blind them to their opportunities and responsibilities, and they may end up with *nothing* to show for their servitude.

That is the paradox that the preacher wants to hold up: That fear of the Master's judgment may be the greatest obstacle to faithful service. Those who dread his return have good reason to dread his return; those who are busy at the work the Master has set them to do have nothing to fear! In the words of FDR "The only thing we have to fear is fear itself."

One who is not familiar with the lectionary as read in Lutheran congregations is bound to ask: Why was this passage chosen for this last Sunday before Advent? Not only is it lacking in clear, compelling metaphors, but it bristles with scholarly problems. Many commentators regard vs. 1–3 as belonging to a lengthy poem, 51:9–52:2. Some doubt that vs. 4–6 are even from the hand of Second Isaiah. One can tell, just by looking, that these latter four verses are prose and the first two verses of the passage are poetry.

Why was this passage chosen to be read and expounded in churches on the final Sunday before Advent? Without having access to the history of this passage in Lutheran churches, one has to make an educated guess. Perhaps it was chosen because of the reference in vs. 1 and 2 to Jerusalem putting on beautiful garments, adorning herself as a bride preparing to meet her husband. That, of course, brings to mind Revelation 21:1–2 (NRSV): "Then I saw a new heaven and a new earth; for the first heaven and the first earth had passed away, and the sea was no more. And I saw the holy city, the New Jerusalem, coming down out of heaven from God, prepared as a bride adorned for her husband."

In those verses from Revelation are the concepts of Jerusalem as a focal point for God's saving work, of Jerusalem as the bride, of Jerusalem as holy. All three concepts are present in the passage from Isaiah.

For the sake of getting on with the interpretation, let us assume that Isaiah 52:1–6, despite scholarly reservations, is indeed from the hand—or the school—of Second Isaiah. Then it was written in Babylon, shortly before the conquest of Babylon by Cyrus and the release of some Jews to return to Judah. Then it is an oracle about the liberation of Jerusalem. Jerusalem, too, will be redeemed, set free. Just as the Babylonians paid nothing for the city, so they will get nothing for her release! When the city is liberated, it will not be defiled again by the Babylonians. (The reference to "the uncircumcised and the unclean" is surely a reference to the Babylonians, not to all Gentiles.)

This liberation will come at the hand of God, who twice before freed the chosen people from oppressors—the Egyptians and Assyrians (v. 4). God will do this to vindicate God's glory, which has been profaned by those who rule the captives. In the day of liberation, the Israelites shall know that it is God who has once again acted to save them.

That is well enough, but the interpreter begins to get skittish when thinking about projecting this message forward to the New Testament and thence into contemporary affairs. The city of Jerusalem may serve nicely as a metaphor for the new age of shalom. Today it is anything but a symbol of peace; it is rather a center of conflict and controversy. Three faiths—Christianity, Islam, and Judaism—claim it is *their* holy city, so that one wants to be very, very judicious in what is claimed for Jerusalem in Christian theology and preaching.

Suppose that the **preacher** does not choose to relate Isaiah 52:1–6 to the vision of Revelation 21:1–2, or to other statements about Jerusalem in the New Testament, or to the present political and ecumenical issues surrounding the city. Suppose that the preacher sticks to the historical context of the passage and what the passage says in response to that context. How might such a sermon be developed?

The message that then seems to arise from the passage is that Jerusalem, the civic and cultic center of Jewish life, is promised redemption along with its former inhabitants. Salvation, then, is not limited to individuals. Salvation is not somehow spiritualized and atomized. Places as well as persons will be restored to former freedom and purity. God does not act to snatch people out of history, to carry them up and away from historical institutions and geographic locations, but quite the opposite. God's salvation is particular, historical, geographical, institutional.

If one wants to project that truth into the present, one might simply say: The promise still holds; Jerusalem will be redeemed; God does not choose and then cast off "holy" places. There is a great tendency among Christians to regard anything and everything in the Old Testament as disposable: for example, the Ten Commandments, the Jews, Jerusalem, the Holy Land, or the Sabbath. It is almost as if all of this history were biodegradable—once useful, but now dissolved and returned to the elements from which it came. Jesus is, as it were, like a flower on a plant; we can pick the flower and throw away the plant. On this last Sunday before Advent, it is perhaps necessary to remind people that the One who is to come is the Messiah promised to Israel.

See also Epiphany 8.

In 1930 Gustav Aulen, a Swedish theologian, delivered a series of lectures, which were later published under the title of *Christus Victor.* The subtitle tells what the lectures were about: "An Historical Study of the Three Main Types of the Idea of the Atonement." Aulen's thesis was that the "classic" view of the atonement, held by the early church fathers, was one in which Christ won a victory for humankind over evil, over the enemies of God. Since the early days of the church, two other ideas of the atonement had developed. One he called the objective view. This is the view put forward by Anselm, in which the dominant metaphor is a forensic one: Christ makes satisfaction for the sins of humankind. The other view Aulen called the subjective. Christ's actions reveal the true character of God and dissipate human beings' mistrust of God.

The interpreter will do well to **read** (or reread) Aulen's book or at least review his or her understanding of "atonement." A theological wordbook would be helpful for this task.

1 Corinthians 15:54–58 is one of those passages which clearly support Aulen's notion of redemption as God's victory over the enemies of humankind: sin, death, and law. In *Letters to Young Churches* J. B. Phillips makes this clear by this paraphrase of v. 57: "[Christ] has delivered us from the fear of death, the power of sin and the condemnation of the Law." Jesus is seen as *Christus Victor,* triumphing over death and powers of death.

One probably ought not go so far as to list the law as one of the enemies of humankind, for after all, the law represents the expression of God's righteousness! Rather, as Phillips has properly noted, it is the "condemnation of the Law" that does us in. As Paul argues in Romans, sin brings death (Rom. 5:12; 7:13), but it is the law that gives sin its power over us (7:5). That is why he can say in v. 56, "the power of sin is the law." So one ought to say that Christ is victor over sin and death—but not ignoring the role of the law in bringing us to an awareness of the awful strength of sin.

Note the reference to "immortality" in v. 54. This is not the Hellenistic view that humans have immortal souls. Rather, immortality is something that is put on when God raises humans from the dead.

Note also Paul's use of the Old Testament. He quotes from Isaiah and Hosea, although he departs considerably from the Hebrew Scriptures: "[The Lord] will swallow up death forever" (Isa. 25:7, NRSV); "O Death, where are your plagues? O Sheol, where is your destruction?" (Hos. 13:14).

This emphasis on *Christus Victor* is an appropriate one for **preaching** on this final Sunday in the season between Pentecost Sunday and the First Sunday of Advent. This is *not* an appropriate time, of course, to argue theories of the redemptive work of God in Christ. The work by Aulen was cited in order to underscore the importance of this text from Paul—not to suggest that one ought to make a three-point sermon based on three possible views of the atonement! If one wants three points, then deal with Christ's saving us from sin, death, and the condemnation of the law!

However, this is one of those texts which ought not be made to yield up a three-point sermon. Three-point sermons tend to be didactic. This is a Sunday for celebration, proclamation, heroic narrative. "Victory" is one of the sweetest words in the language; Christ as victor is one of the grandest of theological concepts. Use the imagery of warfare: Jesus going hand to hand with the devil in the desert; Jesus wrestling with the powers of death in raising Lazarus from the grave; Jesus overpowering evil spirits; Jesus banishing leprosy and blindness and epilepsy—those ancient plagues of humankind. It is this Jesus whom God raised from the dead. Those were real victories, not just symbolic acts of kindness. Do not shrink from linking disease and death with sin as somehow its consequences. When Jesus says to us, "My children, your sins are forgiven" that has consequences beyond the grave. Forgiveness is indeed therapeutic, but it is also triumphant.

Theological Reflection

Are there common themes in the prophet's summons to Jerusalem to rouse herself to liberation, in Jesus' parable of the pounds, and Paul's salute to *Christus Victor*? Perhaps it is well to remember that in the biblical narrative, the central character and the chief actor is always God. The purpose of the narrative is to reveal God's intentions and actions—and in revealing those intentions and actions, to reveal God's "nature." In all three of the passages for this Sunday, the chief actor is God: God will deliver Jerusalem; God is like a returning nobleman who expects faithful service from those to whom treasure was entrusted; God has acted in Christ to give us victory over our ancient enemies. God is Liberator, Judge, Redeemer. And these "roles," if we may call them that, are not mutually exclusive, but rather, complementary.

Children's Message

Tell the story of the poor wretch in Jesus' parable of the pounds who hid his money in a cloth out of fear of his master. How typical he is! How readily we identify with him! And how totally he was betrayed by his own fear! We can all identify with him; we can all sympathize with him. But, poor fool, he is convicted out of his own mouth. He let fear run away with his own best conclusions. He admits that he knew he would have to give answer for his stewardship, but he did not do the least thing to make sure he could answer in the affirmative. How fear makes fools of us! How foolish to let fear rule our relationship to God!

Hymns for Pentecost 27

Thine Is the Glory; Onward, Christian Soldiers; We've a Story to Tell to the Nations.

Christ the King   *(November 20–26)*   **329**

Ordinary Time 34
Proper 29

Psalm 95 (C)	**Colossians 1:11–20 (C) (E)**
	Colossians 1:13–20 (L)
2 Samuel 5:1–5 (C)	**Colossians 1:12–20 (RC)**
2 Samuel 5:1–3 (RC)	
Jeremiah 23:2–6 (L)	**John 12:9–19 (C)**
Jeremiah 23:1–6 (E)	**Luke 23:35–43 (L) (RC) (E)**

Meditation on the Texts

O God, whom we call king, although we have thrown off the rule of all earthly kings and princes; whose coming kingdom we hail, although we have lost faith in political and economic utopias: How shall we greet you aright? Shall we refurbish the old imagery? Shall we seek new images of splendor and glory? Or shall we fall into wondering silence? Teach us how we may best praise you, how we may sing our hosannas, how we may give you the honor due you. We would not honor you less than the Passover pilgrims, not less than the prophets who gloried in your promised One, not less than the apostles, who strained the language in praise of Christ. In Jesus' name we pray. Amen.

Commentary on the Texts

John 12:9–19 (C)

Luke gave us Christmas; John gave us Palm Sunday. The writer of the Fourth Gospel is the one who places the triumphal entry on the fifth day before the Passover. That puts it on Sunday. And that has led to the liturgical celebration of the Sunday before Easter as Palm Sunday. However, in the lectionary the triumphal entry appears also on the final Sunday before Advent, which is by some celebrated as the Festival of Christ the King. Since the Johannine account is unmistakably that of Jesus' reception as the messianic king, 12:9–19 is suitable for this Sunday as well as for Palm Sunday.

Review the Palm Sunday event as described in the Synoptics and in John.

In John's account Jerusalem was crowded with pilgrims who had come for the Passover. When they heard that Jesus was on his way from Bethany to Jerusalem, they went out to meet him. Believing him to be the promised Messiah (the one anointed King of Israel), they took with them palm branches, which were the symbol of regal triumph. And they shouted the words traditionally used by the priests to bless the incoming pilgrims: "Hosanna! Blessed is the one who comes in the name of the Lord." (John 12:13, NRSV).

The welcome was further enhanced by the presence and testimony of Jews from Jerusalem who had been present when Jesus raised Lazarus from the dead. This great and wonderful sign was further proof that indeed Jesus was the promised Ruler.

In describing the excitement of the crowds and mobs that gathered in Leningrad in the months of 1917, the narrator of a documentary film said: "They believed that at last they had become participants in history." Something of that same kind of excitement must have swept the crowds on Palm Sunday. After being for so long the pawns and victims of history, how heady to feel oneself a participant, a mover and shaker!

The response of Jesus to the royal welcome was to procure a young donkey and ride upon it. This was both an affirmation of the crowd's perception and a correction of it. It was, as one commentator remarks, a conscious fulfillment of Zechariah 9:9–10, in which the promised king comes in peace and humility—not as one prepared for battle.

The welcome of the crowd wrecks, for the time being, any plans of hostile opposition to seize Jesus and do away with him.

Preachers who elect John 12:9–19 as their text for this Sunday have their work cut out for them. Not only are most congregations unprepared for a Palm Sunday sermon in November, but the metaphor of "king" bristles with problems. The militant feminists do not like it, because it is masculine. The Greek word "Christ" is a translation of the Hebrew word "Messiah," which in turn means "the Anointed One" (the chosen king). Yet, as John 12:9–19 shows, it is inappropriate to take the usual notion of king and apply it to Jesus. When the crowds did so, Jesus took evasive action. Besides, kings have become passé; they are ceremonial figures in contemporary societies—not rulers in any true sense. If that were not enough, the distinction between the horse of the warrior king and the donkey of the unwarlike king is one that has to be explained. Once signs and symbols have to be carefully explained, they lose a lot of their power.

What do modern congregations care for the claims and counterclaims of "kingship"? Not very much. So what is the preacher to do? Why not follow the structure of the narrative and talk about how "the true light . . . came to what was his own, and his own people did not accept him" (John 1:9, 11, NRSV). Let the pilgrims to Jerusalem, the witnesses to Lazarus' raising, the chief priests, and the hostile Pharisees represent humankind. People have many and varied reactions to God's attempts to assert dominion: They actively resist (in the name of God, of course); they misunderstand; they get wildly excited by signs and proofs; they retreat and wait for a more opportune time to carry out their own visions of peace and justice. God always must do what Jesus did—find some way to assert dominion that is not overpowering, bruising, warlike. God must woo us with gentleness; God must find some way to break the image we have of the divine power as force, might, unstoppable energy.

Luke 23:35–43 (L) (RC) (E)

See also Lent 6, (L) (RC) (E).

The scene is the crucifixion; the focus is on Jesus' "kingship." One commentator asks us to note that the term "king" is used by the soldiers and by Pilate, but the leaders of the Jews use the Jewish titles "Messiah of God" and "Chosen One." The reaction of the two criminals illustrates the possibility of unbelief and of belief: The unbelieving demand miracles, signs, proofs before they will acknowledge Jesus as the Christ; the believing accept judgment on their sins, assert Jesus' innocence, and hope for a place in his realm. Jesus' response to the penitent criminal's hope of a distant kingdom is to speak of a present salvation.

Do a brief study of the various titles given to Jesus by his contemporaries. Which, for example, is favored by each Gospel writer?

In **preaching** on this passage, one might do well to compare and contrast the titles given—or denied—to Jesus and the attitudes of the two criminals. Jesus is best understood as God's Christ rather than as a king like Herod; his realm is best understood as a present relationship rather than simply a future utopia.

2 Samuel 5:1–5 (C)

2 Samuel 5:1–3 (RC)

The anointing of David as head of a united monarchy is one of those key narratives which needs to be seen in its literary context. It is part of the books of Samuel (a literary unity in the Hebrew Scriptures), which in turn is part of the Deuteronomic history, Joshua through 2 Kings. The viewpoint of this history is called by some scholars prophetic, because the authors see God as the true King of Israel, with earthly kings ruling by God's permission and under God's sanctions.

The books of Samuel tell the story of the rise of the monarchy in Israel. They begin with the birth of Samuel and cover the careers of Samuel, Saul, and David. Despite the title, the central figure of the narrative is David. In 2 Samuel 5:1–5 there is the account of how he became head of the united monarchy. Following the death of Saul, David gathered his people at Hebron; there he was anointed king of Judah. Abner, Saul's commander, made Ishbaal, a surviving son of Saul, king of Israel, the ten northern tribes. There followed a long and bitter war between the house of David and the house of Saul, which was ended when Abner defected to David and Ishbaal was assassinated. The northern tribes, deprived of leadership, turned to David; and in 5:1–5 there is the brief account of how the elders from those tribes came to David and made a covenant with him and anointed him king of Israel as well as of Judah.

The language of the northern peoples is interesting. They quote a prophecy to the effect that David is to be Israel's king, and they admit their need for a "shepherd." Presumably they are driven by the same needs that prompted the elders of Israel to demand their first king from Samuel (compare 1 Samuel 8). Without a king to protect them from their enemies, they are like sheep without a shepherd—scattered and at risk.

As one commentator remarks, we would love to know the content of the covenant that the elders of Israel made with David. What were the terms? Who promised what to whom? Perhaps it is more important that David was made king at the request of and by the actions of the people. There is no "divine right of kings" theology operating here!

2 Samuel 5:1–5 is one of those texts which is important both in and of itself and also for the use that later peoples made of it. The uniting of the monarchy under David is no doubt a significant event, with far-reaching consequences for Israel. Yet, the meaning of the narrative is not exhausted by its place in the cause and effect sequence of human affairs. It has what might be called symbolic or metaphorical meaning as well. Note the concepts that later are important metaphors in Christian rhetoric:

1. The ruler as *shepherd*
2. *Anointing* as the acknowledgment of God's prior choice (The term "messiah" means "the anointed one")
3. *Elders* acting on behalf of the whole people of God
4. A *covenant* between ruler and ruled
5. The people choosing a single head of state, a *king*

One has only to thumb through a hymnbook to see how pervasive these metaphors have become in Christian thinking: "Praise Ye the Lord, the Almighty, the King of Creation!"; "O Worship the King, All Glorious Above"; "The Lord's My Shepherd"; "The King of Love My Shepherd Is"; "Hail to the Lord's Anointed, Great David's Greater Son!"

Do a **brief study** of the concept of shepherd as applied to Israel's kings. Use a Bible dictionary to help you with this.

In **preaching** on 2 Samuel 5:1–5, how shall one do justice both to the significance of the event within the story of God's people and to its contributions to Christian theology? It might be useful, for example, to rescue the term "shepherd" from the limited meaning of one who looks after sheep. It might also be useful to remind hearers that "Christ" is not Jesus' last name, but the designation of one who was promised to Israel as a deliverer. The notion of king as absolute ruler also needs some attention; in the narrative it is clear that a king has a limited function and as a ruler has a two-way covenant relationship with the ruled. Also, the concept of covenant cannot be too often explained. As this passage reminds us, a covenant is not the same as a contract between equals.

Few congregations will sit still for a lesson in semantics. They will be patient for explanations of original meanings, and of derived meanings, *only* if the preacher can show how these concepts, which have such a rich history, are meaningful today. So the preacher has to ask himself or herself, Which of these metaphors is the most lively and interesting for people right now? and then focus in on that metaphor, showing how it is enriched by its history, and how it is useful for us today.

For example, one could use 2 Samuel 5:1–5 as the occasion for a sermon on Jewish-Christian relations, with the focus on the act of anointing. What does it mean, one might ask, that we Christians believe Jesus to be the Anointed One of Israel? This passage from 2 Samuel might be linked, then, with the account of Peter's confession at Caesarea Philippi, when he says, "You are the Messiah" (Mark 8:29, NRSV).

Or the focus could be on the concept of the ruler as shepherd, who guards the people against the external enemies, whose leadership is essential for their safety and well-being. It would not hurt, on this Sunday which is sometimes called the Festival of Christ the King, to link the terms "shepherd" and "king." That linkage gives strength to the shepherd image and nurturing to the king image. People tend to be divided among those who see God as some kind of celestial sheepherder, whose only concern is the fatness and security of the human flock, and those who see God as a warrior-king, leading the troops against the forces of darkness. (You may call these two groups doves and hawks if you go in for those metaphors.)

Jeremiah 23:2-6 (L)

Jeremiah 23:1-6 (E)

Every so often it is useful to ask of a Bible passage the routine questions of the working journalist: Who? What? Why? When? Where?

The words of Jeremiah 23:1-6 are from the man who gave his name to the jeremiad, whose constant message was this: Judah is doomed; and that doom is Yahweh's righteous judgment on Judah for her sins. The location is Jerusalem, most likely in the years between the first deportation in 597 B.C.E. and the second deportation and the destruction of the city in 586 B.C.E. The words are addressed to Judah, to King Zedekiah and the nobles who had him under their thumbs, and the message is one of censure: The rulers have been faithless shepherds, who have not properly tended their flocks. Therefore Yahweh will "tend to them," and when they have been properly punished, Yahweh will himself be the Shepherd, gathering the scattered flock. And then new and faithful rulers will be raised up to care for Judah. In particular, there will be a scion from the stock of David, who will rule justly.

Commentators call our attention to two lovely word plays in these verses. The rulers have not properly "cared for" the people; Yahweh will "take care" of them! And in v. 6, the name of the promised Branch is a Hebrew phrase that translates as "Yahweh is our righteousness," whereas the name Zedekiah in Hebrew means "Yahweh is my vindication."

What does all this mean for us? It is obvious why this passage was chosen for lectionary purposes, for this Sunday called the Festival of Christ the King. Verses 5-6 are an announcement of the coming of a future, ideal king from David's line. He is called "the true Shoot (Branch)" to distinguish him from those who are falsely claimed as David's heir. Later Branch became a technical term for the messianic king. (See Zech. 3:8; 6:12.) So it is proper to see Jeremiah 23:1-5 as a messianic prophecy.

The **preaching** value of Jeremiah 23:1-5 does not lie in its literary form as a messianic prophecy. For Christians, messianic prophecies in the Old Testament are not "proofs" of Jesus' Lordship; Jesus is not the Christ because such a One was predicted, but because God vindicated Jesus as Lord and Christ by raising him from the dead. Probably the preaching value is in the false hopes that one can read between the lines. In the awful situation between 597 and 586 B.C.E. some people were looking at Zedekiah as a Savior! Put people in a historical pressure cooker, and they will dream up almost anything. To these messianic hopes that attached to the king, Jeremiah said in effect: It is precisely because of such rulers (shepherds) as Zedekiah that catastrophe has come upon you. He used the occasion to call to mind the promise implicit in the covenant with David, that one day a true King would be given, but not the present caricature of a king!

The trajectory of kings that began with Saul and rose to such heights with David and Solomon would shortly, in the deportation and death of Zedekiah, run itself into the ground. The normal processes of history, by which one king succeeds another, could not produce a winner, anymore than today we may trust the processes of democracy to produce ideal rulers. The words of Psalm 146 come to mind: "Do not put your trust in princes, in mortals, in whom there is no help. When their breath departs, they return to the earth; on that very day their plans perish" (vs. 3-4, NRSV).

Once we have accepted the futility of resting our hopes on earthly rulers, we may be open to hearing the good news of the coming of the true Shoot of David.

Colossians 1:13–20 (L)

Colossians 1:12–20 (RC)

Colossians 1:15–20 is one of the crown jewels of the New Testament. It is worthy to stand alongside of those other great christological statements: John 1:1–17; Philippians 2:6–11; and Hebrews 1:1–4. As a summary statement of the centrality and sufficiency of Jesus Christ, it is unsurpassed.

The setting for this jewel is a letter from Paul, written from prison in Rome, to a congregation that he had not organized and had probably never even visited. This church in Asia was under the threat of new teachings, which evidently had to do with assigning Christ a less-than-central role in creation and with special feasts, festivals, and rituals. Paul wrote to assert the supremacy and sufficiency of Christ, in a letter that was intended to be read aloud to the faithful and to circulate among several congregations in Asia Minor.

Colossians 1:15–20 is best dealt with as a credo, a hymn, a poem, rather than as a theological statement that can be parsed and analyzed. Not that the things attributed to Christ cannot be found in most Christologies; but rather that the whole statement loses something of its magnificence when dissected and argued over.

It is better to compare and contrast it with the other jewel-like Christologies of the New Testament, such as John 1:1–17 and the others mentioned above—and with the christological parts of the Nicene Creed, and with some of the great hymns of the church. Look, for example, at the correspondence between the ascriptions of Colossians 1:15–20 and these from the original version of "Crown Him with Many Crowns":

> Crown him with many crowns, The Lamb upon his throne . . .
> Crown him the Virgin's Son, The God incarnate born . . .
> Crown him the Lord of love . . .
> Crown him the Lord of peace; Whose power a scepter sways from pole
>   to pole . . .
> Crown him the Lord of life, Who triumphed o'er the grave . . .
> Crown him the Lord of years, The Potentate of time . . .
> Crown him the Lord of Heaven, Enthroned in worlds above . . .
> Crown him, ye kings, with many crowns, For he is King of All.

Why not **make four columns** on a sheet of paper and write out Colossians 1:15–20; John 1:1–17; Philippians 2:6–11; and Hebrews 1:1–4. What do they all have in common? What features are *special* to Colossians 1:15–20?

If you choose to **preach** on this text, you may well want to make your sermon a hymn or poem of praise to Christ, drawing upon not only such hymns as Philippians 2:6–11 but also such hymns as "Crown Him with Many Crowns," "Fairest Lord Jesus," "At the Name of Jesus," "When I Survey the Wondrous Cross." The original Palm Sunday crowd may not have had a proper understanding of Christology when they went out to greet Jesus upon his entry into Jerusalem, but they certainly hit upon the right word: *Hosanna!* It is an untranslatable cry of adoration and joy, and that is what we ought to be concerned with on the Sunday set aside as a Festival of Christ the King—adoration and joy, not analysis and semantics!

Theological Reflection

For many years one of the highest accolades that could be given to Jesus was that of "king." Not only was the Davidic king the symbol of God's rule and promise, but contemporary kings were the utmost in splendor and power and majesty. Even when the divine right of kings ceased to have much currency, the symbolic role of the king as head of state still had some cash value. But now, in the interest of inclusive language, "king" is replaced in many hymns and prayers and lectionaries by "ruler." Since most rulers arrive at their status by popular election, "ruler" isn't a very potent symbol. What shall we use in the place of the biblical word "king"? There are no easy answers. Some would say, Good riddance to metaphors of power and force and absolutism; bring on metaphors that honor God as tender, sustaining, nurturing, healing, freeing, empowering. What do you think?

Children's Message

There cannot be any argument about which passage to use this Sunday. Use John 12:9–19. This is your chance to tell how Jesus responded to the enthusiastic crowd by procuring a young donkey for his entry into Jerusalem. Put to children the choices that were his: He could continue to walk into Jerusalem; he could procure a horse (which warriors rode); or he could go for the young donkey. All three choices had some scriptural precedents: Joshua and his troops marched around Jericho on foot; the Pharaohs who pursued the Hebrews as they left Egypt had horses and chariots; and there was the rather obscure reference in Zechariah to the messianic ruler mounted on a donkey. The three choices make a wonderful story.

Hymns for Christ the King

Crown Him with Many Crowns; Hail to the Lord's Anointed; Fairest Lord Jesus.